Doing Business Internationally
The Resource for Business and Social Etiquette

FIFTH EDITION

Princeton Training Press

600 Alexander Road • Princeton, New Jersey 08540 U.S.A.
Tel: 609-951-9319 • Fax: 609-951-0395
Email: ptp@tmcorp.com
Website: http://www.tmcorp.com

Printed in the United States of America

Library of Congress Cataloging-in-Publication Data

Doing Business Internationally
The Resource for Business and Social Etiquette – 5th ed.
Includes bibliographical references
ISBN 1-882390-16-4
March 1999

TABLE OF CONTENTS

INTRODUCTION

Conducting business effectively across cultures requires mastering the ability to communicate with people from cultures other than our own. With the continuing trend toward globalization, every member of an organization must acquire some degree of cross-cultural competence. Whether traveling to other countries to meet with clients, vendors or people in our own organizations, working in multicultural project teams or arranging meetings for others at home or abroad, our effectiveness in our many-faceted roles as businesspeople will inevitably hinge on the willingness and ability to learn about business practices, norms and expectations in other places.

When confronted with different ways of doing business, whether in the form of, for example, greetings, attending meetings or negotiating, it is easy to dismiss these differences as unimportant, inconsequential or, at worst, wrong. This initial impulse is common, but must be avoided at all costs. If we wish to be successful when doing business with people from cultures other than our own, there are four essential components to acquiring cross-cultural competence. The first is the conscious decision to keep an open mind. Only when we maintain an openness to difference in others can we secure the ability to learn continuously, extend respect and understanding, value diversity and difference as opportunities for mutual growth, and improve ourselves both personally and professionally.

Next, we must learn about ourselves and the culturally determined behaviors we engage in. This allows us to understand both that our business practices are deeply ingrained expectations of others and that these expectations may not be met in our cross-cultural business interactions. Simultaneously, we must strive to acquire knowledge about other cultures in as many ways as possible. This is achieved by, among other things, talking to people from all walks of life, observing quietly without judging, and consulting as many sources as possible on the country's background as well as on current political, economic, social and cultural trends. Lastly, we must adapt our personal and professional skills continuously in order to meet the challenges before us.

This book is a reference tool that provides a point of departure for articulating our own culturally determined business behaviors and expectations, for learning about the history and cultures of other countries, and for beginning to acquire the skills we will need to do business in those countries. This, the fifth edition of *Doing Business Internationally: The Resource for Business and Social Etiquette*, provides guidelines for conducting business in 100 countries.

The topics covered for each country include:

Population

Languages

Religions

Currency

Historical Overview

Business Practices

   Hours of Business

   Dress

   Introductions

   Meetings

   Negotiating

   Entertaining

Social Values, Customs and Tips

This edition offers several improvements over the last. It has been reorganized for ease of use; rather than being organized regionally, the 100 countries are arranged alphabetically. The population, languages spoken, religions practiced and the name of the country's currency have been added and are listed at the top of each country entry for quick reference. The Historical Overviews have been rewritten and updated. The Business Practices section has been augmented significantly, especially as regards the negotiating tips, which did not appear in the last edition. Finally, the section entitled Social Values, Customs and Tips provides additional information on important cultural values and protocol in each country.

One way of using this resource book is as a springboard for conversation with someone from another country. As researchers of cross-cultural communication, we have found that people truly enjoy discussing the background, importance or even the validity of a given point.

While we strive to present the most accurate information possible, we also recognize that cultures change and that cultural boundaries are not always equivalent to national boundaries. That is, one country comprises many different cultures, and by engaging in dialogue with others, we can start to appreciate the finer points of the multicultural makeup of any place on the globe. We also view this resource book as a work in progress and are always glad to receive comments or suggestions from our readers in preparation for the next edition.

Should you be interested in gaining a deeper understanding of culture and doing business across cultures, Training Management Corporation offers the Cultural Orientations Model (COM)™, which provides a comprehensive conceptual framework and a neutral vocabulary for grasping, discussing and engaging in continuous learning about cultural values, norms, attitudes and behaviors. Additionally, we have developed the Cultural Orientations Indicator (COI)™, an assessment tool for individuals who wish to expand their knowledge of their own cultural preferences and the roles they play in working effectively across cultures. For information on the COM™, the COI™, our newsletter, *Perspectives for Global Leadership*, or our training seminars, contact us at:

Training Management Corporation
600 Alexander Road
Princeton, NJ, USA 08540
Email: info@tmcorp.com
Website: http://www.tmcorp.com

NOTE:

In composing this publication we have made every effort to provide the most accurate and up-to-date information available and to give our readers as comprehensive a guide as space would permit. Given the fluidity and fast pace of today's business world, change is inevitable and keeping data completely accurate and current is therefore extremely difficult. The publishers take no responsibility for errors that have arisen because the information they were provided was either inaccurate or has, in the meantime, become obsolete.

ACKNOWLEDGMENTS

Training Management Corporation is fortunate to have worked with some extraordinarily talented and resourceful people during the creation of this resource book. The main team members on this project were:

Talia Bloch: A multitalented **writer** and **editor,** who brought gentle wisdom, fortitude and her countless other gifts to the project, and not only rewrote most of the Historical Overviews, but also edited every entry, created the **graphics** for this publication and offered excellent advice whenever it was needed.

Danita Kolb: A remarkable person who not only filled the roles of **writer, researcher** and **proofreader**, but organized projects, people and resources, prepared the manuscript for printing, and delighted us endlessly with her perspicacity and wit from the very beginning of the project to its completion.

Shana Semler: An exceptional **researcher**, **writer** and **proofreader** who organized all of us even when we didn't know we needed it, and whose perseverance, integrity and boundless energy were an inspiration to all of us.

We are also grateful for the significant contributions of the following individuals:

Susan Gaissert: A proofreader who was always there when we needed her.

Craig Schontz: A proofreader and aspiring writer, to whom we wish the best of luck.

Elaina Battista: A researcher who exhibited admirable flexibility when asked to jump in at the last minute and assist in a variety of tasks.

Terri Goldsmith: An intern who made many of our electronic changes.

Susan Scherer: Our program coordinator who has taken charge of the final details to get the manuscript ready for the press.

Stefani Milne: Our marketing coordinator who, with great patience and clear instructions, ensured that this book reached the printer in tip-top shape.

We are indebted to each of you.

Monique Rinere, Chief Editor

Danielle Walker, President, Training Management Corporation

COUNTRY-SPECIFIC INFORMATION

Minimize Regret: This principle should act as your guide as you seek to do business with people from another country. A single wrong gesture or remark may not cause you to lose a deal but continual rudeness and a lack of empathy might well do so. Prepare for a cross-cultural encounter with purpose and thoroughness. Take nothing for granted. *Build relationships and your business will build itself.*

Throughout this section, we have used the term "host" to refer to either a man or a woman who is hosting a business guest or guests. The exception to the use of "host" in a gender-neutral manner is in some Middle Eastern and Asian countries, where the host is almost always a male.

AFGHANISTAN

Population: 24,792,375 (July 1998 est.); Pashtun 38%, Tajik 25%, Uzbek 6%, Hazara 19%, minor ethnic groups (Aimaks, Turkmen, Baloch and others) 12%

Languages: Pashtun 35%, Afghan Persian (Dari) 50%, Turkic languages (primarily Uzbek and Turkmen) 11%, 30 minor languages (primarily Balochi and Pashai) 4%

Religions: Sunni Muslim 84%, Shi'a Muslim 15%, other 1%

Currency: afghanis

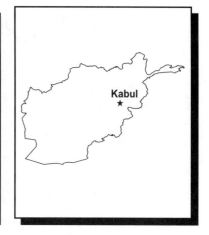

HISTORICAL OVERVIEW

- The area of present-day Afghanistan was part of Cyrus the Great's Persian empire during the sixth century B.C. In the fourth century, it fell to Alexander the Great. The region was divided after Alexander's death and ruled by a succession of peoples.

- Around the beginning of the Common Era the Asiatic Kushans appeared. They built a great empire in which the arts and trade flourished. Buddhism was brought into the region. After the Kushan Empire fell a new succession of nomads came through and conquered the area. The Afghan princedoms then came under the influence of Hinduism and India, but by around 870, Islam took firm hold.

- The Mongols invaded Afghanistan under Genghis Khan in 1219. Once this empire collapsed, Afghanistan became a collection of principalities. The southern part of the country, toward the Indus and Ganges Valleys, became part of the Indian Mughal Empire and the eastern region became part of the Persian Safavid Empire.

- In the early 18th century, all of Afghanistan came under Persian rule and the Afghans of Kandahar revolted. This led to the founding of the Afghan nation under Ahmad Khan, who united the separate parts of Afghanistan into one country.

- Beginning in 1818 Dost Mohammed swept through Afghanistan establishing the Mohammedzai dynasty. The Mohammedzais concentrated on controlling a smaller territory rather than overextending themselves as the previous dynasty had done.

- During the 19th century, both Russia and Great Britain attempted to exercise control over the country. There was a series of wars with Great Britain (1839-42; 1878-80; 1919) but the population would not be subdued and Afghanistan basically remained independent.

- Amanullah succeeded as Amir in 1919 and, in 1928, announced a plan of social and educational modernization. This caused a tribal revolt enabling another branch of the Mohammadzai family to take power, which introduced some further modernization programs.

- In 1964, the Afghan king drew up a new constitution for Afghanistan, providing for a legal system not based solely on Islamic law. He also established a representative legislative body.

- Afghanistan had achieved a modicum of stability between 1930 and 1970. But the political situation deteriorated and, on 17 July 1973, the army seized power with the support of the leftist Pareham (Flag) Party. A republic was proclaimed, but the new president and prime minister proved unpopular, and in a day-long battle in Kabul in 1978, he and many of his ministers perished at the hands of Soviet-trained members of the Afghan army.

- The new communist government, led by Nur Mohammed Taraki, adopted sweeping reforms that caused rebellions in the countryside. These rebels were called the Mujahidin. In 1979, a Soviet force seized control of the country to avert a likely defeat of communism. A bloody conflict began between the Soviets and the Mujahidin. The guerrillas led a successful resistance campaign in which they held the countryside while the Soviets held the cities. Millions of Afghan civilians fled to neighboring Pakistan and Iran.

- By 1986, the Soviets decided to loosen their grip on the government and, by February 1989, all troops were withdrawn. The rebels eventually took power in April 1992 and installed an Islamic government, but civil war continued, and changes in leadership occurred one after another.

- As anarchy threatened in 1994, a group of religious scholars, the Taliban (students), formed a protest movement espousing Islamic laws. These "students" were recruited from Afghan refugees in Pakistan and were probably operating with Pakistani support. By 1995 they had taken control of the western half of the country. Struggles between opposing factions for Kabul continued until 1996 when the Taliban finally captured the city and deposed the post-Communist government.

- In June 1997, Taliban leader Mohammad Omar Akhund was named Commander of the Faith. By this time the Taliban controlled 60 percent of Afghanistan.

- Although the Taliban's promises to establish order in the country originally won them much popular support, they soon lost this support when they began targeting civilians with their rockets. Once in power the Taliban enforced very strict Islamic laws forcing men to wear beards and women to stay at home.

- The years of civil war have taken a tremendous toll on the civilian population and the nation's economy. After over 20 years of fighting, the warring factions agreed to negotiate a peace accord.

BUSINESS PRACTICES

Hours of Business

Offices and banks are open from 8:00 a.m. to 5:00 p.m. throughout the year. Grocery stores are open from 7:00 a.m. to 8:00 p.m. from March through October, and from 9:00 a.m. to 3:30 p.m. throughout the rest of the year.

During Ramadan (the Muslim holy month of fasting), offices close at 2:00 p.m. daily.

Dress

Afghan men often wear a *Perahan tunban* (a knee-length shirt) over baggy trousers.

Common footwear includes sandals, sneakers and boots, all of which are removed for prayer.

Men wear a *kolah* (turban cap) on the head as a means of protection from the harsh winter weather. Another form of headdress is the *qarakuli* (cap), made from the skin of the *karakul* (sheep).

Women rarely appear in public, but when they do, they usually wear a *chadiri* (head-to-toe covering) or a *chador* (shawl-veil). Women may also wear a short jacket, a long coat or a shawl.

Silver and gold jewelry, often made with local semi-precious stones such as lapis lazuli and garnet, is worn. A *tawiz* (white amulet) is worn on the arm by many people because it is believed that white offers protection against evil and misfortune.

Introductions

Men and women greet each other with *Assalaamu alaikum* (Peace be upon you). The appropriate response is *Waalaikum assalaam* (And peace be upon you also). This greeting is accompanied by a hand-shake and a pat on the back.

Afghans also greet each other with the Dari (a form of Persian) phrase *Khubus ti* (How are you?) or the Pashto (one of Afghanistan's major languages) equivalent of "Good-bye," *Sanga ye? Khoda hafiz.*

Although greetings may vary by region or by ethnic group, *Assalaamu alaikum* is universally accepted. Women and men do not shake hands or touch in public, although a man may greet a woman verbally or in an indirect way. Women greet each other by shaking hands, embracing and giving a kiss on alternating cheeks three times.

Special titles are used when formally greeting and are reserved for academics or professionals. A person who has made the pilgrimage to Mecca is referred to as *Haji* (pilgrim). *Haji* or *Khan* (sir) is also used based on a person's social and economic status.

Titles are often combined with names, as in *Umm* (mother of) Muhammed or *Abu* (father of) Alam. First names or nicknames are used to address a friend.

Negotiating

Traditionally, you must be accepted as a friend before any business will be transacted. Keep in mind that business in Afghanistan must be done in person.

Entertaining

The Afghan people are known for their hospitality, and generosity is considered a sign of social status. Hosts serve guests food as well as tea depending on the time of the day. Business discussions begin after refreshments have been served.

Guests are expected to drink at least three cups of tea and are not expected to bring gifts.

Men and women are segregated when visiting or when being entertained.

Some Afghans only eat at home, while others choose to dine in restaurants occasionally. Some restaurants have booths for families, and some have separate dining areas for women.

Afghans are, for the most part, Sunni Muslim and are forbidden by their religious beliefs to drink alcohol and eat pork.

Belching after a meal is considered a sign of satisfaction.

Afghans in rural areas eat breakfast and dinner and occasionally a light lunch. Families generally eat together, except when entertaining a non-family member.

The left hand is never used to eat or to pass food; instead, the right hand is used to serve oneself.

Regardless of whether people eat with their hands or use utensils, they first wash their hands. Everyone eats from a common plate located in the center of the floor or table. Rural families may eat from a communal dish, usually without eating utensils.

Afghan dishes are influenced by the foods of South and Central Asia, China and Iran. The cuisine consists of *pilau* (rice mixed with meat and/or vegetables), *qorma* (vegetable sauce), *kebab* (skewered meat), *ashak* or *mantu* (pasta dishes) and *nahn* (flat bread). *Chai* (green or black tea) is served in *piallas* (bowls) with every meal.

SOCIAL VALUES, CUSTOMS AND TIPS

The Afghan people have very strong family ties. The elderly are cared for at home and are highly respected by all.

Afghans participate in a variety of sports. The national sport, *buzkashi*, is a game played by two teams on horseback that compete by carrying the headless carcass of a calf the distance of one-half circle to a spot, then returning it to the circle. Afghans also enjoy wrestling, soccer and volleyball.

Private cars are rarely used because of the high cost of fuel. Villagers either walk or ride donkeys, horses or horse-drawn carts. There are no railroads; buses run between major cities.

Urban areas have telephone networks, but they are largely unreliable. Public phones are widely used. Most people have televisions and radios, but newspapers and television broadcasts must be received from neighboring countries. The BBC is listened to regularly.

Community life in rural areas centers on daily prayers at the mosque. Local celebrations, festivals and religious activities also take place there.

Afghan people are generally friendly, hospitable and courteous. They place high value on piety, loyalty and identity with the family, kin group, clan and tribe.

Strict and inflexible codes are common within a group to ensure responsibility and roles. Disputes are not easily resolved because of the need to protect a group's strict codes of honor.

Land ownership and herd size define a rural person's wealth, but urban residents view wealth in terms of money or possessions, which they consider equal to education in status.

Although Islam dominates the life of virtually every Afghan, the religion has not overcome ethnic differences. A belief in fatalism helps people to accept and deal with the harshness of life in many areas.

It is considered impolite to pass an item with the left hand since it is reserved for personal hygiene purposes.

Major industries include agriculture, pastoralism and mining.

Large shops and bazaars (markets) are divided into many smaller shops and are grouped together by the products they sell.

Together, Afghans speak 32 languages and dialects.

The gesture of pointing the palm downward is used to call someone. Afghans *du'a* (supplicate) before a meal, a trip or any transaction. To *du'a*, the palms of both hands are held up to chest level and opened like a book.

Afghans very seldom use their hands while speaking; instead, men handle *tasbe* (prayer beads) during a conversation.

The national holidays include *Id al-Fitr* (the feast at the end of Ramadan), *Ashura* (the martyrdom of Imam Husayn), *Roza-Maulud* (the Prophet Mohammed's birthday), *Nooruz* (New Year's Day), Muslim National Day (April 28), Remembrance Day (May 4) and Independence Day (August 18).

ALGERIA

Population: 30,480,793 (July 1998 est.); Arab-Berber 99%, European less than 1%

Languages: Arabic (official), French, Berber dialects

Religions: Sunni Muslim (state religion) 99%, Christian and Jewish 1%

Currency: Algerian dinar

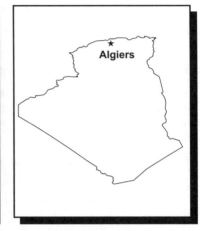

HISTORICAL OVERVIEW

- The earliest inhabitants of Algeria were the Berbers, who still account for a significant minority of the population. The region was later controlled successively by the Phoenicians, the Romans and the Vandals.

- The Umayyads (Arabs) invaded the country in 600 A.D. and introduced Islam to the Berbers. The cities of Algiers, Oran, Constantine and Annaba developed during the period of Arab conquest. When the Berbers regained control in the eighth century, they established their own Islamic Empire. Several Berber empires flourished until the 13th century.

- In the 1200s, Bedouins migrated to the area and the local population adopted the Bedouin nomadic lifestyle. From the early 1500s, the area was part of the Ottoman Empire. Since Algeria was quite far from the center of the empire (Turkey), however, significant local control and relations with neighboring European powers developed.

- France invaded in 1830, which resulted in the establishment of Algeria's present borders in 1902. A fierce independence movement developed and open warfare eventually broke out in 1954. Finally, Algeria became an independent state in 1962. When the French army withdrew, nearly one million European colonists evacuated.

- The new government was led by Ahmed Ben Bella, a member of the National Liberation Front (FLN). A leftist, Ben Bella nevertheless outlawed the Communist Party and shortly thereafter was elected president. He undertook a number of reforms, including the redistribution of land.

- Ben Bella moved toward the elimination of all opposition and a complete takeover, but Colonel Houari Boumedienne thwarted his plans in June 1965 and took over the government. Boumedienne then promptly dissolved the National Assembly and suspended the constitution. In 1976 a new constitution was adopted, and a year later National Assembly elections were finally held.

- Boumedienne died in December 1978 and was succeeded by Colonel Chadli Bendjedid, who took up land reform and redistributed large estates among the peasants.

- In 1988 large-scale riots by Muslim fundamentalists put the government in jeopardy. Unemployment climbed and corruption in the government was widespread. Many people turned to Islamic fundamentalism. In the 1990 local elections the Islamic Salvation Front (ISF) gathered clear majorities. Elections for 1992 were suspended shortly before they were to take place and the FLN dissident, Mohammed Boudiaf, was installed. Five months later he was assassinated by an FIS member.

- During the ensuing years violence in Algeria escalated as government security forces battled Islamic opposition from FIS as well as other fundamentalist groups. The government used drastic and harsh measures, often violating human rights. By 1995 a virtual civil war had broken out in the country.

- In 1996 during a flawed popular referendum, the government received approval for proposed changes to the constitution. The first parliamentary elections since 1992 were held in June 1997. This resulted in the first multiparty parliament to be elected in Algerian history. At the same time, massacres continued in Algeria's hinterlands.

- In 1998, the Algerian government allowed representatives from the EU to visit Algeria to discuss the present situation. Government officials did not allow an investigation into the deaths caused by the violence; rather they requested foreign help in finding means to eradicate terrorism.

- The political crises in the 1990s have had a devastating effect on the Algerian economy, causing a downturn in the growth of the real GDP. By 1997 there was some improvement.

BUSINESS PRACTICES

Hours of Business

During the winter, business hours are Saturday to Thursday, 8:00 a.m. to noon and 2:00 to 5:30 p.m. During the summer, business hours are 8:00 a.m. to noon and 3:00 to 5:30 p.m. During Ramadan, business hours are 9:00 a.m. to 4:00 p.m.

Dress

Business attire for men is a suit and tie. Women should wear a simple but elegant suit and comfortable shoes (not high heels).

Introductions

A warm and firm handshake is the most common greeting. You should keep in mind, however, that religious men never shake hands with women. A handshake is sometimes accompanied by an embrace.

Close friends of the same sex often kiss each other when greeting.

When addressing someone, one should use the last name preceded by the English title "Mr.," "Mrs." or "Miss." It is also a good idea to use professional titles, such as "Doctor," "Professor," "Engineer," "Architect" or "Attorney," when appropriate. One may also use the French titles *Monsieur* (Mr.), *Madame* (Mrs.), *Mademoiselle* (Miss), *Docteur* (Doctor), *Professeur* (Professor), *Avocat* (Lawyer), etc.

If one uses an Arabic title, the title should be used with the first name. Arabic titles include *Say-yeéd* (Mr.), *Zów-gah* (Mrs.), *Oo-stéz* or *Profes-or* (Professor), *Doctór* (Doctor) or *Moo-háhn-dis* (Engineer, Architect or Attorney). There is no Arabic equivalent for "Miss." Instead, simply use the French title *Mademoiselle*.

In small gatherings, it is polite to greet each individual. Elders are greeted first.

Meetings

Try to make appointments well in advance (one or two months), even if your Algerian colleagues resist making such a commitment. Be aware that most Algerian businesses use telexes instead of fax machines. Most hotels, however, offer fax machine service.

It is advisable to try to arrange appointments between 9:00 a.m. and noon. Even though Algerian businesspeople tend to be late for appointments, you should be punctual. This will impress your colleagues, and it is especially important when dealing with top-level executives.

The first business meeting will usually begin with a general discussion about your respective companies, rather than a direct discussion of the business at hand. You should express interest in the Algerian company and be prepared to talk about your own. You should emphasize your company's accomplishments and completed projects as well as the benefits that Algeria will realize by working with your company.

You should have your business cards translated into either French or Arabic. Also, have any materials you plan to use in presentations translated into French.

It is advisable to hire an interpreter if you are not fluent in French and your counterparts are not fluent in English.

Negotiating

You should be prepared to make several trips to Algeria to accomplish your goal. Almost all business dealings involve Algerian government organizations, which can be very bureaucratic. Both the State Planning Secretariat and the Ministry of Finance must approve all contracts with foreign companies. Above all, approval requires some Algerian investment (100 percent foreign-owned companies will not meet with much success).

It is advisable to have contacts in Algeria for making introductions to Algerian companies. The Commercial Section of the U.S. Embassy in Algeria, the National U.S.-Arab Chamber of Commerce and the Algerian Mission at the United Nations can be helpful for establishing contacts.

Algerian contracts will be written in great detail. Performance requirements, deadline dates and other obligations will be included. To protect yourself, it is advisable to pay a good deal of attention to the details of the contract and to allow twice as much time for a project as you would in the U.S. or Europe. It is common for a contract to require a foreign company to pay a penalty if obligations are not fulfilled. This requirement must be met even if the Algerian company has not fulfilled its own obligations to the foreign company.

Be aware that alcohol, including Algerian wine, is available only in international hotels. If you are in a restaurant with an Algerian with whom you are negotiating and you are not sure if the person drinks alcohol, refrain from ordering an alcoholic beverage. Such a faux pas could cause you to lose the deal.

Do not be surprised if you are invited to stay with your Algerian colleague's family once your contract is signed. He will not issue such an invitation before negotiations are complete, however, so as not to show favoritism during the negotiating process.

While traditional attitudes toward women may prevail in Algeria, businesswomen should expect to be accepted and treated with respect in Algiers.

Entertaining

Business dinners are more popular than lunches because of the intense midday heat. Customarily, the person who issues an invitation to a restaurant pays the entire bill.

There are a variety of restaurants in Algeria, including those that serve French and Algerian cuisine as well as others that serve Thai, Chinese and Vietnamese food. To entertain a businessman, it is best to take him to a restaurant in one of the best hotels or to a seafood restaurant near the beach.

If you are a businessman traveling with your wife, feel free to ask an Algerian businessman if he would like his wife to join both of you for dinner. He may refuse, but he will not be offended that you asked.

If you are invited to dinner in a home by members of the older generation, it is recommended that you bring pastries such as napoleons or *millefeuilles*. If the invitation is from young people, it is appropriate to bring flowers. Good choices are pink or red roses or tulips. You should not bring violets since they are associated with sadness.

Appreciated gifts from abroad include cameras, instant coffee, jeans, good-quality sunglasses, T-shirts, running shoes, good-quality chocolates, whiskey (if you know that the person drinks alcohol) or cigarettes.

For a meal at a home or a party, men should wear suits and ties. Women should wear dinner or cocktail dresses that fall below the knee. Women should remember not to wear anything revealing.

Since the state owns most restaurants, the quality of service can vary. You can call the waiter by saying *garçon*. At restaurants, a 15 percent service charge is normally included in the bill. Any extra tip is optional.

Breakfast, served between 7:00 and 8:00 a.m., consists of baguettes, *galettes* (a thick Syrian bread), croissants or brioches with butter or jam. Lunch, the main meal of the day, is served between noon and 2:00 p.m. Dinner is normally served at about 7:00 p.m. in the winter (December to February) and 8:00 or 8:30 p.m. in the summer (June to August). Dinner is a light meal.

There is a great variety of Algerian food, which has a strong Gallic flavor. Lamb, chicken, stews and pastas are popular. The most popular Algerian dish is couscous, a pasta-like semolina cooked with lamb or chicken and vegetables. Muslims do not eat pork.

People usually drink water, milk or a kind of buttermilk called *l'ben*. You should only drink bottled water and similarly you should not use ice cubes or eat raw fruit or vegetables that cannot be peeled.

Different styles of eating are used in Algeria. Some people sit on low couches with a big table in the middle; some sit on mats on the floor around a low table; still others sit on chairs around a standard western dining table.

Some people eat with cutlery, while others use the right hand. The use of utensils usually depends on the dish being served. Couscous is always eaten with a large spoon. Steak is eaten with a fork and knife. Stew is eaten with a fork while the sauce is scooped up with bread.

It is impolite to refuse food or refreshments. If a guest is unable to eat what is offered, he/she may ask for a substitute.

Appetizers and drinks are very rarely served before a meal. Also, when guests are present at a meal, men and women will dine apart. Do not expect a special seat, even if you are the guest of honor.

Algerians are complimented when a guest leaves a little food on his/her plate, as this is a sign of the host's ability to more than adequately provide for his guests.

Normally, guests do not leave immediately after dinner. They usually remain up to two hours after the meal.

SOCIAL VALUES, CUSTOMS AND TIPS

Algeria is not only the largest country in the Maghreb (Algeria, Morocco and Tunisia), but it is also the most conservative. The population is almost entirely Muslim. The three main languages are Arabic (the official language), French (the language of the administrative and intellectual elite) and Berber. People often mix these languages when speaking.

Algerians are formal and traditional. They are also quite expressive and individualistic. Expressiveness, courtesy, individualism and formality are all key attributes of the Algerian character.

The society is male dominated and sex roles are clearly defined. Only about ten percent of the labor force is female. Nevertheless, some women do fill important positions in public and private professions.

One should not discuss a person's family or members of the opposite sex unless the host suggests this topic. Algerians will appreciate comments on the beauties of the country or the quality of the food. Algerians will also appreciate hearing interesting stories about life in your country. Considerable time is usually spent discussing weather, health or the latest news. Soccer is a favorite sport in Algeria; discussing it is a good way of starting a conversation.

Avoid bringing up anything that has to do with France since most Algerians are sensitive about their colonial past. Also avoid mentioning religion or any Middle East situation.

Because Algeria is predominantly Muslim, remember to use only the right hand to touch food or people or to pass objects. The left hand is reserved for personal hygiene. The right hand or both hands together may be used when passing or receiving objects.

In Algiers, there are a lot of French-style cafés. Women may go into these cafés either alone or with friends. In other towns in Algeria, however, women should not go into cafés, even with friends.

While western-style clothing is common, especially in urban areas, traditional North African Muslim clothing is also prominent. In public, it is proper for all to dress conservatively and modestly. For casual dress in public, women should not wear jeans, shorts or slacks. Instead, it is advisable for them to wear skirts and tops with sleeves. In some areas, women are veiled. Also, men should not wear shorts.

Men and women are separated at public and private gatherings. Women should never go to the beach or to sporting events alone. Even if a woman is escorted to a sporting event, she may feel conspicuous since Algerian women are rarely in attendance.

Women should be aware that young men often verbally harass Algerian women. As a foreigner, a woman can deal with similar harassment by saying, *Sib-nee fi-hah-lee*, which means "Leave me alone." Women are less likely to encounter harassment away from the main tourist areas. In such places, however, women are more likely not to be treated as equals.

Bargaining is acceptable and even expected everywhere except in grocery stores.

Ask for permission before photographing people. Many Algerians are very sensitive about having their pictures taken. Also be aware that there are certain areas (such as defense zones) where taking pictures is forbidden.

If you are in Algeria during the Muslim holiday of Ramadan, you should know that many restaurants remain open for non-Muslims even though Muslims are fasting. During this holiday, however, you may want to avoid eating in public since this might offend others.

It is acceptable for non-Muslims to visit mosques, but not during prayer time or during Ramadan.

Using the fingers to point at objects or people is considered impolite. Also, care is usually taken not to let the sole of the foot point toward another person.

ARGENTINA

Population: 36,265,463 (July 1998 est.); white 85%, mestizo, Amerindian or other non-white groups 15%

Languages: Spanish (official), English, Italian, German, French

Religions: Roman Catholic 90% (less than 20% practicing), Protestant 2%, Jewish 2%, other 6%

Currency: nuevo peso argentino

Buenos Aires

HISTORICAL OVERVIEW

- Before the Spanish colonized Argentina in the 1500s, the country was populated by various indigenous groups. Colonization first started slowly, as it was met by strong local resistance. The momentum of colonization increased late in the 1700s, however.

- Argentina was first part of the Viceroyalty of Peru, and then in 1776 Buenos Aires was made the capital of the Viceroyalty of the Río de la Plata, including Uruguay and Paraguay.

- A revolt, which started in 1810, resulted in a declaration of independence from Spain in 1816. The declaration became reality under the leadership of José de San Martin, who marched an army across the Andes to free Chile. He also led his forces to capture the city of Lima, the first step in the liberation of Peru. When San Martin later returned to Argentina, he found a country divided in a conflict raging between the central government and the provinces regarding how Argentina should be governed. These internal conflicts lasted for years. Modern Argentina was not unified until 1862.

- Industrialization and economic prosperity came to Argentina in the latter half of the 19th century, largely due to British investment. Argentina became a major exporter of agricultural products to Europe. Labor unions also formed during this period, and these unions began to challenge the historic domination of the ruling elite. In 1912, the unions were successful in bringing about a democratization of the electoral laws.

- In 1916, the new laws paved the way for a Radical Party (RP) victory over the large landowners and industrialists. The RP ruled for 15 years, but its programs fell short of expectations, and in 1930, power was restored to the conservatives.

- A group of pseudo-fascist army officers seized power in 1943, but they were disorganized, and political confusion ensued. Out of the turmoil emerged Colonel Juan Domingo Perón. With the support of the labor unions he, along with his glamorous wife Maria Eva Duarte, who became popularly known as "Evita," united the country and implemented significant social reforms.

- Gradually, however, economic problems began to mount. In 1955, a military insurrection ended Perón's rule. The military then ruled until 1973 (an 18-year period during which Argentina often bordered on anarchy), when Perón returned to power in a landslide victory. Upon regaining power, he immediately began a program of leftist foreign policy and conservative domestic policy. He died in 1974, however, and was succeeded by his second wife, Isabel. She was ousted in a 1976 military coup. The military then conducted a seven-year-long "Dirty War" in which many civilians lost their lives or disappeared.

- The military temporarily restored the economy, but by 1982, the country was gripped by a recession. To deflect attention and increase its popularity, the military seized the Malvinas (Falkland Islands) in April. The British, who also claimed the islands, defeated the Argentine army. In 1983, with the military having lost its credibility, democratic elections were held in which the Radical Civil Union was victorious. The economic picture worsened, and in 1988 the Peronista Movement nominated Carlos Saúl Menem for president. Menem won in 1989 and, once in office, he began a program of privatization that helped turn the economy around.

- Despite having lost support because of some austere economic measures, Menem was re-elected in 1995. In 1996 he faced continued labor unrest and strikes.

- Foreign competition is very strong in Argentina. U.S. superstores are opening throughout the country, and foreign investors, such as France and the Netherlands, have proven to be shrewd competitors.

- Menem has worked to change the former Peronista focus on labor unions to the issue of productivity. By 1997 real GDP had grown by nine percent. Unemployment, although still high, had dropped from previous years.

BUSINESS PRACTICES

Hours of Business

Although most businesses are open from 9:00 a.m. to 7:00 p.m., some government offices are open only in the morning while others are open only in the afternoon. Be sure to check the hours of the office you wish to visit.

Be prepared for the business day to extend until 10:00 p.m.

Avoid the two weeks before and after Christmas and Easter for a business trip. In addition, be aware that the summer vacation period is January to March.

Dress

Conservative business clothing is appropriate, although dress may vary from region to region.

Introductions

When introduced, men shake hands with other men. If men and women are introduced by a woman friend, they sometimes kiss, but usually they shake hands. Women usually kiss other women on the cheek when they're introduced.

When greeting, close male friends hug one another in an *abrazo* (a brief hug). This may include a few hearty pats on the back.

Female friends shake hands with both hands and kiss one another on both cheeks. Male and female friends usually kiss.

Use titles with last names, as they are considered important. Examples are "Doctor," "Professor," "Architect," "Lawyer" or "Engineer."

At large parties, introduce yourself. At small parties, you will be introduced by the host or hostess. Shake hands and say "Good-bye" to each person when you leave.

Meetings

Always make appointments well in advance. Appointments, however, may not be kept as scheduled.

Appointments may begin around 9:30 a.m., but do not be surprised if your counterpart arrives late. Allow extra time before the next appointment.

An Argentine may be quite willing to meet with you in his office as late as 7:00 or 8:00 p.m.

Most business is done face-to-face, rather than over the telephone.

Have your business cards and documents translated into Spanish.

You will generally be offered espresso or tea at a business meeting.

Do not expect to complete your business in a single meeting. It is important to have patience.

Negotiating

Contacts are extremely important when dealing with both government and private business.

During the negotiation process, both formal and informal approaches are used. The formal approach is primary and may give way to the informal as the negotiations progress. Of primary importance are presentation style and posturing, mutual positive regard and, ultimately, trust.

Interpersonal trust is absolutely fundamental. It precedes business matters and can override such tangibles as pricing, delivery and quality of goods and services.

Argentine negotiators prefer to negotiate with people they trust. Frequent or many changes in the composition of the negotiating teams will probably cause delays. Showing a strong interest in Argentine culture will be appreciated.

Flexibility and patience are very important. Firm schedules and fixed agendas are not likely to be followed. Foreigners, however, are expected to be punctual.

Argentines value the process of negotiating as well as the results. They have a high-context approach to negotiating and respond to both verbal and nonverbal cues.

Discussions can be very heated and emotional. Your counterpart expects to be treated as a business equal and will not take kindly to being treated otherwise.

Negotiations are seen as serious and challenging bargaining sessions in which it is usually expected that the parties will insist on their positions. Concessions may thus be made at a slower pace than in other cultures and negotiations may last longer.

Lively discussions are also seen as part of the process of establishing relations.

Argentine negotiators are selected on the basis of their demonstrated work and speaking skills, social class, education, charisma and connections.

Relations within teams, among its various members, may be intricate and complex.

Compatibility of styles may be more pivotal than objective issues.

Your negotiating counterpart will most likely focus on the larger picture of the project involved, and relegate future details to subordinates.

Persuasive arguments are based on common sense and may be laced with much fervor.

Risk is generally avoided. Even projects that might succeed but are seen as potential threats to a person's prestige or power may be avoided.

The negotiating team may include the actual decision makers, or it may serve an entirely intermediary or utilitarian role. The final important decisions may be made by higher-level executives or by a sole decision maker the team is reporting to. Nevertheless, it is important to maintain a positive regard for and position with regards to the actual negotiating team.

Entertaining

Women should avoid giving gifts to male colleagues as even the most innocuous present might be misconstrued as a personal overture. Gifts for children from both men and women are welcomed.

Business gifts should not be given until a friendly relationship has been established. If you plan a return visit, ask your colleague if he/she would like you to bring something in particular from your home country.

Avoid giving 13 of anything (considered bad luck), anything in black or purple (a reminder of the solemn Lent season), knives of any kind (which cut off a relationship) or handkerchiefs (associated with tears).

Business lunches are important, although more for introductory purposes than for getting business accomplished. Argentines do not generally transact business during a meal.

Argentines keep late hours and do not conduct business early in the morning.

Dinner is served about 10:00 p.m., later on weekends.

Argentines will rarely invite you to their homes unless you are a relative or a very close friend. If invited to a meal in a home, men should wear jackets and ties and women a skirt and blouse or a dress. Men and women should wear nice casual clothes to an *asado* (an outdoor barbecue).

If you are invited to dinner in a city, drinks may be served in the living room before dinner. In rural areas, guests generally go directly to the meal.

Do not admire a possession of your host to excess as he or she may insist on giving it to you and you will have to accept.

Expect meals to last a relatively long time.

Formal wear for men is a tuxedo and, for women, mid-calf dresses. Formal wear is for special events, such as an opera, theater opening or political inauguration.

Dinner guests should bring a small gift, such as flowers, candy or pastries. Bird of Paradise flowers are considered particularly elegant. Do not bring wine, as it is readily available, but you may bring French champagne or a bottle of high-quality Scotch.

When dining in a formal restaurant, men should wear a jacket and tie and women should wear a dress or a skirt and blouse.

Argentines use the continental style of eating, with the knife in the right hand and the fork in the left.

Hands, but not elbows, should always be above the table, not in the lap.

Using a toothpick in public is considered bad manners. So is blowing one's nose or clearing one's throat at the table.

Restaurant waiters are summoned by raising the hand with the index finger extended. Tipping is not required, but is becoming customary in many restaurants.

Among the national dishes are *churrasco* (a thick grilled steak) and *parrilada mixta* (a mixed grill). *Arroz con pollo* (chicken with rice), *puchero de gallina* (chicken, sausage, corn, potatoes and squash, all cooked together), *milanesa* (breaded and fried beef or chicken), *empanada* (a meat pie) and pasta dishes are other popular items. Argentina's national drink is *maté*, a tea made from the young leaves of an evergreen tree.

It is not appropriate to include an Argentine wife in an invitation to a meal in a restaurant unless you have met her.

To show that you have finished eating, place your knife and fork on the plate, crossed, with the tines of the fork facing down.

SOCIAL VALUES, CUSTOMS AND TIPS

Argentines pride themselves on their European heritage (mainly Italian, British, Spanish and German). You may notice a tendency to look down on the indigenous peoples.

Spanish is the official language. Italian and German are spoken as second and third languages. Argentine Spanish contains many distinct phrases, idioms and terms not used in other Spanish-speaking countries.

When talking to one another, Argentines generally stand closer together than do Europeans or North Americans. Additionally, an Argentine man may touch the arm, shoulder or lapel of a man with whom he is speaking.

Argentines are generally conscious of fashion. They like to keep up with fashion trends, especially those from Europe.

Women may be asked personal questions, such as "Do you have children?" As a follow-up, "Why not?" would not be an unusual next question.

Do not take offense if someone makes critical comments about someone's physical appearance in front of others (such as, "Are you going to lose weight?"). It is considered friendly banter and not meant as an insult.

A head tap generally means "I am thinking" or "Think."

Never discuss politics or government when first meeting someone. Passions run high about Argentina's recent past, especially the Perón years. After you have known someone for a while you may be asked your opinion of Argentine politics. Before arrival, read up on Argentine history, especially recent history and current events. Be aware that Argentines use and prefer the Argentine name Malvinas to refer to the Falkland Islands.

Among good topics of conversation are sports (especially soccer), opera, culture, home and children. Avoid personal conversation unless it is initiated by your Argentine counterpart.

Although Argentine women do not work outside the home in great numbers (about 30 percent), foreign businesswomen should not experience problems as long as they are professional in manner.

It is improper for a man and a woman to show affection in public.

Avoid yawning without covering the mouth. Placing one's hands on the hips is considered rude.

Eating when on a street or on public transportation is considered inappropriate.

Hats should be removed in buildings, houses, elevators and in the presence of women.

Argentines consider eye contact important during conversation.

It is customary to show respect to the elderly and to women, following the traditions of Spain and Italy.

Men frequently cross their legs knee-over-knee. Women do not.

There is a strong Italian heritage in Argentina. You may notice many gestures similar to those commonly observed in that country.

AUSTRALIA

Population: 18,613,087 (July 1998 est.); Caucasian 92%, Asian 7%, Aboriginal and other 1%

Languages: English (official), native languages

Religions: Anglican 26.1%, Roman Catholic 26%, other Christian 24.3%, non-Christian 11%

Currency: Australian dollar

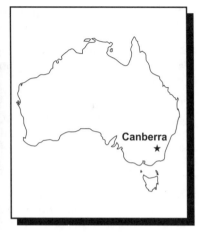

HISTORICAL OVERVIEW

- Aboriginal peoples have inhabited Australia for at least 40,000 years. The Dutch were the first to land in Australia in 1616. They explored the continent until 1644 when it was named New Holland.

- The British appeared in 1668, and in 1770, Captain James Cook took formal possession of the country for Britain. Small settlements were established and immediately, starting in 1788, the British founded penal colonies, mainly in present-day Sydney, Hobart and Brisbane. As a result, many of the early settlers of Australia were prisoners or soldiers.

- Free settlements were then established in Melbourne, Adelaide and Perth. The number of people immigrating to Australia increased rapidly after copper and then gold were discovered in 1842 and 1851, respectively. The successful breeding of sheep, which created an export product (wool) for Australia, also caused the economy to grow but caused the displacement of many Aborigines.

- In 1868, the transportation of convicts to Australia was ended, and convicts were declared free. By that time, six colonies had been established, each with some measure of self-rule: New South Wales (N.S.W.), Tasmania, Western Australia, South Australia, Victoria and Queensland. While the colonies shared a common language (English) and common customs, each one developed differently according to different local laws.

- In 1901, the six colonies became states, when they agreed to join together as the Federal Commonwealth of Australia with Canberra as its capital. A constitutional government was created in which powers were split between the central government and the states. Western Australia's attempts to secede from the Commonwealth in the 1930s failed. Complete autonomy from Great Britain was officially established in 1942 by the passage of the Statute of Westminster Adoption Act.

- Although Australia fought alongside Britain in World War I, during World War II a distancing between the two nations took place, and Australia developed closer ties with the U.S. Since World War II, Australia has been active in global politics.

- After the war, a substantial number of immigrants came to Australia, but due to discriminatory policies most were Caucasian. In 1966, immigration laws were changed, yet in the 1970s the overall immigration rate was reduced.

- Between 1949 and 1972, the country was governed by a coalition of the Liberal Party and the Country Party, which for 17 years was under the leadership of the colorful Sir Robert Menzies. The Labor Party returned to power in 1972, but the economy did badly under its leadership, and the Liberal Party took control again in 1975 and ruled until 1983. In that year, Labor won the election and remained in power until 1996, when a coalition of the Liberal Party and the National Party won a landslide victory giving them a wide margin in Parliament.

- In the latter half of the 20th century, Australia assumed a leadership position in Asian and Pacific affairs. Domestically, the Aboriginal movement grew from the 1960s onward, and the Aborigines were successful in gaining rights to some tribal lands. There was a shift from assimilationist policies to educating the Aborigines in their own culture. Environmental activism also became important on the Australian political scene.

- Severe forest fires ravaged Eastern Australia during the winter of 1997-98.

- In April 1998, Australia was affected by a large-scale strike of dock workers. The National Maritime Union of Australia held a sympathetic strike and soon Japanese dock workers were tying up traffic along the Asian-Pacific coastlines by refusing to deal with non-union staffed Australian ships.

BUSINESS PRACTICES

Hours of Business

The workweek is Monday to Friday 9:00 a.m. to 5:00 p.m. and Saturday 9:00 a.m. to 12:00 p.m.

Dress

Customary business dress is similar to that worn in North America and the United Kingdom. A suit is necessary for both men and women in Sydney, Perth and Melbourne. In Brisbane, dress is generally more casual. A lightweight suit is appropriate for visitors at a first meeting. Thereafter, men may wear a shirt, tie and shorts.

Introductions

People shake hands upon introduction as well as at the beginning and end of meetings. The handshake should be firm and friendly.

When addressing business colleagues, even senior managers, the business title is generally not used.

First names are widely and quickly used in Australia. It is wise, however, to wait to use first names until invited to do so. Many visitors have found themselves surprised by the speed with which Australians adopt the first name as the way of addressing their visitors. This should not be mistaken as a sign of real friendship – it only indicates a friendly informality. Australians are generally quite informal. Avoid being too stiff or overly courteous.

As a member of the Commonwealth, Australia has its share of British titles and honors. As is the case in the United Kingdom, holders of such titles in Australia may or may not use them. In case of doubt, the general term "Sir" may be used to formally address anyone with respect.

Use business cards when being introduced to business associates.

Meetings

Punctuality is highly regarded. Appointments are necessary. Preferably, they should be made one month in advance. Always arrive on time for an appointment, and handle correspondence as promptly as possible.

Meetings are usually easy to schedule with anyone, at all business levels.

Negotiating

Australians are motivated to work hard by affiliation and quality of life. This may contrast markedly with other countries where status and money are viewed as key incentives.

Because of the great distances within the country, it is important to have contacts in Australia. There is an Australian version of the "Old Boy" network among senior industrial executives, and it is helpful to have connections with and introductions from one of these key individuals.

At meetings, preliminary exchanges (on sports, cultural events, Australian sights, etc.) should be brief. Business is attended to fairly immediately.

Presentations should be complete and not conceal any possible problems that may arise.

Communication is very direct. Critiques and directly expressed opinions should not be taken personally, but responded to with confidence and good humor.

Negotiations should not be overly extended but kept to a reasonable amount of time as Australians do not like to negotiate for very lengthy periods of time.

Any attempts at manipulation would be poorly regarded and could cause a breakdown in negotiations.

Price haggling is common. Once a contract is drawn up, however, it should be adhered to faithfully. Australian commercial law is very thorough and detailed.

Because of Australia's geographical isolation, Australian businesspeople are well traveled. You can expect them to have a thorough knowledge of your country of origin and its business practices. Knowing something about Australian history and culture is always appreciated.

The vast majority of Australians speak English only. Visitors who have difficulty with English will find interpreters easy to engage, but hosts do not routinely provide this service.

Australians are, first and foremost, pragmatic. Time is viewed as a precious commodity, not to be wasted. Delays are viewed as ineffi-cient.

Decision making in Australia tends to be concentrated at the top echelons of a company. Sometimes the need to get approval from those in higher positions cause delays. It is counter-productive to pressure public officials or employees for responses faster than they can be generated through normal channels.

Informality reigns in matters of etiquette. People are seated in random fashion and there is generally no special seat of honor. Seniors in company status may be treated with gestures of respect, but such a display of respect is a formality only. Australians do not practice deference. They have a deeply ingrained sense of equality.

Entertaining

Business is often conducted over drinks. Buy only when it is your turn, as it is considered rude to buy out of order. It is advisable not to mention your business dealings until your Australian counterparts initiate that part of the conversation.

Once a social relationship has been established, a businessperson may invite his/her contact to lunch.

Dinner is usually served around 6:00 p.m. It is appropriate to arrive half an hour early or to be on time. Arriving late is considered rude. Guests sometimes bring flowers or wine, but no other gifts. A "Thank you" upon leaving is all that is expected.

More formal evening entertaining is in order when a visitor is meeting with upper managers or once a business relationship has been established.

Formal occasions are likely to take place in a club. Clubs are often formed around athletic events, but may also be oriented toward profession or social class.

Invitations to an Australian's home are not common and should be considered special. Since this kind of entertaining could be formal or informal, it is best to ask the host about appropriate dress. Often such visits will center around a casual outdoor barbecue and will include all family members. On such occasions a modest gift for the host's home would be unexpected but appreciated. Otherwise, the practice of giving gifts is unwelcome in Australia; it might even be considered taboo.

The business visitor should not propose entertainment events over the weekend period. Australians like to keep their weekends free.

The main meal of the day is eaten in the evening. It is usually called dinner, but may be called tea if it is a smaller meal.

Table manners are European, but viewed informally and flexibly. While it is considered proper to hold the fork in the left hand while eating, it is not considered to be the only way.

Indicate that you have finished eating by laying your knife and fork parallel on your plate.

At a restaurant, use a simple hand gesture to get the waiter's attention.

Beer is the most popular national drink.

SOCIAL VALUES, CUSTOMS AND TIPS

Australians have a frank and direct manner.

There are many words and phrases unique to Australian English.

It is best to avoid making comparisons between the United States and Australia or between Great Britain and Australia.

Unsolicited advice or comments are not appreciated, as is any affectation or "airs." Australians are suspicious of pretension and status-conscious behavior, and they are critical of affectation.

Men are fairly quick to call another man "mate" if they take a liking to him.

Australians have a healthy sense of humor. Barbs may be directed at a visitor in a good-natured way. The international visitor should not take such teasing to heart, but in a self-confident manner and with a friendly demeanor. He or she should reply with good humor. Australians also frequently use humor when they are under stress.

Australians enjoy controversy and love to discuss subjects about which they disagree. Fairness is an important principle in Australian life.

Australians do not give praise easily. When they do, it is often done in a sarcastic, joking manner.

With regard to manner, Melbournians are slightly more conservative than their peers elsewhere in the country.

While Australians may at times use strong language, they do not appreciate it when an international visitor does likewise.

Winking at women is considered inappropriate, as are public displays of affection. When yawning, you should cover your mouth and then excuse yourself.

The "thumbs up" gesture is considered rude in Australia.

Sports are very important to most Australians. Among the most popular are Australian football, soccer, rugby, cricket, basketball, cycling, hiking (or bush walking) and tennis. Good sportsmanship is considered very important.

AUSTRIA

Population: 8,133,611 (July 1998 est.); German 99.4%, Croatian 0.3%, Slovene 0.2%, other 0.1%

Languages: German

Religions: Roman Catholic 78%, Protestant 5%, other 17%

Currency: schilling, euro

HISTORICAL OVERVIEW

- Austria was invaded in 400 B.C. by the Celts who, in turn, lost the region to the Romans between 200 and 15 B.C. The country became Romanized and prospered. When the Roman Empire began to crumble, Austria became vulnerable to invasions by Germanic Hun and other tribes. By the sixth century the Slavic Avars and the Germanic Bavarians had settled the region. The Frankish King Charlemagne conquered the area in 799, destroying the Avars and leaving the area fully Germanic and Christianized.

- Otto I, who later became Emperor of the Holy Roman Empire, began his rule of Austria in 955 and is often considered to be the real founder of the country because of the borders he established. In 962, Austria became a part of the Holy Roman Empire.

- In 1156, Austria became an autonomous territory under the control of an aristocratic family, the Babenburgs. Vienna was its capital. In 1278, the Hapsburg dynasty came to power when Rudolf IV of Hapsburg defeated the duke of Aurma. This initiated the 600-year rule of Austria. The Habsburgs reached the height of their power in the 19th century when they helped defeat Napoleon. After the Napoleonic Wars the Holy Roman Empire was dissolved and the Austrian Empire was created.

- Austria was, however, unable to deal with the many ethnic minorities within its borders. At the same time Prussia was growing in power. After losing a war in 1866, Austria was forced to split its empire, resulting in the formation of the Austro-Hungarian Empire. By 1914, the empire covered present-day Austria, Hungary, the Czech Republic, Slovakia, Slovenia, Croatia, Bosnia-Herzegovina and parts of Poland and Romania.

- In 1914, Archduke Franz Ferdinand of Austria was assassinated by a Serbian revolting against Austrian rule. This event quickly developed into World War I as the European powers became involved. The war led to the dissolution of the Austro-Hungarian Empire, as the new countries of Yugoslavia and Czechoslovakia (which have since further divided) were created from parts of the old empire.

- The first Austrian republic was established in 1918 and lasted until 1938 when Hitler annexed the country. After World War II, Austria was divided into four zones, each of which was governed by one of the four allied powers (Great Britain, France, the U.S. and the Soviet Union).

- Austria became an independent democratic republic in 1955 when allied forces withdrew on the condition that Austria declare itself permanently neutral. Since 1955, the country has been economically and socially stable. In addition, Vienna has developed into an important United Nations city. Vienna and its International Center are the headquarters of the Organization of the Petroleum Exporting Companies (OPEC), the International Atomic Energy Agency, the UN Industrial Development Organization (UNIDO) and the UN Relief and Works Agency (UNRWA). There has been a sharp increase in immigrants to Austria in the 1990s and a simultaneous rise in right-wing nationalist positions in politics.

- In 1989, Hungary tore down the barbed wire fence along the Austrian-Hungarian border because of the economic ties between the two countries and the great numbers of people forcing their way out of Eastern Europe. This act has been recognized as a key event in pushing Eastern Europe toward political reform. Once the fence was down, a stream of people began emigrating from Eastern Europe to the West.

- In 1990, Austria applied for membership to the EU and revoked its own neutrality. It was inducted into the EU on 1 January 1995.

- In July 1998 Austrian President Thomas Klestil began his six-month term as President of the European Union.

BUSINESS PRACTICES

Hours of Business

Large stores are open from 8:00 a.m. to 6:00 p.m. on weekdays and from 8:00 a.m. to noon on Saturdays. Large chain stores remain open on Saturdays until evening. An increasing number of stores are open on Sunday.

Small, private shops might still close for the traditional *Mittagspause* (midday break), the two- or three-hour break for the main meal, which was once the rule rather than the exception.

Banks close at 4:30 p.m. daily.

Most family vacations are taken in August. Small family-owned shops might be closed the entire month while the family is away.

Dress

It is important to dress properly for all events. Austrians generally dress fashionably, both at work and at social events.

Men should wear dark conservative business suits. Women should wear business suits or dresses.

Introductions

Austrians shake hands when greeting and parting. Even children shake hands with adults when greeting, as this is an important social courtesy.

In Vienna, a man may kiss the hand of a woman when introduced to her.

Common greetings include *Grüß Gott* (pronounced "gruess got," May God greet you), *Guten Morgen* (good morning), *Guten Tag* (good day) and *Guten Abend* (good evening).

Austrians do not ask *Wie geht es Ihnen*? (pronounced "Vee gate ess eenen," How are you?) unless they wish to hear a detailed account.

Professional titles – such as *Rechtsanwalt* (lawyer), *Magister* (indicating possession of a Masters degree), *Doktor* or *Diplom Ingeneur* (engineer) – are important among adults, and are used whenever known. Otherwise, titles such as *Herr* (Mr.), *Fräulein* (Miss) and *Frau* (Mrs. or Ms.) are combined with family names when addressing acquaintances and strangers. Close friends and young people use first names.

Present business cards to everyone you meet in your counterpart's office when introduced.

Meetings

Always be punctual. Your Austrian counterpart will allow a grace period of 10 to 15 minutes before finding tardiness rude.

Schedule all meetings well in advance. Confirm them in writing as soon as possible after arranging them.

Business cards should be exchanged, and one should be given to the secretary of the person you are meeting. If the person has more than one title listed on his/her business card, ask which one is the most appropriate to use.

Negotiating

Expect very little small talk at the beginning of a meeting. Business will begin shortly after all involved have gathered.

Be patient. Austrian businesspeople pay close attention to detail, and these details play a role in their decision making.

If your Austrian counterparts extend an invitation to lunch during negotiations, you should do the same before leaving Austria.

Bring copies of all your documents for all participants. Make sure that presentations, contracts and other documents are thorough and comprehensive. After negotiating meetings, confirm all requests in writing.

Be aware that a promise or a contract is sacred to Austrians and must always be carried out.

Entertaining

Although Austrians enjoy entertaining in their home and having guests, it is impolite to drop by unannounced.

Punctuality is important. Invited guests should arrive on time.

Men stand when a woman enters the room or when talking to a woman who is standing.

Invited guests bring flowers, candy or a small gift (such as a hand-crafted item or something appropriate for the occasion).

Gifts are given to the wife, or perhaps the children, but not the husband – even if the gift is for the family.

Flowers are given only in odd numbers (even numbers are bad luck), and they are unwrapped in the presence of the hostess. Red roses are only given as a sign of romantic love. Giving purchased flowers is more polite than giving flowers from one's own garden.

Customarily, guests remove their shoes when entering a home. In homes where the hosts expect guests to remove shoes, guest slippers are usually visible near the door.

To show courtesy to the hosts, guests should not ask to use the telephone (all calls are billed, even local ones, and the cost is high). Offer to help make preparations only when well acquainted with the host or if the hostess seems not to have everything under control.

The hostess will almost always offer second helpings, but a polite *Danke, nein* (Thank you, no.) is gracefully accepted.

Most Austrians prefer to entertain in the home, but they also socialize in restaurants and other public places, especially in large cities.

For many people, especially those residing in small villages, it is a custom on Sunday after church service for the women to go home and fix dinner while the men go to a *Gasthaus* (pub) to do business, exchange ideas and drink. This socializing is less about drinking and much more about networking and socializing with male friends.

Do not gesture with utensils or put your elbows on the table while eating, but keep hands above the table.

Austrians eat in the continental style, with the fork in the left hand and the knife remaining in the right.

The bill is paid at the table to the server, and a service charge is usually included. Most people round the bill up to the nearest schilling as a tip.

Austrian cuisine is drawn from various cultures that once comprised the Austro-Hungarian Empire.

Specialties vary by region, but include such favorites as *Wienerschnitzel* (breaded veal cutlet), *Sachertorte* (a rich chocolate cake with apricot jam and chocolate icing), *Knödel* (moist potato dumplings) and *Goulasch*.

A typical day begins early with a light breakfast of coffee or hot chocolate, rolls, bread and jam or marmalade. Later in the morning, some eat a second, heartier breakfast including *Goulasch* or hot sausages.

The main meal, especially if eaten in the evening, may include soup, meat (often pork) with potatoes or pasta, vegetables, a salad and often dessert (such as a homemade pastry). If it is eaten at midday, it may consist of cold cuts, eggs, cheese, rye bread and other breads and a salad. In this instance, families have *Abendbrot* (evening bread) in the evening.

Jause (afternoon tea) may include sandwiches, pastries and coffee.

SOCIAL VALUES, CUSTOMS AND TIPS

The official language is High German, but each area has its own dialect.

English is a required language in high schools and is spoken by many people.

Austrians are known for their *Gemütlichkeit*, a relaxed and happy approach to life. A good-natured sense of frustration and bittersweet attitude toward reality are considered unique national traits.

Austrians are not Germans and should not be referred to as such. It can be considered an insult. While Austrians and Germans speak the same basic language (with important differences in dialect), they have a different historical and political heritage. They also differ in customs, values and attitudes.

Austrians are generally more religious than people in many other Western European countries.

Cultural arts play a key role in Austrian society.

Austrians celebrate New Year's Day, *Heilige Drei Könige* (Three Kings, January 6), Easter (Saturday-Monday), Labor Day (May 1), Flag Day (October 26; this is the national holiday), All Saints Day (November 1) and Christmas (December 25-26), as well as various other holidays throughout the year.

Austrians love the outdoors. *Ein Spaziergang* (taking a walk) is a national pastime.

Most families own at least one car since it is important for daily transportation. The public trains, buses and streetcars are also heavily used, especially in large urban areas. Buses reach even the most remote areas, and a good system of trains crisscrosses the country.

On the expressway, there is a speed limit of 80 miles per hour (130 km per hour). Seat belt laws are strictly enforced. Children under age 12 must ride in the back seat.

Hand gestures are used conservatively in polite company, as verbal communication is preferred.

It is impolite for adults to chew gum in public.

Motioning with the entire hand is more polite than using the index finger.

Tapping one's forehead or temple with one's index finger is considered an insult, because it is used to indicate that someone or something is crazy.

Yawns and coughs are covered when they cannot be avoided.

AZERBAIJAN

Population: 7,855,576 (July 1998 est.); Azeri 90%, Dagestani peoples 3.2%, Russian 2.5%, Armenian 2.3%, other 2%

Languages: Azeri 89%, Russian 3%, Armenian 2%, other 6%

Religions: Muslim 93.4%, Russian Orthodox 2.5%, Armenian Orthodox 2.3 %, other 1.8%

Currency: manat

HISTORICAL OVERVIEW

- The country of Azerbaijan is adjacent to the Iranian region of Azerbaijan, and their ethnic origins are the same.

- In the first century B.C. present-day Azerbaijan was composed of two countries, Atrapatakan and Caucasian Albania (unrelated to present-day Albania). Both countries had their own languages and well-developed economies.

- Beginning in the seventh century A.D., the area was dominated by Arabs who introduced Islam, which soon became the dominant religion. The Arabic language was introduced, and Arabic script was used.

- Most of the population was Persian (Iranian), but by the 11th century a heavy influx of Turkic peoples made the population heavily Turkish and the dominant language a Turkish dialect. Yet, unlike Turkish Sunni Muslims, the Azeris adopted Shi'ite Islam.

- Arabs, Turks, Mongols and Iranians each had control over the region at one time during the centuries that followed. As a result of several wars involving Russia, a 1828 treaty granted northern Azerbaijan to Russia and southern Azerbaijan to Iran. This division profoundly affected the region.

- While Azerbaijan declared itself independent from Russia in 1918, the Red Army suppressed its efforts and made Azerbaijan part of the Soviet Union. In 1922, it was joined by Georgia and Armenia to form the Transcaucasian Soviet Socialist Republic. In

1936, under Stalin's new constitution, this republic was dissolved and the Azerbaijan Soviet Socialist Republic was formed.

- The new Azerbaijani leaders favored a policy of edging out non-Azerbaijanis and replacing them with Azerbaijanis. This policy targeted Armenians among other minority populations. The Armenians who inhabited the area of Nagorno-Karabakh agitated for administrative unification with Armenia. The Armenian Republic supported the move, while the Azerbaijanis opposed it. Civil strife broke out and lasted from 1989 to 1991.

- On 18 October 1991, the Supreme Soviet passed a law reestablishing Azerbaijan's independence. Soon thereafter, war broke out between Azerbaijan and Nagorno-Karabakh. The Azerbaijanis were unsuccessful in keeping the area. Full-scale war broke out and lasted from 1992 to 1993. In 1992, Abulfaz Elchibey was elected president. His inability to defeat the Armenians made him so unpopular that he was forced to flee, leaving a political vacuum in the capital of Baku.

- In new elections, Eidar Aliyev was elected president.

- In 1994, a last cease-fire was signed between the Armenians and Azeris. The war took a great economic and political toll on the country.

- President Aliyev was forced to put down two armed insurrections against his government in 1995.

- Iran proposed linking Caspian oil fields with the Persian Gulf by building a pipeline through Azerbaijan and Iran. This new pipeline would be economically advantageous for the Azeris, but if the deal were completed, Azerbaijan would be subject to U.S. sanctions, because of its dealings with Iran.

BUSINESS PRACTICES

Hours of Business

Offices are open weekdays from 8:00 or 9:00 a.m. to 5:00 or 6:00 p.m. Stores and shops are also open on Saturday, but they often close an hour each afternoon for dinner.

Introductions

When greeting each other, men shake hands and say *Sulh* (Peace). Women also say *Salem*, but they do not shake hands.

Female friends or relatives might hug and kiss.

Another common greeting is *Sagh ol* (Be well), which is also used when parting.

If people are acquainted, *Nejasiniz?* (How are you?) follows the greeting. It is customary to ask after the health of the other's family.

People of the same age call each other by first names.

It is common to use *Hanum* (Miss or Mrs.) or *Hala* (Aunt) after the given name of a woman, and *Ami* or *Dayi* (Uncle) after a man's given name. *Bey* (Mr.) is also used after a man's given name at social gatherings or at work. Its use was banned in 1920 when Russia invaded Azerbaijan, but it is once again becoming a preferred way to address men.

Entertaining

Eating at restaurants is not common; it is generally reserved for special occasions. When eating at a restaurant, however, the host pays the entire bill and the tip.

At meals, the fork is held in the left hand and the knife in the right.

Guests do not serve themselves. They are served by others.

Visitors, especially those who have adopted Russian customs, often take gifts, such as flowers, candy or pastries, to their hosts. A wrapped present is not opened in the presence of the giver.

Guests are often invited for a meal or for "tea," which is a mid-afternoon affair that includes pastries, fruit preserves (not jam), fruit, candy and tea. At other times, guests may be offered tea and sweets. Tea is served in *armudi stakan* (small, pear-shaped glasses).

In the summer, it is best to drink boiled or bottled water rather than tap water.

The most popular dish, *pilau*, is made of steamed rice topped with a variety of foods. *Kebab* is grilled pieces of meat or fish (lamb, chicken or sturgeon) on a stick. *Piti* is a lamb broth with potatoes and peas cooked in clay pots in the oven. *Dovga* consists of yogurt, rice and herbs and is served after the main meal at celebrations.

Popular spices in foods include cilantro, dill, mint, saffron, ginger, garlic, cinnamon and pepper. Azeris refer to their cuisine as "French Cuisine of the East."

SOCIAL VALUES, CUSTOMS AND TIPS

Men and women generally wear western clothing.

Women in urban areas do not practice the traditional roles of Muslim women. Nevertheless, it is a sign of courtesy to dress conservatively. Revealing or flashy clothing may attract unwanted attention.

It is common during social gatherings to recite poems of native poets.

It is impolite to speak loudly to one's colleagues.

Azeris recognize various Muslim holidays, the most important being the feast to end the month of Ramadan. During that month, Muslims fast from sunrise to sunset and eat only in the evenings. Forty days later, *Kurban Bairami,* the holiday of sacrifice, commemorates the pilgrimage season.

Many Azeris can speak Russian, and many of the country's publications are in Russian.

It is impolite to cross one's legs, smoke or chew gum in the presence of elders.

The right hand is used in handshakes and other interactions. It is rude to use the left hand unless the right hand is occupied.

One may point at objects but not people with the index finger. Shaking the index finger while it is vertical is used to reprimand or warn someone. The index finger is also used to attract a listener's attention.

Shoes are removed before entering mosques.

When an older person or a woman enters a room, those present stand to greet him or her.

The "thumbs up" gesture is used for "fine" or "okay." Rounding the finger to touch the thumb tip and form a circle (the traditional U.S. gesture for "okay") is an obscene gesture.

Since hospitality is part of the culture, visiting relatives or friends is popular and often occurs without prior notice.

Azeris value family over the individual, and family needs come first. Men are protective of women in the family. An Azeri man will commonly swear by his mother, the most highly valued person to him.

BAHAMAS

Population: 279,833 (July 1998 est.); African 85%, European/North American Descent 15%

Languages: English, Creole (among Haitian immigrants)

Religions: Baptist 32%, Anglican 20%, Roman Catholic 19%, Methodist 6%, Church of God 6%, other Protestant 12%, none or unknown 3%, other 2%

Currency: Bahamian dollar

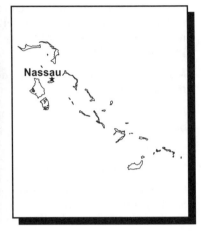

HISTORICAL OVERVIEW

• The Bahamas Islands were originally inhabited by the Lucayan Indians. The first contact with Europeans occurred in 1492, when Columbus landed at San Salvador. Since the Spanish chose to settle in Cuba and Hispaniola instead, the islands of the Bahamas remained relatively obscure until the 17th century.

• In 1648, a group of Puritans migrated from Bermuda in search of religious freedom. In 1656, the British colonized New Providence Island (the site of the present-day capital of the Bahamas). They granted the area to the six Lord Proprietors of Carolina in 1670.

• The Lord Proprietors took little interest in the islands, and the Bahamas entered a half-century of anarchy in which many took to piracy as a way of life. The first royal governor, Woodes Rogers, arrived in 1718 and remained there until his death in 1732. During that 14-year span, he followed a motto of "Pirates Expelled, Commerce Restored." After his death, illegal trade and piracy returned and flourished until the American Revolution.

• During the American Revolution, British loyalists came to the island to establish cotton plantations. The islands were prosperous for a while, but when slavery was abolished in 1834 and the soil could no longer support crops, economic depression set in.

• During the American Civil War, the islands prospered again when they became a central meeting point for blockade runners. The Bahamas received another economic boost during the Prohibition (1919 to 1933) when bootlegging became very profitable.

- During World War II, the Bahamas served as a flight training center for both the U.S. and British Royal Air Forces.

- In the postwar period, wealthy investors recognized the potential of the Bahamas as a tourist destination. Since then, tourism has played a vital role in the economic development of the Bahamas. It now accounts for about 70 percent of the gross national product.

- In 1973, the Bahamas became an independent and sovereign nation and a member of the British Commonwealth of Nations.

- After independence, illegal drug trafficking became a problem.

- Citrus groves have replaced dairy farming as the most important sector of agriculture with much of the fruit being shipped to the U.S. Other major exports are rum and salt.

- In the 1980s, the Progressive Liberal Party dominated the political scene under the leadership of Prime Minister Lynden O. Pindling. In 1992, the opposition Free National Movement prevailed in elections, resulting in the installment of Prime Minister Hubert A. Ingraham.

- In comparison to all Latin American countries, the Bahamas has the highest per capita income, which continues to grow.

BUSINESS PRACTICES

Hours of Business

Business hours are 8:30 or 9:00 a.m. to 5:00 or 5:30 p.m.

Dress

Conservative dress is required for business meetings. Men should wear suits, and women should wear suits or dresses.

Introductions

Basic pleasantries are expected when meeting. Handshakes are appropriate between two men as well as between men and women, but not usually between two women.

Surnames with the appropriate forms of address are used. Due to the large number of North Americans in the country, there is a tendency in some areas to use first names, especially among senior managers.

Bahamians are less formal than people in other Caribbean countries. Business cards are used but there are no particular formalities associated with them.

Meetings

Be on time even though your Bahamian counterpart may arrive later than the exact meeting time.

Meetings frequently take place over lunch, but rarely over dinner.

Negotiating

U.S. banks are highly visible and provide useful contacts.

Very few of the members of a business team have the power to make decisions. Much negotiating must take place within the Bahamian company itself before a deal is finalized, and only the highest-ranking individuals can make the decisions needed to finalize a deal.

Entertaining

Business entertaining is frequently done in the home. Luncheons and banquets in restaurants and hotels are also popular.

A gift, such as fruit or flowers, is appropriate for the host and his/her family.

Continental manners (the fork held in the left hand and the knife in the right) are most commonly used. Good table manners are considered a sign of "good breeding."

Conversation at the table is lengthy, and it usually covers a wide range of subjects.

SOCIAL VALUES, CUSTOMS AND TIPS

Bahamians are open and good-natured when conversing, and physical gestures and contact are common.

Religion is taken very seriously. In most cases, it may be preferable to avoid discussion of this topic.

The Bahamian tax system attracts many North American and European firms. Business practices on the islands have in turn been influenced by the presence of these companies.

There is a more stringent adherence to schedules than found in other parts of the Caribbean.

People are fashion conscious and dress in western-style clothing, jewelry and makeup.

Dress in tourist resorts is informal.

BAHRAIN

Population: 616,342 (July 1998 est.); Bahraini 63%, Asian 13%, other Arab 10%, Iranian 8%, other 6%

Languages: Arabic, English, Farsi, Urdu

Religions: Shi'a Muslim 75%, Sunni Muslim 25%

Currency: Bahraini dinar

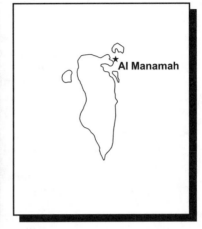

HISTORICAL OVERVIEW

- Over the centuries, Bahrain has attracted the attention of many traders and invaders. Assyrian, Persian, Greek and Roman sources all make mention of the archipelago in their records.

- In the seventh century, the country was controlled by Persians. The Abbasids conquered Bahrain in the eight century, and it remained under Arab control until 1521. In 1521, the Portuguese captured Bahrain and ruled it until 1602. After they were pushed out of the region, the islands were alternately controlled by Arab and Persian groups. In 1783, the Arab Utub tribe expelled the Persians. The Al Khalifa family (part of the Utub tribe) took control of Bahrain. This family has maintained control ever since.

- Beginning in the early 1800s, the Al Khalifa family periodically turned to Great Britain for aid against local threats. In 1816, Bahrain became a British Protected State and the ruling sheikh shared control with a British adviser. The British also established a shipping and trading outpost in Bahrain, which was to remain until 1971.

- In 1968, the British announced their intention to withdraw their military forces by 1971. That same year, Bahrain joined the states of Qatar and the Trucial States (now the United Arab Emirates), which were also under British protection, to form the Federation of Arab Emirates. The interests of Bahrain and Qatar proved to be incompatible with those of the others, however, and they withdrew from the federation.

- In 1971, Bahrain became a fully independent state headed by Emir Shaikh Issa bin Salman Al Khalifa. At the time of independence, the country signed a treaty of friendship with the United Kingdom. The Emir had been the Bahraini monarch since 1961, and he became the full sovereign leader at the time of independence.

- Territorial disputes with Iran subsided in 1970, when Iran accepted a report commissioned by the United Nations which showed that the citizens of Bahrain overwhelmingly favored complete independence over union with Iran. Nevertheless, present-day Iran still maintains a claim to Bahrain and has renewed that claim as recently as 1993.

- Bahrain is pro-western in foreign affairs and it gained international approval when it signed the Nuclear Nonproliferation Agreement in 1988. It has also become increasingly allied with Saudi Arabia, especially since the 1986 opening of the causeway linking the two countries.

- The introduction of representative democracy has begun in small steps. In 1993, a *shura* council was formed by the emir and the prime minister. It is composed of citizen members appointed by the country's leaders. While the council does not criticize the Al Khalifa government directly, it has increased democratic opportunities for the people.

- In recent years, the tension between Sunni and Shi'a Muslims has increased. Since independence, the minority Sunni have ruled the country.

- In 1994, disturbances in Shi'a areas led to many deaths and arrests. Protests and riots were led by Shi'a Muslims seeking economic and political reform. In response, security forces closed down a number of Shi'a mosques and suppressed protesters on the street who spoke out against the government. Although the protests died down by the end of 1995, a series of bombings occurred in 1996.

- Detainment of Shi'a opposition leader, Sheikh Abdul Amir Al-Jamri, increased the friction between the two groups.

- Tension between Bahrain and Qatar arose after Qatari spies were found in Bahrain in December 1996.

- As of 1998, the Bahraini government remained supportive of U.S. pressure on Saddam Hussein in Iraq.

BUSINESS PRACTICES

Hours of Business

Business is generally conducted from Saturday through Thursday. Friday is the Muslim Sabbath.

Dress

In business settings, men should wear suits. Women should wear modest dresses (nothing sleeveless).

In villages, dress is traditional. Men wear long robes and their heads are covered by a light cloth headdress kept in place by a heavy cloth ring. Women wear long black robes and many cover their hair and much of their faces. In urban areas, you will usually observe a combination of traditional and western dress.

Introductions

The most common greeting in Bahrain is *Assalam alikum* (the peace of Allah be upon you). The correct reply is *Alikum essalam*, meaning virtually the same thing.

Handshakes are common in Bahrain and may last the length of the conversation. This exemplifies friendliness, as does a hand lightly grasping the person's arm. Good friends of the same sex may kiss a number of times on both cheeks.

Women, especially those from traditional rural families, generally look down in the presence of men. Therefore, a man should not greet a woman unless the greeting is part of business protocol.

It is customary to use the title *Shaikh* (for a man) or *Shaikha* (for a woman) in front of the name of a member of the royal family. *Bin* in the middle of a name means "son of."

Formal and informal nicknames are common. Among formal nicknames, you will find *Abu*, which means "father of" when used before the given name of the oldest son, such as *Abu Mohammed* (father of Mohammed). Similarly, *Ibn* means "son of," as in *Ibn Rashid* (son of Rashid).

Do not address a Bahraini by his/her first name until he/she addresses you by your first name.

Meetings

Try to make appointments well in advance of your arrival.

Before conducting business, it is usual to spend time on greetings and light conversation.

Serious business may not even be discussed during the first couple of meetings. Coffee is generally served at business meetings, although tea or soft drinks may also be offered.

Arrive for business and social appointments on time, but do not be surprised if your host is late. Your meeting may be interrupted several times.

Religion plays a central role in Bahraini culture. Work may be interrupted at prayer times.

Business cards should be printed with English on one side and Arabic on the other. Present the card with the Arabic side facing up.

Shake hands at the beginning as well as at the end of a meeting.

Arabic is the official language of Bahrain. English is also widely used, especially for business. It is common for people in Bahrain to speak two or more languages.

Negotiating

Expect interruptions during the negotiating meetings.

If possible, the same people from your organization should begin, see through and complete the negotiating.

Bahraini businesspeople are more likely to work with you and compromise once a good personal relationship has been established.

Decisions are usually made by a single person at the top level of the company.

Entertaining

At a party, expect to be introduced to each person individually. Shake hands with each one.

Do not ask for an alcoholic drink unless it is offered.

When invited to a Bahraini home, do not bring a gift for the hostess or ask about her. You may, however, bring a small gift – such as chocolates, flowers or Arab sweets– for the host. You may also bring a gift for the children of the host.

Bahrainis like to feed their guests well, so be prepared to eat large amounts. It is polite to leave a small amount of food on your plate.

Do not invite a businessman to a meal unless he has already offered you an invitation.

Do not offer to entertain an Arab at a nightclub or a bar. Instead, suggest a hotel restaurant.

Eating with the right hand is most common; do not use the left. The left hand is associated with personal hygiene needs.

Traditionally, people eat while seated on an Arabian sofa that rests on the floor. Everyone eats out of communal dishes using their hands.

Pork is not eaten by Muslims.

Popular dishes include *beryanii* (rice with meat), *machbous* (rice, meat, tomatoes and lentils) and *saloneh* (mixed vegetables). Fish and seafood are also staples. *Halwa* (a starch pudding mixed with crushed cardamom seeds, saffron sugar and fat) is a traditional dessert. Dates are served with meals.

SOCIAL VALUES, CUSTOMS AND TIPS

Extended family ties are strong in Bahrain. The father is the ultimate authority in the home. The elderly are given respectful and loving treatment.

Bahrain's citizens receive a very good and extensive education. Bahrainis have contact with people from many foreign cultures because their country is a key trading and banking center.

Do not admire a possession of your host to excess. He/she may insist upon giving it to you.

You may see men holding loops of beads called "worry beads." They serve as tension relievers and have no religious significance.

The phrase *Insha'allah* (Allah [God] willing) is often used.

Sit so that the soles of your shoes are not showing.

Public displays of affection are frowned upon.

BELGIUM

Population: 10,174,922 (July 1998 est.); Fleming 55%, Walloon 33%, mixed and other 12%

Languages: Flemish 56%, French 32%, German 1%, legally bilingual 11%

Religions: Roman Catholic 75%, Protestant or other 25%

Currency: Belgian Franc, euro

HISTORICAL OVERVIEW

- Present-day Belgium was inhabited by Celtic and Germanic tribes when the Romans invaded in the first century B.C. The name "Belgium" comes from the name of one of the tribes, the Belgae.

- In the fifth century A.D., the area fell to the Frankish Merovingians and was subsequently ruled by the Carolingians from the eighth to the ninth century.

- After Charlemagne's death and the breakup of his empire, independent principalities developed, which roughly correspond to Belgium's provinces today. Toward the end of the 14th century, the French dukes of Burgundy began to consolidate territory and eventually gained all of what is now Belgium. In 1504 Belgium came under Spanish Hapsburg rule.

- At this time, what is present-day Belgium was part of a group of territories that included the Netherlands. Both areas were not considered countries but merely territorial possessions of the Spanish Hapsburgs. The southern, Flemish parts remained Roman Catholic while the northern Dutch Netherlands turned to Protestantism in the Reformation.

- By the end of the 16th century the northern provinces, now known as the Netherlands, had broken away and declared themselves independent. Flanders, however, continued to be ruled by the Spanish Hapsburgs and then by the Austrian Hapsburgs. Belgium was briefly reunited with the Netherlands after the Napoleonic invasions. In 1830, the territories of Belgium revolted and, in 1831, they gained independence from the Netherlands and became a constitutional monarchy. Although the territories were now politically united, they were divided based on language and culture. French was spoken in the south by people of Celtic origin, and Flemish was spoken in the north by people of Germanic origin.

- A period of economic growth ensued. Under Leopold II (1865-1909) Belgium became an imperial power with colonies in Africa. King Albert I (1909-34) introduced many social reforms. Belgium was occupied by the Germans in both World Wars. The Belgians led strong resistance movements during both wars.

- Since the 1940s, Belgium has had a strong inclination toward European cooperation and integration. It was a founding member of the North Atlantic Treaty Organization (NATO), and Brussels serves as that alliance's headquarters. Brussels is also home of the European Union headquarters and is an important business and diplomatic center both within Europe and in a global context.

- In 1960, Belgium granted independence to its African colony once called the Belgian Congo.

- Tensions between the Flemish- and French-speaking populations increased after World War II. In the 1960s attempts at reconciliation were begun, and cultural autonomy in the Flemish and Walloon regions was introduced in the 1970s. In 1993, Belgium established itself as a federal state with three autonomous regions: the primarily French Wallonia, the primarily Flemish Flanders and Brussels, of both French and Flemish origin.

- In the 1990s, a system for shared governing of mixed communities was introduced around the country.

- On 31 July 1993, King Baudouin died after 42 years on the throne and his brother Albert was proclaimed king.

- In 1997 Belgium's government deficit was four and a half percent of the Gross Domestic Product (GDP) and its public debt was 135 percent of the GDP.

BUSINESS PRACTICES

Hours of Business

Businesses are generally open from 9:00 a.m. to 6:00 p.m. with a one- or two-hour lunch break. Once a week (usually Friday), most businesses remain open until 9:00 p.m.

Bourse days are Mondays in Antwerp and Wednesdays in Brussels. This is when professionals from different firms meet to discuss new developments in their fields.

Dress

Suits are standard for both men and women in office settings. It is also common for women to wear dresses or skirts with blouses.

Men wear shoes that tie, and all shoes are kept polished.

Introductions

Belgians greet each other with a quick, light handshake. Firmer handshakes are given in some areas. When you shake hands, you should repeat your name.

If you have not been introduced to someone in the group, you should introduce yourself and shake hands.

Close friends or young people greet each other with three light kisses on the cheeks (alternating). Men who know each other well may embrace.

The phrases used for greeting depend on the region. English greetings are quite common in Brussels and some other big cities.

Last names should always be used following the title "Mr.," "Mrs." or "Miss." Only friends and relatives are greeted using first names. Professional titles are not necessary.

When leaving, Belgians usually shake hands and bid farewell to each person in the group.

Meetings

Appointments are necessary. When you write or phone to make an appointment, the Belgian firm will usually set the time. If the appointment is scheduled for 11:30 a.m., you should presume that you will be invited to lunch. You should try not to schedule afternoon appointments before 2:30 p.m.

When you arrive at an office for a business meeting, you should shake hands with everyone there including the secretaries. You should do the same when you leave.

Punctuality is expected and observed.

Do not schedule appointments for a Saturday.

Negotiating

You should be aware that the first meeting with a Belgian businessperson is primarily used for introductions as well as for getting acquainted. You should exchange business cards and answer questions about yourself.

You should bring plenty of business cards since they are widely used. Have the cards printed in English and the language in which you are doing business. Always be sure to have your counterpart's language facing him when giving him a card.

Belgians must trust you before they will have confidence in your company. You will come across as pushy if you try to do business immediately. Take cues from your counterparts.

You should avoid using the same business contact in both French and Flemish Belgium.

A strong work ethic is important to Belgians.

Give all of the facts about a product and your company and let them sell themselves. Belgians appreciate this tactic more than a persuasive sale.

Be aware that a contract is only binding in the regional area where the language of the contract is spoken.

Entertaining

Belgian businesspeople enjoy spending the evening at home with their families. Lunch dates are preferred when entertaining a Belgian businessperson. The typical business lunch lasts from 1:00 to 3:00 p.m. If you do invite a businessperson to dinner, you should be sure to include the spouse in the invitation.

Business entertaining at home has become increasingly popular in Belgium, but it is still not very common. If you are invited to a home, a small gift (flowers, candy, etc.) is appreciated. If you bring flowers, you should avoid chrysanthemums since they are associated with funerals.

When U.S. businesswomen entertain Belgian businessmen, they should make arrangements to pay in advance or they should indicate that their company is paying. Under any other conditions, a Belgian businessman will not allow a woman to pay.

Punctuality is important for social events. Arriving more than 30 minutes late is considered rude.

At a large party, you should rely on the host or hostess to introduce you to the entire group. It is not necessary to shake hands with each person.

In restaurants, cafés and bistros, one pays at the table. Usually the tip is included in the bill. If the service is especially good, you may leave an extra three to five percent. If the tip is not included, you should leave a tip of about 15 percent. In an elegant restaurant, you should tip the *somelier* (wine steward) ten percent of the wine bill if he assists you in selecting a wine.

Meals are social as well as cultural events and they are usually quite lengthy.

The continental style of eating, with the knife in the right hand and the fork in the left, is most common.

It is considered rude not to finish one's food.

Breakfast is light. It usually consists of a hot drink with rolls or bread with jam. Sometimes it is accompanied by cold cuts or cheeses. A larger meal is eaten at midday. Dinner is usually at 7:00 or 8:00 p.m.

Belgium is famous for mussels, chocolates, 300 varieties of beer, waffles and French fries (which Belgians claim to have invented).

Wine, beer or mineral water is often served with meals. While the water is generally safe, Belgians prefer bottled water. If you entertain Belgian colleagues in a restaurant, a French wine is appropriate.

If your host offers a before-dinner drink, wait for him/her to name the selection and do not ask for something other than what is offered. Aperitifs, such as vermouth or Cinzano, are usually offered rather than mixed drinks.

At a dinner in a home, the host and hostess will seat everyone. Husbands and wives are never seated together. The host and hostess usually sit at either end of the table, with the male guest of honor to the right of the hostess and the female guest of honor to the right of the host.

Wrists should be kept on the table during the meal. You should not put your hands on your lap.

When dining out, never order tea or coffee during a meal. Wait until the meal has ended.

When finished eating, place your fork and knife horizontally across the top of the plate, with the tines of the fork and the point of the knife facing left. It is impolite to cross your knife and fork.

It is recommended that you stay between a half hour to an hour once the meal has ended.

SOCIAL VALUES, CUSTOMS AND TIPS

The Walloons and the Flemish can be distinguished by their manner in personal relations. The Flemish are more reserved, while the Walloons exhibit great personal warmth. Both have a love for life and live it to the fullest, however, enjoying both hard work and good entertainment.

Belgians tend to be quite cautious with new people. Once you become acquainted, however, you will be treated with genuine warmth.

Personal privacy is important. Discussions about personal matters or the linguistic divisions in Belgium should be avoided. You may also want to avoid discussing issues relating to religion or to immigrants in Belgium. Due to some recent problems in integrating immigrants into society, the issue is quite volatile.

You should avoid confusing Belgians with the French or discussing French-Flemish rivalries.

A good topic of discussion is the Belgian cultural heritage. World-renowned artistic masters such as Brueghel, Van Eyck and Rubens came from Belgium. Van Gogh lived in Belgium for 20 years. While Flemish architecture reflects a clear Germanic influence, Wallonian architecture maintains a French flavor.

Other good conversation topics include movies, recent and popular books, theater and sports. Cycling, football (soccer) and game sports are popular (Belgium's national soccer team competed in the 1994 and 1998 World Cups). It is acceptable to discuss political topics, but you may want to avoid taking sides.

Belgians appreciate your knowledge of and curiosity about the region that you are visiting.

Belgians follow European fashion and tend to dress well in public. Tattered or extremely casual attire is usually not worn outside of the home. Men who wear hats remove them when entering a building. On Sundays, Belgians tend to dress more formally, wearing their best clothes to go walking or visiting.

It is considered rude to talk with something in your mouth (food, toothpick, gum) or with your hands in your pockets.

Good posture is important, and people do not put their feet up on tables or chairs.

Snapping fingers, pointing with the index finger, blowing your nose, scratching, yawning or using a toothpick in public are all avoided.

Men usually allow women to be seated first, enter rooms first, etc. Men usually stand when a woman enters a room.

BELIZE

Population: 230,160 (July 1998 est.); mestizo 44%, Creole 30%, Mayan 11%, Garifuna 7%, other 8%

Languages: English (official), Spanish, Mayan, Garifuna

Religions: Roman Catholic 62%, Protestant 30%, none 2%, other 6%

Currency: Belizean dollar

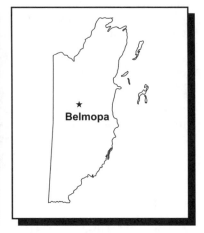

★
Belmopa

HISTORICAL OVERVIEW

- Between the third and the ninth centuries A.D., Belize was part of the Mayan Empire, which included Guatemala, Honduras, Mexico and El Salvador.

- Little is known about the period after the decline of the Mayan Empire until the arrival of the first Europeans in the 16th century.

- During the 16th century, the Spanish came to the area looking for gold, but had little interest in Belize when they did not find any there.

- In the 17th century, British pirates lived and flourished along the Belizean coast. Shortly after their arrival, British woodcutters followed, bringing slaves to help in logging the forests. Some pirates also turned to woodcutting. The mahogany trade flourished for these British, who became known as the "Baymen."

- Spain retained sovereignty over the area and Guatemala later laid claim to the region, although they never settled in the location. The Spanish repeatedly tried to expel the British settlers. In 1798, the "Baymen" fought back Spanish invaders and Belize became a colony in all but name. There followed disputes between Great Britain and Guatemala, which claimed to have inherited the Spanish claim. In 1884, Belize was made a separate crown colony.

- There were several slave revolts in the 19th century. When the old economy declined in the middle of the century, the Creole freedmen remained very poor. Elective government was introduced in 1936.

- In 1964, the British granted Belize self-government. Nevertheless, the country was called "British Honduras" until 1973.

- In 1981, through an independence movement and the support of the United Nations, Belize became a sovereign country within the Commonwealth of Nations.

- Although Belize became a sovereign nation, British troops remained in the country to protect its borders. After Guatemala relinquished its claim to Belize in a 1992 agreement, however, Great Britain announced the withdrawal of its troops in 1994.

- Belize's relationship with Guatemala has remained tenuous. Basing its campaign largely on opposition to Guatemala, the United Democratic Party took control in 1993 and continues to rule under the leadership of Prime Minister Manuel Esquivel.

- Drug trafficking from Colombia to the U.S. via Belize was a problem in the early 1990s, but this problem has abated.

- For many years, forestry and logging were the most important sectors of the economy, but because of dwindling timber supplies, sugarcane-growing has become more significant and is now the leading industry. There is also an attempt to develop tourism and to attract wealthy retirees to the country.

- Since 1996, Belize has been classified by the United States as a country that is working to combat the production and sales of illegal drugs.

- The U.S. and Great Britain are Belize's major trading partners. The country is also currently a member of the Caribbean Free Trade Association (CARIFTA) and the Caribbean Community (CARICOM).

- In July 1998, the government of Belize granted The National Development Foundation of Belize (NDFB), a non-profit organization, $4 million to promote the growth of business enterprises.

BUSINESS PRACTICES

Hours of Business

Businesses are usually open from 8:00 or 9:00 a.m. to 5:00 p.m., Monday through Friday.

Dress

Suits and ties are appropriate for businessmen and dresses are appropriate for businesswomen. Some Belizean men wear *guayaberas* (untucked cotton shirts that are sometimes embroidered).

Introductions

Men shake hands when they are introduced. Although women do not usually shake hands with other women, men and women sometimes shake hands. A man should wait for a woman to offer her hand first.

Close friends and relatives of both sexes hug each other when greeting. Older women sometimes give each other a one-armed hug and a pat on the back. Friends sometimes shake by clasping the palms and locking thumbs, by locking all fingers or just pressing fists together.

The use of titles is very important, reflecting the earlier British influence. "Doctor" is used for a Ph.D., a lawyer or a medical doctor; "Professor" is also used when appropriate. First names are usually used in informal settings.

With a group of ten or fewer, you should expect to be introduced to each person by your host. You should shake hands with each. With a larger group, you will probably be introduced to the group as a whole.

Meetings

Appointments should be made from abroad at least one week in advance.

Punctuality is expected, but may not always be practiced. The pace of life is regulated by people and events, rather than by the clock.

Negotiating

It is a good idea to have a contact in Belize to ensure success in business. The Belize Chamber of Commerce can be helpful in obtaining contacts.

Keep in mind that business decisions are made by only a few high-ranking people in any given company.

Time estimates for completing projects usually change as the project progresses. Be patient.

The building and maintenance of business relationships is essential.

Entertaining

Belizeans are very hospitable. Socializing (often unannounced) usually takes place in the home. It is considered impolite for the host not to offer refreshments or for the guest not to accept.

When invited to a meal in a home, it is appropriate to bring wine or a dessert. Although gifts are not expected, they are appreciated.

Good gifts from abroad include crystal vases or ashtrays, French perfumes and cosmetics, pocket calculators, blank videocassettes, cassettes of western-style music, Scotch or a liqueur.

It is only necessary to include the business associates with whom you are negotiating, but not their spouses and other members of the firm, when entertaining.

If you suggest dining in a restaurant, be prepared to pay for the meal. If a group informally decides to go out to lunch, each person may pay individually.

Women are not allowed to pay for men. A foreign businesswoman who wants to pay for the meal may want to entertain in her hotel restaurant so that she can make arrangements to have the meal paid for in advance by her company.

Belizeans do not dine out often. In small restaurants, you should not expect a wide variety of dishes.

For more formal occasions, men should wear dark suits and women should wear dresses. Formal clothing (e.g., tuxedos) is rarely worn.

To call the waiter, say "Miss" or "Mister" while raising your hand. Never shout loudly.

At a restaurant, it is customary to leave a ten to 15 percent tip.

For breakfast, people usually eat eggs or beans, tortillas made of corn flour and thin oatmeal made like a drink.

Lunch, served at about noon, typically consists of rice or beans (cooked with coconut milk, the national dish) with chicken, meat or fish. The evening meal, served between 6:00 and 8:00 p.m, is usually a lighter meal than lunch when it is eaten at home.

At a dinner party in the city, cocktails and appetizers are sometimes served. "Rum and Coke" is a popular before-dinner drink. Dessert and coffee are generally not served after a meal.

Seafood and fish are abundant and inexpensive. Local Belizean specialties include a number of Creole dishes: for example, conch fritters, stewed turtle, "Johnnycakes" (flour, shortening and coconut cream mixed and then baked), conch soup with okra, stewed chicken or iguana.

Other local specialties include *tamales* (chicken or pork rolled in cornmeal dough and wrapped in banana leaves or aluminum foil), *panades* (ground corn filled with fish or refried beans and then shaped into half-moons), *gornachas* (fried tortillas spread with refried beans, onions and Edam cheese) and *relleno* (a thick soup made of boiled chicken and vegetables).

The most common staple is white rice and kidney beans. Fruits (bananas, oranges, mangoes, papayas, limes, etc.) are abundant and are part of the daily diet, while vegetables are more limited and often imported.

Although cutlery is used for most dishes, a number of foods may be eaten with the hands. It is common to tear up your tortilla and pick up food with the pieces.

It is considered impolite to refuse any food or drink offered to you. Also, make an effort to finish everything on your plate.

To indicate that you are finished, push your plate forward a bit after placing the silverware on it.

If you are at a dinner party in someone's home, leave about 30 minutes to an hour after the meal if conversation is the only after-dinner activity. If your hosts expect you to stay longer, they will suggest playing games, watching a video or looking at photographs.

SOCIAL VALUES, CUSTOMS AND TIPS

English is the official language of Belize. A Belizean Creole dialect of English is widely spoken. Spanish is common in the north.

Although Belize is located in Central America, its citizens claim that the country is part of the Caribbean, as the culture is more closely linked to that of the Caribbean than to that of Central America.

One attitude, however, that some Belizean men share with their Central American neighbors is machismo (a man's habit of demonstrating or claiming his manliness through macho acts or sexually oriented language). Women in Belize generally ignore this behavior and accept it as part of everyday life.

The people of Belize take great pride in their country. It is greatly appreciated when foreigners demonstrate their knowledge of or take an interest in Belize. Compliments on the country as a whole or favorable comments regarding the specific area visited are also welcomed.

Avoid discussing politics, race and religion. Do not ask personal questions of a business associate.

People in Belize are nonconfrontational and generally fun-loving, happy and relaxed. Equality and coexistence are important concepts.

While prejudices exist in their multicultural country, they do not exist in the form of hatred.

Belizeans are generally very animated in conversation. Nonverbal communication plays a vital role; hand and facial gestures are varied and sometimes complicated.

Western-style and casual clothing are worn. Jeans and other less formal wear are acceptable for both men and women. Belizeans consider the way a person is dressed as an indication of taste and status. Provocative clothing is not acceptable. This generally means that women should avoid shorts, short skirts and revealing dresses.

It is polite to ask permission before you photograph people. Do not be surprised if some people request a fee. Also, you should not photograph airports since army troops often use them for maneuvers.

Bargaining is common in the markets, but expect to pay set prices in stores.

Women will usually not be harassed when walking alone. It is also safe for women to take taxis alone. It is unwise, however, for women to hitchhike or to walk alone after dark.

It is considered impolite not to greet even slight acquaintances or not to return a greeting, even when passing on the street. When entering places of business, it is appropriate to greet the clerk or receptionist.

When passing on the street, a simple nod of the head or a wave is acceptable for strangers, and it might be accompanied with "Hey, how?" or "Y'aright?" for acquaintances.

Staring or pointing at someone is rude. Belizeans might indicate a person or direction with the head or lips.

Sucking air through one's teeth can mean "Give me a break."

People might hiss to get someone's attention. This is considered offensive, especially by women.

BOLIVIA

Population: 7,826,352 (July 1998 est.); Quechua 30%, Aymara 25%, mestizo (Amerindian and white) 25%-30%, white 5-15%

Languages: Spanish (official), Quechua (official), Aymara (official)

Religions: Roman Catholic 95%, Protestant (Evangelical Methodist) 5%

Currency: boliviano

HISTORICAL OVERVIEW

- By the mid-15th century, the area was mostly controlled by the Aymara Indians. Although eventually brought into the Incan Empire, the Aymara retained their language.

- The Spanish began their conquest of the country in 1532. By 1538, all of Bolivia, known at that time as Upper Peru, was under their control. From the 16th to the 18th centuries, Upper Peru was one of the wealthiest and most densely populated areas of Spain's American empire.

- The Bolivian cities of Chuquisaca and La Paz were two of the first to rebel. Political uprisings occurred frequently in the 18th century, but they were always quelled.

- After a War of Independence that lasted for 16 years, the area gained independence in 1825 under the leadership of Marshal Antonio José de Sucre and Simón Bolívar, for whom the country was named.

- Sucre was made the first president, but he was soon ousted, and decades of factional strife, revolutions and military dictatorships followed. The economy, too, rapidly declined as it was unable to keep up the level of silver export of colonial times.

- Portions of Bolivia's original territory were lost in wars with Chile and Brazil. As a result of the War of the Pacific (1879-1884), Bolivia lost its access to the ocean to Chile. This has had extensive repercussions for Bolivia's economy. An autonomist rebellion (1889-1903) led Bolivia to sell territory to Brazil in 1903.

- The country came under a period of liberal rule in 1899-1920, which brought it much necessary calm.

- In 1920 the Republican Party took over and was immediately riven by factionalism. In the 1920s, the tin industry had an enormous output, but it was made in the face of falling demands. For more than 400 years, Bolivia's economy had been based on its mineral resources, especially tin, but mismanagement and the decline of world demands for its minerals have crippled the economy in the 20th century.

- In 1932, a border incident with Paraguay led to the protracted Chaco War in which 100,000 Bolivian men were killed, wounded, captured or deserted. Bolivia lost more territory to Paraguay than Paraguay had previously claimed. The unrest and dissatisfaction resulting from the war brought on the overthrow of the civilian government in 1936.

- After 15 years of disorder, Victor Paz Estenssoro was elected president in 1951. A military junta intervened, but a popular revolution overthrew the junta, and Paz Estenssoro returned as president until 1956. He was reelected in 1960, but was overthrown in 1964 shortly after beginning a third term. A series of military governments followed, interspersed by civilian rule.

- In April 1952 began the so-called Bolivian National Revolution, which was one of Latin America's most important revolutions. It introduced far-reaching land reforms and made the Indian peasants of Bolivia a powerful political force.

- Victor Paz Estenssoro was reelected as president in 1985, and he imposed a stabilization program for the economy. His term ended peacefully in 1989 when Jaime Paz Zamora was elected as his successor.

- In 1993, Gonzalo Sánchez de Lozada was named president.

- The export of coca paste, chiefly to the Cali cartel in Colombia, has become a major industry in Bolivia, despite U.S. attempts to stop it due to its illegality.

- Sánchez' economic program called for both the decentralization of the government and the privatization of major industries. In 1996, Sánchez reached a landmark decision giving Indians the right to sell land.

- All major presidential candidates in the 1997 elections supported Sánchez' reforms. Hugo Banzar won after declaring that he would embrace Sánchez' reforms and "humanize" them.

BUSINESS PRACTICES

Hours of Business

Business hours are usually Monday through Friday from 9:00 a.m. to noon and 3:00 to 7:00 p.m. Government offices are also open on Saturday from 9:00 a.m. to noon.

Many businesspeople vacation during the months of January, February and March. Avoid business trips during *Carnaval* (a week of feasting and celebration preceding Lent) and during early August as Bolivian Independence Day is celebrated on August 6.

Dress

Business clothing varies from city to city. In La Paz, men wear dark, three-piece business suits. In Santa Cruz, a lightweight suit or a *guayabera* (a dressy shirt) is worn. In Cochabamba, a two-piece business suit is customary.

Women may wear a suit, dress or skirt and blouse for business. Be sure to wear stockings. Miniskirts and other revealing clothing are not advisable.

Introductions

Greetings are usually accompanied by a handshake.

The title of *Señor* (Mr.), *Señora* (Mrs.) or *Señorita* (Miss) is added for first-time introductions or when greeting a stranger, such as a store owner. *Señorita* is used for any woman, unless she is older or the speaker knows that she is married.

The *abrazo* is a hug, a handshake, two or three pats on the shoulder and another handshake. It is used frequently by close friends and relatives.

Women friends often embrace and kiss each other on the cheek.

Professional titles – such as *Doctor* (used for Ph.D.'s as well as medical doctors), *Arquitecto* (Architect), *Ingeniero* (Engineer) and *Abogado* (Lawyer) – are important.

Common greetings include *Buenos días* (Good morning), *Buenas tardes* (Good afternoon) and *Buenas noches* (Good evening). Less formal greetings, such as *Cómo estás?* (How are you?) and *Hola* (Hi), are also common.

Common phrases for farewells are *Hasta luego* (Until later) and *Hasta mañana* (Until tomorrow). Friends may use the more casual *Chau*. *Adiós* generally implies a longer separation. It might be used when seeing someone off on a trip.

Spanish, Quechua and Aymara are all official languages. Spanish is used in government, education and business.

Always present a business card printed in Spanish.

At large parties, you should expect to introduce yourself, rather than be introduced by another.

Meetings

Make appointments two to three weeks before your arrival. Arrive a day or two before your first appointment as you may need to become acclimated to the altitude.

Visitors should always be punctual, even if your Bolivian contact is often late.

Always make eye contact when conversing; avoiding another's eyes may be interpreted as showing suspicion or lack of trust as well as shyness.

Tea will be served in offices promptly at 4:00 p.m.

It is a good idea to make copies of your proposal before entering Bolivia. Copies can be made but they may take up to a week. Paperwork should be in English and in Spanish.

Negotiating

Several trips to Bolivia will most likely be necessary in order to accomplish your goals. If your company has a representative in Bolivia, however, the process will probably move along more quickly.

The chamber of commerce in major cities can help you set up a contact. If you speak Spanish, use Bolivia's Ministry of Commerce and its Ministry of Finance.

Charts and visuals are viewed as quite appealing and should be included in your presentations.

Never be pushy or demanding in sales meetings. Alleviate any feelings of pressure, if possible.

Entertaining

Businesspeople are most often entertained in a restaurant for lunch or dinner. Spouses are not usually invited.

It is recommended that you bring flowers or a small gift for the hostess when visiting a home. Avoid yellow flowers (which signify contempt) or purple flowers (associated with funerals). Gifts will not be opened in your presence, as it is considered rude to do so.

Visitors may also be presented with a gift: do not open it in the presence of the giver.

Visitors are usually offered a drink or light refreshment upon arrival. It is impolite to refuse.

If invited to dinner at someone's home, it is suggested that you arrive 15 to 30 minutes late.

If you are a special guest, you will be served first. Otherwise, the father of the family is served first.

When invited to dinner, a guest is expected to try all the dishes offered. Compliments on the food are appreciated. Do not take a second helping until invited to do so. It is polite to first refuse.

It is courteous to stay about 30 minutes after the meal is finished. Do not leave immediately after eating, but do not stay too long either.

Guests should address their hosts by the honorific *Don* (for men) or *Doña* (for women) followed by their first name (for example, *Don Pedro* or *Doña Maria*).

Always use utensils, not your hands, even when eating fruit.

Keep your hands above the table at all times during a meal, resting the wrists lightly on the edge of the table.

Summon a waiter by raising your hand, clapping two or three times or snapping your fingers softly.

Do not pour wine with the left hand or "backhanded" (turning the hand so that the palm faces upward).

The host will usually insist upon paying for the meal.

Restaurants generally include a service charge in the bill, but it is recommended that a small additional amount be given to the waiter.

Lunch is usually the main meal of the day. Water is generally served with all meals. On special occasions, beer or wine is served. Coffee is served after the meal.

Many families do not have dinner, but repeat the 4:00 p.m. tea at about 9:00 p.m.

Potatoes, rice, soups and fruits are staples of the Bolivian diet. Many foods are fried and are usually very spicy.

Local specialties include *sopa de maní* (roasted peanut soup), *empanada salteña* (meat turnovers), *silpancho* (very thin breaded steak served with rice, fried potatoes, fried egg and tomato), *picante de pollo* (a spicy chicken dish) and *fricassé* (pork cooked in a hot sauce with potatoes and white corn).

SOCIAL VALUES, CUSTOMS AND TIPS

Bolivians stand relatively close to one another during conversation. They often use hands, eyes and facial expressions to communicate.

Bolivians enjoy visiting one another and often drop by unannounced.

Avoid using "America" when you mean "The United States."

Good topics of conversation include Bolivian culture, families, soccer, car races and food. Avoid praising Chile while in Bolivia. The two countries have had a dispute over borders for more than a century.

People in urban areas generally wear western-style clothes.

Women friends frequently walk arm in arm.

It is considered bad manners to eat on the street.

Do not bargain in stores with fixed prices. In open markets, however, people love to haggle over prices.

A common gesture is the raised hand, palm outward and fingers extended, twisting quickly from side to side. This is a way of saying "no," sometimes used by taxi drivers to indicate that their vehicles are full or by vendors in a marketplace to indicate that certain items have been sold out.

Always cover your mouth when you yawn or cough.

Indian women do not like being photographed as they believe that the camera will capture their souls. Indian men usually do not mind, but they will sometimes ask for payment.

Do not whisper to anyone when you are in a group.

Friday night in the city is called *viernes de soltero* (bachelor Friday). Men go out drinking with male friends and women never accompany them.

Both men and women wear jeans for casual wear, but not shorts. You may not be allowed into churches and official buildings if you are wearing shorts.

BRAZIL

Population: 169,806,557 (July 1998 est.); white (includes Portuguese, German, Italian, Spanish, Polish) 55%, mixed white and black 38%, black 6%, other (includes Japanese, Arab, Amerindian) 1%

Languages: Portuguese (official), Spanish, English, French

Religions: Roman Catholic (nominal) 70%

Currency: real

Brasilia

HISTORICAL OVERVIEW

- Brazil was first colonized by Portugal, whose explorer Pedro Álvares Cabral first visited the country in 1500. Both France and the Netherlands tried to establish colonies, but were driven out by the Portuguese. A somewhat feudal system was established in which first Indians were employed as manual laborers on the sugar plantations and then African slaves were brought in.

- Colonization took a number of decades, and expansion did not really begin until the latter half of the 17th century.

- Fearing the advance of Napoleon, the Portuguese royal family fled to Brazil in 1808. They then established Rio de Janeiro as the seat of the Portuguese Empire. This made Brazil a part of the United Kingdom of Portugal, Brazil and the Algarves.

- When King João VI returned to Lisbon in 1821 leaving his son, Dom Pedro I, to govern Brazil, the king wanted to make Brazil a colony once again. Brazilians refused and Dom Pedro I declared Brazil's independence in 1822. He was then crowned emperor of Brazil. His son, Dom Pedro II, followed, ushering in a period of stability and growth under his almost 50-year rule. He was deposed in 1889 by a military coup, following the abolition of slavery in Brazil.

- The period of the "Old Republic" (1889-1930) followed, a time of further expansion and increased prosperity.

- In the 20th century, immigration increased, manufacturing prospered and military coups and dictatorships were frequent. A dictator, Getúlio Vargas, came to power in 1930 and ruled until 1945. After him, elected presidents governed. A coup in 1964 gave the military control once again.

- Brazil's relatively honest, nonpolitical military government imposed austere economic measures in order to control inflation. The government was interested in industrial development. Social programs and the upholding of human rights were low priorities.

- A civilian president was appointed by an electoral college in 1985. A new constitution was ratified in 1988.

- Elections in 1989 brought Fernando Collor de Mello to power as the first directly elected president in 29 years. Collor began an austerity campaign to revive Brazil's economy, but he resigned in 1992 before he was impeached on corruption charges. This event marked the first time in Brazil's history that a leader was removed from office by legal, constitutional means.

- Itamar Franco, Collor's vice president, assumed the presidency and was widely regarded as ineffectual and unintelligent. His dynamic finance minister, Fernando Henrique Cardoso, however, developed a sweeping economic program that managed to reduce inflation drastically. Cardoso subsequently ran for president and won the election of 1994. He proceeded with an aggressive program of privatization, and productivity in Brazil rose dramatically.

- Major concerns exist regarding the continuing destruction of the Amazon rain forests. In March and April of 1998 fires raged through the northern Amazon. Destruction through fire, pollution, and other means is sure to incur future ecological problems. In addition, many groups indigenous to the area are being displaced.

- Although President Cardoso is well liked, he faces many problems, from rapid population growth and a high illiteracy rate to political corruption.

BUSINESS PRACTICES

Hours of Business

Business hours are Monday through Friday, 9:00 a.m. to 5:00 p.m. Offices close from 12:00 to 2:00 p.m. for lunch.

Government offices open from 9:00 a.m. to 4:30 p.m., Monday through Friday.

Dress

Executives traditionally wear three-piece suits, while other office workers dress in two-piece suits. Men should always wear long-sleeved shirts. Businesswomen should wear elegant suits or dresses. Short-sleeved blouses are acceptable. Many women also wear dressy pantsuits in the office. This attire is for professional women. Women in lower positions wear more casual clothing.

Introductions

Handshakes are the usual form of greeting, although they tend to be light.

When visiting an office or business establishment, shake hands with everyone present. People also customarily shake hands with everyone when parting from a small group. Men who know each other well may add a pat on the back or shoulder to the handshake.

Women customarily greet each other with a kiss on both cheeks. (Actually, they put their cheeks together and kiss the air). Good friends often embrace when they meet.

Brazil is the only country in Latin America in which Portuguese, not Spanish, is the official language. English, German and French are also spoken by many Brazilians. Spanish is understood by Portuguese speakers, but they may be offended if you deliberately speak to them in Spanish. A visitor should try to learn and speak some Portuguese.

Unlike in Spanish-speaking countries, the father's name appears as the last name in Portuguese, and is the surname. Many people refer to each other by title and first name, such as *Senhor Antônio* (Mister Anthony) or *Doutor Paulo* (Doctor Paul) or *Dona Regina* (Mrs. Regina).

Brazilian informality allows you to choose whether to call colleagues by their first names or by their surnames, but only after you have gotten to know them.

Business cards are a necessity in Brazil, since surnames are extremely varied and often difficult to pronounce. Always offer a business card when first meeting. It should be printed in both English and Portuguese.

Meetings

When visiting a Brazilian office, expect to be offered a small cup of coffee, called *cafézinho*. It is drunk black with sugar or sweetener. It is polite to accept even if you do not drink the entire cupful. You may also be offered tea, soft drinks, freshly squeezed juices or bottled water.

Presenting a gift such as liquor to your Brazilian business contact is an excellent way of beginning a meeting.

Be aware that frequent interruptions may occur during the course of a business meeting.

Make appointments at least two weeks in advance of your trip. The best times for appointments are mid-morning and mid to late afternoon. Do not schedule many appointments in one day, as Brazilians do not keep strict schedules. Brazilians may come at least 30 minutes later than the scheduled meeting time. The demands of the relationship and the business at hand may cause the meeting to continue longer than expected.

Negotiating

When beginning a business conversation, it is customary to discuss first the weather, local sights or other light conversational topics for 15 to 30 minutes. Do not touch on personal topics, such as questions about age or salary, but you may ask if your host has any children, as Brazilians are very proud of their children. Expect to keep constant eye contact during a conversation.

Be prepared to make several trips to Brazil when negotiating a business deal.

Negotiators prefer to negotiate with people they know. When confronted with a new negotiating team, they will endeavor to establish interpersonal relations before proceeding with negotiations. During the negotiation process, both formal and informal approaches are common. Compatibility of negotiating styles and mutual trust are of primary importance.

Firm schedules and detailed agendas are less likely to be adhered to.

Decision making is highly bureaucratic during business discussions.

Brazilians value the process of negotiating just as much as the result.

Negotiators will make suggestions rather than attempt to impose their will. This generally results in protracted sessions.

Discussion is often lively and includes debate, as this is considered to be an important way to develop relationships.

Negotiators are selected on the basis of a combination of social class, educational background, charisma, connections, work performance, and speaking abilities.

You may notice that negotiations often include competition between members of your counterparts' team.

Your negotiating counterpart will focus on the larger picture of the project involved and delegate details to subordinates.

Eye contact is important. Touching during conversations is common.

Arguments are made based on common sense, but they are often accompanied by expressive words, tone of voice and gestures.

Being risk-averse, Brazilians are not convinced by the future potential for monetary gain alone. The effects of a deal upon prestige, power and recognition are also taken into account.

The negotiating team generally serves an intermediary role, with decisions made by higher-level executives.

Be philosophical in your approach, and stress the benefits of your proposal to your audience.

State general principles as well as technical details.

Brazilian contracts are often more general than North American ones, stating the overall agreement in broad terms. Detailed and lengthy contracts may seem overwhelming and can be perceived as demonstrating a lack of trust.

Contracts are rarely perceived as being the end point of the negotiation process. Negotiations will often continue to work out specific details, timing and legal responsibility. The contract – no matter how detailed – is an expression of the *character* of the commercial relationship and its guiding principles. Details may change during the course of implementation.

Entertaining

Business entertaining often occurs at very high-quality restaurants, which are only moderately expensive. São Paulo is cosmopolitan and has numerous restaurants specializing in international cuisine.

If you are invited to a private home, it is customary to send your hostess flowers the following day. Do not include purple flowers as they are associated with death. Alternatively, you can bring candy or a bottle of liquor or wine to the dinner. Guests normally arrive 10 to 15 minutes later than the appointed time and stay at least two hours. Dinner parties may begin at approximately 10:00 p.m. with drinks and appetizers. The main meal may not be served until midnight.

It is customary for the guest of honor to sit at the head of the table. The host and hostess sit on one side of the table.

Brazilians eat continental style, holding the knife in the right hand and the fork in the left. They wipe their mouths each time before drinking. Do not use your hands to pick up food. If you must pick up food (such as a sandwich) with your hands, use a napkin.

Never use the side of your fork to cut food, even soft food. Always use a knife.

Both hands should be kept above the table at all times. Elbows should never rest on the table.

Place your utensils horizontally across your plate to indicate that you are finished eating.

At a restaurant, the waiter is beckoned by holding up the index finger or by saying *garçon* (pronounced "garsohn"). The check is requested by saying *conta, por favor* (pronounced "kohn-tuh, por fah-vor").

Dinner dress should be casually formal even though a tropical jacket may be too warm in summer (November through March). Men usually wear earth tone colors and keep their shoes well polished.

Breakfast is usually bread and cheese or marmalade and butter, accompanied by *café com leite* (coffee with milk).

Lunch and dinner are the main meals of the day. These meals typically include beans, rice, meat, salad, fruit, potatoes and bread. A common dish is *bife* or *frango com arroz e feijão* (steak or chicken with rice and black beans). The national dish is *feijoada* (a black bean stew) made with various meats and served with *arroz* (white rice), *couve* (kale), *farofa* (fried manioc flour), *vinagrette* (vinaigrette made with chopped tomatoes, onions and green peppers) and *laranja* (sliced oranges to cleanse the palate). A southern specialty is *churrasco*, a barbecue with a variety of meats.

Water, carbonated beverages, fruit punch or beer is served with meals. Beverages are always drunk from a glass, never from a bottle or can.

A popular drink besides coffee is *maté* (an herbal tea). The national drink is *caipirinha* made from *cachaça*, a Brazilian rum, with fresh lime juice, sugar and crushed ice.

Fruit is often served after lunch and dinner. It should be peeled, sliced and eaten with a fork and knife.

Brazilians generally wait to smoke until the meal is finished.

SOCIAL VALUES, CUSTOMS AND TIPS

The vast majority of Brazilians are Roman Catholic, although Protestant churches are growing rapidly.

Brazilians tend to be blunt about personal characteristics, such as whether you are fat or thin. These comments are meant as observations and are not intended as insults.

Brazilians are fashion conscious, especially in the cities. They generally prefer European fashions.

Brazilians have a relaxed attitude toward time, although less so in São Paulo.

Family ties are very strong in Brazil, and their obligations can affect many aspects of business.

Brazilians tend to stand closer to each other than do North Americans when talking or standing in line.

Brazilians tend to express their opinions forcefully. This should not be misinterpreted as anger.

Brazilians tend to dress casually, except for such formal events as attending the opera. Invitations to lunch during the weekend are very informal, and jackets and ties are rarely worn.

If a woman receives unwanted attention from men on the street, it is best for her to simply ignore it.

A first-time visitor to Brazil should not rely on taxi drivers to find an address. Obtain directions from the hotel concierge or porter, who will usually give the taxi driver directions on how to find the destination.

It is considered obscene to make the U.S. "okay" sign, where the forefinger and thumb touch and the other fingers are extended. Punching your fist into a cupped hand is also a rude gesture.

Brazilians use the "thumbs up" gesture to show approval.

A Brazilian may pinch his earlobe between his thumb and forefinger to indicate appreciation, such as after enjoying a meal.

Do not chew gum or eat while walking on the street.

Brazilians are passionate about *futebol* (soccer). Brazil's soccer teams are among the finest in the world. Some businesses and schools close during the World Cup tournament or important national competitions.

Carnaval (a week of feasting and celebration preceding Lent) is the most famous holiday in Brazil, marked by street parades, dancing, parties, drinking and costumes.

A symbol of good luck is a fist with the thumb sticking out between the second and third fingers. Amulets and charms depicting this gesture are sold .

Be sure to ask permission before photographing anyone.

Shorts may be worn along the beach, but not in the cities.

BRUNEI

Population: 315,292 (July 1998 est.); Malay 64%, Chinese 20%, other 16%

Languages: Malay (official), English, Chinese

Religions: Muslim (official) 63%, Buddhist 14%, Christian 8%, indigenous beliefs and other 15%

Currency: Bruneian dollar

Bandar Seri Begawan

HISTORICAL OVERVIEW

- In the early 15th century, Brunei became a sultanate and developed into the cornerstone of a Muslim state that included most of northern Borneo and the Philippines. The Portuguese Ferdinand Magellan landed in 1521, and by the early 17th century, the empire had been seriously weakened. By 1700, the Dutch dominated the East Indies, and by 1800 the sultanate of Brunei was confined to Sarawak, present-day Sabah and present-day Brunei.

- In exchange for helping the sultan put down a revolt in 1841, British soldier James Brooke was made governor of Sarawak. The Englishman appointed himself Rajah or "king" of the region and was succeeded by his nephew and the latter's son until 1946.

- The sultan attempted to enter into a trade agreement with the U.S. in 1865, but the venture was soon abandoned by the U.S. The British set up the North Borneo Company, which acquired the assets of the U.S. firm and forced more land concessions from the sultan. In 1881, Brunei was reduced to its present size, and in 1888, it was placed under British protection.

- Brunei continued to depend on British protection, and in 1906 permitted a British counselor to reside in the country. The counselor's job was to advise the sultan in all matters of state.

- In the years 1910 to 1919, the economy began to grow, largely due to the cultivation of rubber. In the 1920s, huge oil reserves and natural gas were discovered in the western part of the nation.

Offshore deposits were discovered in the 1960s, paving the way for enormous wealth.

- In 1963, the Federation of Malaysia was established as a bulwark against Indonesian imperialism and the possibility of a Communist takeover in Singapore. The sultan rejected the plan in fear that his power and his country's wealth would be diminished.

- Brunei regained its full independence on 1 January 1984 and became an Islamic sultanate. Brunei became a member of the British Commonwealth and has joined the United Nations (U.N.) and the Association of Southeast Asian Nations (ASEAN). The sultan became prime minister.

- The present sultan took over after his father's abdication in 1968. He has invested funds in many different countries in an effort to diversify the economy. In the past several years the Philippines have claimed nearby Sabah, but this has never been seriously pursued. Brunei has remained politically stable, which the government credits to the widespread distribution of wealth among its people. Brunei is one of the world's wealthiest nations.

- Environmental problems are growing, however, as are domestic tensions caused by ethnic conflicts.

- In the early 1990s the sultan introduced a program of MIB (Malay, Islam, monarchy) to strengthen monarchical rule. It became part of secondary school curricula in 1992.

- Prince Al-Muhtadle Billah was named successor to the throne of Brunei in August 1998, and he will assume the position of absolute monarch upon his father's death.

BUSINESS PRACTICES

Hours of Business

Businesses and government offices are open Monday through Thursday from 7:45 a.m. to 12:15 p.m. and from 1:30 to 4:30 p.m. and Saturday from 9:00 a.m. to 12:00 p.m. Friday is the Muslim day of worship and thus a non-workday.

It is advisable not to travel to Brunei during the monsoon season, which takes place between November and April.

Dress

Both men and women should wear business suits. Women should keep their heads, knees, and arms covered.

If business must be conducted during the monsoon season, adequate rain gear should be brought.

Introductions

Full names are used in Brunei, and titles are considered very important.

The titles *Haji* (for men) and *Hajjah* (for women) are given to those who have completed the pilgrimage to Mecca.

Negotiating

English is the language of business used by and with all non-Malay speakers.

If a company would like to invest or build in Brunei, it must first obtain approval from the Ministry of Industry and Primary Resources.

Since Brunei wishes to expand its private sector, all negotiations will be speedily expedited by the government to bring about a successful deal.

Entertaining

Nightlife is almost nonexistent in Brunei. Therefore, expatriates create their own entertainment, such as *karaoke* singing (singing along to background music using special audio/visual equipment) or home-video viewing.

Bruneians customarily eat with their fingers rather than with utensils. Eating is always done with the right hand, because the left hand is considered unclean.

It is polite to accept food and drink when it is offered, even if accepting only a little. When refusing anything offered, it is polite to touch the plate lightly with your right hand.

Brunei caters to international tastes. A favorite local dish is a Malay-style *satay* with tangy peanut sauce. *Rendang*, a beef in coconut milk and local spices, is also popular.

SOCIAL VALUES, CUSTOMS AND TIPS

Ethnically, over 60 percent of the people are Malay. Yet, many cultural and linguistic differences make Brunei Malays distinct from the larger Malay populations in Malaysia and Indonesia. Brunei also contains a sizable minority of ethnic Chinese. The official language is Malay, although English is widely understood and is used in the business community.

Although Islam is the official religion, freedom of religion exists. Brunei has in the past several years, however, moved closer toward Islamic fundamentalism. Alcohol was banned in 1991, and stricter dress codes were enforced.

Brunei is currently redoing its infrastructure and marketing itself in a manner as to attract international investment.

Approximately half of Brunei's 90,000 jobs are held by foreign expatriates.

Giving and receiving are done with the right hand.

Many Malay women wear a *tudong* (a traditional head covering). Men who have completed the *Haj*, the pilgrimage to Mecca, wear a white *songkok* (a sheet-like covering for the body).

Bruneians generally sit on the floor, especially when there is a large gathering of people. Women typically sit with their legs tucked to one side, while men often sit with their legs folded and crossed at the ankles. It is considered rude to sit with one's legs stretched out in front, especially if someone is sitting in front of you.

It is considered rude to eat or drink while walking in public, or in the presence of Muslims during Ramadan, the month of fasting.

Islamic doctrine strictly prohibits a non-Muslim from being alone in the company of a Muslim of the opposite sex. Even in an open setting, casual contact with the opposite sex will make Muslims uncomfortable. Bruneians are also prohibited from singing or dancing in public.

When walking toward someone, especially an elder or one of higher social rank, it is respectful to bend down slightly towards the person, while keeping one arm straight down along the side of your body.

Several gestures that are acceptable in the West are considered offensive in Brunei. For example, leaning on a table or a chair where someone is seated, especially when visiting an official or a colleague, is considered rude, as is resting one's feet on a table or a chair.

Touching or patting anyone on the head, including a child, is regarded as disrespectful.

Do not motion to someone with the index finger. The polite way to beckon someone is to use all four fingers of the right hand, with the palm down, and to motion them toward oneself.

National Day is celebrated on February 23.

BULGARIA

Population: 8,240,426 (July 1998 est.); Bulgarian 85.3%, Turkish 8.5%, Gypsy 2.6%, Macedonian 2.5%, Armenian 0.3%, Russian 0.2%, other 0.6%

Languages: Bulgarian, secondary languages closely follow ethnic breakdown

Religions: Bulgarian Orthodox 85%, Muslim 13%, Jewish 0.8%, Roman Catholic 0.5%, Uniate Catholic 0.2%, Protestant, Gregorian-Armenian and other 0.5%

Currency: lev

HISTORICAL OVERVIEW

- The oldest known inhabitants of the region that is now known as Bulgaria were Thracians. In the fifth century B.C., they founded the Odrisaw kingdom, but during the first century A.D., Bulgaria was taken over by the Roman Empire.

- All of the Balkans suffered from invasions by Huns, Bulgars, Goths and Avars beginning in the third century and by the sixth, Slavic farmers dominated the area. In the seventh century, the central Asian Bulgars crossed the Danube, fought the Avars and took over the southern part of the Balkans corresponding roughly to Bulgaria today. In 681, a Bulgarian state was recognized by the Byzantine Empire.

- In 864 King Boris I adopted Orthodox Christianity, bringing the Bulgars closer to the majority Slavic population. The Bulgar language and culture soon died out, and the Bulgars were absorbed by the Slavic tribes.

- There were two Bulgarian empires, from 893 to 927 and from 1185 to 1396. From 1018 to 1185 Bulgaria was under Byzantine rule, and in 1396 it was conquered by the Ottoman Turks.

- The Ottoman Empire controlled Bulgaria from 1396 to 1878, destroying its elite classes and enserfing its peasants. There was no attempt, however, to stamp out the indigenous culture. This period is known as the "Turkish yoke," and it gave rise to a cultural renaissance at the end of the 18th century.

- In 1878, part of Bulgaria became independent as a result of the Russian-Turkish War.

- Bulgaria was then briefly divided into two kingdoms, the independent Bulgaria and the Ottoman Eastern Rumelia, but it was reunited in 1885 and declared its own independence in 1908.

- Bulgaria fought two Balkan Wars in 1912 and 1913 in attempts to gain portions of Macedonia and Thrace from Turkey. Bulgaria won some territory in the first war but lost it again in the second. In its continued quest for more territory, the country sided with Germany during both World Wars.

- In 1944, Soviet troops marched into Bulgaria at the same time that a Communist-inspired coalition took control of the government. A nationalist hero, Georgi Dimitrov, who fought the Nazis in World War II, became the first communist leader of Bulgaria.

- Todor Zhikov came to power in 1954 but resigned in 1989, when Bulgaria got caught up in the wave of reforms sweeping through Eastern Europe at the time. The Communists renamed their party the Socialists and won the 1990 parliamentary elections. A new constitution was approved, making Bulgaria a parliamentary republic and granting its citizens a range of freedoms.

- Yet in October 1991 the opposition Union of Democratic Forces won the elections and established Bulgaria's first noncommunist government since 1946. Zhelyu Zhelev, a popular dissident, was named president.

- Faced with serious economic difficulties, the new government privatized industry and seized land from former Communists.

- Political stagnation and the economic crisis grew. In addition, the Turkish minority protested for a greater voice in government. In 1994 the Socialist (former Communist) Party was voted back into office. Their 35-year-old leader, Zhan Videnor, was made prime minister. He too could not relieve Bulgaria's problems, however. People took to the streets to demonstrate and, by 1997, the opposition was in power once again.

- In July 1998, the Bulgarian prime minister signed an agreement with the International Monetary Fund for a loan to help with more structural reforms. The IMF stopped loans in late 1996, due to Bulgaria's instability.

BUSINESS PRACTICES

Hours of Business

Offices are open from 9:00 a.m. to 12:30 p.m. and 1:00 to 5:30 p.m. in most cases. Private shops often have additional hours.

Some businesses close for the midday meal.

Many businesses close by noon on Saturday, and most are closed all day Sunday.

Dress

Professional women usually wear a skirt, blouse or sweater and high heels to work.

Professional men wear suits and ties to work, although older men prefer trousers and a sweater.

Introductions

Bulgarians usually shake hands when meeting someone. The handshake might be accompanied in formal situations by *Kat ste?* (How are you?) or *Zdraveite* (Hello). The informal terms for these greetings, *Kak si?* and *Zdrasti* or *Zdrave*, are used among friends, relatives and colleagues.

Close female friends might kiss each other on the cheek.

Handshakes are not used when saying *Dobro utro* (Good morning), *Dober den* (Good day), *Dobe vetcher* (Good evening) or *Leka nosht* (Good night).

First names are used in informal settings. Otherwise, titles and family names are used to address people. *Gospodin* (Mr.), *Gospozha* (Mrs.) or *Gospozhitsa* (Miss) are common titles. Professional titles are also used.

It is polite to greet each person individually, beginning with the eldest, at a small gathering.

In rural areas, it is considered polite to greet strangers on the street, but this is uncommon in urban areas.

Meetings

Expect to start making arrangements for a meeting in Bulgaria at least three months in advance. You must go through the public relations department to make sure that protocol has been met. If you need an interpreter, one will be provided for you.

A good time to schedule a meeting is either 10:00 a.m. or 11:00 a.m. or 2:00 p.m. or 3:00 p.m.

Negotiating

It is important to build a strong personal relationship with your Bulgarian counterpart, but be aware that Bulgarians must first warm up to you, so repeated trips will be necessary to finish a deal.

No agreements are written in stone. Bulgarians may change their minds at short notice due to forces outside the Bulgarian firm (e.g., elections).

Always accept the liquor given to you during a meeting, but be careful not to drink quickly if you do not want any more as an empty glass will always be filled.

Entertaining

At a home, guests are usually offered refreshments, even if not invited for a meal.

Invited guests often bring flowers for the hostess, a bottle of alcohol for the host and candy for the children. An odd number of flowers is appropriate, as even numbers are reserved for funerals.

Many professional organizations, schools and local governments own lodges in the mountains where their members can stay for minimal cost.

Bills are paid at the table. Diners round the bill up to the next lev (Bulgarian currency) as a tip.

The continental style of eating is most common, with the fork in the left hand and the knife in the right. It is polite for guests to accept second helpings. An empty plate or glass will usually be refilled.

A small amount of food left on the plate (usually after second helpings) indicates that one is full.

Bulgarians eat pork, fish or lamb with most main dishes.

Popular main meals include *moussaka* (pork or lamb casserole with potatoes, tomatoes and yogurt) and *nadenitsa* (stuffed pork sausage). Other common dishes include *kfteta* (a fried meat patty), *sarmi* (a pepper or cabbage stuffed with pork and rice), *shopska* (a salad made with Bulgarian cheese, cucumbers and tomatoes), and *baklava* (a thin, layered pastry with a syrup and nut filling). Espresso or Turkish-style coffees are usually served.

SOCIAL VALUES, CUSTOMS AND TIPS

Socializing is an important part of life and friends and neighbors commonly drop by unexpectedly. Beyond close friends and relations, it is more typical for an invitation to be extended first.

Bulgarians generally respect those who are open, strong, capable, good-humored and are loyal to family and friends.

Bulgarians take pride in their heritage and culture, which have been preserved despite centuries of foreign domination.

Women usually enter a home before men.

Evening visits usually start after 8:00 p.m. and may last until after midnight (3:00 a.m. for special occasions). It is considered rude to leave early.

Be aware that toilet paper is not always available in public restrooms.

The official language is Bulgarian, and nearly all inhabitants speak it. About half of the Turkish population (which makes up eight and one-half percent of the population) speak Turkish and Bulgarian.

European and U.S. fashions are popular.

In rural areas, guests remove their shoes upon entering a home. This courtesy is also practiced in many urban homes. Slippers are sometimes offered to guests.

"Yes" is indicated by shaking the head from side to side and "No" is expressed with one or two nods of the head.

One might shake the index finger back and forth to emphasize the "No" and even add a "tsk" sound to express displeasure.

Hands are not generally used to replace or emphasize verbal communication.

It is impolite to point with the index finger.

It is impolite for men to cross their ankles over their knees.

In a line or crowd, it is not impolite or uncommon for one to touch or press against another person.

Bulgarians often touch while conversing. Female friends might walk arm in arm down the street.

Public holidays include New Year's Day, National Day of Freedom and Independence (March 3), Labor Day (May 1-2), the Day of Bulgarian Culture and Science (May 24) and Christmas Day (December 25). Religious holidays such as Easter are popular, but they are not public holidays.

CANADA

Population: 30,675,398 (July 1998 est.); English 40%, French 27%, other European 20%, Amerindian 1.5%, other (mostly Asian) 11.5%

Languages: English (official), French (official)

Religions: Roman Catholic 45%, United Church 12%, Anglican 8%, other 35%

Currency: Canadian dollar

Ottawa ★

HISTORICAL OVERVIEW

- Canada's first inhabitants were the Intuit Indians and other Native Americans. Several explorers from Iceland and Greenland landed in Labrador and Newfoundland as far back as 1000 A.D., but they failed to establish viable communities.

- In 1497, French explorer Jean Cabot discovered Newfoundland. When Jacques Cartier sailed into the Gulf of St. Lawrence and up the St. Lawrence River in 1534, the French made a claim to the territory. In 1605, the French established a settlement called Acadia in present-day Nova Scotia.

- In 1610, Henry Hudson of England discovered the Hudson Bay and James Bay.

- The French began serious colonization in the mid-1600s with the establishment of the Company of New France. The settlers developed a huge fur-trading network throughout the Great Lakes region and down the Mississippi Valley. The region became known as New France.

- The British responded by setting up Hudson's Bay Company in 1670. British and French rivalry over the interior of upper North America continued throughout the 1600s.

- The French first lost territory in 1713 when Nova Scotia and Newfoundland were handed to the British. France's attempts to further expand its holdings led to the French and Indian War. At its conclusion in 1763, France lost all its North American hold-ings east of the Mississippi to Great Britain, except for two small islands. Its holdings west of the Mississippi eventually became part of the U.S. via the Louisiana Purchase in 1803. New France became the colony of Québec.

- In the peace treaty of 1783, after the American Revolution, Great Britain retained its holdings north of the 13 new United States. English loyalists fled north and settled in Canada. The increased number of English in Québec led Britain to divide it into Upper and Lower Canada, later Québec and Ontario.

- By 1848 the Canadian colonies were self-governing. In 1867, the British North America Act created the Dominion of Canada out of Nova Scotia, New Brunswick, Québec and Ontario. Much of the west was purchased by Canada in 1870. This land was acquired through treaties with the indigenous Indians, who were pushed onto reservations. British Columbia joined in 1871 and Prince Edward Island in 1873. Newfoundland remained a separate colony until 1949.

- In the late 19th century Canada prospered greatly, but political and cultural tensions between the English and French persisted.

- In 1931, Great Britain relinquished its formal authority over Canadian affairs, retaining only the right to have the last word on constitutional matters. In 1982, it gave up that right and Canada's constitution was changed to reflect its full sovereignty.

- Although the British monarch is represented in Canada by a governor general, all of Canada's affairs, foreign and domestic, are conducted independently of Great Britain.

- French separatism has been an issue in Canada in the second half of the 20th century. The separatist Parti Québecois was formed in the late 1960s, and there were two referendums held on secession, in 1980 and again in 1995. Although the measure lost both times, the votes were very close in 1995.

- In 1991, the Canadian government announced plans to make good on treaties with Native Americans, which they had ignored for over a century. In 1992, a measure was approved to split the northeast territory into east and west. By 1999, the eastern portion would become "Nanavut," a region in which the Intuit would exercise self-rule.

- Jean Chrétien has been serving as prime minister since 1993.

- Canada entered into the North American Free Trade Agreement (NAFTA) with the U.S. and Mexico in 1994. Since then, Canada has also signed free trade agreements with Chile and Israel.

- Chrétien eliminated the budget deficit. A native of Québec, he gave it more rights and officially recognized its "unique character" while, at the same time, pointing to the difficulty of secession.

BUSINESS PRACTICES

Hours of Business

Business hours are usually 10:00 a.m. to 6:00 p.m., Monday through Friday.

Shops are open from 10:00 a.m. to 6:00 p.m., Monday through Saturday. Some shops remain open until 9:00 p.m. and some provinces have laws regarding Sunday store hours.

Dress

Canadians usually dress formally for social occasions. If attending dinner at a restaurant or a colleague's home, men should wear suits or jackets and ties, and women should wear dresses. On less formal occasions, Canadians dress casually.

Introductions

Throughout Canada, people usually shake hands when meeting and when departing. A nod of the head may take the place of a handshake in an informal situation. Men should shake hands with women if they offer their hand.

Introductions vary from region to region, depending upon the person's cultural background.

In Québec and other French-speaking areas, the traditional French greeting *Bonjour* (Good day) and a firm handshake are the usual introductions. Use the polite *vous* (you) pronoun rather than *tu*, which is generally reserved for family and very close friends. Among close friends, both men and women greet each other by exchanging kisses on both cheeks, although close women friends may also embrace.

When first introduced to Canadians, it is proper to use surnames. First names should only be used after being invited to do so. Titles are used with new acquaintances and on formal occasions.

Meetings

Morning appointments are generally preferred.

Because of strong cultural ties to Europe (particularly France), and by law, all writing on packaging must be printed in both French and English. It is also best to prepare advertising and promotional materials in both languages.

Refreshments are generally offered during business meetings, but it is not considered impolite to refuse them.

Negotiating

Business is conducted in a direct, forthright and concise manner. The Canadian business community values clarity and thoroughness in the exchange of information.

Business communications tend to be more formal in Ontario and Atlantic Canada than in Québec and the West.

Never exaggerate the qualities of your product.

The Canadian business pace may be a little slower than in the U.S.

Entertaining

Business entertaining is usually conducted in restaurants and clubs.

The dinner hour varies. Dinner may be served as early as 5:00 p.m. or as late as 7:00 p.m., and it usually lasts from two to three hours.

Continental dining style is used in Canada, with the fork held in the left hand and the knife in the right. Some people, however, use the style common in the U.S. where the fork is transferred back and forth between the two hands.

Traditionally, the host will indicate where dinner guests should sit.

At a formal meal, it is considered impolite to reach across the table. Instead, ask that items be passed to you.

In French-speaking areas, one should keep both hands above the table during a meal. Women rest their wrists on the table, men their forearms. Elbows can be placed on the table after the meal is finished. Proper etiquette is to wipe the mouth before drinking.

At the end of the meal, guests should place utensils on their plate.

Because of Canada's varied multi-ethnic make-up, there is a wide variety of foods and eating habits in the country, especially in the largest cities. Seafood and fish are most popular on the coasts. Food in Québec reflects a definite French influence.

To beckon a waiter, raise your hand at or above head level. In Québec, beckon a waiter by nodding the head backward slightly or raising your hand discreetly. To signal that you would like the check, make a motion with your hands as if you were signing a piece of paper.

A holiday unique to Québec is the two-week *Carnaval de Québec*, usually held in February.

If you are entertained in a private home, it is courteous and recommended to bring or send flowers to your host/hostess and follow up with a thank-you note. Avoid sending white lilies since they are associated with funerals. An alternative to flowers is candy or wine.

In general, dress habits are similar to those in the U.S., but a bit more conservative and formal.

SOCIAL VALUES, CUSTOMS AND TIPS

Canada has a strong identity, which is quite different from that of the United States, although many people in the U.S. tend to emphasize the similarities between the two countries and overlook the differences. Canadians resent these exaggerated comparisons. They have their own heritage and culture and are not "U.S.-type" people who happen to live in Canada. Canadians value the preservation of their culture, especially against undue influence from the United States.

Canadians take great pride in their country as a whole as well as in the individual provinces. They welcome favorable comments about their country and people.

The majority of Canadians have a British, French or other European heritage, but there are many other ethnic groups as well. The population of Vancouver, for example, is 15 percent Chinese, most of whom have emigrated from Hong Kong. Native Intuit groups live mainly in the more northern areas of the country.

English and French are both official languages in Canada. While most government employees are bilingual, only about 15 percent of the population actually speaks both languages well. French is the official language in the province of Québec, where many people are not fluent in English. If you are traveling to Québec, a working knowledge of French is essential. In the province of New Brunswick, about a third of the population speaks French as their first language.

Canadian English differs somewhat from the U.S. English. British spellings, such as "theatre" instead of "theater," are used.

Three facts about Canada should be kept in mind. It is the second-largest country in the world by land mass, and it is the largest trading partner of the United States. In addition, more than 75 percent of Canadians live within 100 miles of the U.S. border.

Sports are a good topic for conversation. Ice hockey is very popular all over Canada, as are many other winter sports. Boating, fishing, swimming, soccer, baseball, rugby, tennis, golf and lacrosse are also popular.

The topic of partition (separation into French-speaking and English-speaking states) should be treated delicately. Avoid taking sides on this issue.

Two important forms of communication, eye contact and smiles, are always welcome.

In social situations, men will usually rise when a woman enters a room.

The U.S. sign of "thumbs down" (meaning no) is an offensive gesture in Québec and should be avoided. It is also considered offensive to belch in public, even if one excuses oneself.

English-speaking Canadians from Ontario tend to be more reserved than both French Canadians and English-speaking Canadians from the western provinces. They do not welcome body contact or gestures in greeting or in conversation. Generally, people with a French heritage are often more outgoing and open than those of British descent.

Etiquette and politeness are valued by both French- and English-speaking Canadians. It is accepted practice for a man to open a door or give up his seat for a woman.

In Québec, it is improper to eat on the streets unless you are sitting at an outdoor café or standing outside of a food stand.

CHILE

Population: 14,787,781 (July 1998 est.); white and white-Amerindian 95%, Amerindian 3%, other 2%

Languages: Spanish (official)

Religions: Roman Catholic 89%, Protestant 11%, Jewish 1%

Currency: Chilean peso

HISTORICAL OVERVIEW

- Ferdinand Magellan was the first European to sight the Chilean shore after he successfully navigated around the southern tip of South America in 1520.

- The Spanish first landed in Chile in 1536 looking for "another Peru." Finding neither gold nor an advanced civilization, they quickly left again. In 1540, they returned and began conquest of the territory. They were met with strong resistance from the local population, which continued to resist until the 1800s.

- Very few mineral reserves were found in Chile, and the colony therefore quickly became agricultural.

- Chile formed part of the Viceroyalty of Peru but its relative poverty resulted in isolation from and neglect by the viceroyalty.

- Chile began to fight for independence from Spain in 1810. In 1817, the Spanish were defeated with the help of armies under the leadership of José de San Martín of Argentina. One of the heroes of the revolution, Bernardo O'Higgins, became the country's new leader.

- The policies of O'Higgins' government were not popular with the landed aristocracy, and he left office and the country in 1823. A period of political anarchy and financial chaos followed.

- In 1829 a collegial government was installed but the actual power resided with Diego Portales, who governed as a dictator. A new constitution was instituted, which lasted until 1925. The relative stability that ensued allowed for economic improvements and progress toward modernization.

- From 1861 through 1891, the country experienced a growth in political parties that favored political change through peaceful means and secularization of the state, as well as an increase in European influences.

- From 1879 to 1883, Chile fought the War of the Pacific against Peru and Bolivia. Chile was victorious and annexed three provinces whose main attraction was their saltpeter mines, which were also of interest to many European powers.

- The first half of the 20th century was generally a period of growth and peace, although there was some turmoil during the 1920s and early 1930s. President Eduardo Frei, elected in 1964, introduced reforms that brought greater political power to the poor.

- In 1970, Salvador Allende was elected, becoming the first freely elected Marxist president in South America. By the end of 1972, however, the country faced economic disaster. In 1973, General Augusto Pinochet Ugarte led a military coup that ended Allende's socialist government.

- Pinochet ruled by decree. In 1980, a new constitution gave him the right to rule until 1988, when he held a plebiscite (a direct vote by the people) to determine if he should continue to rule or allow free elections. He lost the plebiscite and called for elections in December 1989. The Pinochet government was guilty of many human rights violations. It did, however, manage to turn around the ailing Chilean economy.

- Patricio Aylwin Azócar became the first elected president since 1970, although Pinochet retained his position as head of the army. Aylwin was succeeded by Eduardo Frei, elected in December 1993.

- Chile's economy has continued to prosper due to free trade and foreign investment. The country has also managed to all but wipe out corruption in its government.

- In 1997, the unemployment rate was four percent. New jobs continue to open up, which introduces other problems, including a greater influx of other South Americans seeking work.

- With a highly literate workforce, low wage costs, and a stable political environment, foreign investors grow increasingly attracted to the prospect of locating in Chile.

BUSINESS PRACTICES

Hours of Business

Business hours are generally from 9:00 a.m. to 6:00 p.m. In many areas, a midday *siesta* (a rest after the midday meal), when offices and shops close, is still common.

Vacations are generally taken in January and February, the Chilean summer.

Dress

Business dress is conservative. Men generally wear suits and ties, not sports jackets, for business and social events. Do not wear anything on the lapel. Women should wear a suit and heels for business and a dress for dinner.

Introductions

Men shake hands with other men when they are introduced. After they know each other well, they also pat one another on the back. An *abrazo* (an embrace) is also common.

Women kiss one another on one cheek when they know each other well. Men and women who know each other well will also do this.

Men should stand when a woman enters a room. Be prepared to shake her hand if she offers it. A seated woman, however, is not obliged to rise or offer her hand when a man enters.

At a small party, greet each person individually. At a large party, saying "Hello" to the whole group is acceptable.

Professional titles such as *Doctor* (for a medical doctor) and *Profesor* (Professor) are used regularly when greeting someone.

People use either their full name (including both the father's family name and the mother's family name) or their father's family name, which is the official surname. An example would be Eduardo Jose Peres Garcia, who would be known as *Señor Peres* or *Don Eduardo*.

Meetings

It is important to use Spanish in all business documents and trade literature. Business cards should be bilingual.

Prior appointments are necessary, preferably made at least two weeks in advance.

Your first meeting will, for the most part, be an introduction to discuss your company and your position. Much of the time will be spent on conversation unrelated to business.

Chileans respect punctuality.

Negotiating

Develop a strategy for your negotiations and a plan for their execution. Hold a pre-meeting planning and rehearsal session and do a post-meeting analysis. Come to each meeting with an agenda and a summary (or the minutes) of the previous meeting.

Business decisions are usually made by a few people at the top of an organization. Status and level of negotiators are important. Do not send a mid-level person to deal with a top executive or owner of a firm.

When negotiating with those who are not top-level decision makers, expect issues to require "final approval" by a person in a position of higher authority. Once that approval is obtained, negotiations reopen.

Avoid showing impatience with delays and with the time needed for decision making.

Promptly answer all correspondence, preferably in Spanish.

Building a business relationship is important. A hard-nosed, aggressive approach will offend your Chilean counterpart.

Courtesy is vital to the process. You can advance negotiations if you pay great attention to protocols that show politeness and respect.

Expect a "Little us" versus "Big you" comparison to be used at times to explain why they can not give more but you can.

Do not expect "tit-for-tat" concessions. An agreement on your part to "meet them halfway" may not make your counterpart feel obliged to match your offer.

Be alert to arguments advocating that things be done or granted "for the sake of friendship" or "to show good faith."

Casual conversations during breaks, lunch, or at drinks after work are considered part of doing business. These may be used at times to get you to lower your guard, let information out, or make concessions.

Do not permit the usage of vague language that your counterpart promises to "clarify" later.

Have all translations that are not done by your translator checked by a third party.

Study your counterpart's history (personal and company). Learn all you can about the players at the table and those whom they represent, including other agreements made by your counterpart with other companies.

Get everything in writing.

Your counterpart may consider it fair to attempt to reopen negotiations after you consider them closed simply because, for example, "circumstances have changed."

If somebody says that something is prohibited by local law or regulation, confirm the veracity of this statement. Get a copy of the legislation or regulation, and then find someone knowledgeable who can interpret it for you.

Never cause your counterpart to "lose face."

Be alert to what factors motivate your counterpart. The motivation may not be solely financial. On the other hand, be cautious of a statement such as, "It is the principle, not the money." This may indicate a primarily financial motivation.

Unless it is to your advantage not to do so, make all agreements contingent upon arriving at a final agreement.

Entertaining

Women should avoid giving gifts to male colleagues. Even the most innocuous present might be misconstrued as a personal overture. Gifts for children from both men and women are welcomed.

Business gifts should not be given until a friendly relationship has been established. If you plan a return visit, ask your colleague if he would like you to bring something particular from your home country.

Avoid giving 13 of anything (considered bad luck), black or purple (a reminder of the solemn Lent season), knives (which, symbolically, cut off a relationship) and handkerchiefs (associated with tears).

Business entertaining is generally done at major hotels and restaurants.

If you are invited to a meal by a Chilean businessperson, he/she will pay. If you issue the invitation, you will pay. Splitting the check, even in a group, is unusual and is called "American treat."

The main meal of the day is generally lunch. A lighter meal is eaten between 8:00 and 10:00 p.m. Teatime, called *onces*, usually consists of small sandwiches, beverages and cookies or cakes.

Do not expect spouses to be included in a business lunch. For business dinners that are primarily social, it is appropriate to include spouses.

When invited to dinner at someone's home, arrive 15 minutes after the stated invitation time. If invited to a party, arrive 30 minutes later than stated.

Greet the head of the family first.

Bring a gift, such as flowers or chocolates, for the host.

Do not admire a possession of your host to excess. He/she may insist on giving it to you, and you must accept.

It is considered impolite to ask for second helpings. Even if second helpings are offered, guests are expected to decline. Take more food only if the host insists.

It is impolite to leave immediately after eating. You should plan to stay for conversation after the meal.

If you invite Chileans to a business lunch, ask them to suggest a restaurant. For dinner, entertain at your hotel's restaurant.

Chileans seldom eat anything with their fingers.

The continental style of eating is used, with the fork in the left hand and the knife in the right.

Both hands are kept above the table at all times during meals.

Chileans are very proud of their local wines, especially white wines. When toasts are made, raise your glass, look at your host and others present and say *Salud* (To your health). Never pour wine with the left hand.

National dishes include *cazuela de ave* (a stew of chicken, potatoes, rice and green peppers), *empanadas de horno* (turnovers filled with raisins, olives, meat, hard-boiled eggs and onions), *empanada frita* (a fried meat pastry) and *pastel de choclo* (a casserole of meat, onions and olives, topped with cornmeal and baked). There are many local seafood dishes, especially conger eel, *paila chochi* (a kind of bouilla-baisse) and *parrillada de mariscos* (grilled mixed seafood).

Except for ice cream, it is not polite to eat while walking in public.

Café con leche is made by pouring hot milk into a cup that has a single spoonful of coffee in it. *Té con leche* is a small amount of tea with hot milk.

SOCIAL VALUES, CUSTOMS AND TIPS

Avoid talking about local politics and religion. Good topics include family, children, Easter Island and history.

People tend to stand closer together than they do in North America.

Good eye contact and good posture are important during conversations. Respect and courtesy are quite important in general.

Neatness and cleanliness are important to Chileans, and this is reflected in how they dress. European fashions are followed.

Nearly 30 percent of the labor force is female. Many women have important political and business positions.

Formal dress is rare, even for weddings.

About 70 percent of Chile's population are of mestizo (mixed white and native Indian) origin.

Fútbol (soccer) is very popular, as are skiing, swimming and fishing. Theater, music and movies are also popular.

In areas where cattle have been important, rodeo is very popular. Chilean rodeo is very different from the version enjoyed in the U.S.

Spanish, called *Castellano*, is the official language. Some terms common to Chile, however, will not have the same meaning in other Spanish-speaking countries. In addition, the final syllables of words are often eliminated.

Yawns should be stifled or covered with your hand.

Only a waiter should be beckoned with hand gestures.

Making a fist and slapping it up into the palm of the other hand is a rude gesture.

Holding the palm upward and then spreading the fingers means that someone is stupid.

CHINA (PRC)

Population: 1,236,914,658 (July 1998 est.); Han Chinese 91.9%, Zhuang, Uygur, Hui, Yi, Tibetan, Miao, Manchu, Mongol, Buyi, Korean and other 8.1%

Languages: Mandarin, Yue (Cantonese), Wu (Shanghaiese), Minbei (Fuzhou), Minnan (Hokkien-Taiwanese), Xiang, Gan, Hakka dialects, minority languages

Religions: Daoist, Buddhist, Muslim 2-3%, Christian 1%

Currency: yuan

Beijing

HISTORICAL OVERVIEW

• China is one of the world's oldest continuous civilizations. Throughout most of its history, China was ruled by a series of dynasties.

• The Shang dynasty, the earliest dynasty for which there is known historical evidence, was already present in the 18th century B.C. Under the Shang, a writing system and calendar were already in use. The Zhou dynasty succeeded the Shang in 1111 B.C. and ruled until 255 B.C. Confucius dates from this era. He lived from 551-479 B.C.

• In 221 B.C. the Chin dynasty came to power and unified China, giving China its name. The Han dynasty quickly followed, however, in 206 B.C. and ruled until 220 A.D. The Han adopted the teachings of Confucius as the official national philosophy. After the fall of the Han, Buddhism began to gain followers in China.

• The Chinese empire reached its zenith under the T'ang dynasty (618-907 A.D.) which perfected China's civil service system. China's military strength and culture under the T'ang had a profound influence on neighboring Japan, Korea and Vietnam.

• A period of warfare followed the fall of the T'ang until the Song dynasty (960-1279 A.D.) came to power. The Song period was marked by rapid economic and commercial development. In 1279, however, the Mongols under Genghis Khan and his grandson Kublai Khan conquered the Song dynasty and hence China.

The Mongols built their capital at Beijing and ruled a vast domain, but they could never properly integrate with Chinese institutions and in 1369 they were overthrown by the Ming.

- The Ming brought China into a period of strict isolationism. In 1644 Manchurians from the north invaded and began the Qing dynasty.

- During the 19th century China was severely weakened by foreign commercial intrusions. The Opium War (1839-42) with Britain, the Taiping Rebellion (1851-64), and the Sino-Japanese War (1894-95) were some of the major events that shook the Qing dynasty. It fell in 1911 in a revolution inspired by Sun Yat-Sen.

- Sun Yat-Sen established the *Kuomintang* (KMT) Political Party in an effort to unify China, which was being fragmented by opposing warlords during the 1920s.

- Chiang Kai-shek took control of the KMT in 1927 and ousted the once-allied Communist Party (CCP). Some unity of the country was achieved.

- Japan seized Manchuria in 1931 and then invaded North China proper in 1937. The Japanese occupied most of northern and eastern China until 1945.

- From 1934-35 Mao Zedong led the Communists on their "Long March" across China to regroup and fight the KMT for control of China.

- After World War II, with the defeat of the Japanese, civil war resumed and Mao's forces gained control. Chiang's army fled to Taiwan.

- The People's Republic of China was proclaimed on 1 October 1949, and Mao Zedong ruled China from 1949 to 1976.

- Mao died in 1976. His wife, Jiang Quing, and three of her colleagues, known as the "Gang of Four," attempted to seize power. After being arrested and tried, Jiang Quing was executed.

- The violence and chaos engendered by Mao's cultural revolutions discredited him and his policies after his death and brought the more moderate Deng Xiaoping to power.

- Major reforms were instituted in the early 1980s, primarily aimed at raising the standard of living. These reforms were known as the "Four Modernizations": agriculture, industry, national defense and science and technology. The Chinese government legitimized free market forces and opened the country to western investment and cultural influences.

- In 1989, students demonstrated in Tiananmen Square after the death of Hu Yaobang, leader of the Chinese Communist Party.

They demanded greater freedom, an end to government corruption and relief from overcrowded conditions within Chinese universities. After six weeks, many others had joined in the protests. On 3 June 1989, military troops rolled in and put a stop to the demonstrations. Many protestors were killed or injured. As a result, China lost many foreign investments and tourism declined. The government returned to stricter measures to reassert control. By 1922, however, it was again trying its hand at economic reform.

- In February 1997, Jiang Zemin became president.

- On 1 July 1997, China regained control of Hong Kong, which became a Special Administrative region of China.

BUSINESS PRACTICES

Hours of Business

Business and government offices are open from 8:00 a.m. to 5:00 p.m. Stores are open from 9:00 a.m. to 7:00 p.m., but remain open longer in Shanghai. Everything closes from noon until 2:00 p.m.

Dress

Formal dress for men is a suit and tie. Pantsuits are appropriate for businesswomen, since Chinese women often wear pants. Dress styles are changing rapidly in China. You should dress fashionably, but be conservative in all your accessories. Do not wear very short skirts or low necklines. For business meetings or dining out, women should wear a suit or a dress and as little makeup as possible. Jewelry should be modest and of excellent quality.

Introductions

In China's larger cities such as Beijing or Shanghai and in business situations, the customary greeting is a handshake. You should wait for your counterpart to extend his/her hand first, since not everyone uses this greeting. The handshake is usually light, but may last several seconds. Throughout the rest of China, the most common greeting is a nod or slight bow.

If you bow, never do so with a hand or hands in your pockets.

Business cards in Chinese and English are essential. Present your card with both hands after the handshake. Receive your counterpart's card with both hands and take a moment to examine the card and what it says, even if it is printed only in Chinese characters.

In Chinese names, the family name always comes first (for example, in the name Chen Wu, Chen is the family name and Wu is the given name). He should be addressed as Mr. Chen. Only family members or close friends use first names.

The Chinese often will not look you straight in the eye when greeting you. They sometimes lower their eyes slightly as a sign of respect. Looking directly into a Chinese person's eyes may make them uncomfortable and make you seem rude.

Meetings

Business appointments are necessary and punctuality is important.

When entering a business meeting as a group, the highest-ranked person should lead the group. Conventionally, the senior members of the Chinese and foreign teams head the discussion. It is not usually expected for junior members of your group to interject.

Negotiating

"Economic value" is the basis for negotiations.

Negotiators are selected on the basis of political understanding and Confucian virtues.

Teams are large and lawyers are rare. Chinese prefer to deal with groups rather than an individual negotiator. Be sure to have technically competent engineers and other experts on your team.

Chinese negotiators prefer to host negotiations in order to help secure a favorable outcome for their group.

Give your counterparts advance notice as to what you would like to accomplish in China. This is a courtesy they appreciate and reduces any concerns they may have about being surprised by your intentions.

Although a no-compromise approach is initially taken during the process of negotiations, flexibility emerges.

Chinese negotiators are characterized by the "soft sell" and the "hard buy". Give yourself plenty of room to negotiate and to give concessions.

Although your Chinese counterpart will probably seek specific terms and conditions, he or she might not be as willing to grant them himself.

Impatience on your part will usually be met with delays.

A network of personal connections is very important. This is called *guanxi*. Little or no distinction is made between business and personal relationships. To succeed in China, you must establish close personal ties with your Chinese business colleagues. Respect and trust must be earned before business can be negotiated.

Never do or say anything that might embarrass your counterpart. Be subtle and sensitive in your disagreements. Try not to ask direct questions. Be reserved and dignified in your personal style.

Presentations should be detailed, technical and factual. Speak often of trust and cooperation between you and your counterparts. Focus on long-term benefits.

Be patient and persistent. Several trips to China will probably be necessary before you reach a business agreement. Keep your return plans flexible.

The hierarchy within a Chinese organization is complicated. It is often difficult to identify who makes the final decision. Thus, treat everybody with equal respect and be prepared to present your material to many different people at varying levels of authority.

Expect slow decision making that must work its way through a cumbersome bureaucracy. Remember that your negotiating counter-part may not be able to make a decision to go forward on a project although he/she may be able to veto a decision or slow down progress.

Be aware of the Chinese tactic of "shaming," whereby your counter-part might suggest that you have broken the bond of friendship if you do not agree to the final contract proposals they have made.

Chinese businesspeople will usually not come out directly and say "No" to a proposal. They will find indirect ways to indicate a negative response.

Part of Chinese negotiating strategy involves being an excellent host. You should not misinterpret this as an indication of their attitude toward you or your project.

Periods of silence during business or dinner are a sign of politeness and of thought. Do not be quick to fill the silence with words. Take care not to interrupt during a conversation.

Avoid using maps showing a British Hong Kong or an independent Taiwan.

It is considered inappropriate to give an individual a business gift. It would be more appropriate to present a modest gift from your company division to the Chinese unit with which you are dealing. It should be presented to the most senior person in the Chinese unit. Gifts might include books about your country, records, a magazine subscription, pens, notepads or calendars. If suitable, wrap the gift in red, which is considered a lucky color, and present it at a banquet. It is common for the Chinese to refuse a gift or other offering two or three times before accepting it. It is not necessary for foreigners to go through the same ritual.

Entertaining

Keep track of all favors done for you, small gifts received, etc. You will be expected to reciprocate in the future.

As a foreign businessperson, you will be treated to an evening banquet. You should reciprocate the invitation as soon as possible, preferably on the same trip. When you are in China, it is polite to allow your Chinese counterpart to issue the first invitation.

All members of your delegation should arrive for a banquet at the same time. Be punctual.

In making the invitation list for your banquet, include everybody with whom you have interacted because it is often difficult to tell who the ultimate authority figure is. Do not risk excluding the most important person. If your spouse co-hosts a banquet, be sure to include the spouse of the principal guest in your invitation.

An invitation to a Chinese home is rare. If you are invited to someone's home, bring a small gift such as a fruit basket or flowers. A memento from your home country is also appreciated. Gifts for the children are welcomed, as is perfume for the wife.

Business is generally not discussed during meals, although indirect references to business are common practice.

Seating arrangements are important, whether for business meetings or for dining. The principal guest sits next to the host when dining. Guests will be shown where to sit. At meetings, the main guest is seated facing the door and the host with his back to the door.

Tipping is officially illegal in China. Some people, however, will accept tips in private.

A wide variety of cuisines are represented in the different regions of China.

If you are invited to a restaurant, dinner will be served at a round table with dishes in the center. The table will probably be set with a soup bowl, several pairs of chopsticks (to take food from serving plates to individual bowls), a wine cup, a rice dish and a dish for shells and bones.

Banquets may consist of 10-12 courses.

Begin eating only after your host picks up his/her chopsticks.

The host may serve you. Otherwise, use chopsticks for reaching the food rather than passing around the serving dishes. If there is more than one pair of chopsticks at your place setting, use a different pair of chopsticks from the one you are putting in your mouth. Otherwise, use the other end of the chopsticks. It is considered polite to take what is close to you in the serving dish. Do not pick through items.

Eat one dish at a time using the chopsticks. Never touch food with your fingers.

Refusing food may be considered rude. If you don't want to eat a particular item, just move it to the side of your dish.

Meat dishes may have small bones. Remove the bones from your mouth using your chopsticks. It is rude to use your hands.

To eat rice, bring the bowl to your mouth and shovel the rice into your mouth with your chopsticks. Do not stick your chopsticks upright in your rice. Some Chinese people believe a superstition that this might bring bad luck.

Chinese people generally do not drink alone. They propose a toast so that others will join them.

Indicate that you have finished eating by placing your chopsticks parallel across your plate. Do not worry about leaving a little food on your plate. It is polite to leave some food to show that you have eaten your fill and that the host has provided more than you can eat.

Tea is much more common than coffee. At a meal, if you do not want more tea, leave some in your cup.

Soup is sometimes one of the last courses served. The serving of fruit signals the end of the meal. Your host will probably rise to show that the banquet has ended. If not, wait ten minutes after tea is served and hot towels have been distributed before leaving.

SOCIALS VALUES, CUSTOMS AND TIPS

The Chinese are known for their good manners, hospitality and reserve.

Confucianism has had a great influence on attitudes and actions. The basic tenets of Confucian thoughts are obedience to and respect for superiors and parents, duty to family, loyalty to friends, humility, sincerity and courtesy.

Respect and status increase with age. Older foreign businesspeople will likely be received with greater respect and will be regarded more seriously than will younger businesspeople.

Good conversation topics include personal questions, tourist sights, Chinese culture, shopping and life in western countries. Topics to avoid include government, politics and Taiwan. You may be asked how much money something costs or how much you earn. If this seems awkward, you may wish to explain that things cost a lot more in your country so that your purchasing power is not as high as it may seem.

China should be referred to as the People's Republic of China (PRC). Among the mainland Chinese, Taiwan is called the Province of Taiwan, never the Republic of China.

The concept of "face" is important in understanding the Chinese people. Be careful to avoid causing someone to "lose face" by insulting, criticizing or embarrassing him/her in front of others, or by treating the person with less than the proper respect due his/her status in the organization.

Chinese people generally stand closer to each other than do Europeans and North Americans.

When nervous or embarrassed, Chinese people may smile or laugh and cover their mouths with their hands.

When touring a factory, for example, you may be greeted by a group of people with applause. Returning the applause is the proper response.

It is rude to put your hands in your mouth. As a result, you should refrain from biting your fingernails or using your nails to remove food from your teeth. It will disgust the Chinese.

Public displays of affection are rare. Chinese people do not touch each other much in public.

Good friends of the same sex may walk hand in hand (a sign of friendship).

Direct eye contact or staring in public places is not common in large cities. In smaller towns, a Westerner may be greeted with curiosity and stares.

Good posture is important. Do not put your feet on a desk or a chair. Do not use your feet to point at something or to move objects.

Always ask permission before taking photographs of anyone.

Pointing is done with an open hand, not with one finger. The gesture for beckoning someone is done with the palm facing down and the fingers moving in a scratching motion.

COLOMBIA

Population: 38,580,949 (July 1998 est.); mestizo 58%, white 20%, mulatto 14%, black 4%, mixed black-Amerindian 3%, Amerindian 1%

Languages: Spanish

Religions: Roman Catholic 95%

Currency: Colombian peso

HISTORICAL OVERVIEW

- The first permanent Spanish settlement was made at Santa Marta on the Caribbean coast in 1525. Cartagena was founded in 1533. Bogotá was founded in 1538. In 1549, an administrative and judicial governing body, called an *audiencia*, was established to govern the area. The Indian population was greatly decimated, but there was little political unrest.

- Spain established four viceroyalties to govern its holdings in South and Central America. Colombia, along with present-day Ecuador and Venezuela, were combined to form the viceroyalty of Nueva Granada with its capital at Bogotá in 1740. Power was centralized, and the economy and culture began to flourish.

- In 1794, Antonio Nariño translated into Spanish the French Declaration of the Rights of Man and set in motion the movement toward independence from Spain.

- In 1808, when Napoleon replaced Ferdinand VII of Spain with his own brother, Joseph, there were several revolts in Colombia, first against French rule and then for Colombian independence. After Napoleon's fall from power in 1815, Spain attempted to reassert its authority over Nueva Granada, but Simon Bolívar assembled an army and defeated the Spanish troops in 1819. After the defeat of the Spanish, Neuva Granada was renamed the Republic of Gran Colombia.

- The Republic of Gran Colombia was a political union between

Colombia, Venezuela and Ecuador. The union began to dissolve when Venezuela broke away in 1829, and Ecuador followed in 1830. The remaining provinces were then named Nueva Granada. Not until 1863 was the name Colombia restored.

- A liberal revolt in 1899 turned into a civil war, The War of a Thousand Days, which cost many lives. The Liberals were defeated in 1903.

- In 1903, Panama declared its independence from Colombia.

- The strife between Conservatives and Liberals flared up again from 1948 to 1962 in a period known as *La Violencia* in which some 200,000 lives were lost and the economy suffered significantly. This conflict was ended by a political truce, which required the presidency to alternate between the Liberal and Conservative political parties until 1974. Since then, elections have been held regularly.

- Guerilla movements and drug cartels caused unrest and violence throughout the 1980s. During the 1990 election, the candidates of the Liberal Party and the *Unión Patriótica* were assassinated by drug traffickers. César Gaviria Trujillo was elected president.

- A new constitution took effect in July 1991. This constitution encourages political pluralism and secures the rule of law and special rights for the local indigenous peoples.

- In 1994, Ernesto Samper Pizarro of the Liberal Party was elected president. Evidence shows that his campaign was substantially financed by the Cali drug lords. U.S. President Clinton placed Colombia on a list of countries that fail to adequately combat drug trafficking, and this move severely hurt Colombia's economy.

- In 1995-96, the government broke the Cali drug cartel and arrested its main leaders. Samper also attempted peace talks with the Revolutionary Armed Forces of Colombia (FARC), the oldest rebel group in Latin America, but no definitive agreement was reached.

- On 23 June 1998, Andres Pastrana was elected president. Prior to the elections, Colombians peacefully protested the political violence that had traditionally broken out before elections.

- Having never been accused of corruption or favoritism, Pastrana desired to establish peace between the government and the FARC. He continues to develop plans to eliminate underground drug trafficking by rebel groups and to seek alternate crops for coca farmers.

BUSINESS PRACTICES

Hours of Business

Business hours are Monday through Friday, 7:00 a.m. to 6:00 p.m. There is a break for lunch between noon and 2:00 p.m. Shops generally close at midday for a lunch break.

Businesspeople usually vacation in December and January. In Barranquilla, they also vacation during June and July. Avoid visiting during the week before and after Easter and during the two weeks before and after Christmas.

Dress

Inland businesspeople dress more formally than those in the coastal regions. Foreigners are expected to dress formally in business environments, no matter how hot it is. Jacket and tie for men and a suit or dress for women are appropriate.

On social business occasions, men wear a jacket and tie and women wear cocktail dresses.

Introductions

A handshake is the most common greeting. Men often shake hands with everyone when entering a home, greeting a group or leaving.

Women who are acquainted with each other often kiss on the cheek. Otherwise, they offer a verbal greeting. Sometimes they will grasp each other's forearms instead of shaking hands.

Young people will also kiss on the cheek if they are good friends.

The *abrazo* (hug) is common between close friends and relatives.

Titles are important during introductions. People who have a university degree should be addressed as "Doctor." Be sure that your business cards include your title on them.

It is customary for a child to bear two family names. The last name is the mother's family name, and the next-to-last name is the father's family name. People use either their full names or their father's family name, which is the official surname. Someone named Jorge Lopez Muñoz would be called "Señor Lopez."

At parties, the host will introduce you individually to the others present. When leaving, say "Good-bye" to each guest.

Meetings

Make business appointments at least a week in advance. Arrive a day or two before your appointment in Bogotá. The altitude may affect you, and you will need time to get acclimated.

Be punctual for appointments, but do not expect Colombians to be on time.

You will most likely be offered coffee when you arrive for a meeting. Be sure to accept it.

Expect not to discuss business directly during your first or perhaps even your second appointment. Do not begin to discuss business until your Colombian counterpart initiates the conversation. Be knowledgeable or show interest in Colombian culture and achievements.

No matter how hot it is, men should wear a jacket in a business meeting until invited to remove it.

If you meet workers in a factory, shake hands with those nearest you when you are introduced and when you leave. Do not participate in any manual labor as status is very important in Colombia.

Negotiating

Negotiating is a relatively lengthy process in Colombia, allowing more time for concessions to be made. Businesspeople should be ready to give in, but always ask for something in return. If you concede without getting something in return, Colombian negotiation teams will immediately ask for another concession. Delays are to be expected. High-pressure selling or aggressive tactics are not well received.

While negotiating, try to stay with one individual rather than the group as a whole, since personal relationships are important in making business decisions. If you can convince middle managers that your proposal will make their work more efficient and thereby benefit their superiors, they will hear you out and lobby on your behalf.

Protocol and courtesy are highly valued. Take your cues from your Colombian counterparts.

Verbal and written communication are both conducted in an elaborate and indirect manner.

Individuals play a decisive role in negotiations. Keep your negotiating team the same from beginning to end.

Often what occurs outside the negotiating room and outside negotiating hours is as important as what occurs within them.

Colombian society is conscious of hierarchy, and status plays an important role. It is polite to show respect to higher-status people present by speaking to them first when entering a group. Learn their titles and use them. It is also beneficial to have a person of status introduce you.

Attempt to make your Colombian colleague look good. Do not embarrass him/her in front of others.

To initiate and maintain relationships, you may have to do things that are frowned upon back home, like taking longer trips to socialize and develop trust, bestowing "favors" that your Colombian colleague can use to bolster social prestige, and showing patience when deadlines are missed.

Hiring a local contact will prove beneficial, if not essential, in order to establish the business relationships imperative for the negotiation process.

Entertaining

You may be invited to a business associate's home. Colombians like you to meet their spouses and families. If time permits, send a gift of fruit, flowers or chocolates before you arrive. If not, send a gift afterwards along with a note of appreciation.

When invited to dinner at someone's home, a man should wear a suit and tie and a woman should wear a skirt and blouse or dress.

The major occasions for formal wear are weddings and graduation parties. An invitation will specify formal dress.

You will probably be offered a before-dinner drink, such as Scotch, vodka, gin, etc. Wine may be served with the meal as a dinner for guests is a special occasion. If you do not drink, ask for soda water. Hors d'oeuvres will be served with before-dinner drinks.

It is considered polite to leave a small amount of food on your plate to indicate that the host has provided abundantly for his/her guests. To show that you have finished eating, place the knife and fork horizontally across your plate.

Reciprocate an invitation to someone's home by hosting a dinner in a restaurant.

Lunch is frequently the main meal of the day. When possible, the family gathers for this meal. In urban areas, there is a trend toward having the main meal in the evening.

Colombians use the continental style of dining, with the knife held in the right hand and the fork in the left.

To give a toast, raise your glass, look at the people around you and say *Salud* (To your health).

Soup, rice, meat, potatoes, salad and beans are staples. *Arroz con pollo* (chicken with rice) and *sancocho* (stew with meat and vegetables) are popular national dishes. *Arepas* (cornmeal pancakes) are popular at breakfast. Other specialties include *hallacas* (meat stuffed into ground corn dough and wrapped in banana leaves) and *pabellón criollo* (shredded beef with rice, black beans and plantains).

Colombian coffee is the favorite beverage. Black coffee is called *tinto*. Coffee with milk is called *café perico*. A cup of milk with a little coffee added is called *café con leche*.

SOCIAL VALUES, CUSTOMS AND TIPS

Colombians will seldom turn down an invitation directly, although they may plan not to attend. They will say something like "I'll try to come." You will have to learn how to pick up their cues.

Friends often drop in on each other unannounced.

The family is an important part of Colombian society.

Good conversational topics include sports, especially *fútbol* (soccer), art, Colombian coffee and the scenic countryside. Bullfighting is popular in Colombia. Do not make negative comments about it.

Women should be careful not to make any glances or gestures that could be construed as flirtatious or provocative.

Do not yawn in public or eat on the streets.

Beckon someone by extending the arm palm down and moving the fingers in a scratching motion.

Colombians do not usually form lines (for example, when waiting for a bus).

When you visit a church, do not use flash photography.

Do not wear shorts when visiting churches or while walking on the street. Jeans should be stylish and clean.

In open markets you may bargain, but not in stores.

In Colombia, there are particular gestures for showing the size of things. To show how tall an animal is, the flat palm is held downward. To show the height of a person, the flat palm is held sideways with the thumb on top. To show the length of something, hold the right arm out, the palm flat with thumb on top and use the left hand to mark off the length along the right hand, wrist or forearm. You would offend Colombians by holding out your two hands and pointing with the two index fingers to indicate the distance between the two fingers as the correct length.

COSTA RICA

Population: 3,604,642 (July 1998 est.); white (including mestizo) 96%, black 2%, Amerindian 1%, Chinese 1%

Languages: Spanish (official), English spoken around Puerto Limón

Religions: Roman Catholic 95%

Currency: Costa Rican colon

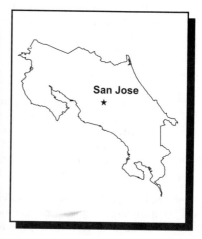

San Jose ★

HISTORICAL OVERVIEW

- A variety of native peoples lived in present-day Costa Rica before Columbus arrived in 1502. The indigenous populations had been influenced by the Mayan civilization in the north and by other South American groups in the south.

- Beginning in 1522, Spain colonized the Costa Rican area along with most of the rest of Central America. The Spanish intermarried with the native peoples, who were then assimilated into the Spanish culture. Nevertheless, because of its lack of mineral wealth, Costa Rica was largely ignored by the Spanish crown and remained quite isolated.

- In 1821, Costa Rica joined Mexico and other Central American countries in declaring independence from Spain during a nonviolent revolution.

- In 1823, Costa Rica helped form the United Provinces of Central America, which was ruled by Mexico. Conflict within the other states in the federation, however, caused Costa Rica to leave the organization and declare independence in 1938.

- Costa Rica has one of the most stable governments in Central America. It had only one major experience with a dictatorial government, when Tomás Guardia came to power in 1870 and led the country until 1882. In 1890, Jose Joaquin Rodriquez came to power in the first free election in Central America. Only three subsequent attempts were made to seize the government unlawfully. These occurred in 1917, 1932 and 1948.

- The 1948 attempt to seize the government is the most recent instance of political unrest. In that year, a civil war erupted for six weeks after a dispute over elections. José Figueres Ferrer led an interim government until 1949 when the election dispute was settled. Figueres, who was elected president in 1948 and again in 1970, abolished the army in 1948 and established a civil guard. A new constitution was introduced in 1949, and Costa Rica has enjoyed peace ever since.

- In the 1980s, Costa Rica faced severe economic problems and communist infiltration of the Labor Party from within. In addition, the country found itself surrounded by armed conflict in Nicaragua, El Salvador and Guatemala. Oscar Arias Sánchez was voted president in the 1986 elections. Arias (who left office in 1990) attempted to broker peace in his neighboring countries and was a creator of the Central American Peace Plan, for which he won a Nobel Peace Prize.

- Rafael Calderón Fournier was elected president in 1990. He implemented measures to modernize the economy and reduce the size of government. José Maria Figueres Olsen was elected in 1994.

- Figueres introduced a series of highly successful economic reforms. He was most successful at attracting multinational corporations by promoting his country's literate workforce and low labor costs. Despite his successes, Figueres was rather unpopular, partly due to low-level scandals in his administration and his neglect of the nation's infrastructure.

- Figueres did not run in the 1998 presidential elections. Miguel Angel Rodriquez Echeverría, who had lost to Figueres in the 1994 elections, was elected.

BUSINESS PRACTICES

Hours of Business

Businesses are open Monday through Friday, 8:00 a.m. to 5:00 p.m. and Saturday, 8:00 a.m. to 11:00 a.m.

Government office hours are 8:00 a.m. to 4:00 p.m., Monday through Friday.

Avoid planning business trips during December and January, as these are the most popular vacation times.

Dress

Dress for business meetings is formal. Ties and jackets should be worn. Women should wear conservative dresses. Men should keep their jackets on throughout the business meeting.

Introductions

A strong but friendly handshake is appropriate each time you meet acquaintances or friends, especially when arriving or leaving a meeting place.

Among Costa Ricans, first names are used quickly, usually after the first meeting, but only among equals of similar status and age. Foreigners should wait for a signal from their counterparts before using first names. Business acquaintances are usually addressed by the first name with the prefix *Don* or *Doña* (which denotes respect) or with the term *licenciado* (which refers to a college degree or doctorate) before the last name.

Among women, a full embrace and pats on the back are very common. Kisses on the cheek are customary among female friends.

Costa Ricans, popularly known as *ticos*, follow the Spanish tradition of full names (first name, middle name, father's last name and mother's last name, in that order).

Meetings

Appointments should be arranged well in advance. Businesspeople from the private sector are usually very punctual for appointments, while government officials can be as much as a half an hour late for meetings.

It is customary to engage in informal conversation before discussing business matters. Coffee is offered at most meetings.

Business lunches can last up to three hours. It is recommended to leave any business until the end of the meal. Take your cues from your counterparts.

Have business cards and any sales literature printed in both Spanish and English.

Negotiating

For the new or infrequent business visitor, a good lawyer is a prerequisite for conducting business. There are many lawyers in Costa Rica who speak English.

Establishing a personal relationship before entering into business negotiations is imperative in Costa Rica. This will take time. Do not try to rush the process.

Several visits to Costa Rica will be necessary before any agreement is finalized.

Equality and individual honor are very important in Costa Rican society. Therefore, avoid any comments that may embarrass someone or cause them to "lose face."

Decisions are made on a consensus basis. Although this may slow the negotiation process, be patient. Impatience may break down the trust established between you and your Costa Rican counterpart.

Women are accepted in the Costa Rican business world to a much greater extent than in other Latin American countries.

Costa Ricans are known for having a very flexible view towards their payment due dates.

Entertaining

It is customary to invite visitors to restaurants. Although they are very private about their families, Costa Ricans may occasionally invite business acquaintances to their homes. When invited to a private home, it is customary to arrive half an hour late and to bring a gift for the host. Flowers are an appropriate gift.

It is wise for women to accept only business lunch invitations from men. Invitations to dinner should be accepted only if the meal will be attended by a group of people.

Invite spouses, both foreign and Costa Rican, to business dinners.

The preferred style of eating is U.S.-style (knife in the right hand and fork in the left when cutting, then switching the fork to the right hand for eating), not continental.

It is considered polite to linger for about an hour after the meal is finished before leaving.

SOCIAL VALUES, CUSTOMS AND TIPS

After you have come to know a Costa Rican, any topic is appropriate for conversation (except taboo subjects such as sex or very personal matters).

People stand no more than two feet apart when speaking.

English is accepted and widely spoken among business executives.

Dress is usually informal, especially in hot weather. Men can wear short-sleeved shirts and do not need to wear ties, unless it is a formal occasion. Jackets are not usually worn. If worn, however, it is best to wait for a sign from the host before removing it.

Men usually give their seats to women in crowded waiting areas and public places.

CÔTE D'IVOIRE

Population: 15,446,231 (July 1998 est.); Baoule 23%, Bete 18%, Senoufou 15%, Malinke 11%, Agni 12%, foreign Africans 19%, non-Africans (mainly French and Lebanese) 2%

Languages: French (official), 60 native dialects with Dioula the most widely spoken

Religions: Muslim 60%, Christian 12%, Indigenous 25%

Currency: Communaute Financiere Africaine franc (CFA franc)

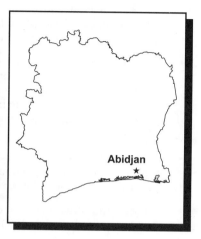

Abidjan

HISTORICAL OVERVIEW

- The early history of Côte d'Ivoire is virtually unknown. Ivory and slaves attracted Europeans to the area beginning in the 15th century. France made its initial contact with Côte d'Ivoire in 1637 when missionaries landed near the Ghana border. By the end of the century, France had trading posts in Assini and Grand Bassam.

- In the 18th century, the country was invaded by two related ethnic groups, the Agnis, who occupied the southeast, and the Baoules, who settled in the central section.

- During 1843-1844, Bouet-Williaumez signed treaties with the kings of the Grand Bassam and Assinie regions, placing their territories under a French protectorate. French explorers, missionaries, trading companies and soldiers gradually extended the area under French control inland from the lagoon region.

- The Mandingo people, led by Samory Toure, resisted French expansion in the region. While able to sign treaties with coastal chieftains, the French also met with fierce resistance from the Ashanti people in the west. Eventually, however, the French prevailed, and Côte d'Ivoire, which was made a colony in 1893, was completely conquered by 1918.

- The country suffered throughout the Great Depression, as the price of its agricultural exports dropped. During World War II, Côte d'Ivoire was under control of the pro-German Vichy administration that had been established in France.

- After the war, colonial rule continued, but there was a rapid rise in nationalism among natives in Côte d'Ivoire. In 1947, the inhabitants of the north separated and formed the nation of Upper Volta (now Burkina Faso). Faced with rebellion in Vietnam and Algeria, France was in no position to oppose the nationalist demands and, in 1956, passed the Overseas Reform Act, which gave the African colonies internal autonomy.

- Félix Houphouët-Boigny peacefully led Côte d'Ivoire to independence, which it achieved in 1960. He became the first president. He developed the country into an industrious, comparatively wealthy republic. One key to his success was that, unlike the leaders of many newly independent African nations, he was able to avoid tribalism.

- Houphouët-Boigny ruled until his death in 1993. For the first time, the Côte d'Ivoire Democratic Party (PCDI) was the sole political party. (The PCDI remains dominant today.)

- The constitutional successor to the presidency, Henri Konan Bedie, assumed office in 1995.

- Prior to 1996, Côte d'Ivoire assumed an open-door policy that allowed non-citizens to live within its borders. Under Bedie, the government closed its borders and allowed in only citizens who could prove that both their parents and grandparents had been born in the country. Documentation is difficult because Côte d'Ivoire was not yet a country when many of the older generations were born.

- In 1994, the currency was devalued. Since then, however, the GDP has steadily increased and inflation continues to shrink. The continuing worldwide coffee surplus and the AIDS epidemic are major concerns in present-day Côte d'Ivoire.

BUSINESS PRACTICES

Hours of Business

Weekday business hours are from 8:00 a.m. to noon and from 2:30 to 6:00 p.m. On Saturday, hours are from 8:00 a.m. to noon.

Dress

Men should wear a suit and tie, and women should wear a suit or dress.

Because of the extreme climate (warm and humid), lightweight and linen suits with a tie are required for men. For women, cotton or light knit dresses or suits are appropriate.

Introductions

A handshake is customary when meeting for the first time. If meeting more than one individual, make sure to give your name and your company name to each.

Ivorian businessmen will greet you at the airport and drive you to your hotel. A handshake and a formal greeting of either *Comment allez-vous?* (French) or *E-kah kay nay wah?* (local tribal language) meaning "How are you?" is customary.

You should refer to your host as *Monsieur* or "Mr.," or *Madame* or "Mrs." Some Ivorian names are long and complicated. Seek advice on pronunciation.

Once you get to know your host personally, you can expect to be greeted with a hug and what seems like a kiss, but is more a touch on the cheeks, first the left, then the right, then the left again.

It is best to send letters of introduction through a courier or parcel service that specializes in service to West Africa. Usually, a third party should provide an introduction, but local firms, for the most part, are receptive to unsolicited business proposals.

Meetings

One month prior to visiting Côte d'Ivoire, write, fax or call ahead several times to confirm appointments. Advise your counterpart that you will be in the country for less time than you had planned. Reconfirm appointments once you have arrived.

If you do not speak French, you will need an interpreter, although some Ivorian businesspeople do speak English (usually with difficulty). Almost all high-level businesspeople speak English.

Be punctual for meetings. Meetings may begin with non-business-related conversation as a way of getting acquainted.

It is not uncommon for African businessmen to have sunrise meetings over breakfast and coffee.

Avoid making appointments during the Muslim fasting month of Ramadan.

Negotiating

Engagement of a local agent or representative is essential to conducting business successfully, although the law does not require one to be appointed.

There are two types of Ivorian executives, French nationals and Ivorian nationals – many of whom have been educated in France.

Both tend to be formal in their approach toward business.

Personal relationships will be the foundation of any business agreement. Ivorians rarely do business with a person who is not within the extended family or a friend. The personal relationship will develop through a series of invitations to eat together or to visit your host's home, or perhaps through a trip to the Ivorian countryside.

The business pace in Côte d'Ivoire is relatively slow. Therefore, be patient when conducting negotiations.

Decisions are largely made by a few top executives. If the Ivorians you are negotiating with have familial connections with those at the top, however, a decision will be finalized more rapidly.

Married women are more respected by Ivorian businessmen than single women are. If your company sends a woman, be sure that she is experienced in foreign negotiations and is extremely professional.

Entertaining

Gift-giving is common, and gifts are usually presented to the family as a whole. Never present a gift to the wife only. Chocolates, electronic gadgets or a small memento of your country are always welcome.

Ivorians are not flamboyant, but they do have the French flair for enjoying the finer things in life. Generally, they do not drink wine without food or eat a meal without wine.

Entertaining is a way of promoting the friendship necessary for a good business relationship.

Most western food is imported and therefore expensive, so business entertainment may not include western cuisine.

When meal invitations are extended, acceptance is expected.

If invited to your host's home, expect dinner to be informal. It is appropriate to bring flowers or a gift.

Ivorians enjoy dancing at a local nightclub after dinner. Nightlife usually begins around 10:30 p.m. and lasts until 3:00 or 4:00 a.m.

If your host takes you to a restaurant, it will most probably be one that offers either French cuisine or hot and spicy Ivorian specialties.

The traditional Ivorian restaurant for lunch or dinner, a *maquis*, is popular. Your host will invite you to sample a favorite Ivorian specialty, Ivorian rice with sauce.

Ivorians love fish – the spicier the recipe, the better. Fish dishes are served with a variety of sauces: coconut and cream or hot and spicy with chili and peppers.

Braised chicken and fish smothered in onions and tomatoes, served with *attieke* (the national dish of the Ivory Coast) are popular dishes. Although it resembles couscous, *attieke* is in fact grated manioc, a type of cassava. Some Ivorians also favor beef brochettes and chicken *redjenou* (the local specialty).

To hurry through a meal or to eat copious amounts is considered vulgar.

To ask for a second helping of food is considered impolite.

SOCIAL VALUES, CUSTOMS AND TIPS

Ivorians, as well as many other Africans, are very sensitive about "westernized superior attitudes." Be careful not to make remarks that may be taken as disparaging of Ivorian culture or as assuming western superiority. Make sure to recognize Ivorian achievements and economic development. Discuss the culture and the country. A genuine interest in local food, music, art and customs is always welcome.

Ivorians are extremely cordial and may spend a lot of time becoming better acquainted with you.

Ivorians are impressed with French culture and customs. They strongly believe that the best clothing, for example, bears a "Made in France" label.

Criticism of the Ivorian president, colonialism, government and politics in general should be avoided.

Do not expect favors in return for those given. All personal actions are taken as an investment in friendship.

CUBA

Population: 11,050,729 (July 1998 est.); mulatto 51%, white 37%, black 11%, Chinese 1%

Languages: Spanish

Religions: Nominally Roman Catholic 85%, Protestant, Jehovah's Witness, Jewish, Santeria

Currency: Cuban peso

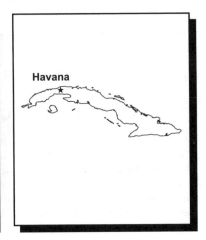

Havana

HISTORICAL OVERVIEW

- Cuba was discovered by Christopher Columbus in 1492 and became a Spanish colony in 1511. It was used by Spain as a staging area to launch expeditions into Central America. By the end of the 1500s, most of the indigenous population died from exposure to European diseases.

- In the 18th century, tobacco and sugarcane production flourished on the island. In 1762, the British invaded Havana but did not penetrate the interior and left less than two years later.

- In 1830, Spain began to tighten its grip on Cuba through heavy taxation and denial of fair representation of the Creole population. In 1867, Spain dismissed a Cuban delegation in Madrid. Later that year the Cuban independence movement, led by Carlos Manuel de Céspedes, began. The rebels failed to take Cuba from Spain, and after ten years of guerrilla warfare, the Spanish and Cubans reconciled with the hope of Cuban reforms.

- After reforms failed to take shape, the Cubans, under José Martí, revolted once more in 1895. The U.S. joined their cause after a mysterious explosion aboard the USS Maine in Havana Harbor. By the end of the war, all of Cuba's plantations had been completely destroyed, and Cuba was under U.S. military control.

- In 1902, the U.S. military occupation of Cuba came to an end. Cuba adopted a constitution, and, under Tomás Estrada Palma, Cuba became a free nation.

- Between 1902 and 1959, the U.S. intervened in Cuba's political affairs repeatedly in order to ensure a democratic succession of presidents. In 1935, Fugencio Batista was elected president of Cuba, and though corrupt, he stabilized the economic and political systems. After being out of office, Batista led a military coup that restored him to power in 1952. Batista's lack of popular support resulted in the formation of revolutionary forces. Fidel Castro and his troops entered Cuba in 1959.

- Castro's 16th of July Movement promised to restore Cuba's democratic policies to those of the 1940 constitution and to hold free elections. Shortly thereafter, however, Castro began to consolidate his power freely, align himself with the Soviet Union and pass communist reforms.

- Cuban expatriates, backed by the CIA, attempted to invade Cuba at the Bay of Pigs in 1961. The revolt failed. In 1962, the Soviet Union sent Cuba missiles to be pointed toward the U.S. This became known as the Cuban Missile Crisis. The Soviet Union withdrew its missiles after the U.S. and the Soviet Union came close to war. After six years of harboring revolutionaries and backing guerrilla revolutions in Latin America, Cuba accepted Soviet Communism in 1968.

- Cuba sent troops to many parts of the world to aid communist revolutions, particularly in Angola and Latin America. Cuba also accrued a large foreign debt to the U.S.S.R. Both of these factors debilitated the economy. In 1986, Soviet President Gorbachev cut almost all aid to Cuba and the Cuban economy was in severe decline by 1992.

- In the 1990s, waves of Cuban refugees entered or attempted to enter Florida and Castro threatened to send more if the long-lasting U.S. embargo against Cuba continued. The U.S. position remained unchanged, in spite of disagreement and pressure from its allies and the international community as a whole.

- In 1995, Cuba and China began to renew relations and to conduct trade. For the first time since the Cuban communist revolution, Cuban and Chinese heads of state met.

- Pope John Paul II visited Cuba in January 1998. After his visit Castro released many political prisoners, and the U.S. lifted some sanctions against the country.

BUSINESS PRACTICES

Hours of Business

Government offices and businesses keep the same hours: Monday through Friday, 8:30 a.m. to 12:30 p.m. and 1:30 p.m. to 5:30 p.m.

Dress

For businessmen, a suit and tie is not necessary for regular business meetings. Casual business attire is acceptable. For businesswomen, a light dress or suit is appropriate.

For formal evening business engagements men should wear a suit and women a cocktail dress.

Introductions

A handshake is an acceptable greeting for both men and women upon arrival and departure.

When meeting someone for the first time, official titles should be used. Professional titles used alone are the preferred forms of address. People who do not have professional titles should be addressed as *Señor* (Mr.), *Señora* (Mrs.) or *Señorita* (Miss), followed by the surname. People also use *Usted* (the formal form of "you") when meeting someone for the first time.

Most people in Cuba have two surnames, one from the father (listed first) and one from the mother. Normally, the father's name is used when addressing someone. For example, Hernan Antonio Martinez Garcia is addressed as *Señor Martinez* and María Elisa Gutierrez Herrera is addressed as *Señorita Gutierrez*. When a woman marries, she usually adds her husband's surname and goes by that surname. For example, if the two people in the above example married, the woman would be known as Señora María Elisa Gutierrez Herrera de Martinez. She would be addressed as Señora de Martinez or, more informally, Señora Martinez.

Cubans will often address one another as *compañero*.

Upon being introduced to your Cuban counterpart, remember to present your business card.

Meetings

It is best to schedule a business trip to Cuba between November and April.

Business appointments should be scheduled well in advance.

Meetings begin on time. It is important to be punctual.

Negotiating

Cuban businesspeople prefer working with groups rather than with individuals.

Since almost all commercial businesses in Cuba are state-owned, you will most likely be dealing with government officials when conducting business in Cuba.

Knowing something about Cuban culture will impress and please your Cuban counterpart.

Entertaining

Restaurants are usually not able to offer all of the items listed on the menu because of food shortages.

Some local dishes include omelets, suckling pig, chicken and rice and beans. Rum is also readily available.

If you are invited for a meal in your Cuban counterpart's home, it is appropriate to bring a small gift.

Nightclubs are available at the many tourist resorts in Cuba.

In Cuba, the average tip is 20 percent.

SOCIAL VALUES, CUSTOMS AND TIPS

The Ministry of Culture was founded to promote the arts in 1959. Cuba has a bustling cultural life that includes film, dance, theater, ballet, music and literature.

Cubans are very hospitable to and cautious of foreigners because of the network of government spies throughout the island.

Cuba's national sport is baseball, but *fútbol* (soccer) is also very popular. All sporting events in Cuba are free.

Businesswomen should wear cotton dresses and pants when not attending business functions. Shorts and bathing suits should only be worn when at the beach or pool.

Cuban men typically wear a *guayabera*, a casual pleated shirt worn over the pants.

CZECH REPUBLIC

Population: 10,286,470 (July 1998 est.); Czech 94.4%, Slovak 3%, Polish 0.6%, German 0.5%, Gypsy 0.35%, Hungarian 0.2%, other 1%

Languages: Czech, Slovak

Religions: atheist 39.8%, Roman Catholic 39.2%, Protestant 4.6%, Orthodox 3%, other 13.4%

Currency: koruna

★ **Prague**

HISTORICAL OVERVIEW

- Until 1918, when what is now known as the Czech Republic united with Slovakia, its history was largely that of Bohemia. The first settlers were the Celtic Boií, followed by Germanic tribes. Slavic tribes, including the Czechs, began settling in the region in the fifth century, and, by the middle of the ninth century, they lived in a loose confederation with Slavs around the Morava River known as the Great Moravian Empire. The Moravian Empire was destroyed in the late ninth century by invading Magyars from Hungary, but Bohemia managed to keep its independence and remain intact.

- The first Bohemian kingdom lasted from 895 to 1306 under the leadership of the Premysl rulers. The Luxembourgs took over in 1306, and in 1346 Charles I became king. He made Prague a cultural and political capital, ushering in a golden age. In 1355 Bohemia became part of the Holy Roman Empire. In the 15th century, Jan Hus led a Protestant reform movement that had nationalist overtones.

- When the Roman Catholic Hapsburgs took over the Bohemian crown in 1536, the Hussites agitated against them and led a revolt in 1618 that precipitated the Thirty Years' War. The defeat of the Bohemians in 1627 reduced Bohemia to the status of a province within the Austro-Hungarian Empire.

- With the collapse of the Austro-Hungarian Empire after World War I, Czech and Slovak lands were united to form a new Czecho-

Slovak state. (The hyphen in the name was dropped in 1920, and the name changed to Czechoslovakia.) Democracy and the economy of the new state flourished.

- In 1938, Hitler annexed the Sudetenland, a German-speaking area of Czechoslovakia and, by 1939, all of Czechoslovakia was under German occupation with Slovakia a puppet state. Over 350,000 Czechoslovak citizens (250,000 Jews) lost their lives.

- At the end of World War II, Czechoslovakia came under Soviet domination, and in 1948 the Communist Party seized total control. Rapid industrialization was promoted during the 1950s. In the 1960s, due to a decline in the economy, the government began to liberalize, and there were discussions about easing political restrictions. Alexander Dubcek, who became president in 1968, initiated more open reforms under the title "socialism with a human face." The short period of liberation that followed is known as the Prague Spring. In August 1968, however, the Soviet Union and its Warsaw Pact allies marched into the country, crushed all reforms and conducted a series of purges.

- The regime that followed built up the economy but was also one of the most repressive in Eastern Europe.

- In 1989, many people took part in peaceful demonstrations and general strikes. The Communist Party finally gave in and introduced reforms. A multiparty system was written into law, the former dissident Vaclav Havel became president, and in 1990 free elections to the Federal Assembly were held. This became known as the Velvet Revolution.

- Full multiparty elections were held in 1992, and Havel remained president, Vaclav Klaus became prime minister of the Czech national government, and Vladimir Meciar became prime minister of the Slovak national government. Disagreements between the Slovak and Czech leaders over economic policies and Slovak nationalist sentiments led to a dissolution of the country into a Czech and Slovak Republic in 1993. The breakup was peaceful, and ties between the two nations remain strong. Klaus launched an impressive program of economic reform in the Czech Republic.

- In the 1990s Czechs were allowed to buy shares of state companies through a coupon system. At the same time the Prague Stock Exchange opened.

- In 1996 the Czech Republic was asked to become a member of NATO, and in 1997 full membership talks began, with the goal of making the Czech Republic a part of the European Union.

BUSINESS PRACTICES

Hours of Business

Business hours are usually from 8:00 or 8:30 a.m. until some time between 4:00 and 5:15 p.m. during the week.

Dress

Business dress is conservative. Businessmen wear dark suits, ties and white shirts. Businesswomen wear dark suits with white blouses or dresses. Follow the lead of your colleagues with regard to removing ties or jackets.

Nowadays one may see young Czech businessmen wearing brightly colored suits.

Introductions

Upon introduction, people shake hands firmly and say their last names, followed by a verbal greeting, such as *Tesi mne* (Pleased to meet you) or *Dobry den* (Good day). Women and older people extend their hands first when greeting others.

It is customary to shake hands with everyone present upon arrival and upon departure at both social and business occasions.

To show respect, it is important to address both men and women by their professional titles (Engineer, Doctor, Professor), followed by the last name. If the people you are meeting are not professionals, you may use the titles *Pán* (pronounced "Pahn") which means "Mr.," *Pani* (pronounced "PAH-nee") which means "Mrs." or *Slecna* (pronounced "SLEH-chnah") which means "Miss."

It is also common when greeting someone to precede a professional title with *Pán* or *Pani* . For example, you can say, *Dobry den, Pan Doktorko Cekan* (Good day, Mrs. Dr. Cekan).

Normally, first names are only used among relatives, good friends and young people, who also sometimes hug each other in greeting.

To say good-bye, the formal *Na shledanou* or the informal *Cau* (pronounced like "Ciao") are used. *Ahoj* can be used as an informal "Hi" and "Bye."

Meetings

Avoid planning business trips for July or August, as most people take vacations during the summer months.

Make appointments well in advance (at least ten days) of a meeting.

Negotiating

When doing business in the Czech Republic, be aware that the country has just made the transition from a planned economy to a free market. Both small and large private companies are opening and developing. Additionally, people are generally eager to do business and to encourage foreign investment. You should not be surprised, however, if your Czech colleagues seem very cautious, since new business laws and customs are being introduced and developed. In fact, it is advisable to hire a Czech business lawyer, since radical changes in business law have created considerable complexity in doing business.

The "soft-sell" technique will work best when dealing with new Czech firms.

It may take some time for first introductions. If you are sending a letter from abroad, you should send it at least a month in advance. When writing a letter to a Czech company, you should address the letter to the firm, not to an individual.

Czechs typically converse before conducting business, and it is acceptable to ask your Czech associates personal, but nonpolitical, questions. Drinks and Turkish coffee are often offered at business meetings. It is polite to accept these refreshments. If a toast is made, it is polite to reciprocate.

Expect decisions to be made much more slowly than in the U.S. Many Czechs have adopted the German style of conducting business, which involves slow, methodical planning.

Have business letters sent in English as well as in Czech to make an extremely good impression.

Keep in mind that although English is becoming more and more widely spoken, an interpreter may still be necessary.

Bring plenty of business cards, as they are used abundantly. It is appreciated if your card is printed both in English and in Czech. Czechs respect education. Therefore, you should be sure to include on your card any degrees you have beyond a bachelor's.

Eye contact is very important in conversation. Gestures are also used extensively for emphasis.

The Czech republic still has an extensive bureaucracy. Allow sufficient time during negotiations to overcome bureaucratic hurdles.

Emphasize your company's position in the West, and point out how your company can train your Czech counterpart's company in technological and managerial skills.

Entertaining

Entertaining rarely takes place in the home, since Czechs consider the home to be strictly private. Normally, people socialize in pubs, coffeehouses and wine bars, and dinners take place in restaurants. If you are invited to a home, even for a drink or coffee, you should consider this an honor.

Do not expect to have much contact with your business associates outside of the office. While Czechs are very hospitable, it may take a long time to establish a close business relationship. Historically, business meetings have been confined to offices, but Czechs are becoming more accustomed to western habits, including the business lunch.

Meal reservations should be made in advance since the number of good restaurants for business entertaining is limited, and they are generally very busy.

Business is generally discussed before and after, but not during, a meal.

It is appropriate, but not necessary, to include spouses in invitations.

Czechs remove their shoes and leave them in the entryway when entering a home.

If you are invited to a home, it is polite to bring flowers. Bring an odd number of flowers (but not 13) to the host, since an even number of flowers is associated with a funeral. Avoid chrysanthemums or calla lilies (which are associated with funerals as well) and red roses (which are associated with romance). Unwrap the flowers before presenting them. Liquor (wine, whiskey or cognac), chocolates or gifts for the children are also appreciated.

Generally, businesspeople do not give or expect to receive expensive gifts. Acceptable business gifts include good-quality pens, pocket calculators, cigarette lighters or imported wine or liquor.

At formal parties, your host should introduce you to the other guests. In fact, at such parties it is impolite to speak to someone unless you have been introduced. At informal parties, however, it is acceptable to introduce yourself if your host has not introduced you.

Wait until everyone has been served a drink before picking up your glass. Toasting is common both at formal and informal events. As a guest, you should feel free to offer a toast in honor of the celebration.

When dining in a home or in a restaurant, men should wear casual slacks, a shirt and a sweater (optional), while women should wear dresses or skirts and blouses. In more formal restaurants, men should wear suits and ties.

A tip is not usually included in the bill at a restaurant. It is customary to round the bill up to the next whole number or leave a five to ten percent tip on the table.

Czechs generally eat three meals a day as well as a mid-morning snack. For most people, lunch is the main meal with breakfast and dinner being lighter.

Breakfast, which is served early, usually consists of rolls, coffee cake, butter, jam and coffee. Lunch usually begins with a hearty soup, followed by a main dish of meat and potatoes or bread dumplings. A common dish is *vepro-knedlo-zelo* (pork roast, dumplings and sauerkraut). The mid-morning snack, eaten at about 10:00 a.m., usually consists of sandwiches or hot sausages and yogurt. At 4:00 p.m., there is often a break for sandwiches and Turkish coffee.

Supper is usually served between 5:30 and 6:30 p.m. If lunch was a full meal, supper will be lighter. The meal will be heavier at a dinner party. *Slivovitz* (plum brandy) or *becherovka* (herb brandy) may be served before the meal.

Czechs usually prefer a hot meal to a cold one, even in hot weather. Popular dishes include *franecek* (herring), *sardinky* (sardines), *husa* (roast goose) and *svickova na smetane* (filet of beef with sour cream).

At a dinner, guests are usually served first, although the oldest woman at the table is sometimes served first.

People eat in the continental style, with the fork in the left hand and the knife remaining in the right. You should not put your knife and fork down between bites.

Hands, but not elbows, should be kept above the table during meals (even once the meal has been finished and people are talking).

Conversation is not abundant during meals and is usually only encouraged if guests are present or if the head of the household speaks first. After the meal, people will stay at the table and talk.

Normally, second or third servings are offered. It is not impolite to decline the food graciously. On a first offer for a second serving, however, it is polite to accept a little food after initially refusing.

To indicate that you have finished, you should place your utensils together at one side of the plate. If you want to signal that you are just taking a break, you should cross your utensils on the plate.

SOCIAL VALUES, CUSTOMS AND TIPS

Czech is a Slavic language, related to Polish, Croatian and Russian. It uses a Latin alphabet. Czechs also often speak German, Russian or English, depending on their generation. German is the most commonly spoken foreign language among the older generation.

Czech society emphasizes conformity and cooperation over individuality. Community leaders are held in high esteem, and the youth are encouraged to participate in community and sports clubs. Czechs can be highly individualistic in stating their opinions or personal beliefs and wishes, however.

While the vast majority are ethnic Czechs, there are a number of other minorities that may exhibit other customs and values. Among them are the Roma Gypsies, who represent a sizable minority of the population.

Sports, especially soccer, tennis and ice hockey, make good conversation topics, as do the countryside and area you are in, since Czechs have a love of nature and enjoy a number of outdoor activities. Music (including Czech composers Dvorak and Janacek) and Czech literary and architectural history are other popular topics of conversation.

Do not discuss politics, especially socialism and the former Soviet Union. If your host brings up political matters, feel free to participate, but avoid criticizing the government.

It is perfectly acceptable to ask personal questions about someone's job or family, even if you have just met the person.

Speaking loudly is considered impolite.

Czechs will commonly look at or even stare at people in public. This should not be taken amiss.

Svejk is one of the national folk heroes of the Czech Republic. He represents the Czech ideal of rejecting authority.

Avoid taking pictures in museums or galleries or photographing policemen, military installations, airports and railroad stations.

European fashions are commonly worn in the Czech Republic. Younger people, in particular, wear the latest styles. Casual wear, including jeans and T-shirts, is popular. Adults do not normally wear shorts on city streets (only in parks). Members of the older generation may dress more formally.

It is acceptable to beckon others and point using the index finger. To gain someone's attention, raise your hand, palm facing out, with only the index finger extended. You should avoid waving.

When sitting, you should cross one knee over the other, rather than resting your ankle on the other knee. You should not prop your feet up on furniture.

It is impolite to converse with your hands in your pockets or while chewing gum.

Bargaining is not acceptable anywhere in the Czech Republic.

DENMARK

Population: 5,333,617 (July 1998 est.); Danish 97%, Turkish 0.5%, other Scandinavian 0.4%

Languages: Danish (official), Faroese, Greenlandic, German

Religions: Evangelical Lutheran 91%, other Protestant and Roman Catholic 2%, other 7%

Currency: Danish krone

HISTORICAL OVERVIEW

- It was around 14,000 years ago that continuous settlement of Denmark began. At the turn of the millennium, trade by sea brought the peoples in the area now called Denmark into contact with other civilizations. Denmark then came under the control of the Vikings, and the inhabitants were organized into small communities governed by local chieftains.

- Under the Vikings (750-1060 B.C.), Denmark became quite powerful. When Viking King Harald I Bluetooth came to power, he united all of Denmark and Christianized it. Canute I the Great commanded a vast empire that included England until 1042. During this era, Danish seamen raided European coastal towns and spread terror through much of Western Europe.

- In 1387, Margaret I became queen, and in 1397 she united Denmark, Norway and Sweden under one monarch in the Union of Kalmar, making Denmark politically dominant.

- Sweden left the Kalmar Union in 1523, and during the 16th, 17th and 18th centuries, Denmark engaged in costly wars, particularly against Sweden. In 1814, Denmark lost Norway to Sweden. In 1864, some additional territory was lost to Prussia (Germany). Despite these territorial losses, Denmark itself remained stable. In 1849, King Frederik VII signed a liberal constitution, making the country a constitutional monarchy rather than an autocracy.

- Denmark was neutral during World War I. Although it also declared neutrality during World War II, Nazi Germany marched in and occupied it. After the war, Denmark was one of the founding members of the North Atlantic Treaty Organization (NATO) in 1949, and in 1973 it joined the European Union (EU).

- During the 1970s and 1980s, government policies focused on helping the economy and on maintaining its social welfare system.

- During the 1990s, Denmark has been gradually moving toward greater integration with its European Union partners. In 1992, the Danish rejected the Maastricht Treaty, later accepting a modified version in 1993, which allows the country greater flexibility in its interactions with other EU nations. Denmark, along with Great Britain and Sweden, refused to adopt the EU currency: the euro.

- The current queen of Denmark, Margaret II, is the first queen since Margaret I ruled the country in the 14th century. Denmark has had 53 kings but only two queens. 1997 marks the 25th anniversary of the reign of Margaret II.

- After finding large Arctic oil reserves off of its coast in 1997, Greenland, a Danish territory that has had home rule since 1979, threatened to declare independence.

- In 1998, the Great Belt bridge connecting Copenhagen to the Jutland Peninsula was opened. The Osresund bridge connecting Norway to Denmark and the rest of Europe is expected to open in 2000.

BUSINESS PRACTICES

Hours of Business

Businesses are usually open from 8:00 or 9:00 a.m. to 5:00 p.m., Monday through Friday.

You should avoid scheduling business trips between June 20 and August 15 (summer vacation) as well as around Easter, April 16 (the Queen's birthday), June 5 (Constitution Day) and Christmas.

Dress

For business, men should wear suits or sports jackets and ties. Pants should be neatly pressed and shoes should be polished. Women should wear skirt suits or dresses.

Introductions

When you are introduced, you should rise and shake hands, whether the occasion is business or social. You should make eye contact, nod and say "Hello" or "Good Day." Feel free to introduce yourself if necessary.

You should shake hands heartily when you meet someone you know as well as when you leave.

Generally, you should use last names following a title (e.g., "Mr.," "Mrs." or "Miss"), but if your Danish colleague switches to first names in conversation, you should feel free to do the same.

If you wish to be very polite, use professional titles (e.g., Doctor, Professor, etc.), especially with older people.

Young people and close acquaintances may nod and wave and say, *Dav* or *Davs* (pronounced "Dow"), which is like saying "Hello." The youth often also say *Hej* (pronounced "Hi") when greeting or parting. The term for "Good Day" is *Goddag*.

Meetings

Appointments are necessary. Try not to schedule an appointment on a weekend.

Punctuality for business appointments is practiced and expected.

Negotiating

Eye contact is important in conversation.

The Danish people respect tradition, so it is useful to mention the age and history of your firm (if it is well established).

The pace of business is slow and efficient. The Danes have a love of details, and presentations should address all details of a business proposal.

As soon as both parties sit down to negotiate, the meeting begins. There is usually very little, if any, small talk. A direct, straightforward manner of communicating is the norm.

Bringing a small gift to your Danish counterparts (e.g., a book about your country or region) at the beginning of negotiations will be greatly appreciated.

Entertaining

Danes enjoy entertaining visitors in their homes and making guests feel welcome. Refreshments are almost always served.

If you are invited to a Danish home for the evening, do not assume that dinner will be served, unless your host specified this in your invitation.

When visiting, conversation about one's personal life is avoided.

If you are invited to a dinner in a home, you should be punctual. There is no pre-dinner cocktail hour and you may be seated in the dining room immediately.

Appropriate gifts include liquor (particularly appreciated since taxes on alcoholic products are very high in Denmark), wrapped flowers (tiny roses, anemones or flowers of the season), a product typical of your hometown, a book describing your home area, etc.

Alcohol may be ordered in a bar or restaurant 24 hours a day, unlike in other Scandinavian countries.

If you are invited to a casual dinner, you may wear clean jeans. At a more formal dinner, men usually wear jackets and ties; women wear dresses, blouses and skirts or dressy pants. It is advisable for businesspeople to pack formal wear since senior businessmen in Denmark sometimes host black-tie dinners.

In restaurants, men customarily handle all affairs. A waiter can be summoned by raising the hand and index finger.

It is not necessary to leave a tip, as a service charge is included in the bill. Some people, however, leave a small additional gratuity.

Dinners are usually long and slow with a lot of conversation. People will stay at the table talking long after the meal is finished.

Breakfast (served about 8:00 a.m.) is a light meal consisting of cereal, *ymer* (a type of yogurt) or soft-boiled eggs, bread or hard rolls, cheese and a hot drink or milk. A midday meal, consisting of open-faced sandwiches with beer or soft drinks and coffee, is eaten between noon and 2:00 p.m. Dinner is served between 6:00 and 8:00 p.m.

Danes usually take a coffee break at 9:00 or 10:00 a.m., a tea break at 3:00 p.m. and, often, an evening snack of pastries and fruit around 9:00 or 10:00 p.m.

Usually, the host and hostess sit at either end of the table with the guest of honor seated beside the host. Everyone is seated and served before anyone starts eating.

Toasting in Denmark involves quite formal etiquette. You should not taste the wine until the host makes the first toast. Before you take your first sip of wine, lift your glass and look around at everyone, toasting them. After you have tasted the wine, look around at everyone again. Although the guest may propose subsequent toasts, a guest should never toast the host or a person senior in age until that person toasts him/her first. If you are the guest of honor, you may propose a toast by tapping your glass with a spoon. An appropriate toast would be to say, "Thank you for having this dinner in my honor." During dessert, the person seated to the left of the host should propose a toast. The person seated on the right should make a brief speech of appreciation.

The Danish eat in the continental style, holding the fork in the left hand and the knife in the right.

At a dinner, the food will usually be passed around several times on platters. You may want to take small portions the first time, since it is considered insulting not to take a second helping of at least some dishes.

It is considered impolite to leave food on your plate. If you did not like a particular dish, however, do not feel obliged to take a second helping of it.

To show that you have finished eating, you should place the knife and fork, tines up, side by side vertically on the plate. Placing the fork with its tines down indicates that you would like more food.

Do not get up from the table until the hostess has done so. It is proper to thank her for the meal before leaving the table. Very often, the dinner party will move to the living room for after-dinner cocktails. Guests often stay as late as 1:00 a.m. after dining.

Danish specialties include: *bøf tartare* (raw ground sirloin on white bread with a raw onion ring and raw egg yolk on top of it), *flæskesteg* (roast pork served with red cabbage), *frikadeller* (meatballs), *øllebrød* (rye bread mixed with black beer, sugar and lemon, with a soup-like texture), *rødspætter* (sole), *sild* (herring), *lagkage* (layers of sponge cake with custard, strawberries and whipped cream) and *rødgrød* (fruit compote).

The *frokostbord*, a cold buffet of many different foods, is very popular in Denmark. This kind of meal can last several hours.

SOCIAL VALUES, CUSTOMS AND TIPS

Danish is the official language of the country and German is spoken in small communities along the border of Germany. English is widely studied, understood and spoken, although less so in rural areas and by older people.

Danes are quite reserved but are very friendly and informal. They do not generally show their emotions in public or use hand gestures in conversation.

The Danes pride themselves on having a progressive society in which many types of people and points of view are tolerated. The standard of living is quite high and heavy taxes support a very extensive social welfare system.

Good topics of conversation include food, Danish culture, your own hometown or area, the area in which you are staying and current events. Danes also enjoy discussing scientific or cultural topics. They are generally well educated. Recent and popular books and sports are also good conversation topics. Soccer is particularly popular.

Avoid discussing income, religion, divorce or any other personal subject. Commenting on someone's clothes, even if you are making a compliment, is considered odd.

The Danes do not like to be confused with Norwegians or Swedes.

Danes follow general European fashion trends. Due to the climate, which is cool and rainy, coats and woolen clothes are essential. Casual dress is generally appropriate and fashionable. Both men and women often wear slacks and sports shirts or sweaters. Sloppy clothes are inappropriate, as neatness and cleanliness are valued.

Touching others is considered inappropriate.

Men usually allow a woman to be seated first, enter a doorway first, etc. Men usually stand when a woman enters the room. Going up stairways, men should go first; going down stairways, women should go first.

It is common for women to go topless at the beach.

DOMINICAN REPUBLIC

Population: 7,998,766 (July 1998 est.); white 16%, black 11%, mixed 73%

Languages: Spanish

Religions: Roman Catholic 95%

Currency: Dominican peso

Santo Domingo

HISTORICAL OVERVIEW

• In pre-Columbian times, the indigenous Arawaks occupied the island of Hispaniola now comprising the Dominican Republic and Haiti. When Columbus arrived in 1492, the island was inhabited by Caribs who preyed on the Arawaks. Columbus established Santo Domingo in 1496. Diseases and Spanish brutality decimated the native population by 1520. As the indigenous labor force was destroyed, West Africans were imported to provide cheap labor for the mines, sugar plantations and cattle farms.

• The importance of the island declined in the 16th and 17th centuries. In 1697, the western third of the island of Hispaniola (now known as Haiti) was given to France, and in 1795 the rest of the island was ceded to France.

• In 1809, the eastern two-thirds of the island was returned to Spain, and in 1821 the colony declared independence as the Dominican Republic. It was then immediately overrun by Haitian troops, who remained in power there until 1844. This domination left a legacy of mistrust and strained relations that still endures.

• In 1844, the Dominicans declared independence from Haiti, although Spanish rule returned intermittently during the 19th century. Convinced that the republic could not survive without outside support, the Dominicans negotiated a treaty providing for U.S. annexation in 1869. Although the Dominican electorate supported the treaty, the U.S. Senate refused to ratify it. After a series of corrupt and inept governments, the country fell deeply in debt to the U.S. In 1905, the U.S. assumed control of Dominican customs and a U.S. military government was established in 1916. In 1924, a constitutional government replaced it.

- Beginning in 1930, the country was controlled by a military dictatorship under the elected President Rafael Leonidas Trujillo. The country improved economically and was politically stable, but at the cost of brutal repression. The dictatorship was brought to an end when Trujillo was assassinated. In 1965, U.S. Marines and other peacekeeping forces supported by Latin American countries entered the country in an effort to quell the unrest. In 1966, stability was restored, elections were held, and the constitutional government was reestablished under Joaquín Balanguer.

- Balanguer's reelection in 1970 and 1974 reflected the power of business and industry. In 1978 Balanguer was defeated by the opposition but reforms were implemented only slowly.

- Hurricane David devastated the country and the economy in 1979.

- Salvador Jorge Blanco succeeded in 1982. To bolster the economy, he introduced austerity measures, which provoked riots and strikes and led to the reinstatement of a more authoritarian regime.

- Leonel Fernández was elected president in July 1996. He sought to improve the economic situation.

- From 1990 to 1997, the inflation rate dropped from 100 percent to seven percent. The GDP grew steadily during the same period. The unequal distribution of wealth continued to be a serious issue, however.

- In April 1998, the Dominican Republic restored diplomatic relations with Cuba. Relations had been severed in 1962 after Cuba was ousted from the Organization of American States.

- In September 1998, Hurricane Georges devastated the country, leaving more than 100,000 people homeless and undoing years of economic progress.

BUSINESS PRACTICES

Hours of Business

The usual workweek is from Monday through Friday. Offices open and business is conducted early so as to avoid the oppressive heat during the day. Appointments may begin as early as 7:30 a.m. with the last meeting of the day beginning no later than 4:00 p.m.

Avoid business travel during the Christmas season. Festivities start early in December and continue through January 6 (Epiphany).

Dress

Men wear business suits. Women may wear tailored suits or dresses.

Introductions

It is customary for both men and women to shake hands in greeting or when departing.

Friends often hug each other and women may exchange a kiss on the cheek.

At social functions, the host will generally introduce each guest individually.

Have business cards printed in Spanish and English, although the majority of Dominican businesspeople speak English.

Meetings

Always make appointments in advance and confirm them upon arrival in the country. Dominicans tend to be informal and may assume that appointments made some time ago are no longer valid.

There is usually some light social conversation before business is discussed.

Negotiating

Contacts are extremely important for conducting business with the government and private companies. It is recommended that you use your bank or embassy if introductions are needed.

Do not expect to complete your business in one meeting. More than one will almost certainly be required.

Decisions are primarily made by top executives. Cultivate relationships with your counterparts no matter the place in the hierarchy, however, as this will influence the final decision makers.

Historically, women have had no place in the Dominican workplace, but nowadays there are many women working in the business world. Foreign women should experience few problems.

Entertaining

Business lunches are important, although more for getting acquainted than for actual detailed negotiations.

Do not bring a business gift until a friendly relationship has been established. After that, exchanging gifts and favors is common and aids the business relationship. Never go to someone's house empty-handed.

Women should avoid giving gifts to male colleagues, as this might be misconstrued as a personal overture.

Gift-giving should follow business. A less formal setting, such as lunch, is more appropriate.

Gifts for children, from both men and women, are appreciated.

If you are planning a return visit, it is polite to ask your Dominican counterparts if they would like you to bring them something from your home country.

Avoid giving 13 of anything (bad luck), an item or items that contain the color black or purple (associated with Lent, a somber season), knives (they cut off relationships) or handkerchiefs (associated with tears).

Do not admire to excess any particular item owned by your host. He or she will insist on giving it to you.

Restaurants generally include a service charge on bills. It is customary, however, to leave an extra ten percent tip.

The Dominican national dish is *sancocho* (a stew of beef, chicken, pork, root vegetables and herbs). Other favorites include *chicharrones de pollo* (pieces of fried chicken) and *pastelitos* (meat pies). *Arroz con habichuelas* (rice and beans) is a frequent part of the Dominican diet.

Dominican coffee is of very high quality. It is customary to order some with your dessert.

Local beers are also very popular.

SOCIAL VALUES, CUSTOMS AND TIPS

Spanish is the official language of the Dominican Republic and is spoken by virtually the entire population.

Social dress is casual, and clothes are usually made of cotton and light materials. Shorts are not permitted in church.

There are many open markets where shopping takes place.

Avoid discussing issues that focus on the social difficulties that exist within Dominican society.

ECUADOR

Population: 12,336,572 (July 1998 est.); mestizo (Amerindian and Spanish) 55%, Amerindian 25%, Spanish 10%, black 10%

Languages: Spanish (official), Amerindian languages (especially Quechua)

Religions: Roman Catholic 95%

Currency: sucre

HISTORICAL OVERVIEW

- The area called Ecuador today was once inhabited by various indigenous Indian populations. Some time after 1450, the Incas conquered the territory. The Incas ruled Ecuador briefly, but dynastic rivalry weakened them, allowing the Spanish to conquer the region in 1534. The Spanish colonized the central mountainous region of Ecuador, where they established large estates worked by Indian laborers. Ecuador remained relatively peaceful under Spanish control until the 19th century.

- The first uprising against Spanish rule occurred in 1809. In 1822, Antonio José de Sucre invaded from Colombia and led a campaign against the Spaniards. The country, along with Colombia and Venezuela, gained independence and became part of "Gran Colombia," a federation that was dissolved only a few years later. Ecuador declared itself a republic in 1830.

- Increasing tensions developed between the largely aristocratic Sierran capital town of Quito and the coastal, more liberal, modern commercial town of Guayaquil. Since independence, politicians and army generals have played off of this rivalry, causing great political instability and frequent changes in the government. Up through the early 20th century, authoritarian rule prevailed. Post-war Ecuador, by contrast, has been relatively stable, governed by constitutional rule for long periods of time.

- In 1941, Peru invaded Ecuador in the southern Amazon region. Global politics and World War II forced Ecuador to sign a treaty that gave Peru half of its territory (almost all of its Amazon jungle). Ecuador still claims this ceded territory, and the issue has caused violence to erupt between the two nations.

- In 1948, President Galo Plaza Lasso became the first freely elected president to serve a full term. Although his presidency was followed by two other peaceful administrations, military rule was reinstated from 1963 until 1966 and again from 1972 through 1979. The figure who dominated the political scene in Ecuador during these decades was Jose Maria Velasco Ibana. He was elected to the presidency five times but only completed one term. Tremendously popular with the people, his rule was nevertheless so erratic that he was never in office long enough to ensure social and economic progress.

- In the 1970s, the economy was greatly boosted by profits from the oil industry. Depressed oil prices plus earthquake and rainstorm damages caused another recession in the 1980s.

- In 1992, Sixto Duran Bellen became president. He instituted much-needed economic reforms. The poor, however, were largely ignored.

- In 1995, skirmishes over the border with Peru erupted into a small war, which ended after six months.

- In 1996, Abdala Bucaram won the presidential elections, but once in office his popularity plummeted because a series of austere economic measures were imposed. Congress removed Bucarum from office on account of his "mental incapacity." The treasury produced evidence that Bucaram had embezzled as much as $80 million from the treasury during his six months in office. Congress appointed Fabian Alarcon Rivera as the interim president.

- Elections were held in August 1998, and Jamil Mahuad won the presidency.

BUSINESS PRACTICES

Hours of Business

Business hours are 9:00 a.m. to 6:00 p.m., Monday through Friday. Offices usually close from 1:00 p.m. to 3:00 p.m..

Dress

In inland areas, men should wear suits, and women should wear suits or dresses. Although Ecuadorian businesspeople may dress less formally in the coastal regions, foreigners are expected to dress more conservatively for business meetings.

Introductions

It is customary to shake hands when making someone's acquaintance for the first time.

Close friends appear to kiss each other on the cheek. They are in fact "kissing the air" while brushing or touching cheeks.

If men know each other well they will often embrace.

It is considered proper to address people by a title (*Señor, Señora, Doctor, Doctora,* etc.) upon introduction.

Among friends, the title *Don* or *Doña,* followed by the first name, is a common greeting that indicates respect and friendship.

Buenos días (Good day) or *Cómo está?* (How are you?) are common greetings.

Meetings

Appointments should be made two weeks prior to the desired date.

Arrange meetings to start after 10:00 a.m.

Punctuality is important, although your Ecuadorian colleague may arrive late.

Have business cards and any materials printed in both Spanish and English. Bring copies with you or be prepared to wait as long as a week for copies to be made.

Spanish is generally used in business meetings, although English is spoken in some private businesses.

Negotiating

It will take more than one business trip to finalize a deal in Ecuador.

Building a relationship of trust is necessary for doing business with Ecuadorians and will affect decisions made in the long run.

Hire a local contact and/or a lawyer before beginning the negotiation process. This is essential to the success of your negotiations.

Ecuadorians are not formal in their negotiations.

Be patient, as delays are common.

Women should be reserved and non-aggressive in their business approach.

Maintain the same negotiating team throughout the business exchange. Ecuadorians feel that they are dealing with people rather than with a corporation. Changing team members may breach the trust established and bring negotiations to a halt.

Entertaining

If you invite a guest to a restaurant, you are expected to pay the bill. Young people will often split the bill. Splitting the bill is referred to as "doing as the North Americans."

When a guest is invited to visit someone's home, the arrival time is stated. It is considered bad taste, however, to specify an ending time. Guests are not expected to arrive on time and can be anywhere from ten minutes to an hour late.

Evening socials sometimes end after midnight, especially on the coast. The evening will consist of eating, drinking and dancing. The meal is usually served later in the evening, after which some guests leave while others stay.

At smaller gatherings, it is customary for arriving guests to greet each person they know. The host will then introduce them to the rest of the guests. Guests who do not say "Hello" to those they know are considered rude as they are not placing enough value on relationships.

There are three daily meals. The midday meal is by far the most important.

The *Serranos* (people from mountainous areas) favor corn and potatoes, while the *Costeños* (people from the coastal region) favor rice, beans and bananas.

Fresh fruits are abundant, and fish is a staple. Soup is almost always served at both the midday and evening meals. A popular afternoon snack is hot bread.

Some favored dishes include *arroz con pollo* (fried chicken with rice), *locro* (soup made with potatoes, cheese, meat and avocados), *llapingachos* (cheese and potato cakes), *ceviche* (raw seafood marinated in lime and served with onions, tomatoes and spices), *fritada* (fried pork) and *empanadas* (pastries filled with meat or cheese).

Both social and business conversation is appropriate at meals.

SOCIAL VALUES, CUSTOMS AND TIPS

Ecuadorians are proud of their country and their history. Ecuador is still a developing country, but the people do not appreciate being considered inefficient or inferior.

The *Serranos* are more formal, conservative and reserved than the *Costeños*. The *Costeños* are cosmopolitan, open and liberal (most of the businesspeople of Ecuador are *Costeños*). These two groups are distrustful of each other and are political rivals.

Indigenous people (Indian groups from the Sierra, Coastal and Amazon areas) prefer to remain in their own communities and retain their own traditions.

Avoid discussing political issues that involve the relationship between Peru and Ecuador.

Food and eating habits are an important part of Ecuadorian culture. Holidays are associated with certain kinds of food, and each town has a specialty dish.

Family is important, and the elderly are highly respected. Many families live modestly in small homes or apartments, and several generations may reside together.

It is customary for a family who opens its doors to a guest to leave the door open.

Yawning in public, whistling for someone's attention or pointing with the index finger are considered impolite gestures. They display a lack of respect for others.

Ecuadorians might point by puckering their lips, and by lifting or lowering their chin.

Hand gestures are used to emphasize verbal communication. Touching is important and shows friendly concern.

To indicate "Sorry, the bus is full" or "Sorry, we are out of tomatoes," or something similar, stick out your hand, as if to shake hands, and move it in a manner similar to waving.

EGYPT

Population: 66,050,004 (July 1998 est.); Eastern Hamitic (Egyptians, Bedouins, Berbers) 99%, Greek, Nubian, Armenian and other European (primarily Italian and French) 1%

Languages: Arabic (official)

Religions: Muslim (mostly Sunni) 94%, Coptic Christian and other 6%

Currency: Egyptian pound

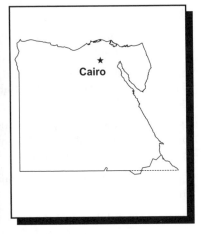

HISTORICAL OVERVIEW

- Egypt has endured as a unified state for more than 5,000 years and has one of the world's oldest continuous civilizations. The earliest recorded Egyptian dynasty united the two kingdoms of Upper Egypt and Lower Egypt around 3100 B.C. Egypt was then ruled by Pharaohs for many centuries. Egypt's ancient history is divided into the Old, Middle and New Kingdoms, which include 31 dynasties and extend until 332 B.C.

- Egypt came under Persian control in 525 B.C. and was then conquered by Alexander the Great in 332 B.C., initiating a Hellenic period in Egypt during which time the city of Alexandria was a center for Greek and Semitic learning and scientific scholarship. The Roman emperor Augustus established direct Roman control over Egypt after Queen Cleopatra's death, initiating almost seven centuries of Roman and Byzantine rule.

- Egypt was one of the first countries to adopt Christianity. Egyptians followed their own Coptic patriarch and eventually were subjected to religious persecution by the Byzantines. As a consequence, Egyptians welcomed the Muslim invasion that began in 642 A.D. By the eighth century, Egypt had become an Arab-speaking country with Islam as the primary religion.

- Egypt was then ruled by a series of Arabic caliphates. In 1517, Egypt came under Ottoman rule and Egypt was associated with the Ottoman Empire until World War I.

- Napoleon Bonaparte of France invaded Egypt in 1798. The three-year sojourn of Napoleon's army and French scientists opened Egypt to direct western influence. Throughout the 19th century, France and Britain vied for influence over Egypt.

- After the completion of the Suez Canal in 1869, France and Britain increased their control of the country. Britain made Egypt a protectorate in 1914.

- Egypt was given independence in 1922, but Egyptians regard 1952 as the beginning of real independence. In that year, a revolution overthrew the British-supported monarchy.

- Gamal Abdel Nasser became the first president, and the first native Egyptian ruler in 2,000 years, in 1954. He was an influential leader and governed until his death in 1970. During Nasser's reign, Egypt waged two wars against Israel (1956 and 1967) and lost the Sinai Peninsula to Israel in 1967. Nasser also nationalized the Suez Canal and built the Aswan High Dam.

- Nasser was succeeded by his vice president, Anwar el-Sadat. His government led a war against Israel in 1973 in which it regained a foothold in the Sinai. Sadat signed a peace treaty with Israel in 1979 that returned the Sinai to Egypt. He was assassinated in 1981 by fundamentalists opposed to his policies.

- Sadat's vice president, Hosni Mubarak, succeeded him and became an important leader of moderate Arab nations.

- In the late 1980s, several serious problems emerged: falling oil revenues, lowered receipts from canal revenues and a drop in tourism. This drop was due to the rise of fundamentalist violence. Mubarak expanded a campaign to end the violence.

- In 1996 and 1997, Egyptian extremist groups launched three major attacks in the Nile Valley region. The groups targeted tourist areas in order to endanger the country's economy and to destabilize the government. Several tourists lost their lives. As a result, Egyptian authorities have increased security in these areas.

- A major extremist group known as *al-Gama'a al Islamiya* (Vanguards of Conquest) seeks to make Egypt a state governed strictly by Islamic law.

- Since the late 1990s, President Mubarak and his government have sought to strengthen economic ties with Sub-Saharan Africa.

BUSINESS PRACTICES

Hours of Business

The typical workweek is from Saturday through Thursday.

Business hours often vary. Usual summer hours are 8:00 a.m. to 2:00 p.m., and usual winter hours are 9:00 a.m. to 1:00 p.m. and 5:00 p.m. to 7:00 p.m.

Dress

One should dress conservatively in Egypt. Many women cover their hair and bodies completely, leaving only their faces and hands exposed. Men wear modest clothing and skullcaps. A beard can be a sign of religious faith, but it can also signify membership in certain political organizations. In large cities, western-style clothing is popular as long as it is modest.

Business representatives generally wear business suits. Men should wear long-sleeved shirts buttoned up to the collarbone. Business-women should not wear pantsuits, but long skirts and shirts with long sleeves.

Introductions

Greetings in Egypt are often elaborate and warm. Friends of the same sex usually shake hands and kiss on both cheeks. If the friends have not seen each other for a long time, they may repeat the kisses and add a kiss to the forehead.

A man will shake hands with a woman only if the woman extends her hand first. Otherwise, he will greet her verbally only.

Titles are important. Do not use first names unless invited to do so. Good friends use first names in social settings, but may add an honorific title to the first name in more formal settings.

It is acceptable for men to shake hands with both men and women. Women may only shake hands with other women.

Meetings

Business visits usually begin with light conversation and coffee or tea.

Arabic is the official language in Egypt, although English and French are widely used in business and in education. Bilingual business cards are helpful.

It is not unusual for a meeting to be interrupted frequently by telephone calls, visitors and many cups of tea or coffee.

Appointments are always necessary.

Negotiating

The two dominant styles of negotiating are the *suq* model, which is the marketplace haggling approach, and the tribal model, reflecting the Bedouin tribal dispute resolution process of posturing, lofty rhetoric, ritualized confrontation, extensive use of mediation and face-saving activities.

Opening positions are generally far from the final settlement.

There is an expectation of high levels of involvement and protracted discussion to establish the seriousness of the parties.

Egyptians are sensitive regarding their treatment by representatives of powerful foreign countries.

Positions may change radically as a result of a change in direction from the leader.

Egypt is infamous for its abundant "red tape." You need to be patient, as things move relatively slowly, especially when the government is involved.

Prepare a clear agenda before negotiating. Egyptian businesspeople usually take a reactive stance in dealing with foreign companies.

Aggressive bargaining is not only expected but its absence may be taken as an insult.

Contracts are viewed as guidelines rather than definitive transactions. Although detailed, they will often be modified numerous times throughout negotiations. Avoid forcing your Egyptian counterpart into making a decision; this could prove detrimental to the negotiations.

Building personal relationships with the right people is imperative prior to and during the negotiation process. Do not underestimate the importance of social interaction. Business negotiations are greatly influenced by affinity and trust.

Egyptian Arabs follow the *Hijrah* (Arabic) calendar, which has only 354 days. When forming written agreements, use two dates, both western and Arabic.

"Yes" may often be used to mean "possibly."

Entertaining

Egyptians prepare elaborate meals when they entertain guests.

To refuse anything is an insult to the host.

When eating a meal, do not feel that you have to finish everything on your plate. Leftover food is a symbol of abundance and a compliment to the host for providing so well.

Lunch is the main meal and is usually served from 2:00 to 4:00 p.m. Dinner may not be served until 10:30 p.m. or even later.

When invited to dine at someone's house, bring a gift of flowers or chocolates. Do not bring alcohol.

During the month of Ramadan (which occurs at different times each year due to the lunar calendar), Muslims will not eat or drink between sunrise and sunset.

Finger food is eaten with the right hand only. When western utensils are used, they are used in the continental style, with the fork in the left hand and the knife remaining in the right hand.

The *Qur'an* (the holy scriptures of Islam) prohibits eating pork and drinking alcohol.

The staples of the Egyptian diet have changed little over the centuries. The walls of tombs show paintings of garlic, beans, leeks and rice. These remain the staples for Egyptians today.

Traditional foods include flat Egyptian bread, skewered meats and fava beans. *Tahina* (sesame seed paste), tomatoes, yogurt and cucumbers are often eaten with meals.

The national dish is *molochaia* ("green herb" cooked with chicken broth, tomatoes and garlic).

SOCIAL VALUES, CUSTOMS AND TIPS

One of the most important pastimes in Egypt is visiting others because personal relationships with friends and relatives are paramount.

Married children often visit parents on Fridays (the Islamic day of rest and worship) and holidays.

Egyptians like to relax and enjoy life. Their phrase *Ma'alesh* can be translated as "Do not worry" or "Never mind."

Over 90 percent of the country belongs to the Sunni sect of Islam. Egyptian life is therefore thoroughly infused with Islamic philosophy, which has an impact upon the country's laws, business relations and social customs.

The concept of *Insha'allah* or "Allah (God) willing" dominates all aspects of Muslim life. This calls for a lot of patience, as Egyptians view events in an extended time frame.

Egyptians are known for their sense of humor, especially their love of riddles, jokes, sarcasm and wordplay.

Avoid discussing the politics of the Middle East region.

Appropriate conversation topics include Egyptian advancement and achievement, Egyptian cotton and Egypt's ancient civilization.

Avoid showing the sole of your shoe or inadvertently pointing it at someone. The sole of the shoe is considered the dirtiest and lowest part of the body.

Pointing at a person is considered impolite.

You may see men fingering loops of beads that are similar to a Catholic rosary. These are tension relievers called "worry beads" and have little or no religious significance.

Smoking in public places is very common.

The distance between men while conversing is fairly small, but it is much further apart for members of the opposite sex. It is common for males to hold hands with each other in public as a sign of friendship.

Remove your shoes when entering a mosque. Do not plan to visit mosques between noon and 1:00 p.m. on Fridays. At this time, mosques may be restricted to Muslims and if you are not Muslim, you will not be allowed to enter.

Two gestures to be aware of: the right hand held up with the palm facing away from the body and the fingers waving up and down means "Come here;" the hand and palm facing toward you with all fingertips touching and the hand moving up and down can mean "Wait a minute," "Shut up!" or "Take it easy!"

When you enter an elevator, always greet the people in it.

EL SALVADOR

Population: 5,752,067 (July 1998 est.); mestizo 94%, Amerindian 5%, white 1%

Languages: Spanish (official), Nahua (among some Amerindians)

Religions: Roman Catholic 75%

Currency: Salvadoran colon

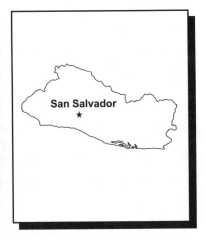

San Salvador
★

HISTORICAL OVERVIEW

- In 1524, Pedro de Alvarado, a Spaniard, led a group of Mexican soldiers in the conquest of El Salvador. He then divided the region into San Salvador and Sonsonate and united both with the colonial territory of Guatemala. The Spanish settlers intermarried with the native Pipil Indians and established agricultural estates in the fertile valleys of the volcanic uplands.

- On September 15, 1821, San Salvador declared its independence from Spain along with the other countries of Central America. In 1823 San Salvador was reunited with Sonsonate and entered into a short-lived federation of Central American nations. El Salvador was the last to withdraw in 1840.

- In 1871 a liberal government came to power, bringing 60 years of peace, stability and economic growth to the country. First indigo and then coffee production was the major economic base. The coffee growers came increasingly to form the ruling elite until the 1929 depression brought them down completely.

- In 1931, Hernández Martínez seized power, beginning a series of brutal dictatorships that lasted until 1979. A year later, his regime suppressed a peasant uprising, leaving 20,000 people dead. Martínez remained in power until 1944 when protests forced him to resign.

- A series of short-term military dictatorships followed. In 1961 Adalberto Rivera of the National Conciliation Party (PCN) came to power. He proved a capable administrator, encouraging the development of light industry and supporting participation in the Central American Common Market.

- The PCN stayed in power for the next 18 years. In 1969 El Salvador fought a bitter war with Honduras and, in the 1972 elections, José Napoleón Duarte of the Christian Democratic Party seemed to have defeated the PCN candidate Colonel Arturo Armando Molina, but the "official" government count gave Molina the victory. When, in 1977, the PCN candidate, General Carlos Humberto Romero, was declared the winner by the same means, riots broke out. In 1979, with El Salvador descending into chaos, a group of liberal army officers led by Colonel Adolfo Arnoldo Majano ousted Romero.

- By 1979 El Salvador was wracked by a civil war that would continue into the 1990s. The U.S. supported the reforms of the new government with economic and military assistance, but when right-wing violence escalated, aid was cut off in late 1980. This led to a political crisis, out of which emerged a new four-member junta led by José Napoléon Duarte of the Christian Democratic Party.

- Duarte held elections in 1982, and arch conservatives won a majority. The newly formed Constituent Assembly excluded the Christian Democrats from power and elected a new president, Alvaro Alfredo Magaña. The government soon turned its attention to wiping out the guerrilla movement. In response, the nation's five Marxist groups joined under a single organization, the Farabundo Marti National Liberation Front (FMLN). Having decided that the Soviet Union was backing the guerillas, Ronald Reagan led the U.S. to supply $4 billion in aid and extensive training to the military.

- By 1991, the FMLN had weakened, and peace negotiations began. A cease-fire was prepared in 1992 by "neutrals" from other countries who called for a purge of the military. The U.S. endorsed this purge, which angered and confused the military. In 1994, the National Republican Alliance (ARENA) candidate Armando Calderón Sol was victorious. The fighters of the FMLN were promised jobs and stipends, but this has not materialized, and the former revolutionaries have split into numerous factions, all of which engage in thievery, kidnapping and extortion.

- Since the peace accords, the government has turned over 250,000 acres of land to an organization that has successfully distributed land to farmers. A major portion of the government's budget previously devoted to military spending is now being spent on health and welfare programs.

- In 1998, the per capita income increased 18 percent from the year before.

BUSINESS PRACTICES

Hours of Business

Businesses are usually open from 9:00 a.m. to noon and then from 2:00 to 6:00 p.m., Monday through Friday. They are often open from 8:00 a.m. to noon on Saturday.

The best time to schedule appointments is between February and June or between September and November. This avoids peak vacation times.

Dress

Most businessmen wear conservative, lightweight suits and ties. Businesswomen wear equally conservative blouses and skirts or dresses.

Introductions

A handshake is the customary greeting. A slight nod of the head is sometimes used instead of or along with the handshake. Salvadoran handshakes may last longer and be less firm than U.S. handshakes. You should adjust your grip accordingly.

Women often pat each other on the right forearm instead of shaking hands. Women who are good friends may also hug each other, especially if they have not seen each other in a long time.

Salvadoran men normally will only shake hands with a woman if she extends her hand first. Foreign men should also wait for a Salvadoran woman to initiate the handshake.

Titles should be used to show respect, particularly when greeting older people. The first name or family name alone is all that is used among close friends. Professional titles, used alone, are the most appropriate forms of address. A Ph.D. or a physician is addressed as *Doctor*, teachers use the title *Profesor*, engineers go by the title *Ingenerio*, architects by the title *Arquitectô*, and lawyers are addressed as *Abogado*. If a person does not have a professional title or if you are not sure of it, you may use *Señor* (Mr.), *Señora* (Mrs.) or *Señorita* (Miss).

Most Salvadorans have two surnames, one from their father (listed first) and one from their mother. Normally, the father's name is used when addressing someone. For example, Hernan Antonio Martinez Garcia is addressed as *Señor Martinez*, and María Elisa Gutierrez Herrera is addressed as *Señorita Gutierrez*. When a woman marries, she usually adds her husband's surname and goes by that surname. For example, if the two people in the above example married, the woman would be known as María Elisa Gutierrez Herrera de

Martinez. She would be addressed as *Señora de Martinez* or, more informally, as *Señora Martinez*.

Common greetings include *¡Buenos días!* ("Good day" or "Good morning"), *¡Buenas tardes!* (Good afternoon) and *¡Buenas noches!* (Good evening).

It is appropriate to stand when meeting others and when being introduced.

At parties, it is customary to greet and shake hands with each person in the room.

Meetings

Although Salvadorans may treat appointment times flexibly, they appreciate and expect punctuality from foreign visitors.

Appointments should be made well in advance (at least one month).

Negotiating

It is important to establish a personal rapport with your Salvadoran counterparts before commencing business discussions. It is very helpful as well to have a Salvadoran contact (through an embassy, bank, etc.) who can arrange introductions before you travel to the country.

Business generally takes place at a slower pace than in the U.S. Delays are fairly common and several trips to El Salvador may be necessary to complete a transaction.

When negotiating, bear in mind that Salvadorans may value their feelings about associations with the issues and facts involved. They may place greater weight on personal perspective (including faith or political ideology) than on particular rules or factual information. They may also be skeptical about information provided by outsiders or by those who support the opposite side of an issue. Nevertheless, many Salvadoran businesspeople have been educated in the U.S., and they may view matters in a manner more akin to the U.S. approach.

You may find that while Salvadoran businesspeople assume individual responsibility and take initiative, the best interests of the group (i.e., the organization, business team, nation, etc.) may be considered to be of greater importance than those of the individual. Salvadorans are collectivistic and base their self-identity in relationships within social groups. Individual expertise is considered less important than the ability to work within the group.

It is quite unusual to find women in upper levels of business although this is gradually changing. Visiting businesswomen should act very professionally and should emphasize that they are representing their company rather than themselves alone.

Entertaining

It is appropriate, but not necessary, for small gifts to be exchanged with first-time visitors. Good gifts include books about your country, crafts from your area, distinctive pens and pocket calculators.

Business may be discussed during a meal. It is not discussed in the home or around family, however. If you are invited to a home, the visit is strictly for socializing.

If you are invited to a meal at someone's home, it is appropriate to bring a gift of candy or flowers. Avoid bringing white flowers, since they are associated with funerals.

Salvadorans appreciate sincere compliments about their homes, children or gardens when a guest pays a visit. Similarly, if you are invited to a meal in a home, complimenting the host or hostess on the meal is also appreciated. This is understood as a sign that the guest feels welcome.

Salvadoran food is less spicy than that of many other Latin American countries. Basic foods of the diet include *frijoles* (black beans), refried beans, thick *tortillas* (thin, round unleavened bread made from cornmeal or wheat flour), rice, eggs, meat and fruit.

The main meal of the day is at noon. This meal usually includes black beans or meat with tortillas and fruit or vegetables.

If you are invited to a meal in a home, each person usually serves himself or herself. It is polite for guests to try some of every dish served. You may want to use discretion in selecting food since it is considered rude to take food and leave it untouched on your plate. At the same time, leaving a little food on your plate is considered good manners.

Men should stand when a woman leaves the table.

SOCIAL VALUES, CUSTOMS AND TIPS

Spanish is the official language, although English is widely spoken in big cities, tourist centers and among well-educated members of the population.

The country as a whole or the area you are currently visiting make good conversation topics. Salvadorans love their country and are proud of its accomplishments. Now that the 12-year civil war has ended, people are optimistic about the future of their country and about establishing a democracy.

Family and work are also good conversation topics as is sports, especially soccer. Some consider El Salvador the sports capital of Central America. Salvadorans excel in a number of sports, and most towns have a gym and an athletic field.

Avoid discussing political unrest, violence, religion and U.S. intervention in Latin America.

While women may work side by side with men, a sense of equality may be forgotten at home. Visitors may be faced with macho behavior or comments. This behavior is usually ignored and accepted as a part of life.

You should be careful not to refer to U.S. citizens as "Americans." Latin Americans also consider themselves to be Americans and are very sensitive to the use of this term.

Personal honor is very important to Salvadorans. Avoid criticizing or embarrassing someone or pulling rank in public.

Friends and acquaintances usually stand very close to each other when conversing. You might offend a Salvadoran if you step back. It is considered poor manners to use excessive hand gestures in conversation or in expressing feelings. Salvadorans tend to speak softly. Try to match the volume level of the people with whom you are speaking.

Because of the warm climate, light summer clothing is appropriate year round. People take care to have a neat and clean appearance in public. For both men and women, short pants or jeans are not appropriate attire. Women usually wear skirts and blouses; they very rarely wear pants. Revealing clothing may offend some people.

Traditional courtesy is expected in El Salvador. For example, it is appropriate to stand when a woman enters the room. If a yawn cannot be suppressed, cover your mouth with your hand.

It is not appropriate to point feet or fingers at anyone. Only close friends are beckoned with a hand wave (wiggling the fingers with the palm down).

ESTONIA

Population: 1,421,335 (July 1998 est.); Estonian 64.2%, Russian 28.7%, Ukrainian 2.7%, Byelorussian 1.5%, Finnish 1%, other 1.9%

Languages: Estonian (official), Russian, Ukrainian, other

Religions: Evangelical Lutheran, Russian Orthodox, Estonian Orthodox, Baptist, Methodist, Seventh Day Adventist, Roman Catholic, Pentecostal, Word of Life, Seventh Day Baptist, Jewish

Currency: Estonian kroon

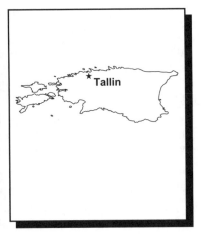

HISTORICAL OVERVIEW

- Present-day Estonians are descendants of an ancient Finno-Ugric tribe that inhabited the region for thousands of years. Before the 13th century, predominantly rural Estonians lived in a loose association without an aristocracy of any kind.

- In the 1200s, German and Danish crusaders invaded the region and eventually dominated it. This invasion introduced an aristocracy to the region. Baltic Germans remained the ruling class until well into the 20th century.

- In 1561, northern Estonia came under Swedish control while southern Estonia, or Livonia, went to Poland. In 1629, most of Livonia was ceded to Sweden as well, and in 1721, Peter the Great acquired both Livonia and Estonia for Russia.

- In the 19th century, landholding reforms were introduced, and Estonians were subjected to extensive Russification.

- In 1918, Estonia took advantage of the chaos created by Russia's Bolshevik Revolution and gained its independence. Although the Red Army invaded at this time, it was defeated in the Battle of Vonnu.

- After 22 years of independence, Estonia was invaded by the Soviet Union in 1940, under the secret German-Soviet Nonaggression Pact between Germany's Hitler and Russia's Stalin. Hitler then broke his pact with Stalin, and Germany occupied the territory of Estonia from 1941 until 1944.

- At the end of World War II, the Russians reestablished their power and incorporated Estonia into the Soviet Union. Estonians were subjected to repressive Russification and mass deportations during the first years of Soviet occupation.

- When Soviet leader Mikhail Gorbachev instituted reforms in the mid-1980s that changed the Eastern bloc's political climate, Estonia's desire for independence became more visible internationally. A number of large demonstrations took place throughout Estonia during the 1980s.

- When the Soviet Union finally collapsed in 1991, Russian President Boris Yeltsin accepted Estonia's declaration of independence.

- In 1993, the Baltic republics – Latvia, Lithuania and Estonia – established a free trade zone and agreed to coordinate their trade and defense policies. In contrast to most other republics of the former Soviet Union, there is political and economic stability in Estonia and in the other Baltic republics.

- Since 1995 the Estonian government has made it much easier for its Russian residents to become citizens.

- In 1996, President Lennart Meri won re-election by the electoral college.

- In 1998, the presidents of Latvia, Lithuania and Estonia signed an agreement with the United States with a view toward future NATO and EU membership.

BUSINESS PRACTICES

Hours of Business

Business offices are open from 8:00 or 9:00 a.m. to 5:00 p.m. Offices close for lunch, but shops and restaurants remain open.

On weekdays and weekends, food stores are open until 9:00 p.m. Some stores open on Saturdays, but close by noon.

Dress

Conservative business suits, preferably of a European cut, are acceptable for both men and women.

Introductions

When beginning a conversation, Estonians commonly say *Kuidas käsi käib?* (How are you?), or *Kuidas läheb?* (How is it going?). Another popular greeting is *Tere* (Hello). Shaking hands is common.

Among friends and relatives, the informal *Sina* (you) is used, but when greeting someone for the first time, the formal *Teie* (you) is used as a courtesy.

In a group, the elderly are greeted first, and a conversation usually begins with *Terre hommikust* (Good morning) or *Tere Õhtust* (Good evening).

It is polite to greet people while standing, and you should maintain eye contact during the greeting. It is also polite to offer a greeting when passing someone on the street.

Gentlemen tip their hats upon meeting someone.

Meetings

Always be punctual, and schedule appointments well in advance.

Expect the first meeting to be rather reserved, but once relations have been established, subsequent meetings should become less restrained.

Negotiating

Contracts may be verbal. Expect to be held to your word if you make a verbal agreement.

Remain formal in your manners and posture, even if you are using first names.

Many businesspeople speak English, but do not take this for granted. Always check to see if a translator is necessary.

Presentations should be precise, detailed and straightforward. Know your subject very well.

Entertaining

People eat breakfast before work, have a light lunch during the day, and eat the main meal after work.

Punctuality is expected. People usually bring flowers when visiting someone for the first time.

Many Estonians enjoy having friends to their homes. Tea or coffee is usually offered to guests.

A host gives departing guests a bouquet of flowers as a token of friendship, and guests thank the host for his/her hospitality.

Hands are kept above the table during meals, and no one leaves the table until everyone is finished. A request for a second helping is considered a polite gesture.

Alcohol is consumed with gusto. Someone will always be there to fill your glass, but you may opt out of drinking after a couple of rounds.

Dinner is eaten after 6:00 p.m., and usually consists of soup (bouillon, cabbage or pea) or stew, and a main dish of meat or fish and potatoes.

Dessert consists of cake, ice cream, fruit or preserves. The most commonly served fruits are apples, cherries, pears and wild berries.

Vodka is popular as are *rosolje* (a Russian dish), *verivorst* (blood sausage), *pirukas* (a pastry of meat and vegetables) and *sült* (head cheese).

SOCIAL VALUES, CUSTOMS AND TIPS

Although Estonians are reserved in manner, they tend to speak quite frankly. They are strongly individualistic and have a great love of solitude. At the same time, Estonians are friendly and helpful.

Estonians speak Finnish, English and Russian. English is very popular among young people and is taught in school.

The Russian language was imposed on the Estonian people during the Soviet era. Estonian, however, became the official language in 1991, after the country's independence.

Even though many ethnic Russians do not speak Estonian, they are now required to pass a language test for citizenship.

Most Estonians are not actively religious as a result of many years of Soviet communist rule. Various Christian denominations are active, but most people are Lutheran, which is the dominant Christian faith in Estonia.

Religious freedom is guaranteed, and the government is not tied to a particular religion; prayers, however, are sometimes offered at official functions.

Every city has a theater or community playhouse. Western plays and local plays are often performed.

Many families own cars; trains and buses run between cities. In urban areas, public transportation – such as buses, streetcars and private cars – are used.

Electric trains are used in suburban areas, and train service is available between Estonia, Finland, Sweden and Germany. Elderly Estonians ride free on public transportation.

Estonians identify with the Scandinavian way of life and values; they are patriotic and proud, and they cherish freedom as well as their traditional culture.

Estonia is proud of its representation in the Olympics and has produced a number of Olympic champions.

Several types of music, sports and recreation are enjoyed by Estonians.

Among the most popular sports are soccer, basketball, volleyball, sailing, cycling, cross-country skiing, swimming, ice skating and ice boating. The favorite summer pastime is picking wild berries and mushrooms in the forest.

Hand gestures are not common among Estonians, although they do use the "thumbs up" gesture to indicate that things are going well. Pointing the index finger or talking with one's hands in one's pockets is considered impolite.

Men dress well in public and very formally when going out to eat, to the theater or to visit friends.

Women prefer dresses to slacks; young women, however, are now wearing slacks more frequently. In general, young people prefer European fashions.

In rural areas people dress in a more relaxed manner than in cities.

Traditional clothing is worn for special occasions, holidays, weddings and festivals.

Estonians celebrate New Year's Day (January 1), *Vastlapäev* (February 15), Independence Day (February 24) and Fools Day (April 1), commemorate Stalin's deportation of Estonians in 1949 (June 14), and celebrate Victory at Võnnu Day (June 23), *Jaanipäev* (Midsummer's Day, June 24), Kadri Day (October 25), All Souls Day (November 2), Mardi Day (November 10) and Christmas (December 24-26).

FINLAND

Population: 5,149,242 (July 1998 est.); Finnish 93%, Swedish 6%, Lappish 0.11%, Gypsy 0.12%, Tatar 0.02%

Languages: Finnish (official), Swedish (official), Sami, Russian

Religions: Evangelical Lutheran 89%, Greek Orthodox 1%, none 9%, other 1%

Currency: Markka, euro

HISTORICAL OVERVIEW

- The first known inhabitants of Finland were the Sami (Lapps), who go back to 7200 B.C. The ancient Finno-Ugric tribe, which crossed the Gulf of Finland each year to hunt and fish, gradually settled in the southwestern corner of Finland during the first millennium B.C., pushed the Lapps northward and eventually became dominant.

- Finland became a battleground between Sweden and Russia from the 12th century onwards. In about 1155, Swedish crusaders invaded the region, bringing Christianity to the area. The Danes then invaded in 1191 and in 1202. When the Swedish king counterattacked, he was given the title to the lands. In the meantime, the Russian Orthodox church tried to gain a foothold in eastern Finland. After a further series of wars, what is Finland today was made part of the Swedish kingdom in 1323.

- Under Swedish rule the various tribes were encouraged to think of themselves as a unified entity. A Finnish literary language was established and Lutheranism was imported from Germany.

- During the 18th century the power of the Swedish kingdom declined and it began to lose its hold on Finland. In addition to attacks by Russia, some Finns themselves supported the idea of freedom from Sweden under Russian protection. When Sweden lost a war to Russia during the Napoleonic Wars in 1809, it ceded Finland to the Russians. Russian Tsar Alexander I granted Finland extensive autonomy, and the region became a unified entity.

Under Russian control, a Finnish nationalist movement led Finnish to be placed on equal footing with Swedish as the language of government. Until the 1890s, Russia respected Finland's special position within the empire and supported institutions that led to ever greater autonomy.

- In 1899, however, growing Russian nationalism led to Russification. These policies were resisted in Finland. Before violent rebellion developed, however, Russia's Bolshevik Revolution broke out. Finland took advantage of the chaotic situation and declared its independence in 1917. After a brief civil war ending in 1918, the Finns adopted a republican constitution in 1919.

- During World War II, Finland fought the Soviet Union – first in the 1939-1940 Winter War, forcing it to cede one-tenth of its territory to the Soviets (the province of Karelia and a strip of Lapland), and then in the War of Continuation (1941-44) when it fought with German troops. Nevertheless, Finland avoided Soviet occupation and preserved its independence. Since World War II, the country has maintained its neutrality.

- In 1948, Finland signed an agreement with the Soviet Union, which included a mutual defense provision. Finland was not permitted to join any organization hostile to the U.S.S.R. This treaty created a situation in which the Soviet Union was able to influence Finnish foreign policy.

- In 1989, Soviet President Mikhail Gorbachev officially recognized Finnish neutrality and, in 1992, Russian President Boris Yeltsin signed a treaty with Finland's president to void the 1948 agreement. The new treaty recognizes Russia's and Finland's equality and sovereignty and establishes positive economic relations.

- In 1993, Finland decided to more fully integrate with Europe by applying for membership in the European Union (EU). Finland became a member in 1995.

- Martti Ahtisaari, a member of the Social Democratic Party, became president in 1994.

- In the mid-1990s, Finland had one of the most rapidly expanding and prosperous economies in the industrialized world. In 1997, spending was cut to begin to prepare the economy for the euro.

- In March 1997 Finland hosted the U.S.- Russia Summit between Presidents Clinton and Yeltsin.

BUSINESS PRACTICES

Hours of Business

Avoid planning a business trip during July or August since most people take vacations at this time.

Businesses are open from 8:00 or 8:30 a.m. to 4:00 or 4:30 p.m., Monday through Friday.

They tend to open only for a half-day on the day before a holiday.

Dress

Women wear dresses or suits for business, while men wear suits and ties.

Introductions

Both men and women shake hands firmly when greeting. You should shake hands when being introduced, when greeting someone you know and when parting. Sometimes both hands will be offered to shake simultaneously.

When introduced, people state their full name or a title and last name. Traditionally it has not been appropriate to use first names until invited to do so, but it is now quite common to use a first name even on a first meeting, especially among young people. You may want to wait until your Finnish colleague uses your first name or invites you to use his/her first name so as not to offend anyone.

Finns kiss and hug only very close relatives and friends whom they have not seen in a long time.

The titles "Mr.," "Mrs." or "Miss" may be used. Most businesspeople, however, prefer to use their occupational title with the last name. If you are not sure of someone's title, you can use *Johtaja*, which means "Director."

The general term for greeting is *Hyvåå påivåå* (Good morning/afternoon) or simply *Påivåå*. Another expression for "Good morning" is *Hyvåå huomenta*.

The presentation of business cards is very important. You should present one to everyone you meet while conducting business.

Meetings

Appointments are necessary and should be scheduled at least two weeks in advance. Try to arrange meetings with the managing director of a firm, since he/she is usually the decision maker.

Punctuality is very important.

Negotiating

Finns maintain high ideals of loyalty and reliability. They take promises and agreements seriously.

There is very little small talk during negotiations. Business is attended to immediately. You should try to do all of your negotiating with the managing director of the firm. He is the head of the firm and will make all decisions.

Do not be disturbed if there are long pauses in your counterpart's replies or if there are periods of silence during a meeting. This is normal. Finns like to think over what has been discussed and will always take a moment to think before they speak.

Never be ostentatious or boastful during a meeting. Always remain calm.

Entertaining

The most popular way of entertaining is to invite people to a "coffee table" in the afternoon or evening. Cookies and cake are served with coffee. It is polite to taste each of the pastries.

Finns are more likely to entertain foreign visitors in restaurants than in their homes.

Spouses should be included in invitations to business dinners.

If you are invited to a meal, it is appropriate to bring cut flowers as a gift for the host. The bouquet should not be large, as this would be considered ostentatious. A bottle of wine or a box of chocolates is also appropriate. A gift may also be sent afterwards to thank the host.

You should wait until the host has taken a first sip before you begin drinking, even if you are simply having refreshments.

At a small party, the host will introduce the guests to each other. At a large party, you should introduce yourself.

Do not be surprised if you are asked to spend some time in the sauna with your host. Spending time in the sauna is a national pastime. An invitation to a sauna is less likely if you are a businesswoman dealing with businessmen. (There are usually separate saunas for men and women.) Business discussions may even take place in the sauna. In fact, after a business deal is concluded, there is usually a long lunch, often followed by a sauna.

While it is common for Finns to take their saunas naked, they will not feel uncomfortable if you do not do the same. Bathing suits or a towel wrap may be worn. Snacks are often served after a sauna. A beverage called *Kalja* (similar to beer, but non-alcoholic) may be served.

A 15 percent service charge is usually included in the bill, although most people also leave an additional gratuity on the table. If the service charge is not included, you should leave a ten to 15 percent tip.

The check is never split in Finland. Therefore, if you invite someone to a restaurant, you should pick up the check.

Guests are seated by the host when invited to a dinner at someone's house. The host and the hostess usually sit at opposite ends of the table and guests sit along the sides. Often women sit on one side and men on the other.

At a dinner in someone's home, women should wear dresses and men should wear suits and ties.

The Finns eat in the continental style, with the fork in the left hand and the knife in the right. Do not eat anything with your hands. Even fruit should be peeled and sliced using a fork and knife.

Guests begin eating after the host does and they also leave the table after he/she has. Guests should refrain from drinking until the host proposes a toast. It is inappropriate for guests to toast the host(s).

It is rude to leave food on your plate.

At the end of the meal, you should approach your host and thank him/her. This does not, however, signal the end of the evening. Guests stay for about one-and-a-half to two hours after the meal.

It is considered bad luck to pass salt hand to hand. Instead, put the salt shaker down on the table and let the next person pick it up.

Finnish cuisine has been influenced by many cultures, from French to Russian. It includes a number of Finnish specialties using seafood, wild game and vegetables. Reindeer steak and salmon are traditional specialties. The *smørgåsbord*, a Finnish buffet, is also very popular. Coffee and milk are the most common beverages.

For breakfast, which is served between 7:30 and 9:00 a.m., people eat hot cereal, *pulla* (yeast bread) and either open-faced sandwiches or yogurt and fruit, with coffee. Lunch, between noon and 1:00 p.m., is a light meal consisting of soup, sandwiches, salad and milk or butter-milk. Coffee breaks are normally taken at 10:00 a.m. and 2:00 p.m. Dinner is served at 6:00 or at 7:00 p.m. for a dinner party. An informal dinner will consist of meat, potatoes, vegetables or salad, and pudding with milk.

You should be aware that large quantities and, often, a great variety of alcoholic beverages are consumed during dinners in Finland.

SOCIAL VALUES, CUSTOMS AND TIPS

Although Finland has two official languages, Finnish and Swedish, Finland has two small minorities, who respectively speak Sami and Russian. English is a popular second language, especially among young people, the educated and businesspeople.

In many ways, Finland is very different from the other countries commonly grouped together as Scandinavia. While Finns reflect Scandinavia in customs and lifestyle, they are linguistically and racially different from Scandinavians.

Finnish people are quite reserved and appreciate general courtesy. They avoid showing emotions in public and are quiet.

Eye contact is very important during conversation, although touching and gesturing are uncommon. Folding one's arms while talking is interpreted as arrogant and prideful.

Finnish people are very proud of their heritage and national identity. Despite the country's small size, it has been a leader in peace conferences and initiatives. It also has the cleanest environment in the world and is a leader in women's rights. In fact, there is no such thing as feminism in Finland, since women are involved in all spheres of life. The Finns stress and appreciate the values that maintain these elements of life.

Because Finland has survived centuries of domination by other powers, Finns are not only proud of their national identity but have developed a wry humor and a cheerful sense of fatalism.

Conversation can cover a wide range of topics. Religion or politics is not avoided, but you may want to be cautious in taking sides. You may want to avoid discussing socialism or Finnish neutrality as well as asking personal questions of your host (i.e., questions about someone's family, job or religion, etc.).

Sports and hobbies make good conversation topics, since recreation and general fitness are important to the Finns. Favorite hobbies include fishing, hunting, camping, skiing, soccer, *pesåpallo* (Finnish baseball), ice hockey, cycling and boating. Finns also enjoy picking wild berries and mushrooms and taking vacations in the woods. The sauna is a traditional and popular way to relax. In fact, *sauna* is a Finnish word that has been adopted by English and other languages.

Good topics of conversation also include the history, sights and architecture of the area you are visiting.

Finnish fashion standards are very high and internationally recognized. People may dress quite formally and follow European fashion trends closely. Also, a variety of native costumes are worn at festivals, weddings or graduation balls.

Hats are very often worn by men in the winter. All men in Finland, even teenagers, wear ties and hats when they dress up. Men remove their hats when they enter a building or elevator or when they are speaking with another person. Men may also raise their hats to greet people from a distance.

It is considered impolite to talk with your hands in your pockets or with something in your mouth (toothpick, food, gum, etc.). Also, if a yawn cannot be suppressed, cover your mouth.

Finns will wave in greeting if they see at a distance someone whom they know.

It is preferable to cross your legs with one knee over the other, as placing one ankle over the other knee is inappropriate.

Loud talking and noise are avoided in public places. Also, it is inappropriate to eat food (except for ice cream) while walking down the street.

FRANCE

Population: 58,804,944 (July 1998 est.); Celtic and Latin origin 91%, Slavic, North African, Indochinese and Basque minorities 9%

Languages: French (official)

Religions: Roman Catholic 90%, Protestant 2%, Jewish 1%, Muslim 1%, unaffiliated 6%

Currency: French franc, euro

HISTORICAL OVERVIEW

- Around 1200 B.C. the Gauls settled in what is modern-day France. Julius Caesar conquered Gaul in 58-52 B.C., establishing Roman dominance over all of Gaul, which ended with the barbarian invasions and the fall of the western Roman Empire. The Franks, from whom France gets its name, came to power in the early sixth century.

- In 800 A.D. the Frankish king Charlemagne had himself crowned Holy Roman Emperor, and he set about attempting to recreate the Roman Empire. He absorbed what is now France into a huge political unit encompassing much of present-day Europe. This empire did not survive his death.

- The Capetians, who came to power after the Carolingians, chose what is now the city of Paris as their capital around 1000 A.D.

- During the 14th and 15th centuries, French-English rivalries culminated in the Hundred Years' War. During the late 16th century, wars of religion raged between Catholics and Protestants. Under the absolute monarchy of Louis XIV (The Sun King), 1661-1715, royal authority reached its zenith.

- The 18th century became known as the Age of Enlightenment, an era when absolutism was questioned and rationalism championioned. In 1789 the French Revolution introduced radical political reform based on the principles of "equality, liberty, and fraternity." The first republic was established. Napoleon was named emperor in 1804, and the restoration of the monarchy followed in 1815.

- The 19th century was marked by a number of revolts and the establishment of the Second Empire under Napoleon III. The Third Republic was established in 1875, and it lasted until 1940. The Alsace and Lorraine regions were lost to Germany (Prussia) following military defeat in 1871. They were regained by France after World War I.

- France was occupied by Germany during World War II.

- War in Vietnam (Indochina), a French colony, broke out when France tried to reestablish its authority in Vietnam following World War II. Algeria, formerly a French colony, rebelled against French rule in 1954 and gained independence in 1962.

- Charles de Gaulle became president of France in 1958 and founded the Fifth Republic. He remained in office for two terms. De Gaulle expanded educational opportunities, stabilized the currency, helped bring about a rise in real wages and expanded the social security net. His real interest, however, was foreign policy, and he set out to create an independent foreign policy for France and to diminish Soviet and U.S. influence in Europe.

- In 1968 a series of student riots rocked France and set off a series of worker and trade union strikes. Discontent among the people was high and, after making some concessions, de Gaulle resigned in 1969 and was succeeded by Georges Pompidou, who continued with similar policies. Pompidou died in 1974, and Valery Giscard d'Estaing won the presidency in a narrow victory over Socialist leader François Mitterand. Giscard d'Estaing reorganized industrial priorities and introduced modest social reform, but voters upset with economic woes put Mitterand into office in 1981. Mitterand's two major reforms were the nationalization of certain industries and the decentralization of the French political system.

- Public sentiment shifted to the right in the late 1980s, and Prime Minister Jacques Chirac fought President Mitterand on a number of privatization issues. In 1995, Chirac won the presidency. Once in office his economic austerity programs led to the worst demonstrations and strikes since 1968.

- France rejoined NATO in 1995.

- During their 1995-96 military testing exercises in the South Pacific, France came under attack from environmentalist groups and in 1996 France signed the Nuclear Test Ban Treaty.

- In July 1997 France and the U.S. joined forces to help bring an end to the Democratic Republic of Congo's civil war and in 1998 France began negotiations to bring self-rule to New Caledonia, a French territory in the South Pacific.

BUSINESS PRACTICES

Hours of Business

A business day usually lasts from 8:30 a.m. or 9:00 a.m. to 6:30 p.m. or 7:00 p.m. with as long as a two-hour lunch break.

Dress

Dress in France, even casual dress, is more formal than in the U.S. Much attention is paid to dressing fashionably.

Men should wear conservative business suits, with colored, striped or white shirts and a tie. Women should wear business suits or conservative dresses.

Business attire should be well tailored and of good quality.

Introductions

Upon introduction, it is customary to shake hands with a single, quick shake using light pressure, rather than the firm U.S. pumping handshake, which is considered boorish. It is also customary upon leaving to shake hands with all those to whom you were introduced.

It is best to address everyone as either *Monsieur* (Mr.), *Madame* (Mrs.) or *Mademoiselle* (Miss), without adding the surname. In business circles, first names are rarely used, even among colleagues, unless they are close friends. Use of first names can be initiated by the eldest person present or the one with superior rank.

Women who know each other very well kiss each other on both cheeks. Men will also do this with relatives. Rather than an actual kiss, it is more like touching cheeks and kissing the air.

Always carry business cards, as they are exchanged often.

A letter of introduction by a mutual friend or colleague or a formal, elegant letter (or fax) introducing yourself is helpful and appropriate. Your letter should be written in impeccable formal French.

Meetings

Business appointments are necessary. Mid-morning and mid-afternoon are the preferred times.

Always be punctual for your business appointments. Give your business card to the secretary or receptionist when you arrive.

It is always prudent to confirm your appointment a few days in advance.

Do not expect meetings to begin on time, and expect interruptions during meetings.

The first meeting with a French businessperson will be a session in which to get acquainted, and it is based on their sense of personal relations that a French businessperson will decide whether to continue further contact and negotiate.

Negotiating

Business presentations should be made in a formal, subdued and unemotional manner.

Business negotiations in France tend to take longer than those in the U.S. The French apply reason and logic to negotiations, and they do not hesitate to argue a point. At times, they may seem to disagree for the sake of discussion.

Decisions often follow lengthy deliberations, so be patient. Trying the U.S.-style "hard sell" could cause you to lose a customer. An agreement may be reached orally; written contracts may follow, however, after approval by top management.

It is advisable to have a local agent or representative present to conduct business. It may be necessary to create joint ventures, branch offices or even a network of distributors throughout France to ensure your success.

If you need to give a business gift, items that appeal to the intellect or aesthetics, such as recordings, art prints and books, are particularly prized.

Even if negotiations become tense, always keep your emotions under control and remain calm and reserved.

The French do not always adhere to deadlines. They have a more fluid attitude toward time.

Negotiating takes time. The French enjoy a large amount of general conversation before the actual objectives are discussed. Do not rush this process, as it could hurt the deal. But if it is time for a decision to be made, it will be made even if not all of the necessary French businesspeople are present during the meetings.

Entertaining

Business entertaining is usually conducted in restaurants. You will probably be invited to someone's home only after you have become friends as well as business associates.

Bring a gift, such as a box of candy, cookies or flowers, when invited to a French home for dinner. If you bring flowers, avoid chrysanthemums or red roses and always bring an odd number of flowers. Only bring wine to a very good friend and then make sure it is a very high-quality wine.

Whether you are entertained at home or in a restaurant, your host would appreciate receiving a telephone call or brief note the following day expressing your thanks.

French restaurants are frequently very expensive. You should refrain from ordering the most expensive items on the menu, as this might embarrass your host. Also, avoid the temptation to overeat – or worse – overdrink.

Wine usually accompanies lunch and dinner. You may choose to drink mineral water instead of, or in addition to, the wine. Do not drink until your host has poured wine for everyone and has proposed a toast.

Spouses are seldom included at business meals. As a rule, your spouse should only be invited when you have already met your colleague's spouse.

In France, cultured dinner conversation is valued as highly as delectable food. When attending a business meal, avoid discussing business until your host indicates that it is appropriate to do so. Dinner conversation is very important. The French enjoy sitting and talking for hours at the table.

The French eat in the continental style, with the fork in the left hand and the knife in the right.

Since it is considered impolite to point with the hand and the fingers, beckon a waiter by tipping the head back slightly and saying "*Garçon*" (Waiter).

Smoking between courses is frowned upon. Always ask permission before you smoke.

Keep both hands on the table. It is considered impolite to keep your hands in your lap, even when you are not eating.

Breakfast is customarily *café au lait* (coffee with milk) or *chocolat chaud* (hot chocolate), bread or croissants, butter and jam.

Lunch has traditionally been the main meal of the day. It was common for a businessperson to go home for a long lunch rather than dine at a restaurant. This is becoming less common, however, as more women work outside the home. *Demi-tasse* coffee (strong black coffee in small cups) is served after the meal.

Dinner traditionally has been simpler, comprising perhaps soup, a casserole and bread. If it is a social occasion, however, it will be more elaborate, similar to lunch.

Break your bread with your hands; do not cut it with a knife. If there is no separate bread plate it is appropriate to put the bread directly on the tablecloth.

It is considered rude and wasteful not to finish everything on your plate.

Cheese and fruit are frequently served at the end of a meal. Help yourself to the cheese only once. Peel the fruit with a knife and eat it with a fork.

SOCIAL VALUES, CUSTOMS AND TIPS

Follow the same advice about conversation topics that would apply in the United States. Sports (especially soccer), local history and culture are generally safer topics than politics, money or personal matters.

The French are very proud of their history and their culture and will be delighted if you are knowledgeable in this subject.

The French are very private people. Questions about their families are considered too personal for business conversation.

The French are modest when given a compliment. They will often respond with a self-deprecating remark instead of "Thank you."

If you are invited to someone's home, you will probably not get a tour of the entire house. You will probably be entertained in the living room and will not be encouraged to enter other rooms.

Keep in mind the French motto *Toujours la politesse* (Always be polite). Courtesy is valued.

It is not considered polite to chew gum or speak or laugh loudly in public. If you need to blow your nose, do it discreetly and always use a handkerchief or tissue. In addition, yawning in public is avoided.

Do not keep your hands in your pockets when speaking.

The U.S. "okay" sign (rounded index finger and rounded thumb touching at the fingertips) means "zero" in France. The French use the "thumbs up" sign for "okay."

Sit straight in a chair with knees together or with legs crossed at the knees. Never place your feet on tables or chairs.

Do not be surprised to see nude or topless bathers at public beaches and swimming pools, especially near the Mediterranean, as this is very common.

Many stores, restaurants, theaters and businesses close during August for vacation.

GEORGIA

Population: 5,108,527 (July 1998 est.); Georgian 70.1%, Armenian 8.1%, Russian 6.3%, Azeri 5.7%, Ossetian 3%, Abkhaz 1.8%, other 5%

Languages: Georgian (official), Russian, Armenian, Azeri, other

Religions: Christian Orthodox 75% (Georgian Orthodox 65%, Russian Orthodox 10%), Muslim 11%, Armenian Apostolic 8%, unknown 6%

Currency: laris

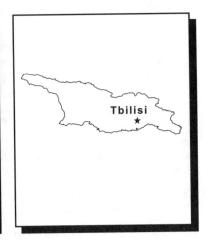

HISTORICAL OVERVIEW

- Human activity has been in the region known as Georgia since 3000 B.C. The modern Georgian people appeared around 1000 B.C. and converted to Christianity in 337 A.D. For the next three centuries the area was fought over by the Persian and Byzantine Empires. In 654, Georgia was invaded by expanding Arab caliphates. Their capital was at Tbilisi. The Georgians requested the help of the Armenian Bagritad dynasty, which unified the Georgian lands and linked them to Armenia from the eighth to the 12th centuries. Georgia reached its height under the reign of Queen Tamara (1184-1213) who created a pan-Caucasian empire.

- In the 13th and 14th centuries Georgia was invaded by the Mongol tribes, which dealt severe blows to Georgian cultural and economic life. After the Ottoman Turks came to power in 1453 Georgia was repeatedly invaded by the Turks and the Persians for the next 300 years. Tsar Alexander I incorporated Georgia into the Russian Empire from 1801 to 1864. With Russia's help Georgia became a prosperous region.

- In the late 19th century, Marxist political groups began to form in Georgia and political uprisings were common. Joseph Stalin, later to become president of the Soviet Union, was born in Tbilisi during this time.

- Because of the confusion and disorder after the Russian Revolution of 1917 the Soviet Transcaucasian committee declared Georgian independence on 22 April 1918. The state was then periodically under German or British control until it was taken over by the Soviets and made a part of the Transcaucasian Soviet Socialist Federal Republic in February 1921. In 1936 Stalin declared Georgia an individual republic and full member of the Soviet Union.

- Georgia, which had been an agricultural state, was transformed into an industrial one.

- Georgian nationalism arose when, in the late 1980s, Soviet President Mikhail Gorbachev instituted reforms and permitted free elections in the Soviet Union. A noncommunist coalition threw its support behind Zviad Gamsakhurdiya, who was elected the leader of the Georgian Supreme Soviet. In April 1991 Georgia became an independent country with Gamsakhurdiya as president. He soon proved more of a dictator than a democratic ruler and, in the fall of 1991, Gamsakhurdiya was overthrown. A military oligarchy took over. New elections were held in October 1992 and Eduard Shevardnadze won.

- Georgia joined the Commonwealth of Independent States (CIS) in 1994. This decision helped Shevardnadze's government control separatist fighting that had plagued Georgia in the early 1990s.

- The most serious of these separatist movements was the Abkhazia movement. President Yeltsin tried to negotiate peace between Georgia and Abkhazia, but he was unsuccessful, and in 1997 the United Nations began to take action. There has been no progress in Georgia-Abkhazian relations.

- In 1995, political and economic stability came to the region. A new constitution was signed creating a parliamentary government with a president as head of state. Shevardnadze was re-elected president.

- Although Gamsakhurdiya committed suicide in 1992, his supporters were many and they continue to agitate. In 1998, there was an assassination attempt on President Shevardnadze by Gamsakhurdiya's supporters.

BUSINESS PRACTICES

Hours of Business

The typical Georgian workweek is Monday through Friday, from 9:00 a.m. to 6:00 p.m.

All government offices and some businesses close a half day early before a national holiday.

Dress

Both businessmen and women should wear business suits, and men should wear subdued ties.

For their safety, women should not wear flashy jewelry.

Introductions

Business associates should introduce themselves with their titles and surnames. Only friends use first names.

Meetings

Meetings must be arranged months in advance because of visa procedures and transit time.

The best time to schedule appointments is between 10:00 a.m. and 4:00 p.m. during the workweek.

Negotiating

Western capitalism is new to Georgians. They may thus enter into agreements to which they later feel that they cannot adhere. Before making any agreements, explain all terms involved to your Georgian counterparts.

Despite the fact that women hold many jobs in the government, they are still viewed in a traditional manner. Foreign businesswomen must overcome this disadvantage.

When dealing with Georgian businesspeople, it is advantageous to have an interpreter present.

Entertaining

Georgians enjoy entertaining foreign businesspeople and will usually prepare a great feast in their home. You can expect to eat well.

During the course of a meal, there are many toasts, usually made with local Georgian wines.

Unlike other aspects of Georgian culture, Georgian food survived Soviet rule in its traditional form.

Walnuts are a staple crop in Georgia and are used in almost all dishes.

Some traditional Georgian dishes are *churchkhela* (strung walnuts dipped in grape juice and dried), *chakhokhbi* (a stew of tomatoes, herbs, and paprika), *lobio* (bean and walnut salad), *khachapuri* (layers of flat bread and melted cheese), *pkhali* (young spinach leaves and spices pounded together) and *basturma* (cured meat). Pickled vegetables are also popular.

A meal usually consists of both hot and cold dishes.

Georgia also has many restaurants and cafés in comparison to other former Soviet republics.

When visiting someone's home it is customary to bring a small gift. Flowers, chocolates or alcohol are all appropriate.

SOCIAL VALUES, CUSTOMS AND TIPS

Smoking is common and widespread in Georgia.

It is not unusual for Georgian men to carry weapons, since family feuding (an ancient tradition still alive today) and crime are commonplace.

As a guest in Georgia, you should refrain from going out after dark, but if you must go, carry as little as possible.

National holidays are as follows: New Year's Day (January 1), Christmas (January 7), Baptism Day (January 19), Mother's Day (March 3), Memorial Day (April 9), Recollection of the Deceased (May 2), Independence Day (May 26), August Day of the Virgin (August 28), *Svetitskhovloba* (October 14) and St. George's Day (November 23).

GERMANY

Population: 82,079,454 (July 1998 est.); German 91.5%, Turkish 2.4%, Italian 0.7%, Greek 0.4%, Polish 0.4%, other 4.6%

Languages: German

Religions: Protestant 38%, Roman Catholic 34%, Muslim 1.7%, unaffiliated or other 26.3%

Currency: Deutsche Mark, euro

HISTORICAL OVERVIEW

- Parts of present-day Germany were first occupied by the Romans, under Julius Caesar in 58 B.C. The movement of the Hunnic peoples drove the Germanic peoples into the Roman Empire, and by 476 A.D. this wave of invasions by Germanic tribes caused the downfall of the western half of the Roman Empire.

- One of the main Germanic tribes was the Franks. By the 730s the Carolingians had become the ruling dynasty of the Franks, and their King Charlemagne conquered the Saxons, another Germanic tribe, thus expanding his kingdom eastward. Charlemagne eventually claimed the title of Holy Roman Emperor and used alliances with various dukes and archbishops who ruled the cities and provinces to keep his empire functioning and unified. In 843 the empire was divided up and Charlemagne's grandson, Louis the German, came to rule over most of present-day Germany. By the ninth century, however, the German kingdom began to disintegrate.

- Thereafter, the absence of any strong, centralizing power in Germany prevented the development of a unified German nation for six centuries. Various alliances were formed and then dissolved again. Competing territorial and religious claims caused the Thirty Years' War (1816-1848), which devastated the economy, population and political structures of the German provinces.

- In 1862 Otto von Bismarck became prime minister of Prussia. In 1866 Prussia annexed most of the northern German states, and in

1871, it added the southern German states (excluding Austria) to form the German Empire.

- Germany was allied with Austria-Hungary and Turkey in World War I. After its defeat in 1918, Germany was required to pay reparations and cede some of its territory. The Weimar Republic, a democratic government, was established in 1918.

- The Weimar Republic had little popular support and was troubled by economic woes. Adolf Hitler, leader of the Nazi Party, became chancellor in 1933 on a platform of right-wing nationalism and anti-Semitism. In 1934 Hitler declared himself *Führer* (leader) of what he called the Third Reich. Hitler's actions soon led to World War II and the Holocaust. The Nazis occupied much of Europe, killing millions of people in concentration camps and warfare. Germany was defeated by Allied forces in 1945.

- The victorious Allies divided Germany into four zones of occupation. Disagreements between the Soviet Union and the other Allies brought about the creation of the Federal Republic of Germany (FRG) in the West and the communist German Democratic Republic (GDR) in the East, commonly known as West Germany and East Germany. The city of Berlin, which was in the GDR, was divided into East and West Berlin.

- With thousands of people fleeing the east through Berlin, the GDR built the Berlin Wall in 1961 to close off access to West Berlin. In 1989 a peaceful revolution overthrew the East German government and the wall came down.

- The two nations became reunited as the Federal Republic of Germany in October 1990. Chancellor Helmut Kohl was successful in leading Germany through its dramatic reunification.

- The Bonn government was faced with transforming the socialist economy of the East and integrating it into the capitalist economy of the West. Change was slow and required raising taxes in the West to pay for subsidies. The deficit grew and foreign trade problems developed. In addition, Germany's neighbors were concerned about a bigger, reunited Germany in Europe.

- From 1991 to 1997, western Germany gave $700 billion in aid to the East. Unfortunately, instead of making the East stronger economically, it has resulted in greater dependence on subsidies and has incurred mutual resentment between western and eastern Germans.

- Neo-Nazi groups gained strength in the 1980s and 1990s, and attacks against non-Germans living and working in Germany increased in number significantly.

- In the late 1990s Kohl and his party began to lose popularity. On 27 October 1998, Gerhard Schröder, the Social Democratic Party candidate, became the new chancellor of Germany.

BUSINESS PRACTICES

Hours of Business

Everyone in Germany takes at least four weeks of vacation per year. Many people take long vacations during July, August or December, so check first to see if your counterpart will be available. Also be aware that little work gets done during regional festivals, such as the Oktoberfest in Munich or the three-day Carnival before Lent.

Business hours are 8:00 or 9:00 a.m. to 4:00 or 5:00 p.m., Monday through Friday, except for Long Thursday when business hours extend until 8:30 or 9:00 p.m.

Store hours are 8:00 or 9:00 a.m. to 5:00 or 6:30 p.m., Monday through Friday. On Saturday, most shops close by 1:00 p.m., except for the first Saturday of the month, when they remain open until 4:00 p.m. Legally, store hours have been extended to 9:00 p.m., Monday through Friday, but most stores outside of urban areas still maintain the earlier closing hours.

Dress

Both men and women should wear conservative business suits. Blue, gray, or black suits (with white blouses for women and a white shirt and subdued tie for men) are acceptable.

Top management dresses more conservatively than middle management and nonprofessionals.

Conservative business attire is appropriate for most formal social events such as parties, dinners and the theater. Remember that one is obliged to check one's coat in German theaters. Therefore, if you tend to get cold easily, bring a sweater. On the opening night of an opera, concert or play, men are expected to wear their best dark suit or tuxedo, and women a long evening gown.

Introductions

While customs vary in different regions of Germany, the general rule is to shake hands both upon meeting and upon departing.

Always shake hands, firmly but briefly, when introduced to a German man. When introduced to a woman, wait to see if she extends her hand first before offering to shake.

When several people are being introduced, take turns shaking hands. It is impolite to reach over someone else's handshake.

Never keep your left hand in your pocket while shaking hands with your right.

Traditionally, only family members and close friends address each other by their first names. It will take time to establish a close enough relationship with a German to be on a first-name basis. Wait for him or her to initiate it.

It is very important to use professional titles. Attorneys, engineers, pastors and other professionals will expect you to address them as *Herr* (Mr.) or *Frau* (Mrs.) plus their title. This goes for anyone with a Ph.D. as well, e.g., *Herr* (or *Frau*) Doktor Professor. Make sure that you know the correct professional title.

When speaking to people who do not have professional titles, use "Mr.," "Mrs." or "Miss," plus the surname. In German, these titles are *Herr* (Mr.), *Frau* (Mrs. or Ms.) and *Fräulein* (Miss). *Fräulein* is used only for very young women (under the age of 18) nowadays. Any businesswoman you meet should be addressed as *Frau* (plus surname), whether or not she is married.

The order of names in Germany is the same as in other western countries (the first name followed by the surname).

In accordance with German formality, it is better to be introduced by a third person than to introduce yourself. If no one is available, however, it is acceptable to introduce yourself.

When you are the third person making an introduction between two parties, give the name of the younger (or lower-ranking) person first.

Meetings

Punctuality is of the utmost importance. Arrive five minutes before the appointed meeting time, if possible. If you are late, apologize sincerely.

It is acceptable to leave work on time, but it is customary to work beyond official hours.

Business appointments should be made far in advance (at the very least, two weeks in advance), and everything must be planned. The best time to schedule an appointment is between 9:00 a.m. and 1:00 p.m. or between 3:00 and 5:00 p.m. Friday afternoons should be avoided.

During meetings very formal agendas are followed and the introduction of new topics outside of the agenda is usually frowned upon. Do not diverge from the agenda set, if possible.

Negotiating

Business is conducted with great attention to detail, order and planning. Discipline and restraint are encouraged and duty, obedience and loyalty are highly valued.

Germans make a point of laying a proper foundation prior to explaining something in detail. Consequently, explanations tend to be lengthy and somewhat complicated.

Business negotiations in Germany are done in a technical and factual manner. You should be aware that it is best to avoid humor, little anecdotes, surprises and the "hard-sell" approach.

German managers tend to keep office doors closed for privacy. You may enter an office, but never open a door without knocking first.

Humor is used only in certain settings and the workplace is not one of them. As a rule, the more formal the occasion, the less humor is accepted. Germans may feel uncomfortable joking among strangers or new acquaintances. In some countries, people feel that they can relax more as they gain seniority; in Germany, the opposite is the case. At the same time, there is banter and joking among close colleagues, in private.

A German negotiation team will present a unified mindset. If you and your team do not present a similarly unified mindset it could jeopardize your meeting and a positive outcome.

For important negotiations it would be best to have an interpreter present. It is normal to have an interpreter for both parties during crucial negotiations.

Many decisions will be made outside of the conference room by a team of informed advisors or experts that you and your team have never met.

Entertaining

If you are invited out to lunch, you may offer to pay, but expect your host to decline your offer. Insist on paying only when you have made the invitation.

Be on time for social events. Drinks are served before the meal, usually with a few appetizers. The meal itself will start soon thereafter.

Gifts should be of good quality but not of exorbitant cost. Appropriate gifts include good-quality pens or imported liquor.

The only article of clothing considered an appropriate gift is a scarf. Other clothing, perfume or soap, for example, are considered too personal.

At everyday restaurants, people find their own seats. There is no host to seat customers. Do not be surprised if someone you do not know joins your table if there is an empty seat. Additionally, you have to get the waiter's attention since the bill will not be brought to you automatically at the end of the meal.

When invited to dinner at a German home, always bring a bouquet of unwrapped flowers (remove the wrapping before entering the house) for your host or hostess. The bouquet should not be showy and overly large and should have an uneven number of flowers (but not 13). Red roses are reserved for courting, and calla lilies are for funerals. Also do not bring carnations as they are considered to be cheap. Remember that heather should never be included in a bouquet in Northern Germany (because of its hardy nature, heather is often planted on graves, and deemed bad luck to bring into a house).

A gift of a locally available wine can be interpreted as saying that your host's wine cellar is inadequate. A good wine brought from your home country (one not sold in Germany) or a top-quality imported red wine will be appreciated, however. Since Germans make some of the finest beers in the world, it is unlikely that you could bring a foreign beer that would be of interest to them.

Consider it an honor to be invited to a home. Do not expect to be given a tour of the house, however.

A German meal customarily begins with saying *Guten Appetit* to everyone present before eating. Drinking is preceded by the host's toasting the guests with *Prosit* or *zum Wohle*. If someone raises a glass to you personally, you should reciprocate some time during the meal.

When dining out in Germany, keep your hands on the table throughout the meal.

When eating, always use utensils. Very few items are eaten with the hands. Even sandwiches and pizza are eaten with a knife and fork. Place your utensils vertically side by side on the plate when you are finished.

At all meals except breakfast, bread or rolls should be broken with your hands rather than cut with a knife. Potatoes are eaten with a fork only and not cut with a knife.

It is considered wasteful to leave food on your plate.

Smoking should be saved until the end of the meal, after the last person has finished eating and coffee or brandy is served. Always ask for permission to smoke.

Breakfast usually consists of rye bread, rolls, butter and jam served with coffee and milk.

Lunch is usually a large meal. Soup, a main dish featuring meat, potatoes and vegetables, and a salad may be included. Rye bread (without butter) and beer usually accompany the meal. Coffee and pastry are generally consumed at a late afternoon break.

The evening meal is generally simple, except on special occasions and at parties. It will often consist of open-faced sandwiches.

The Germans keep the fork in the left hand and the knife in the right hand. Use the knife to push food onto the fork. Hold onto the knife even when you are not using it.

Some German food specialties include: *Wurst* (sausage), *Wienerschnitzel* (a veal dish), *Sauerbraten* (marinated beef pot roast cooked with raisins and crumbled gingersnaps) and *Spätzle* (noodle dumplings).

SOCIAL VALUES, CUSTOMS AND TIPS

In most regions of Germany, men stand when women enter a room. Women need not rise. As long as a woman remains standing, any man talking to her will probably remain standing as well (unless the man is elderly or of much higher social rank).

Sports are a good topic of conversation. Many Germans are passionate *Fußball* (soccer) fans. Skiing, hiking, cycling and tennis are also popular. The collapse of the state-run East German Olympic sports program may be an uncomfortable subject, however.

Embarrassing political comments should be avoided. Keep in mind that politics and the Second World War may be sensitive topics. Open-ended questions and asking for explanations are appreciated.

Germans tend to be well informed about politics and to have firm political opinions. They are also honest and may tell you their opinions about your country (or its actions), even if these opinions are negative.

Expect to be hushed if you so much as cough while attending an opera, play or concert. German audiences remain extraordinarily silent, rarely even shifting in their seats.

Be aware that Germans have a strong sense of privacy. Their personal space tends to be greater in size than that of people in the U.S.

As a rule, Germans answer the phone by giving their name.

Casual clothing is essentially the same as in the U.S. Jeans are quite common, but they should not show signs of wear.

On correspondence and other dated papers, remember that Germans, as well as many other Europeans, write the day first, then the month and then the year (e.g., December 3, 1999, is written 3.12.99). Before writing the date, Germans will also write the place from which the correspondence is originating (*München, den 3. December 1999*).

When entering or leaving a shop, it is considered polite to say "Hello" and "Good-bye" to the sales clerk.

If you smoke, always offer cigarettes to others with you before lighting up.

While Germans are open and generous with close friends, they tend to be formal and reserved in public. You will not see many smiles or displays of affection on German streets.

The avoidance of public spectacles is reflected in the way that Germans will wait until they get quite close to each other before they will offer a greeting. Only young or impolite people will wave or shout at each other from a distance.

The eldest or highest-ranking person enters a room first. If their age and status are the same, men enter before women.

When speaking with someone, do not keep your hands in your pockets or chew gum.

When a man and a woman walk down a street, the man walks closest to the curb.

Germans will look you directly in the eye; they do not like to touch, however. Also, they do not smile readily, and their gestures are often restrained.

To get someone's attention, raise your hand, palm facing out, with only the index finger extended. Do not wave or beckon, as it is considered rude.

There are often no lines in places such as banks and post offices. Usually the boldest person goes to the counter and is helped next.

GHANA

Population: 18,497,206 (July 1998 est.); Black African 99.8%, (major tribes: Akan 44%, Moshi-Dagomba 16%, Ewe 13%, Ga 8%), European and other 0.2%

Languages: English (official), African languages (including Akan Moshi-Dagomba, Ewe and Ga)

Religions: indigenous beliefs 38%, Muslim 30%, Christian 24%, other 8%

Currency: new cedi

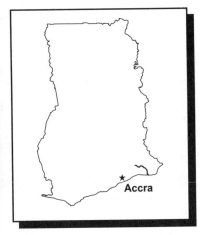

Accra

HISTORICAL OVERVIEW

- Ghana, formerly the Colony of the Gold Coast, was the primary source of gold for the large West African inland trading empires that flourished from the fourth to the 11th centuries A.D. Modern Ghana takes its name from the Ghana empire that existed in the region until the 13th century A.D.

- After the 13th century A.D. various African peoples moved into as well as around what is modern-day Ghana. The Akan founded their first states in the 13th century. Gold-seeking Mande traders arrived in the 14th and Hausa merchants in the 16th centuries. From the 15th through the 17th centuries the Mande set up various states. The Asants, a powerful branch of the Akan, set up an empire in the interior that reached its height in the 18th and 19th centuries.

- In 1487, the Portuguese established a fort at Elmina as their headquarters for the gold trade. Competition among the European powers for gold and slaves led to the establishment of numerous bases on the Gulf of Guinea coast where Ghana is located. In 1874, Great Britain took control of the Gold Coast. After several years of battles with the Asante tribe, it gained control of present-day Ghana in 1901.

- Opposition to British rule increased after World War II. Kwame Nkrumah led the independence movement. The Colony of the Gold Coast, along with British Togoland, became Ghana, which was granted independence in 1957.

- Three years later the country became a republic with Nkrumah as its president, but in 1966 he was deposed by a military coup.

- Ghana gradually returned to civilian rule, but a second military coup in 1972 deposed Prime Minister Kofi Busia, abolished the presidency and dissolved the national assembly.

- In June 1979, an air force lieutenant named Jerry Rawlings led a successful revolt against the military government. Rawlings turned power over to a newly elected president and a new national assembly, but was not satisfied with their performance and again seized power in 1981. The constitution was again suspended and the national assembly dissolved. Rawlings appointed a seven-member Provisional National Defense Council (PNDC).

- In 1988, a new national assembly was established, but members could not belong to political parties. Ghana returned to democratic rule with national elections in 1992. Rawlings was elected president and Ghana officially became a multiparty democracy.

- In the early 1990s, Ghana was economically depressed. The banking system was nearing massive failure, the currency had been greatly devalued and the inflation rate was in excess of 80 percent annually. The bloated government bureaucracy employed 400,000 people, whose salaries made up 43 percent of state spending.

- Rawlings tried a program of privatization, which led to economic growth. Germany and Libya made large concessions on debts owed them by Ghana, while diamond, gold and agricultural production greatly increased.

- Rawlings was reelected in the 1996 presidential elections.

- In September 1997, the National Economic Forum met to draw up a plan to bring economic stability to Ghana by 2020. The forum addressed the problems of high inflation and interest rates and the large budget deficit. They were also concerned with educating the entrepreneurial class so as to create a competitive global market. Although the forum generated good ideas, the proper government operations are not yet in place to implement them.

- In 1998, Ghana experienced greater economic and political stability than many of its African neighbors. Rains proved beneficial for the agricultural sector. Because political violence has waned, the government has been able to turn its attention to initiatives to better living conditions.

BUSINESS PRACTICES

Hours of Business

Most businesses are open Monday through Friday from 8:00 a.m. to noon and from 2:00 to 4:30 p.m. Some are open on Saturday morning as well.

Dress

Business dress is conservative. Men should wear suits that are neatly ironed, and shoes should be shined. Women should wear a business suit or dress.

Introductions

Ghana has many different ethnic groups, each having its own distinct language, culture and customs. Because of these pronounced differences, there is no one greeting or introduction that is a standard all over the country.

English greetings and handshakes are common due to the country's long colonial affiliation with the British Empire.

Several greetings are recognized for getting someone's attention so that they continue to listen to what is said after one says such things as "Good morning" or "Good evening."

Titles and family names are used to address new acquaintances.

Friends and family members often use given names.

Children refer to any adult who is well known to the family as "Aunt" or "Uncle," even when they are not related.

Meetings

Since not everyone speaks English you may need to hire an interpreter.

Meetings need to be confirmed in person because there are very few phones. Allow for extra time to reach your destination. Traffic jams occur frequently.

Ghanaian businesspeople have a very fluid sense of time and therefore often arrive later than the scheduled appointment time.

Negotiating

Formal government agencies may not be very helpful when conducting business negotiations.

Personal relations are considered very important in the culture, in general and when conducting business. Developing a personal rapport with your Ghanaian counterparts and others who might aid in negotiations will therefore greatly benefit your project.

Entertaining

Casual dress is the rule in most circumstances. A shirt, tie and suit for men and a dress for women, however, are required for formal occasions.

Hospitality is important, and Ghanaians work hard to please their guests. Most visits occur in the home, and it is polite to bring at least a small gift for the children. Be aware that some hosts prefer that guests remove their shoes when entering the home.

Guests are nearly always served refreshments. It is considered impolite to refuse.

With most Ghanaians, western etiquette is practiced when eating.

The diet consists mainly of yams, cassava (a starchy root), maize, plantains and rice.

Ghanaians enjoy hot and spicy food, and most meals are accompanied by a pepper sauce. Foreigners generally require some time to become accustomed to the spiciness of the food.

Specialty dishes include *fufu* (a doughlike combination of plantain and cassava), *ampesi* (a green vegetable dish) and palm or peanut oil soups and sauces.

Most large restaurants serve western food as well as native Ghanaian food. Although a tip is usually included in the bill, it is polite to leave a small additional gratuity as well.

SOCIAL VALUES, CUSTOMS AND TIPS

The most popular day for visiting is Sunday, and many people like to dress up for the occasion.

Visitors are usually welcome to stay as long as they wish. It is polite to avoid visiting during mealtimes, but an unexpected guest would be invited to share the meal.

When the visit is over, guests are accompanied or given transportation to their home. It is impolite to let them leave on their own.

Ghanaians are proud of their status as the first sub-Saharan colony to gain independence from a European power.

The Ghanaian people generally have a relaxed disposition.

Tipping for personal services is an opportunity to extend *dash* (from the Portuguese *das*, a form of the verb meaning "to give"). Ghanaian compensation may be in the form of money, goods or favors for personal services performed.

Although the system of *dash* is discouraged by the government, it is widely practiced and includes anything from watching a car to expediting the movement of goods in and out of the country. Except in restaurants and hotels, *dash* is usually paid before the service is given.

Ghanaians consider it impolite to gesture with the left hand. You should not pass or receive items with your left hand.

It is important to cover your mouth when yawning or using a tooth-pick.

The sole of your foot should not point at another person. It is impolite to place your feet on chairs, desks or tables.

It is considered impolite and an act of defiance for children to have direct eye contact with adults.

GREECE

Population: 10,662,138 (July 1998 est.); Greek 98%, other 2%

Languages: Greek (official), English, French

Religions: Greek Orthodox 98%, Muslim 1.3%, other 0.7%

Currency: drachma

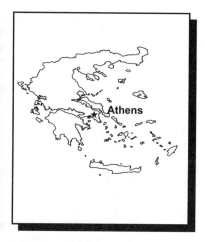

HISTORICAL OVERVIEW

- The history of ancient Greece began around 3000 B.C. From 2000 until 1100 B.C., the Minoan civilization flourished and then fell on Crete while the mainland was still caught up in the Bronze Age. The Mycenaean civilization arose on the mainland around 1600 B.C. and continued until 1200 B.C. As city-states began to form, Greek culture began to flourish. Classical Greece began to take shape in 750 B.C. and was devoted to art, literature, politics and philosophy. It reached its zenith in the fifth century B.C.

- Under the rule of the Macedonian Alexander the Great, ancient Greece developed an empire that covered much of what is now the Middle East, and its culture spread. After Alexander's death in 323 B.C., however, the empire began to decline, and, by 146 B.C., all of its states had been conquered by the Roman Empire. Ancient Greece's rich heritage of architecture, sculpture, science, drama, poetry and government is one of the foundations of western civilization.

- A shadow of the former Greek civilization survived in the Byzantine Empire, which preserved the Greek language and maintained a separate, distinct branch of Christianity. Its capital, Constantinople, was sacked by crusaders in 1204, but the empire recuperated and continued to survive until 1453, when it fell to the Ottoman Turks.

- After four centuries of Turkish rule, the Greeks began a war of independence, supported by Great Britain, France and Russia.

Independence was won in 1832 and, in 1833, Prince Otto of Bavaria was made king of Greece. Prince Otto was replaced by the Dane George I in 1862, who expanded Greece's borders.

- During most of the 20th century Greek government has been marked by instability. In 1923 Greece was made a republic, but 12 years later the monarchy was restored. During World War II, the country was occupied by German and Italian forces and lost one-eighth of its population. After the war ended, a civil war between the government and communist guerillas cost another 120,000 lives. With aid from the U.S., the Greek government reestablished order in 1949.

- Then, in 1967, a group of military colonels staged a coup and the royal family was forced to flee, leaving behind a military dictator-ship that lasted until 1974.

- After the military dictatorship fell, general elections took place and Greece was made a republic. Konstantinos Karamanlis became prime minister and made sure that Greece joined the European Economic Community early. Andreas Papandreou's Panhellic Socialist Movement (PASOK) was democratically elected for two terms, putting him in office from 1981 until 1989. After that, the party lost the majority vote because of various financial and political scandals and because Papandreou was unable to come through on many of his economic promises.

- In 1987 Greece ended many years of strife with neighboring Albania. The New Democracy Party came to power in 1990 and introduced measures to privatize enterprises, cut government spending and prepare Greece for greater integration within Europe. Discontent with the austerity required led to a PASOK Party victory in the 1993 elections, and Andreas Papandreou, in spite of failing health, returned to office. He began to reverse privatization and other economic measures.

- By 1994, Greece had become Albania's largest investor, but a conflict developed after a Greek raid on an Albanian border town. In 1995, Greece and Macedonia began to implement measures to end their quarrel.

- In 1996, Costar Simitis became prime minister. He tried to end corruption in Greece's government by hiring only one new civil servant for every three who retired. Greece's ailing economy began to pick up.

- In January 1997 the delicate peace between Greece and Turkey almost came to an end when the Greek Cypriot government announced its intention to purchase Russian S-300 surface missiles. Turkey threatened military action in response.

BUSINESS PRACTICES

Hours of Business

Work and business hours vary, depending on the season and the type of business. In general, most Greeks work from 8:00 a.m. to 1:30 p.m. and from 5:00 to 8:00 p.m. Some government offices may close as early as 2:30 p.m. Many businesses close early on Wednesday afternoons.

Avoid business trips during the summer (June through August) and the weeks before and after Christmas and Greek Orthodox Easter.

Dress

Men should wear suits and ties in the winter. In the summer, Greeks dress more casually. Wearing a suit will make a good impression, however. Women should wear dresses or suits and heels.

Introductions

When being introduced to either men or women, it is customary to shake hands. One may also receive an embrace and a kiss on both cheeks. A common, more informal way of greeting is to slap a friend's arm at shoulder level.

In Greece, everyone shakes hands almost every time they meet and a firm handshake is considered a sign of good character.

Carry a large stock of business cards and distribute them generously.

Have your business cards printed in English on one side and in Greek on the other and remember to present the cards with the Greek side facing your Greek counterpart.

Wait for your Greek colleague to use first names before you do.

Meetings

The *siesta* (a rest after the midday meal) hour is taken seriously. Do not try to make appointments or call people at home during afternoon closing hours.

Greeks like to "pass" time, not "use" time. They may not be prompt in keeping appointments and consider it foolish to set a specific length of time for a meeting. Foreigners are expected to arrive on time, but do not be surprised if your counterpart is late by a half an hour or more. This may be partly attributed to temperament but most likely is due to the horrendous Athenian traffic and parking conditions.

Negotiating

Do not be offended if Greeks ask you pointedly personal questions, such as how much you earn. If you prefer not to answer, try to make your evasions tactful.

Senior executives in a group make all of the firm's decisions and should be treated with due respect.

Patience and bargaining abilities are two vital skills needed when negotiating with Greeks.

Business gifts are expected during negotiations. Small office supplies with your company's logo on them are always appreciated.

Not drinking the alcohol given to you during meetings is considered impolite.

Entertaining

Greeks have a tradition of hospitality that goes back to ancient times. Ancient Greeks believed that a stranger might be a god in disguise and were therefore kind to all strangers.

Greeks expect personal contact to be part of a business relationship. They may invite you to meals, take you out in the evening or even pick you up at the airport.

Business associates will invariably offer sweet Greek (never "Turkish") coffee accompanied by a glass of cold water.

Drinking and dancing the night away is often considered an inherent part of doing business in Greece.

At home, men traditionally stay with their guests while the women prepare food or serve drinks.

Hosts appreciate compliments on their homes, but one should avoid praising a specific object to excess as the host might insist on giving it to the guest.

A guest may praise the host's children, and, if the parents approve, give them a small gift.

If a Greek host continues to insist on anything (that a guest stay longer or eat more, for example), they mean it and the guest should try to be accommodating.

Greeks often eat dinner (a small meal) as late as 8:00 or 9:00 p.m. The main meal of the day is lunch, served between noon and 2:00 p.m.

At restaurants, a group will often order a number of different dishes for everyone to share. Sometimes Greeks will go into the kitchen of a restaurant and choose their dinner by looking into the pots.

Do not ask about the cost of the dish you are ordering in a restaurant. It will offend the people with you.

While tastes vary between urban and rural residents, certain foods are common to all Greeks. These include lamb, seafood, olives and cheese. Meats and vegetables are grilled or fried in their own juices or with lemon and garlic. *Souvlaki* is a shish kebab with cubes of meat (often lamb), mushrooms and other vegetables. Yogurt is often used in sauces with cucumber, dill, mint and garlic.

Greeks often make a meal out of *mezedes* (hot and cold appetizers) such as *melitzanosalata* (mashed eggplant), *dolmadakia* (meat or rice rolled in grape leaves), *taramoslata* (caviar spread), stuffed peppers and other dishes.

The favorite local alcoholic beverages are *metaxa* and *ouzo*.

A guest may courteously insist on sharing the bill.

A 15 percent service charge is usually added to restaurant and bar bills. If not, leave the waiter 12 to 20 percent on the plate and loose change (five percent) on the table for the busboy.

SOCIAL VALUES, CUSTOMS AND TIPS

While women have gained greater prominence and rights, Greek society is still dominated by men.

Greeks are influenced by European fashion trends. Women wear dresses more often than their North American counterparts. Traditional costumes are worn at folk festivals and on other special occasions.

Men consider it a matter of personal honor to fulfill obligations to their families and others. They may attribute their failures to external circumstances rather than to personal inadequacies.

When eating at a person's home, the host will offer several helpings of each dish. As a general rule, the more one eats, the greater the indication of approval.

A man may praise the food served in his home as especially good, or he may be the hero of his own tales. Such self-praise is not considered bragging.

One should use verbal terms for "Yes" and "No," rather than gestures. A slight upward nod of the head can mean "No" rather than "Yes" and tilting (not shaking) the head to either side means "Yes" or "Of course." This is not always the case, as Greek society is using North American gestures more often now, but the fact that both systems are used can lead to confusion.

The family unit is very strong in Greece. The elderly are respected, addressed by courteous titles, served first and have much authority. Most Greeks care for their elderly parents.

Tip a hotel concierge if he performs a special service, such as obtaining hard-to-get theater tickets.

Coffeehouses are favorite leisure spots for men.

Folk dancing is common, and visitors may be invited to join in. Accepting the invitation is considered a gesture of friendliness and of appreciation of the Greek people.

The U.S. "okay" sign (with the thumb and forefinger forming a circle) is an obscene gesture in Greece. Waving the whole hand, called the *moutza*, is a threatening gesture – particularly when the hand is close to another person's face.

Women visitors may need to take special precautions. To avoid harassment by men, women dining alone should choose one of the more elegant restaurants. For similar reasons, women should take taxis at night unless they know the area they are in very well.

When visiting a church or monastery, women should wear skirts (never pants) and have their arms covered. Women are not allowed behind the altar in a Greek Orthodox church.

GUATEMALA

Population: 12,007,580 (July 1998 est.); mestizo (Amerindian-Spanish) 56%, Amerindian 44%

Languages: Spanish 60%, Amerindian languages 40%

Religions: Roman Catholic, Protestant, traditional Mayan

Currency: quetzal

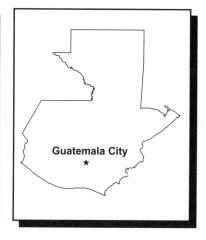

Guatemala City
★

HISTORICAL OVERVIEW

- The Mayan empire flourished in the region now known as Guatemala for more than 1,000 years until it began to decline in 1100 A.D.

- The Spanish ruled Central America, including Guatemala, from 1524 to 1821. After gaining independence in 1821, Guatemala was annexed by Mexico and then very soon became a member of the Central American Federation. This federation was dissolved mainly under pressure from an uprising in Guatemala under Rafael Carrera, who appointed himself military leader of the state in 1838. Carrera became an authoritarian ruler with strong allegiances to the Catholic Church.

- In 1871, a revolution brought Julio Rufino Barrios to power. He focused his efforts on creating a landholding class. Wealth soon became concentrated in the hands of a few.

- From 1898 to 1944, Guatemala was ruled by two more dictatorships, under which the condition of the country's poor, mainly Indian, population continued to decline.

- In 1944, a revolution caused the government's downfall. The two political leaders who followed introduced social and political reforms, giving much more power to the peasants and workers. The new democracy was nevertheless plagued by some rebel activity.

- In 1954, after an elected president was overthrown by a U.S.-backed military coup, rebels began a civil war. Repeated coups and outbreaks of civil war made political stability impossible until 1984. In that year, a constituent assembly was elected to write a new constitution.

- In 1985, civilian rule returned to Guatemala under Marco Vinicio Cerezo Arévalo. Nevertheless, Cerezo continued to use the notorious death squads, and Marxist guerrilla activity increased. The human rights situation continued to decline, and insurgency grew into the 1990s.

- President Jorge Serrano Elías, elected in 1990, began peace talks with the rebels, but his attempts to install authoritarian rule in 1993 cost him his presidency.

- After Serrano left the country, military leaders recalled the Congress, which chose a popular human rights activist, Ramiro de León Carpio, to finish Serrano's term of office.

- Alvaro Arzu Irigoyen won the elections in 1996.

- Arzu required that the rebels give up their arms and tried to bring them into the political realm as a positive force.

- In 1996, government officials and leftist rebels signed a peace treaty, ending the 36-year civil war, the longest civil war in Central America's history. This war, which had pitched military forces in favor of the wealthy elite against rebel guerrillas in favor of the poor, claimed more than 140,000 lives and destroyed 400 villages.

- In 1998, natural disasters took their toll on the country. The Pacaya volcano erupted and spread through the rain forest and rural areas, threatening the largest areas of untouched forest in the country.

BUSINESS PRACTICES

Hours of Business

Businesses are generally open from 8:00 a.m. to 12:00 p.m. and 2:00 p.m. to 6:00 p.m., Monday through Friday. Government offices stay open until 3:30 p.m. or 4:30 p.m. and do not close for lunch.

Dress

Men should wear lightweight suits, and women should wear dresses or suits, never pants.

Introductions

Always offer a handshake when you are introduced to either a man or a woman. Women often pat each other on the right forearm rather than shaking hands. Do not expect – or give – a firm handshake. Such handshakes are used primarily by those from urban areas or those familiar with the U.S.

Men who are good friends give each other an *abrazo* (an embrace with a pat on the back).

Titles are very important. *Licenciado* is used for anyone with a college degree (e.g., B.A.). Other titles include *Arquitecto* (architect), *Ingeniero* (engineer), *Doctor* (medical doctor or lawyer) and *Profesor* (professor).

Meetings

Make appointments at least two weeks in advance if you are traveling from outside Guatemala. If you are in the country, a few days notice is sufficient.

Guatemalans are usually punctual for business appointments. But you may experience unforeseen delays, often caused by the country's power shortages.

Negotiating

It may be necessary to make several trips to Guatemala to complete your business. You must establish a personal relationship with a Guatemalan businessperson before discussing business. A mutual contact can help move the business process along.

Guatemalans do not appreciate loud and brash voices. Ask questions quietly, be patient and never raise your voice or insult anyone.

Learn a little about Guatemala before you visit the country, and show an interest in the history and culture. Avoid discussing politics or "the violence," with which Guatemala has suffered a great deal since 1978. A good subject for conversation is travel, both within Guatemala and abroad. But do not compare Guatemala to other Central American countries or other regions.

It is not necessary to translate business cards into Spanish. Manuals and sales materials, however, should be translated.

Very few Guatemalan women work in high levels of business. A foreign businesswoman should appear very professional and speak on behalf of her company rather than herself.

Entertaining

If a colleague invites you to his/her home for a meal, do not discuss business. If your spouse is accompanying you on the business trip, invite your Guatemalan counterpart and his/her spouse to a social dinner in a restaurant.

There are no set rules or customs regarding whether one person pays for the group or each person pays individually. Offer to pay, but if one person absolutely insists on paying, let him/her follow through and then reciprocate the gesture at the next meal. If a group goes for drinks and not a meal, most often each person will buy a "round."

In Guatemala, business lunches are more popular than dinners. Do not discuss business until you have first spent time addressing non-business topics.

Buen provecho is often said before a meal. (Roughly translated, this means "May it do you good.") After a meal, expect everyone to say *"Muchas gracias"* (Thank you).

It is not appropriate to bring gifts on your first business trip to the country, but for subsequent trips, it is polite to ask people what they would like from abroad.

SOCIAL VALUES, CUSTOMS AND TIPS

Discussions about children, your interests and your job are appropriate. Do not be surprised if people ask about your job and marital status after a very short acquaintance.

Do not wear shorts in the cities or in the highlands. Do not wear jeans in cities. Men should wear pants and a shirt, and women should wear a skirt and a blouse. Indians may be offended to see a woman wearing pants.

Guatemalans find the American "okay" sign (thumb and forefinger forming a circle) offensive.

HONDURAS

Population: 5,861,955 (July 1998 est.); mestizo (Amerindian and European) 90%, Amerindian 7%, black 2%, white 1%

Languages: Spanish (official), Amerindian dialects

Religions: Roman Catholic 97%, Protestant 3%, other less than 1%

Currency: tempira

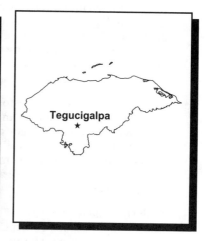

Tegucigalpa ★

HISTORICAL OVERVIEW

- The Mayan Empire flourished in the region now known as Honduras until about 800 A.D., when the Mayan population in the area declined. A number of small empires then controlled the region until the arrival of Spanish explorers.

- In 1502, Columbus arrived and named the region *Honduras* (meaning "depths") because of the deep waters off the north coast. The indigenous people fought against Spanish occupation until 1539. In that year, the last of the indigenous chiefs was killed, and the Spanish settled a city at Comayagua. After 1570 Honduras was incorporated into Spain's Captaincy General (colony) of Guatemala. The Spanish population began to grow, especially after silver was discovered in the area in the 1570s.

- At the request of the Mosquito Indians, the British occupied the Mosquito region of the country beginning near the end of the 16th century, withdrawing only in 1859.

- In 1821, Honduras and four other Central American provinces declared independence and joined together as a federation under the Mexican Empire. The period under this new empire was short-lived, however. In 1838, complete independence was declared, and the republic of Honduras was established.

- In Honduras' 161 years as an independent country, it experienced 385 armed rebellions, 126 different governments, and 16 constitutions. By the end of the 19th century, due to internal instability, the country came under Nicaraguan influence.

- Internal political instability continued in Honduras until Tiburcio Carías Andino took power in 1932 and ruled as a benevolent despot. Carías did more to advance the social and economic well-being of the country than any of his predecessors, although he maintained his power only by jailing or exiling his critics. Carías' military rule lasted until 1948, when he peacefully surrendered power following elections. Nevertheless, even once Carías stepped down, military leaders continued to exercise control. Military rule, a number of coups and corruption marked the period between the 1950s and 1980s.

- Finally, in 1982, elections restored civilian rule. Free elections and civilian rule continued, and the elections of 1989 marked the third free election in a decade as well as the first peaceful transfer of power to a political opposition party in half a century. The military, however, continued to exercise a great deal of power, and many citizens felt there was too little popular participation in the political process.

- In the late 1980s, after years of involvement in local area conflicts, Honduras joined other Central American governments in a cooperative movement for peace.

- Carlos Roberto Reina, who was elected and took office in 1994, promised to attack corruption and to reduce the military's budget. In 1996, he reduced the role of the military by abolishing the draft and ending military rule over the national police. He faced many difficult issues, however, regarding discontent from indigenous groups.

- In November 1997, Carlos Flores was elected president.

- Although issues of land reform, unemployment, military and civilian discontent still remain prevalent in Honduran society, the move toward peace throughout Central America has allowed the Honduran government to focus more on the social needs of the population.

BUSINESS PRACTICES

Hours of Business

Business hours are usually from 7:30 a.m. to 4:30 p.m., although some offices close for the *siesta* (a rest after the midday meal). Businesses are often open on Saturdays from 8:00 a.m. until sometime between noon and 2:00 p.m.

The best time for business travel is between February and June, since the rainy season lasts from May to November, and December and August are popular vacation times.

Dress

Businessmen generally wear a conservative suit or a *guayabera* (a decorative shirt instead of a shirt and tie). Businesswomen generally wear a skirt and blouse or a dress.

Introductions

A handshake is the most common form of greeting for both men and women. Women sometimes pat each other on the arm or shoulder instead of shaking hands. Be aware that handshakes are not as firm as those given in the U.S. and you should adjust your grip accordingly.

Middle- and upper-class women kiss male and female friends on the cheek. The *abrazo* is a warm embrace shared by close friends and relatives.

When people meet for the first time, a person's official title should be used. Professional titles used alone are the preferred forms of address. People who do not have professional titles should be addressed as *Señor* (Mr.), *Señora* (Mrs. or Ms.) or *Señorita* (Miss), followed by the surname. People also use *Usted* (the formal form of "you") when meeting someone for the first time.

Most Hondurans have two surnames, one from their father (listed first) and one from their mother. Normally, the father's name is used when addressing someone. For example, Hernan Antonio Martinez García is addressed as *Señor Martinez*, and María Elisa Gutierrez Herrera is addressed as *Señorita Gutierrez*. When a woman marries, she usually adds her husband's surname and goes by that surname. For example, if the two people in the above example married, the woman would be known as María Elisa Gutierrez Herrera de Martinez. She would be addressed as *Señora de Martinez* or, more informally, *Señora Martinez*.

When you meet a small group of people, you should greet and say good-bye to each person individually.

Have your business cards printed in both English and Spanish, and present the card to Hondurans with the Spanish side up.

Meetings

Punctuality is generally not highly valued in Honduran society, but people in cities as well as in business settings tend to be more punctual. Despite this, scheduled appointments may still be delayed. Punctuality is, however, expected of foreign visitors. It is still always best to make appointments well in advance and confirm them upon arriving in Honduras.

Using graphs and other visual aids in presentations makes a very good impression.

Negotiating

While doing business, you should try to establish a long-term relationship based on mutual trust and reliability. If several trips are made, it is important that the same person be involved each time.

Extensive negotiations may be necessary to complete your transaction. An emotional approach, emphasizing trust, mutual compatibility, the benefits to a person's pride, etc., will be more effective than the logical bottom line of a proposal.

Hondurans place importance on their emotional reactions to projects and the people involved in them.

Hondurans also place great importance on the collective group and their role within the social system. The decision-making process is strongly affected by the need to maintain group harmony, which is often considered to be above innovation or showing initiative or expertise.

Business may progress at a slower pace than in the U.S. Speedy progress is not a major goal, and Honduran businesspeople tend to exhibit somewhat laid-back behavior. This is true even in high-paced situations, partly to reduce anxiety.

It is better to phrase questions in a way that will require more detailed responses than a simple "Yes" or "No." It is important to get all agreements in writing, since a verbal "Yes" may be considered simply polite, rather than binding.

Avoid saying "No" in Honduras. Instead, milder responses, such as "Maybe" or "We'll see," will be understood as a "No." Similarly, remember that if your Honduran counterpart seems particularly hesitant or noncommittal, this may indicate a "No."

If there is a disagreement, be aware that a compromise may be difficult to reach, as this will be seen as weakness.

It is rare for women to occupy top positions in Honduran companies. A foreign businesswoman may also face an initial lack of respect. She should respond to this by acting extremely professional and by emphasizing her role as a representative of her company.

Hondurans are very status conscious. It is therefore a good idea if at least one member of the foreign negotiating team is from a higher level of management.

Entertaining

It is very common for business meetings to take place over breakfast, lunch or dinner. It is best to let your Honduran counterpart suggest the time for a business meeting over a meal.

Foreign businesswomen should never invite a Honduran business-man to a dinner unless spouses also attend. If a businesswoman invites a Honduran businessman to lunch, the man will not let her pay. If she wishes to pay, it is a good idea for her to invite him to eat at her hotel and arrange in advance to have the bill added to her hotel tab.

Hondurans are courteous and generous to guests in their homes, even when guests arrive unannounced. Refreshments are almost always offered. Even if a guest does not feel like eating, the host may wrap up a little food to send home with the visitor.

If you are invited to a home or if a spouse is included in an invitation, you should not expect to discuss business. The engagement will be purely social.

While social events may have official starting times, it should be understood by both hosts and guests that this time is flexible. It is not uncommon for people to be up to an hour late for a social engage-ment. In fact, it is generally considered polite to arrive about 30 minutes late for social engagements.

When in someone's home, you should be careful not to admire the person's belongings too much as they may feel obligated to give them to you.

When leaving a home, guests should be especially respectful of the head of the household and should say good-bye to each person.

At more formal restaurants, a ten to 15 percent tip is appropriate. Tips are not usually expected in less formal restaurants.

Breakfast is served between 6:00 and 8:30 a.m. The main meal of the day begins around noon. A light evening meal is eaten between 6:00 and 8:00 p.m. Dinners with guests tend to be larger and will be served at about 8:30 or 9:00 p.m.

Beans, corn, *tortillas* (thin, round unleavened bread made from cornmeal or wheat flour) and rice are staples. The most common fruits and vegetables are bananas, pineapples, mangos, citrus fruits, coconuts, melons, avocados, potatoes and yams. Coffee (often with milk) is a common drink that is usually served with the main meal of the day.

Both hands, but not elbows, should be kept above the table when seated for a meal.

Continental manners, with the fork in the right hand and the knife remaining in the left, are the most commonly used. Pieces of *tortilla* may also be used to move or pick up food, however.

At the table before a meal, one always says *Buen provecho* (Enjoy your meal). In a restaurant, a person approaching or passing a table also says *Buen provecho* to the people at the table.

SOCIAL VALUES, CUSTOMS AND TIPS

Spanish is the official and dominant language, although English is widely understood in urban and tourist centers and in business circles.

In Honduras, as in many other Latin American countries, the social philosophies of fatalism, machismo and *hora latina* play a role in daily life. Machismo reflects the fact that Honduran society is male-dominated and that there are clear and traditional role differences between the sexes. *Hora latina* refers to a concept of time, in which individuals are considered to be more important than schedules. Being late for appointments is very common.

Christian beliefs as well as environmental values (ties to the land and agriculture) are very important to Hondurans. You should be careful not to offend these values.

You should avoid openly criticizing or embarrassing someone or pulling rank.

Good topics of conversation include Honduran tourist sites, your family and your job. You should avoid talking about local politics or the unrest in Central America.

Sports, which are extremely popular in Honduras, make good topics of conversation. *Fútbol* (soccer) is the national sport. Wealthier Hondurans also enjoy cycling, baseball, golf, tennis and swimming.

Be careful in referring to U.S. citizens as "Americans." Hondurans also consider themselves to be Americans and are sensitive to the use of this term. Use more exact terms such as North Americans, Central Americans and South Americans.

People stand close together when conversing. Stepping away will offend the person with whom you are speaking.

Hand and body language are very important forms of communication. Clasping both hands indicates strong approval. Waving the index finger is often used to say "No."

It is considered inappropriate for men and women to wear shorts in public, except in coastal areas where it is hot and humid. It is considered inappropriate for women to wear revealing clothing, and a woman may even offend some people by wearing pants.

It is customary to give a general greeting when entering a room.

When you pass someone in the street, you should say *Adios* (Goodbye), which is used as a general greeting in this situation.

Placing the finger below the eye is used as a warning to be cautious.

A hand placed under the elbow usually means that someone is thought to be stingy.

To express enthusiasm, Hondurans place their middle finger and thumb together and shake their hand, producing a snapping noise.

It is rude to beckon someone with the index finger. Beckoning is done by waving the hand with the palm facing down.

Bartering is common in marketplaces and shops where prices are not posted. Otherwise, prices are fixed.

Older people are given preference. For example, if you are standing in line do not be surprised if an elderly person is served before you.

Honduran men are very warm and friendly with each other. It is considered an insult to withdraw from such contact.

HONG KONG

Population: 6,706,965 (July 1998 est.); Chinese 95%, other 5%

Languages: Cantonese (official), English (official), Mandarin

Religions: Buddhist, Taoist and Confuncianist majorities, Christian, Muslim, Hindu, Sikh and Jewish minorities

Currency: Hong Kong dollar

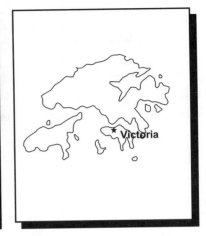

HISTORICAL OVERVIEW

- Prior to British settlement, Hong Kong was inhabited largely by fishermen and pirates.

- The British East India Trading Company began using Hong Kong harbor for trade with China as early as 1699.

- Hong Kong was acquired by Great Britain from China in three stages: Hong Kong Island in 1842, the Kowloon Peninsula in 1860, and the New Territories in 1898, under a 99-year lease.

- Hong Kong quickly became a very prosperous trading center, and Chinese immigrants were drawn to the island.

- Hong Kong was occupied by Japan from 1941-1945.

- The population greatly increased following the victory of the Communists in China in 1949. Over one million refugees arrived immediately following China's civil war.

- Hong Kong's importance as a free port grew after World War II, when it became a leading commercial port and tourist center. Industry moved from textile manufacturing in the 1960s to electronics, finance and trade.

- During the 1980s, Hong Kong became a destination for Vietnamese refugees.

- Chris Patten, a Conservative, was appointed by the British as governor of Hong Kong in 1992. He took steps to strengthen Hong Kong's democratic process.

- Under the Sino-British Joint Declaration, issued on 19 December 1984, China regained control of Hong Kong on 1 July 1997. Hong Kong is now a Special Administrative Region (SAR) of China. While China remains responsible for foreign affairs and defense policies, Hong Kong is allowed to maintain its own governing and economic policies.

- Hong Kong's first new chief executive, Tung Chee Hwa, was elected in 1996.

- Although protests occurred during the transfer, it was more peaceful than had been expected. The major difficulties facing Hong Kong stem from the Asian economic crisis of 1997.

- Hong Kong's economy functions with little government intervention. While manufacturing takes place in Hong Kong, the service sector accounts for the vast majority of the GDP. Much of the country's income also derives from the heavy use of ports for shipping and from its elevated position as a leading financial center.

BUSINESS PRACTICES

Hours of Business

Business hours are 9:00 a.m. to 5:00 p.m., Monday through Friday, and 9:00 a.m. to 1:00 p.m. on Saturdays. Some offices close from 12:00 to 2:00 p.m. for lunch.

Holidays are based on the lunar calendar and may fall on different days each year. The Chinese New Year, the most important holiday, is often in February.

Dress

All styles of clothing are worn in Hong Kong, from traditional to modern. Men wear western-style suits for business, and women wear suits or dresses.

Introductions

Both English and Chinese greetings are common in Hong Kong. Therefore, shaking hands when meeting is appropriate and acceptable, and should be done when leaving as well. A handshake is usually quite light, but may last as long as ten seconds.

Business cards are essential. They should be printed with English on one side and Chinese on the other. Present and receive business cards with both hands. Then take a few moments to look over the business cards you have received.

The Chinese do not look people directly in the eye when greeting them. Sometimes they lower their eyes as a sign of deference and respect.

Following introductions, polite conversation will include inquiries about one's health, business affairs or school activities.

Make a special effort to greet and show respect to older people.

In Chinese names, the family name precedes the given name. In Hong Kong, some Chinese people adapt western first names for use in international business settings.

Meetings

Tea may be served during business meetings. If so, do not drink until your host does. If your host leaves his or her tea untouched for a lengthy period of time, it may indicate that the meeting is over.

Businesspeople are generally punctual for appointments.

Be modest and patient in your presentations.

Negotiating

Personal connections are indispensable to doing business in Hong Kong. Little distinction is made between business and personal relationships.

The people of Hong Kong place great value on reliability and trustworthiness. Permanence of a relationship is very important, and therefore the emphasis in doing business is on promoting long-term mutual benefits.

Although the pace of life is fast, business transactions are seldom made in a hurry, and much attention is paid to detail.

Concessions are generally requested toward the end of the deal.

Show no aggression during negotiations, and take care not to cause one of your Chinese colleagues to lose face.

Do not address an issue of potential embarrassment or conflict in public. Appearances are very important.

"Yes" does not necessarily mean agreement, but rather often suggests acknowledgment of what has been said.

Maintain the same negotiating team throughout the process. This will express loyalty to your company and team members, a quality that Chinese businesspeople find very important.

Entertaining

Gifts are often given to individuals in Hong Kong. A good gift would be something not available in Hong Kong, such as an item made in your home area or town. If gifts are given to a number of people, make sure that they are of roughly the same value, although the chief executive's gift should be of greater value.

Business is often conducted during lunch or dinner. Guests are expected to arrive on time.

Lavish restaurant meals are traditional for special events among people in the Chinese community. Additionally, those of European heritage may hold dinner parties at their homes.

At a restaurant, the guest of honor usually rises at the end of the meal and thanks the host on behalf of the entire group.

If you are invited to someone's home, take along a small gift of fruit or candy. A picture book about your home area is a welcome item, as is perfume for the hostess and toys for the family's children.

Red and gold are considered lucky colors, and gifts are often wrapped in paper of these colors. Avoid using black or white wrapping paper, as these are considered mourning colors.

As with business cards, present and receive a gift with both hands.

Unwrapping a gift in front of the giver is not done unless the giver encourages it.

Be aware that a Chinese person may refuse a gift two or three times before finally accepting it. It is not necessary, however, for a foreigner to go through the same ritual.

Shoes are not generally removed when entering a home, although the custom is widespread in other parts of Asia.

You should be seated when invited to do so. Always maintain good posture.

Rice is the main staple of meals. Chinese dishes are often prepared with fish, pork, chicken and vegetables.

In the home, chopsticks are used for eating most meals. Dishes are usually placed in the center of the table. Everyone helps themselves to a portion of food from the main platter with chopsticks and places it in their own personal bowl of rice. In some families, it is acceptable to use the same chopsticks for serving and eating.

The proper way to eat is to hold the rice bowl close to your mouth.

Your host will offer to refill your bowl with more rice and other food until you politely refuse.

You may find both chopsticks and western utensils at a meal, which is a reflection of Hong Kong's heritage as a British Crown Colony. When using a knife and fork, the continental style is followed, keeping the knife in the right hand and the fork in the left.

When someone pours you tea at a meal, indicate "Thank you" by lightly tapping your fingertips on the table.

Always leave some food in your dish to indicate that your host has provided more food than you could possibly eat.

In restaurants, a service charge is often included in the bill. It is customary, however, to leave an additional tip.

Signal a waiter that you want the check by making a writing motion with your hands.

Reciprocate a toast made by your host. A common time for toasts in a multi-course meal is when the shark's fin soup (often considered the highlight of the meal) is served. Toasts can also be made when a new dish is served and before people start eating that dish.

SOCIAL VALUES, CUSTOMS AND TIPS

Hong Kong has two official languages: Chinese (Cantonese) and English. Although dialects from all parts of China are heard, the Cantonese dialect is predominant and is officially recognized. Street signs, telephone directories and government documents are written in both languages.

The Chinese people are reserved and show modesty when dealing with others. Humility or self-demeaning comments are generally used to describe oneself or one's accomplishments. They will usually deny praise, although sincere compliments are given and appreciated.

Strong elements of Taoism, Confucianism and Buddhism form part of the religious background of many Hong Kong residents.

The Confucian ethics of proper social and family relationships form the foundation of Chinese society.

The Chinese are very conscious of social position. Anything you can do to enhance their opinion of your social position is worthwhile, so long as you do not appear arrogant or haughty.

A person's actions reflect on the entire family. "Saving face" and avoiding embarrassment, shame and dishonor are very important. Never do or say anything that could cause someone to "lose face."

Expect to be asked personal questions, especially about your family, how much you earn, how much your watch cost or what type of car you drive. It is not necessary to answer such questions if you do not feel comfortable.

The Chinese prefer to be indirect when they need to say "No." They may say something is inconvenient or difficult or that it is under consideration.

Laughing or smiling may indicate embarrassment.

Although the influence of the British over the last century has left its mark, you should expect to observe many traditional Chinese customs.

When sitting, place your hands in your lap and keep your feet on the floor. Traditional Chinese do not cross their legs, but it is all right for women to do so.

Winking at someone is considered impolite.

An open hand, not just the index finger, is used for pointing. Beckon someone with the palm down and all fingers waving.

Eating on the streets is considered inappropriate.

The Chinese do not usually show affection in public, although this is changing somewhat among younger people.

Friends of the same sex may walk hand-in-hand.

Mahjong, a traditional game played with tiles, is a popular pastime.

Favorite sports include ping pong, soccer, squash, tennis, swimming and boating.

HUNGARY

Population: 10,208,127 (July 1998 est.); Hungarian 89.9%, Gypsy 4%, German 2.6%, Serb 2%, Slovak 0.8%, Romanian 0.7%

Languages: Hungarian (official), other

Religions: Roman Catholic 67.5%, Calvinist 20%, Lutheran 5%, atheist and other 7.5%

Currency: forint

HISTORICAL OVERVIEW

- Part of Hungary became part of the Roman Empire in 14 B.C. as the provinces of Pannonia and Dacia. When Rome lost Pannonia in the fourth century A.D., it was inhabited first by Germanic tribes and then by Slavs. Probably in 896, the Magyars, led by Arpád, entered en masse. In 906, they conquered the resident Moravians and then, in 907, occupied Pannonia.

- Arpád's great-grandson, Géza, introduced Christianity in the late tenth century. When Géza's son, Stephen, became Hungary's first king in 1000 A.D., he converted the people to Christianity. The 14th century was a golden age for Hungary as well as for many of its neighbors.

- Most of the country was conquered by the Ottoman Turks in the 16th century and was subsequently ruled by the Austrian Hapsburgs in the 17th and 18th centuries.

- In 1848, the Hungarians rebelled against Hapsburg rule, but they were defeated after two years. In 1867, a system for sharing power between the Austrians and Hungarians in Central Europe, known as the Dual Monarchy, was established. Internal ethnic conflicts, however, caused by the increasing desire for self-rule among the Empire's Slavic minorities, contributed to the beginning of World War I, which in turn, led to the dissolution of the Austro-Hungarian Empire.

- Following World War I, according to treaty settlements, Hungary became an independent republic but lost much of its territory to neighboring countries.

- During World War II, Germany invaded Hungary in 1944, and for the remainder of the war Hungary fought as a German ally. After the war, the Soviets briefly occupied the territory. Following an armistice, free elections reestablished a republic in 1945.

- Yet in 1947, the Communist Party, supported by the Soviets, seized control of the country and, in 1949, declared Hungary a socialist state called the People's Republic of Hungary. Communist reformer Imre Nagy came to power in 1953 and tried to bring about systemic changes. He withdrew Hungary from the Warsaw Pact and declared the country neutral in 1956. In response, the Soviets attacked Hungary, repressed the movement and executed Nagy.

- After Nagy's death, János Kádár was the leader of the Communist government until he was forced to resign under pressure for reform in 1988. By 1989, the Communists lost their hold on the government and the country was renamed the Republic of Hungary. Nagy was subsequently reburied as a national hero.

- In 1990, free elections were held and József Antall became the new prime minister. Antall died in 1993 and was briefly replaced by Peter Boross. Antall's and Boross's party, the Hungarian Democratic Forum, lost the May 1994 election due to popular disillusion with economic reforms. A newly formed Socialist Party (consisting of former Communists) gained the parliamentary majority, and Gyula Horn became prime minister. Problems with privatizing old state-owned industries caused Prime Minister Horn to dismiss his privatization commissioner and his finance minister in 1995.

- In December 1995, the U.S. set up a NATO facility at Taszar Air Base in Kaposvar, Hungary. The base was used to help mobilize U.S. troops headed for Bosnia. Many Hungarian military families were uprooted in the process, but operations went smoothly.

- In July 1997 Hungary was invited to become a NATO member, and in March 1998 negotiations began to make Hungary a member of the EU. Hungary should be a full NATO member within a few years.

BUSINESS PRACTICES

Hours of Business

The workweek is Monday through Friday, 8:30 a.m. to 5:00 p.m., and Saturdays, 8:30 a.m. to 1:30 p.m.

Business appointments should not be scheduled for July or August because of the summer vacation, or from mid-December to mid-January because of the Christmas holiday.

Dress

For business meetings, men wear suits, white shirts and ties. Women typically wear suits or dresses.

Introductions

It is customary to shake hands when first being introduced. People shake hands upon meeting and departing. A man should wait for a woman to extend her hand.

Hungarians address each other using their appropriate titles preceded by "Mr." or "Ms." The surname should not be used when using a title, e.g., "Mr. Engineer" would be correct. If someone does not have a title or you are uncertain, address that person by "Mr.," "Mrs." or "Miss" followed by his/her last name.

It is common for two men who are close friends and who have not seen each other for some time to shake hands and embrace, making cheek-to-cheek contact, first the left and then the right. Close women friends embrace.

In business settings or at formal parties, you should wait to be introduced by your host. In more informal settings, it is acceptable to introduce yourself.

First names should only be used after being invited to do so by your Hungarian colleague.

Business cards should be distributed liberally.

Meetings

Meetings begin on time, and punctuality is valued highly.

You will need a Hungarian contact who will schedule your appointments and accompany you to them. All appointments should be scheduled in writing at least two weeks in advance.

Never schedule an appointment on a Saturday.

Negotiating

Unless you are fluent in Hungarian, it is best to write all business letters in English. Businesses expect to translate letters written in other languages.

Consider hiring an interpreter if you do not speak Hungarian or German well enough to conduct business. If the business you are visiting is in an outlying area, you will almost certainly need an interpreter.

Hungarians often review their decisions, so meetings tend to last longer than in North America. Be patient. Once they have agreed to a contract Hungarians will keep their word and fulfill the agreement. Agendas are treated very flexibly and are not necessarily adhered to.

Brandy is usually served during negotiations. It is impolite to refuse. If you do not wish to drink, simply place it on the table while negotiating.

Stress how your company can help Hungary advance technologically and assume an important role in the global marketplace. Hungarian businesses are particularly interested in this at the present time.

It is not customary to say "No" to something outright. Use "Maybe" or change the topic instead.

Always do business face-to-face if you intend to establish trust and a lasting business relationship.

Entertaining

If your business dealings are successful, consider hosting a cocktail party for your Hungarian colleagues. Guests should be greeted at the door, and you should be prepared to give a short speech.

If you want to have a meal with business associates, you can suggest meeting them for lunch.

After you have developed a personal relationship with a business colleague, you can entertain at a dinner and include spouses.

Most business entertaining is conducted at restaurants because homes are often too small to accommodate entertaining.

If you are invited to dinner at someone's home, western liquor or wrapped flowers are appropriate gifts. Avoid bringing chrysanthemums.

The host and hostess sit opposite one another, with the guest of honor seated to the hostess's right.

Before starting to eat, it is customary to wish everyone a good appetite. Hungarians say *Jóèt vagyat* (Enjoy the meal).

After each course is served, it is polite to wait until your hostess begins to eat before you start.

If wine is served, it is a Hungarian custom for the guest to propose a toast, saying "To your health."

Hungarians eat continental style, with the fork in the left hand and the knife in the right. Push food onto the back of your fork with your knife.

When eating fish, use only a fork or the hostess will think the fish is not tender enough.

It would be wise to taste the food before adding seasoning, or you could insult the hostess. Begin by eating small portions of various dishes. The food tends to be very rich, and you are expected to finish everything on your plate. If you must leave something, apologize to your hostess.

Breakfast usually consists of bread with butter and jam. Espresso will be served with hot milk. Lunch is the main meal of the day. It may include soup, a main course and salad. The evening meal is usually light, consisting of open-faced sandwiches or salad and cold cuts. A dinner party, however, will be more like the midday meal.

Popular main dishes include *pörkölt* (pork stew with paprika), *töltött káposzta* (stuffed cabbage) and *fátanyéros* (mixed grill of meats and sausages served on a wooden platter). *Palacsinta* (crepe-like pancakes) are used with various courses. They can be part of a main dish or a dessert.

Desserts can be elaborate, such as *dobos torta*, a twelve-layer cake with chocolate filling. Other popular items are marzipan balls dipped in chocolate and glazed chestnuts.

Hungary is famous for its sweet dessert wine, called *Tokay*.

SOCIAL VALUES, CUSTOMS AND TIPS

It is common during conversation for the subject to be changed rather abruptly. Hungarians often have an "official" opinion and also a very private opinion. Changing the subject could either indicate that you have said too much or that you have touched too closely on an unacceptable political topic.

Hungarians can be very modest and self-effacing. If you pay them a compliment, it is not unusual for them to belittle their achievement.

Hungarians enjoy hearing visitors describe what they have seen in other parts of the world, since their travel has been restricted. They have a strong sense of both personal and national pride, and relish discussing what you like about Hungary as well as other topics such as food and wine.

It is customary for a man to walk to the left of a woman or an honored guest of either sex.

Do not wear shorts except on country outings or at the beach.

INDIA

Population: 984,003,683 (July 1998 est.); Indo-Aryan 72%, Dravidian 25%, Mongoloid and other 3%

Languages: English is the most important language for national, political, and commercial communication, Hindi, 14 other official languages (Bengali, Telugu, Marathi, Tamil, Urdu, Gujarati, Malayalam, Kannada, Oriya, Punjabi, Assamese, Kashmiri, Sindhi, Sanskrit), numerous other languages and dialects

Religions: Hindu 80%, Muslim 14%, Christian 2.4%, Sikh 2%, Buddhist 0.7%, Jain 0.5%, other 0.4%

Currency: Indian rupee

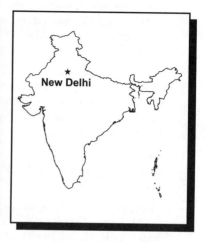

HISTORICAL OVERVIEW

- The Indian subcontinent was the site of the Indus Valley civilization more than 5,000 years ago. Around 1500 B.C., Aryans arrived from Central Asia. They gradually pushed the native Dravidians to the south. The Aryans gave India many of its basic institutions, such as the caste system, and introduced Hinduism and Sanskrit.

- Buddhism developed in the sixth century B.C. Alexander the Great invaded India in 327 B.C., but his influence was short-lived. The first great Indian empire was the Maurya, established shortly after Alexander's invasion. It was this empire that unified the entire north and spread Buddhism throughout the region. The influence of Buddhism later waned, and Hinduism became more dominant. Hindu philosophy and legal codes were developed under the Mauryas and succeeding dynasties.

- The fourth to sixth centuries A.D. are considered a golden age of science, literature and the arts and of greater political unity under the northern Gupta Empire. There were also several great empires in southern India, which developed separately. They established a maritime trade that spread throughout the East.

- Arab, Turk and Afghan Muslims ruled successively in various parts of the Indian subcontinent from the eighth to the 18th centuries. This provided some basis for the historical animosity between Hindus and Muslims. Most notable among the Muslim rulers were the Mughals, who founded their empire in 1526.

- Their power extended over most of India by the end of the 17th century. Portuguese, Dutch, French and British traders established bases in India, starting with the landing of Vasco da Gama in 1498. Until 1757 there was not much foreign conquest, but when the British defeated the French and the Mughals in this year they quickly spread throughout India. The last kingdom to be defeated was the Sikh kingdom in 1849. The British assumed political control of the country in 1858.

- Nationalist feelings quickly found a voice in the Indian National Congress in 1885. After World War I, Mahatma Gandhi led a series of nationalist movements advocating civil disobedience and passive resistance to British rule. India gained independence from Great Britain in 1947.

- Pakistan was established as a separate Muslim country due to religious rivalry and violence. Bangladesh broke away from Pakistan in 1971.

- Violence, including the assassinations of Mahatma Gandhi (1948), Indira Gandhi (1984) and Rajiv Gandhi (1991), has marked Indian politics. Religious and caste strife divided the country throughout the 1990s and continues to divide it today.

- In the 1990s the Congress Party, in power since 1947, saw its support erode while the Hindu nationalist Bharatiya Janata Party (BJP) gained much support.

- In 1992 the BJP and militant Hindu groups were implicated in the destruction of a mosque at Ayodhya, causing an outbreak of religious fighting that quickly spread.

- The economy was in a deep crisis in the early 1990s but reforms, encouraging foreign investment, were instituted in 1993. India has six operational nuclear facilities, several car manufacturing and industrial plants and huge mineral deposits.

- In early 1996, a number of high-ranking government officials stepped down as a result of corruption scandals, further chipping away at support for the Congress Party and bolstering the BJP.

- Regional, class and caste loyalties continued to grow and the BJP won the 1996 Parliamentary elections under the leadership of the more moderate Atal Bihari Valpayee. Unable to form a coalition, however, Valpayee was soon forced to resign. The prime ministership then passed back and forth between various parties over the next two years until the BJP won the elections in March 1998 on a platform that promoted protecting domestic industry against international competition and developing nuclear weapons to counter China and Pakistan.

- In May 1998 India conducted several nuclear tests, bringing upon it the condemnation of the international community and provoking Pakistan to respond in kind.

BUSINESS PRACTICES

Hours of Business

Business hours are weekdays from 9:30 a.m. to 5:00 p.m. Lunch is usually from 1:00 p.m. to 2:00 p.m.

Dress

Men should wear a suit on the first business visit and for all government visits; afterwards, you may follow the lead of your host. Men usually wear slacks and short-sleeved sports shirts to the office. Similarly, women should wear a suit for the first visit. Women generally wear casual dresses or pants outfits for daytime, and cocktail dresses, suits or long dresses to evening receptions and to more formal restaurants.

Introductions

Greeting in the proper manner is important. The traditional Indian greeting is called *namaste* – a ritual where one presses the palms together (fingers up) below the chin and inclines the head slightly, while saying the word *namaste*. Do not bow. Greet the oldest person in the group first, not the host. When greeting a man, shake hands. When greeting a woman, make a *namaste*. Indians usually will not shake hands with a woman. If meeting a man and woman together, make a *namaste*.

Titles are important. Don't use first names unless you know someone well. Use "Mr.," "Mrs." or "Miss." Use titles such as "Professor" and "Doctor," and use "Sir" with a superior.

You may have a garland of flowers placed around your neck as a sign of affection and respect. Accept it and remove it immediately to show humility.

Be aware that Indian businessmen may graciously pat or slap you on the back. This signifies cordiality and friendship.

Meetings

Your Indian colleagues will speak perfect English. Although Hindi is the predominant language, English is the language of commerce and administration.

Make appointments at least 30 days in advance. Most Indian executives prefer their meetings in the late morning or early afternoon. Construct your schedule with enough flexibility to accommodate extra days in India for unforeseen meetings or delays.

Though Indians are impressed by punctuality, they are often late. Do not be surprised if Indian businesspeople are somewhat vague about a commitment since they do not like to be pressed for exact times.

Business cards may be in English. You may add your academic credentials by identifying degrees and disciplines and even the name of the institution if it is particularly distinguished.

Negotiating

Focus is on a win/win relationship, but compromise is an acceptable form of negotiating.

Connections are important.

Facilitation payments are not uncommon.

Indian negotiating teams are led by management and supported by technical experts. Decisions are made by high-level management who may not be represented on the team. Try to make contacts at the highest levels and provide incentives for middle managers and assistants to help make your concerns or proposals a top priority.

Be deferential when dealing with bureaucrats.

Promotional and sales materials should be printed in English and Hindi to reach wide markets.

After sales, service and credit are important items.

Concern for maintaining harmony may result in an Indian negotiator responding with words that he/she believes the other party would like to hear.

Self-control and fatalism (based upon the concept of predestination) play a large role in decision making. Risk-taking is allowable since events are all predetermined.

Allowing the Indian negotiating team to set the lead may help foster the necessary establishment and building of trust.

Generally, business is conducted at a slow pace. Be prepared for a good deal of discussion, followed by a long wait for a final decision. Be patient and enjoy the pleasantries and conversation that are typical during business transactions.

While a handshake signals an agreement, contract disputes are settled in court so contracts should include all necessary details.

Business contracts will usually be scrutinized very carefully, sometimes taking weeks or months.

Phrase questions carefully. Indian responses can be ambiguous so as to avoid upsetting a person.

Indians are tolerant of others. Be cautious in giving criticism, however, as Indians easily take offense. Indians prefer seriousness mixed with warmth and genuineness.

Entertaining

The prelude to most business meetings is a cup of tea.

Business can be discussed during meals, but let your host initiate the discussion. Business meals usually take place in the evening. The traffic and humidity limit luncheon meetings.

When offered refreshments or snacks in or out of the home, it is polite to initially refuse and then to accept. If it is not to your taste, simply leave it.

Food and religious belief are interwoven in Indian culture. The giving of food is considered a spiritual act.

Most Hindus and all orthodox Muslims abstain from alcoholic drinks.

To thank an Indian host after a meal is considered an insult because Indians take it as a payment. Instead, you should reciprocate with an invitation.

When invited to dine at an Indian home, do not arrive early. It is wise to have a snack before you arrive, because dinner may not be served for quite some time. Leave immediately after dinner has concluded.

Bring a gift of sweets and pastry or fruit and flowers. Avoid frangipani flowers, which are used for funerals.

The religion of your hosts will determine the menu. Muslims eat beef, but not pork or shellfish. Many Hindus are vegetarians. Those who are not will never eat or serve beef since the cow is considered sacred.

In rural homes, women may be seated separately. Even when the guests are mixed, the sexes usually talk only to each other.

In traditional homes, you may sit cross-legged on floor mats at low tables. Expect to be seated first, but there is no particular place of honor.

Always wash your hands before and after meals. In Hindu homes, you will be expected to wash your mouth as well. If so, swirl some water around in your mouth and then spit it into the sink.

Always wait to be served. Guests and men will be served first.

Indians are fastidious about cleanliness. It is advisable never to touch a common dish or serve with your fingers or with a utensil that you have used. Always use serving spoons.

Unless you are offered a fork, eat with your hands just as the Indians do.

Your Indian host will likely entertain you at a private club, a prestigious hotel or in a restaurant, rather than at home. Wives are generally invited, except for Muslim wives, who are kept from public view.

The guest of honor should be seated to the right of the host. Otherwise, there are no seating formalities.

Indians rarely split the bill for a meal. The party that issued the invitation will pay.

The tip for meals is usually ten percent of the bill.

There is no such spice as "curry;" the word simply means "dish" or "culinary preparation." In northern Indian cuisine, there are a variety of breads such as *chapatti, nan* and *paratha.* Southern cuisine is accompanied by rice. Some specialties include *tandoori* chicken (marinated and then cooked in a clay oven) and *samosas* (fried pastry triangles with a meat or vegetable filling). A large variety of vegetarian dishes are also popular.

After eating, it is customary to consume *pan,* a mixture of spices rolled in a betel leaf, as a digestive.

Do not offer anyone, even a member of your family, food from your plate. It is considered socially offensive. Hindus do not let anyone outside their caste or religion touch their food.

SOCIAL VALUES, CUSTOMS AND TIPS

Indian people are very family oriented with strong religious and spiritual ties. Physical and spiritual purity are highly valued, and humility and self-denial are respected. Fatalism is widespread and a component of the major religion (Hindu).

British manners prevail in India. Be subdued. Self-control is favored over impulsiveness. A quiet, self-confident demeanor breeds trust and respect. Be friendly and communicative, as well.

Public displays of affection, even among married couples, are not considered proper.

Hindu culture and heritage are good topics of conversation, except with individuals from a Christian, Muslim or Sikh background. In general, Indians enjoy talking about their rich artistic and architectural heritage as well as life in other countries. Ask about India's thriving motion picture industry. Bombay, known as "Bollywood," has the largest movie industry in the world. Soccer, cricket and hockey are popular sports, as well as good conversation topics.

Avoid discussing sex, salaries, poverty, beggars, famines, snake charmers and widow-burning. Other sensitive topics to avoid are India-Pakistan relations, the weather (which is often extremely hot and humid), politics and comparisons of Hinduism or Islam with Christianity.

You will often be asked about yourself, your family, your hobbies and whether or not you like sports. You should show curiosity about your host's family and bring pictures of your own family.

Do not be surprised if the Indians you meet, even very casually, ask for your home address. They do not want the address so that they can visit you; the gesture signifies a desire to be accepted as a friend.

Be sure not to touch the head of an Indian as the head is considered a sacred part of the body.

When accepting anything, including food, or when eating, always use your right hand. In India, the left hand is used for personal hygiene purposes.

Expect to be overwhelmed by hospitality. Never refuse an invitation, but do not make an explicit commitment unless you are genuinely sure that you can keep it.

Thanking someone repetitively connotes superficiality.

Indians use the words "thank you" to signify the end of a transaction, for example, when purchasing an item in the market.

Women should dress conservatively, covering up as much of the body as comfort permits. Indian women usually wear a sari (a long, colorful wraparound dress). Both single and married women may wear a *bindi* (a dot) on their foreheads.

It is considered inappropriate for a man to compliment a woman who is not a close relative.

Before entering a home, ask if you should remove your shoes.

Whistling is considered very impolite.

One's feet or shoes should never touch another person. If they do, an immediate apology is necessary. Keep feet flat on the floor.

Beckon with the palm turned down, flexing fingers rapidly a few times.

In the south, you will notice people moving their heads slightly from side to side repetitively. This means "Yes."

Bargaining is common only in certain shopping districts; in others it is totally unknown.

When visiting a mosque, temple, Sikh *gurdwara* or other religious place, be sure to cover your arms and legs. Women should cover their heads. Normally, shoes are removed outside of a place of worship. Be aware that some shrines do not permit foreigners to enter. Additionally, photography is usually forbidden at religious sites.

INDONESIA

Population: 212,941,810 (July 1998 est.); Javanese 45%, Sudanese 14%, Madurese 7.5%, coastal Malays 7.5%, other 26%

Languages: Bahasa Indonesian (official, modified form of Malay), English, Dutch, local dialects (Javanese is the most widely spoken)

Religions: Muslim 87%, Protestant 6%, Roman Catholic 3%, Hindu 2%, Buddhist 1%, other 1%

Currency: Indonesian rupiah

HISTORICAL OVERVIEW

- Indonesia is made up of 13,760 islands that stretch across 3,200 miles, but only 6,000 of the islands are inhabited. More than 300 ethnic groups, speaking 250 languages, live on them. The Javanese people form the largest group.

- Around the beginning of the Christian era, early Indonesian culture was influenced by India's Buddhist and Hindu traditions. At the same time, commercial relations with China began.

- During the 13th century Islam was brought to northern Sumatra by Indian Muslim traders, and in the following two centuries the religion spread through the rest of Indonesia.

- During the 16th century newly formed Muslim trading kingdoms contended among themselves. Europeans, led by the Portuguese, arrived at the time and exploited the rivalries to seize control. They then built fortresses to protect their spice trade.

- The Dutch East India Company eventually gained control of Java, Sumatra and the Moluccas, and in the 18th century, the Dutch came to rule most of the islands.

- Dutch rule transformed the Indonesian economy and also introduced something of a caste system clearly drawn along racial and ethnic lines. In the early 20th century, the Dutch attempted to rectify social and political injustices.

- After Japanese occupation during World War II, Indonesia declared independence from the Netherlands in August 1945. A republic was formed under President Sukarno. The Dutch tried to regain control, but in 1949 they finally granted Indonesia independence.

- The original constitutions put into place were federal and parliamentary, but a quick succession of governments and growing political factionalism discouraged the populace. In broad terms, parties were divided between the hierarchical rice-based society of Java and the commerce-dominated Muslim areas. Sukarno became increasingly dissatisfied with his role as figurehead and attempted to gain more power for himself by interfering with constitutional laws.

- Sukarno indulged in grand projects intended to bolster national unity, while ignoring their devastating effects upon the economy.

- In 1962 he was finally successful in regaining Irian Barat, a portion of Indonesia retained by the Dutch after independence.

- Following the murder of six army generals on 30 September 1965 and an attempted coup against the president, General Suharto, commander of the army's strategic reserves, began to take over. In the following months anywhere from 80,000 to one million Communists were killed and Sukarno was put under house arrest.

- Indonesia made great economic strides under Suharto. Foreign capital was brought into the country and industry grew. Nevertheless, Suharto's regime was one that kept a tight political control, severely limiting personal rights and freedoms.

- In the 1990s, there was some liberalization of Suharto's authoritarian political system. These changes were partly due to the impact of democratic developments in the Philippines and South Korea. Severe political repression continued in East Timor, however. In 1991, a pro-independence demonstration in East Timor was violently suppressed by the army.

- In May 1998, student protesters broke into the government's Assembly Hall and forced Suharto to resign. Former Vice President Bacharuddin Jusuf Habibie immediately assumed the presidency.

- Many are skeptical of Habibie's ability to improve Indonesia's economic situation. Much of the country's wealth is linked to Suharto and the government he created.

- Habibie pledged to hold elections as soon as possible. Protests and riots demanding further change continued after Suharto's resignation.

BUSINESS PRACTICES

Hours of Business

Do not schedule business trips to Indonesia during July or August since most businessmen take their vacations at this time. Check the dates of holidays before planning your trip, as most vary from year to year.

Most Indonesian businesses close for two to three hours in the middle of the day. Business and government offices close at midday on Friday for worship.

Dress

For a business meeting, men should wear a white shirt, tie and slacks. A safari suit, common throughout Asia, is also acceptable. Jackets are not necessary except for meetings with government officials. Women should wear a dress or a skirt with a blouse.

Introductions

Indonesian culture is based on honor and respect for the individual. Respect should always be shown when greeting others.

Elders are introduced before younger people and women before men.

People usually shake hands only when introduced for the first time or when congratulating someone. On other occasions, it is not customary to shake hands. When first meeting someone, shake hands lightly and state your name . If someone touches her/his heart while shaking hands, that means that the greeting is very heartfelt and that the person being greeted is very special. It is appropriate to bow slightly when greeting an older person. Women usually do not shake hands.

Except for handshaking, physical contact is usually avoided in greetings. Smiling, bowing or nodding is considered more gracious.

Bring business cards. They should be exchanged at the first meeting. Do not hesitate to use very sophisticated-looking cards. They are appreciated. Use the acronyms for whatever degrees you hold.

If a person has a title, use it in greeting and in general conversation. A man may be referred to as *Bapak* (Father) either instead of or in addition to his name. Similarly, a woman may be referred to as *Ibu* (Mother) in the same fashion.

Many Indonesians have only one name.

Guests are welcomed warmly. At a party, expect to be introduced individually. Do not be surprised if your host and other guests make welcoming speeches and call upon you to give a speech as well.

Simply acknowledge that you are happy to be at the party and to have met everyone and thank the host for the invitation.

Meetings

Punctuality is important, but is not emphasized over personal relations. Indonesians tend to arrive late. Keep mentioning the time of an appointment, or arrange it for about a half an hour earlier than when you want it to start. Foreigners are expected to be punctual.

The atmosphere of most business meetings may be informal. Do not voice criticism at a meeting. It is always given in private.

Research the business backgrounds of the people you will be meeting. Make sure that your proposal is solid and that you have something very tangible to offer.

All written materials should be translated into Bahasa.

Negotiating

Plan to spend a minimum of a week negotiating the simplest agreement. Business dealings tend to be slow and may cause frustration to people accustomed to a faster pace.

Indonesians do not conduct business transactions or make decisions in a direct fashion. Businesspeople should be prepared to spend a good deal of time with clients before getting to the business at hand. Patience is the key. Never lose your temper or show strong emotions. Consensus, rather than confrontation, is necessary for successful negotiation.

Indonesians do business with people with whom they have an established relationship or who are part of their social network. Developing a rapport and a friendship is crucial. While quality and price are important, they remain secondary to the personal interaction of the business partners. There are no sales without face-to-face negotiation.

An Indonesian virtue is not to speak directly. "Yes" does not necessarily mean "Yes." Indonesians use the indirect approach, often taking their time before getting to the point. The word "No" is rarely used. They will say *Belum* (Not yet) instead.

Indonesians take product, service, price criteria, delivery arrangements, and how good they feel about the interpersonal contact into account before reaching a decision. They also want to know that you are making a long-term commitment to their company.

Indonesians view contracts as a reference point and the key to starting up operations or a joint venture. Maintain a close relationship with your Indonesian counterpart so that you are constantly aware of any progress or changes.

Although the nature of business is informal, the signing of documents is taken seriously.

After returning home, follow up with business contacts by fax. Then be prepared for a long response time or no response at all, even though some Indonesian managers insist that employees answer faxes within 24 hours. Indonesians can have difficulty communicating from a long distance. Generally they communicate much better face-to-face.

Be prepared to encounter managers and business owners from the People's Republic of China or of Chinese descent in Indonesia.

Many, but not all, government and business representatives are used to dealing with foreigners.

Entertaining

Unannounced visits are common in Indonesia. Visitors wait to be invited to sit, and stand when their host/hostess enters the room. Drinks may be served. Visitors should wait to drink, however, until invited to do so. If hors d'oeuvres are offered, eat a little bit to avoid insulting your hosts.

Expect to be entertained by Indonesian business counterparts. Be sure to reciprocate on the same trip.

If a businesswoman wishes to entertain, she should say, "It would give me great pleasure to invite you to dinner," and then arrange payment beforehand by giving the maitre d' her credit card.

In Java, business lunches are more popular than business dinners. A man should not invite a Javanese businessman's wife to attend a meal unless his own wife will be present. A businesswoman, however, should include a Javanese man's wife in the invitation.

Gifts are not expected by traditional Indonesians. More westernized Indonesians will appreciate flowers or candy brought by dinner guests. Any gift you give will be accepted graciously since it is considered impolite to refuse anything. The gift will not be opened in the presence of the giver, with the exception of "official" gifts such as those given at the end of a lecture or official visit.

In Muslim homes, neither alcohol nor pork is served. Indonesians, however, tend not to be as strict as other Muslim societies, such as those in the Middle East. Drinking alcohol in front of your host does not usually present a problem.

Many westernized Indonesians use a fork and a spoon to eat, but more traditional families eat with their hands. If using a fork and spoon, hold the fork in the left hand, hold the spoon in the right and eat from the spoon.

Keep both hands above the table while eating.

Rice is the main staple. Vegetables, fish and spicy sauces are often served with rice. The national dish is *nasi goreng*, which is fried rice with egg, spices and vegetables.

Many Indonesian dishes are highly spiced. One spicy dish, containing coconut milk, is known as *padang*. It was named after the city on Sumatra where it originated. Other popular dishes are *satay* (grilled skewered meat with a spicy peanut sauce) and *gado gado* (a salad with a peanut sauce).

Tea and coffee are the most common drinks.

By finishing a drink, you are sending a signal for the glass to be refilled. Similarly, leave some food on your plate if you do not wish to be served more.

Bread with butter and sugar on it is served as a dessert. Fresh fruit is also often served as dessert.

Beckon a waiter by raising your hand. To ask for the check, make a writing motion with both hands.

Tipping is not common. At restaurants, a service charge is usually included in the bill.

Guests should wait for the host to invite them to begin eating. During the meal, do not worry if there is not much conversation. Indonesians like to concentrate on eating their meals.

SOCIAL VALUES, CUSTOMS AND TIPS

Families are a major source of conversation topics. Personal questions are often asked, even on short acquaintance. Good topics of conversation might include food and the beauties of Indonesia.

In Java, avoid personal questions about such subjects as job, age, salary, prices and religion. Also avoid any discussion of material goods.

Nearly 90 percent of Indonesians are Muslim, which represents the largest population of Muslims in the world. Be aware of when the holy month of Ramadan occurs each year (the dates are based on the lunar calendar). At that time, Muslims do not eat or drink from sunrise to sundown. The people of Bali are mostly Hindu.

Indonesians greatly value a quiet voice, an unassuming attitude and agreement by consensus. Disagreement and criticism should be handled privately, as it is a great insult to embarrass someone publicly. Confrontation and disharmony are to be avoided.

Indonesians often laugh to cover their anger, shock, embarrassment, or other negative sentiments.

Indonesians dress modestly whether they are dressed in western styles or traditional clothing. The traditional dress for women is called a sarong, which is a long wraparound dress with an intricate batik pattern. Batik is a traditional handicraft using molten wax to create designs on cloth. Batik clothing may be worn by both men and women for formal situations.

It is disrespectful to be affectionate with members of the opposite sex in public.

Do not beckon with a single finger. Signal with the whole hand down, palm open, waving your fingers toward you.

Pointing is done with the thumb in Indonesia.

Never use your left hand to touch others, take or give money, signal a waiter or pass food. The left hand is reserved for personal hygiene purposes.

Do not touch anyone's head. It is the seat of the soul and is sacred.

Shoes are removed when entering carpeted rooms and holy places, especially mosques.

Avoid standing with your hands in your pockets or on your hips. It is felt to be a sign of defiance or arrogance.

Indonesians do not usually cross their legs. If you do, one knee should be over the other or you may cross your ankles. Never cross your legs by placing one ankle on the other knee. Also avoid having your foot or the sole of your shoe face another person.

It is considered inappropriate to eat while walking on the street.

Soccer is very popular. Badminton, volleyball and tennis are also enjoyed.

IRAN

Population: 68,959,931 (July 1998 est.); Persian 51%, Azerbaijani 24%, Gilaki and Mazandarani 8%, Kurdish 7%, Arab 3%, Lur 2%, Baloch 2%, Turkish 2%, other 1%

Languages: Persian and Persian dialects 98%, Turkic and Turkic dialects 26%, Kurdish 9%, Luri 2%, Balochi 1%, Arabic 1%, Turkish 1%, other 2%

Religions: Shi'a Muslim 89%, Sunni Muslim 10%, Zoroastrian, Jewish, Christian and Baha'i 1%

Currency: Iranian rial

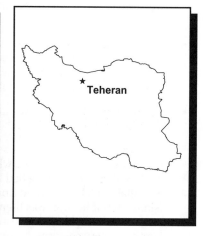

HISTORICAL OVERVIEW

- Iran, known as Persia until the 20th century, began to emerge with the rise of the Medes tribe in the mountainous area east of the Tigris River. The Medes were eventually conquered by the Persians in 550 B.C. Under Cyrus the Great the Persian Empire stretched from the borders of Greece to eastern Asia. By the fourth century B.C., the Persian Empire was significantly weakened and then conquered by Alexander the Great. Nevertheless, the native Parthians created a great Greek-speaking empire. In 226 A.D. they were conquered by the Sasanians, an Iranian people. Zoroastrianism was established as the official religion.

- A weakened Sasanian Empire was completely conquered by Arab Muslims by 640 A.D. With brief interruptions, Persia (Iran) was subsequently governed by non-Iranian Muslim princes for the next 850 years. During the 13th and early 14th centuries Persia faced Mongol invasions.

- Modern Iranian history and culture took shape with the ascendancy of the Safavid dynasty in the 16th century. The Safavids established Shi'ite Islam as the official religion. The end of the Safavid dynasty in 1736 was marked by internal conflict and, by 1779, the Qajars emerged as rulers.

- By this time, however, European colonial expansionism was well underway and Iran found itself in the midst of a struggle between Russia and Great Britain. It remained in a semi-colonial state until the early 20th century.

- In 1921, a coup brought Reza Khan to power. He deposed the Qajars in 1925, but he himself was forced to abdicate in the 1940s because of his collaboration with Nazi Germany. His son, Mohammad Reza Shah Pahlavi, took over. Pahlavi's policies to westernize and modernize Iran alienated the country's religious leaders.

- After political problems in the early 1950s, the Shah began to enforce dictatorial policies. The National Security and Intelligence Organization (SAVAK) was set up to control Islamic fundamentalism, opposing political parties and the press.

- Opposition to Pahlavi grew, and in the 1970s there were many demonstrations against him.

- By 1978, there was great unrest among the lower classes of the country and rioting became widespread. The Shah's government collapsed, and in 1979 he fled Iran. Rehollah Khomeini, a Shi'ite ayatollah, quickly returned from exile in Paris and set up an Islamic republic. Iran was then ruled strictly by Islamic law. Iraq declared war on Iran in 1980 and invaded. The resulting Iran-Iraq War was a very costly and prolonged stalemate that devastated the economies of both countries and took many lives. The war was ended in 1988.

- Khomenini died in 1989 and was succeeded by Ali Khamenei as the new spiritual leader. Ali Akbar Hashemi Rafsanjani was elected president. Rafsanjani was a moderate who introduced economic reforms and moved toward a rapprochement with the West.

- During the Gulf War, Iran began to gain international recognition for its cooperation with the UN sanctions against Iraq and its aid to Iraqi refuges.

- In 1998, border tensions between Iran and Afghanistan increased after members of the Taleban militia killed nine Iranian diplomats. In response, the Iranians increased the number of troops and military exercises along the Iran-Afghanistan border.

BUSINESS PRACTICES

Hours of Business

Business hours in Iran are Saturday though Wednesday, 8:00 a.m. to 4:00 p.m. and on Thursday from 9:00 a.m. until 12:00 p.m.

Some businesses remain closed on Thursdays.

Dress

Business suits and ties are acceptable attire for businessmen.

Women should dress extremely conservatively, making sure to keep their legs and arms covered.

Introductions

Your Iranian counterpart should be addressed by his or her title and surname.

Handshaking is a common form of greeting in Iran, but only among members of the same sex.

Meetings

Appointments should be made well in advance. Meetings begin promptly at the scheduled time.

It is customary to accept the tea offered during a business meeting.

Negotiating

Formal British English is the language of international business in Iran.

Only senior executives exchange business cards with each other.

Business gifts are not mandatory but will be greatly appreciated by your Iranian counterparts.

The United States currently has a trade embargo against Iran, but it is ignored by most other nations.

Iran's main trading partners are China, the new Asian states, Turkey, Russia and Germany.

In recent years Iran's manufacturing capabilities have advanced technologically.

Entertaining

Iranians enjoy entertaining and will offer tea when a visitor calls upon them. It is customary to accept.

Formal attire should be worn to formal social occasions or to fine restaurants.

Iranians usually eat with a spoon and fork, but when eating a western-style meal, eating in the continental style is also acceptable.

Alcoholic beverages are unavailable in Iran because Islamic law forbids the consumption of alcohol. Tea, fruit or vegetable juices, and mineral water are usually served with meals or as refreshments.

Rice accompanies every meal in Iran. Some popular dishes include *chelo khoresh* (rice, vegetables and meat in a nut sauce), *aclas polo* (rice with meat and lentils), *a bgusht* (stew) and *mast-o-khier* (cold yogurt soup with mint, cucumber and raisins). Western-style dishes are also available.

In hotels, it is acceptable to tip between ten to 15 percent.

SOCIAL VALUES, CUSTOMS AND TIPS

Avoid discussing the United States, the United Kingdom, or the westernization of Iran. These are very sensitive topics.

There are many western-style hotels and sporting centers in and around the Teheran area including a golf course, tennis courts and swimming pools.

Since the Shah's ousting from office, Iran has been governed mainly by Islamic law.

During the month of Ramadan drinking, smoking or eating in public is forbidden from sunrise to sunset. The larger hotels in the Teheran area, however, keep their restaurants open for those not observing Ramadan.

IRELAND

Population: 3,619,480 (July 1998 est.); Celtic, English

Languages: Irish (Gaelic), English

Religions: Roman Catholic 93%, Anglican 3%, none 1%, unknown 2%, other 1%

Currency: Irish pound, euro

HISTORICAL OVERVIEW

- The Celts first conquered the region in the fourth century B.C. Saint Patrick arrived in the region in 432 A.D., bringing Christianity with him, and the monastic life became widespread. In 795, the Norse invaded Ireland, destroyed many monasteries and libraries and established a number of seaports along the coasts. They were eventually defeated in 1014.

- In 1171, King Henry II of England invaded with the backing of the church and declared himself overlord of the entire island. The Anglo-Norman invaders were soon assimilated into the Gaelic Irish community and by the 15th century only a small group of English crown loyalists remained. The real power was in the hands of the earls of Kildare, who were officially deputies for the English crown.

- Following the English Reformation in the 16th century, Ireland was subjected once again to tighter English and now Anglican reign. Parliament passed several ecclesiastical decrees, and many Catholics were prohibited from owning land.

- Under Elizabeth I there were three serious rebellions against the English crown, all of which were defeated, thus ensuring Irish obedience but not Irish loyalty.

- Under James I many Irish Catholic earls fled the country and were replaced by English landowners, many of whom settled in the north of Ireland. By 1691 Anglicans, who comprised only one-tenth of the population, gained control of most of the land and political rule.

- In 1801 the United Kingdom of Great Britain and Ireland was established under English rule.

- The union was very unpopular, and the rift between Catholics and Protestants grew. Its disastrous economic effects were greatly exacerbated by the great potato famine (1846-1851), during which at least one million people died and another two million emigrated to other countries, including the U.S. Political conflict and agitation for independence intensified after the famine.

- During the early years of the 20th century various groups formed within Ireland, some favoring home rule and others favoring a continued union with Great Britain. It was during this period that Sinn Fein, and then somewhat later, the Irish Republican Army (IRA), were founded. By 1920, virtual civil war had broken out. The British Parliament passed an act dividing Ireland into North and South, and in 1921 the Irish free state was established. Six northern counties, with a Protestant majority, were allowed to remain in the United Kingdom as Northern Ireland.

- In 1937, a new constitution changed the country's name to *Éire* (Ireland) and the country began to decrease its association with the British Commonwealth. Finally, in 1949, Ireland formally withdrew from the Commonwealth and became completely independent. While Britain recognized the new republic, it declared that Northern Ireland could only be considered independent if its parliament voted on it. The new republic turned its attention to stimulating economic growth.

- Since independence, talks have taken place between England and Ireland on returning Northern Ireland to Irish sovereignty. Ireland became increasingly concerned over outbreaks of violence in Northern Ireland. A 1985 agreement established a consultative role for the republic in the affairs of Northern Ireland.

- The early 1990s were marked by political instability as Ireland's coalition government continuously broke down and reconstituted itself. In 1994 John Bruton was made prime minister. He was succeeded by Bertie Athen in 1997.

- In 1994 the IRA declared a cease-fire. The cease-fire endured until 9 February 1996 when an IRA bomb exploded. Throughout 1996 Ireland was preoccupied by attempts to keep the peace process going in Northern Ireland.

- In July 1998, residents of Northern Ireland and the Irish Republic voted on an agreement for a power-sharing government in Northern Ireland. A large majority in both areas voted "yes," but further violence and confrontation on both sides in subsequent months placed the agreement in jeopardy.

BUSINESS PRACTICES

Hours of Business

Business hours are usually 9:00 a.m. to 5:00 p.m., Monday through Friday, with an hour break for lunch in all but the major cities.

You should avoid making business trips to Ireland during the first week in May (when most people are busy with trade fairs), in July and August and during the Christmas and New Year periods, when people are on vacation.

Dress

Business attire is very conservative in Ireland. Men should wear suits and ties or tweed sports jackets. Women usually wear suits or wool blazers and wool skirts. Both men and women wear subdued colors for business.

Introductions

The Irish are somewhat reserved when greeting people, although they are generally very friendly. A firm handshake is appropriate for both men and women. You should wait for a woman to extend her hand first.

The traditional Irish greeting *Céad míle fáilte* (which means "One thousand welcomes") is used to greet visitors. Otherwise, usual English greetings, such as "Hello" or "How are you?," are used.

Last names are used, following the title "Mr.," "Mrs." or "Miss," as an appropriate form of address. The only occupational titles commonly used are "Doctor" and "Professor."

First names should only be used if you are invited to do so or if your colleague begins using your first name. Although it is common to use first names after even a short acquaintance, you should use last names whenever your Irish colleagues address you using your last name.

At a large party, you should introduce yourself. Allow your host to introduce you at small parties.

Meetings

Business appointments should be made by letter or by phone.

You should be punctual for business appointments even though the Irish may not be punctual. This may require some patience. Someone who offers to meet you in five minutes is more likely to appear in a half an hour.

English is always used in business transactions. There is no need to make arrangements for an interpreter to translate discussions into Gaelic.

Business cards are not as commonly used in Ireland as in other countries, but it is a good idea to bring some with you so that you can leave a card with a secretary if the person you want to see is unavailable.

Negotiating

Avoid being demonstrative when you are making presentations. While the Irish have a reputation for being friendly and hearty, they are not very demonstrative and are not comfortable with people who are overly vehement.

Negotiations are conducted as serious and challenging bargaining sessions in which all parties are called upon to use their persuasive tactics to the best of their ability. Irish businesspeople are generally very persuasive negotiators.

Irish businesspeople are highly educated and will expect an educated, thorough and well-prepared presentation.

The Irish are well read and very social. They may know more about your country than you do. When discussing anything, whether business-related or not, remember that the Irish enjoy long conversations and do not fear confrontation.

The Irish are perceptive in business negotiations. Any attempts at deception will be recognized and pointed out.

Do not treat your Irish colleagues as less than equals. If you offend them in this regard expect a candid statement to that effect.

Although drinking is common and accepted among business negotiators, getting inebriated at a social function is not considered businesslike.

Entertaining

The Irish are a warm and hospitable people. It is not common, however, to invite foreigners to one's home for dinner.

Gift-giving is not common when conducting business in Ireland. If you are invited to a dinner, however, a gift of flowers, chocolates, wine or cheese is usually appreciated.

There are no set rules about including spouses in dinner invitations. If you intend to include the spouse of an Irish colleague in an invitation to a dinner party, you should be specific. Similarly, if you are invited to a dinner, you should take note as to whether spouses are included in the invitation, or you may ask the host specifically.

Irish people like to have conversations in "pubs" (public houses). Some say that conversation is the national pastime. Many pubs feature folk music as entertainment. Pubs usually have two sections, the bar and the lounge. Women usually frequent the lounge.

You should be aware that refusing a drink is a serious insult in Ireland. If you really do not care to drink, explain that you do not drink for health reasons. If you accept a drink, you should raise the glass and say "Cheers" before you take a sip.

Drinks are not served with ice, but it is perfectly acceptable to request ice.

There are customs associated with the size of the drink you order. Women are expected to order half-pints (ten ounces) of beer or stout. In fact, some pubs will not even serve full pints to women. On the other hand, if a man orders a half-pint, comments or jokes about his virility may be heard.

If you are with a group, men are each expected to buy a round of drinks. Women are generally not permitted to buy a round.

In restaurants, a service charge is usually included in the check. You may want to leave some extra change for exemplary service. If a service charge is not included, you should leave a ten to 15 percent tip on the table.

Traditional Irish dishes are hearty and simple. Fresh dairy products, breads, seafood and vegetables are widely available since Ireland is an agricultural country. Potatoes are a staple. Smoked salmon is considered an Irish specialty. The main meats eaten at dinner include chicken, pork, beef and mutton. Tea is the most popular drink.

Breakfasts are usually large, often including bacon and eggs. Lunch, served between 1:00 and 2:00 p.m., usually consists of hot dishes, such as steak and kidney pie or boiled bacon and cabbage. Dinner is usually eaten between 5:00 and 8:00 p.m. A light dinner, sometimes called "tea," may consist of cold cuts and salads or a "fry-up" (eggs, grilled sausage, bacon, tomatoes and black pudding cut up and grilled). A more formal meal is usually served later in the evening and consists of several courses preceded by drinks.

Dining etiquette is neither formal nor strictly adhered to in Ireland. The Irish eat in the continental style, with the fork in the left hand and the knife remaining in the right.

When you eat at someone's home, it is common for your plate to be brought to you with food already on it. You should try to eat everything on your plate.

If there is a small plate next to your dinner plate, be aware that it is not for bread, but for peelings, which should be removed from boiled potatoes (you should not eat them). Bread is usually not served with dinner.

SOCIAL VALUES, CUSTOMS AND TIPS

The Irish can be quite reserved. Personal space is valued. Hands are not used often during conversation.

Although Irish (called Gaelic) is the first officially recognized language, it is only spoken in small areas of the western seaboard. English, recognized as Ireland's second language, is spoken and used everywhere (with accents varying as you move through the country).

The Irish are easygoing, lighthearted, good-humored and cheerful. They are also quick-witted, appreciate a sense of humor and enjoy lively conversation. They particularly enjoy telling British jokes (just as the British enjoy telling Irish jokes).

The Catholic faith has a strong influence on the values of the Irish people. Traditions are important and material goods do not have the same priority as they do in other countries.

Both the Republic of Ireland and Northern Ireland have similar cultural roots and similar customs and values. The main differences are religious and political. The majority in the Republic of Ireland are Catholic and very nationalistic. The majority in Northern Ireland are Anglican and consider themselves to be part of Great Britain, not Ireland.

Good topics of conversation include the beauty of the country, Gaelic culture, Irish handicrafts and the weather. You should avoid discussing the division of the country, Ireland's relationship to the U.K., religion, politics and feminism. Avoid making pro-British comments or being unkind, which will offend the Irish.

Another good topic of conversation is sports, as the Irish are very sports oriented. Gaelic football (a cross between soccer and basketball) and hurling (played on a soccer-type field with wooden sticks and a small leather ball) are two national pastimes. Soccer, rugby, fishing, sailing and horse racing are also favorite activities.

General courtesy and politeness are valued. The Irish are very easygoing and informal, however, and it is difficult to offend anyone by using the wrong fork or shaking hands at the wrong time.

Long lines are common and expected. Pushing and shoving when waiting in line for buses, in theaters and in shops or barging into line is unacceptable and considered extremely rude.

Although most gestures used in Ireland are the same as those used in the United States, gestures that specifically use the fingers (e.g., pointing or summoning with the index finger, etc.) are not as common and should be avoided. You should be aware that the reverse "V for victory" sign is especially offensive.

ISRAEL

Population: 5,643,966 (July 1998 est.); Jewish 82%, (Israel-born 50%, Europe/Americas/Oceania-born 20%, Africa-born 7%, Asia-born 5%), non-Jewish (mostly Arab) 18%

Languages: Hebrew (official), Arabic used officially for Arab minority, English most commonly used foreign language

Religions: Jewish 82%, Muslim (mostly Sunni Muslim) 14%, Christian 2%, Druze and other 2%

Currency: new Israeli shekel

HISTORICAL OVERVIEW

- By the end of the 13th century B.C., the Israelites had come to occupy most of what was later to be called Palestine. Under King David and Solomon in the tenth century, further expansion took place. Solomon's reign was a golden age marked by the building of the First Temple in Jerusalem. After his death, however, the kingdom split into the northern kingdom of Israel and the southern kingdom of Judah.

- Israel was destroyed by the Assyrians in 722 B.C., and in 587 B.C. the Babylonians destroyed Judah, exiling many of its inhabitants.

- The Persians, under Cyrus II, allowed the Jews to return to Jerusalem and build the Second Temple. Invasion by Alexander the Great brought the Jews under Greek control.

- Independence was gained in 141 B.C. but then lost again to the Romans in 65 B.C. After the Romans crushed two Jewish revolts, they crushed a third in 135 A.D. in which the Jewish population was decimated and Israel (formally Judah) ceased to exist as a political entity.

- In the seventh century A.D., Palestine fell to the Muslims and, except for the times when it was ruled by crusaders, it remained under Arab rule until 1517 when it passed to Ottoman rule. From the 16th century until World War I the Ottoman Turks controlled Palestine.

- In 1882, the first Zionist settlers came. In 1890, Theodor Herzl established Zionism as an international movement to restore Palestine to the Jews. The British took over Palestine after World War I.

- During World War II, Jews began to emigrate to Israel in large numbers to escape the Holocaust. In 1947, the United Nations voted to divide the area into two states – one Arab and one Jewish – but the plan was rejected by the Arabs. In 1948, the state of Israel was proclaimed, the British withdrew, and a war immediately broke out. Wars were fought again in 1956, 1967 and 1973. In 1979, Egypt and Israel signed a peace treaty, as Egypt became the first Arab nation to recognize Israel's right to exist. Throughout the 1980s, Arab terrorism and border wars with Lebanon were serious problems. The conflicts focused on the status of territories occupied by Israel since the 1967 war.

- In 1988, the Palestine Liberation Organization (PLO) declared an independent Palestinian state in the occupied West Bank and Gaza with Jerusalem as its capital. The declaration was rejected by Israel and riots broke out beginning the *intifada* or "uprising." Israel agreed to discuss plans for peace with its Arab neighbors, and the Middle East peace process began in 1991. Peace talks frequently broke down, as internal dissent and violence on both sides broke out, until secret talks in Norway between Israeli Prime Minister Yitzhak Rabin and PLO leader Yasser Arafat led to a breakthrough in 1993. The agreement involved limited autonomy in parts of the occupied territories and by mid-1994, Gaza and Jericho (in the West Bank) had achieved autonomy. In 1994, Israel and Jordan signed a peace agreement.

- In November 1995, Rabin was assassinated by a fundamentalist Jew. Rabin's partner in the peace process, Shimon Peres, became acting prime minister. A series of suicide attacks in early 1996 by Islamic terrorists changed the minds of many Israelis, and support increased for Benjamin Netanyahu and his wish to slow the process. Netanyahu became prime minister in the May 1996 election.

- Land contention continued throughout 1997. Netanyuha refused to listen to western suggestions of compromise. He maintains Jewish territorial demands, but in late summer 1998, moves toward reopening negotiations began.

- Agriculture, industrial goods (especially armaments) and tourism comprise the majority of the economy's mainstay. Technological and scientific achievements continue to spur economic growth as well, and Israel maintains favorable trading relations abroad.

BUSINESS PRACTICES

Hours of Business

General business hours are Sunday through Thursday, 9:00 a.m. to 1:00 p.m. and 4:00 to 7:00 p.m.

Government buildings are open 9:00 a.m. to 1:00 p.m. Sunday through Thursday.

Dress

Men should wear a sports jacket and tie, while women should wear a suit, dress or skirt and blouse. Israeli businessmen often wear shirts with open collars, but business suits and ties are becoming more popular.

Introductions

English is used frequently in business and is spoken by most Israelis.

The usual greeting is *Shalom*, which means "peace." *Shalom* is said upon departing as well. Israelis also use the word when answering the phone.

Greetings are informal and handshakes are common.

Some men who are good friends may pat each other on the back or shoulder when greeting each other.

First names are commonly used once someone has been introduced. Titles are not necessary, and even military officers are referred to by their first names.

Meetings

You should make appointments prior to your arrival in Israel.

It is important to know with whom you are doing business and what their style of working is. Some Israelis are quite formal while others are very informal.

Subordinates often challenge the boss's decisions. It may therefore be difficult to know who is the final decision maker.

Expect frequent interruptions during a meeting.

Avoid small talk prior to business meetings.

In Israel the product is much more important than the presentation.

Be prepared to be interrupted when speaking. If Israelis do not interrupt or ask questions, it may mean that you are not capturing their attention. Interest in the product can be measured by how much discussion it has generated.

After every meeting, put everything in writing to avoid cross-cultural misunderstandings. As the business relationship progresses, exchange informal memos to keep track of where agreement has been reached. Convert these memos into formal documents only once all sides are ready to make a serious commitment of time and resources.

Negotiating

Israelis are experienced negotiators. They are known for being tough but fair.

Israelis tend to speak bluntly, assertively and honestly when negotiating. It can mean that your Israeli counterpart is showing you respect and thinks that you have the integrity to take straightforward discussions. It can also mean that he thinks you want action, rather than empty words. Avoid using high-sounding rhetoric. You will be respected for your concise and explicit language.

Be prepared for your Israeli counterpart to anticipate what you might do next. He/she is probably very adept in strategic planning. Anticipate in advance which angles might arise so that you are not surprised. Assume that your counterpart has figured out your game plan.

When bargaining or negotiating, Israelis often start off with an extreme position and gradually work toward a compromise.

Israelis tend to be spontaneous. Be ready to change your plans as you receive new information.

If you feel that the negotiations are moving too rapidly, say that you need time to think.

If you are convinced that you are right, be assertive and stand up for what you want. Israelis respect those who stand by what they want and think is right. If they think that you will be a good partner, they will be willing to compromise.

Finish the negotiations with a written agreement. Hire an experienced Israeli lawyer who knows your culture and language. Beware of loopholes in the law, but keep the agreement as short as possible.

Entertaining

Israelis are very friendly and informal, and they often invite new friends to their homes. A gift is not necessary, but it is appreciated. Books, candy or flowers are appropriate.

You will more likely be invited to a business lunch than to a business dinner.

Eating habits vary, as Israelis have a diverse cultural heritage.

Generally, continental manners are used, with the knife kept in the right hand and the fork in the left. Some foods are eaten by hand.

Your host or the oldest person will generally begin the meal.

The main meal of the day is eaten in the early afternoon. Evening meals are generally light.

Israeli food specialties include *falafel* (pita bread filled with balls of fried chick-pea batter), vegetable salads, *kebabs* (skewered meats) and other foods that reflect the varied heritage of today's Israelis.

Many people observe the traditional kosher dietary laws that prohibit milk and meat from being eaten during the same meal. Under these laws, pork and shellfish are also forbidden at any time.

Restaurants may add a service charge to the bill. It is suggested that you leave something extra for the waiter if service was good.

Israeli wines are of high quality.

SOCIAL VALUES, CUSTOMS AND TIPS

Punctuality is expected for important occasions. For informal events, it is permissible to arrive 15 minutes late.

Visits to see a friend may be made without an invitation. Israelis often stop by a friend's home for conversation.

Israelis are very civic minded and involved in their community.

They are inquisitive and avid readers who enjoy frank discussions.

Israelis are devoted to their culture and their nation. Jewish immigration from around the world is encouraged.

Except among Orthodox Jews and traditional Muslims, western-style clothing is worn, and dress is casual. Men wear shirts unbuttoned at the neck. Ties and suits are worn only for formal occasions.

Orthodox Jews observe the Jewish Sabbath – from sundown Friday to sundown Saturday.

Holidays are important in Israel. Businesses close and public transportation stops. The Jewish calendar is based on the lunar cycle, so dates for holidays vary yearly.

The family is central to Israelis. Family ties remain strong as the children grow into adulthood. Married children are expected to live near their parents or other family members and they are also expected to care for their elderly parents.

Gestures are often used in conversation to emphasize a point.

Pointing at someone with the index finger is considered rude.

Women should not wear shorts in areas populated with Arabs or religious Jews. In addition to being stared at, they may be reprimanded and will not be admitted to any of the holy places.

Soccer and basketball are the favorite sports in Israel.

ITALY

Population: 56,782,748 (July 1998 est.); Italian (includes small clusters of German-, French-, and Slovene-Italians in the north and Albanian- and Greek-Italians in the south)

Languages: Italian (official), German, French, Slovene

Religions: Roman Catholic 98%, other 2%

Currency: lira, euro

HISTORICAL OVERVIEW

- One of the first civilizations to flourish in Italy was that of the Etruscans beginning in the ninth century B.C. During the fourth and third centuries B.C., the Roman Empire slowly conquered the Etruscans and by 264 B.C. a good part of present-day Italy was under Roman rule.

- This Roman Republic continued to grow, ultimately expanding to become an empire that extended from Britain to Africa to the Euphrates by 180 A.D. The Roman civilization has had a tremendous impact on modern legal, social, political and military structures throughout the western world and extending into the 20th century.

- The Roman Empire in the west fell to barbarian invaders in the fourth and fifth centuries A.D. and the peninsula was then divided into several separate political regions. Parts of Italy were conquered by the Byzantines. Other parts fell to the Ostrogoths, then Lombards and Byzantines and then the Franks. Southern Italy was eventually invaded by the Normans and the north was divided up into very competitive city-states.

- Despite the persistence of this political fragmentation throughout many centuries, Italy was the western cultural center from the 13th to 16th centuries. The Italian Renaissance gave rise to one of the greatest artistic flowerings in western history.

- Beginning in the 15th century Italy was once again subject to renewed invasions from foreign powers, beginning with the French, moving to the Spanish and Austrian Hapsburgs and ending with Napoleon.

- By 1815 Italy was once again an assortment of independent states. *Risorgimento*, the Italian unification movement, began at this time and in 1861, unification was declared by the first Italian parliament in Turin. Victor Emmanuel II was named king. Unification was completed by the annexation of Venetia in 1866 and of Rome in 1870.

- Italy fought with the allies in World War I. From 1922 to 1943, Italy had a fascist dictatorship under Benito Mussolini, and the country allied itself with Hitler in World War II. In 1943, the allies invaded, Mussolini fled and Italy surrendered. After the war, a republic was established in 1946 and coalition governments became the norm. The economy revived slowly, but at a steady pace. Political violence and terrorism marked the 1970s, and the 1980s were marked by frequent collapses of the government.

- In the 1990s, the Italian government was rocked by political scandal. Voting patterns changed to favor new parties, many of them right-wing. Oscar Luigi Scalfaro was elected as president by parliament in 1992, but the government was weak due to the coalition politics. By 1994, 6,000 individuals were under investigation for corruption. Finally, the parliament was dissolved and early elections were held. Silvio Berlusconi's Forza Italia party won by promising a government without corruption and an improved economy.

- Berlusconi's strong business ties, in addition to charges of corruption brought against him, quickly made his government unpopular. In April 1996, a national election, in which the center-left Olive Tree Alliance won a near majority of seats, brought Italy closer to stability.

- Since 1997 Italy has been hit with several natural disasters. On 30 October 1997, an earthquake shook central Italy, and in May 1998, mudslides ravaged southern Italy.

BUSINESS PRACTICES

Hours of Business

Businesses in southern and northern Italy keep different hours. In the north the working day lasts from 8:30 a.m. until 12:45 p.m. and from 3:00 p.m. until 6:00 p.m. In the south the hours are 8:30 a.m. until 12:45 p.m. and from either 4:30 p.m. or 5:00 p.m. until either 7:30 p.m. or 8:00 p.m.

As in most of Europe, many businesses are closed for vacation in August.

Dress

Italians dress elegantly and fashionably for both business and social occasions. Dark suits with ties for men and classic dresses or suits for women are recommended.

Introductions

The Italian custom is to shake hands when meeting or departing. Italians tend to use more physical contact than many other Europeans, so do not be surprised if a colleague or a client greets you with a hug after you have become familiar.

Italian businesspeople usually address each other by surnames. Do not use first names until you are asked to do so. Use *dottore* or *dottoressa* plus the last name if a person has a college degree.

When addressing a woman who is a professional, use *Signora* (Mrs.) or *Signorina* (Miss) plus her title; i.e., *Signorina Avocatessa* (Miss Lawyer). *Dottoressa* can be used if you are uncertain of her marital status, regardless of her profession.

Bring business cards with you and exchange them when first introduced to new people, after you have shaken hands and are seated.

If no formal introductions are made (for instance, at a party), introduce yourself by saying your name and shaking hands.

People who know each other well greet each other with a kiss on each cheek, which is really "kissing the air."

Meetings

Northern Italians tend to respect punctuality, while people in the south have a more relaxed attitude about time. Since meetings may be cancelled on short notice, always confirm an appointment by telephone just prior to the meeting.

Good times for business appointments are between 10:00 and 11:00 a.m. or after 3:00 p.m.

Make all meeting arrangements by fax or letter well in advance of your arrival in Italy. Shortly before your visit reconfirm your appointment.

It is important to send ahead a list of those who will be attending along with their ranks and titles.

Negotiating

Your team leader should be fluent in Italian.

General conversation is typical before the meeting actually begins.

Keep in mind that Italian business is very hierarchical and all decisions come from the top. You may not be meeting with the person who will make the final decisions involved in your negotiations.

In Italy, there is a clear distinction between business and pleasure. At business meetings, the focus is on business. You should not spend much time making light conversation, and jokes are considered out of place. At your first meeting, however, it is appropriate to take time to get to know each other before transacting any business.

The time for lighter conversation is during drinks or dinner, where you can safely discuss a wide range of subjects.

Work is not usually discussed at social functions. Therefore, only after you get to know your client well should you meet for lunch to discuss business.

Italians prefer not to take work home.

Your client will expect you to be very knowledgeable about your product/service and how it is used worldwide.

Your client may not indicate his/her disinterest in your product or service with a definitive "No," but instead may be somewhat tactful in rejecting a proposal or business plan, etc.

The formal meeting is not usually used for deciding significant matters, but rather to ratify them and to communicate them to other levels of management. Major decisions are made more privately.

The person presiding over the meeting may or may not be the most senior person. He/she may be the second in rank so that the proceedings will not be disrupted should the senior person be called away.

When negotiating in Italy, do not display any urgency, as it will weaken your bargaining position. Also, when an agreement seems near, be aware that Italians sometimes bring in a large number of new demands.

The custom of giving business gifts is very common. Give a small gift to any staff members who were especially helpful to you.

Entertaining

Most business entertaining is done in restaurants. It is unusual to be invited to a private home.

If you have a lot of business to conduct with one person, invite him/her to dinner and possibly to a club after the meal. You should treat this as a strictly social occasion and include spouses.

Sometime during the course of a business relationship you may be invited to a sporting event, but the usual invitation is to a restaurant for dinner. It is important to reciprocate.

If you are invited to a colleague's home, a gift of chocolates, individual pastries or flowers would be appreciated. If you bring flowers, buy an odd number and never purchase chrysanthemums. Italians often appreciate gifts from your home state or region.

At an Italian meal, the host is always the first to begin eating. Wait to see if you should pass food around the table or if the hostess will serve everyone.

It is considered impolite to smoke between courses because Italians believe that it ruins the taste of the food.

Italians eat in the continental manner, keeping the fork in the left hand and the knife in the right. Pasta should be eaten by twisting it around your fork using the sides of the pasta plate, not by twirling it around your fork with a spoon.

Keep your hands above the table during a meal.

Allow the host to pour the wine. If you do not want more, keep your glass almost full by taking small sips. Take care not to get drunk, as it is considered very offensive.

The host and hostess generally sit opposite one another at the table. The most important male guest is seated to the left of the hostess and the second most important male guest to her right. Female guests are seated similarly next to the host.

It is considered polite to refuse a second helping when it is first offered. If your hostess insists, then it is polite to accept. If you really do not want more, say that you really cannot eat any more.

Indicate that you are finished by placing the knife and fork parallel on the plate, with the fork tines facing down.

To beckon a waiter or waitress, raise your hand slightly and say *Camariere* or *Signorina*.

Expect that the person who extends an invitation to a meal will pay for it. The guest should try to reciprocate within a few days. When inviting an Italian to a meal, ask him/her to recommend a restaurant.

Breakfast usually consists of bread and butter, served with *cappuccino* (strong coffee with hot foamy milk) or hot chocolate. Lunch is traditionally the main meal of the day, although less so now than in the past. It usually begins with a pasta course, followed by a meat course (frequently veal). Italians will end the meal with *espresso*.

Espresso is not lingered over; it is consumed rapidly.

The evening meal is usually lighter than the midday meal unless it is a dinner party.

Fruit is eaten with a knife and fork, except for grapes and cherries, which you may eat by hand.

SOCIAL VALUES, CUSTOMS AND TIPS

Italians always appreciate when a foreigner can speak a few words in Italian.

Italians are very family oriented, and they generally appreciate discussing each other's families.

Food, wine and restaurants are savored, and people enjoy conversing about them. Other good conversation topics include sports, especially soccer and bicycling.

Italians tend to be demonstrative and use frequent hand gestures.

In adherence to Italian custom, always stand when an older person enters or departs from the room.

Do not wear shorts or old jeans in cities, especially when visiting churches.

In Italy, men often walk arm-in-arm with other men, as in Latin America.

Always ask permission before photographing someone. Italians are usually pleased to cooperate.

JAMAICA

Population: 2,634,678 (July 1998 est.); black 90.4%, East Indian 1.3%, white 0.2%, Chinese 0.2%, mixed 7.3%, other 0.6%

Languages: English, Creole

Religions: Protestant 61.3%, Roman Catholic 4%, other 34.7%

Currency: Jamaican dollar

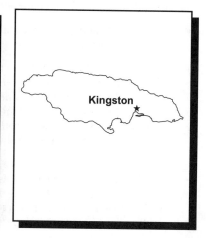

HISTORICAL OVERVIEW

- Jamaica's original inhabitants were the Arawak Indians, who called the island Xaymaca, meaning "land of wood and rivers." In 1494, Columbus landed on the island, and Spanish colonization followed. The Arawaks were virtually wiped out within 50 years of Spanish occupation due to the harsh treatment they received as slaves as well as the many diseases brought from Europe.

- The English captured Jamaica from the Spanish in 1655 and began colonizing it. They hoped to use the island as a base for the conquest of Central and South America. Most of the Spaniards fled to Cuba or Hispaniola (now known as the Dominican Republic), while their former slaves fled to the hills from where they began to wage guerilla warfare. Under British rule, buccaneers, who combined piracy with the merchant profession, turned Jamaican ports into the richest and most active ports in the Caribbean. With the pirates' help, the new colony flourished. The British government supported the pirates, knighting their leader, Henry Morgan, and appointing him lieutenant governor of the island. By the end of the 17th century, the buccaneers were suppressed.

- The British had established sugarcane plantations on the island and were importing large numbers of Africans to be slaves, making Jamaica one of the largest slave markets in the world.

- Jamaica reached its greatest prosperity in the 1700s, based on the sugar and slave trades. Yet the plantation system began to collapse with the abolition of slavery in Jamaica in 1838. The Spaniards who had stayed in Jamaica after the British conquest mixed with the African peoples.

- In 1866, Jamaica gained the status of a British Crown Colony (as opposed to being a simple colonial possession).

- In the 1930s, Jamaicans began to call for self-determination. In 1938, serious social unrest erupted because of long-standing injustices and economic problems exacerbated by the worldwide depression. This resulted in the formation of labor unions and political parties associated with them. Alexander Bustamante and his aide, Norman Manley, were at the forefront of these changes.

- In 1944, a new constitution was written, providing for adult suffrage, and rule by the British Crown Colony government was ended. Nevertheless, Jamaica remained under nominal British rule until it gained full independence in 1962.

- Jamaica was run by a socialist government during the 1970s. This government was then replaced by a conservative one in the 1980s.

- In 1989, by promising to reduce the national debt, the Socialists again took control in the national elections.

- In 1993, P.J. Patterson, the head of the People's National Party, won on a campaign that appealed directly to race and racial loyalists. He got a large majority of the black vote and won the elections.

- Jamaica's economy has improved, but the picture is still bleak, with the external debt exceeding the annual gross national product.

BUSINESS PRACTICES

Hours of Business

Business hours are generally 8:30 a.m. to 4:30 p.m., Monday through Friday. Government offices stay open until 5:00 p.m.

Dress

Business attire is somewhat less formal than in many countries. Men wear lightweight suits or sports coats. Women wear conservative dresses or suits but stockings are usually not necessary.

Introductions

Greetings range from a nod or bow to a handshake or a slap on the back to a kiss, all depending on the people involved and the occasion.

When people are introduced, however, a handshake is customary.

Jamaicans are formal in their introductions, using titles and surnames.

Children generally refer to adults other than family members as "Sir" or "Miss."

Meetings

Arrive at meetings on time, although your Jamaican colleague may have a more relaxed view of time.

Negotiating

Decision makers usually exist at the highest echelons of a company.

Cultivate relationships at all levels. Even if your immediate counterpart does not make the ultimate decision, what he/she thinks of you will still affect the outcome of the transaction.

Entertaining

Visitors in homes are usually offered a drink and sometimes a meal. Guests often bring a small gift for the host or hostess. Appropriate gifts include fresh produce, flowers or a bottle of wine.

Meals are relaxed social occasions, even when formal.

Buffet meals are popular.

It is common to be invited to breakfast or brunch.

Eating outdoors is popular, especially in gardens and on patios.

Continental manners are used, with the knife kept in the right hand and the fork in the left.

Street vendors selling food are plentiful and relatively inexpensive. Food may be eaten on the spot.

Restaurants generally add a service charge to the bill.

Many Jamaicans say grace before or after a meal.

Jamaican food is usually quite spicy.

Ackee and salt fish, the national dish, is usually eaten for breakfast.

Fish and various curries are popular. Another favorite food is jerk – spicy barbecued pork or chicken, often served with a hard-dough bread.

Coffee and tea are popular drinks, and it is common for all hot drinks to be called "tea" (i.e., coffee, cocoa, etc.).

Women usually do not drink alcohol in public.

Bammy (cassava/manioc bread) is a standard food still prepared in the style of the Arawak Indians. *Bammy* with fried fish is a common combination.

SOCIAL VALUES, CUSTOMS AND TIPS

Jamaicans are lively, friendly and hospitable. They may, however, be more reserved when first meeting strangers.

Informal visitors are greeted at the gate of the house. People do not approach the house door until greeted and invited past the gate.

Surprise guests are almost always welcome. Unannounced visits are common since many rural Jamaicans do not have telephones.

Attitudes toward time vary according to lifestyle. It is not uncommon for events and appointments to start later than arranged.

Jamaicans do not appreciate being asked personal questions.

Jamaicans are fashion conscious and like to wear jewelry. Western-style clothing is most frequently worn, but traditional clothing is also worn.

Beckoning is done by clapping the hands or by making a "pssst" sound.

Jamaicans use an abundance of hand gestures, and their voices may be loud and excited during discussions.

Cricket and football (soccer) are the most popular sports in Jamaica.

JAPAN

Population: 125,931,533 (July 1998 est.); Japanese 99.4%, other (mostly Korean) 0.6%

Languages: Japanese

Religions: Shinto and Buddhist 84%, other 16% (including Christian 0.7%)

Currency: yen

HISTORICAL OVERVIEW

• According to legend, the first emperor was Jimmu in 660 B.C., but historical records place the first unified Japanese state in the late fourth or early fifth century A.D.

• Japan came under the cultural influence of China in the sixth century A.D. with the import of Buddhism and the Chinese writing system. It also modeled its governmental and cultural institutions on the Chinese Tang Dynasty. By the ninth century, however, Japan began to separate itself from China.

• A powerful military class developed and took power from the emperors. The first military government or shogunate came to power in the 12th century. Shoguns then held control until the late 19th century. Portuguese traders and missionaries arrived in the 16th century, followed by the Dutch and the British. The Tokugawa shogunate expelled all foreigners in the early 17th century with the exception of a few on Deshima (an island off the coast of Nagasaki). Japan then proceeded to isolate itself for the next two centuries, during which time its culture flourished but society stagnated.

• In 1853, Matthew Perry (U.S. Navy) renewed western contact with the Japanese.

• The shoguns lost power in the 1860s, and the emperor was restored, but real political control was in the hands of a group of young leaders who radically modernized Japan from 1868 to 1912.

- In the late 19th century, Japan began an imperialist quest that led to a war with China (1894-95), a war with Russia (1904-05) and the annexation of Korea (1910).

- Involvement in World War I brought Japan increased global influence. At Versailles, Japan was one of the "big five" (one of the five nations to have representatives on the Council of Ten) that negotiated the terms of peace.

- Japan took possession of Manchuria, renaming it Manchuko, in 1931.

- During World War II Japan was allied with Germany, and on 7 December 1941 Japan launched an air attack on U.S. naval forces at Pearl Harbor in Hawaii.

- After its defeat in World War II, Japan was occupied by military forces (mainly from the U.S.) from 1945 to 1952.

- In 1947, a new constitution was adopted that declared Japan a democracy.

- Once occupation of Japan ended, a period of tremendous economic growth and expansion followed. From the end of World War II until the early 1990s, the Liberal Democratic Party (LDP) controlled politics in Japan.

- The current emperor, Akihito, ascended to the throne in 1989. He is the head of state, but has no governing powers.

- During the 1990s Japan was beset by political scandals and crises. Bad debt caused a banking crisis early in the decade resulting in a recession. In the political arena problems included factionalism, corruption, the dominance of big business and "money politics."

- When Ryutaro Hashimoto became prime minister in 1996, this represented the fourth change in government since 1993.

- A scandal emerged in 1998 involving the finance minister and various other officials in the Ministry of Finance. Confidence in the government then dropped to such a low point that the LDP lost a major parliamentary election and installed yet another prime minister, Keizo Obuchi.

- The Asian financial crisis that rocked Asian markets beginning in the summer of 1997 had serious repercussions for Japan, which is considered the second-largest economy in the world.

BUSINESS PRACTICES

Hours of Business

Business hours are 9:00 a.m. to 5:00 or 5:30 p.m. Workweeks are usually 48 hours and span five and one-half days.

Many Japanese businesspeople return after the evening meal and work until 9:00 or 10:00 p.m. They rarely take work home, however. After work, executives frequently go to bars to drink and have informal business discussions. It is seen as an extension of the regular workday.

The most popular vacation periods are mid-December to mid-January (especially near the New Year) as well as in July and August. Many offices also close during "Golden Week," which extends from late April into the first week of May.

Dress

Always dress in conservative business suits and ties. Businesswomen should use makeup, perfume and jewelry sparingly. Make sure that your shoes are polished. Slip-on shoes are generally more convenient than lace-up shoes since you may need to remove them in certain places. You may be provided with slippers to use indoors except in rooms in which the floors are covered in straw tatami mats, where you are expected to walk in your stocking feet. Always remove your overcoat in the hall before entering an office.

Introductions

Japanese people tend to be rather reserved, and customarily adhere to traditional Japanese rituals. When formally introduced, it is proper to bow, although recently the combination of a bow and a handshake has become more widespread. The depth and length of your bow indicates the degree of respect.

Meishi koukan (business card exchange) is an important aspect of business etiquette. Present your card with both hands and bow slightly. Receive a business card with both hands and take a moment to study it before bowing or shaking hands. Place the card in front of you on a table or desk for reference and as an additional sign of respect. Do not quickly stuff it into a pocket or wallet. Do not write on business cards you receive. Print your business card in your own language and in Japanese with one language on each side of the card. When written in Japanese, the surname comes before the given name(s).

When addressing people, always use Mr., Ms., Mrs., Miss or the Japanese suffix *san*. Mr. Hanafusa, for example, would become *Hanafusa-san*. The Japanese often address someone by using their title, for example, *Ogushi* plus the Japanese word for manager (*Ogushi-bucho*).

Be aware that physical contact is not used when greeting others in public, no matter how close the relationship. Younger people often shake hands with Westerners, while more cosmopolitan Japanese men and women may combine a bow with a handshake. Take your cue from the Japanese person with whom you are meeting as to whether you should bow or shake hands.

When meeting someone, a Japanese person will lower his/her eyes out of politeness and respect. He/she will not make the same degree of direct eye contact as would a Westerner.

Meetings

The only acceptable way to approach a Japanese firm is through an introduction by a third party, preferably someone who knows you, your background, your company and the Japanese company with which you want to transact business. This introduction could be made either by letter or in person.

Although English is studied in school, knowledge of the language is often more academic than conversational. If you are having trouble communicating, you may find that it is helpful to write down your questions, since it is often easier for people to understand written rather than spoken English.

Surprises are not appreciated. It is best to prepare your counterpart for upcoming presentations or discussions by sending them written material well in advance. Arrange for several copies of any written material you plan to use to be printed – translated into Japanese. This will allow each member of the team to have a copy, which will in turn speed the decision-making process.

If possible, prepare visual aids such as charts, drawings, samples, slides and films for use in your presentation.

Make business appointments as far in advance as possible. Punctuality is very important in Japan. Be sure to allow ample time between appointments.

At meetings, the most senior person will usually sit furthest from the door and the most junior person nearest the door. Wait until you have been shown where to sit before sitting down.

Negotiating

Harmony in relationships is the basis for Japanese negotiations. Taking the time required to build such relationships is key to working effectively with the Japanese. Relationships are built on shared experience, sincerity, showing vulnerability, and accepting and giving help.

A business relationship is based more on personal relations than on the cost of the product. The Japanese first want to become acquainted and familiar with you, learning vital facts including your age, the university you attended and details about your firm. Business comes later. Your Japanese counterparts will appreciate you showing the same interest in their backgrounds.

A key concept to remember when negotiating with the Japanese is that there is a high value placed on the concept of "face." The Japanese will avoid directly saying "No" in order to save their own "face" or that of the people with whom they are dealing. Many non-Japanese feel that they are misled by the use of the word "Yes," when in fact they are not reading the nonverbal cues that further explain how the "Yes" was meant.

To build teamwork, try to involve others in a task instead of doing it yourself. Japanese may ask for help even if they are capable of performing a task, in order to build a relationship. People in addition to the officially responsible individual or team may be connected to a project or situation.

The decision-making process can be very slow in Japan. Input from workers at all levels of a company is considered. The process involves many face-to-face discussions, and the contract must be approved at each level of the company and is often renegotiated. Patience is considered a virtue. Once a decision is made, however, implementation is immediate.

Subordinates may not take initiative and may expect to be taken care of by their managers.

It is customary to repeat the same question several times.

Extensive preparation and documentation is the norm and is generally requested.

Japanese negotiating teams often consist of five men selected on the basis of age, seniority and knowledge. Deference is given to the person with the highest authority (generally the oldest).

The senior negotiator is seated in the center, with key decision makers seated to the immediate right and left.

Informal discussions following formal sessions are considered very important.

The desire to avoid failure often causes high risk avoidance.

To demonstrate courtesy and an interest in others, ask other people their opinion before expressing your own.

Be prepared for periods of silence during a business meeting. Silence may indicate that your counterparts have not come to a decision and are thinking. It may also mean that something has been done to displease them. Be patient and allow your counterparts to speak first.

A Japanese person may show concentration by closing his/her eyes and slightly nodding the head up and down.

Be very careful not to interrupt when someone is speaking. While Westerners have a tendency to do this, it is not well received in Japan.

Entertaining

When you begin a business relationship with a Japanese firm, you will be given a gift. After receiving it, present your Japanese associations with a group gift, such as an item that represents your company, fine wine, rare Scotch, golf balls, books about your area of the country or a subscription to a magazine. Avoid garish wrapping paper, bows and ribbons. It is advisable to have the present wrapped by someone at the store from which it was purchased.

Remember to receive or give a gift with both hands and to bow slightly. The recipient of a gift is not expected to open it immediately. Avoid giving an even number of something, especially four. (The word for "four" sounds like the Japanese word for "death.") An exception to the rule of preferring odd numbers is the number nine. The word for "nine" sounds like the Japanese word for "suffering." Therefore, avoid giving nine of anything.

Business deals are sealed with dinner in a restaurant or a drinking session at a bar. In Japan, the lengthy business lunch is rare and lunchtime drinking is unusual. After business has been concluded, allow the Japanese executive(s) to issue the first invitation to a dinner. As at meetings, the seat of honor in a restaurant is usually furthest from the door. Wait to sit until you have been shown where to be seated.

Always reciprocate hospitality by inviting the most important members of the Japanese team to dinner. It is best to invite your Japanese business colleagues to a Chinese or western-style restaurant, preferably in a large hotel. It is suggested that Westerners not entertain their guests in a Japanese restaurant unless they are very familiar with the subtleties of Japanese dining and can act as proper hosts. Wives rarely accompany their husbands on business-oriented social occasions.

Prepare to be taken to a nightclub called a *karaoke* (singing along to background music using special audio/visual equipment) bar. The standard drink offered is called a *mizuwari* (Scotch and water). If you do not wish to drink much, leave your glass half full and then act tipsy when offered more to drink. One way of avoiding a refill is to cover your glass with your hand when others are trying to pour you another drink.

After being invited to a *karaoke* bar, reciprocate by inviting your Japanese colleagues to a restaurant. Japanese businesspeople, however, do not expect you to take them to *karaoke* bars.

It is an honor to be invited to play golf with your Japanese hosts.

If you are invited to a Japanese home, bring a gift of fruit or a cake to the host/hostess. Since the Japanese rarely entertain in their homes, it is a great honor to be invited to an individual's home.

The traditional Japanese diet consists largely of rice, fresh vegetables, seafood, fruit and small portions of meat. Rice and tea are part of nearly every meal.

When dining either at someone's home or in a restaurant, you will receive a set of disposable chopsticks in a paper wrapper. Western utensils are generally used only when eating western foods.

Traditional etiquette emphasizes humility. If you are offered tea or fruit, before accepting you should express a slight hesitation. It is also courteous to deny compliments graciously and to avoid extending excessive compliments on the decor. Understated compliments are more appropriate.

Japanese people generally consume food in a certain order. For example, first a chopstick full of rice is eaten, then one of the side dishes and then more rice. It is considered rude to eat just one dish at a time.

After being seated, you will be given an *oshibori* (damp cloth) for cleaning your hands. Remember not to use this on your face, neck or arms. Put it back on the tray from which it was served when you are done. Handkerchiefs are often used in place of napkins during a meal.

Tipping is virtually nonexistent in Japan, and a tip may very well be refused. At hotels and restaurants, be prepared to have a service charge added to your bill.

When eating all dishes except rice, use chopsticks to bring the food to your mouth. If you do not know how to use chopsticks, your Japanese hosts will enjoy showing you how. Do not use your chopsticks for pointing.

For rice dishes, it is proper to bring the dish up toward your mouth, rather than bending over it. Do not mix sauces or other foods with the rice.

Wait until your host/hostess picks up his/her chopsticks before you touch yours, but do not wait until he/she starts eating. The highest-ranking guest is the one who should start eating first. The custom is for the host to bow to the guest and for the guest to say *Itadakimasu*, which means literally "I receive this feast." A variation is for your host to bow and say the same. You should then reply with the same word and start eating.

Soup is usually served before the main course and is consumed quietly. Pieces of tofu or fish that are in the soup should be picked out using chopsticks. Pickles should be eaten only after you have finished eating other food.

If you want more rice, leave a few grains of rice in your bowl and the waiter or waitress will refill it. If you do not want any more, be sure not to leave any grains of rice in the bowl. Generally, only second helpings of rice are offered, and it is considered impolite to ask for more food.

When you have finished, leave the chopsticks on the chopsticks rest. Never leave them standing in a bowl of rice or other food. When taking food from a communal serving bowl, reverse your chopsticks and use the blunt ends to be polite. It is rude to directly transfer a piece of food from your chopsticks to another person's chopsticks.

Drinks are refilled by your host or other guests. Never refill your own glass. When someone pours a drink for you, reciprocate by filling his/her glass. When a drink is being poured into your glass, hold your glass up off the table.

Green tea is the most popular drink in Japan, although coffee has become more common in recent years.

Sake, a traditional alcoholic drink in Japan, is made from rice. It is served slightly warmed in tiny cups. A *sake* cup should be held with one hand underneath the cup and the other around it.

Toasting is common. To toast someone, raise your glass and say *"kanpai"* (which literally means "drain the cup").

If you are sitting at a meal and have to blow your nose, it is polite to get up, excuse yourself and leave the table. Use a paper tissue to blow your nose, not a handkerchief. A handkerchief is used for wiping the fingers or the brow or as a napkin during a meal.

The main meal of the day is eaten in the evening.

To beckon a waiter/waitress, catch his/her eye and then nod your head downward.

At many restaurants, it is customary for men to sit cross-legged on the floor. Women either sit on their legs or tuck their legs to one side.

Conversation at meals can be intermittent and there may be periods of complete silence, but do not be surprised if the atmosphere suddenly becomes lively. Do not rush to fill the silences.

SOCIAL VALUES, CUSTOMS AND TIPS

Spoken Japanese is not closely related to the spoken Chinese language, but written Japanese is based on Chinese ideographs (characters). The Japanese also use two phonetic alphabets simplified from the ideographs. A third phonetic alphabet uses Roman letters.

Traditionally, most Japanese people have practiced a combination of Buddhist and Shinto religions. Shintoism as well as Confucian thought have been important in forming Japanese social values.

Although it has been customary and, indeed, very common for a person to be employed by one company throughout his/her working life, you should be aware that recent changes in Japanese attitudes toward employment now include more job flexibility than previously.

Japanese people enjoy social conversations, especially those that express a curiosity about their culture and country. Suggested topics for conversation include your reactions to Japan (of great interest to the Japanese), Japanese food, sports (especially baseball and golf), other countries you have visited and questions you have about Japan.

Friendships are not casual but carry long-term obligations and responsibilities. Close relationships may resemble relationships between parent and child.

Age and tradition are highly honored in Japan. Show respect for age, rank and status.

Wa (harmony) and courtesy are very important to the Japanese. They avoid saying "No" directly. They may instead say something like "I will think about it" or "It may be difficult." "Yes" may only mean "Yes, I'm listening."

Know that harmony and politeness do not pertain to crowded public situations, such as those encountered on the subway.

Japanese society is very group oriented. Loyalty to the group and to your superiors takes precedence over personal feelings. A popular proverb in Japan that illustrates this point is, "The nail that sticks up gets hammered down."

The concept of "face" is extremely important. Never do anything to embarrass, criticize or question the knowledge of a Japanese person in front of others.

In Japan, laughter or a smile does not necessarily signify joy or amusement. Instead, it can be a sign of embarrassment or distress.

Outward style is very important in Japan. For example, gifts are carefully wrapped, food is displayed artfully, etc.

Showing an open mouth is considered impolite. Therefore, cover your mouth if you must cough or yawn.

Do not stand with your hands in your pockets, especially if you are speaking to someone, as it is considered rude.

Pointing is done with the entire hand, palm down. Beckoning is done in the same way, but with wiggling all the fingers.

It is not proper to chew gum in public. Although many young people eat while walking in public, it is not considered good manners. If you purchase food or drink at a street stand, eat or drink it at the stand.

Good posture is important, especially while seated. Sit up straight in a chair with both feet on the floor. You may cross your legs at the knee or at the ankles, but do not place an ankle over a knee.

Public displays of affection are frowned upon, although some young people disregard this sentiment. Foreigners create a bad impression when they engage in this type of behavior.

Shoes are removed before entering a Japanese home. Place them together, pointing away from the house.

Men and women do not wear shorts, except at resorts or while jogging.

Traditional sports include sumo wrestling, judo, kendo (fencing with bamboo poles) and karate. Baseball has been played in Japan since the 1870s and is considered a national sport.

JORDAN

Population: 4,434,978 (July 1998 est.); Arab 98%, Circassian 1%, Armenian 1%
Languages: Arabic (official), English widely understood among upper and middle class
Religions: Sunni Muslim 96%, Christian 4%
Currency: Jordanian dinar

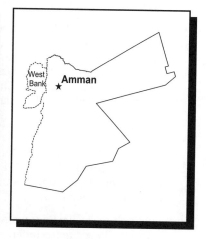

HISTORICAL OVERVIEW

- Jordan's history has been closely linked to that of Israel because both have occupied the area historically known as Palestine. The early settlers of the area included the Gideonites, Edomites, Maobites and Ammonites. Much of present-day eastern Jordan was conquered by the Kingdom of Israel under Solomon and David. It then passed on to the Assyrians, the Babylonians, the Persians and the Seleucids in succession, when these conquered other parts of the Middle East. In 64-62 B.C. it fell to the Romans.

- In the seventh century, the Arabs invaded the area, and while Christian crusaders ruled for a time, the region has been largely Muslim since the Arab invasion.

- The Ottoman Turks ruled for many years, until the Great Arab Revolt of 1916, in which the Arabs were supported by the British. In 1920, the British made Jordan, then known as Transjordan, a British mandate ruled by the Hashemite Prince Abdullah.

- The British slowly turned control of the region over to local Arab officials, and Transjordan became independent in 1927 although the British mandate did not end until 1948. In 1950, the name of the country was shortened to "Jordan," and in this year, Jordan also annexed the West Bank of the Jordan River. In 1951, Abdullah was assassinated and his son Talal was proclaimed king, but because of poor health, he was deposed by government officials. Talal's 17-year-old son, Hussein, became the new Jordanian monarch.

- During the 1967 War, Jordan lost the West Bank to Israel, and many Palestinian refugees fled to Jordan. This sudden influx of immigrants caused unrest and violence. Members of the Palestinian resistance (*fedayeen*) were expelled from Jordan after an assassination attempt on King Hussein.

- After the War of 1967, Jordan considered the people of the West Bank part of its population and provided for Palestinian representatives in the Jordanian parliament. In 1988, however, King Hussein announced that Jordan no longer would claim the West Bank as its territory. As a result, strains between the Jordanian government and the Palestinian Liberation Organization (PLO) relaxed.

- Elections for the new parliament took place in 1989, and a new legislature was convened with a greater number of opposition groups represented. In 1991, King Hussein restored multiparty democracy. He also lifted a number of martial law provisions that had existed since 1967.

- Full multiparty elections were held in 1993. A strong voter turnout allowed many independents to gain seats in the new parliament. This election weakened the political parties' control in the Jordanian parliament.

- In 1994 Jordan signed a peace treaty with Israel and an economic accord with the PLO. Opposition resulted from the peace treaty with Israel. Some Arab-run companies prohibited business dealings with Israelis.

- Political tension rose before the 1997 parliamentary elections. There was opposition to the treaty, dissatisfaction with restrictions to the press and the government's seeming favoritism of rural areas. Because the Islamic Action Front and other opposition groups boycotted the elections, major opposition existed outside the legal system.

- In August 1998, Fayez al-Tarawnak became prime minister. Educated as an economist, he created a cabinet whose principal goal is to pull Jordan out of its economic troubles.

- Unemployment and poverty are prominent social and economic problems. In recent years, however, the World Bank has contributed to investment endeavors, and the government has released numerous shares of its enterprises to private and foreign-owned companies.

BUSINESS PRACTICES

Hours of Business

Government offices are usually open from 9:00 a.m. to 2:00 p.m., Saturday through Thursday.

Businesses are open from 8:00 a.m. to about 2:00 p.m. and from 4:00 to 7:00 p.m.

Most businesses close on Friday, the day of worship for Muslims. Christian businesses close on Sunday as well.

Dress

Men should wear a business suit and women should wear a conservative plain dress or suit. Formal dress is required for diplomatic affairs.

Introductions

Greetings are important, and Jordanians greet people they know and newcomers warmly.

A handshake is the most common greeting. It is usually accompanied by verbal greetings and inquiries about each person's health.

Friends of the same sex often exchange a kiss on either cheek.

A common term for "Hello" is *Mar-haba.*

A term used to welcome someone is *Ahlan wa sahalan. Ahlein mar-haba* might also be used as a welcome greeting.

When entering or leaving a room, it is customary to shake hands with each person (except, of course, at large gatherings).

Remember that first names are not used between strangers when greeting.

Business cards may be printed in English.

Meetings

The best time for business appointments is between 9:00 a.m. and 12:00 p.m.

Patience is a valuable asset. Punctuality is not as important in Jordan as in the West. Jordanians believe that paying attention to interpersonal relationships is more important than schedules. Individuals in the private sector, however, are usually more time conscious than those in the public sector.

Accept the cups of coffee that will be offered you during business meetings.

You may want to suggest discussing business in a small restaurant or coffee shop to avoid the interruptions that often occur in an office.

Negotiating

In contrast to other people in the Middle East, Jordanian businesspeople usually negotiate in a direct manner and the bureaucracy is not as prevalent.

Many Jordanians are familiar with North American business practices. Depending on the degree of your counterpart's education and adaptability, business can move more quickly or more slowly than in the U.S.

Jordanian businesspeople want to know you well before any transaction takes place. Be prepared for a number of preliminary meetings before starting to discuss a contract, for example.

Always be on time with your deliveries. Otherwise, you will lose the Jordanian company's trust and business.

Although it may take a little time for Jordanian businessmen to get accustomed to negotiating with a foreign businesswoman, a professional woman with whom they must do business will be treated with respect.

Entertaining

Visiting and entertaining play a fundamental role in Jordanian society.

Guests are greeted by both husband and wife.

Invited visitors may bring gifts of flowers or sweets, but never alcohol (which is forbidden by Muslim law).

It is customary for a person who has had enough to drink to shake the empty cup back and forth.

Guests not originally invited for a meal may be expected to remain. It is polite to decline the offer initially before accepting, but it is impolite not to accept the offer in the end. Some guests will refuse the invitation up to three times before accepting it.

A Jordanian will entertain in his/her home more often than at restaurants because it is a greater honor for a guest to be invited to a home.

Visitors should avoid excessive admiration of any object owned by the host because the host may feel obligated to offer it to them. In most cases, it is wise to remember that an offer is made only as a gesture intended to demonstrate the host's generosity. It is therefore expected that the admirer will decline the item. If the host insists several times, the guest must accept it or risk embarrassing the host.

In any situation where gifts are given, the recipients should not immediately accept them.

Excessive praise of children is considered bad luck for the family.

When invited to a home for a meal, it is polite to leave a little food on the plate. This tells the host that the guest has eaten well and that the host has been generous.

Keep in mind that Islamic law prohibits the consumption of pork and alcohol, and most Muslims are careful to obey these restrictions.

Most meals include meat and bread, along with vegetables and fruits that are in season.

Jordan's national dish is *mansaf,* a large tray of rice covered with chunks of stewed lamb (including the head) and *jameed* (yogurt sauce). It is eaten by hand from the serving tray.

Coffee is important at all meals. *Qahwah Saadah* (Bedouin coffee) is sipped slowly from small cups. Arabic or Turkish coffee is sweeter. It is deliberately not stirred so as to keep the thick coffee grains at the bottom of the cup. It is considered impolite for a person to leave before the coffee is served.

SOCIAL VALUES, CUSTOMS AND TIPS

Islamic values and laws are an integral part of Jordanian society.

Each religious community has the right to regulate personal matters such as marriage, divorce and inheritance.

Although many Palestinians residing in Jordan hold Jordanian citizenship, they consider themselves Palestinians first. Some do not consider themselves Jordanians at all and resent being called Jordanians. These people strongly support the establishment of a Palestinian homeland. Visitors should be aware of their views.

Women comprise only about ten percent of the workforce.

Jordanian employers look after the interests of their employees and are responsible for a wider area of concerns than western employees are. In many cases, an employer is regarded as being more like an uncle or a father than a boss.

Most men wear western-style clothing, often accompanied by the traditional white or red-checkered headdress.

Some women also wear western clothing, but many continue to wear traditional Islamic floor-length dresses, head scarves and veils. Either way, clothing is always conservative and never revealing. Jewelry is an important part of a woman's wardrobe.

Visitors should dress conservatively. Cotton clothing is most comfortable due to the desert heat. Shorts are not worn, except during athletic events.

It is improper to pass or accept objects or eat with only the left hand. The left hand is traditionally reserved for personal hygiene purposes.

It is impolite to show the sole of one's foot or shoe to another person. For this reason, crossing one's legs is generally avoided.

Good posture is important, especially at social events.

It is improper to be affectionate in public.

Hand gestures are used a great deal in conversation.

Jordanians love children and they lavish a great deal of time and attention on them. Likewise, the elderly are greatly respected and cared for by their children.

To be able to help another member of the family is considered a great honor as well as a duty. Gender roles in the family follow traditional lines.

National holidays follow the western (Gregorian) calendar and fall on fixed dates. They include Labor Day (May 1), Independence Day (May 25), Arab Revolt and Army Day (June 10), King Hussein's Accession to the Throne (August 11) and King Hussein's Birthday (November 14).

Although Christians celebrate Easter and Christmas, they are not national holidays.

Islamic religious holy days follow the lunar calendar, which is a few days shorter than the western calendar. One important holiday is *Eid al-Fitr*, a three-day feast at the end of the month of Ramadan. During Ramadan, Muslims do not eat or drink from dawn to dusk.

Eid al-Adha is known as the Feast of Sacrifice and comes after the pilgrimage to Mecca. The birth of the prophet *Moulid al-Nebi* (Mohammad) is also celebrated.

Jordan has a good transportation system.

Water is not potable. Remember that boiled water must be used not only for drinking but for brushing teeth, in ice cubes and so forth.

Ask permission before taking a picture of anyone. Do not take pictures of people praying.

KENYA

Population: 28,337,071 (July 1998 est.); Kikuyu 22%, Luhya 14%, Luo 13%, Kalenjin 12%, Kamba 11%, Kisii 6%, Meru 6%, other African 15%, non-African (Asian, European, Arab) 1%

Languages: English (official), Swahili (official), numerous indigenous languages

Religions: Protestant (including Anglican) 38%, Roman Catholic 28%, indigenous beliefs 26%, Muslim 6%, other 2%

Currency: Kenyan shilling

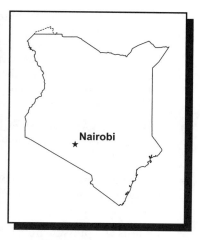

HISTORICAL OVERVIEW

- Kenya's many and diverse ethnic groups can be divided into three main language groups: Bantu, Nilotic and Cushitic. The Bantu group, which lives mainly in the south, accounts for two-thirds of the population. The Nilotic, who are spread throughout, account for approximately one-quarter, and the Cushitic, in the extreme north, for only three to four percent of the population. Thus, many languages are spoken in Kenya, but the lingua franca is Swahili, which evolved along Kenya's coastline. It is a mixture of various Bantu languages and Arabic, Persian, Portuguese, Hindi and English.

- Before the 19th century little is known about most of Kenya. The only significant records are those concerning the coastline along which trade with Arabia was conducted for centuries.

- After 1740, Arabs ruled the Kenyan coast from the island of Zanzibar. In the 19th century, Arab and Swahili speakers traveled into the interior in search of ivory. Their advance beyond the central plains was checked by the powerful Masair, who had migrated down from northern Kenya during the century prior.

- The first Europeans to travel to Kenya's interior were the Germans, who briefly controlled the country until the British assumed control. In 1887, the British East Africa Company leased the Kenyan coast from the Sultan of Zanzibar. Kenya became a British protectorate in 1890 and was organized as a British Crown Colony in 1920.

- Great Britain granted Kenya its independence in 1963 after a period of violent uprisings called the Mau-Mau Rebellion. Since then it has remained in the Commonwealth as a sovereign republic.

- Jomo Kenyatta, the leader of the independence movement, became Kenya's first president. Kenyatta organized a strong central government under one political party, the Kenya African National Union (KANU). He was succeeded, as president and as leader of the KANU, by Daniel Arap Moi. He remained in power until his death in 1978 and brought the country political stability and sustained economic growth.

- In 1982, the KANU was proclaimed the only legal political party. Free elections were still held, but all candidates had to register with the KANU.

- Kenya faced an economic downturn in the 1980s due to rising oil prices and a population growth that outstripped employment opportunities.

- Protests and pressure from other countries eventually led Moi to change his one-party policy, and in 1991, he rescinded the constitutional provision that gave the KANU its dominance.

- Dozens of political parties formed in anticipation of the 1992 national elections, but Moi kept the opposition weak by exploiting the differences among the various parties.

- Moi's reign increased terror and oppression in Kenya, and his corrupt government accumulated a large foreign debt.

- During 1996 and 1997 there were confirmed reports of various human rights violations under Moi's regime. Increased violence on the streets caused a sharp drop in tourism.

- After the IMF suspended funds to Kenya in 1997, Moi pledged to fight government corruption and to reduce violence in the country. He also initiated talks to reform the constitution but shunned all opposition groups.

- In 1998, Moi was re-elected president by a slim margin.

- In August 1998, the United States embassy in Nairobi was bombed, killing many Kenyans and several foreign nationals.

BUSINESS PRACTICES

Hours of Business

Business hours are from 8:00 a.m. to 5:00 p.m. Monday through Friday, and from 8:30 a.m. to 3:00 p.m. on Saturday.

Dress

Conservative lightweight business suits for men and cotton or linen dresses for women are the usual attire because of the year-round warm climate. Women are advised never to wear dresses above the knee.

Introductions

Kenyans are friendly and greet people with warmth. Politeness is essential in greetings.

In Kenya, physical contact is important. Handshakes are used often and are considered a gesture of trust and peace. They are common and an important part of a greeting throughout the country.

Because most people speak Swahili, the term, *Hujambo, habari?*, meaning "Greetings! How are you?," is often used. English greetings are also acceptable.

Greeting customs may differ between ethnic groups since Kenya is inhabited by more than 30 different ethnic groups.

Kenyans will introduce themselves with their surname first and given name last. Since English is the principle business language, a Kenyan man is addressed as "Mr.," a married woman as "Mrs." and a single woman as "Miss."

Meetings

Business correspondence, catalogs and advertising material prepared in English are readily understood by most potential buyers.

Schedule meetings at least two weeks prior to entering the country.

Be punctual. Most Kenyan businesspeople familiar with international negotiations are punctual for appointments.

Personal visits are warmly welcomed and are generally regarded as the most efficient method of establishing new trade contracts.

Business cards are both presented and received with your right hand. Avoid using the left hand because it is seen as unclean and unlucky.

When receiving a business card, it is considered appropriate to pause and read it thoroughly before putting it away.

Meetings are generally informal. Kenyans are well known for being casual, humorous and seemingly carefree. Business procedures may vary according to race, tribe and religion, but the strong British influence is noticeable in formality and manners.

Plan to arrive in Kenya a day before your first meeting and reconfirm your appointments when you arrive.

Negotiating

Correspondence and personal calls play a significant role in conducting business in Kenya. Therefore, expeditious handling of correspondence is expected and greatly appreciated.

Contacts are very important. You can find them at the Rotary Club or Lions Club in Kenya, if you are a member. The Kenya National Chamber of Commerce and the Nairobi Chamber of Commerce are also helpful.

Be patient. Your Kenyan colleague will want to get to know you before doing business. The first meeting will often involve a lengthy period of small talk. Take your cues from your counterpart.

Build a network of references and personal relationships when beginning the negotiating process in Kenya.

Decision making is largely carried out by a few top executives.

Entertaining

Since Kenyans are very hospitable, be prepared for many business and social gatherings to center around meals.

If you are a first-time visitor, you will probably be taken to a restaurant by your Kenyan host. It is recommended that you reciprocate soon after by taking your host to your hotel's restaurant.

Lunch and dinner are both appropriate for business meals. Your spouse is not generally welcome, but, with advance notice, plans can be arranged to include him/her.

It is best to give gifts to your host at dinner or if you are invited to a Kenyan's home. Flowers and candy are suitable for Kenyan women, toys and western music for children.

Breakfast is usually served between 7:00 and 8:30 a.m., lunch between noon and 2:00 p.m. and dinner between 7:00 and 9:00 p.m.

Kenyan cuisine is a cross between Indian, European and various tribal influences.

The staples of Kenyan cooking are meat (goat, beef and mutton) and starches (potatoes, rice or *ugali,* a cornmeal cooked like porridge).

The Abaluhya menu might consist of groundnut soup, *ugali, m'baazi* (pea beans); *ndizi* (bananas steamed in leaves) or *m'chuzi wa kulu* (chicken in a coconut dish). The Kikuyu's menu is different because the meal centers around the *irio*, which is a seasoned puree of corn, peas and potatoes.

The most popular after-dinner drink is *mazuva ya kuganda*, a sour skimmed milk served cold. Coffee and tea are also available.

Kenya is well known for its lively brewing industry, and beer is consumed in great quantities.

One Kenyan wine to sip carefully is the ubiquitous papaya wine. It is an acquired taste for many people.

SOCIAL VALUES, CUSTOMS AND TIPS

Because of strong family ties and friendships, visiting is a common activity among Kenyans. Sunday is the most popular day for visiting relatives and friends.

The Catholic Church has been a powerful influence in the last century.

Kenyans are proud of their country, and it is not wise to offer gratuitous or condescending advice about national or local affairs.

It is best to speak in a low-toned and mild-mannered voice. It is considered an insult to shout at anyone, even with words of praise.

Never use the word "blacks" when describing Kenyans.

Kenyans place great importance on keeping in touch with visitors and friends. Sending birthday and holiday cards will be remembered for years.

Kenya is dominated by a society of upper-class and wealthy families. Long-established families control much of the business in the country.

Patriotism is evident in people's respect for the national flag. Whenever the flag is raised or lowered, Kenyans stop to observe the short ceremony.

Public displays of affection are not acceptable in most areas, although they are becoming increasingly common in the capital city of Nairobi.

It is common for men to hold hands while walking in public. A man and a woman, however, would not do so.

Eye contact is important to Kenyans as it both conveys and instills a sense of trust.

Kenyan society has a great deal of respect and appreciation for age. Thus older family members carry the most status.

KUWAIT

Population: 1,913,285 (July 1998 est.); Kuwaiti 45%, other Arab 35%, South Asian 9%, Iranian 4%, other 7%

Languages: Arabic (official), English

Religions: Muslim 85% (Shi'a 40%, Sunni 45%), Christian, Hindu, Parsi and other 15%

Currency: Kuwaiti dinar (KD)

Kuwait City

HISTORICAL OVERVIEW

- Although remains on Faylakah Island in Kuwait Bay suggest that Kuwait was already inhabited by an early civilization in the third millennium B.C., modern Kuwaiti history can be traced back to the 18th century A.D., when the Anizah tribe wandered eastward looking for better pasture and water. They established Kuwait City in 1710. The name "Kuwait" is an Arabic word, meaning "fortress built near water."

- In 1756, the place was established as an autonomous sheikdom under the Al Sabah family, who still rule the country. In about 1775, Kuwait established relations with the British. The Kuwaitis looked to the British for support in maintaining their autonomy. When both Germany and the Ottoman Empire pushed to extend their influence over Kuwait, Kuwait and Britain formalized their relations in a treaty in 1899. From 1914 to 1961 Kuwait was a British protectorate.

- Although oil was discovered in 1937, its exploration had to be delayed until the end of World War II. Once exploration started, Kuwait flourished economically. In 1976, the Kuwaiti government nationalized oil operations that were originally granted jointly to British Petroleum and Gulf Oil.

- Although Kuwait has managed to maintain a delicate diplomatic balance in the Middle East, it has nevertheless been affected by local conflicts, especially the Iranian revolution and the Iran-Iraq War. During the war it remained nonbelligerent. Kuwait did provide financial support for Iraq, however, since the most severe threat to Kuwait and its oil shipments came from Iran and its sympathizers.

- In 1983, Shi'ite terrorists based in Iran bombed the U.S. and French embassies in Kuwait City. When it was found that several native Shi'ites were responsible for subsequent hijackings intended to force Kuwait to release the convicted terrorists, a Sunni backlash removed Shi'ites from sensitive positions in the oil industry, army and police.

- Talks between Iraq and Kuwait on the repayment of war debts and other issues broke down in 1990 and Iraq marched into Kuwait. The Kuwaiti government fled to Saudi Arabia and, after international sanctions were ineffective in driving out Iraq, the U.S. along with other powers attacked in what became the Gulf War. Iraq soon retreated, but not before destroying nearly half of the country's oil wells. Kuwait spent the next few years rebuilding what had been destroyed by the war. Although progress was quick, it placed a great strain on the economy.

- The National Assembly was reestablished in 1992 after having been suspended by the emir in 1967. Although political parties were forbidden, opposition groups formed and won more than 50 percent of the seats. Prime Minister Sheikh Saad Abdallah Al-Sabah then appointed six "opposition" members to his cabinet.

- In both the 1992 and 1996 elections, women protesters demanded the right to vote.

- Through 1998, tension between Iraq and Kuwait continued.

BUSINESS PRACTICES

Hours of Business

Businesses are usually open from 8:30 a.m. until 12:30 p.m. and from 4:30 until 8:30 p.m., Saturday through Thursday. Businesses are closed on Fridays for observance of the Muslim Sabbath.

Avoid scheduling business meetings during the month of Ramadan, when most businesses are closed during the day for religious observance. The dates of Ramadan are set according to the lunar calendar and thus change every year on the solar calendar. It is therefore best to check when they are before arranging your visit.

Dress

In the summer (April to September), Kuwaiti businessmen usually wear lightweight suits (linen or cotton). The winter months are cooler and rainy, but not cold. Business attire during this time is generally conservative: a dark suit and tie with a white shirt for men and a dark suit or skirt with a white blouse for women. Suits should be cut conservatively and jewelry (e.g., cufflinks, watch, ring, etc.) should be kept to a minimum. If jewelry is worn it is preferable that it be gold.

Introductions

The most common form of greeting is a handshake, especially in business. Foreign businesswomen should wait for a Kuwaiti businessman to offer his hand. Similarly, a foreign businessman should wait for a Kuwaiti businesswoman to offer her hand.

Kuwaitis may also greet you with a short, quick bow. In a more traditional form of greeting, Kuwaitis may extend one hand to a visitor's shoulder, grasp the visitor's hand with the other, kiss both cheeks and then hold the visitor's hand for a moment.

It is very important to use titles in Kuwait. If someone has a doctorate, you should address them as "Doctor," followed by the last name, unless otherwise requested. If you are addressing a government official who has a title, you should use the title, followed by a last name. A *sheik* (pronounced "shake") should be addressed as "Your Excellency" or as *Sheik*, followed by the given name.

If the person you are addressing does not have a title, you should use "Mr.," "Mrs." or "Miss," followed by a last name. First names should not be used unless your host requests that you use it and a closer relationship has been established.

Business cards are very important since it is standard practice for people to have unlisted phone numbers in Kuwait. The card is also used as a tool of presentation. It should look conservative and professional (with no color unless there is color in your company's logo). If you have a university degree above a bachelor's degree, it should be included on your card. Your position or title within your firm should also be printed. Business cards should be printed in both English and Arabic and should be presented with the Arabic side up, using the right hand. When receiving a card, it is considered polite to read it thoughtfully and then to nod at your counterpart before putting it away.

In order to conduct business in Kuwait, foreign firms must appoint a Kuwaiti representative or agent. The agent introduces the foreign business to potential markets and government officials.

Letters of introduction should be forwarded by a third party – the Kuwaiti Chamber of Commerce, a banker or your agent – accompanied by a letter from a senior official from your firm.

Meetings

Making firm appointments is extremely important. "Dropping by" unannounced at an office makes a very poor impression.

While your counterparts may arrive late or a meeting may be delayed, it is very important to arrive on time in order to make a good impression.

Very often, the first meeting (or first few meetings) will simply be spent on polite small talk. While they may seem unnecessary, these preliminary meetings should be taken seriously. During this time, your Kuwaiti counterpart will be evaluating you and your firm to see whether or not business should take place in the future. Often, after an initial talk, your counterpart will end the meeting and will invite you to another meeting where the actual business discussions will be conducted. The Kuwaiti executives will indicate when they are ready to start discussing business.

Your Kuwaiti counterparts may take time to pray during a meeting. It is Muslim practice to pray five times a day. It is out of place to ask a Muslim to interfere with this practice. The period of prayer usually lasts about 20 minutes and the flow of conversation is readily picked up again when the prayers have been concluded.

Visual aids used during presentations make a good impression. Presentations should be concise and direct, particularly when you are dealing with senior executives. Lengthy presentations are customary when junior-level executives take over to discuss technical details.

Business meetings are rarely private. It is important to be patient since there are often numerous interruptions for phone calls and visitors. Since people come in and out of meetings, you may be asked to deliver the same presentation a number of times.

Negotiating

It is unwise to bring along lawyers during initial meetings since this will be interpreted as a sign of distrust. It is appropriate, however, to include lawyers in the final stages of a negotiation. Contracts should be simple and concise and should be translated into Arabic. It is advisable to hire a Kuwaiti lawyer who is familiar with local laws and with the subtleties of the Arabic language.

Kuwaitis do not speak loudly, and they tend to stand close together when conversing. A calm demeanor is taken as a sign of intelligence. Maintaining eye contact is also very important. If you shift eye contact away from your host, it may be interpreted as a sign that you are not trustworthy.

Since maintaining personal honor is very important, one should avoid embarrassing or criticizing anyone. Compromises may sometimes be necessary in order to maintain someone's sense of honor.

Business may proceed at quite a slow pace in Kuwait since negotiations can be slow and a great deal of time is spent on reinforcing personal relationships.

Establishing a personal relationship of depth and trust is one of the most important elements of conducting business in Kuwait. You should allow plenty of time for conducting transactions. At times, several days may pass between meetings and it is not acceptable to try to close deals by phone or fax communication.

Rank and status are very important in conducting business in Kuwait. Subordinates are expected to defer to senior management. The use of titles is also very important. People of high rank will amply display their wealth with lavish offices and expensive cars. Personal relations and strong (often familial) connections play an important role within the small Kuwaiti business community.

In negotiating, a calm but firm, sincere and personal approach works best. Kuwaiti businesspeople do not appreciate a "hard-sell" approach or being hurried. Instead, it is very common for there to be lengthy haggling.

You should be aware that Kuwaitis do not like dealing with lower-level executives when negotiating, since decisions are made only at the top levels of Kuwaiti firms. While lower-level management may be involved in some parts of the negotiation process, the senior executive is expected to make final decisions. The decision maker in a Kuwaiti firm may speak very little and, instead, quietly observe negotiations to come to a decision.

Since Arabic is a language that makes frequent use of hyperbole, a "Yes" very often means "Maybe."

More so than in other Islamic countries, women occupy positions in both business and government. At the same time, foreign businesswomen may encounter some initial disrespect since Kuwaiti businessmen are not accustomed to dealing with female executives who are decision makers. Nevertheless, these traditional beliefs are gradually changing as more and more women are entering high-level management and decision-making positions in Kuwait.

Entertaining

Lunch, the largest meal of the day, is the most common business meal in Kuwait and is usually taken between 12:30 and 2:00 p.m. Business dinners, which are less common and tend to be lighter meals, usually take place between 8:00 and 9:00 p.m. Business is usually not discussed during the first meal together or during dinners. Business meals are perceived as a social opportunity to establish trust and personal rapport between the executives working together on a transaction.

If you invite your counterparts to a meal, it is appropriate to dine in your hotel restaurant or to ask them to choose a restaurant for you. If possible, pay the bill in advance. Keep in mind that it is inappropriate to take your Kuwaiti guests to a bar or nightclub.

It is considered an honor to be invited to a Kuwaiti's home. It is considered very rude to decline such an invitation.

Even when the meal takes place in a home, spouses are rarely included in business entertainment. It will be specified if they are. If you are unsure, check in advance.

Gift-giving is not an important part of doing business in Kuwait and giving a gift may be misinterpreted since laws against bribery are seriously enforced. Expensive gifts should never be given during negotiations or when bidding on contracts if there is any chance that they may be misinterpreted as a bribe.

Gifts that have the company logo on them are most appropriate, since it is unlikely that they would be interpreted as bribes. Avoid presenting gifts to your host when you are alone. If you give gifts to a group of businesspeople, be mindful that each gift matches the status of each individual within the team.

To congratulate your Kuwaiti business counterpart or when visiting a home, flowers are the most appropriate gift. It is also appropriate to have flowers sent to the home before a dinner party. If you are invited to a home for a meal, be aware that your host will be insulted if you bring food or drink as a gift (which would be taken to imply that you think your host is not generous). Avoid giving a gift solely to your host's wife. It will seem too personal. Remember not to bring alcohol (which is prohibited by Islam).

Any kind of book or gift for your host's children is considered appropriate. Gold pens, finely made compasses (so that your host will always know where Mecca is), business card cases and cigarette lighters make appropriate business gifts.

Avoid gifts that portray people or animals. Images of the human body are frowned upon according to Islamic custom, and certain animals are considered unclean or symbolize negative characteristics.

The greatest compliment you can pay your host is to acknowledge his generosity. Similarly, when offered a gift by a Kuwaiti, it is impolite to refuse.

Avoid admiring an object or any other possession of your host's to excess, or your host may feel obliged to give it to you. It would then be impolite to refuse.

Even if your Kuwaiti host encourages you to drink alcohol, it is advisable not to do so. While a host may feel obligated to offer you alcohol, he may also feel offended if you do not respect local custom.

When entering a house or tent, keep in mind that you may be asked to remove your shoes.

Rice is a basic element of the Kuwaiti diet. *Couscous* (grain-like pasta) is also popular. The main spices of Kuwaiti cuisine are turmeric, ginger, cardamom, nutmeg, parsley, rosewater, pepper, saffron and ground citrus fruits. Ground limes are used in many dishes and are called *loomi*. Cucumbers, tomatoes, chick-peas, eggplant, onions and olives accompany many dishes. Broiled lamb, barbecued fish, chicken and prawns are also common.

Desserts are usually made with a light, flaky dough, stuffed with raisins, nuts and honey. The dough is then baked or fried. Sweet drinks made from yogurt and fruit juices also make popular desserts. Arabic coffee is served in very small cups. You are expected to drink two or three cupfuls.

It is polite both to sample all the dishes offered and to consume large amounts of food. This will be understood as a compliment to local cuisine and to your hostess. It is also appropriate and even appreciated if you ask your host to describe certain unfamiliar foods to you.

Dining style varies depending on the particular home. In some homes, guests may be seated western-style (on chairs around a table). Otherwise, guests may be seated on the floor next to a low table. Food may be eaten with utensils or with the right hand only, using Arabic bread to pick up food or move it on the plate. Sometimes a jug of water is passed around to each diner before a meal so that each person may wash his/her hands.

It is polite to wait for your host to seat you. It is likely that you will be seated to the right of your host or at the head of the table. All dishes are usually served at the same time and guests help themselves to the food, which is presented on communal trays.

Kuwaitis may toast with fruit juice, mineral water or iced tea. The host may say *Mah-bruk*! (Congratulations!) or *Sahatak*! (To your health!), depending on what is appropriate.

During meals, conversation is usually minimal. After the meal, guests usually gather in a smoking room to smoke from a water pipe, to have coffee or mint tea and to converse.

SOCIAL VALUES, CUSTOMS AND TIPS

While Kuwait has been successfully modernized and urbanized, it still observes Muslim traditions and faith. The customs of Islam dominate all aspects of daily life. Nevertheless, Kuwaitis are more open to the outside world, more tolerant of difference and more progressive in comparison to some other Muslim countries.

Kuwaitis are generous and amiable. They communicate with a modest demeanor rather than with a pragmatic and outgoing manner.

Good topics of conversation include sports, technology and travel. Soccer, horse and camel racing and hunting are popular sports. Kuwaitis also enjoy hearing praise of their country and its accomplishments.

To avoid topics that Kuwaitis find too personal, follow the lead of your host. While you should not specifically ask or talk about a man's wife or daughters, you may inquire about the family or children in general.

Avoid discussing Middle Eastern politics or Israel.

Be aware that Kuwaitis demonstrate trust and comfort with small gestures, such as tapping the shoulder or back. It is appropriate to smile and nod your head approvingly as a response. Similarly, it is quite common for men to hold hands. You should not be taken aback or embarrassed if your Kuwaiti colleague grasps your hand.

The left hand is considered unclean. Only use the right hand for passing objects or for touching food or people.

While women's clothing styles are more relaxed in Kuwait than in other Muslim countries, women should still avoid wearing revealing garments and should keep makeup and jewelry to a minimum. Knee-length or longer skirts with at least elbow-length sleeves are appropriate, and women should always cover their shoulders. Shirts should be buttoned up to the neck. Neither men nor women should wear shorts in public. As a foreign visitor, you may offend some Kuwaitis if you wear traditional Kuwaiti clothing.

Good posture is expected when you are sitting. You should be especially careful not to point the sole of your shoe towards anybody, especially if you cross your legs. Generally, it is best to keep both feet flat on the ground.

It is not appropriate to get too physically comfortable with those around you. You should not rest your arm on someone else's chair, pat someone on the back, gesticulate or touch people (other than a handshake).

Avoid coughing, sneezing or clearing your throat in public. If it cannot be avoided, you should try to muffle it.

It is considered impolite to point at another person.

The "thumbs up" gesture is considered to be very rude.

KYRGYZSTAN

Population: 4,522,281 (July 1998 est.); Kyrgyz 52.4%, Russian 18%, Uzbek 12.9%, Ukranian 2.5%, German 2.4%, other 11.8%

Languages: Kyrgyz (official), Russian (official)

Religions: Muslim 75%, Russian Orthodox 20%, other 5%

Currency: som

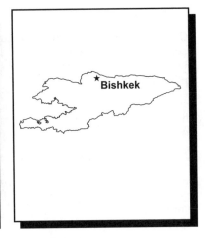

HISTORICAL OVERVIEW

- The Republic of Kyrgyzstan is located on a western spur of the Tien Shan mountains. The Kyrgyz people have dwelled in the area and its surroundings since at least the first century B.C. and have, until very recently, led a nomadic life. For centuries they were a forest-dwelling people who practiced shamanism. By the ninth century they had become Turkic speakers, and by the 16th century they had retreated to the Tien Shan mountains.

- The Kyrgyz people came under the nominal control of the Ching (Manchu) dynasty of China in the 18th century. Between 1825 and 1830 they were conquered by the Muslim Khanate of Kokand. Islam was gradually adopted by some of the Kyrgyz, but never as more than a veneer.

- Soon thereafter, two Kyrgyz tribes waged a fratricidal war that divided the country and drew in the Russians. In the second half of the 19th century, Russian peasants emigrated to Kyrgyz areas and took the winter pasturelands, thus seriously threatening Kyrgyz existence.

- The Kyrgyz revolted in 1916, but the revolt was brutally put down by the tsar. Following the Russian Revolution, this area became part of Soviet Turkistan. After several changes in classification, it was finally recognized in 1936 as a constituent republic and named the Kyrgyz Soviet Socialist Republic.

- During the Soviet years, nomadic life ended as the people were forced onto collective and state farms. Industrialization and mining increased the number of urban jobs, although these were mostly occupied by non-Kyrgyz residents. The Kyrgyz people generally preferred to remain in agriculture.

- Perestroika did not affect Kyrgyzstan until 1990, when ethnic riots broke out along its border with Uzbekistan. The riots damaged the standing of Absamat Masaliev, the Kyrgyz Communist Party leader. The opposition organized itself into a new party, Democratic Kyrgyzstan, led by Askar Akayev, who in the 1991 elections defeated Masaliev and became president.

- In August 1991, local Communists tried to depose President Akayev but were unsuccessful. Akayev subsequently banned the Communist Party from government offices and declared Kyrgyzstan an independent nation.

- Despite the drop in the standard of living since the breakup of the Soviet Union, Akayev remained very popular. He pushed democratic reforms and moved to create a market economy. He also made plans for 27 new universities.

- Under Akayev a new legislature was instituted by way of referendum, and, in 1995, elections were held with about 80 percent of the candidates running as independents.

- Between 1995 and 1996, thousands of Russians left Kyrgyzstan to return to Russia, leaving many technical jobs unfilled.

- Because of its democratic reforms, Kyrgyzstan has received more per capita U.S. aid than any of the other ex-Soviet republics, and it has received an additional $240 million from the World Bank.

- Kyrgyzstan and Tajikistan entered into a dispute over the boundaries of the Isfara Valley in the late 1990s.

BUSINESS PRACTICES

Hours of Business

Business offices are open from 8:00 a.m. to 5:00 p.m. and food stores are open from 7:00 a.m. to 8:00 p.m.

Dress

Men wear western-style clothing, but they also wear a *kolpak* (a traditional white wool pointed hat), which protects the wearer's head and is a national patriotic symbol as well. The high point of the *kolpak* represents the mountains.

Introductions

Business cards are exchanged, and it is advisable to have cards printed in Russian on one side and in English on the other.

The Kyrgyz greet each other with the standard greeting of *Salamatsyzby* (Hello) and a handshake. Adult men greet each other with *Assalamu alikum* (Peace be upon you). The correct response is *Waalaikum assalaam* (And peace be upon you also).

Women in business greet each other with a handshake, while older women embrace each other and kiss. A Kyrgyz woman bows to an older man, particularly to her husband's relatives.

When addressing an older person by his/her first name, you should add the patronymic (father's first name with the suffix *-ovich* for son or *-ovna* for daughter). For example, if a man's name is Vladimir son of Ivan, he would be addressed as Vladimir Ivanovich, or if a woman's name is Maria daughter of Yuri, she would be addressed as Maria Yurinova.

Another custom is to greet a person by his/her father's first name followed by *uulu* (son) or *kyzy* (daughter) and then by the person's own given name, for example, Kadyrbek uulu Ulan (Kadyrbek's son, Ulan).

Special titles such as *Agai* or *Baikay* (older brother) or *Ejay* (older sister) are used with the title placed at the end (e.g., Salamatsyzby, Gulsara Ejay).

Kosh (Good-bye) or *Rakhmat* (Thank you) are customarily said when departing.

Meetings

Traditionally, personal relations have been considered more important than time schedules. This attitude is changing, however, with the newest generation of bankers, students and merchants.

Tours of facilities and factories are common at initial meetings.

Usually, all officials who are involved in your business negotiations will attend one large meeting rather than having many separate meetings. Often, however, only the senior person will speak.

Business meetings often lead to invitations to meals. These meals can last many hours and include countless courses and many toasts.

Negotiating

Kyrgyz culture places a high value on establishing social relationships during business negotiations. Casual and extended conversation over tea or a long dinner is an important part of conducting business.

Two of the major industries in Kyrgzstan are agriculture (cotton and tobacco) and mining (gold, antimony, uranium, coal and natural gas).

Entertaining

The Kyrgyz are known for their hospitality. A guest is given *tapochki* (slippers) upon removing his/her shoes when entering a room.

Fruit, books, candy or items with your company's logo are all appropriate business gifts.

When invited to someone's home, it is advisable not to arrive before noon.

The Kyrgyz are, for the most part, Sunni Muslim, and the consumption of alcohol and pork is strictly prohibited by Muslim law. Nevertheless, many Kyrgyz families drink alcohol.

Kyrgyz families eat three meals a day together, as their schedule allows. The farthest seat facing the entrance is reserved for the most honored individual. Women sit with their legs tucked under, or folded to the side and covered by their skirts.

Many popular Kyrgyz dishes consist of *nahn* (flat bread) served with lamb, carrots, onions and garlic. Commonly eaten vegetables are potatoes, tomatoes, cucumbers, carrots, peppers and squash, and among fruits, grapes, melons and apples are common. *Chai* (tea) is served in *piallas* (bowls) with every meal.

SOCIAL VALUES, CUSTOMS AND TIPS

The two major dialects of Kyrgyz are northern and southern Kyrgyz, but various regional dialects are also spoken.

The Kyrgyz are soft-spoken, hospitable and courteous people.

Family ties are very strong. The nuclear family includes husband and wife, brothers and sisters, children and grandparents. The elderly are cared for at home and are greatly respected. The Kyrgyz business, social and political network is structured along extended family lines. The family network structure is often referred to as "tribalism" and is gradually changing to include non-family members.

Socializing occurs at home or in the office, but never in a restaurant. There are several types of homes ranging from modest single-family dwellings or apartments to *bohzooi* or *yurtas* (round tents).

Community life in rural areas centers on daily prayers at the mosque, where local celebrations, festivals and religious activities all take place.

The Kyrgyz enjoy a variety of sports. They engage in *Aht Chabysh* (long-distance races), *Dzhorgosalysh* (betting races), *Oodarysh* (wrestling on horseback), *Tyin Enmei* (falconry on horseback) and *Kyz Dzharysh* (girls' races).

It is important to wash one's hands before meals. Everyone eats from a common plate located in the center of the floor or the table. Rural families may eat from a communal dish *pa kirghizi* (without utensils).

Pointing with one's finger is considered impolite. Gestures to call someone, to point or to beckon are made with the entire hand.

Blowing one's nose in public, chewing gum, yelling and yawning are all considered impolite.

During the winter, men generally wear a *tumak* (Russian fur hat). A *tebetei* (fur hat decorated with a fox tail) was once commonly worn. Though this style has become expensive, it is still very popular.

Traditional Kyrgyz clothing (colorful silk dresses and head scarves) are worn by women in rural areas. Silver jewelry is preferred over gold because it is closer in color to white, and it is believed that the color white brings good luck. The Kyrgyz also believe that silver protects against misfortune.

Most people who live in rural areas do not own cars because of the cost of fuel. Instead, they walk or ride donkeys, horses or horse-drawn carts. Buses run between major cities, and many areas are connected by train.

Urban areas have a network of telephones, but they are often unreliable. Most people own a television and a radio, but broadcasts are received from neighboring countries.

The national holidays include New Year's Day (January 1), *Orozo Ait* (feast at the end of Ramadan), International Women's Day (March 8), Victory Day (May 9, for the end of World War II), *Kurban Ait* (Day of Remembrance), Independence Day (September 9), Constitution Day (May 5), Christmas (January 7) and Easter.

LATVIA

Population: 2,385,396 (July 1998 est.); Latvian 56.5%, Russian 30.4%, Byelorussian 4.3%, Ukarainian 2.8%, Polish 2.6%, other 3.4%

Languages: Lettish (official), Lithuanian, Russian, other

Religions: Lutheran, Roman Catholic, Russian Orthodox

Currency: lat

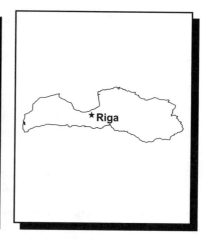

HISTORICAL OVERVIEW

- The people living along the southern shores of the Baltic have occupied the area of present-day Latvia for more than 2,000 years. In the ninth century, the Vikings established control in the region.

- The Baltic people continued their pagan religion for many centuries. A Christianizing effort by German missionaries in the 12th and 13th centuries was followed by invasions of crusading knights. The most significant of these was the invasion of the Teutonic Knights, who conquered the area of present-day Latvia in 1225. For the next three centuries the Germans functioned as a landowning class ruling over Latvian peasant serfs.

- The spread of the Protestant Reformation in the 16th century led to the conversion of Latvian serfs to Lutheranism. Latvia was partitioned between Poland and Sweden from the mid 16th to the early 18th century.

- Peter the Great defeated the Swedes in the early 18th century and gained control in the region. By the end of the century all of Latvia was under Russian rule. The Russians industrialized the region and fostered the spread of the Orthodox Church.

- In the early 20th century Latvian nationalism grew. By 1905, illegal nationalist political parties were operating. When World War I broke out, these parties at first supported the Russian war effort, but then became dissatisfied and began pressing for their own governments. The Bolshevik Revolution further alienated the Baltic peoples. They were able to withstand both the Bolshevik threat as well as the threat of German annexation, however. In August 1920, the Bolsheviks signed a treaty recognizing Latvia's independence. Latvia moved toward a totalitarian regime in the 1920s as the economic situation worsened and the premier, Karlis Ulmanis, argued convincingly that he needed additional powers to defend Latvian democracy.

- Latvia was weakened by this totalitarian turn, and in 1939, the German-Soviet Nonaggression Pact stipulated that Latvia and the Soviet Union would provide each other mutual assistance. A year later the Red Army invaded and noncommunist parties were outlawed. A program of agricultural collectivism was begun. Extreme Russification was imposed and many Latvians were deported under Stalin. Over the next 35 years, the Soviets tried to integrate Latvia into the union. Branch factories were located in the area, education was restructured to include Soviet indoctrination and non-Baltic nationalists were relocated to Latvia.

- Latvians were among the earliest supporters of *glasnost* (Gorbachev's program of reform and liberalization). The Popular Front of Latvia (PFL) won 75 percent of Latvia's 1989 elections to the USSR Congress of People's Deputies. The move toward independence was at first resisted by Gorbachev, but negative international reaction, coupled with mounting pressure from all the Baltic Republics, led to the recognition of Latvian independence in 1991. Since then, there has been tension and debate over the position of the substantial Russian ethnic minority in Latvian society.

- Parliamentary elections in 1995 produced a heavily fragmented assembly with nine political blocs. Although the political scene was unstable, Latvia made significant progress in moving toward a market economy.

- In January 1997, Prime Minister Skele resigned, but was then renominated by President Ulmanus.

- In 1998, the presidents of Latvia, Lithuania and Estonia signed an agreement with the United States strengthening their position with a view to NATO and EU membership.

BUSINESS PRACTICES

Hours of Business

Office hours are typically 9:00 a.m. to 6:00 p.m., Monday through Friday. Many shops are open late, some until 11:00 p.m. There are quite a few 24-hour convenience stores.

Dress

During the winter it is advisable to wear extremely warm business clothing. Be aware that in the winter the days are very short and there is not much daylight.

Introductions

The word used for greeting in Latvia on formal and informal occasions is *Sveicinati* (Hello). The Italian word *Ciao* (meaning "Hello") is used quite often, though only among good friends and on informal occasions.

Shaking hands upon meeting is customary.

Latvians love flowers, and they are typically given during the first welcome meeting at the airport. They are also regarded as an essential part of a present on important occasions and celebrations.

Latvian businesspeople usually have business cards printed in Latvian on one side and English on the other.

Meetings

Appointments should be made in advance.

Negotiating

Presentations should be precise, detailed and straightforward. Efforts to be diplomatic may be misunderstood as hesitation or dissatisfaction with negotiations.

Contracts can be verbal, especially if the matter is relatively minor. Expect to be held to your word if you have assented verbally.

Many Latvians in business speak English or German. These languages are considered appropriate for official business, so do not hesitate to use them.

Negotiations usually begin immediately, without introductory social conversation. Conversations about family, culture, country, etc. should be left for after the working day.

If you are not very familiar with your Latvian business partner, it is wise to avoid conversations or correspondence in Russian. This may be construed as a lack of respect for Latvia's own culture and an offensive reminder of the Soviet Union's occupation of the country. Latvians usually prefer to talk about their future rather than their past.

Before World War II, Latvia had a well-established European business culture. Now that the Soviet Union has been dissolved and Latvia has been liberated, it is going through a reintegration process into the European Community. As a result, the business culture is European with strong influences from the Soviet era.

Latvians are traditionally known for their diplomatic skills.

Since corruption from the Soviet era has not been totally eliminated, reassure yourself that those with whom you are doing business are legitimate so that your deal can be completed.

It is advisable to have extremely clear and detailed contracts drawn up since regulations concerning business contracts have only recently been instituted, and new contracts are often used as tests of and guidelines for these regulations.

Entertaining

Depending on the situation, lunch may or may not include alcohol. It is polite to take a taste but it is not necessary to finish your glass.

Often, the Latvian business partner acting as host will pay for your accommodations, evening entertainment, etc. This should be regarded as hospitality. Keep in mind that Latvian businessmen visiting your country may expect similar treatment.

Restaurants begin serving lunch at about noon, and dinner is served after 6:00 p.m.

Service charges are usually included in the bill. Keep in mind that men's bathrooms are marked by a triangle pointing downwards and women's bathrooms by a triangle pointing upwards.

Latvians eat in the continental style, with the knife kept in the right hand and the fork in the left.

Local specialties include cabbage soup, grilled pork ribs, smoked fish and grey peas with fat.

Water is not customarily served with meals, but it will be brought if requested.

A popular liquor is Riga's Black Balsam, an herb concoction that can be consumed with small sips or used to make cocktails. Latvians are very proud of their brewing traditions. Local beers include Aldaris, Cesu Alus and Rigas Alus.

SOCIAL VALUES, CUSTOMS AND TIPS

Latvians are somewhat reserved at first but are generally very hospitable people. It is important to know that Latvians do not smile often, and so one should not misinterpret a serious expression as indicating dissatisfaction.

Cultural heritage, especially folklore, is a source of tremendous pride to Latvians. There are folk artists everywhere. One form of folk art is *daina*, a four-line song form that reflects the morals and lifestyle of Latvia's past. The Song Festival, held each year since 1873, features much choral singing and dancing and is an important symbol of Latvian nationalism.

During the existence of the Soviet Union, Latvians were the most frequent visitors to theaters, concerts and museums. Presently, due to economic difficulties, cultural life has decreased.

Extended families are found mostly in rural areas. One-third of all marriages are ethnically mixed.

Most Latvians consider themselves Nordic, though Eastern Latvians retain Polish and Russian cultural and linguistic influences.

Riga is home to one-third of the Latvian population. It is a diverse city, including large numbers of Russians, Ukrainians and Belorussians.

Evangelical Lutheranism and Roman Catholicism are the most widely practiced religions, but there are also sizable minorities of Russian Orthodox and Baptists.

The society is highly literate, with free and compulsory education until the age of 18.

All parts of Riga are accessible by public transportation.

Taxi drivers, room service personnel and others should be tipped according to the quality of service.

There are two types of days celebrated in Latvia: holidays and commemorative days. Holidays are usually observed by all Latvians and are official days off. Commemorative days acknowledge important events in history, but people generally work on these days.

The following days are official holidays: January 1 (New Year's Day), Good Friday, Easter, May 1 (Labor Day and anniversary of the Constitutional Convention of 1922), June 23-24 (Midsummer's Eve celebration), November 18 (Independence Day), December 25-26 (Christmas), December 31 (New Year's Eve).

The following are commemorative days: March 25 (commemorative day for victims of communist terror), May 8 (commemorative day for victims of WWII), 2nd Sunday in May (Mother's Day), June 14 (commemorative day for victims of the 1941 Soviet deportations), July 4 (commemorative day for victims of anti-Semitic genocide), November 11 (*Lacplesis Day* [Veterans' Day]).

LEBANON

Population: 3,505,794 (July 1998 est.); Arab 95 %, Armenian 4%, other 1%

Languages: Arabic (official), French (official), Armenian, English

Religions: Muslim 70%, Christian 30%

Currency: Lebanese pound

Beirut

HISTORICAL OVERVIEW

- Much of present-day Lebanon was the historic home of the Phoenicians, who arrived in the area around 3000 B.C. They soon linked Phoenicia both commercially and religiously to Egypt. Phoenicia was periodically invaded and controlled by other groups in the area including the Egyptians and the Assyrians.

- In 538 B.C., it was conquered by the Persians and then in 332 B.C. by the Greek Alexander the Great.

- Throughout most of the first millennium B.C. the city of Tyre was a great commercial center and trading post, but Alexander the Great's arrival put an end to Tyre's prominence. The Romans conquered Phoenicia and made it part of Syria in 64 B.C.

- Lebanon passed into Byzantine control, and in the sixth century A.D. a Christian group fleeing persecution in Syria settled in northern Lebanon, gained local converts and set up the Maronite church. Arab tribes, fleeing the Muslim conquest of Syria, settled in southern Lebanon in the seventh century. Four hundred years later many of them brought their beliefs together in the Druze religion. Many coastal villagers became Sunni Muslims.

- Between the 15th and 18th centuries Lebanon developed social and political institutions of its own, while at the same time European and especially French influence grew. Syria came under Ottoman control in 1516. Over the next several hundred years tensions between the Druze and Maronites escalated. After the 1860 massacre of Maronites the French intervened, forcing the Ottomans to set up an independent Christian province.

- During World War I Lebanon was given to France in the Sykes-Pilot Agreement, but it was not until 1923 that France gained total control of the country. The French withdrew in 1945, and Lebanon officially became independent the following year.

- According to an unwritten power-sharing agreement, Lebanon's president was a Maronite, the prime minister a Sunni Muslim and the speaker of the National Assembly a Shi'ite Muslim. This worked quite well for approximately two decades and Lebanon prospered. In 1958, however, Lebanon's Muslims staged an insurrection that was put down by the government with help from the U.S. Fuah Chebab was subsequently elected president. He helped restore peace and prosperity.

- As a result of the Arab-Israeli War of 1948-49, several hundred thousand Palestinian refugees came to southern Lebanon. Lebanon stayed out of Arab-Israeli conflicts initially, but in 1970 the Palestinian Liberation Organization (PLO) transferred its headquarters to Lebanon.

- The PLO then led attacks from its seat in Lebanon, causing the rift between Muslims and Christians to widen as the Christian-led Lebanese government tried to curb attacks while the PLO endorsed the Lebanese Muslims. By 1975 a civil war had begun.

- Fearful of Israeli intervention, Syria sent troops to help the government, but in 1982 Israel invaded in order to drive out the PLO. When Israel withdrew in 1985 the conflict was still unresolved, and parts of the country had been reduced to ruins by the long civil war.

- In 1988, General Michel Aoun came to power and attempted to end the militia fighting and Syrian occupation in Lebanon. He was replaced in 1989 by Elias Hrawi. Hrawi was able to gain sufficient control over Lebanon to improve daily life there. In 1990, 15 years of civil war finally came to an end.

- In 1992, Hrawi appointed Rafiq Hariri to the position of prime minister. Hariri worked to establish a stable business environment and make social services widely available once again. At the same time, Hariri allowed Syria to keep its stronghold on Lebanon.

- On 24 November 1998 General Emile Lahoud replaced Elias Hrawi as Lebanon's president.

BUSINESS PRACTICES

Hours of Business

Businesses and government offices traditionally keep separate hours in Lebanon. Businesses are usually open from 8:00 a.m. to 6:00 p.m. Government offices are open Monday through Saturday 8:00 a.m. to 1:00 p.m. June through October and 8:00 a.m. to 2:00 p.m. November through May.

Dress

Businessmen should wear a sports jacket and tie to all business engagements.

When attending a business dinner at a relatively expensive restaurant or hotel, guests are required to dress for dinner.

When sightseeing with your Lebanese business associates, casual business attire is acceptable.

Introductions

Handshaking is the typical form of greeting throughout Lebanon.

When offering your hand in introduction to a Lebanese woman, it is her choice whether to reciprocate or not.

Always present your business card when being introduced to your Lebanese associates.

Meetings

It is best to plan a business trip to Lebanon between October and December or February and June.

Appointments are necessary and courteous. Make them well in advance, and reconfirm upon arrival.

Negotiating

Lebanon is currently undergoing a massive reconstruction process to regain the strong economy it had before its 15-year civil war.

When working with a Lebanese Arab counterpart it is necessary to establish a strong personal relationship before discussing business affairs.

Patience and trust are two necessary factors for doing business in Lebanon. You must never rush your counterpart to make a decision and you must gain your counterpart's trust before a deal can be concluded.

Entertaining

When invited to a Lebanese home expect your hosts to be very hospitable. You should reciprocate the same level of hospitality if you want to be seen as a viable business partner and friend.

When invited to a Lebanese home for dinner it is appropriate to bring a small gift. Present the gift with both hands. Do not expect it to be opened in front of you.

Always try to accept and eat the food given to you by your Lebanese host, at least until the third helping is offered.

Always use the right hand to eat.

Some national Lebanese dishes included *kibbe* with *burghul* (lamb or fish paste served with cracked wheat), *meza* (a series of up to 40 hors d'oeuvres served simultaneously) and *lahmmishwi* (lamb, peppers, onions and tomatoes). Many dishes are served with rice and vegetables. Fruit is always served at the end of a meal.

Due to the large Muslim population in Lebanon, alcohol is not available throughout the country.

When going out to dinner, your Lebanese counterpart will often insist on paying the restaurant bill. A tip of between ten to 15 percent is expected only in restaurants.

Going to nightclubs or the movies are popular activities among those living in Beirut.

SOCIAL VALUES, CUSTOMS AND TIPS

Many Lebanese dress in western style but maintain their traditional values.

Many Lebanese practice the Maronite religion, a form of Christianity with strong ties to the Roman Catholic Church.

Education is highly valued in Lebanon, and educated women do not follow the traditional roles of women practiced throughout the Middle East. In some parts of Lebanon, however, gender roles are strictly defined.

Religion and politics are not good topics of conversation.

Allowing the soles of your feet to be seen by another is a sign of disrespect.

Lebanese men will always stand when a woman enters a room and will allow her to enter a room first when arriving together.

When conversing with a Lebanese always have good posture and refrain from having your hands in your pockets.

Souks, traditional outdoor markets, can be found throughout Lebanon. Popular purchases for foreigners include gold and silver jewelry, cutlery, kaftans, *abays* (embroidered evening wear) and copper goods. There are also many western shops that are open Monday to Saturday 8:00 a.m. to 7:00 p.m.

Along Lebanon's Mediterranean coast, water sports are very popular along with skiing in the mountains. Equestrian and football (soccer) events are quite common.

LIBYA

Population: 5,690,727 (July 1998 est.); Berber and Arab 97%, Greek, Maltese, Italian, Egyptian, Pakistani, Turkish, Indian and Tunisian 3%

Languages: Arabic, Italian, English

Religions: Sunni Muslim 97%

Currency: Libyan dinar

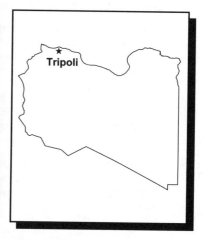

HISTORICAL OVERVIEW

- Modern-day Libya is comprised of three ancient regions: Cyrenaica, Tripolitania and Fezzan. In the seventh century B.C. both Phoenicians and Greeks settled in North Africa, including in present-day Libya. Trade routes were established and several cities built. The Romans conquered the area during the first century B.C., and once their empire collapsed the Byzantines took control.

- Muslim Arabs took over the region beginning in the seventh century. Tripolitania was ruled by Berber Almohads from Morocco, and Cyrenaica was ruled by Egypt.

- In the 16th century the Ottoman Turks united the three regions of Libya into one country ruled from Tripoli. In 1911 Libya was invaded by Italy and the Italians remained in control of the country until 1942. After World War II the country was divided into French and British allied zones. Libya became an independent state in 1951 under King Irdis I. King Irdis was a monarch from the Sanusiyah Islamic religious order, established in 1837, which had considerable influence on Libyan politics in the late 19th and early 20th centuries.

- The discovery of oil in 1959 brought wealth to the Libyan monarchy. In 1963, a new constitution was ratified, but in 1969 Lt. Muammar al-Qadhafi led a successful military coup against King Irdis I on the platform of Arab unity.

- Qadhafi has attempted to form alliances with almost all of the Arab nations but has been unsuccessful. In 1976 he annexed part of northern Chad and supported the rebellion in that nation. With France's help, Chad was able to expel the Libyans. In 1977 Libya and Egypt came into conflict.

- Since 1979 Libyan and Western European relations have remained strained. During the Cold War Libya was a large supplier of hard currency to the Soviet Union and its allies in exchange for weapons.

- Since taking power Qadhafi's government has initiated several terrorist bombings in Europe. For his militant actions in the Mediterranean and in response to various terrorist attacks, the U.S. carried out numerous air strikes against Libya in the 1980s.

- Beginning in the late 1980s, Qadhafi seemed to be adopting a more conciliatory stance toward the West and other Arab nations. In 1989, Libya became a member of the Union of the Arab Maghreb.

BUSINESS PRACTICES

Hours of Business

Business is normally conducted from 7:00 a.m. to 2:00 p.m. Saturday through Thursday in the summer. During the rest of the year, business hours are generally 8:00 a.m. to 1:00 p.m. and 4:00 p.m. to 6:30 p.m.

Dress

A dress shirt is acceptable for men doing business in Libya during the summer. Suits are worn in the winter and at all formal occasions.

Businesswomen should dress very conservatively and should keep their heads and arms covered when visiting holy sites.

Introductions

All government officials should be referred to as "Your Excellency."

Business cards are an important part of all business introductions. Have all business cards printed in Arabic on one side and in your native language on the other side.

Meetings

Appointments are required for all business meetings in Libya.

It is best not to schedule a business meeting during the Muslim month of Ramadan when businesses are closed during the day for religious observance.

Negotiating

Business may be conducted in English, but all documents must also be drawn up in Arabic for them to be official.

Entertaining

In restaurants it is customary to eat with one's hands, using the right hand only. Utensils are available upon request, however.

A tip of between ten and 20 percent will be included in both your restaurant and hotel bills.

Islamic law prohibits the consumption of alcohol or pork products. Both are prohibited throughout Libya.

During the fasting month of Ramadan it is not appropriate for visitors to eat, drink, or smoke in public between dawn and dusk.

Cinemas are a popular form of entertainment in Tripoli.

SOCIAL VALUES, CUSTOMS AND TIPS

Women have a very traditional role in Libya and are not an active part of the business world.

Islamic rule pervades the customs and culture of all Libyans.

It is disrespectful to point the soles of your feet at others.

Souks, traditional outdoor markets, can be found throughout Libya.

Swimming, tennis, golf, bowling, horse racing and football are all popular sports in Libya.

Photography is prohibited in Libya.

The smuggling of alcohol into Libya is a crime punishable by death.

Libyan holidays include Evacuation Day (March 28), Evacuation Day (June 11), Revolution Day (SPLAS [September 1]) and Evacuation Day (October 7) in addition to the regular Islamic holidays.

LITHUANIA

Population: 3,600,158 (July 1998 est.); Lithuanian 80.6%, Russian 8.7%, Polish 7%, Byelorussian 1.6%, other 2.1%

Languages: Lithuanian (official), Russian, Polish

Religions: Roman Catholic (majority), Russian Orthodox, Lutheran, Protestant, Evangelical Christian Baptist, Muslim, Jewish

Currency: litas

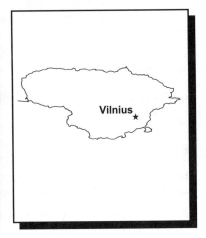

HISTORICAL OVERVIEW

- In 1236, Duke Minaugas first united the lands then inhabited by the Lithuanians, the Yatwingians and the Couronians to form the Grand Duchy of Lithuania.

- In the 14th century, the state was ruled by strong monarchs who annexed neighboring lands. By 1323, Vilnius was the capital. In 1386, in response to a serious threat from Germanic invaders, the Grand Duke of Lithuania married the Polish crown princess, uniting Lithuania and Poland. This allowed them to defeat the German (Teutonic) invaders in 1410.

- For the next 400 years Poland and Lithuania remained closely allied with one another, Poland being the dominant member of the union. The Lithuanians adopted Roman Catholicism and began to adopt western culture. The association between Poland and Lithuania was solidified in 1569 with the Lublin Union.

- After a gradual partition of the Polish-Lithuanian state (in 1772, 1793 and 1795) by its neighbors, Lithuania came under the control of the Russian Empire. A number of attempts to gain independence in the 19th century proved unsuccessful.

- Germany occupied Lithuania in World War I. But in 1917, after the Russian Revolution, the Germans allowed Lithuania to elect its own officials, who then declared Lithuania an independent state in 1918.

- In January 1919, the Russian Red Army invaded. Determined to regain sovereignty, the Lithuanians drove most of the Soviets out by mid-1919. Simultaneously, Poland sought to regain all territory it had claimed before 1795, including Lithuania, and was fighting the Soviets. In response, Lithuania signed a peace treaty with the Soviets that recognized Vilnius as Lithuania's. The treaty was also signed with Poland, which was to give up its claim to the region. Nevertheless, the Polish army seized Vilnius, and Kaunas became the capital of Lithuania.

- From 1920 to 1940, Lithuania was an independent and prosperous nation. After invading Poland in 1939, the Soviets began to tighten their grip on Lithuania and, by 1940, occupied the nation. Armed partisan fighters, called "Forest Brothers," fought unsuccessfully for independence between 1940 and 1954. Lithuania suffered mass deportations, because of the Nazi occupation and Stalin's purges. When relations within the Soviet Union relaxed in the 1960s, Lithuania continued to seek independence.

- In 1990, the freely elected legislature declared independence, and after the Soviet Union collapsed, Russia officially recognized Lithuania's independence. The government, led by the Sajudis political movement, implemented aggressive economic and political reforms. Yet the transition was slower than hoped and voters rejected the Sajudis in 1992 and voted instead for the former Communists. The new government was committed to democracy, but slowed privatization and other reform measures. In late 1993, the leaders effected a full withdrawal of Russian troops from the country.

- President Algirdas Brazauskas, of the Democratic Labor Party, was a nationalist who maintained, but slowed down, the transition to a market economy. Inflation caused the government to begin issuing currency based on the gold standard, which was modeled after that of neighboring Estonia.

- In 1996, Prime Minister Adolfas Slezevicius was asked to step down and was replaced by several different prime ministers in succession.

- In 1998, the presidents of Lithuania, Latvia and Estonia signed an agreement with the United States strengthening their position with a view to NATO and EU membership.

BUSINESS PRACTICES

Hours of Business

Businesses are open from 9:00 a.m. to 6:00 p.m. with an hour break for lunch at 1:00 p.m. Banks are open from 9:00 a.m. to noon.

Dress

Businesspeople generally dress conservatively.

During the winter it is advisable to wear extremely warm business clothing. Be aware that the days are very short in winter and there is not much daylight.

Lithuanians place importance on dressing neatly. Clothing styles are taken mainly from Europe and from the U.S. Hats are commonly worn in winter. Handmade clothes are often worn, especially in rural areas. Older rural women often wear scarves on their heads.

Introductions

It is customary to shake hands with men and, to some extent in business settings, with women when greeting. Men sometimes kiss the extended hand of women in greeting. Good friends of both sexes may kiss cheeks.

A handshake is almost always used with professional contacts.

When introducing a man, use the term *Ponas* (Mr.) before the last name. For a woman use the term *Ponia* (Mrs.) or *Panele* (Miss). When applicable, also use the professional title before the last name.

First names are not used among adults until an invitation to do so is extended.

Men raise their hats or nod to greet someone at a distance.

The most common phrases for greeting are *Laba diena* (Good day), *Labas rytas* (Good morning), *Labas vakaras* (Good evening), *Labas* (Hello) and *Sveikas* or *Sveiki* (How do you do?).

Meetings

Punctuality is expected at both business meetings and social visits.

Negotiating

Business is usually kept separate from socializing.

Keep in mind that, since the Lithuanian transition from communism to a free market system in 1992, business has generally operated along free market lines with state coordination only in key areas.

It is good policy to assure yourself of the legitimacy of the business with which you are negotiating since not all firms have been set up with complete legal backing.

It is advisable to have extremely clear and detailed contracts drawn up since business regulations have only been recently instituted and new contracts are often used as tests of and guidelines for these regulations.

Entertaining

Because of the limited public space for social engagements outside the home, entertaining in Lithuanian homes is popular.

Dinner guests often bring flowers and wine as gifts to the host. Unwrap the flowers before presenting them. White flowers are usually reserved for brides.

For even a brief visit, one should bring flowers, but be sure to bring an odd number of them. Your host will be offended if you bring an even number of flowers (appropriate only when there is a death in the family). Be aware that carnations are associated with mourning.

Guests are always offered refreshments, which may be coffee or tea and cake or cookies.

In formal situations, guests wait to sit down until they are invited to do so or until the host sits.

The length of an evening visit will depend on the occasion. The host may accompany a guest outside when he/she leaves if the hour is late.

It is considered impolite to leave food on your plate; it implies that the food was not good.

Tipping has not been customary, but is becoming more common.

The continental style of eating is used, with the knife kept in the right hand and the fork in the left.

The midday meal (dinner) is the main meal of the day. Most businesses close for the meal and people either go home or eat at worksite canteens.

Toasting is common at dinner and at supper.

Lithuanian specialties include smoked sausage and *cepelinai* (meat cooked inside a ball of potato dough, served with a special sauce). Soup and local fruits and vegetables often accompany meals. Rye bread and dairy products are eaten regularly.

SOCIAL VALUES, CUSTOMS AND TIPS

Lithuanian is the country's official language. Most Lithuanians also speak Russian, however, and English is becoming popular.

Lithuanians are proud of their heritage, except for the period under the Soviet Union. Lithuania only completed its transition from communism in October 1992. Many people are frustrated with the current transition and uncertain about the future.

Lithuanians are somewhat reserved, but are sincere and full of emotion. They mask their feelings to maintain privacy. Lithuanians are often openly critical of public institutions. They are also very self-critical. They are generally optimistic, patient and hardworking, however.

Lithuanians appreciate skill, intelligence and punctuality. They value education, family and loyalty to one's nationality.

Spontaneous visits are not common, even between friends and neighbors. Unannounced guests will be welcomed, however.

Visiting, gardening, watching television and attending cultural events are the most common leisure activities.

It is impolite to talk with your hands in your pockets.

Using the hands a great deal during conversation or using hand gestures instead of speech is generally inappropriate.

Eye contact is important during conversation.

Adults should not chew gum in public.

Favorite sports in Lithuania include basketball and soccer.

LUXEMBOURG

Population: 425,017 (July 1998 est.); Celtic base (with French and German blend), Portuguese, Italian and other European immigrants

Languages: Luxembourgish (official), German (official), French, English

Religions: Roman Catholic 97%, Protestant and Jewish 3%

Currency: Luxembourg franc, euro

Luxembourg
★

HISTORICAL OVERVIEW

- Luxembourg formed part of both the Roman and the Carolingian empires. In 963, Count Siegfried of the Ardennes built a castle in present-day Luxembourg and founded the Luxembourg dynasty, making the area independent. He built an impregnable fortress that some called the "Gibraltar of the North." In fact, the word "Luxembourg" means "little fortress."

- The domain of Luxembourg was increased in subsequent years through marriage, treaties, conquests and inherited lands. Charles Luxembourg became the king of Bohemia in the 14th century and strove to make Prague (now in the Czech Republic) as beautiful as Paris. In the same century, Luxembourg's duke, Henry VII, was crowned Holy Roman Emperor.

- In 1441, the region was conquered by the Duke of Burgundy and, subsequently, was ruled by foreign powers for more than four centuries. After the War of Spanish Succession in 1714, the Austrian Hapsburg family ruled Luxembourg. At the Congress of Vienna in 1815 Luxembourg was made a Grand Duchy in the Dutch kingdom.

- In 1830, the Luxembourgers supported the Belgians in their revolt against Dutch control. After the revolt, the French-speaking western part was made part of Belgium, and the rest of Luxembourg remained under Dutch rule.

- In 1867, the Treaty of London declared Luxembourg (the part that had come under the control of the Netherlands) an independent neutral state. Under the international agreement, according to which Luxembourg was to remain neutral and unarmed, the powerful battlements that Count Siegfried had built into the cliffs where Luxembourg's present capital city is located were destroyed.

- Once independent, Luxembourg began tapping into its iron ore and developed a great steel industry. Luxembourg continued to maintain close ties with the Netherlands.

- Although a neutral nation, Luxembourg was invaded by Germany in both World Wars. Luxembourg served an important part in the "Battle of the Bulge" in the Ardennes forest when General Omar Bradley of the allied forces used Luxembourg City as the allied headquarters for the battle. After its liberation, Luxembourg ended its neutrality and joined the Western European alliances, including NATO, in 1949.

- In 1957, Luxembourg was one of the six founders of the European Economic Community (EEC).

- In 1964, the Grand Duchess Charlotte abdicated, allowing her son, Grand Duke Jean, to become the country's ruler. He has proven to be a very popular monarch. Since that time, Luxembourg has enjoyed peace, economic growth and beneficial relations with other European nations.

- After Switzerland, Luxembourg has the highest per capita GDP in the world and the highest GDP of all EU nations.

- Jean-Claude Juncker was elected Luxembourg's prime minister in 1995. In the second half of 1997 Luxembourg held the EU presidency. Luxembourg also hosts many EU meetings and conferences, and houses the Secretariat for the European Parliament, the European Coal and Steel Community (ECSC), the European Court of Justice, the European Audit Court, the European Investment Bank and the European Currency Union.

BUSINESS PRACTICES

Hours of Business

Customary business hours are from 8:30 a.m. to 5:30 p.m., Monday through Friday. Some shops and recreational facilities are open longer.

Dress

Men should wear business suits with well-polished shoes. Women can wear either suits or dresses.

Introductions

A gentle handshake is appropriate when greeting acquaintances or meeting someone for the first time.

Close female friends will sometimes hug each other three times as well as kiss each other on the cheek three times.

Common greetings include *Moien* (Morning), *Gudden Owend* (Good evening) and *Wéi geet et?* (How are you?). The French *Bonjour* (Good day) is also used.

Luxembourgers tend to be reserved with strangers but are loyal and affectionate with their friends. Acquaintances use titles and surnames while friends and relatives use given names or nicknames. High-ranking persons may be greeted using more than one title, such as *Här* Minister (Mr. Minister).

Always present business cards upon being introduced in a business environment.

Meetings

Make contact with your Luxembourg counterpart well in advance and allow them to suggest a meeting time. If an appointment is scheduled for 11:30 a.m. expect it to be over lunch.

If you must schedule an appointment, never schedule one on a Saturday or Monday through Friday before 2:30 p.m.

Negotiating

First meetings are normally for acquaintance purposes only; usually negotiations do not begin until the second meeting.

It is appropriate to bring a business gift for your Luxembourg associates or counterparts.

Entertaining

When dining in a restaurant, service is normally included in the bill. An extra tip is not necessary but is appreciated. If service is not included, then it is customary to leave a ten to 15 percent tip.

Most restaurants serve German-style food. Menus are usually written in French and German.

Luxembourgers often visit friends and relatives at home, but rarely without notice. Dinner guests bring flowers, chocolates or a bottle of wine to their hosts. Among younger people, it is common for the guests to bring dessert.

Hosts expect guests to ask for second helpings and some cooks believe that the food has not been enjoyed if guests do not ask for seconds.

Traditionally, the main meal of the day is lunch, but dinner has become the main meal for those whose work does not allow them to return home to take a long lunch.

Guests are not usually invited to a home to discuss business. This is done in public places such as restaurants, cafés and offices.

Popular dishes are *Judd mat Gaardebounen* (smoked collar of pork with broad beans), *Bouneschlupp* (bean soup), *Kachkéis* (a soft cheese), *Quetschentaart* (plum tart), *Fritten Ham an Zalot* (french fries, ham and salad), *Träipen* (black pudding) and freshwater fish (usually trout). Sausages, potatoes and sauerkraut are important parts of the diet.

The continental style of eating is used, with the fork in the left hand and the knife remaining in the right hand.

It is impolite to rest your hands in your lap during a meal. Belching at the table is also unacceptable.

SOCIAL VALUES, CUSTOMS AND TIPS

Although the native language is Luxembourgish, German is often used for newspapers and French is the official language of the civil service, law and Parliament. English is also widely understood.

Luxembourgers, an ethnic mix of French and German origins, account for about 75 percent of the population. The rest consists of guest and worker residents, primarily from Portugal, France and Italy.

Although Luxembourgers descend from various nationalities, they have a strong feeling of national pride that is reflected in their national motto, *Mir wëlle bleiwe wat mer sin!* (We want to remain what we are!).

Through invasion and through peaceful exchange, Belgium, France and Germany have all influenced the customs of Luxembourg. Yet, there are ways in which Luxembourg is distinct from its neighbors. For example, the pace of life is not as hurried as it is in neighboring countries. Still, Luxembourgers are hardworking and productive.

Family ties are strong. Parents are legally required to pay for their children's education and adult children must meet certain financial obligations to their parents if they are in need.

The nightlife is modest, even on weekends. There are a few well-patronized pubs in the capital and the neighborhood café is often a hub of social activity.

Luxembourgers are reserved in public; it is impolite to yawn, shout or use offensive language. Luxembourgers are attentive to neatness and cleanliness in their dress and overall appearance.

The education system is well developed and the literacy rate is 99 percent.

National holidays include New Year's Day, Labor Day (May 1), the Grand Duke's Birthday – also called National Day (June 23) – and Fair Day (early September). Fair Day occurs in an ancient shepherds' market and focuses on shepherding. Religious holidays include Shrove Tuesday (February), Easter (including Monday), Ascension, Whitmonday, Assumption (August 15), All Saints' Day (November 1), All Souls' Day (November 2) and Christmas (December 24-26).

MALAYSIA

Population: 20,932,901 (July 1998 est.); Malay and other indigenous peoples 58%, Chinese 26%, Indian 7%, other 9%

Languages: Malay, English, Tamil, other

Religions: Muslim 53%, Buddhist 17%, Chinese folk-religions 12%, Hindu 7%, Christian 6%, other 5%

Currency: ringgit

HISTORICAL OVERVIEW

- Malaysia has two different and distinct land regions: the Malaysia Peninsula and East Malaysia, which are located on the island of Borneo.

- At the time when Indian adventurers first arrived in the second or third centuries A.D., small Malayan kingdoms already existed in Malaya (present-day Malaysia). India exercised cultural and political influence over Malaya for over 1,000 years.

- In the 15th century, Sumatran exiles founded the city-state of Malacca under Chinese protection. It flourished as a center for trade and Islam, but in 1511 it was captured by the Portuguese, who ended its golden age.

- The Dutch followed the Portuguese in 1641, and were, in turn, followed by the British, who acquired the island of Penang in 1786. In the meantime, new immigrants from Sumatra in the late 17th century brought a matrilineal culture with them and 18th-century immigrants from the island of Celebes established two sultanates of their own. By 1795, the British had taken over most of the Malay peninsula's west coast. Chinese immigrants began coming to the territories in the late 19th century. By the early 20th century, Britain had gained control of all the Malay states, including those on Borneo, as colonies or protectorates.

- The British developed the region as a center for the rubber industry.

- The Japanese occupied Malaya during World War II. When the British attempted to organize Malaya into a single state after World War II, Malayan nationalism was born.

- The United Malays National Organization (UMNO) was formed to agitate for independence. And in 1948, the predominantly Chinese Communist Party of Malaya began a 12-year guerilla war against the British. Attempts to mitigate the strength of the communist insurgency failed until the British addressed social ills in the country. In 1957, with the struggle abating, Britain granted Malaya independence.

- Six years later the Federation of Malaya and the former British colonies of Singapore, Sarawak and North Borneo (Sabah) united with Malay to become Malaysia. Tension between the Malay-dominated government in Malaya and the Chinese-dominated government in Singapore led to the creation of an independent Singapore in 1965.

- The government subsequently advocated the cause of national unity by attempting to make Malay culture the dominant, official one. Government attempts to increase Malay wealth and power, as well the rise of Islam, led to concern and protests among other ethnic groups in the country.

- Ethnic tensions persisted throughout the 1970s and 1980s. The UMNO remained in power throughout most of this period.

- In 1981 Mahathir bin Mohammed became prime minister, and in 1988 he took advantage of a split in the UMNO to create a new party, the UMNO Baru.

- By 1988 Malaysia had developed a prosperous, diversified economy and literacy rates had risen dramatically. In addition, the growing middle class was becoming ethnically ever more diverse.

- Politics in Sarawak and Sabah (East Malaysia) proved turbulent in the 1980s, with ethnic tensions heightened by a rise in Islamic fundamentalism.

- In 1993, Anwar Ibrahim was elected deputy president of UMNO thus making him heir apparent to Mahathir. Since he is an East Malaysian, he made those in Mahathir's government uneasy.

- In 1994, the radical Islamic al-Arquam sect, which had recruited possibly up to 100,000 Malaysians, was prohibited from holding public meetings and disseminating information.

- In the second half of the 1990s Malaysia faced serious environmental pollution. Its three main rivers were polluted, its rain forest was shrinking and forest fires in Indonesia in 1997 caused a dangerous haze to settle over the country.

- Malaysia was hit hard by the Asian economic crisis, which came to a head in 1998. Political tensions in the country grew over the IMF bailout. In addition, a Malaysian petroleum company signed contracts with foreign companies to look for off-shore oil.

BUSINESS PRACTICES

There are three distinct cultures in Malaysia – Malay, Chinese and Indian. The official religion is Islam, although the Chinese population is mostly Buddhist and the Indians mostly Hindu. Each culture has its own social, business and greeting customs. As a result, the best guideline is to follow the example of your host and others around you.

Hours of Business

Businesses are generally open from 8:30 a.m. to 5:00 p.m., Monday through Friday. Some businesses are open on Saturday. In many cases, businesses close for one hour at lunch.

Dress

Appropriate business dress is a jacket, a long-sleeved shirt, a tie and trousers for men. Light fabrics will add to your comfort. Because of the climate, jackets are not necessary, except for meetings with high government officials or at receptions. Women wear modest light short-sleeved dresses. Women should not wear slacks, shorts or sleeveless dresses and should avoid loud or garish colors or patterns.

Since it rains very frequently in Malaysia, it is advisable to bring appropriate rain gear, such as an umbrella.

Introductions

Generally, a simple, not overly firm handshake is the customary greeting. A lengthy greeting is a sign of an old friendship.

Women should be greeted with a nod and a smile. Chinese people of both sexes will shake hands, but Malays and Indians will not. If a Chinese woman wishes to shake hands, she will extend her hand first. Handshakes between men and women are particularly rare among members of the older generation. Generally, if you are a businessman, avoid initiating contact with Malaysian businesswomen, but you may shake a woman's hand if she offers it. If you are a businesswoman, nod and smile.

Malays will often bow slightly when greeting others. Men may engage in a salaam ritual, in which they offer both hands outstretched, touch each other's hands and then bring them back to touch their own chests.

Indians may greet you with the *namaste* (placing the hands in a prayer-like position, chest high and bowing slightly).

Using "Mr." and "Mrs." is appropriate in addressing others. Titles are often used, as in the case of the prime minister, who presents himself as "Dr. Mahathir Mohammed," but is referred to as "Mr. Prime Minister."

In traditional Malaysian names, the family name comes first. For example, "Osman bin Mohammed" would be called "Mr. Osman."

You can address a Moslem man as *Encik* or a woman as *Cik*, followed by the individual's name, to show respect.

A common greeting is *Salamut pagi* (Good morning). A more casual greeting is *Halo* (Hello).

Meetings

At the first business meeting, it is customary to present business cards to all in attendance. Remember that visitors should handle or receive papers, cards and samples with the right hand only.

It is best to schedule meetings at least two weeks in advance.

Small talk and the exchange of personal information will most likely dominate the conversation at the first meeting. Do not be surprised if you are questioned about your health, family or children. Wives, however, are not an acceptable conversation topic.

Include enough time in your itinerary to schedule a second business meeting with your Malaysian counterpart since business is not concluded after an initial meeting.

Be prepared for frequent interruptions during a business meeting. Some of these interruptions may even include calling participants out of the meeting to see superiors or to answer the phone. It is important to maintain a good sense of humor throughout the process.

Strict punctuality is not valued by Malaysians. You may find yourself waiting, perhaps for as long as half an hour, for your appointment. Therefore, it is important to be patient. Punctuality is expected, however, and scheduling appointments is advisable. It is best to arrive on time as a sign of reliability and practicality.

The best time to schedule appointments is usually after 2:30 p.m.

Negotiating

Respect is extremely important among Malaysians. Malays recognize rank and status when dealing with each other. In their own language, they carefully differentiate status by using special terminology or honorific terms. Visitors are expected to show respect, if not outright humility, toward the host.

Be careful not to appear condescending to your Malaysian business counterparts. Never underestimate their knowledge of any topic.

In Malaysian business negotiations, human relations are integrated into the bargaining process and weigh heavily in business transactions. When Malays field a team of negotiators, they enjoy the cooperative effort involved, which can overshadow their competitive interests or their desire for economic gain.

Negotiations are conducted in a spirit of friendship, civility and pleasantry. Be aware, however, that Malays can appear manipulative, and they will take offense at the slightest loss of self-esteem, which can present a challenging situation for the visitor. It is more important to get along than to be effective.

During business conversations, the host may serve nonalcoholic beverages. It is best to accept this sign of hospitality by drinking at least some of the beverage offered.

It is also quite acceptable to weave business and personal topics together. This will project a favorable image.

You will discover that a consensus has been reached by the enthusiastic response among lower-level negotiators. Actual notification will come from the decision maker at a higher level. Either party may propose drafting a written agreement. The deal is firm when both sides sign the contract.

Presentations should be complete. Take nothing for granted. An audio/visual presentation will be impressive to your Malaysian counterparts. Malay businesspeople are most likely to be impressed with projects that build their company's image or are proven concepts.

Build a trusting rapport with your Malay partners. It is of greater significance to them than a contract.

Always include an escape clause in your contract in case negotiations do not go as planned.

Although English is the most commonly spoken business language in Malaysia, it is best when negotiating with government officials to have a Bahasa Malay interpreter present.

Malaysians will never publicly disagree or say "No" to something. Instead, they will give an affirmative answer with exceptions or negative suggestions attached.

It is not common to present gifts, but most Malaysians would appreciate receiving an item from your company or country. Gifts should not be presented on the first visit, and alcohol as well as inexpensive mementos should be avoided altogether. Never present a gift to the wife of your Malay host.

Entertaining

Malays appreciate entertainment, which they believe enhances personal relationships. Therefore, entertainment is an important part of business arrangements. In fact, important meetings should be followed by a dinner or a lunch.

It is rare to be entertained in someone's home. Business entertainment usually takes place at a restaurant.

Business lunches are quite common, although it is not considered polite to discuss business during the meal. Eating is considered private and will be accompanied by very light conversation. Speeches are sometimes expected at dinner.

Dinners are usually for larger groups and will not include women. Business is not discussed. You should reciprocate by hosting events such as lunches or dinners.

Spouses are rarely included in business entertaining.

It is a good idea to send a thank-you note or flowers following a meal.

When seating guests at a Malay table, the seat of honor is to the right of the host. If seated on the floor, men should sit cross-legged and women should sit with their legs tucked under themselves.

Do not begin eating until invited by the host to do so.

In Malaysia, cuisine varies. Hindus and some Buddhists do not eat beef. Muslims do not eat pork. Alcoholic beverages are forbidden to Muslims and are generally not offered to guests, although it is not necessary that you abstain.

When toasting or when handing a dish to another person, use the left hand to support the right arm as a sign of respect.

Follow the lead of the host in deciding which hand to use to eat food. Malays use only their right hand and spoons. You may use a fork in the left hand to push food onto a spoon held in the right hand. Indians use the fingers of the right hand (never soiling their fingers above the first knuckle). Guests will usually be provided with a fork and spoon. Using the left hand to eat is acceptable among the Chinese. When in doubt, use only your right hand.

When dining among the Chinese, be aware that placing your chopsticks across your plate indicates that you are still hungry. (To indicate you have had enough to eat, place them on the small stand instead.) Waving chopsticks in the air to gesture is considered rude, and sticking a chopstick upright in a bowl of rice is considered to be a bad omen. Slurping soup and belching during a meal are acceptable.

Leave food on your plate to indicate that you are full or you will be given more.

To get a waiter's attention, raise your hand. Avoid shouting or pointing.

SOCIAL VALUES, CUSTOMS AND TIPS

Malaysia is a multiethnic country: the Chinese live predominantly in urban areas, and Malays (mostly Muslim) live predominantly in rural areas. Those of Chinese origin are heavily represented in business.

Business activities and attitudes toward work are often affected by folk beliefs, customs and a belief in fate.

English is commonly spoken, but is second to Malaysian.

Many Malay are fatalistic. In addition, a person's ancestral background is often considered to be important to social status and to future opportunities.

It is important to note that Indians indicate agreement by moving their head quickly from side to side. (Many Westerners misread this gesture as meaning "No.")

The Malays are proud of their people and culture. They appreciate comments about their country, city or enterprise. Family, sports, food and travel are also good conversation topics. Your host's business or social achievements are excellent topics of discussion.

Avoid discussing matters that are religious, political or racial in nature. Additionally, do not compare standards of living in Malaysia with those in the West.

The left hand is reserved for personal hygiene and is therefore considered "unclean." It should not be used for touching others, for eating or for passing along gifts or other objects.

If you see a small rug that is made of either silk or wool and has a decorative design of floral patterns in a Muslim's office or home, be certain not to stand on it or touch it with your feet, as it is most likely a prayer rug.

To cover up their feelings of embarrassment, people in Malaysia may smile or laugh at someone else's discomfort or misfortune.

Visitors should demonstrate restraint by avoiding broad gestures, loud outbursts or a show of emotion.

It is considered rude to blow your nose or clear your throat at the dinner table or in public.

If you are invited to someone's home, be aware that it is proper etiquette to remove your shoes and sunglasses before entering the house. Shoes are also removed before entering a mosque.

The Malay culture is predominantly and officially Muslim. Women are treated with deference and should dress modestly.

Elderly people are given great respect.

Casual touching between men and women should be avoided.

People do not line up for things (buses, etc.). Instead, pushing and crowding are both common and acceptable.

Avoid touching the head of a Malay or Indian person. That is where they believe the spirit or soul resides.

Pointing the sole of the shoe at someone is considered rude. Therefore, try to keep your feet flat on the ground and avoid using your feet to move objects.

Malays consider it a sign of anger if a person stands with their hands on their hips.

Do not smack your closed fist into the palm of the other hand. It is considered a rude gesture.

Malays consider it rude to point with the forefinger. Instead, point with the thumb with the other four fingers curled into the palm.

MALTA

Population: 379,563 (July 1998 est.); Maltese

Languages: Maltese (official), English (official), Italian, Arab, British, Phoenician

Religions: Roman Catholic 98%

Currency: Maltese lira

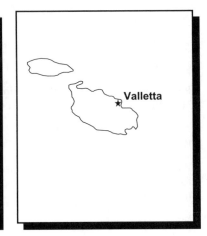

Valletta

HISTORICAL OVERVIEW

- Civilization on the island of Malta dates back to 3800 B.C. Malta was settled by the Phoenicians, Greeks and Carthaginians before being conquered by the Romans in 218 B.C. In 60 A.D., the Maltese converted to Christianity, and after the fall of the Roman Empire, Malta became a territory of the Byzantine Empire. In 870 A.D. it was conquered by the Arabs.

- Christianity was reinstituted on the island in 1091 when the Norman nobleman, Roger I, arrived and defeated the Arabs. A feudal system gradually took hold. In 1530, the islands came under the control of the Order of the Hospital of St. John of Jerusalem. These Knights of Malta were a religious and military order established, in part, to stop piracy in the area and to harass Turkish commerce. The Knights succeeded in both of these and, with the money accrued from the raids on the Turks, built great fortresses and palaces, which are architecturally significant.

- In 1798, Napoleon conquered the islands, but an 1802 treaty returned them to the Knights. Malta became an official part of the British Empire as a result of the Paris Treaty of 1814. From that time until 1964, a British governor ruled Malta. Since 1814 the Knights of St. John have only played a symbolic role on the island. They still convene each year in Malta for ceremonial purposes.

- Under British rule, Malta's status frequently changed with constitutions granted and then revoked again. The economy became tied to British military needs. The islands were subjected to severe bombings during World War II.

- Malta became an independent nation within the British Commonwealth in 1964 and in 1974 it left the Commonwealth. Since then, Malta has been a parliamentary democracy.

- The Labor Party (LP) led by Prime Minister Dom Mintoff had almost continuous control of the Maltese Parliament from 1971 until 1985. Since 1967, the LP has had many clashes with the Catholic Church because of the government's desire to make Catholic schools and hospitals part of a state-run welfare system. This conflict was finally resolved in 1985.

- From 1987 to 1996, the Nationalist Party (NP) was in control of the parliament under the leadership of Prime Minister Eddie Fenech Adami.

- Since the end of the alliance with Britain in 1979, Malta has maintained its neutrality. It has signed economic agreements with Libya and Italy. Malta decided not to join the EU in 1996.

BUSINESS PRACTICES

Hours of Business

Business hours are Monday through Friday 8:30 a.m. to 12:45 p.m. and 2:30 p.m. to 5:30 p.m., and Saturday 8:30 p.m. to 12:00 p.m.

Dress

Business suits are considered acceptable attire for both men and women. Maltese business dress is rather conservative.

In the summer, clothing of a lightweight material is most appropriate, but during the cooler winter months, layering is the best means of adjusting to the weather.

Introductions

Male friends tend to hug when greeting one another.

The Maltese are a very private people. They respond to foreigners only once the foreigner has introduced himself/herself.

Acceptable greetings are *Bongu* (Good Morning and Hello) and *Il-lejl-it-tajjeb* (Good Evening). *Sahha* means "Good-bye."

Meetings

It is best to schedule all business appointments from the month of May through October.

It is important to be punctual for appointments.

Negotiating

Learning a few words of Maltese will be greatly appreciated by your Maltese counterparts.

Most business negotiations are conducted in English, but it will be helpful to know some Arabic or Maltese for non-business situations.

Some of the older British firms in Malta tend to follow British business customs.

The Malta Development Corporation serves as a direct liaison between foreign businesses and the Maltese government. All proposals for foreign investment must first be sent to the Malta Development Corporation for approval.

There are many incentives given by the Maltese government to foreign investors who wish to set up a production base in Malta.

All negotiations are very relaxed and informal and do not usually follow a rigid protocol.

Entertaining

Malta has all the modern fast-food conveniences of any other European country. National dishes include *fenek* (rabbit in wine), *lampuki* pie and *bragoli*. Pork and fish are also popular. Malta is known for its fine fruits and vegetables.

Waiters and waitresses, along with hotel attendants and taxi drivers, should be tipped ten percent when a gratuity is not included in the bill.

Maltese nightlife is rather active, especially in St. John.

SOCIAL VALUES, CUSTOMS AND TIPS

Smoking is prohibited in many public areas.

The Catholic Church plays an important role in Maltese society. When visiting a church, dress conservatively and remember to keep shoulders and knees covered.

Football (soccer) and water sports are very popular in Malta.

All visitors to Malta should drink only bottled water.

MEXICO

Population: 98,552,776 (July 1998 est.); mestizo (Amerindian-Spanish) 60%, Amerindian 30%, white 9%, other 1%

Languages: Spanish, various Mayan dialects

Religions: nominally Roman Catholic 89%, Protestant 6%

Currency: New Mexican peso

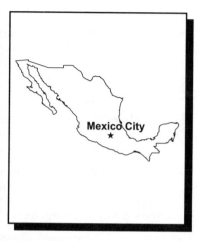

HISTORICAL OVERVIEW

- The early history of Mexico includes a long line of advanced Indian civilizations whose achievements rival those of the Egyptians and the early Europeans. The Olmecs are thought to have been among the area's earliest inhabitants at around 2000 B.C., followed by the Mayan, the Toltec and the Aztec.

- The Mayans built technologically advanced cities throughout North and Central America. Their civilization fell in the 12th century because of internal rivalry and warfare.

- The Aztecs, who became prominent around 1200 A.D., were the last great empire. In 1521, they were conquered by the Spanish, who destroyed the Aztec civilization and all remnants of Mayan culture.

- Mexico constituted part of the viceroyalty of New Spain from its establishment until its independence. The movement for independence began in 1810, led by Miguel Hidalgo y Costilla, a Mexican priest. A second insurrection occurred in 1814-1815. Both were crushed and the independence movement devolved into a guerrilla war. Independence was achieved in 1821. The country then included parts of the present-day western U.S. A constitution was adopted in 1824.

- In 1833, Antonio López de Santa Ana came to power in a liberal revolt and ruled until 1855. In 1836, Texas seceded from Mexico and declared itself independent. Although Mexico was initially successful in its attempt to reconquer Texas, it lost eventually. In 1845, the U.S. annexed Texas. Disputes with Mexico over the border provoked the Mexican War (1846-1848) in which Mexico lost today's Arizona, western Colorado, Nevada, Utah, Texas, California and New Mexico.

- In the early 1850s there were moves toward political reform. In 1857, under Benito Juárez, a new constitution was adopted making Mexico a representative republic. Conservatives and the church were both strongly opposed and civil war broke out. Juárez was victorious in 1861, but various factors, including conservative intrigue, led to a French invasion. In May 1864 the Hapsburg Maximillian was made emperor of Mexico. His attempts to reconcile the opposing political factions failed and the French withdrew in 1867.

- Porfirio Díaz led a rebellion in 1876 putting him in power until 1911. He was an autocratic ruler who established order. Yet, in the later years of his rule a significant gap began to develop between the wealthy and the poor.

- After 1911 there was a series of coups, spurred on by peasant and labor demand for reform. In 1929, the National Revolutionary Party (PNR) took power. Renamed, in 1949, as the Institutional Revolutionary Party (PRI), it has governed Mexico since.

- Mexico's economy experienced a period of steady growth following World War II, bolstered by its oil exports. In the early 1970s, however, its foreign debt rose and farm output failed to keep pace with population growth. A sharp drop in oil prices in the 1980s brought Mexico to the brink of financial crisis.

- In December 1988, amid cries of election fraud, candidate Carlos Salinas de Gortari was inaugurated president. In 1992, Salinas signed the North American Free Trade Agreement (NAFTA) with the U.S. and Canada. His successor, Ernesto Zedillo Ponce de Leon, also won amid rumors of fraud. Foreign investment increased until the catastrophic devaluation of the peso in 1994.

- In the same year, a ten-day war broke out between the Zapatista National Liberation Party (EZLN) in the state of Chiapas and the PRI. Since then, the conflict continues to result in violence and deaths. As of June 1998, both government troops and pro-PRI paramilitaries occupy Chiapas, resulting in occasional clashes.

- In the July 1997 elections, the PRI lost the majority in the lower house of Mexico's parliament, resulting in the formation of a four-party coalition.

- As a result of El Niño weather patterns in 1998, a drought severely damaged the cattle and coffee industries. Mexico is also saddled with a large national debt and a high poverty rate.

BUSINESS PRACTICES

Hours of Business

Businesses are open five days a week, generally from 9:00 a.m. until 6:00 p.m. There is an extended lunch break from about 1:00 to 4:00 p.m. Banks are open from 9:00 a.m. to 1:30 p.m., and the official working hours for government offices are from 8:30 a.m. to 2:30 p.m.

Dress

Lightweight business suits are generally advisable, although winter-weight suits may be worn in the evening or during colder times of the year.

Dress relatively conservatively. Inappropriate dress will reflect badly on you and will convey disrespect to your Mexican business associates.

For dinner, a dark suit is appropriate.

Never wear shorts or tank tops when visiting churches or religious sites.

Introductions

When introduced to business colleagues or friends, it is customary to shake hands. People usually shake hands each time they meet. People often shake hands both on arrival and on departure. Men should let the woman make the first move toward handshaking.

Women often greet each other with a kiss on the cheek.

For closer acquaintances, an *abrazo* (a full embrace with a pat on the back) is common between men. After two or three meetings with your Mexican colleagues, you might be greeted this way. This does not mean that you may call your colleague by his first name, however; wait until invited to do so.

When addressing someone, use the surname unless you know the person well. *Señor* (Mr.) is used when speaking with a man and *Señora* (Mrs.) or *Señorita* (Miss) should precede the surname of a married or unmarried woman, respectively. *Doña* is a term of respect used before a first name, somewhat like "Dame" in Britain. Also, always refer to a female secretary as *Señorita*, regardless of her age or marital status.

Titles are considered to be an important part of business protocol. Common titles are *Doctor, Profesor, Químico* (chemist), *Ingeniero* (engineer) and *Arquitecto* (architect). *Lic.* following a person's name in writing means that he or she has a bachelor's degree.

Spanish names usually include the mother's family name after, not before, the father's family name, although the father's family name is considered the surname. For instance, a man named José Rodriquez Ortega would be called *Señor* Rodriquez. A married woman or widow usually uses her maiden name in the middle position.

Meetings

Business is often conducted during the long midday break and many appointments are set between 10:00 a.m. and 1:00 p.m. Meetings can also be scheduled at uncommon hours – for example, at 8:30 p.m.

It is a good idea to have your business cards printed in both English and Spanish. Make sure that your university degree and your title follow your name.

Mexicans have a relaxed attitude toward time and do not place a high premium on punctuality. It is not unusual for a colleague to arrive half an hour late for a business meeting. You should always be on time for meetings, however, and should not complain about tardiness.

You should make appointments at least two weeks in advance. It is common for government officials to reschedule at the last minute.

People are considered to be more important than schedules. In Mexico, it is considered appropriate to meet with an unexpected business visitor first, even when a scheduled visitor has arrived first. Be prepared for interruptions. If a visitor drops in, you should give him/her your full attention.

In Mexico, the business atmosphere is friendly, gracious and easygoing.

Many business meetings are held during breakfast or lunch. Business lunches are often quite lengthy and are held between 2:00 and 4:00 p.m. These are social meetings for the most part, and business is conducted only in the last few minutes. Take your cues from your Mexican colleagues.

Business is rarely conducted at dinner. (Most restaurants do not serve dinner until 9:00 or 9:30 p.m.) Younger executives, however, may suggest meeting at 7:00 p.m. for snacks and drinks.

Negotiating

Initial contact with a Mexican firm should be made between the top managers from both the foreign and Mexican companies. The foreign manager should make the initial trip to Mexico (accompanied by members of the firm's staff).

One of the fastest ways to alienate your Mexican counterpart is to enter into negotiations with a sense of superiority. Do not be overly demanding or aggressive. Courtesy, friendliness and an easygoing manner are well received.

Demonstrating respect is paramount. Show respect to your Mexican colleagues and, likewise, expect respect from them.

Mexicans generally prefer win-win situations over compromises. You will gain more trust if your actions suggest that you want what is best for your Mexican counterpart's company.

Patience is considered important and you should avoid showing anger (for example, when encountering delays or interruptions).

It is helpful to have either a contact in Mexico or a letter of introduction. The introductory letter should be written in Spanish, and you should indicate in the letter whether or not you speak Spanish.

Mexicans will appreciate it if your presentation materials have been translated into Spanish prior to your meeting. Scientific displays (e.g., charts, graphs, three-dimensional models) are highly valued and appreciated.

Mexicans do not appreciate hasty decision making. Be prepared to have social discussions before commencing business transactions. You should remain flexible regarding deadlines.

It is very rare to find a woman in a top business position. A businesswoman should strive to be extremely professional and to instill respect.

Entertaining

Mexicans view entertaining as an important and enjoyable part of business. Mutual invitations are essential, and one should always reciprocate.

Entertaining in the home is reserved for closer acquaintances.

Gifts are not expected but they are welcomed. Gifts should be wrapped and presented. For women, popular brands of perfume or personal accessories are appropriate. For men, popular brands of personal or office accessories (e.g., books, calculators, clocks, etc.) are appropriate. It is customary to present all secretaries and support staff involved in a business transaction with small gifts. Unique items related to the art or history of your homeland are appreciated.

If you are invited to a private home, flowers or wine are appropriate gifts. Also, if you know the family has children, bring small gifts for them. If you bring flowers, remember that, according to popular beliefs, purple and yellow flowers connote death. (Similarly, avoid purple clothing or gifts in which purple is the primary color.) Red flowers cast spells, and white ones lift spells.

On a business trip, try to stay in the best possible hotel or entertain in the best possible restaurants. Make a point of dressing neatly and elegantly. These are important elements in enhancing your prestige in the eyes of Mexicans.

Popular drinks are tequila (the maguey worm in some brands of tequila is considered a delicacy), beers and margaritas. Wines are not popular because vineyards do not thrive in Mexico. Mexicans appreciate Scotch, both when abroad and when given as a gift.

A foreign businesswoman should never make dinner appointments with Mexican male colleagues unless they are accompanied by their spouses.

If a businesswoman entertains a Mexican businessman at lunch, she should arrange to have the lunch in her hotel's restaurant so that she can have the check added to her bill in advance. If the check is presented at the table, a man will not allow her to pay.

Restaurant bills usually include a service charge. It is customary to contribute an additional five percent tip.

During the meal, both hands should be kept above the table.

Guests do not usually leave immediately after a meal.

Toasts are common. Allow the host to toast first.

Even at finer hotels or in restaurants, people often order mineral water because it is not advisable to drink the tap water.

The midday meal, eaten from about 1:00 to 4:00 p.m., is the main meal of the day.

Bread and rice are eaten with spicy foods and with a pinch of salt to relieve the burning sensation. Very spicy food is called *picante*, while hot, temperate food is called *caliente*.

Some foods are eaten with utensils, others with the hand. Tortillas (thin, round unleavened bread made from cornmeal or wheat flour) are often used as scoops for sauces. Observe your host or others dining with you for guidelines.

SOCIAL VALUES, CUSTOMS AND TIPS

English is spoken by most members of the business community and in larger cities. (Many Mexicans at the managerial level also speak French.) Mexicans, nevertheless, appreciate visitors' efforts to speak Spanish.

Mexicans are very proud of their country and appreciate it when visitors compliment Mexico's progress and achievements. Avoid comparisons with the U.S.

Mexicans are generally open and expressive people.

Good topics of discussion are Mexican culture, history, art, museums, fashion and travel.

Sports such as soccer, bullfighting, jai alai (a type of handball), *charreada* (a Mexican type of rodeo), baseball, tennis and volleyball are popular.

Avoid discussing religious or political subjects, earthquakes or poverty. Jokes about "Montezuma's revenge" (diarrhea and/or upset stomach) are inappropriate.

Mexicans refer to people from the U.S. as North Americans and call them *Americanos*. They also like to remind U.S. citizens that they are not the only Americans and that Mexicans are also North Americans.

Mexican people typically stand close to each other while they talk. Many Mexicans are "touch-oriented," meaning that they will linger over a handshake and casually touch the forearm, elbow or lapel of the other person's suit. These touches signify a willingness to be friendly. If you withdraw, Mexicans may take offense and you will immediately establish an emotional distance and communicate a lack of trust.

Refrain from placing your hands in your pockets while conversing, as it is considered impolite.

To beckon someone, extend the arm, palm down, and make a scratching motion.

When passing an object, hand it to the other person; never toss it. Similarly, when paying for a purchase, place the money in the cashier's hand, not on the counter.

A distinctive, very rude gesture in Mexico is a "V" sign, made with the index and middle fingers placed under the nose with your palm against your face.

Hand and arm gestures are often used in conversation.

Many gestures commonly used in North America are understood and even used in Mexico (e.g., the "thumbs up" gesture can be used to show approval).

A sweeping or grabbing motion toward your body means that someone is "stealing" or "getting away with something."

Other than verbally, "No" can be indicated by shaking the head from side to side and extending the index finger with the palm outward.

Placing your hands on yours hips can suggest aggressiveness.

MOROCCO

Population: 29,114,497 (July 1998 est.); Arab-Berber 99.1%, other 0.7%, Jewish 0.2%

Languages: Arabic (official), Berber dialects, French (esp. in business, government, diplomacy)

Religions: Muslim 98.7%, Christian 1.1%, Jewish 0.2%

Currency: Moroccan dirham

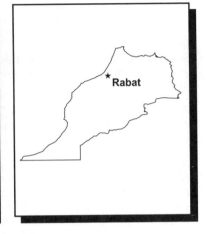

HISTORICAL OVERVIEW

- The earliest settlers of Morocco were the Berbers, who arrived toward the close of the second millennium B.C. Phoenician traders set up trading posts along the coast in the 12th century B.C. They were followed by the Carthaginians in the fifth century B.C. Once Carthage fell, Morocco became a strong ally of Rome. In 46 A.D. Rome annexed Morocco and Christianized it widely. Locally, Morocco was ruled by the Berbers.

- The Arabs invaded in the late seventh century A.D. and introduced Islam to Morocco. The Berbers revolted against Arab rule in 740 and established an independent kingdom. After several centuries of battles and shifting control, Morocco was completely under the control of the Berbers, who also conquered Muslim Spain and parts of North Africa in the 11th century.

- The Arab Marnid dynasty forced the Berbers out of Spain and took over Morocco in the 13th century. The Marnids ruled until the mid 15th century and introduced Muslim mysticism, called Sufism, to Morocco.

- In 1787, Morocco became one of the first nations to sign a peace and friendship treaty with the newly formed United States of America.

- European nations became involved in Morocco in the 19th century, particularly after France invaded Algeria in 1830 and demanded that Morocco help in capturing the Algerian leader

Abdelkader in 1846. France made the country a protectorate in 1912.

- The French ruled until 1956, when growing Moroccan nationalism forced France to grant the country independence.

- Morocco is ruled by a constitutional monarchy. The current king, in power since 1961, is Moulay Hassan II. He is a direct descendent of Alawi kings of the Alawi dynasty, which had ruled beginning in 1660.

- A new constitution, adopted in 1972, increased the size of the Chamber of Representatives, giving it more legislative power. Several attempted military coups disrupted the installation of a parliament. In 1977, new parliamentary elections finally led to the formation of Parliament, in which the crown's supporters were in the majority.

- In 1975, Morocco reclaimed the Spanish Sahara (now the Western Sahara) as its territory. Spain was forced to withdraw its troops. Neighboring countries, especially Algeria, objected to Morocco's development of the area, and a guerilla war ensued. A cease-fire went into effect in September 1991. A referendum on independence or annexation by Morocco, sponsored by the U.N., has continuously been postponed due to a disagreement over who is qualified to vote. In 1994, some progress was made as voter registration offices were opened.

- The increasing mechanization of agriculture has allowed for the export of large quantities of produce and citrus to Europe each year. Increased privatization of the country's economy has attracted over two billion dollars in foreign investment since 1992. Morocco is now attempting to spur on the growth of its fishing industry.

- The regime of Hassan II became less repressive in the 1990s, but direct criticism of the king is still prohibited and may still result in a prison sentence.

- As a result of constitutional reforms in 1996, a bicameral legislature replaced the former unicameral one, adding the Chamber of Advisors to the already existent House of Representatives. In addition, every seat in the House was made an elected position.

- Lack of employment has caused many Moroccans to attempt illegal emigration to Spain. Many have died or been arrested on their journey.

BUSINESS PRACTICES

Hours of Business

In Tangier, businesses are open Monday through Friday, 9:00 a.m. to noon and 4:00 p.m. to 8:00 p.m. In the rest of the country and in Casablanca, business hours are 9:00 a.m. to noon and 3:00 p.m. to 6:00 p.m.

Dress

It is important to dress well and conservatively in order to gain respect. Businesswomen should avoid low necklines, bare shoulders, short skirts and short sleeves. It also suggested that women wear long sleeves for business entertaining. Women with long hair should wear their hair up.

Introductions

The practice of shaking hands when greeting or when being introduced is widely accepted in Morocco. Handshakes are made with the right hand only.

It is common for women or good friends – both male and female – to greet one another by kissing each other on each cheek.

Less than fervent greetings are considered rude.

Whether in conversation or when greeting, women should never make eye contact with men whom they do not know (as it may be construed as an invitation).

Placing your hand over your heart signifies personal warmth or pleasure in seeing the person being greeted. Older people usually partake in this custom.

Titles are always used in formal situations as well as when being introduced to acquaintances. When meeting anyone for the first time, use French titles – *Monsieur, Madame, Mademoiselle.* You should greet doctors and professors (M.D. or Ph.D.) by their title, followed by their last name.

Be aware that there are two titles of importance – *Haj* (masculine) and *Haja* (feminine) – which signify that the individual has been to Mecca. It is suggested, however, that Westerners do not use this title when addressing someone.

At a party or group gathering, expect to be introduced to each person individually. Make sure that you shake hands with everyone you meet.

Meetings

In order to do business in Morocco, you must obtain a letter of credit. Usually your country's embassy in Morocco can provide this.

Business is usually conducted in French.

The Moroccan business atmosphere tends to combine Middle Eastern and French styles. Both styles tend to be formal.

It is acceptable to contact Moroccan firms directly by sending several letters before your arrival, stating the purpose of your visit and giving an account of your company's history and the scope of the business at hand.

Bring business cards printed both in English and in Arabic.

Make appointments well in advance, when possible. Your host may not arrive on time for a meeting, but you are expected to be punctual.

Be aware that business discussions may occur in hotels and restaurants, but final deals are always made in an office.

To contact people, it is best to go to an office directly since it can take up to an hour for a telephone call to go through from one place to another within the same city.

Negotiating

Work with a Moroccan representative for help with the legalities of business transactions.

There are many international banks in Morocco that can provide useful contacts.

Several trips to Morocco may be necessary to accomplish your goals.

The Moroccan government is more open toward foreign enterprises than it was in the past.

Moroccans place a lot of emphasis on establishing strong personal relations between those involved in business negotiations. Successful business in Morocco requires at least one or two visits by a senior executive. Sending a few executives along on the trip indicates the seriousness of your proposal.

It is considered impolite to say "No" directly. Expect Moroccans to say "Yes" even when they do not mean it.

The business organization structure is very precise, centralized and structured, so there is little room for error. Prior to your appointment, find out who the top-level negotiator is as well as who will be making final decisions.

Although a written contract is necessary, Moroccans view a person's word as more binding than a contract. When a transaction is finalized, shake hands with your colleague as a symbol that you will honor your word.

Entertaining

Be prepared to participate in the customary drinking of tea, without which business is never conducted.

Do not give a gift to someone when you first meet. It may be interpreted as a bribe. Be especially careful about giving alcohol as a gift since consumption of liquor is prohibited by the Muslim religion.

The giving of gifts is not taken lightly in Morocco. Moroccans place great emphasis on respect for tradition and manners. Do not expect a gift to be accepted with profuse expressions of gratitude, as Moroccans do not like to appear materialistic.

When invited to a meal by a family living in the city, gifts are not expected. If you do bring gifts, nuts, dates, candy, flowers or small toys for the children are welcome. Appropriate gifts from abroad for children and teenagers include soccer balls, solar calculators, CDs of popular U.S. music or clothing, especially T-shirts with a city or university insignia.

It is impolite to refuse refreshments when offered (even if a token refusal is made before accepting the offer).

Often only men socialize in public coffeehouses, especially on weekends or in the evenings. As a businesswoman, you should not go into a coffeehouse unless you see other women inside.

It is common for Moroccan businessmen to invite colleagues to their homes for feasts, but you will rarely meet their wives.

You should offer to remove your shoes before entering a Moroccan home. Enter a home with your right foot first.

If you eat at someone's house, you will please your host by complimenting the home.

In restaurants or cafés, snapping one's fingers is the method used to call a waiter/waitress.

In restaurants, a service charge is usually included in the bill, which is paid by the host. If a service charge is not included, leave a gratuity of about ten percent.

Most Moroccans prefer to eat at home. If they do dine out, however, they favor French and Italian restaurants.

Breakfast is served between 7:00 and 8:00 a.m. and usually consists of mint tea or French roast coffee and bread with honey. Lunch is served at around 2:00 p.m. and is the main meal of the day. It is also the preferred business meal. Dinner is eaten between 8:00 and 11:00 p.m. and is usually a light meal with the exception of special business meals. Dinner is typically a snack of cheese and bread or pasta and salad.

It is common for a meal to be eaten with the fingers (of the right hand only) from a communal dish. You should eat from the section of the dish directly in front of you. Never reach beyond the closest area, and do not touch the meat until your host pushes it toward you.

A basin of water is usually available in the eating area. Each person washes his/her hands before and after eating. It is important to wash your hands in front of everybody.

Moroccans dine while sitting on low banquette seats (large overstuffed pillows). Men and women usually eat separately.

Cumin is the main spice in Morocco. Two versatile staples are *couscous* (grain-like pasta that is the national dish of Morocco) usually accompanied by chicken, lamb and vegetables, and fish such as tuna, whiting, red mullet and perch. Fruits and soups are also popular in Moroccan cuisine.

The serving of tea requires a particular ceremony in Morocco. When women are serving, they must pour in a manner that produces a ring of bubbles (called a *fez*) around the inside rim of the glass. If you are asked to pour tea, you may want to decline unless you feel that you have the necessary skills to produce *fez*.

Remember to use only your right hand for handling food. The left hand is to be kept in your lap while eating.

In homes it is generally considered impolite for the guests to finish eating before the host, as this can imply that the food did not taste good. Licking your fingers is a sign that you are finished.

SOCIAL VALUES, CUSTOMS AND TIPS

Most Moroccans are bilingual, speaking both Arabic (in the Moroccan dialect) and French. Spanish is also spoken in the north. English is widely studied and is gaining popularity.

Moroccans value family, honor, dignity, generosity and hospitality. Moroccan culture is rooted in a Muslim belief in fatalism, which claims that all events are predetermined by fate and therefore cannot be changed by human beings. This may affect individual attitudes in business.

When meeting someone, remember to ask about that person's family. If the person is a man, do not ask about his wife but about his family in general. Other good subjects to ask about are soccer, track, golf, basketball, Moroccan history, culture and architecture.

Avoid talking about religion, politics in the Middle East or Israel. Do not be surprised if people ask about your views on Islam. If you are not Muslim, it is best to say that Islam has some beautiful customs, but that you are of another religion.

Expect Moroccans to be very formal. Behavior should conform to the social situation, not to a specific individual. French culture is considered the ideal, and anything French is held in high regard.

Be careful about excessively admiring an object belonging to your host, as your host may feel obligated to give it to you as a gift.

Items are passed with the right hand or with both hands, but never with the left hand.

It is impolite to point at people or to show the bottom of one's foot. It is also generally considered improper to cross one's legs.

A businesswoman traveling alone should expect to be asked frequently if she is married. If she is not married, she will be confronted with further inquiries.

It is considered improper for a woman to travel alone at night. If a woman does this, it is likely that she will be harassed.

If you want to use a gesture to say "come here," use the western goodbye wave.

Do not be surprised to see men and men or women and women holding hands. This simply signifies warmth and friendship.

Western-style clothing is becoming more popular in Morocco, but short pants and casual attire are not worn in public. Shorts are only worn on the beach.

When one visits a mosque, clothing that covers the entire body (except the head and hands) should be worn and shoes should be removed. Be advised, however, that foreigners rarely are allowed in mosques.

Each year Muslims observe Ramadan, a month of fasting and prayer. (Because Muslims use a lunar calendar, the dates of Ramadan on the solar calendar change every year.) During this time, no eating or drinking is permitted between dawn and sunset. Visitors are exempt from the fast, but at this time, foreign visitors should exercise discretion when eating in public during the day.

Bargaining is widely practiced and is expected, except in restaurants.

MOZAMBIQUE

Population: 18,641,469 (July 1998 est.); Indigenous tribal groups 99.66% (Shangaan, Chokwe, Manyika, Sena, Makua, and others), European 0.06%, Euro-African 0.2%, Indian 0.08%

Languages: Portuguese (official), indigenous dialects

Religions: Indigenous beliefs 50%, Christian 30%, Muslim 20%

Currency: metical

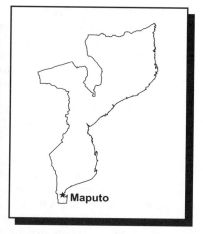

Maputo

HISTORICAL OVERVIEW

- Mozambique's early inhabitants were probably Bantu-speaking peoples who arrived in the third century A.D. Arab traders are believed to have set up outposts in Mozambique as early as the eighth century. They traded in ivory, gold and slaves. Arab settlements developed into independent city-states.

- A distinct Muslim culture was in place by the first contact with the Portuguese in 1498. Islam is still strong in the coastal areas today.

- The Portuguese began by establishing trade posts and settlements. In 1629, the Mwene Matapa, one of the peoples with a city-state, recognized Portuguese sovereignty. Soon thereafter, however, the Roturi city-state conquered the Mwene Matapa and pushed the Portuguese to the southern regions of the country. The Portuguese slowly advanced northward again and by 1752 most of present-day Mozambique was under Portuguese colonial rule.

- Portugal found the colony to be a plentiful source of slave labor. Controlled mainly by Arabs and Swahili-speakers, the slave trade became a keystone to Mozambique's economy. Agriculture was also developed and Portugal established Mozambique as a European transport corridor.

- In ruling Mozambique, the Portuguese sought to spend as little money as possible. They developed a land grant system that failed and, in the end, they chartered parts of the country to private companies. In the first half of the 20th century, the Portuguese reclaimed most company-owned regions.

- Mozambique's struggle for independence began in 1962, when the Front for the Liberation of Mozambique (FRELIMO) was formed. Two years later they began a guerilla movement against the Portuguese. The costs to the Portuguese were too high, and Portuguese army officers revolted in the mid-1970s. In 1974, following the end of the dictatorship in Portugal, a cease-fire was declared and independence was soon granted.

- FRELIMO ruled the newly independent nation. It instituted a rigid socialist economy and supported the struggle for independence in neighboring Rhodesia.

- While FRELIMO enjoyed initial success, its tight control of the economy and especially its establishment of state-run agriculture gave rise to dissident movements (the most significant of which was called RENAMO, the Mozambique National Resistance). The protracted civil war, begun by RENAMO, devastated Mozambique's economy and infrastructure, took many lives and created vast numbers of refugees.

- By 1985, under pressure from the International Monetary Fund (IMF), FRELIMO introduced many reforms that began well, but the war with RENAMO continued to wreak havoc. A series of droughts in the late 1980s compounded matters.

- A new multiparty constitution was drawn up in 1990 and, in 1992, a peace accord was signed. Since then, RENAMO's power has been declining.

- Weather conditions continue to affect agricultural production greatly, and the lack of adequate transportation has continued to cause unnecessary food shortages. In 1995, rioters took to the streets of the capitol to protest this situation.

- In August 1998, the Mozambican government approved approximately U.S. $360 million in investment projects. The majority of projects are domestic initiatives. The government hopes that these investments will spur on the economy and lower the country's debt.

BUSINESS PRACTICES

Hours of Business

Businesses are open from 7:30 a.m. to 12:30 p.m. and from 2:00 p.m. to 5:30 p.m., Monday through Friday.

Dress

Safari suits should be worn during the summer months. Summer suits should be worn during the winter months.

Introductions

A handshake is the proper greeting in Mozambique. The handshake, however, is a three-step process. The two people grasp each other's hands, rotate the wrist up, then resume a normal handshake.

First names are rarely used in professional contexts. Professional titles should be used whenever they are known.

Meetings

Do not make appointments during January because most people are on vacation during this month.

Appointments should be made well in advance.

Business cards are used widely in Mozambique. Be sure to bring them with you to give to others. Your information should be written in English on one side and in Portuguese on the other.

It is best to confirm your meeting on the day it is scheduled. Be advised that you may be kept waiting in an office for quite some time; the higher the management level of the individual you are meeting, the longer your wait may be.

Negotiating

Mozambique has adopted many of Portugal's business practices and procedures. You will most likely find that business agreements require a "stamp of approval" from many different officials and that the decision-making process will take a long time.

It is best to try to understand the many different levels at which business decisions are made in Mozambique. Be sensitive to the hierarchies involved and expect a slower pace of business.

All documents need to be translated into Portuguese. There are some offices that provide translation services in Maputo, but your Mozambican counterpart will be happy to help you find a translator.

Mozambique is a member of the Southern African Development Conference.

The U.S. is one of Mozambique's major trading partners.

Entertaining

Lunch and dinner appointments at local restaurants are appropriate for business meetings. It is uncommon, however, to invite spouses.

Avoid lavish gifts (over U.S. $10). Mozambique is one of the poorest countries in the world (the minimum wage is $13/month) and you may offend or embarrass people if you present them with expensive gifts.

The most popular food in Mozambique is chicken. There are many restaurants that capture the spicy tastes of the local cuisine.

A specialty in Mozambique is tiger prawns, which are shrimp that run from 10 to 12 inches in length.

SOCIAL VALUES, CUSTOMS AND TIPS

Affiliation with one's tribe is very strong in Mozambique. Family ties are very close as well.

Mozambicans are friendly and hospitable to outsiders.

Good topics of discussion include history and culture. Avoid discussing politics and regional disputes.

It is unwise to bring or wear expensive jewelry. Others may take offense at displays of wealth.

MYANMAR

Population: 47,305,319 (July 1998 est.); Burmese 68%, Shan 9%, Karen 7%, Rakhine 4%, Chinese 3%, Mon 2%, Indian 2%, other 5%

Languages: Burmese

Religions: Buddhist 89%, Christian 4%, Muslim 4%, animist beliefs 1%, other 2%

Currency: kyat

HISTORICAL OVERVIEW

- Present-day Myanmar was settled by the Tibeto-Burmese Pyu peoples in the north, between 100 B.C. and 800 A.D., and the Austro-Asiatic Mon in the south. Burmese from Southern China took over the Pyu in the ninth century and set up a kingdom with its capital in Pagan.

- In 1044, Anaurata became king in Pagan and quickly united all of Myanmar into one kingdom, founding the first Myanmar empire.

- The dominance of the Burmese was resented by the Shan people of northeastern Myanmar, who, in the late 13th century, enlisted the aid of the Mongols. A force of Mongol cavalrymen then invaded and destroyed the Burmese kingdom in 1287.

- The Mongols turned rule over to the Shan, who tried repeatedly to establish a permanent state. From the 13th through the mid 18th century, Myanmar endured repeated civil wars between the Shans, Burmese and Mons, with no group emerging victorious.

- In 1759, the popular Burmese leader Alaungpaya came to power, united the country, and established its last dynasty. The kingdom invaded Thailand and, in the early 1800s, also invaded Assam to the west. The British, who controlled Assam at the time, responded by sending troops to push the Burmese out of the region. The British were successful in this first Burmese War, and the Burmese surrendered some coastal land and permitted the installment of a British minister in the capital of Ava.

- Burmese resistance to British rule and interference with colonial commerce led to the second Burmese War in 1852 and the third in 1885-1886, which completely ended Burmese rule. The country was renamed Burma and governed as a province of British India until 1937, when it became a crown colony.

- The Myanmar people were particularly resentful of Britain's cutting state patronage for Buddhism. In addition, Britain's economic policies impoverished many. Resulting peasant uprising caused Britain to separate Burma from India in 1937.

- The Japanese invaded Burma in 1942. After the war, the British tried to resume control, but agreed to Burma's independence in 1948.

- Power was in the hands of the Anti-Fascist People's Freedom League (AFPFL), a left-wing nationalist group. Strife within the party, however, enabled the military, commanded by Ne Win, to take control in 1962. Win suspended the constitution and, within a few years, abolished existing political parties, imprisoned communist leaders and announced that he would make Burma a socialist, although not a communist, state.

- Ne Win was able to withstand Chinese-supported rebels, and his repressive, unpopular and inept government ruled from the 1960s to the early 1980s. Ethnic insurgents, students and urban residents began to press for an end to the dictatorship, and, in 1988, a long series of demonstrations occurred. Martial law was imposed and a new body, the State Law and Order Restoration Council (SLORC), replaced the government.

- Finally, in 1990, the military agreed to free elections, but when the opposition party, the National League for Democracy, won 80 percent of the vote, the army refused to surrender power and kept the opposition leader, Aung San Suh Kyi, under house arrest. Myanmar was subject to strong international condemnation for its actions.

- The military has since been strengthened by arms purchases from China, and the SLORC has neutralized various rebel groups by signing individual cease-fire agreements.

- In 1995, Anung San Suu Kyi was released from house arrest but still faces great opposition, such as in November 1997 when she and her aides were mobbed by a government-approved protest while driving in Rangoon.

- In July 1997, Burma became a member of the Association of Southeast Asian Nations (ASEAN).

BUSINESS PRACTICES

Hours of Business

The workweek is Monday through Friday, typically from 9:00 a.m. to 4:30 p.m.

Dress

Neatness is key for business attire. Men should wear a tie and a long-sleeved shirt, and women should wear suits.

Women normally dress in a sarong (a wraparound skirt) with a short blouse on top. Men also wear a sarong tied in front, often with a western-style shirt.

Introductions

Do not shake hands with a woman unless she initiates the handshake.

Verbal greetings usually take the form of rhetorical questions about one's health and mood. Smiling in return is the accepted response.

The Myanmar are generally curious and will not hesitate to ask personal questions immediately after meeting someone.

Meetings

The initial meeting is a time to start building a trusting relationship and, often, little or no business is discussed.

The Myanmar prefer to do all business face-to-face rather than over the phone. A series of face-to-face meetings will be needed to accomplish most business objectives.

Negotiating

Strong relationships are necessary to accomplish business goals in Myanmar. If someone does a favor for you, it is expected that you will return the favor without needing to be asked.

It is important to use correct names and rank when speaking with government officials, which you will almost surely have to do when conducting business in Myanmar.

The exchange of business cards is standard practice.

Be aware that astrological calculations are sometimes made prior to business negotiations.

Traditionally the Myanmar are uncomfortable on committees, preferring governance by seniority or hierarchy. Egalitarianism is perceived as a threat to harmony.

Entertaining

Business entertaining is usually done in hotels and restaurants. You may, however, be invited to a large feast in someone's private home.

Gifts are expected only on special occasions, such as someone's retirement.

Some popular foods are oil-based curries, salted fish, salad and rice. The Myanmar are not heavy drinkers.

When entering someone's home, take off your shoes at the entrance. An offer to help with the dishes will be appreciated, although it will probably not be accepted. The host will admire any efforts you make to play with and to entertain the children.

Seating arrangements are not important and you will usually seat yourself.

SOCIAL VALUES, CUSTOMS AND TIPS

English is a second language but has recently declined in usage.

The Myanmar are very kind to foreigners, especially if one attempts to speak their language.

Theravada Buddhism is the principal religion and has a profound effect on Burmese life. An important concept is that of *kan* or *kharma*, which holds that actions in past lives affect the present life. Therefore, one should behave according to Buddhist precepts so that future lives will be blessed. *Kan* allows people to attribute shortcomings to powers beyond their control.

Buddhist monks are the exemplars for society and are treated with great respect. They are not allowed to touch females. Nearly all Myanmar men spend some time in a monastery.

The Myanmar will lose respect for you if you show too much emotion. Both anger and affection must not be overtly displayed.

The word *anade* describes the behavioral pattern of withdrawal when faced with the embarrassment of a direct affront. The Myanmar are also embarrassed by compliments. Direct praise and criticism, therefore, can create discomfort and lead to problems. It may be difficult to realize when you have made an error because the Myanmar tend to smile when they are embarrassed.

Buddhist tradition considers discussing money tasteless, and the result is that services and goods are sometimes given for free.

Be careful not to point your feet at someone as it is considered rude.

Loud, boastful body language is offensive, as is hugging or kissing in public.

Teasing is common among friends and is a sign of intimacy.

Staring is accepted and common and is sure to be encountered by Westerners, especially Caucasians.

Be sure to show respect for Buddhist images. Posing for pictures in front of them or climbing such images is considered highly offensive.

Women should never ride on the roofs of boats or other vehicles as this is a sign of looseness or coarseness.

Spitting is the ultimate gesture of contempt.

Independence Day is celebrated on January 4.

THE NETHERLANDS

Population: 15,731,112 (July 1998 est.); Dutch 96%, Moroccan, Turkish and other 4%

Languages: Dutch

Religions: Roman Catholic 34%, Protestant 25%, Muslim 3%, other 2%, unaffiliated 36%

Currency: guilder, euro

HISTORICAL OVERVIEW

- Up until the late 16th century, what is now known as the Netherlands was not a distinct united country but a set of separate entities that shared the same fate as Belgium and Luxembourg and, with them, was known as the Low Countries.

- In the first century B.C., the entire area was conquered by the Romans. At the time, the population was mainly composed of Celtic and Germanic peoples. The Frankish Merovingians succeeded the Romans in the fifth century and, in the eighth century, the Carolingians took control of the Low Countries.

- Between roughly 925 and 1350, the Low Countries saw the emergence, development and ultimate independence of various principalities and countries, both secular and religious. When the French dukes of Burgundy intruded in the late 14th century, they brought about a degree of political unity that fostered economic and cultural unity as well. Control of the Low Countries passed to the Spanish Hapsburgs in the 16th century.

- The northern provinces of the Low Countries converted to Calvinism during the Reformation, and in 1568, Prince William of Orange rebelled against the Spanish crown, in part for religious reasons, beginning an 80-year war for independence. In 1579, the northern provinces broke away and established the United Provinces of the Netherlands. William of Orange became the first head of the new republic and was soon assassinated by order of the Spanish king. The republic was able to resist Spanish efforts to regain control, however, and in 1648, Spain finally recognized the Netherlands' independence.

- In 1602, the Dutch East India company was formed to strengthen and protect trade. Following independence, the Netherlands built a vast overseas empire and became the world's leading maritime and commercial power for a short time. By 1650, the Dutch navy was twice the size of the English and French fleets combined. Numerous wars against England and France, however, drained the Netherlands' resources.

- In 1688, Prince William of Orange and Mary Stuart were invited by the English Parliament to become king and queen of England. In 1795, French forces moved into the Netherlands and by 1810, Napoleon had completely annexed the territory. Napoleon's brother, Louis, was made king, and he gave the country the name of Holland.

- The Congress of Vienna ended the French occupation and the House of Orange was restored under William IV. He created a new kingdom of the Netherlands, which included Belgium and Luxembourg. In 1830, the Belgians established an independent country.

- During World War I, the Netherlands remained neutral, but the country was invaded by Germany in World War II. Many German Jews found refuge in the Netherlands during the 1930s until the Nazi invasion when many German Jews were deported.

- After the war, the Netherlands played an important role in European economic development. In 1958, the Netherlands was one of the six founders of the European Economic Community.

- Postwar governments were led by coalitions of the Labor Party and the Catholic Party. But from the late 1950s until the early 1970s the Catholic Party, renamed the People's Party and including Protestants, was in power. In 1973, the Labor Party won.

- In 1980, Queen Beatrix took power after her mother, Queen Juliana, abdicated the throne. She continues as the head of state today.

- During the 1980's, the Dutch rapidly used up much of their natural gas reserves, causing concern over the future of the economy and the Dutch social welfare system.

- In the 1980's, political parties realigned themselves, forming the Christian Democratic Appeal (CDA). In 1994, the Labor Party won parliamentary elections.

- In 1996, the Dutch once again turned to controlling the seas with a $1.6 billion project to renovate and expand Rotterdam. The expansion includes new pipelines.

BUSINESS PRACTICES

Hours of Business

Business hours are from 8:30 or 9:00 a.m. to 5:00 or 5:30 p.m., Monday through Friday.

The summer months and the Christmas and New Year's holidays are for family get-togethers and travel, so it is best to avoid scheduling business during these times (unless you are encouraged to do so by your Dutch colleagues).

Dress

Dark business suits and white blouses are worn by both men and women. Men should wear conservative ties.

Introductions

A handshake is the appropriate greeting for both men and women when meeting or departing. Adults also shake hands with young children.

When being introduced in the Netherlands, it is customary to repeat your last name while shaking hands. If you are not introduced at a business or social gathering, it is acceptable to introduce yourself and shake hands with each person you meet.

The preferred greeting when being introduced is "Pleased to meet you."

Close friends often kiss three times (alternating cheeks) and embrace when they meet.

Generally, titles followed by last names are used when addressing people. First names should only be used once your Dutch colleagues initiate addressing you by your first name.

A common greeting between those who are already acquainted is *Hoe gaat het?* (How are you?)

Meetings

It is important to plan business appointments, including business entertaining, well in advance. Punctuality is also very important. Once an appointment is scheduled, it is very hard to change the time of the appointment.

Exaggeration and fluff are not appreciated in business proposals. Presentations should focus on the facts and include all pertinent figures.

Upon exiting a meeting, it is customary to tip the attendant in the reception room of a firm if that person has given you something while you were waiting for the meeting to begin.

Negotiating

English is widely spoken in the Netherlands, and the Dutch readily accommodate their English-speaking guests by switching to English for meetings and for formal presentations.

Correct titles should be used when conducting business, especially when writing business correspondence.

The Dutch are extremely experienced in business as the nation is very reliant on foreign trade. As a result, they are generally efficient, open to new ideas and welcoming of foreigners.

Negotiations proceed quickly because the Dutch do not like haggling. A good proposal will make a better impression than will concessions.

In the Netherlands, being organized and attentive will inspire a sense of trust.

Always reply after having received important documents from the Netherlands (e.g., contracts, letters of intent, etc.), even if only to confirm their arrival.

Bear in mind that reaching a decision takes time because Dutch businesspeople like to reach decisions based on a consensus. They will ask everyone whom the decision affects for an opinion. Once this process is completed, expect to move very quickly and efficiently until the project is finished.

Sometimes a Dutch firm will do a background check on your company. The sole aim of such a check is to collect all available information on your firm so that they may make the most informed decision possible.

Entertaining

Dutch businesspeople enjoy entertaining and being entertained. An offer to pay for a meal will usually encounter little resistance.

A tip is usually included in the bill. If not, it is appropriate to leave a 15 percent gratuity on the table.

It is not uncommon to include spouses in business entertaining. If you are invited for a social occasion, you should ask your host whether spouses are included in the invitation.

Punctuality is considered extremely important. It is customary to remain and talk for around an hour and a half after the meal is finished. The meal itself, however, can last quite a long time.

In the Netherlands, toasts are made just before as well as just after the first sip.

It is considered a real sign of friendship to be invited to someone's home. Sending a thank-you note several days after visiting a home is appreciated.

When invited to someone's home for dinner, flowers or chocolates are an appropriate gift. Gifts should be wrapped, but flowers should be unwrapped before being presented to the host.

If you are invited to a businessperson's home, your host will appreciate compliments on his/her home, furniture, artwork, carpeting, etc.

The Dutch use the continental style of eating, with the knife held in the right hand and the fork in the left.

It is proper to eat many types of food, including sandwiches and fruit, with a knife and fork. Dessert is eaten with a spoon.

When dining, both hands should be kept above the table at all times, but you should not rest your elbows on the table.

Make a point of using restrooms either before or after the meal, as leaving the table for personal purposes is considered rude.

It is common for the host to serve. It is impolite to begin eating before others at the table. Expect your host to indicate when to begin eating. It is also impolite to drink before a toast is made.

Take small portions of food and try to taste every dish offered. It is considered impolite not to eat everything on your plate.

Genevre, the local alcoholic beverage, is similar in taste to gin or vodka, but it has a distinct flavor derived from anise.

SOCIAL VALUES, CUSTOMS AND TIPS

The correct name of the country is the Kingdom of the Netherlands. The Netherlands received its nickname, Holland, from two of its provinces: North Holland and South Holland. People from other provinces may object to this name. Therefore, you should refer to the people as Netherlanders or Dutch.

The Caribbean islands of Aruba and the Netherlands Antilles, which have a distinct culture of their own, are part of the Kingdom of the Netherlands.

The official language of the Netherlands is Dutch. French, English and German are taught in secondary schools, however, and are commonly understood and spoken by many.

It is acceptable to discuss Dutch or European politics in the Netherlands. Other good topics of conversation include social trends, sports, travel and vacations.

Avoid discussing money or prices. Do not probe excessively into someone's profession or family as the Dutch value their privacy.

As a small and dependent nation, the Dutch are very internationally minded. Note, however, that the Dutch also take great pride in their work in land reclamation, their art and history and their nation's strong tradition of liberalism.

Jokes about the Dutch queen or the royal family are considered to be in poor taste and are not acceptable.

When answering the telephone, it is customary for both the caller and the receiver to say their names.

The Dutch are not physically demonstrative and generally refrain from touching. Instead, they rely on eye contact and facial expressions.

There is a noticeable difference between the general attitude of people in the southern and in the northern provinces. By reputation, the people in the south are more gregarious than those in the north.

It is best to suppress signs of boredom or irritation.

When entering a shop or train compartment, greet each person present.

It is proper etiquette for the man to walk on the side of the pavement nearest the street when accompanying a woman. Men should stand when a woman enters the room.

People may wave in greeting from a distance, as it is considered impolite to shout.

Shaking the finger while speaking emphasizes a point.

In the Netherlands, a circular motion of the finger around the ear means that someone has a phone call. (In many other cultures, this might be interpreted as "crazy.")

In the Netherlands, tapping the elbow in reference to an individual signifies that that person is unreliable.

If a Dutch person taps his or her thumbnails together (as if applauding), it is a sign that the person does not appreciate what has just transpired (e.g., a joke or comment).

It is considered impolite to chew gum or stand with your hands in your pockets in public.

NEW ZEALAND

Population: 3,625,388 (July 1998 est.); New Zealand European 74.5%, Maori 9.7%, other European 4.6%, Pacific Islander 3.8%, Asian and others 7.4%

Languages: English (official), Maori (official)

Religions: Anglican 24%, Presbyterian 18%, Roman Catholic 15%, Methodist 5%, Baptist 2%, other Protestant 3%, unspecified or none 33%

Currency: New Zealand dollar

Wellington

HISTORICAL OVERVIEW

- The Maori, the first settlers in New Zealand, arrived in a series of migrations from the vicinity of Tahiti about 1,000 years ago. The period of the so-called "Great Migration" of the Maoris took place during the 13th and 14th centuries. Maori culture developed mainly on the relatively warm North Island with little outside interference.

- In 1642, the Dutch explorer Abel Tasman was the first European to discover New Zealand, but his attempts to go ashore were thwarted by the Maori. He called the islands Staten Landt, but the name was later changed by Dutch geographers to Nieuw Zeeland, after the Dutch province of Zeeland.

- The next contact New Zealand had with Europe was when Captain James Cook of England arrived in 1769. Sealers and whalers from Australia were the first to settle in the area, however. As a result of disease as well as the introduction of firearms into Maori warfare, the Maori population began to decline dramatically. At the same time, European settlers began to demand that the British protect them from the Maoris.

- In 1840, the Maoris ceded sovereignty to the British in return for legal protection and rights to perpetual ownership of Maori lands. The British did not honor their obligation to mediate disputes between the settlers and the Maoris, and skirmishes broke out, further reducing the Maori population and weakening the Maori influence in local affairs. In 1860, British troops forced the Maori people off land they refused to sell, and a decade-long war broke out.

- British colonization proceeded rapidly, and by 1852, internal self-government was granted to provincial parliaments that governed the area. The discovery of gold in 1861 brought new waves of settlers. In the early 1800s, the advent of refrigerated ships allowed New Zealand to export produce to England, thus developing its agriculturally based economy. In 1907, New Zealand became an independent dominion within the British Commonwealth.

- New Zealand was one of the most progressive countries at the end of the 19th century. From 1891 to 1912, under the Liberal Party, it introduced old-age pensions, a minimum wage, arbitration courts, child health-care services and women's suffrage. The Reform Party that followed introduced cooperative marketing systems between producer and state.

- New Zealand supported Britain in both World Wars, but after 1941 New Zealand was more concerned with events in the Pacific, where the U.S. played an important role as protector. New Zealand's focus began to change and, in 1951, the ANZUS pact between Australia, New Zealand and the U.S. was signed. New Zealand then assumed a much more active role in southeast Asia. Involvement in Vietnam triggered a national debate on foreign policy, and forces were withdrawn in 1971. Shortly thereafter, New Zealand also withdrew from the Southeast Asia Treaty Organization.

- In recent years, New Zealand has taken a strong antinuclear stand, refusing entry to U.S. nuclear-powered ships and condemning French nuclear testing in the Pacific. As a result, the U.S. dropped New Zealand from the ANZUS treaty agreements and French agents sank a vessel belonging to an antinuclear group in Auckland's harbor.

- Jim Bolger of the mildly conservative National Party was elected prime minister in 1990 and reelected in 1993 and 1995. In March of that year, Bolger met with U.S. President Bill Clinton and overall relations with the U.S. appeared to have been mended.

- New parliamentary elections held in October 1996 were the first that did not follow the British model. Instead, votes were counted in such a manner as to allow for greater minority party representation in parliament.

- Discontent with the government's lack of direction led the NP to appoint Jenny Shipley as prime minister in 1997. Shipley continued to uphold New Zealand's antinuclear testing policies. She recalled New Zealand's ambassador to India after India conducted nuclear tests, and this topic remains a sensitive issue in U.S.-New Zealand relations.

BUSINESS PRACTICES

Hours of Business

Usually, business hours are from 9:00 a.m. until 5:30 p.m., Monday to Friday and from 9:00 a.m. until 12:30 p.m. on Saturday.

It is advisable not to try to organize a business trip during the months of December and January, when most people are on vacation (these are the summer months).

Dress

Business dress is somewhat formal and conservative. Most businessmen wear a dark suit and tie, and businesswomen wear a dark skirt suit with a white blouse.

Introductions

While a handshake is the standard greeting, be aware that styles of greeting can vary a great deal in New Zealand. The manner of greeting can vary from U.S.-style openness and Maori graciousness to British reserve. The style of greeting usually depends on the individuals involved and the circumstances. Generally, New Zealanders wait to be approached, but are very friendly once they are greeted.

In formal situations such as business meetings or dinner parties, a man usually waits for the woman to offer her hand in a handshake.

The somewhat formal greeting, "How do you do?," is often used when people first meet. General verbal greetings include "Good day" (pronounced "Gidday") or simply "Hello" or "Hi."

Titles such as "Mr.," "Mrs." or "Miss" or a professional title followed by the last name should be used at first meetings. Most people use first names after an initial introduction.

People sometimes greet each other with a hug or the traditional *hongi* – pressing the noses together with the eyes closed and making a low "mm-mm" sound. The *hongi* is not used with non-Maoris.

Meetings

Appointments should be arranged in advance. Punctuality is important. In fact, it is advisable for foreign visitors to arrive a few minutes early for any engagement because New Zealanders traditionally arrive five minutes early.

Meetings move rather quickly, but it is expected that information be presented clearly, that proposals be meticulously made and that contracts be written in a clear and succinct manner.

Introductory meetings usually take place in an office but, after that, you may suggest meeting over lunch at a restaurant or in a hotel. Lunch appointments are usually for conducting business, while dinner engagements are more relaxed occasions for socializing. Spouses are normally included in invitations.

Negotiating

Be aware that the accumulation of objective facts is the most important element of negotiating, and little importance is given to subjective feelings. New Zealanders are direct but friendly when negotiating and will not hesitate to say "No" directly.

There is a lot of individualism in decision making, and individual initiative and achievement are emphasized. At the same time, the individual will follow company policy, so that dealing with different executives at different times will not disrupt business.

Rank is minimized in business, and equality is emphasized.

In New Zealand, the pace of business is generally slower than that of the U.S., but faster than in Australia.

Conducting business according to typical North American protocol is considered appropriate in New Zealand.

Entertaining

Entertaining in the home is popular and common. New Zealanders enjoy cooking and will often invite guests for dinner.

Summer barbecues (called "barbies") are very popular and are usually held on weekends. Inviting people for "afternoon tea," at about 3:00 p.m., is also common. Even if not invited for afternoon tea or a meal, guests will always be offered refreshments.

Dinner guests almost always bring a gift. Acceptable gifts include wine, flowers, a potted plant or a box of chocolates. Gifts should be simple since ostentation usually meets with disapproval.

In restaurants, waiters will not hurry unless asked to do so since they consider it their job to let diners take their time.

People avoid talking loudly in restaurants. In fact, little conversation takes place during the meal. Instead, there is conversation afterwards.

A service charge is generally not included in the restaurant bill and tipping is not expected.

Dinner, called "tea," is the main meal of the day. In homes, "tea" is served around 6:00 or 7:00 p.m., although when eating out the meal takes place closer to 8:00 p.m. (Note the difference between "tea" and "afternoon tea," which is served at 3:00 or 4:00 p.m.) Sometimes, a light "supper" is served in the late evening.

The New Zealand diet has traditionally been based on the British one, with hearty meals of meat and potatoes. Recently, however, the diet has been changing to reflect a more health-conscious population. New Zealand also specializes in dairy products. A unique New Zealand food is vegemite (a yeast extract), which is used as a spread for bread.

New Zealanders eat in the continental style, with the fork in the left hand and the knife in the right.

It is best to keep your hands but not your elbows above the table.

To indicate that you have finished eating, place your utensils parallel on your plate.

SOCIAL VALUES, CUSTOMS AND TIPS

English and Maori are the official languages of New Zealand, although Maori is used primarily for Maori ceremonies and other special occasions.

The English language spoken in New Zealand includes several distinctive expressions. Some Maori words have found their way into New Zealand English.

Some distinctive words or phrases are "over the road" (across the street), "pop downtown" (go downtown), "go to the loo" (go to the bathroom) and "come around" (come over). The hood of a car is called a "bonnet," a "lift" is an elevator, a "bathroom" is a place to take a bath, "petrol" is gasoline, "serviettes" are napkins, "napkins" are diapers, and "entrees" are appetizers. If someone says that you are a "mate" or a "hard case," consider it a compliment because he/she means that you are a friend or a humorous person.

New Zealanders are open, friendly and hospitable, and their attitude toward life is relaxed and informal. A New Zealander is more likely to discuss leisure activities and family interests than occupations, incomes or career objectives.

New Zealanders are very proud of their country as well as the high value placed on self-reliance and practicality. The country, the culture and the area in which you are staying make good topics for conversation.

While many Maoris have been integrated into mainstream society, they retain roots to their land and ethnic group. The Maoris are proud of their Polynesian culture, which emphasizes humility, truth and a strong sense of community. Good conversation topics also include sports and politics. Many New Zealanders participate in outdoor, noncompetitive sports such as hiking, fishing or sailing. New Zealanders appreciate lively political discussions, especially with those who maintain strong beliefs or convictions. Hold up your end of the debate without becoming personal or critical.

Avoid bringing up racial topics or the treatment of the Maori as well as religion, personal questions or nuclear energy. Be aware that New Zealanders try to establish a distinct identity from Australia and that there exists a strong rivalry between the two countries. Therefore, make a point never to confuse them. Finally, avoid any praise of Australia or Australians.

New Zealanders do not like to stand close to others or touch each other during conversation. New Zealanders tend to speak softly and do not open their mouths widely when speaking. They maintain more of the traditional British reserve than their Australian counterparts do.

Western-style clothing is the standard, although the Maoris wear a variety of traditional clothing for cultural events. A neat, clean appearance is important in public. Warm clothes and rain gear are common due to New Zealand's temperate climate.

Most offensive gestures used in the U.S. are also offensive in New Zealand. The "V-for-victory" sign is considered obscene, especially when done with the palm facing inwards.

The mouth is covered if a yawn or a cough cannot be suppressed. Chewing gum or using a toothpick in public is considered rude.

NICARAGUA

Population: 4,583,379 (July 1998 est.); mestizo (Amerindian and white) 69%, white 17%, black 9%, Amerindian 5%

Languages: Spanish (official)

Religions: Roman Catholic 95%, Protestant 5%

Currency: cordoba

Managua
★

HISTORICAL OVERVIEW

- When he arrived in 1502, Columbus was the first European to visit Nicaragua. He was followed by Spanish conquistadores, who explored the region. Indigenous groups resisted the Spanish until they were finally conquered in 1522.

- British settlements were established along the Caribbean coast in the 17th and 18th centuries, leading Britain to claim sovereignty over the coast in 1740. Despite the British claim, Spain ruled Nicaragua until 1826, when it declared independence. Upon independence, the country became a member of the United Provinces of Central America, but it chose to become an independent republic in 1838.

- For almost a century after Nicaragua had become a republic, political clashes between liberals based in Léon and conservatives from Granada dominated politics and often led to violence. Beginning in 1909, internal chaos and U.S. economic interests led the U.S. to intervene and press for the installation of a conservative government. During the 1920s and 1930s, guerillas led by Augusto Cesar Sandino fought the U.S. occupation. Sandino was assassinated in 1934 at the instigation of General Anastasio Somoza García, who became president without opposition in 1936.

- General Somoza ruled as a dictator until he was assassinated in 1956. Although the economy grew, its fruits went mainly to the Somoza family. After his death, Somoza's family continued to rule until the 1970s. Meanwhile, in 1962, a revolutionary group called the Sandinistas was formed with the goal of overthrowing the Somozas. They carried out unsuccessful terrorist attacks for fifteen years on Somoza's National Guard, which had been trained and continued to be armed by the U.S government.

- In 1972 an earthquake wreaked havoc on Managua. When the Somoza family took international aid from the victims for itself, the Sandinistas gained support among the middle class. Civil war broke out in 1978 and 50,000 were killed. In 1979, the Somozas were forced to flee while the Sandinistas took control.

- The new Marxist government seized the Somoza fortune, redistributed their lands to the peasants, suspended the constitution and tightened controls, suspending elections until 1984. Anti-Sandinista activity on the part of counterrevolutionaries known as Contras began in 1980. Concerned that the Sandinistas were aiding Marxist rebels in El Salvador, the U.S. suspended aid to the Nicaraguan government in 1981 and began aiding the Contras.

- Sandinista leader Daniel Ortega Saaverda was elected to power in the 1984 general elections. In response, the U.S. imposed a trade embargo on the nation and continued funding the Contras. The results were disastrous for the Nicaraguan economy. A peace plan proposed by the Costa Rican president in 1987 led to negotiations between the Contras and Sandinistas and, while fighting continued, free elections were ensured for 1990.

- In the 1990 elections, Violeta Barrios de Chamorro, the widow of an assassinated newspaper editor, defeated Ortega. The U.S. backed her candidacy and pledged to end trade restrictions. The Contras began to disband in 1990. Severe economic difficulties, however, subsequently contributed to increasing tensions. In 1992, Sandinista soldiers and Contras began to rearm.

- The Sandinista commander in chief of the army, Humberto Ortega, retired in 1995 after considerable pressure from the U.S. He was, however, succeeded by another Sandinista member.

- Chamorro was unable to institute programs to revitalize the economy. Arnoldo Alemán won the presidential elections of 1996. This was the first time in Nicaragua's history that one civilian president consecutively succeeded another. Alemán began talks in 1997 with the Sandinistas, who still had a significant say in the National Assembly and municipal governments. He hoped to gain their support as he attempted to open Nicaragua up to free market capitalism.

- Per capita income has dropped since 1979, and unemployment, inflation and the external debt have risen considerably.

BUSINESS PRACTICES

Hours of Business

Businesses are open from 8:00 a.m. until 6:00 p.m., Monday through Friday and from 8:00 a.m. until noon on Saturday. There is usually a two-hour *siesta* (a rest after the midday meal) for lunch and resting, between noon and 2:00 p.m.

The best time to arrange a trip to Nicaragua is between February and July or between September and November, when people are not on vacation.

Dress

Businessmen customarily wear conservative dark suits and ties. In the hottest summer months, however, they will seldom wear jackets. Businesswomen normally wear dresses or skirts and blouses.

Introductions

When meeting someone for the first time, Nicaraguans shake hands and say either *Mucho gusto de conocerle* (Glad to meet you) or *¿Cómo está usted?* (How are you?). Complete attention is given to the person being greeted. Eye contact and smiles are very important.

Close male friends may greet each other with an *abrazo*, a brief hug. Women usually kiss each other on the cheek and give each other a gentle hug upon greeting.

Titles should be used when addressing Nicaraguans. First names are used only with close friends, family or children. It is preferable to use a professional title. If the person does not have a professional title or you are not sure of it, you may use the titles *Señor* (Mr.), *Señora* (Mrs.) or *Señorita* (Miss), followed by a last name. The titles *Don* and *Doña* are used with men's and women's first names, respectively, to indicate special respect and familiarity or affection.

Most Nicaraguans have two surnames, one from the father (listed first) and one from the mother. Normally, the father's name is used when addressing someone. For example, Hernan Antonio Martinez Garcia is addressed as *Señor Martinez*, and María Elisa Gutierrez Herrera is addressed as *Señorita Gutierrez*. When a woman marries, she usually adds her husband's surname and is addressed by that surname. For example, if the two people in the above example married, the woman would be known as María Elisa Gutierrez Herrera de Martinez. She would be addressed as *Señora de Martinez* or, more informally, as *Señora Martinez*.

Common terms of greeting include ¡*Buenos días*! (Good morning), ¡*Buenas tardes*! (Good afternoon) and ¡*Buenas noches*! (Good evening).

A casual greeting, especially among the youth, is ¡*Hola*! (Hi).

If you are at a small party, it is polite to greet and shake hands with each person individually.

Meetings

It is important to make appointments well in advance (at least one month) from your country, either by telephone or fax.

Because the demands of interpersonal relationships are considered more important than schedules, precise punctuality is often not observed. Being on time, however, is admired, appreciated and expected of foreigners.

Negotiating

Since establishing a personal relationship is so important in negotiating in Nicaragua, contacts are very important. It is essential to try to establish them before you visit and to have them arrange introductions with major clients. You can establish *enchufados* (contacts) through embassies, banks, etc.

Expect business to be conducted at a slower pace in Nicaragua than in North America. A good deal of time will be spent on establishing personal relationships, and delays in schedules are quite common.

In negotiating, be aware that Nicaraguans may be suspicious of information provided by outsiders. They also tend to look at problems and situations from a subjective, personal perspective and seldom rely solely on abstract rules and objective facts in making decisions. Similarly, they will seldom use factual information to prove a point. An emotional appeal (to pride, trust, mutual compatibility, etc.) is generally more common and more successful in negotiating than an appeal to facts and logic.

Individuals tend to be group oriented. Self-identity is based on an individual's position and performance in the group. Individual expertise and initiative tend to be subordinated to personal connections and the individual's ability to be part of the group. Appeals highlighting the benefits of a particular business deal for the group (for example, the company, the negotiating team or the country) tend to be most successful.

Because machismo (the concept that men are superior to women) is quite strong in Nicaragua and because there are very few women in top positions in Nicaraguan firms, foreign businesswomen may encounter an initial lack of respect. They should act very professionally and emphasize that they are representing their firms and not themselves as individuals.

Entertaining

Business breakfasts or lunches are preferred over dinners. If you are invited to a meal in a home or if spouses are included at a meal, it is a purely social engagement. Nicaraguans do not discuss business at home or around family members.

Business gifts are usually not given on the first trip to Nicaragua. It is more appropriate, at the end of your visit, to ask your Nicaraguan counterparts if there is anything you can bring them from your country on your next visit.

It is usually a good idea to bring a gift for secretaries and receptionists. Perfume or scarves make appropriate gifts.

If you are invited to a home, it is appropriate to bring a small gift of candy or flowers. Do not bring white flowers, which are normally reserved for funerals.

It is polite to arrive a few minutes late to all social occasions.

The main meal of the day is at 12:00 noon. It is usually followed by a *siesta*, an afternoon nap.

Beans, rice and corn are the basic elements of the Nicaraguan diet. Typical dishes include *tortillas* (thin, round unleavened bread made from cornmeal or wheat four), *enchiladas* (a tortilla rolled and stuffed with meat and/or vegetables served with chili sauce), *nacatamales* (meat and vegetables with spices), *mondongo* (tripe and beef knuckles) and *baho* (meat, vegetables and plantain). Tropical fruits and fried bananas (*plátanos*) are popular. A typical vegetable dish is called vigorón.

Meals tend to last longer than in North America since eating is accompanied by pleasant conversation. People avoid bringing up controversial topics during meals.

Both hands (but not elbows) should remain above the table at all times.

SOCIAL VALUES, CUSTOMS AND TIPS

Nicaraguan Spanish has many words unique to the Spanish language and is known for its forcefulness. Words considered profane in neighboring Costa Rica are used daily in Nicaragua. Small groups that live along the Caribbean coast speak English and other languages. English will be understood by many in the capital city.

Nicaraguans are particularly hospitable to foreign visitors. They enjoy hearing stories about life in other countries. Nicaraguan tourist sites and culture are also good topics of conversation.

Traditional values support a social hierarchy and machismo. Because it is traditionally considered that only the opinions of those holding power are important, power is highly valued and often sought. Nevertheless, people living in urban areas tend to be less traditional and will accept modern values.

Personal honor is very important and will be defended verbally or even physically. Be careful not to embarrass or criticize someone or attempt to pull rank.

Expressing admiration for material objects is not as important as making compliments on good personality traits.

Good topics of conversation include jobs, history, culture and family. Inquiring about the health of family members demonstrates friendliness between acquaintances. Avoid discussing poverty, politics and religion. Be somewhat diplomatic when discussing U.S. involvement in Nicaragua, since some Nicaraguans love and respect the U.S., but others see it as their enemy.

Sports also makes a good topic of conversation. Baseball is the national sport. People also enjoy soccer, boxing, basketball and volleyball.

Due to the year-round warm climate, cool, lightweight clothes are most commonly worn. Women generally wear cotton dresses or skirts and blouses. In some areas, a woman may offend others by wearing pants. In cities and rural areas, shorts and jeans are inappropriate for both men and women. A woman should avoid wearing revealing clothes. Men sometimes wear the traditional *guayabera*, a lightweight shirt.

Most gestures that are used in the U.S. are also common in Nicaragua, although making a fist with the thumb positioned between the index and middle fingers (the "fig" gesture) is considered vulgar.

To beckon someone, make a scooping gesture with the fingers with the palm facing down.

When Nicaraguans wave good-bye, they sometimes wave with their hand facing out. They also sometimes wave with the palm facing inwards, as if they were fanning themselves.

Be careful when taking photographs, especially of individuals and religious ceremonies. Some people object to having their pictures taken. Avoid photographing transportation depots and bridges, which may have military significance.

Deference is shown to older people. It is appropriate to stand when they enter or leave a room and to give them your seat on public transportation. Do not be surprised if an older person is served before you when you are standing in line.

NIGERIA

Population: 110,532,242 (July 1998 est.); Hausa, Fulani, Yoruba, Ibo, Kanuri, Ibibio, Tiv, Ijaw

Languages: English (official), Hausa, Yoruba, Ibo, Fulani

Religions: Muslim 50%, Christian 40%, indigenous beliefs 10%

Currency: naira

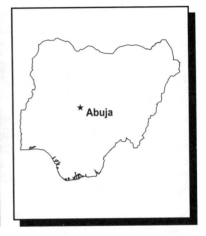

★ Abuja

HISTORICAL OVERVIEW

- Nigeria's history can be dated back to 500 B.C. when the Nok people lived in the area. They flourished until 200 A.D. when the Kanuri, Hausa and Fulani peoples migrated into its northern parts.

- By the end of the 11th century the Karem empire had spread out in the northeast, including across many Hausa lands.

- The Hausa peoples converted to Islam in the 13th century and established a feudal system among themselves. The Karem Empire declined and shrank in the 14th century.

- The Fulani, who had been migrating for centuries to Hausa lands, became rulers in some Hausa states in the late 19th century and proceeded to build an empire.

- In the southwest, the Yoruba established the Kingdom of Oyo and extended its influence as far as modern Togo, while the Ibo in the southwest remained isolated.

- European explorers and traders, first the Portuguese and then the British, made contact with the Yoruba and the Benin peoples at the end of the 15th century. They began a profitable slave trade, although there was no attempt made during this time to colonize Nigeria.

- British influence increased until 1861 when Britain declared the area around the city of Lagos a crown colony. By 1914, the entire area had become the Colony and Protectorate of Nigeria.

- Nigeria became independent in 1960 and a republic in 1963. Tensions mounted among the various ethnic groups. Very bloody clashes between the Hausa and Ibo took place, resulting in the death or flight of thousands of Ibo. The Ibo then attempted to secede and establish the Republic of Biafra in the eastern region of the country. Civil war followed from 1967-1970, and the Ibo were forced back into the republic.

- Since then Nigeria has been ruled by a series of military regimes interspersed with brief periods of unstable civilian rule.

- In 1979, under a new constitution, a civilian government headed by President Shehu Shagari was elected. Yet, in 1983, a military coup placed power in the hands of General Mohammed Buhari, who banned political parties.

- Another coup followed in 1985, and Major General Ibrahim Babangida became the nation's new military leader.

- Babangida's government focused on economic reforms. Although he promised a transition to civilian rule in the 1990s, and even set up a transitional government, he annulled the first elections he held in 1993.

- Chaos ensued and General Sani Abacha took over, abolishing all democratic institutions.

- Abacha did not fulfill his promise to restore a civilian government and instead declared the extension of his reign until 1998. During this time, he exiled, imprisoned and killed many of his political opponents.

- On 8 June 1998, Abacha died. Although the cause of death is unclear, it is attributed to his failing health. Nigeria's military leaders immediately appointed General Abdulsalam Abubakar to assume the position of president.

- That week, 45 of Nigeria's pro-democratic groups demonstrated for the reinstallation of a civilian government headed by Moshood K.O. Abiola, who had won the suddenly annulled 1993 elections. Abiola, however, died as well.

- Suspicions that Abiola's death was not a natural one and the population's continued demand for civilian rule led to widespread protests.

- Continued social and economic disorganization, as well as a high inflation rate, have made trade with Nigeria increasingly difficult.

BUSINESS PRACTICES

Hours of Business

Business hours are weekdays from 8:30 a.m. to 5:00 p.m. In the Muslim areas, business is not done on Fridays or Saturdays for religious reasons.

Dress

To a formal business meeting men should wear a shirt, tie and slacks. Women should wear a dress.

When meeting with top executives, businessmen must wear a business suit with a conservative shirt and tie. Businesswomen must wear a business dress.

It is acceptable and appreciated for businesspeople to wear the Nigerian national dress or business casual clothing to informal business occasions. Women may wear slacks in Lagos. The national dress for men is a pair of cotton pants with a long tunic and a *baban riga* (bah-bahn ree-gah), a long robe. The national dress for women is a six-foot-long cloth cut into three two-foot-long pieces – one piece functions as a skirt, one as a top, and one as a head covering.

Introductions

Nigerians place great value on properly greeting someone, and handshaking is customary. Upon meeting a Nigerian business associate, the greeting is western but formal.

Learning local forms and words of greetings is very much appreciated by prospective business partners. A few words in the local language, even phrased imperfectly, show a willingness to adapt as well as an appreciation for local customs.

Although there is a great diversity of customs, cultures and dialects in Nigeria, be aware that English is widely used when exchanging greetings.

Traditionally, titles are important.

Meetings

It is best to schedule no more than two appointments a day and to allow plenty of time in between. Nigerians do not have a rigid sense of time, and punctuality is not common. An 8:00 a.m. appointment may not show up until 4:00 p.m., if at all. In addition, transportation often does not run on schedule.

Nigerians tend to schedule business appointments well in advance.

Business cards are sometimes called the "compliment card." They often say "with the compliments of" and are given with more meaning than as just a handy reference. Presenting a card indicates that you wish your business initiatives to be taken seriously.

Negotiating

The area in which you are conducting business will greatly determine the type of business environment you will encounter. The Nigerian population is split largely among Muslims and Christians.

Foreign executives should avoid lumping vaguely related cultures together in the same general groupings. The cultures of the Ibos in the largely Christian south and the Hausas in the mainly Muslim north are quite different as are the respective deal-making and business styles of these two ethnic groups. The Ibo people adapted well to westernization during British colonial rule. The Hausas are generally more formal and conservative in their business approach.

In order to do business legally in Nigeria, you must have a Nigerian partner. Be sure to inspect the qualifications and backgrounds of prospective partners carefully.

Sensitivity to the colonial past suggests the use of a mixed-race team. (Males are generally preferred.)

Experience, educational credentials and age are important in establishing credibility. Age is highly respected and associated with wisdom. It is recommended that an older rather than younger person be sent to meet with prospective business partners. Sending a young executive may suggest to Nigerians that their business is not worthy of the attention of the elders who are presumed to head an organization.

After greeting your counterparts, take some time to converse socially before commencing business. Better yet, let them first broach the subject of business. Small talk is considered part of the greeting process.

Middlemen are pivotal for introduction to the business environment.

Rapport is valued over price, quality or other issues in completing negotiations.

In Nigeria, significant business transactions are always conducted in person. Any attempt to conduct business by telephone or by mail is taken to mean that the item of business is trivial or unimportant.

Verbal agreements are preferred, with a follow-up in writing. Regardless of the type of agreement, flexibility is expected.

Communication is open and direct in nature and may appear heated. Nigerians expect hard bargaining to occur on the negotiating table and may reject part of a deal.

Trust is important in maintaining the business relationship. Be sure to follow through on all matters stated in the contract.

Be patient. The bureaucracy's red tape and the relaxed notion of time result in a slow process with many delays.

Dash, a facilitation fee, is usually expected to expedite business. Although the government discourages such fees, they are common throughout Nigeria.

Tolerance for risk varies throughout the country from risk-accepting in the south to risk-averse in the north.

Large prepayments are generally required for services.

Entertaining

Most entertaining, especially in Lagos, is conducted in clubs, hotels or elegant, expensive restaurants. Food and customs in these establishments are very much in the style of the British.

Breakfast meetings are very popular as Nigerians start their day early. Discussing business during breakfast is often very productive.

It is common to continue business over lunch. It is unlikely that you will be invited out for a social evening until a friendly relationship has been established or you are about to close a business deal.

If you are invited to a Nigerian home for a social evening, remember to always bring gifts. Perfume and makeup are acceptable for a woman. Your Nigerian host may enjoy customized stationery or western-style clothing.

The most interesting part of Nigerian entertaining is the music and dancing. Lagos has more nightclubs with live music than most of the rest of Africa combined, and one can expect to be shown the host's favorite discos during a night out. *Juju*, a local style of pop music with strong local flavor and rhythms, dominates many clubs.

Nigerian cooking is often very spicy. Specialties include dried fish and herbs, *alapa* (smothered red snapper), *frejon* (smothered catfish in bean sauce), chicken and beef loaf, chicken *imoyo* (chicken and okra), *jo jo jo* (meatballs), *akara* (bean balls), *puff-puff* (fried bread), *fetri detsi* (spicy chili chicken) and *moyinmoyin* (steamed dumplings stuffed with shrimp).

In Yoruba country as well as other areas of Nigeria, stews are made with *egunsi* – melon or gourd seeds – that are boiled and then soaked several days until fermented.

Nigeria has long been a fertile producer of cocoa, palm oil, cocoyams, tubers, sorghum, millet, rice and other agricultural bounties.

Breakfast is usually eaten between 7:00 and 9:00 a.m. and consists of hot porridge or rice, bread and English tea. Lunch is served from 1:30 to 3:30 p.m., often with a *siesta* around the same time. Dinner typically begins around 8:30 p.m. and may end around 11:00 p.m. or later.

Nigerians often have their meals at home, although small, cozy restaurants featuring traditional foods are also popular settings for eating.

A specialty is a traditional Nigerian buffet, where a savory array is offered for large gatherings. This array includes the local cuisine, with the centerpiece consisting of bananas, surrounded by coconuts, avocados, mangoes, fresh pineapple slices, cucumbers, eggplants and peanuts.

SOCIAL VALUES, CUSTOMS AND TIPS

When conversing, members of the same sex stand much closer to each other than do people in North America.

Good conversation topics include modern and future aspects of the country. Nigerians derive much pride and self-confidence from the belief that their country is in many ways a leader in Africa.

Friendship is a valued commodity among most Nigerians. Hospitality is abundant and generous. Also, relationships develop quickly and tend to be long-lasting.

Family ties are very strong in Nigeria. Family members remain close to each other throughout their entire lives. It is not unusual for family members to expect a relative either to find or create a job for them once this relative is employed.

As in many other cultures, the left hand is considered unclean in Nigeria. It is extremely impolite to extend the left hand to others or to eat with it, even if a person is left-handed.

Although women in the cities and young girls often wear western dress, most women wear traditional long wraparound skirts, short-sleeved tops and head scarves. Traditional dress for men is loose and comfortable.

NORWAY

Population: 4,419,955 (July 1998 est.); Germanic 97%, Lappish 3%

Languages: Norwegian (official)

Religions: Evangelical Lutheran 87.8%, other Protestant and Roman Catholic 3.8%, none 3.2%, unknown 5.2%

Currency: krone

HISTORICAL OVERVIEW

- There is evidence that Norway has been inhabited as far back as 7000 B.C. During the first four centuries A.D. peoples in Norway were in contact with the Romans through Gaul. The period from 800 to 1050 is known as the Viking Age. During this time the Vikings of Norway emerged as great sailors and explorers. They went on many expeditions westward, raiding and settling in the British Isles, Iceland, France and Greenland. They even went as far as modern-day Newfoundland in Canada. Harald I Fairhair united the region of Norway and became the first king of the unified kingdom of Norway in 900.

- King Olaf II Haraldsson became king in 1015. In England he had been convinced of Christianity and he converted many Norwegians. Viking power declined as Christianity grew, foreign trade expanded and political confusion and struggles for power took hold.

- Norway was subject to civil wars between 1130 and 1240 as various claimants contended for the throne, but the victorious King Haakon IV (1217-73) emerged as a very strong king. Through the 14th century the Norwegian monarchy continued to grow in power. Eric of Pomerania became king of Norway in 1389 and then also of Sweden and Denmark. When he was deposed in 1442, Norway was placed under Danish rule, where it remained until 1814.

- In 1814, Norway was given to Sweden as a peace treaty provision to punish Denmark for its alliance with Napoleon during the Napoleonic Wars. Norway immediately declared its independence and drafted a constitution. While the constitution was accepted, Swedish rule prevailed until 1905.

- In 1905, the union with Sweden was peacefully dissolved by referendum and Prince Carl of Denmark was chosen to be King Haakon VI of the new constitutional monarchy.

- Norway remained neutral in World War I. In 1940 during World War II, however, Germany occupied the country until the end of the war. The king and government fled to England, where it assisted the allied effort.

- Despite some setbacks suffered around the Depression, Norway's economy flourished in the first half of the 20th century and many important social programs were introduced.

- After the war, Norway became a member of the North Atlantic Treaty Organization (NATO) and later became a member of the European Free Trade Association (EFTA). The postwar period has been marked by political stability, continued economic development and positive foreign relations.

- The Norwegian Labor Party was in power almost continuously from 1945 to 1965. A right-wing coalition took over from 1965 to 1971. Labor then returned, but not as strong as before, and, after a decade or so, power went back and forth between Labor and the Conservative Party. In the 1981 election, Gro Harlem Brundtland, a Labor Party member, became Norway's first woman prime minister. She was in power on and off through 1996.

- Although the Norwegian government originally signed a membership agreement with the fledgling EEC, voters rejected the agreement and membership first in the EEC and then in the EU.

- In the 1970s Norway became heavily involved in the booming North Sea oil industry. Today, Norway must find a way to balance its investments in the North Sea with other more traditional aspects of its economy so that it is able to sustain a high standard of living while not becoming dependent on oil revenues.

- Gro Harlem Brundtland resigned in 1996 and was replaced by Thorbjørn Jagland, who is also a member of the Labor Party.

- TROLL, Norway's newest gas platform, opened in October 1996. The new gas line will supply one-third of Germany's and France's gas requirements.

BUSINESS PRACTICES

Hours of Business

Businesses are usually open from 8:00 a.m. to 4:00 p.m. Sometimes they may be open later, but all business is generally conducted by 5:00 p.m.

Avoid scheduling business trips during July and August, since Norwegians go on vacation during these months.

Dress

In Norway, business dress is fairly casual. Men can wear sports jackets, but should always wear ties. Women can wear suits, dresses or dress pants.

Introductions

Always remember to shake hands when being introduced, when greeting someone and when you are leaving.

In Norway it is very common for men to be addressed by their surname only (i.e., Good morning, Jones). This is perfectly acceptable and is not considered rude.

When you are first introduced to someone, use the person's first and last name when addressing him/her.

The Norwegians are quite restrictive about using first names only.

Use a person's occupational title before the surname when you are addressing a professor, doctor or engineer. You should not use a title, however, when addressing a lawyer or a clergyman.

Meetings

It is recommended that appointments be scheduled at least a week in advance, and they should be scheduled for between 10:00 a.m. and noon or between 2:00 and 4:00 p.m. It is best to allow the secretary of the Norwegian firm to schedule the meeting.

Punctuality is considered very important. If you are going to be late, it is best to telephone to explain your tardiness. Also telephone ahead to cancel or postpone an appointment.

Negotiating

Most Norwegian businesspeople are fluent in English and are very familiar with other business and trade practices.

At business meetings, avoid becoming too familiar. It is not common to have casual conversations or make jokes at meetings. Presentations should be very clear and emphasize hard facts, include figures and be precise.

Since all business is normally concluded by 5:00 p.m. it is best to set a time limit for your meeting so that it does not run over.

Formality is not stressed in a Norwegian business setting. Feel free to introduce yourself to those present at the meeting, even if they are of a higher rank than yourself. You do not need to wait for the secretary to do so.

Entertaining

In Norway, businesspeople usually eat lunch at their desks. Lunch is normally the lightest meal of the day. If you invite someone to lunch, however, expect the offer to be accepted.

It is very common for a Norwegian businessperson to invite colleagues home for a meal.

If invited to dinner in a home, men should wear suits and women should wear dresses, skirts or dress pants and blouses. If invited to a restaurant, a man should wear a jacket and tie. (A jacket and tie are not necessary in smaller or neighborhood restaurants.)

Be punctual if invited for a meal. Even in a home, it is common for people to go immediately to the table. If there is time set aside for cocktails, it is usually very brief.

At a small party, wait for your host or hostess to introduce you. At a larger party, it is best to introduce yourself. If you are seated, always stand when you are introduced.

If you are invited for a cup of coffee, it is appropriate to bring pastries or chocolates. When invited for a meal, bring wine, chocolates, pastries or flowers.

Liquor is always a welcome gift since it is very expensive in Norway. If you bring flowers, avoid bringing wreaths, carnations or any kind of white flower, since these are reserved for funerals.

Spouses are usually not included in business meals at restaurants.

Toasting is very common, using the expression *Skoal*.

In order to get the attention of a waiter/waitress, raise your hand and extend the index finger. It is considered rude to snap your fingers to get someone's attention.

In restaurants, the tip is included in the bill. It is common, however, to leave an extra three to five kroner if the service was very good.

According to Norwegian eating style, the fork should be kept in the left hand and the knife in the right. The knife is used to push food onto the back of the fork.

Open-faced sandwiches, which are commonly served for lunch in Norway, should be eaten with a knife and fork and should never be picked up with your hands.

At a dinner party, the host and hostess will usually sit at opposite ends of the table. The male guest of honor will be seated to the left of the hostess and the female guest of honor to the left of the host. Food is usually passed around the table on platters.

It is polite to finish everything on your plate and to accept any food or drink that is offered to you. Your host will not be offended, however, if you do not want to eat something after tasting it.

You can indicate that you are finished eating by crossing your utensils in the middle of your plate.

If invited to dinner, you should plan to stay until about 10:00 or 11:00 p.m. It is common for the meal itself to last several hours. Dinner is commonly the largest meal of the day.

It is considered polite to thank the hostess at the end of the meal. This does not signal the end of the evening, however. In fact, it is impolite to leave immediately after the meal.

It is not unusual to have dancing after a dinner party, even in a home. Also, during the summer when it is light until about 11:00 p.m., it is not unusual for your host to suggest taking a walk after dinner. After the walk, it is common to return to the house for a liqueur.

In Norway, fresh fish is very common at meals. In addition, several common delicacies are *fenalar* (cured and baked leg of mutton), *flatbrod* (crisp thin rye bread), *himmelsk lapskaus* (fruit salad with nuts, served with rum and egg sauce) and *rabarbragrot* (rhubarb compote). You may also want to be aware of several unusual foods that are served in Norway. These include *hval biff* (whale meat), *gjetost* (a cheese that tastes more like sweet fudge) and *sylte* (a fatty, gelatinous salami made of innards).

SOCIAL VALUES, CUSTOMS AND TIPS

Norwegians admire self-reliance and the ability to put aside personal interests for the common good. They take great pride in individual and national independence. Tolerance, human kindness and personal independence are also admired. Do not offer any criticism of the people or their customs.

Good topics of conversation include interests, hobbies, politics or sports (especially soccer, skiing, hiking or sailing). Also, Norwegians are very proud of their history, culture and Viking heritage.

Norwegians are usually reserved about themselves. It takes time to get to know people personally. Avoid talking about personal matters. For example, avoid questions such as, "What do you do?" or "Are you married?," etc. You should also avoid talking about employment, salary or social status.

Answer the telephone by giving your last name or phone number.

Speaking in a loud voice and using demonstrative gestures (e.g., slapping someone's back or putting your arm around someone's shoulder) should be avoided.

Courtesy and good behavior are important at all times. It is common for men to offer their seats to women or to the elderly.

OMAN

Population: 2,363,591 (July 1998 est.); Arab, Baluchi, South Asian (Indian, Pakistani, Sri Lankan, Bangladeshi), African

Languages: Arabic (official), English, Baluchi, Urdu, Indian dialects

Religions: Ibadhi Muslim 75%, Sunni Muslim, Shi'a Muslim, Hindu

Currency: Omani rial

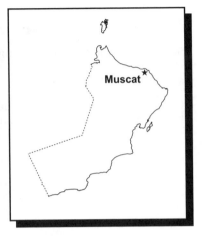

Muscat

HISTORICAL OVERVIEW

- Early inhabitants of Oman manufactured and traded frankincense throughout the Middle East and the Mediterranean. In the ninth century B.C. Arabs began migrating to the country. The rivalry between the two clans that first emigrated, the Qahtan and the Nizar, has affected Omani history ever since. Before the country's conversion to Islam in the seventh century A.D. its history was marked by tribal warfare.

- By 751 the Omanis had all been converted to Islam, and they elected an imam (spiritual leader) to rule them. Oman was ruled by imams until 1154, when kings took over the leadership role. In the 15th century the imams became dominant once again. Nasr ibn Murshid, who became imam in 1624, ended tribal conflict for a period of time.

- Portuguese explorers took over the Omani coast in 1507, but were expelled in the following century.

- In 1744, the dynasty of the Al Bu Sa'id family was established and is still in power today. Ahmad ibn Sa'id was elected as imam in that year by descendants of the Qahtan and Nizan, who had been once again engaging in a civil war over succession since early in the century. Ahmad ibn Sa'id ended the war.

- Throughout the centuries Oman had been engaged in extensive maritime trade, and the successors to Ahmad established an Omani empire in Oman and East Africa in the late 18th and early

19th centuries. Calling themselves sultanates, they located the empire's capital on the East African island of Zanzibar for a time.

- Under Sa'id the Great (1806-1856) clove plantations, along with the slave trade, on Zanzibar flourished. After Sa'id the Great died his two sons divided the Omani Empire into modern day Oman and Zanzibar, which were each ruled separately thereafter. Oman came under British influence but was never made a colony. The British helped prop up the weakening Al Bu Sa'id dynasty against challenges to their rule from the Ibadite imams, who were in the country's interior.

- A degree of stability lasted until 1954 when a new imam, Ghalib, joined forces with two other leaders to oppose the Omani sultan Sa'id ibn Taymur. British troops helped put down the insurrection, but clashes continued. Only once the last Ibadi imam was ousted from the country in 1959 was peace restored.

- In a 1970 palace coup Sultan Sa'id was deposed in favor of his son, Qabus. Qabus' mission was to modernize Oman. His first official act was to change the country's name from the Sultanate of Muscat and Oman to just Oman.

- Qabus began immediately to bring Oman into international organizations such as the League of Arab States and the UN. He renewed and improved relations with Saudi Arabia. With the help of Iranian forces Qabus was able to halt a communist rebellion sponsored by the People's Democratic Republic of Yemen in the Omani city of Dhofar, thus regaining complete control of Oman.

- Oman allowed the United States to use its military bases during the Gulf War and fought in the UN coalition forces against Iraq. In 1994, Oman became the first Gulf country to welcome a state visit from an Israeli prime minister. Relations with South Yemen have been improving as well.

- Since 1970 Sultan Qabus has been working hard to modernize Oman's infrastructure, health care, education system and telecommunications network. The country's oil revenues have been a significant source of funds for these improvements.

BUSINESS PRACTICES

Hours of Business

The average workweek is from Saturday through Wednesday, 8:00 a.m. to 1:00 p.m. and 3:00 p.m. to 6:00 p.m. or 4:00 p.m. to 7:00 p.m.

Banks are open from 8:00 a.m. to 12:00 p.m., Saturday through Wednesday and from 8:00 a.m. to 11:30 a.m. on Thursday.

Dress

It is acceptable for non-Omani men to wear business suits while conducting business negotiations. For women, a conservative business dress is appropriate.

For casual wear, foreign women should pack skirts, knee length or longer, with short-sleeved tops. A man should plan to wear pants and golf shirts when not doing business. In restaurants, women are required to wear a dress, and men must wear suits.

The national dress for an Omani male is called the *dishdasha*. It is a long robe with a wool scarf used as a headdress. For more formal occasions men also wear a silver belted dagger. Women usually wear colorful baggy pants and a long dress with a scarf.

Introductions

Shaking hands with both men and women is a common form of introduction. If a man does not wish to shake a woman's hand because of his religious beliefs he will simply say so and then apologize for his actions.

Sometimes friends of the same sex will greet one another by kissing each other on the cheek up to four times.

The only acceptable titles of address are "Your Highness" for royalty, "Doctor" (physicians only), "General," "Colonel" and "Your Excellency" for civil servants.

Wait until your Omani counterpart initiates relations on a first-name basis.

Have your business cards printed in both English and Arabic. Since education is highly regarded in Oman, be sure to have all of your degrees, past the bachelors, listed on the card after your name.

Meetings

In order to schedule an initial appointment it is best to begin negotiating a time for an appointment at least six to eight weeks in advance. Expect to conduct a lengthy correspondence. Be aware that some businesspeople will not schedule an appointment until you have arrived in Oman.

It is best not to plan a business trip from June through September because many Omanis are on vacation during these months.

Plan to arrive in Oman at least a day before your first appointment.

Punctuality is important. Being punctual is one method used to build trust between negotiating partners.

Try to schedule business meetings in your hotel lobby. This should reduce the number of interruptions typically encountered in an Omani office.

The end of a business meeting is signaled by the serving of coffee.

Negotiating

English is the language of international business in Oman, but you should learn a few Arabic phrases to show appreciation for your Omani counterpart's country and culture.

Omanis, like others living in an Arab culture, tend to have a very relaxed and fluid sense of time.

Government permission must be granted in order to obtain a visa for entry into Oman. In addition, you must have either the Omani company or your Omani counterpart sponsor you and state the reason for his or her desire to do business with you.

It is best to stay in a good hotel and to hire a car and driver. Omanis believe that where one stays reflects one's status.

It is best to send the head of your firm to participate in negotiations, because Omani businesspeople like to deal only with the person who is ultimately in charge when a decision is being made.

Bringing an introductory letter with you written by a joint business associate will help you to initiate a trusting rapport between you and your Omani counterpart.

Establishing personal trust is very important to Omanis, and you may be required to attend several business meetings during your stay in Oman or to make several business trips to Oman to help establish good personal relations.

Expect frequent outside interruptions during negotiations. You may have to repeat your presentation several times.

There are usually three Omanis present at all business meetings: the "gatekeeper" (whose job it is to conduct small talk), the "analyst" and the "decision maker." Try to discover which one is the "decision maker."

Expect there to be long periods of small talk during a meeting.

Have all documents printed in both Arabic and English and refer to all measurements in metric units.

Be aware that Omani contracts are vague in comparison to those drawn up in the West.

Businesswomen in Oman are treated more liberally than in other

Islamic countries. They are allowed to go out with men, especially western men, and to order their own drinks. They should, however, refrain from ordering alcoholic beverages if their host refrains from doing so.

Foreign businesswomen are viewed as acceptable business counterparts by Omani men, except in the oil and gas industry.

It is customary and appropriate to give your Omani counterpart a business gift representing your country or company.

Entertaining

It is best to entertain your Omani counterpart in your hotel restaurant. It is also prudent to pre-order the meal. You should, however, avoid extending a dinner invitation until your Omani counterpart has done so first.

Only eat or present a gift with your right hand.

Those who issue an invitation to a meal in a restaurant will usually pay for the meal. A gratuity is included in all restaurant bills.

If you wish to beckon a waiter in a restaurant say *Lawsah-maht* (Excuse me).

At a party or official dinner the host will introduce you to everyone in attendance. Remember to shake everyone's hand when leaving.

While being entertained or doing business with your Omani counterpart over coffee, expect long periods of silence. Do not feel pushed to fill these silences.

It is impolite to refuse an invitation to an Omani home. Entertaining in the home is quite common in Oman, but you should call before arriving.

If you are invited to a dinner party in your Omani counterpart's home expect to be seated first.

Expect there to be many courses at a dinner party. It is polite to try some of everything served.

Breakfast in Oman is normally served between 6:30 and 7:30 a.m., lunch between 12:30 and 2:00 p.m., and dinner between 8:00 and 9:00 p.m. Dinner is usually a light meal.

Arabian coffee, which is very strong, is normally served after most meals.

Some common Arabic dishes found in Oman include *chanad* (mullet), *mashkoul* (rice and onions), kebabs and *machbous* (spicy lamb with rice).

SOCIAL VALUES, CUSTOMS AND TIPS

The Persian Gulf is known as the Arabian Gulf in Oman.

It is impolite to criticize Islam or make jokes referring to harems.

Mutual friends are always a good topic of conversation.

Do not photograph Omani women or religious ceremonies. Ask permission to photograph Omani men.

Women should not enter a room of only men unless invited to do so. Women should not be seen in public without an appropriate male escort.

Many new restaurants have recently opened in Oman, serving Indian, Oriental, Arabic and continental dishes.

PAKISTAN

Population: 135,135,195 (July 1998 est.); Punjabi, Sindhi, Pashtun, Baloch, Muhajir

Languages: Urdu (official), English (official), Punjabi, Shidhi, Siraiki, Pushtu, Balochi, Hindko, Brahui, Burushaski, other

Religions: Muslim 97% (Sunni 77%, Shi'a 20%), Christian, Hindu and other 3%

Currency: Pakistani rupee

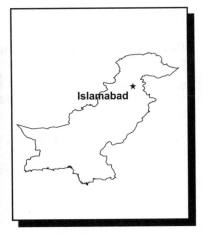

Islamabad

HISTORICAL OVERVIEW

- Pakistan shares much of its early history with that of India. It was part of the Mauryan empire during the third and second centuries B.C., and the Guptas, ruling northern India from 320-540 A.D., were also ruling in Pakistan.

- In the eighth century, Arab traders introduced Islam to Pakistan. In the tenth century, Muslim warriors conquered most of the area, and their power grew until it reached its apex in the 16th century under the Mughal Dynasty.

- By the 19th century, the British East India Trading Company exerted great influence in the area and the British gained dominance in the region. The last Mughal emperor was deposed in 1858 and Pakistan became administratively part of India.

- After World War I, British control of India, Pakistan and present-day Bangladesh was contested by various independence movements, which united for a time under Mahatma Gandhi. In 1940, Mohammed Ali Jinnah, leader of the Muslim League, began advocating separate Muslim and Hindu nations.

- Finally, in 1947, Britain granted independence to the entire area. Fearing that Hindus (the majority) would completely dominate the new country, Muslim leaders pressed for a separate Muslim nation. As a result, each region was given a choice to join either India (under Hindu control) or Pakistan (under Muslim control). The areas that chose Pakistan became East and West Pakistan, separated by 1,000 miles of India. The people of Kashmir (northern India) chose Pakistan, but their Hindu prince chose India. The area remains in dispute today.

- When East Pakistan (inhabited by Bengalis) declared independence in 1971, civil war erupted. Pakistani troops were defeated with the aid of the Indian army and East Pakistan became Bangladesh, under Bengali rule.

- Following the creation of Bangladesh, Zulfikar Ali Bhutto was elected leader of Pakistan. In 1977 during a year of civil unrest, General Mohammed Zia ul-Haq seized control of the government and jailed Bhutto, who was eventually hanged in 1979. Zia instituted *Shari'a* (Islamic law) and suspended civil rights.

- In 1988, Zia was killed in a plane crash and, subsequently, free elections were held. Bhutto's daughter, Benazir Bhutto, won the overall majority and was made prime minister, becoming the first female leader of an Islamic country. Civil rights were restored and reforms were implemented. President Ishaq Khan, who had appointed Benazir Bhutto to be prime minister, dismissed her in 1990 on charges of corruption.

- Nawaz Sharif was elected prime minister in 1990. He began to liberalize the economy and to reform the bureaucracy but he also instituted Islamic law as the highest law. Economic reform and Islamic law often came into conflict, causing foreign investors to leave. As his position became more embattled Sharif turned ever more to Islamic law. In 1993, the president attempted to dismiss Sharif, but this attempt was overruled by the Supreme Court. In the 1993 elections, Benazir Bhutto returned to the office of prime minister. On the basis of her regained political strength, her choice for president, Farooq Leghari, was elected by both houses of parliament and four provincial legislatures.

- Bhutto faced several problems. The debate over Kashmir intensified, violence in Karachi worsened and government officials were increasingly regarded as corrupt, thus strengthening the position of Islamic fundamentalists who promised a moral society.

- The drug trade was burgeoning as well. Ethnic rioting and violence broke out in 1994.

- In 1996, President Leghari again dismissed Bhutto, accusing her government of corruption and nepotism. National elections were held and Sharif was returned to power. His Pakistan Muslim League gained a clear majority in the National Assembly. Pakistan is mired in a recession and has a large budget deficit.

- In response to nuclear tests conducted by India, Pakistan carried out some of its own tests in May 1998. Although these tests won strong support domestically, internationally they brought condemnation and economic sanctions.

BUSINESS PRACTICES

Hours of Business

Most work schedules are determined by the seasons and the crops, since about half of the population is engaged in agriculture.

In urban areas, business hours extend from 9:00 a.m. to 4:00 p.m., Saturday through Thursday. In the summer, the hours change to 7:30 a.m. to 2:30 p.m.

Business trips should not be scheduled from June to September since this is the monsoon season. Avoid the month of Ramadan as well because business hours are subject to change without notice during this period.

Dress

When dealing with government officials, men should always wear a suit and tie. When meeting with businesspeople from private firms, a suit and tie are not required from November to March because of the heat.

Women should wear pantsuits and should always cover their arms.

Formal events require men to wear dark suits, not tuxedos, and for women a dress or skirt of modest length is advisable.

Casual wear for men is usually trousers and a shirt. Women should always dress modestly and shorts are never appropriate.

Introductions

A handshake is the most common form of greeting, although close friends may embrace if meeting after a long time.

Women may also greet each other with a handshake or a hug.

It is not appropriate for a man to shake hands with a woman or to touch her in public, but he may greet another man's wife verbally without looking directly at her.

Verbal greetings often include inquiries about one's health and family. Answering these inquiries may take some time.

In Pakistan, the most common greeting is *Assalaam alaikum* (May peace be upon you). The reply is *Waalaikum assalaam* (And peace also upon you).

The Pakistani phrase for good-bye is *Khodha Haafis*.

Titles and last names are used when addressing someone.

In small groups, each person is greeted individually.

Always present your business card to your associates and counterparts upon introduction.

Meetings

Appointments should be made at least one month before your arrival in Pakistan.

Pakistanis expect clients to be on time even though they have a casual sense of time.

Plan to conduct several meetings if you are meeting with government officials.

Negotiating

Pakistanis believe in focused negotiations, although they do not conduct business at the same fast pace as U.S. Americans.

It is important to build a personal relation with your counterpart before attempting to accomplish your business objectives, but avoid asking direct personal questions. Do not be alarmed if your counterpart takes a strong stand on a business issue or checks and then double-checks all details before making a final decision.

Not accepting tea offered at a meeting is considered impolite.

The government is the largest organization willing to do business in Pakistan. It is a large bureaucracy. More than one meeting is required to solidify a deal.

It is important to note that Pakistanis have special terms when dealing with financial or demographic information. They are the *lakh* (100,000) and the *crore* (100 *lakhs* or 1,000,000). These are Pakistan's units of financial and demographic measure.

Never joke during meetings. It is considered rude.

Contracts should be drawn up in both English and the local language of the region.

Entertaining

Visitors are often treated to coffee, tea or soft drinks and may be invited to eat a meal. Visitors should accept this hospitality, although refusing politely with good reason is appropriate.

Guests often bring gifts if well acquainted with the host or if the occasion calls for a present. Gifts might include something for the children, a decoration for the home, fruit or sweets. Gifts should not be too expensive since that could cause your host embarrassment.

A businesswoman should make arrangements to meet her Pakistani counterpart in her hotel restaurant and prearrange to pay for the bill if she wishes to entertain. Pakistani men will not allow women to pay for the meal.

It is customary to socialize before a meal and then to leave soon after the meal is finished since a meal may be served as late as 11:00 p.m.

In traditional homes, men and women do not socialize together. Rather, men receive their male guests in a special room to enjoy conversation and refreshments.

In urban areas, people may eat with utensils or the hand.

Whenever possible, the whole family eats together, usually sharing the same platter and eating the portion directly in front of him/her.

In large groups, men and women eat in separate areas.

The mainstay of the Pakistani diet is *chapati* or *roti*, an unleavened bread similar to pita bread. *Chapati* is used to scoop up food.

Pakistani food is generally hot and spicy.

Islamic law forbids the consumption of pork and alcohol, and there are strict civil laws regarding the sale and consumption of alcoholic beverages.

Rice is part of most meals and desserts. Two customary dishes include *pillau* (lightly fried rice with vegetables) and *biryani* (rice with meat and spices). *Kheer* is a type of rice pudding.

Tea is the most popular drink.

SOCIAL VALUES, CUSTOMS AND TIPS

Pakistan's population is divided into five major ethnic groups. The Punjabi is the largest group, comprising about 65 percent. The other four groups are the Sindhi, the Baluchi, the Pashtuns and the Muhajir.

The Pashtuns have been referred to as Pathans in the past, but today some consider that name derogatory.

The Muhajir ethnic group is made up of immigrants from India and their descendants.

Pakistan is also home to more than three million Afghan refugees who fled civil war in Afghanistan and live in camps maintained by . Pakistan's government.

Urdu is slowly replacing English as the country's language of business. While only eight percent of the people speak Urdu as a native tongue, most people in the country speak it in addition to their own language.

During the Muslim fasting month of Ramadan, it is impolite for non-Muslims to eat or drink in front of Muslims during daylight hours.

Visiting between friends and relatives is a very important social custom and occurs as often as possible.

Avoid talking about sex, Middle Eastern politics, politics in general, religion and foreign policy.

Insha'allah (God willing) is a term commonly employed to express hope for success on a project, for one's family or for a positive outcome to events.

Hospitality is important and guests are made to feel welcome.

Local transportation consists of donkeys and horse-drawn carts in rural areas. In cities, buses, minibuses and motorized rickshaws are available.

Although 40 percent of the roads are paved, many are in poor condition. Roads in rural areas are not paved and many areas are not accessible by car.

Following the British tradition, traffic moves on the left side of the road.

Most people do not own telephones.

Water is not safe for drinking in most areas.

Although western-style clothing is worn in Pakistan, the national dress, the *shalwar-qameez* (two-piece pantsuit) is more common in both rural and urban areas. Made of cotton, the *shalwar-qameez* differs for men and women. Men wear solid, plain colors. For women, the colors are brighter and patterns bolder.

Women wear a *dupatta* (scarf) around their heads and sometimes another long scarf around their shoulders.

Men usually wear some kind of headdress and it is often possible to determine a man's ethnic group from his headwear.

Despite the heat, Pakistanis cover their legs, arms and heads in public.

Men wear shorts only for athletic events. Women never wear shorts.

If sitting on the floor or if crossing the legs, remember to position your feet so as not to point them directly at another person.

Items are passed with the right hand or both hands.

Using individual fingers to make gestures is considered very impolite, as are gestures with a closed fist.

To beckon, all fingers of the hand are waved, with the palm facing down.

Male friends may walk hand in hand or with their arms over each other's shoulders, but it is inappropriate for members of the opposite sex to touch in public.

Secular holidays include Pakistan Day (March 23); Labor Day (May 1); Independence Day (August 14); Defense of Pakistan Day (September 6); the Anniversary of the Death of Quaid-e-Azam, or Mohammad Ali Jinnah, the nation's founder (September 11); Allama Iqbal Day (November 9); and the Birth of Quaid-e-Azam (December 25). Bank holidays fall in December and July.

Islamic holidays are regulated by the lunar calendar and fall on different solar days each year. The most important ones include *Eid-ul-Fitr*, the three-day feast at the end of the month of Ramadan; *Eid-ul-Azha* (Feast of the Sacrifice), which commemorates Abraham's willingness to sacrifice his son; and *Eid-ii-Milad-un-Nabi*, the feast commemorating the birth of the Prophet Muhammad.

PANAMA

Population: 2,735,943 (July 1998 est.); mestizo (Amerindian and white) 70%, Amerindian and mixed (West Indian) 14%, white 10%, Amerindian 6%

Languages: Spanish (official), English 14%

Religions: Roman Catholic 85%, Protestant 15%

Currency: balboa

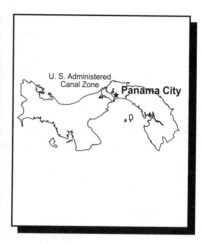

HISTORICAL OVERVIEW

- Originally, Columbus claimed the area for Spain in 1502. It was considered part of what is now Colombia. Panama developed into a transshipment center for Spanish and colonial goods. Trade fairs held in Portobelo attracted British pirates, who attacked the coast until 1688.

- Spanish rule was eventually overthrown in 1821, and Panama became a province of Colombia.

- In the 1880s, France tried to build a canal across Panama, but yellow fever claimed many of the laborers' lives. The canal rights were subsequently sold to the U.S.

- In 1902, Panama declared its independence from Colombia, and the U.S. sent troops to support the new government.

- Construction of the Panama Canal began in 1907 under U.S. supervision. It was completed in seven years and was under U.S. control.

- In 1968, Arnulfo Arias, a fiery nationalist, was elected president. He served only 11 days before he was ousted by the National Guard, whose leader, Omar Torrijos Herrera, subsequently assumed dictatorial power. In 1977, the U.S. signed the Panama Canal Treaty, under which Panama assumed control over the former U.S. canal zone. Operating the canal was to remain a U.S. responsibility until 1999.

- A succession of civilian presidents followed Herrera, with the first popular election in 12 years taking place in 1980.

- Manuel Antonio Noriega, the chief of defense, ousted Eric Arturo Delvalle Henríquez in 1988 after Noriega's rule had been challenged in 1987. He suspended the constitution and civil rights, banned freedom of the press and declared a state of emergency. The U.S. invaded Panama in December 1989 after a Noriega-led assembly declared a state of war with the United States and an unarmed U.S. marine officer was killed. Noriega was eventually taken prisoner and extradited to the U.S. to stand trial for drug-related charges.

- In 1992, the new government, under elected President Guillermo Endara, began the task of rebuilding the nation.

- Endara, however, was not up to the task, and chronic unemployment and rampant corruption persisted. In 1994, Ernesto Perez Balladares, a U.S.-educated former Citibank official, was elected president.

- In June 1996, President Balladares was accused of having received illegal funds from drug trafficking. He denied the charges at first but then admitted that they were true.

- As 1999 drew near, it became clear that Panama was ill-prepared for taking over the operation of the canal. Both the canal and the parallel railroad are in poor shape, and if the tariffs are raised too high to finance repair, tonnage will instead elect to either cross the U.S. by land or go around the South American continent. Despite efforts to diversify the economy, Panama still largely remains dependent on the canal for its income. Panama must also consider how to fund the large payroll the U.S. military bases have been supporting.

BUSINESS PRACTICES

Hours of Business

The business day starts relatively early, in some cases as early as 7:00 a.m., and ends early, usually between 3:30 and 4:00 p.m. Most businesses are also open on Saturday. Government offices are closed on Saturday and Sunday.

Dress

Business executives wear dark suits and ties. Women in Panama dress similarly to women in the U.S. Most urban male workers wear open-necked shirts (*camisillas* or *panabrisas*).

Introductions

A handshake is the appropriate greeting between new acquaintances or business associates.

The most common forms of greeting among male friends are a nod and an *abrazo* (a brief hug). Women friends usually embrace and make a kissing motion on one cheek. These gestures are generally repeated upon departure.

Panama's official language is Spanish, although English is widely spoken.

At large parties, your host will not introduce you. You will need to introduce yourself to each person.

Professional titles are important when addressing someone.

Meetings

Make business appointments at least two weeks before arriving in Panama.

Business cards and materials should be printed in Spanish and English.

Using graphs and visual aids in presentations is advisable.

Negotiating

Panamanian businesspeople prefer to establish personal relations before beginning business negotiations.

It is advisable to demonstrate to your counterpart how your two companies are compatible.

The negotiating process takes longer in Panama than in the U.S. Be patient and be prepared to make more than one trip to finalize the deal. Build your business relationships carefully.

There are few women in the Panamanian business world. Women should emphasize their position as part of a team, rather than their own position in the company.

Panamanian businesspeople will be prepared to bargain. Adjust your pricing accordingly.

Entertaining

When invited to a party, you may arrive up to two hours after the scheduled start time. For a large dinner party, you may arrive an hour after. If you (or you and your spouse) are the only guests, appear no more than 30 minutes after the designated time.

Ending times for visits are not generally given so as not to make a guest feel unwelcome after a certain period of time.

It is not necessary to bring a gift when invited to someone's home. It is expected, instead, that the invitation will be reciprocated.

The host sits at the head of the table during a meal. The guest of honor usually sits at the opposite end of the table.

You will please your host by eating everything on your plate, but you will not offend him/her if you leave some food on your plate.

Generally, hands should be kept above the table.

Restaurants usually do not include a service charge in the final bill total. A ten percent tip to the waiter is customary.

At restaurants the party that does the inviting generally pays for the meal.

Staples of the Panamanian diet include kidney beans, rice, plantains, corn and chicken. Omelets and tortillas (thin, round unleavened bread made from cornmeal or wheat flour) are popular national foods.

Place your knife and fork parallel to each other and across your plate to signal that you have finished eating.

Use the term *Mozo* or *Señor* to summon a waiter; use *Señorita* for a waitress.

The most common dessert is fruit. A specialty is *buñuelos de viento* (fritters served with syrup). Coffee, usually espresso, is served after dinner.

SOCIAL VALUES, CUSTOMS AND TIPS

In the interior of the country, gift-giving among friends is common, but only inexpensive items such as food or seedlings are exchanged. In urban areas, however, gift-giving is not customary.

In Panama, the ideal man is a man of action who seems forceful, daring and virile. The ideal woman is expected to appear well-bred, understanding and feminine. People in large urban areas, however, are less likely to value these more traditional gender roles.

National pride is very strong in Panama. Although relations with the U.S. are generally good, it is best to avoid conversation about U.S. financial aid, the 1989 invasion and the continued presence of the U.S. in the canal zone.

Good subjects of conversation include family, common friends or acquaintances, hobbies and sports such as baseball and basketball.

Nonverbal communication is used more by people outside of urban areas. "No" is indicated by wagging the index finger from side to side. To express "Over there" or "Time to go," people pucker their lips and gesture in the appropriate direction.

Eye contact is important in conversation.

Cover your mouth when you yawn or cough.

Most Panamanians do not wear shorts in public. In general, women should avoid revealing clothing.

Baseball is the most popular sport in Panama. Other favorites include boxing, basketball and soccer.

Ask permission before photographing a Panamanian.

PARAGUAY

Population: 5,291,020 (July 1998 est.); mestizo (Spanish and Amerindian) 95%, white and Amerindian 5%

Languages: Spanish (official), Guaraní (official)

Religions: Roman Catholic 90%, Mennonite and other Protestant denominations 10%

Currency: guarani

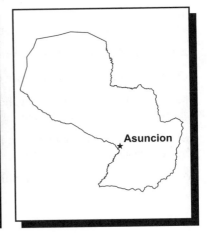

HISTORICAL OVERVIEW

- Spanish explorers first came to Paraguay in 1524 and established Asunción in 1537.

- Spanish colonial rule lasted until the 19th century. Paraguay peacefully gained independence in 1811, and José Gaspar Rodríguez Francia became its first leader. Until 1840, Rodríguez ruled as a dictator and closed the country to the outside world.

- In 1864, Francisco Solano López brought Paraguay into the War of the Triple Alliance against Brazil, Argentina and Uruguay. Eventually this war was lost, along with 55,000 square miles of territory and 500,000 lives. As a result of the war, foreign troops stayed until 1876, and Paraguay remained politically unstable for another generation.

- Paraguay fought Bolivia in the Chaco War, a territorial dispute, from 1928 to 1935. This war was successful in terms of regaining territory, but the victory cost yet more lives and did not stabilize the nation politically.

- The country continued to be marked by political instability and dictatorships. Various dictators and one elected president ruled until 1954, when General Alfredo Stroessner, commander of the army, took control of the Paraguayan government and established a dictatorship. While this period of dictatorship brought about economic development, it was also marked by human rights violations, corruption and oppression.

- A 1989 coup ousted Stroessner, who then moved to Brazil. General Andrés Rodríguez Pedotti led the coup and was subsequently elected as the country's president. Much remained as it had under the Stroessner regime.

- As he had promised, General Rodríguez ended his term in 1993, and national elections were then held. Juan Carlos Wasmosy was elected president.

- Wasmosy tried, unsuccessfully, in 1993 to exclude the military from membership in the main political parties. In 1995, however, Wasmosy told the military commander, General Lino Oviedo, that he must resign, offering him in exchange the office of Secretary of Defense. Popular demonstration against Oviedo convinced him to decline the offer.

- Political stability in Paraguay has allowed it to grow into a prominent banking center. It is considered a good credit risk and a good place for investment due in part to low inflation. Human rights violations are far less frequent than in the 1980s, although the problem of bureaucratic corruption has yet to be dealt with adequately.

- In May 1998, Raul Cubas Grau won the presidential elections, marking the first peaceful transition between civilian governments since the end of Stroessner's dictatorship in 1989.

BUSINESS PRACTICES

Hours of Business

Urban businesses are usually open from 7:00 a.m. until noon and then from 3:00 p.m. until 6:00 p.m., Monday through Friday. There is a *siesta* (a rest after the midday meal) between noon and 3:00 p.m., during which people eat their midday meal and rest or sleep. Some businesses are open on Saturday mornings as well.

The best time to arrange business trips to Paraguay is between June and October, when people are not on vacation or celebrating holidays.

Dress

Business dress is conservative. Men wear dark suits and ties. Women wear white blouses and dark suits or skirts. Women do not usually wear nylons in the summer. Sometimes men remove their jackets and ties due to the hot climate. Foreign businesspeople should follow the example of their Paraguayan counterparts.

Introductions

Men and women always shake hands both when being introduced or when greeting.

Close male friends may either shake hands or embrace each other when greeting. When women greet each other or when a woman greets a man, they will kiss one another on each cheek as well as shake hands.

It is appropriate to use Spanish greetings and titles. The Spanish greeting *¡Mucho gusto!* (Pleased to meet you) is often used with strangers or in somewhat formal situations. Acquaintances use less formal Spanish phrases and greet each other by saying *¡Hola! ¿Cómo estás?* (Hi, How are you?). Friends and family most commonly speak in Guaraní when greeting.

Only close friends, family members and children address each other using first names. Professional titles, followed by the last name, should normally be used to show respect. If the person does not have a professional title, use the titles *Señor* (Mr.), *Señora* (Mrs.) or *Señorita* (Miss) followed by the last name.

Most people in Paraguay have two surnames, one from the father (listed first) and one from the mother. Normally, the father's name is used when addressing someone. For example, Hernan Antonio Martinez Garcia is addressed as *Señor Martinez* and María Elisa Gutierrez Herrera is addressed as *Señorita Gutierrez*. When a woman marries, she usually adds her husband's surname and goes by that surname. For example, if the two people in the above example married, the woman would be known as Señora María Elisa Gutierrez Herrera de Martinez. She would be addressed as *Señora de Martinez* or, more informally, *Señora Martinez*.

At a party, it is important to shake hands with each person individually, both when arriving and when leaving.

Meetings

Many business executives speak English. It is wise, however, to check before your visit and to arrange for an interpreter if necessary.

Arrange appointments well in advance. The morning (between 8:00 a.m. and noon) is the best time to schedule meetings.

Punctuality is not highly valued by Paraguayans. Although business meetings rarely start at the designated time, a foreigner (especially a North American) is still expected to be punctual.

While it is not necessary to translate materials into the Guaraní language, business cards and all presentation materials and brochures should be translated into Spanish.

Negotiating

In Paraguay, the pace of business is generally slow. Delays are common. Paraguayans maintain a relaxed attitude even in fast-paced situations, and a considerable amount of time is spent on establishing personal relationships before transacting business.

Accomplishing a business transaction may require several trips to Paraguay. It is a good idea for the same individual(s) to be sent each time because the establishment of a relationship is important. If your company's representative changes, you will be starting from scratch – a new relationship will have to be built before business can proceed.

Contracts are rarely agreed upon in sections. Until the entire contract is signed, each section is considered to be renegotiable.

When negotiating, be aware that Paraguayans tend to look at problems and situations from a subjective, personal perspective. They seldom rely solely on abstract rules and hard facts in making decisions. Similarly, they will seldom use objective facts to prove a point. An emotional appeal (to pride, trust, mutual compatibility, etc.) is generally more common and more successful in negotiating than an appeal to facts alone. A Paraguayan's concept of what constitutes a solution to a problem may be guided by faith in their nation and religion.

When doing business in Paraguay, be aware that individuals tend to be group oriented. One's identity is based on an individual's position and performance in the group. Individual expertise and initiative tend to be subordinated to personal connections and the individual's ability to be part of the group. Appeals to the good of a business deal for the group (for example, the company, the negotiating team or the country) tend to be most successful.

Since Paraguay is a traditional society with clearly defined hierarchical, gender-based and social roles, decision making is usually based on perceptions of power and hierarchy within the negotiating teams.

Because machismo is quite strong in Paraguay and because there are very few women in top positions in Paraguayan firms, foreign businesswomen may initially encounter a lack of respect. Foreign businesswomen should act very professionally and emphasize that they are representing their firm and not themselves. On the other hand, since Paraguayan men dislike confronting or offending women, it can be useful to include a female business representative on a negotiating team.

Entertaining

Paraguayans enjoy entertaining guests. It is not uncommon for people to drop by unexpectedly.

Gift-giving can be a sensitive matter in Paraguay since corruption and bribery were widespread during earlier regimes. Any gift should be of high quality. If the gift has a corporate name or logo on it, it should be printed discreetly. Avoid giving knives, which are taken to symbolize the severing of a relationship.

Business lunches are atypical since most people go home for the midday *siesta*. As Paraguayan businesspeople are more and more influenced by North American practices, however, they may work through the afternoon and attend business lunches.

Most business entertaining is done during dinner, which is usually served around 9:00 or 10:00 p.m. In fact, many restaurants do not serve dinner before 9:00 p.m., and they stay open until midnight. At the same time, most dinners are considered to be social occasions, and one should not try to discuss business unless the host first broaches the subject.

Urban residents enjoy inviting guests to their homes for a meal, while more rural people tend to extend such invitations only for special occasions.

It is considered polite to arrive 30 minutes late for a special occasion.

If you are invited to a home for a meal, it is not expected but is appropriate to bring a small gift, such as flowers, wine or chocolates.

It is customary in Paraguay to share food and drink. For example, it is unusual to order oneself a drink. Instead, a larger pitcher should be ordered for everyone at the table. Additional rounds are usually ordered by the other diners.

If you are meeting business associates in a casual situation, it is recommended that men wear slacks (avoid jeans) and a blazer. Women may wear pants as casual wear, but should avoid shorts.

In restaurants, service is included in the bill. An additional tip is not expected.

Mealtimes and eating habits vary according to the region and the family. In cities, families usually eat their main meal of the day together. When guests are invited, children might eat before the guests arrive or before they are served.

Breakfast usually consists of *cocido* (yerba tea, cooked sugar, and milk) or coffee, bread and butter, rolls or pastries. Lunch is usually the main meal of the day. Dinner is normally eaten at the end of the workday.

Paraguayans often drink yerba tea, which is either served cold (called *tereré*) or, less commonly, hot (called *maté*).

The most important staples include *mandioca* (cassava), *sopa Paraguaya* (cornbread baked with cheese, onions and sometimes meat), *chipa* (hard cheese bread), *tortillas* (thin, round unleavened bread made from cornmeal or wheat flour) and *empanadas* (deep-fried meat or vegetable pockets).

Guests are usually served full plates of food. Additional portions may be taken from serving dishes placed on the table. Leaving food on your plate is considered an insult to the cook. In addition, hosts usually insist that their guests take several servings.

The hands, but not the elbows, should be kept above the table. Guests should wait for the host to begin eating.

Paraguayans normally do not drink during the meal, but wait until they are finished eating.

Meals can be quite extended. Guests are normally expected to stay after a meal for conversation and tea.

SOCIAL VALUES, CUSTOMS AND TIPS

Spanish is used by people in government, urban commerce and schools. Portuguese is also spoken along the Brazilian border.

Paraguayans enjoy being asked about their country and heritage. They like defining themselves by exhibiting the unique elements of the country's culture (by speaking Guaraní). Paraguayans say that Spanish is the language of the head and Guaraní the language of the heart.

Be aware that Paraguay is a traditional society whose people place a great value on large families, property, beauty, virility, money and status. The ultimate goal is harmony and lack of problems, or *tranquilo* (tranquillity). Deviations from or criticisms of these values are not appreciated.

Avoid making negative comparisons between Paraguay and other countries. Paraguayans do not appreciate stereotypes about poverty and inferiority in developing nations.

Avoid offering any political opinions. Instead, wait until your Paraguayan counterpart has voiced his/her opinion and then choose a position that does not disagree.

Sports is a good topic of conversation. *Fútbol* (soccer) is the most popular spectator sport, while volleyball is the most popular participatory sport. U.S. football (*fútbol americano*), basketball and horse racing are also popular.

Avoid referring to U.S. citizens as Americans since Paraguayans consider themselves to be (South) Americans and are very sensitive to the use of the term. They would rather refer to U.S. residents as *Norteamericano* (for men) or *Norteamericana* (for women), meaning "North American."

Loud, disruptive behavior is inappropriate.

Paraguayans tend to stand much closer together than U.S. Americans do when speaking. If you step away, you may offend the person with whom you are speaking.

Western-style clothing is commonly worn throughout Paraguay, and the youth, in particular, wear North American fashions. A clean and neat appearance is emphasized. Lightweight, natural fabrics are usually worn because of the hot climate. Adults do not wear shorts in public, and men rarely wear sandals. Regardless of economic conditions, women in particular pay attention to their appearance. Styled hair, makeup, jewelry and manicured nails are all considered important.

The most common gesture used in Paraguay is the "thumbs up" sign, which expresses anything positive or encouraging. It is commonly used when a person is answering a question.

Wagging the index finger means "No" or "I don't think so."

The North American "okay" sign, with the tip of the thumb and the tip of the index finger touching to form a circle, is an offensive gesture in Paraguay.

Tapping one's chin with the top of the index finger means "I don't know." A backwards tilt of the head means "I forgot."

Be aware that winking is not used as a casual gesture in Paraguay. It has romantic, even sexual, connotations.

Making a "tsst-tsst" sound is the most common way of getting a person's attention. If this does not work, a Paraguayan might whistle or run after the person, but never shout.

On public transportation, Paraguayan men usually give up their seats to older or pregnant women or women with children. Seated passengers will often offer to hold children or packages for standing passengers.

It is acceptable and common for people to eat in public.

Whenever you have a snack or small meal, it is polite to offer some of the food to whomever is present. If you are offered food by someone, it is polite to decline.

It is common for close friends of either sex to walk arm-in-arm.

Proper posture is important when sitting. Sitting upright connotes interest and attentiveness. It is considered rude to slump or to sit on a ledge, box or table. It is considered very impolite to put your feet up on a table.

PERU

Population: 26,111,110 (July 1998 est.); Amerindian 45%, mestizo (Amerindian and white) 37%, white 15%, black, Japanese, Chinese and other 3%

Languages: Spanish (official), Quechua (official), Aymara

Religions: Roman Catholic 90%, Anglican, Methodist, Peruvian Baha'I minorities

Currency: nuevo sol

HISTORICAL OVERVIEW

- A number of indigenous groups populated the area now known as Peru before the arrival of European settlers. The last of these groups was the Incas.

- In 1532, the Spanish, under the leadership of Francisco Pizarro, invaded Peru and conquered the Incan Empire by 1533. Because of its location and its abundance of minerals, Peru soon became the richest and most powerful Spanish colony in America.

- Peru declared independence in 1821 under the leadership of the South American liberator, José de San Martín. A war ensued that lasted until 1826, when complete independence was finally achieved. In the mid-1800s, Peru's economy expanded greatly as a result of newly-discovered natural resources.

- Spain made a failed attempt to regain its former colonial power over Peru in a war from 1862 to 1883. From 1879 to 1883, Chile, with Britain's help, fought over Peru's nitrate fields in the War of the Pacific. Peru lost this war with devastating repercussions for its economy.

- In 1924 the American Popular Revolutionary Alliance (APRA) was founded. This group, which sought to integrate the indigenous population into Peru's dominant social structure, became a major political force throughout the 20th century.

- Although the 1933 constitution provided for democratic leadership, Peruvian politics from the 1930s to 1970s were marked by power struggles between dictators, the military and the APRA. Political instability coupled with the effects of the worldwide depression created significant economic problems. In 1968, military forces once again took over the civilian government, beginning 11 years of military rule. Despite reforms, including land reforms aimed to benefit peasants, little popular support existed for the regime. After another military coup in 1975 failed to restore the economy and eliminate political unrest, a constitutional government was instituted in 1978.

- In 1980, the *Sendero Luminoso* (Shining Path), a neo-Maoist group, began a decade of violent warfare against the government. They consolidated power in the Upper Huallaga Valley, where drug traffickers paid them for protection and the right to operate.

- Free elections were held in 1978 for the Constituent Assembly, but political and economic problems continued. Alan García (1985-1990) was the first elected president. He nationalized key industries, the foreign debt crisis deepened and relations with the U.S. declined. In 1990, plans for military cooperation between Peru and the U.S. to fight drug trafficking were implemented.

- In 1990, Alberto Fujimori, a son of Japanese immigrants, was elected as García's successor. He vowed to reinstate civil rights and to improve the economy by imposing austerity measures.

- Fujimori suspended the constitution in April 1992 and dissolved congress, citing Shining Path insurgency, government corruption and legislative inefficiency as his reasons. He took emergency powers and restricted civil liberties. While some supported the move, domestic and international pressure soon mounted, and Fujimori quickly announced a return to democracy.

- In 1992, Shining Path leader Abimael Guzmán was captured and sentenced to 40 years in prison. Within a year, Guzmán began encouraging former followers to make peace with the government. Many thus deserted the organization in 1993.

- A new constitution, guaranteeing a free market economy and a democratic system, was put into effect after the 1995 elections. In the same year, Fujimori won a second term as president.

- In December 1996, the terrorist group Tupac Amaru invaded the home of the Japanese ambassador in Peru, took 72 hostages and demanded reforms. Refusing to give in to their demands, Peruvian troops stormed the residence in April 1997, killing all rebel soldiers and one hostage. Thereafter, terrorist acts in Peru declined.

- In January 1998, flooding, resulting from *El Niño* weather patterns, killed many Peruvians and left others homeless.

- In August 1998, unresolved territorial disputes continued between Ecuador and Peru after Peru claimed that Ecuadorian troops had crossed over Peruvian borders. Fujimori and Ecuadorian President Mahaud are seeking to solve this issue peacefully.

- Peru's economy continues to improve with the real GDP steadily growing since 1990.

BUSINESS PRACTICES

Hours of Business

Businesses are generally open from 8:30 a.m. to 12:30 p.m. and from 3:00 p.m. to 6:30 p.m., Monday through Friday.

Avoid planning business trips during the January to March period, when most businesspeople are on vacation.

Dress

In winter, businessmen wear dark wool suits and, in summer, they wear dark lightweight suits or blazers and slacks. Businesswomen should wear a dress or a skirt, a blouse and a jacket.

Introductions

Both men and women shake hands when greeting and when departing. Sometimes when a man and a woman or two women are introduced, they kiss one another on the cheek.

Men who are close friends may embrace each other or pat each other on the back. Women who are close friends usually kiss one another on the cheek.

Officials or elders should be greeted with their last name, preceded by a title. Common titles are *Doctor, Profesor, Arquitecto* (architect) or *Ingenerio* (engineer). First names are only used among friends.

Meetings

Business appointments should be made from abroad at least two weeks in advance. You will have more success in scheduling business meetings in the morning than in the afternoon. Most businesspeople take lunch breaks from 1:00 until 3:00 p.m. Be aware that morning appointments usually lead to lunch invitations. Therefore, it is usually advisable to avoid scheduling two consecutive morning appointments.

Foreigners are expected to be punctual for business engagements even though Peruvians do not adhere to strict timetables.

Charts or visual aids in presentations will be well received in Peru.

Carry business cards printed in both English and Spanish.

Negotiating

Local contacts can help guide you through the methods and details of businesses and government and act as mediators.

Building business relationships personally is very important in Peru. A Peruvian businessperson usually feels more comfortable proceeding when he/she is interacting with an individual rather than a corporation.

Business may proceed very quickly since foreign investment is welcomed.

You should proceed subtly, as Peruvians do, when negotiating. Take your cues from your Peruvian mediators or counterparts. Avoid confronting people with questions that require a "Yes" or "No" response. Most Peruvians will tell you what they think you want to hear rather than what they really believe.

Every aspect of a contract will be meticulously reviewed by your Peruvian counterpart. The contract will be discussed in its entirety, rather than point by point. Be patient and nonconfrontational.

It is very difficult for foreign businesswomen to succeed in Peru as traditional roles are ascribed to women. As an indication of the nature of women's roles, it is interesting to note that a married woman still needs her husband's consent in order to open a bank account.

Entertaining

When invited to a dinner at a home, men should wear a sports jacket and a tie and women should wear a dress or skirt and blouse. If the occasion is a party at a home, men should wear a suit and tie and women a dress or skirt and blouse. If an invitation says that dress is formal, men should wear tuxedos and women should wear cocktail dresses.

Lunches are more appropriate for discussing business, while dinners tend to be more social affairs.

If you are invited to a meal, it is appropriate to arrive 30 minutes late. Most dinner invitations are scheduled for 9:00 p.m., although dinner is often not served until 10:30 p.m.

The person who issues the invitation to a meal at a restaurant should pay for the meal.

If you are entertaining in order to hold a business discussion, it is appropriate to invite only those with whom you have been negotiating directly. When the deal is completed, however, feel free to invite everyone who has been involved in any given project to a meal.

Peruvian businesspeople like to be entertained at luxurious restaurants. They will be particularly impressed if you invite them to a restaurant that caters to luxury dining. It is recommended that you ask someone in the firm for suggestions or call a tourist office to get names of appropriate restaurants.

When invited to a meal at a Peruvian's home, it is recommended that you bring wine, liquor or chocolates as a gift. Your host will not expect anything, but any gift will be appreciated. If you bring or send flowers, choose roses. In Peru, other flowers are so inexpensive that they are not highly valued.

Other good gift items include perfume, scarves, elegant neckties or costume jewelry. Avoid giving people synthetic clothing as Peruvians prefer natural fabrics. Inexpensive cameras, calculators and good pens also make excellent business gifts.

When dining in a home or at a restaurant, refrain from drinking tap water or any cold drinks containing tap water. Also avoid eating raw shellfish and raw fruits and vegetables that cannot be peeled.

Restaurants usually add a ten percent service charge to the bill. If the service is outstanding, you may add another five percent.

Breakfast is a simple meal of rolls with ham, cheese or jam and *café con leche* (coffee with milk). Lunch, served from 12:30 or 1:00 p.m. to 3:00 p.m., usually consists of a pasta course followed by steak, chops, chicken or fish with salad and rice. At 6:00 p.m., people routinely have cake and cookies with tea. At 8:30 or 9:00 p.m., dinner is served, which includes soup with noodles and *guiso* (vegetables pureed with spices) served with rice. The meal ends with coffee or an herbal tea.

The main staples in the Peruvian diet are rice, beans, fish and tropical fruits. Corn, native to Peru, is also popular. *Cebiche* (raw fish seasoned with lemon and vinegar) is popular on the coast. Potatoes, onions and garlic are frequent ingredients for dishes in the highlands.

The host and hostess usually sit next to one another. A male guest of honor sits to the right of the hostess, and a female guest of honor sits to the right of the host.

The continental style of eating is used, with the fork held in the left hand and the knife in the right. If fish is served, you should use the fish knife and fork provided.

Keep your hands (but not your elbows) above the table during a meal.

You should not feel obliged to eat a large amount or to finish everything on your plate – in fact, it is polite to leave a little food (indicating that you are satisfied).

To indicate that you have finished eating, place your utensils either diagonally or vertically across the plate.

You should stay only about 30 minutes after a meal ends, although your host will probably urge you to stay as a gesture of politeness.

SOCIAL VALUES, CUSTOMS AND TIPS

Jokes about the Peruvian lifestyle, especially coming from foreigners, are considered offensive. Personal criticism, if necessary, is expressed in a positive manner.

Peruvians welcome foreigners very warmly. Do not be surprised if people discuss family and occupation as soon as they meet you. Peruvians may also ask you a lot of questions about your country's government. Discussing salary or how much something costs is generally avoided.

Avoid discussing Peruvian government and politics, even if you hear complaints and criticisms about Peru's government. Avoid asking Peruvians about their ancestors. They generally feel more comfortable being associated with their Spanish colonial heritage than with their Indian heritage.

It is appreciated if you ask questions about the area you are visiting or ask for advice about sights to see or places to eat. Soccer and other sports also make good topics of conversation.

In Peru, people stand close to each other when conversing. If you back away, you may offend those with whom you are speaking.

Western-style clothing is worn regularly in most urban areas, although more traditional clothing may also be seen. For casual attire, men should wear slacks and an elegant shirt. Women should wear a skirt or pants and a blouse.

It is common for people of the same sex to walk arm-in-arm as a sign of warmth and friendship. Do not be surprised if someone takes your arm when you are walking with them.

Always offer cigarettes to the people around you if you light one for yourself.

To beckon someone, wave your hand back and forth while holding it vertically, palm facing out.

Women should cross their legs at the knee, while men should cross their legs by placing one ankle on the knee of the other leg.

Be discreet when taking pictures of Indians; some object to having their pictures taken and others might become angry if they are not offered a tip. Similarly, you should not photograph airports, military installations or industrial plants.

PHILIPPINES

Population: 77,725,862 (July 1998 est.); Christian Malay 91.5%, Muslim Malay 4%, Chinese 1.5%, other 3%

Languages: Filipino (official), English (official)

Religions: Roman Catholic 83%, Protestant 9%, Muslim 5%, Buddhist and other 3%

Currency: Philippine peso

Manila

HISTORICAL OVERVIEW

- The Philippines is a collection of 7,107 islands. Many of these islands are uninhabited and the majority of the population resides on 11 main islands, of which Luzon and Mindanao are the largest.

- At the beginning of the 15th century the Filipinos were semi-nomadic agriculturists, hunters and fishermen with animistic beliefs. Later on in the century Islam was introduced. Magellan made the first western contact with the Philippines in 1521 and claimed the area for Spain. Spain colonized the islands, forcing conversion to Roman Catholicism. It maintained control for almost 400 years, fending off attempts by China, Japan and other countries to conquer the Philippines.

- Manila, the capital, grew into an international trade center. Mexican silver and Chinese silks were traded there and European demands for sugar and abaca led to the growth of domestic agriculture. The resulting wealth went into the pockets of the Spanish descended elites.

- Nationalist sentiment developed and in 1896 José Rezal, writer and patriot, inspired an unsuccessful revolt against Spain. The Philippines were ceded to the U.S. after its victory in the Spanish-American War of 1898.

- Unable to reconcile ideals of American democracy with imperialism, the U.S. used training the Filipinos in self-rule as a pretext for their occupation.

- Japan occupied the Philippines during World War II. On 4 July 1946, the Philippines became an independent republic with a constitution modeled on that of the U.S.

- Throughout the 1950s and 1960s, social unrest over inequalities threatened the stability of the government. In 1965, Ferdinand Marcos was first elected president and in 1972 he declared martial law. He ruled by decree until 1986.

- In February 1986, Marcos lost the presidential elections, but nevertheless declared himself the winner. His opponent, Corazon Aquino, widow of political rival Benigno S. Aquino, Jr., who was assassinated in 1983, led a peaceful "People's Power Revolution" that eventually led to Marcos's downfall.

- In 1992 peaceful elections brought Aquino's successor, Fidel V. Ramos, to power.

- Also in 1992, the U.S. Navy turned over the naval base at Subic Bay to the Philippines, ending a long-term U.S. military presence.

- Ramos was faced with demands from several Islamic groups, some of whom were advocating for independent rule and had been conducing guerrilla warfare since 1972. A peace treaty was signed in 1996 and peace talks continue.

- There was substantial economic growth in the early 1990s, especially in agriculture, and Ramos' administration turned over more land to the peasants.

- In May 1998, Joseph Estrada, former vice president and film actor, was elected president by the largest vote margin in a free election in the history of the Philippines. Estrada has promised to improve the lives of the mostly poor population of the country.

BUSINESS PRACTICES

Hours of Business

Business and government offices are usually open Monday through Friday from 8:00 a.m. to 5:00 p.m. and some are open for a half day on Saturday. Normally businesses close for *siesta* break at lunchtime.

Dress

In the Philippines, status and an appearance of authority are strongly valued, and conservative, appropriate and neat business dress is very important. Men should wear a jacket and tie. Women should wear a dress or a skirt and blouse and, despite the heat, panty hose. In general, people are very fashion conscious.

After repeated visits to a firm, feel free to wear a *barong*, the national dress shirt (a white or pastel-colored embroidered shirt that is worn over pants). For business meetings, however, men should remember to wear a coat and tie.

Introductions

On first and subsequent meetings, the appropriate greeting is a handshake – for men and men, women and men or women and women. Foreign men should wait for Filipino women to extend their hands.

In the Philippines, the presentation of business cards is quite important. As a foreign visitor, you should present your card first.

If your company is not well known, bring letters of introduction from mutual friends or business associates.

The eldest person should be greeted first as a sign of respect. To show special honor when greeting older persons, especially relatives, the terms *lolo* and *lola* are used.

At a party, expect to be introduced to each guest individually. Shake hands with each person as you are introduced.

Address business superiors as "Sir" or "Ma'am" or by their title or profession (e.g., Congressman, Attorney). Use "Mr.," "Mrs." and "Miss" with business peers.

You may see Filipinos greet each other by making eye contact and then raising and lowering their eyebrows.

Do not use your finger to beckon someone. Rather, with the palm of your hand down, move your four fingers toward you.

Meetings

Make business appointments about a month in advance. Schedule appointments for the morning or late afternoon, since there is a midday *siesta* break. While punctuality is not always observed in the Philippines for social occasions, punctuality is expected for business meetings.

Realize that you will almost certainly have to make more than one trip to conclude a business deal in the Philippines.

Confirm all meetings or appointments 72 hours in advance.

At the beginning of the meeting present an overview of the objectives to be discussed as well as a packet outlining the objectives in detail.

Negotiating

Be aware that English is the usual language of commercial correspondence. Many of the leading businesspeople have traveled to the West.

Present the main objectives of the negotiations early because business is conducted at a slower pace in the Philippines than in the U.S. This may be due to a concern on the part of Filipino businesspeople with maintaining group harmony. You will make a bad impression if you try to rush things.

When doing business in the Philippines, be aware that Filipinos often react to decisions, rather than participate in making them. Filipino businesspeople often will not want to disagree with you openly or present a problem or make a request directly. Blunt and emphatic words are avoided. Pay attention to what may be expressed indirectly.

Filipinos avoid saying "No"; direct disagreement can cause shame or embarrassment. Building trust and long-term relationships is of the utmost importance. To maintain clarity, however, at each stage of your negotiations you may want to try to get a written agreement.

When conducting business in the Philippines, do not show impatience or act condescendingly. Filipinos do not react well to pushiness.

Do not be surprised when Filipino businesspeople laugh at a crucial point in the meeting. In Filipino culture, people tend to laugh at tense moments to release tension without confrontation.

Businesswomen should behave in a highly professional manner, without being overly aggressive or impolite. Take cues from your counterparts.

Like people in other East Asian countries, the Filipinos believe in "saving face". They will never lose their temper in public and their foreign counterparts should not either. Both parties, while negotiating, should practice *pakikisama* (smooth relations).

Although group harmony is preserved during negotiations, all decisions are made by the senior executives of the Philippine company.

Facilitation payments are common and may be included in a contract. Foreigners should not involve themselves in this process but should allow their Philippine facilitators or advisors to handle the matter.

Bear in mind that information is passed along private channels. Any information might be used in negotiations by the decision makers, whether or not you are made aware of it.

Entertaining

In the Philippines, business entertaining is very important since business relationships are often highly personalized. It is appreciated if you show genuine interest in Filipino culture and make an effort to interact with your Filipino colleagues. Filipinos entertain with ease, warmth and joy.

Learning a few Filipino phrases or words shows your counterparts that you understand and appreciate their culture.

U.S. practices (style of eating, customs, etc.) tend to prevail in business entertaining.

In the Philippines, when food, drink or cigarettes are first offered, you should refuse. You can accept the item the second time, if you wish.

In public and when dining at someone's house, typically only men drink alcohol (principally beer and wine). Women are usually offered soft drinks such as Coca-Cola, orange juice or *calamansi* (a native drink made of a citrus fruit similar to lemon). It is becoming more common, however, for women to drink wine.

While taking part in business entertainment, you may be asked to engage in solo or group singing. It is appreciated if you join in, no matter how poorly you sing.

A service fee is usually included in a restaurant bill. If this fee is not included, a ten percent tip should be left for the waiter/waitress.

People in restaurants may hiss to gain the waiter's/waitress's attention. It is more polite to beckon with your hand (palm facing downwards).

If you are invited to someone's home, keep in mind that, at some homes, you should remove your shoes before entering. Follow the example of your host.

Remember that Filipinos almost never cook anything by itself, except for fish on occasion, which is broiled or grilled. Chicken, fish, vegetables and noodles are all combined in soups and stews and then served with rice. The rice and food are mixed together on the plate and *bagoong* or *patis* are added. *Bagoong* is a pungent fish or shrimp paste. *Patis* is an amber-colored liquid fish seasoning. In homes, there will be bottles of these two condiments on the table, while in restaurants they are added to the food in the cooking.

Do not expect drinks to be served before dinner.

At your place setting, there will usually be a fork and a spoon. In some homes, knives are also placed on the table. If not, take the spoon in your right hand and the fork in your left. Push food onto the spoon with the fork.

Try a small amount of every type of food offered and leave a little of each item on your plate to show that your host has prepared enough and that you are satisfied.

To indicate that you are finished, place utensils horizontally on your plate.

If invited to a home for a meal, you may bring a gift such as flowers, which should be given upon arrival. Thank-you notes are also appreciated. You may even send a small gift of thanks to a host following a dinner.

SOCIAL VALUES, CUSTOMS AND TIPS

In the Philippines, 80 different languages are used, including some Spanish. While Tagalog (or Filipino) has been declared the official language, it has failed to replace English as the country's unifying language. English is widely spoken and is the de facto national language in law, commerce, government and popular entertainment.

Filipino culture has been influenced by the Chinese, Malaysian, Spanish and U.S. cultures. Over time you will notice many different aspects of these different cultures in Filipino culture.

A sense of propriety, a need to maintain social harmony and a consciousness of social obligation are central to Filipino culture.

Filipinos tend to be very sensitive to others and to the way one presents oneself. Confrontation is avoided. When in the Philippines, strive to be sensitive and tactful at all times.

Great importance is placed on the role of the family, relationships to authority and maintenance of harmony. Appearances and a sense of dignity within the community are essential to the continuity of social networks. Filipinos also have a strong sense of hierarchy.

Younger people defer to older people in the family, in social life and at work.

Good topics of discussion include culture, history, business, the place you are from, your job or your family. Filipinos are very family oriented, so children are a good topic of discussion. In fact, expect to be asked many personal questions, even at first business meetings.

Avoid discussing Filipino politics, corruption, foreign aid and religion. Never criticize a person, his or her family or an established institution.

Filipinos respect a quiet, attentive, unassuming attitude and a cheerful disposition.

Note that someone may touch you lightly on the elbow to gain your attention.

Do not be surprised to see men or boys holding hands with one another (or women with women). The gesture has no sexual implications. In contrast, physical contact with members of the opposite sex in public should be avoided.

Remember that raising the eyebrows means "No" in the Philippines.

Instead of pointing to an object, Filipinos will shift their eyes towards it, purse their lips and point with the mouth.

Do not be surprised if a Filipino smiles when upset or embarrassed. This is the Filipino way of changing the atmosphere during a difficult moment or situation.

Never show anger in public. Note that placing your hands on your hips is interpreted as a sign of anger or confrontation.

Filipinos are very respectful of women and elders and tend to be very reserved in mixed company.

Be aware that customs related to food are extremely important. If a clerk in a store you are visiting is having a snack or a coffee break, prepare to wait a long time for service. If you eat in the presence of others, it is advisable to offer them some food.

Although Filipino women seldom smoke or drink in public, it is acceptable for foreign women to do so.

Before taking a picture, look for any signs indicating that photography is forbidden. Feel free to photograph people, but be courteous and ask for permission first.

People seldom form orderly lines and crowding is both acceptable and expected.

POLAND

Population: 38,606,922 (July 1998 est.); Polish 97.6%, German 1.3%, Ukrainian 0.6%, Byelorussian 0.5%

Languages: Polish

Religions: Roman Catholic 95%, Eastern Orthodox, Protestant and other 5%

Currency: zloty

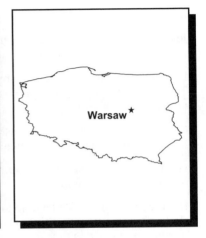

HISTORICAL OVERVIEW

- The Poles are descendants of Slavic tribes that settled in the Vistula River region as far back as the second millennium B.C. From here the Slavic tribes spread out and became differentiated. West Slavs, inhabiting the area around Poznan, formed states and united them under the Piast dynasty. The inception of the Polish nation is dated to 966 A.D. when the Piast King Miesko I adopted the Roman Catholic faith.

- In 1047, the western region of Poland united with the southern state. During the reign of Piast King Kasimir the Great, Polish culture flourished. In 1386, the Piast dynasty came to an end when a royal marriage united Poland and Lithuania under the Jagiellon dynasty, which ruled until 1572.

- Under the Jagiellons Poland became a major power in central Europe, extending its rule as far as Hungary and Bohemia. Monarchs succeeding the Jagiellons after 1572 were weak and ineffectual and ever more power went to the landed nobility. The strength of the Polish-Lithuanian Commonwealth steadily declined as a result, and the year 1655 marked the start of a series of Swedish and Russian invasions of the country.

- The Polish social order and economy continued to decline until Poland was subject to three different partitions: in 1772, 1793 and 1795. Each time, Poland lost land to Russia, Prussia and Austria until, in 1795, the state of Poland had completely disappeared and been replaced by Russian, Austrian and Prussian sectors.

- During the 19th century the Russian sector was subject to strict Russification, while Bismarck forced Germanization of Poles in the Prussian sector. The Polish Catholic Church became the locus for preserving Polish national identity.

- At the end of World War I, Poland became an independent nation again, but political life was neither stable nor strong. Poland was in an uneasy position between the Soviet Union to the east and Nazi Germany to the west. Finally in 1939, the German army invaded. In 1941, all of Poland came under Nazi rule, which aimed at stamping out Polish culture and exterminating the country's large Jewish population. When Germany was defeated at the end of the war, the Soviets were given administrative control of Poland. Although elections were held in Poland after the war, by 1948 a communist government supported by the Soviets was in control, and the country's political system was generally patterned after that of the Soviet Union.

- In 1981, following the formation of the Solidarity Labor Union under Lech Walesa and a series of strikes, Polish leader General Wojciech Jaruzelski declared martial law. He outlawed the Solidarity group and jailed its members. Martial law was lifted in 1983 but Solidarity remained outlawed.

- In 1989, the Polish government legalized Solidarity and agreed to wide-reaching reforms, including the creation of the office of president. Jaruzelski was elected president and stepped down as leader of the Communist Party. Due to pressure for reform, the Polish parliament elected a top Solidarity official, Tadeusz Mazowiecki, as prime minister. This led the way to further political and economic reforms. In 1992, however, the pace of economic reform was slowed down as the transition became too difficult for the population.

- Incumbent Walesa was defeated in the 1995 elections by Aleksander Kwasniewski, who stressed Polish membership in NATO and a further slowdown of reforms.

- In 1997 Poland was invited to join NATO and the EU.

- A new constitution for the country was approved by a public referendum in May 1997.

BUSINESS PRACTICES

Hours of Business

The Polish workday begins at 8:00 a.m. and lasts until about 2:00 p.m.

Dress

Business dress is conservative. Men wear suits and ties while women wear suits or skirts and blouses.

Introductions

People generally shake hands when meeting and when departing.

Use the term *Pan* in front of a man's last name when being introduced and the term *Pani* for a woman. A professional person's title is used along with his/her surname, but in formal conversation or in business contexts, use only the title without the surname.

First names are used by mutual consent between adult friends.

Men will often kiss the extended hand of a woman in greeting. Women greet close female friends with a kiss on both cheeks.

Meetings

Make appointments ahead of time and be punctual.

It is best to schedule an appointment in writing.

Meetings in Poland may be scheduled for as early as 8:00 a.m. and lunch meetings for as late as 4:00 p.m.

Always try to schedule a meeting with the highest-ranking Polish counterpart with whom you wish to do business.

Negotiating

A guest will usually be offered tea or coffee as a refreshment during business negotiations. Acceptance or rejection of this offer is immaterial, and you may refuse if you wish.

Poles have a strong work ethic.

It is to your advantage to have any written materials you bring along translated into Polish.

Although Poles tend to be low-context communicators, concentrating mainly on the contents of a presentation rather than on style and emotional verve, the legality of a certain action is often of secondary importance to how the action will affect relationships.

You should consider having local representatives assist you with handling business arrangements.

Direct communication is used and preferred.

When negotiating with government officials, expect things to take time. The government is still encumbered by a large bureaucracy and several trips to the country might be necessary.

Emphasize your company's position in the world market and demonstrate how your company can help your Polish counterpart technologically, but if you and your Polish counterparts are negotiating a contract, hold your technological negotiations until the end.

Formal financial record keeping is relatively new to Polish business. If your company requires such information, send people ahead of time to obtain it.

Have various strategies worked out for achieving your objectives. The path of particular negotiations may change unexpectedly and you should be prepared for such an eventuality.

Entertaining

Flowers are an appropriate gift, even if your visit is brief. Always bring an odd number of flowers and avoid red roses, which have a romantic connotation. Flowers should be given to the hostess unwrapped.

Consumption of hard liquor is widespread in Poland. Cognac and vodka are especially favored.

Toasting is often part of both formal and informal dinners. Let your host initiate a toast and then reciprocate later.

The main meal of the day is eaten after 3:00 p.m. A light supper is eaten at home after 6:00 p.m.

Since dining in restaurants is expensive, entertaining at home is much more common.

The guest of honor is often seated at the head of the table.

When dining, keep your hands but not your elbows above the table.

Do not start eating until everyone has been served.

Because Poles start their day early, evening visits usually end by 11:00 p.m.

You may be entertained at a *kawiarna*, a café that serves fancy pastries. Visits to a *kawiarna* may last a number of hours.

In Poland the continental style of eating is followed. The fork is held in the left hand and the knife in the right hand.

In restaurants, the bill must be requested from the waiter and paid at the table. Tips are generally expected.

Traditional foods include *pierogi* (dumplings filled with cheese, potatoes or sauerkraut), *uszka* (a kind of ravioli), *bigos* (sausage, mushrooms and cabbage), poppy seed desserts and cheesecake. Pork is a more popular meat than beef.

Table manners and etiquette are similar to those used in the West. It is considered good manners when starting a meal to say *Smacznego* (Bon Appetit). When toasting, one says *Na Zdrowie* (Cheers).

SOCIAL VALUES, CUSTOMS AND TIPS

European clothing fashions are common in the major cities.

The majority of women work outside the home. They make up nearly half of the labor force.

Good conversation topics include Polish national history and culture as well as one's family and its activities. Avoid any reference to World War II.

It is inappropriate for either friends or relatives to visit each other without first planning ahead. It is not appreciated when people "drop by" unannounced.

Poles are generally outgoing and outspoken. They are proud of their cultural heritage and enjoy conversing about their country and customs.

Except among very close friends, Poles do not generally touch each other in public. People generally stand about an arm's length from each other when conversing.

Loud behavior in public is considered rude.

Polish men tend to hold traditional views concerning women. For example, if a woman talks to a man whom she does not know, it may be considered flirting.

When signing their names, Poles sign their family name first and then their given name.

It is considered rude to chew gum while speaking to someone.

Soccer is very popular in Poland.

National holidays include New Year's Day, Easter Monday, Labor Day (May 1), Constitution Day (May 3), Assumption Day (August 15), All Soul's Day, Christmas and December 26.

PORTUGAL

Population: 9,927,556 (July 1998 est.); Mediterranean, small African minority

Languages: Portuguese

Religions: Roman Catholic 97%, Protestant denominations 1%, other 2%

Currency: escudo, euro

HISTORICAL OVERVIEW

- During the first millennium B.C. Celtic peoples migrated to the Iberian Peninsula. Those who settled in present-day Portugal conquered but did not intermarry with the local population. In around 140 B.C. the Celts were conquered by the Romans and during the fifth century B.C. the Germanic Suebi arrived, followed by the Visigoths.

- Portugal and Spain were conquered by the Moors in 711 A.D. The portion of Portugal left in Christian hands became known as the country of Portugal, and it was from here that modern-day Portugal was reconquered by the Christians. Ruled by King Alfonso Henriques, Portugal became an independent nation in 1143. Portuguese reconquest of lands still held by the Moors continued and, by 1270, Portugal's modern continental boundaries were set.

- With the ascent of the house of Aviz to the throne in 1385, Portugal's age of exploration and expansion began. During the 14th, 15th and 16th centuries, Portuguese voyagers traveled to Africa, India, China, the Middle East and South America, setting up colonies and trading posts.

- In the 16th century, when the Aviz line died out, Phillip II of Spain ruled Portugal briefly as Phillip I. Spanish neglect, however, brought the Portugues Bragança family to the throne in 1640. Portuguese power and its grand empire began to decline, in part due to the effects of the Spanish Inquisition and invasions by Spain, England and France.

- In 1807, during the Napoleonic Wars, the Portuguese monarchy was forced to flee to Brazil. Brazil had become so strong by that time that it was elevated to kingdom status in 1815 and united with Portugal. The royal family returned to Portugal shortly thereafter but strife followed between constitutionalists and absolutists for the rest of the century.

- In 1910, Portugal's monarchy was overthrown, and a republic was established. Political instability dominated the country, however, and a military coup replaced the democracy in 1926. From 1928 to 1968, António de Oliviera Salazar ruled as a virtual dictator in what amounted to a fascist political system.

- Salazar's colonial policies met with opposition from military leaders and finally led to his downfall.

- In 1974, a socialist military coup, led by General Antonio de Spinola, took control of the government. In 1975, elections were held, leading to the Third Republic. Under the new left-wing government, the economy was nationalized. The political situation remained somewhat unstable until 1985.

- In the 1985 elections, voting patterns were more concrete than in the past, and Mário Soares, a center-right candidate, won. Under his leadership and that of Prime Minister Aníbal Cavaco Silva, the government implemented privatization efforts and started other reforms. Portugal joined the European Union (EU) in 1986, and since the mid-1980s, the country has been a thriving democracy.

- Due to the popularity of his reforms, Cavaco Silva was reelected in 1991.

- An economic recession, excessive patronage and a 1994 scandal involving wiretapping of the attorney general's office removed Cavaco Silva from favor. The Socialist Party subsequently won the 1995 parliamentary election and the 1996 presidential election.

- Since 1995 the Socialist Party has been in control of the government with António Guterres serving as prime minister and Jorges Sampaio serving as president.

- The formation of the Community of Portuguese Speaking Countries (CPSC) in 1996 fulfilled Portugal's dream of once more reuniting with its former colonies, albeit as independent states. In 1997, Portugal helped negotiate the "Estoril Accord," which ended the civil war in Angola, a former Portuguese colony.

- During the 1990s Portugal spent money donated to it by the EU to improve its infrastructure significantly. Lisbon, the capital, got a particular boost in preparation for the 1998 World's Fair or Expo, which Portugal hosted in the summer of that year.

BUSINESS PRACTICES

Hours of Business

Business hours are generally from 9:00 a.m. to 12:00 p.m. and from 2:00 to 5:00 p.m., Monday through Friday.

Avoid planning business trips during August, when many Portuguese executives take vacations.

Dress

Businessmen usually wear suits and ties, even when it is hot. Sports jackets and slacks are also popular. If your Portuguese colleagues remove their jackets, you may do the same. Businesswomen generally wear conservative skirt suits or dresses with high heels.

Introductions

A warm, firm handshake is the appropriate greeting for both men and women of all ages. Avoid very firm handshakes, since some Portuguese people may not grip very strongly. Gauge your handshake accordingly.

Relatives or close female friends will greet each other by appearing to kiss each other on both cheeks (actually "kissing the air"), starting with the right cheek. Close male friends will greet each other with a hug and a slap on the back rather than by shaking hands.

Men should stand when they are being introduced, but it is not necessary for women to do so. When you are introduced, shake hands with each person, even if you are meeting a large group of people.

First names are only used among friends, with children and with youth. Normally, a title such as "Mr.," "Mrs." or "Miss" should be used followed by a surname when addressing an adult. A person's professional title followed by a surname should be used when addressing a doctor, lawyer, professor or engineer. Sometimes the title is combined with a first name instead of the surname when the relationship has passed from merely professional to a more personal one. Follow the cues of your Portuguese hosts.

Common terms used for greeting are *Bom dia* (Good day) and *Boa noite* (Good evening).

Meetings

The Portuguese consider people and relationships to be more important than time and formalities. As a result, punctuality is usually not stressed, but it is advisable that you be prompt since it will impress your colleagues. Expect other businesspeople, however, to arrive at a meeting 15 to 30 minutes late. Individuals living in urban areas tend to value punctuality more than rural dwellers.

Negotiating

All correspondence, especially regarding business arrangements, should be translated into Portuguese.

When doing business with a small Portuguese company, you may want to consider hiring an interpreter to ensure proper communication with your business counterparts.

When transacting business in Portugal, be aware that the Portuguese are relatively conservative and traditional. Innovation or change is accepted, but only after careful consideration.

The Portuguese are quite reserved. Avoid using a lot of demonstrative gestures when making presentations.

If you are offered refreshments by your colleagues at a business meeting, it is impolite to refuse.

Business cards are not as commonly used in Portugal as in other countries. Ask for someone's business card only if he/she is a senior member of a company. You should have your business cards printed in English on one side and in Portuguese on the other. When presenting the card, always present it with the Portuguese side facing your Portuguese counterpart.

If you are selling a product, maintain steady contact with your client. Make sure to have full customer services available for your client during Portuguese business hours.

Entertaining

Most socializing is done in the home, but it is also common for business associates to go to a restaurant or a café for conversation, sweets and tea or coffee.

When visiting a home, guests wait outside the door until asked inside. Similarly, guests allow the host to open the door when they are leaving.

Homes in Portugal are kept very clean and guests are expected to wipe their feet before entering. Dirty shoes should be removed entirely while still outside.

Punctuality by foreigners at social occasions is appreciated, especially in urban areas.

Since the Portuguese people take great pride in their homes, they sincerely appreciate any compliments offered.

When invited to a home, guests often bring a small gift to their host or send a thank-you note after the dinner engagement. Nevertheless, do not feel obligated to bring a gift. You may simply reciprocate by inviting your host to a restaurant. Expensive chocolates are the most appropriate gift. Flowers are also acceptable, but never bring chrysanthemums (as they are associated with funerals) or inexpensive flowers. Wine does not make a good gift since wine is inexpensive in Portugal and most people have good wine cellars.

If you have established contact with businesspeople in Portugal before traveling there, it is polite to ask them what gift they would like you to bring for them from your home country. People often like to receive technical books or computer programs, which are difficult to obtain in Portugal.

Refreshments are usually served when you visit someone's home. It is impolite to refuse.

If you are invited to a dinner, suits and ties are appropriate for men and dresses are appropriate for women. Even when attending the cinema, men often wear jackets and ties, and women wear skirts and blouses or dresses.

In restaurants, the waiter can be summoned with a raised hand. A service charge is usually not included in the bill and it is customary to round up the bill to the nearest whole number. In a better restaurant you may wish to leave a bigger tip of ten to 15 percent. If a service charge is included in the bill, it is recommended that you leave an extra 50 escudos (Portuguese currency) on the table.

A small breakfast, which includes bread, butter and jam and coffee mixed with hot milk, is eaten around 8:00 a.m. Lunch is eaten between noon and 2:00 p.m. Dinner is usually served between 8:00 and 9:00 p.m. Both are usually warm substantial meals consisting of a main dish (meat or fish), soup, vegetables and dessert.

The staples in Portugal include fish, vegetables and fruits. One of the national dishes is *bacalhau* (dried cod), which is usually served with potatoes and green vegetables. It is served often and can be prepared in a variety of ways.

Corn bread is usually served in the north, and wheat bread is generally served in the south. Olive oil is commonly used in Portuguese cooking, and garlic is the most popular seasoning. Portugal has many pastry shops, as sweets are very popular. The meal normally ends with fruit, dessert (something sweet or cheese and crackers) and coffee.

The Portuguese enjoy lengthy conversation during meals, especially during dinner. In fact, to avoid seeming as if they are in a hurry, diners all try to finish their meals at the same time. At dinner parties, guests usually stay after the meal until about 11:00 p.m. or midnight.

The continental style of eating is used, with the fork held in the left hand and the knife in the right. A special knife and fork are used when eating fish. Never eat with your hands. Even fruit should be eaten with a knife and fork.

When serving, dishes are passed around the table. It is expected that you will help yourself first as you are the guest, and then pass the serving platter to the other diners. At each course, do not begin eating until everyone has been served.

At a dinner party, the host may say a few words to the guests before the meal.

It is important to keep your hands above the table at all times, but only your wrists should be on the table (never your elbows). The napkin should be on your lap and should never be tied around the neck. It is considered impolite to stretch at the table. Stretching is taken to imply that you are tired or bored with the company.

You must cover your mouth when using a toothpick.

To indicate that you have finished eating, place your knife and fork with the tines up vertically on the plate. You should fold your napkin before leaving the table.

If you smoke, it is customary to do so after the meal, but not between courses. You should be sure to ask your host beforehand for permission to smoke.

SOCIAL VALUES, CUSTOMS AND TIPS

Portuguese is the official language, but English, French and German are taught in school and are quite widely understood.

The Portuguese are very warm, friendly and hospitable to people of other nations. They value and cultivate strong and lasting friendships.

Be aware that, while Portugal is an open, liberal society, there is a greater emphasis on moral and religious values (especially Roman Catholic) than in other European countries. Therefore, avoid making remarks that might touch on moral or religious sensitivities.

Showing that you have some knowledge about the area in which you are staying or about their sense of Portuguese culture is appreciated. The Portuguese are proud of their cultural heritage, nationhood and the economic progress they have made. Even urban people have strong links to their hometowns or regions. In addition, political issues (but not parties) are avidly discussed.

It is polite to converse about yourself and your host's family, positive aspects of Portugal, vacations, wines and personal interests and hobbies. Inquisitive personal questions (especially about money issues, such as salaries and the cost of living), however, should be avoided. Popular participatory and spectator sports, including soccer, hockey, roller skating, sailing and Portuguese bullfighting, are also good topics of conversation.

Both in public and in private, you should defer to older people. Always wait until an older person is finished speaking before saying anything. Make a point of walking to the left of an older person, especially when you are going down the street.

The Portuguese generally dress conservatively. People are very careful to be dressed neatly and cleanly in public. Dirty or tattered clothing is considered improper. Leather dress shoes should be worn for most occasions. Tennis shoes are only worn for sports activities.

It is considered impolite for adults to eat while walking in public. Eating an ice cream cone is the only exception to this rule.

Pointing at someone with the index finger is considered rude. To beckon someone, all fingers are waved with the palm facing up.

There are a number of gestures that are commonly used in Portugal. Pinching the earlobe and shaking it gently while raising the eyebrows means that something (e.g., a meal) is very good. Pulling down the skin just below the eye with the index finger can mean "You are perceptive" or "You are kidding me." Spreading the fingers with the palm down and rocking the hand means "more or less." Rubbing the thumb against the first two fingers with the palm facing up is a sign for money. Touching the tips of all fingers to the tip of the thumb with the palm facing up signifies fear or cowardice.

Keep in mind that it is a serious insult to make a "V" sign or to make "rabbit ears" behind someone's head because it connotes a lack of morals.

Bargaining is acceptable at markets, but you should not bargain in shops or food markets.

Women may go into a café alone. Going into a bar alone may bring unwelcome attention, however, since it is not a common practice by local women. Women should also avoid walking alone after 8:00 or 9:00 p.m. when there are not many people on the street.

PUERTO RICO

Population: 3,857,070 (July 1998 est.); Hispanic

Languages: Spanish (official), English

Religions: Roman Catholic 85%, Protestant denominations and other 15%

Currency: US dollar

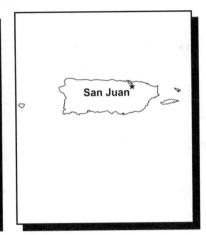

HISTORICAL OVERVIEW

- In 1493, Columbus arrived in the region now known as Puerto Rico and claimed the island for Spain, calling it San Juan Bautista. In 1508, Spanish settlers began colonizing the island, and in 1513 they began importing African slaves. During this period of colonization, the indigenous Arawak Indians were virtually wiped out. First gold mining and then agriculture were the major industries, although Puerto Rico remained largely underdeveloped until the 1700s.

- In 1873, slavery was abolished on the island. In 1897, self-government was granted to Puerto Rico, which became a dominion under Spain. The first leader under dominion status was Luis Muñoz Rivera, who had been instrumental in winning this status for the island.

- In 1898, during the Spanish-American War, the United States invaded the island of Puerto Rico and defeated the Spaniards. Spain ceded the island to the U.S. in that year. Puerto Rico became the first colony of the United States.

- In 1917, Puerto Rico became a U.S. territory, and its people were granted citizenship.

- Puerto Rico was hit hard by the Great Depression in the 1930s, which caused 60 percent unemployment and great suffering. During the same decade, Puerto Rican political life became divided between those supporting independence and those championing U.S. statehood.

- The first island-born governor, Jesus Toribio Pinero, was appointed by U.S. President Truman in 1946.

- In 1952, Puerto Ricans voted to establish the self-governing Commonwealth of Puerto Rico, with its own constitution. The status of commonwealth has meant that a resident high commissioner represents the country in the U.S. House of Representatives, but citizens do not vote in national elections, and they do not pay federal income taxes. Puerto Ricans are subject to the draft, receive partial welfare benefits and elect their own officials.

- The issue of commonwealth status has been volatile and has at times caused violence to erupt, including attempts on former President Truman's life and a shooting in the U.S. Congress.

- From the 1940s to the 1960s, Puerto Rico moved from an agrarian economy to an industrial one.

- Today, Puerto Ricans continue to be divided over the issue of whether to request statehood or remain a commonwealth. In 1993, a referendum regarding Puerto Rico's status took place, and the decision to remain a commonwealth passed by a slim margin. This contrasted with the significantly wider margin by which a similar referendum passed in 1967 and 1981.

- The Puerto Rican economy is fairly good, but agriculture and tourism have suffered, mainly due to an increase in crime associated with burgeoning drug traffic. The economy is also hampered by the large bureaucracy: 28 percent of the populace works for the government.

- Pedro Rosello was elected governor in late 1996 and carried the pro-statehood New Progressive Party to victory.

- In April 1998, the U.S. passed another resolution for a referendum on the issue of statehood. During the referendum in the fall of 1998, Puerto Rico chose to once again maintain its status as a commonwealth.

BUSINESS PRACTICES

Hours of Business

Business hours are usually 9:00 a.m. to 5:00 p.m., often with a one- to two-hour break in the early afternoon for the midday meal.

Banks are open from 8:30 a.m. to 2:30 p.m. and some until 4:00 p.m.

Dress

Dress codes are similar to those on the U.S. mainland, although it is not unusual to see an older gentlemen wearing the traditional *guayabera* (a decorative shirt worn rather than a shirt and tie) during the summer. Women dress professionally in lightweight suits or dresses.

Businesspeople should not wear shorts or bathing suits outside the confines of their hotel pool/recreation area.

Introductions

People generally shake hands when they meet. A firm handshake however, may be interpreted as a sign of aggression. Close friends often embrace, and women may grasp each other's shoulders and kiss each other's cheek when greeting. People stand very close while conversing with each other.

Puerto Ricans often use titles such as *Doctor, Profesor, Ingeniero, Abogado*, etc. Always use a title or *Señor, Señora* or *Señorita* when addressing someone. Sometimes the informal custom of using first names is borrowed from the mainland, but do not call your client or counterpart by his/her first name until invited to do so. Sometimes a single surname is used in business instead of the traditional custom of using both matronymic and patronymic surnames as is often done in Latin America. A business card may simply read "Jose Castillo" instead of "Jose Castillo Contreras", for example. On the other hand, do not be surprised to see both names on the card, as an individual may want to be addressed by both names. In any case, inquire as to your counterpart's preference.

Meetings

Puerto Ricans are spontaneous and warm in their relationships, and this sentiment carries over into business meetings. You may spend time socializing before your business begins. This usually involves discussing family, which is one of the most important aspects of life in Puerto Rico.

Meetings will begin or close at the appointed time, but since Puerto Ricans have a more relaxed lifestyle, there may be delays. These should not be taken amiss.

Negotiating

Personal and interpersonal relationships have a great impact on business. A task may be very important, and it will get accomplished. Personal relationships and the people involved in a task, however, are considered much more important than any task itself.

Business is conducted more slowly in Puerto Rico than on the mainland and it is critical that attempts are not made to rush things.

A Puerto Rican businessperson tends to avoid directly answering "No" to questions. For example, a response such as "I'll see what I can do about that," may really mean "No."

Entertaining

After a meeting, it is customary to invite the client for a drink or to dinner. Business should not be discussed during dinner as this occasion is considered a time to become better acquainted. The pace of dinner is usually relaxed and includes good-natured joking. It is not considered polite to eat and run, and it is customary to linger over coffee.

It should be noted that outside San Juan the pace of business as well as entertainment is slower.

Both the continental European and the U.S. styles of eating are acceptable. An offer of a toast to the health of all and success in all endeavors is appreciated.

You will sometimes hear a hissing sound in a restaurant. This sound is used to call a waiter. Do not comment on it.

SOCIAL VALUES, CUSTOMS AND TIPS

Puerto Ricans object to open criticism of Puerto Rico. They would rather discuss their cultural heritage and their rapid economic growth. Statehood with the U.S. is a hotly debated and divisive issue and is best left untouched. Politics and religious topics should be avoided in conversation and in public addresses. Puerto Ricans are not disturbed by interruptions while conversing. Commenting quietly while others are talking is not generally considered offensive.

Puerto Ricans are generally not disturbed by background noise. They can transact business, listen to one another and carry on a meaningful conversation in spite it.

Most Puerto Ricans are fluent in English. Nevertheless, if you speak some Spanish, it will be appreciated.

ROMANIA

Population: 22,395,848 (July 1998 est.); Romanian 89.1%, Hungarian 8.9%, German 0.4%, Ukrainian, Serbian, Croatian, Russian, Turkish, and Gypsy 1.6%

Languages: Romanian (official), Hungarian, German

Religions: Romanian Orthodox 70%, Roman Catholic 6%, Protestant 6%, unaffiliated 18%

Currency: leu

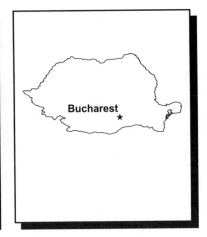

HISTORICAL OVERVIEW

- Romanians are descendants of the Geto-Dacians, an Indo-European people, who came to the area before the seventh century B.C. Around 100 A.D., the Romans conquered most of Dacia and made the area a province to supply grain, gold and cattle. The natives adopted the Roman language and culture. In fact, the name "Romania" means "Land of the Romans."

- The Romans lost control of Dacia in the third century when the Goths invaded. Between 200 and 1100, the land was invaded by Visigoths, Huns, Avars, Slavs, Bulgars and Magyars. Some claim that the Romanized Dacians fled south of the Danube during this time, while others believe they fled to the Carpathians. The Bulgars brought Eastern Orthodox Christianity.

- Transylvania, a region of Romania, became part of the Hungarian Empire during the 11th century. In the 14th century, two separate Romanian states were founded: first Walachia, and then Moldavia, but within another 100 years both had come under Ottoman rule. Thus, the three constituent parts of modern Romania – Transylvania, Walachia and Moldavia – were then under foreign rule up through the 19th century. In 1812 part of Moldavia was ceded to Russia.

- The 19th century was marked by nationalist uprisings in all three regions. In 1856, Walachia and Moldavia became independent, uniting in 1859 to form Romania.

- In World War I, Romania was part of the Allied alliance. As a result, when the war was over, Romania reacquired Bessarabia from Russia and Transylvania from the Austro-Hungarian Empire. These acquisitions doubled the country's size. Although Romanian nationalists were pleased with their new acquisitions many of the minorities in these newly acquired territories were not.

- In 1940, Romania was occupied by Nazi Germany and, in 1941, joined in an attack on Russia. By 1944, however, Romania joined the Allies, and Soviet troops occupied the country. Under Russian occupation, the Romanian monarchy was overthrown and a Communist regime was established.

- In 1965, under the leadership of Nicolae Ceausescu, the country broke away from the Soviet Union. While the 1965 constitution recognized the primacy of the Communist Party in the country, Romania began to carry on an independent foreign policy and relations with the U.S.S.R. became strained.

- The Ceausescu regime took drastic measures to modernize the Romanian economy quickly. While it managed to industrialize the nation, grander plans failed and the country was plunged into great poverty in the 1980s as it attempted to pay off its foreign debt. The secret police became very repressive.

- As communist regimes fell throughout Europe in 1989, large groups of demonstrators protested Ceausescu's regime and rioting broke out when security forces turned on the crowds. The army supported the people, and the government was toppled after only a few days of fighting. Ceausescu and his wife fled but were soon arrested and executed by the provisional government. A group called the Council of the National Salvation Front took control of the government.

- The National Salvation Front organized elections in 1990, and National Salvation Front leader Ion Iliescu won. Iliescu introduced democratic reforms, and a bicameral parliament elected a new constitution, implemented economic reforms and scheduled national elections. In 1992, Iliescu was reelected president. Since then, the Romanian government has been working to improve the country's image and has promoted privatization. Transforming Romania's inefficient industrial base requires tremendous capital, which the country does not have. Furthermore, Romania faces severe environmental problems.

- In 1995, Romania asked to become part of NATO and was granted "most favored nation" trading status by the U.S.

- During the 1996 national elections the Democratic Convention Alliance won a majority in Parliament, and Emil Constantinescu became president.

BUSINESS PRACTICES

Hours of Business

The usual workday begins at 7:00 a.m. for factory workers, but at 8:00 or 9:00 a.m. for office workers. The day ends between 3:00 and 5:00 p.m. depending on the place of work.

Most factories are closed on Saturdays and Sundays, and Friday is usually a shortened workday. With the exception of restaurants, coffee shops and some private shops, everything is closed on Sundays. Stores may be closed for a few hours around lunchtime, but then remain open later in the evening. General department stores remain open all day.

Dress

Conservative business suits are appropriate for men. Female office workers usually wear a skirt and a blouse with a scarf.

Introductions

Adults commonly greet each other with a handshake, but a man usually waits for a woman to extend her hand first. In cities, some men might greet a woman by kissing her hand.

Greetings using the first name are usually made only between close friends and relatives.

When addressing others, use last names and titles. Shake hands each time you meet with someone, and use a firm grip.

When applicable, it is most polite to use a person's title (e.g., Doctor, Professor) in front of the surname.

Be prepared to present your business card to every businessperson you encounter. Remember to have your degrees printed after your name.

Meetings

Appointments should be scheduled beforehand, and punctuality is appreciated. It is best to ask for and receive confirmation of an appointment in writing. Letters should be sent in English, for these will be respected more than documents written in Romanian.

Negotiating

Western-style business is quite new to Romania, and thus Romanian management may be unused to many practices common to western businesspeople. This may be compounded by a general distrust of authority emerging from years of authoritarian rule.

It is worthwhile to examine the business credentials of the firm with which you will be dealing to assure yourself of its legitimacy.

When conducting negotiations and making decisions most Romanian businesspeople will focus on the business facts involved, but emotional attachments and personal relations play a part as well.

It is advisable to bring an interpreter to all negotiations unless you and your Romanian associate both speak a common language. Older Romanians tend to speak French or German, while younger Romanians often speak English.

The pace of business in Romania is very slow, but once a relationship has been established you can expect to have a loyal Romanian business partner for a very long time.

Romanians pay attention to prestige. It is advisable, therefore, to stay in the best hotels in order to contribute to a favorable impression.

Communicate the parameters of your company's abilities and wishes early on so that your Romanian counterparts know what they can and cannot expect.

Once an agreement is reached and a contract is drawn up, it will be subject to approval by the senior executives of the Romanian firm.

The Romanians still practice *baksheen* (tipping), a form of financial supplementation. It is best to allow a Romanian contact or friend to help you with this system, especially when you are negotiating with government officials.

Entertaining

When invited to dinner, it is considered polite for the guest to bring an odd number of flowers (three or more) or a small gift for the host. Red roses are avoided for such an occasion, however, because they are a sign of romantic affection.

Romanians like to receive and pay visits. In the home, guests are usually offered refreshments such as coffee, tea, brandy or wine.

The continental style of eating is used, with the fork in the left hand and the knife in the right.

Toasting is usually part of both formal and informal lunches and dinners.

Evening visits usually end before 11:00 p.m. because work begins early in the morning.

The host or hostess indicates when the meal will begin and when it will end.

Romanians generally consider it a great honor to entertain guests, and visitors will usually be invited out as much as possible.

Popular Romanian food includes distinctive ethnic specialties such as *mititei* (grilled meatballs), *patricieni* (grilled sausage) and *mamaliga* (cornmeal mush).

Breakfast usually consists of eggs, cheese, rolls, breads and coffee.

Lunch is the main meal of the day and usually consists of soup, meat, potatoes, bread and vegetables.

In the past, food shortages were common. Although food is generally available now, remember that people cannot easily afford the much higher prices that many food items may now carry.

A small tip for good service at a restaurant or café is customary.

SOCIAL VALUES, CUSTOMS AND TIPS

Romanians attach importance to their appearance. People generally dress conservatively in public.

When someone sneezes, *Noroc* (Bless you) or *Sanatate* (Good health) is said. *Noroc* is also used when toasting at parties and means "Cheers."

On public transportation, men generally offer their seats to women.

Opinions are openly and freely expressed.

Romanian businesspeople enjoy vacations of two to four weeks, depending on their seniority.

Both hands but not the elbows are kept above the table during a meal.

It is impolite to yawn or cough without covering one's mouth.

Men remove their hats before they enter buildings, except stores.

Romanians use many gestures when speaking, but visitors should be careful about what gestures they use, since gestures taken from another culture may be misinterpreted.

National holidays include New Year's Day (January 1-2), Easter Monday, Labor Day (May 1), National Day (December 1) and Christmas (December 25-26).

RUSSIA

Population: 146,861,022 (July 1998 est.); Russian 81.5%, Tatar 3.8%, Ukrainian 3%, Chuvash 1.2%, Bashkir 0.9%, Byelorussian 0.8%, Moldavian 0.7%, other 8.1%

Languages: Russian (official), other

Religions: Russian Orthodox, Muslim, other

Currency: Russian ruble

HISTORICAL OVERVIEW

- Present-day Russia emerged from the Rus civilization, which first came into its own along the northern Volga River in the eighth and ninth centuries. The Rus expanded their territory south to the border with Byzantium, and during the tenth century the grand prince of Kiev began to unite the Rus lands. His son, Vladimir, continued this unification and converted the Rus to Christianity, establishing the Russian Orthodox Church.

- By 1240 most of Russia had been conquered by the Mongols. Under Mongol rule Moscow grew in prominence, becoming the seat of the Russian throne by the 15th century. Ivan III the Great drove out the Mongols in 1480. Ivan IV the Terrible, who was crowned the first tsar of Russia in 1547, conquered several non-Slavic states for Great Russia.

- The Romanov dynasty, which ruled until 1917, was established in 1613 with the election of Michael of Romanov as tsar.

- Peter I the Great, who came to the throne in 1689, introduced western reforms, secured Russia's position as a major European power, expanded the country to include the Baltic states and declared Russia an empire. His successors Elizabeth (1741-62) and Catherine II the Great (1762-69) continued his reforms and his expansion of the country's territories.

- Opposition to serfdom began in the late 18th century, but the Napoleonic Wars (in which Russia was victorious) early in the next century diverted the tsars' attention from domestic reforms.

- Thereafter, however, social unrest continued to grow. The last tsar, Nicholas II, was forced to establish a parliament or Duma in 1906, but the tsar's unwillingness to institute reforms eventually contributed to the end of the monarchy.

- World War I was devastating to Russia, costing it one million lives.

- In 1917, the tsar abdicated in favor of a provisional government, but in October of that year Vladimir Ilich Lenin, head of the Bolsheviks, led a successful revolutionary coup.

- A civil war between Lenin's Red Army and the Royalist White Army ensued. The Bolsheviks won in 1920 and formed the Union of Soviet Socialist Republics (USSR). In 1922, Armenia, Azerbaijan, Georgia, Ukraine and Belarus were incorporated into the union.

- Lenin died in 1924 and was replaced by Joseph Stalin, who implemented forced industrialization and collective agriculture. Millions of people died under Stalin's autocratic reign. Stalin signed a nonaggression pact with Hitler at the beginning of World War II, but nevertheless, Hitler invaded the Soviet Union in 1941. The Soviet Union helped defeat Germany and emerged a world power, but the war took more than 25 million Soviet lives.

- When Stalin died in 1953, Nikita Khrushchev took his place. Communist hard-liners opposed his reforms, and Leonid Brezhnev replaced him in 1964. Brezhnev sought to expand Soviet influence in the developing world and to reinstate harsher controls. After Brezhnev's death in 1982, the Soviet Union was ruled by two short-lived leaders, Yuri Andropov and Konstantin Chernenko.

- In 1985, Mikhail Gorbachev emerged as the new leader. Gorbachev implemented *perestroika* (restructuring) and *glasnost* (openness). Both the political system and the economy were restructured and a greater range of individual freedoms was granted.

- In June 1991, Boris Yeltsin became the first popularly elected Russian president. An unsuccessful coup in 1991 led to further democratic and free-market reforms.

- On 25 December 1991, the USSR was officially abolished and Russia and ten other former Soviet republics founded the Commonwealth of Independent States (CIS).

- Russia found itself in a state of serious economic and societal disarray. It turned to the West for substantial financial aid.

- In 1993, a power struggle between Yeltsin and the Supreme Soviet, which was still in place, led to Yeltsin's dissolution of the parliament. New elections were held and a new constitution was approved, and Yeltsin managed to keep his position.

- The new Russia also faced growing dissatisfaction from its ethnic minorities. It allowed several federal republics, such as Tatarstan, to adopt a constitution and have a degree of autonomy. In the case of Chechnya, however, Russian troops invaded the area as soon as the Chechans declared independence. The resulting war was bloody and protracted and proved disastrous for Russia. In 1996, a peace was negotiated that allowed Chechnya to apply for independence in five years.

- In early 1997, domestic affairs in Russia looked optimistic. Yeltsin overhauled his cabinet to include several young reformers – including Anatoly Chubais – who planned to restructure housing, welfare and taxation, and to continue liberalizing the economy. The Russian Duma, dominated by old Communists, thwarted these plans at every turn.

- In 1998, Yeltsin was forced to abandon his choice of a young economic reformer for prime minister. The ruble began to decline in value.

- Russia began to slide into a severe economic crisis at this time. Widespread tax fraud prevented the government from collecting enough revenue to pay the many workers on its payrolls. The lack of income, rising prices and food shortages made for a very harsh winter in 1998 and 1999 for many Russians.

BUSINESS PRACTICES

Hours of Business

Businesses are generally open from 9:00 a.m. to 5:00 p.m., Monday through Friday.

Dress

Both men and women wear conservative business suits with white blouses. Men wear ties of subdued colors.

During the winter months it is important to dress very warmly and to bring a pair of boots that will not skid easily.

Layering is a very good way to keep warm in the often very cold fall and winter months. Once inside the warm Russian buildings, layers can be removed as needed.

Introductions

Russian friends will usually embrace one another upon meeting. Strangers will shake hands and state their names.

Russian names follow the western order, but the middle name is a patronymic. For example, Andre Buchovich Romanov is Andre Romanov, son of Bucho. A woman will add an "a" to her last name and her patronymic ending is not "vich" but "nova". For example, Anna Buchonova Romanova is Anna Romanova, daughter of Bucho.

First names are not used in Russia unless a close relationship exists. "Mr.", "Mrs.", "Miss" or a person's title is used followed by the last name. Upon forming a personal relationship a foreigner may begin to call a Russian by his or her first name and patronymic or nickname. Wait until you counterpart initiates a first-name basis of address.

Meetings

Scheduling appointments can be a difficult and lengthy process. Every effort should therefore be made to keep them once they have been scheduled.

Negotiating

Before entering into negotiations with a Russian firm be sure to review the firm's history carefully and have an expert on Russian law explain the newest and most important laws.

Russians respond better to a personal approach to business than to the "hard sell." It is better to know and use some proper Russian phrases well than to attempt to speak Russian poorly, which will insult your Russian counterparts.

Your negotiating team should present a unified front and should present in writing everything your team wants and hopes to accomplish.

You and your team may be asked to sign a *protokol*, a summary of the day's meeting, after daily negotiations are completed. This is not an agreement. In fact, Russians very rarely take "no" for an answer and never conclude deals after only one round of negotiations.

A woman doing business in Russia should enter negotiations with her Russian male counterpart with a specific set of objectives. She should present bilingual business cards with all of her titles on them, and she should be sure to mention her international connections. These will help to enhance her status in the eyes of her Russian counterpart.

All joint ventures with Russians need to be approved by the government, which is steeped in bureaucracy. Expect this phase of negotiations to take quite a long time. To help facilitate this process try to find the highest-ranking official possible in the appropriate government department and present him with a detailed report of your business plans. You should include the history and philosophy of your firm along with details of the project and present it a few weeks before actually meeting with your official in that government office.

In a joint venture be careful not to accept 51 percent of a company since all decisions about the company must be unanimous. Thus 51 percent does not mean control of the company. When drawing up a contract include a clause for third-country intervention in the event that your firm and the Russian firm cannot come to an agreement. The most popular country for this task is Sweden.

Russians will always say "No" before they say "Yes."

Russians may suddenly become expressive or emotional during negotiations. The Russians consider this an expression of their emotional souls, which they call *dusha*. *Dusha* during negotiations is quite normal and will slow negotiations. A Russian may walk out of negotiations quite frequently rather than compromise. (Compromising is seen as a sign of weakness.) Instead they will wait patiently to obtain what they want.

Russians also expect their foreign counterparts to be highly emotional as well and to walk out during negotiations.

All parts of a deal should be agreed upon before the contract is drawn up. Once a contract has been finalized negotiation is not possible.

It is customary for Russian businesspeople and professionals to ask for help in making connections to their counterparts in your country in order to expand their knowledge in their field of expertise.

Russian firms may ask for a cash advance on occasion, because they need the hard currency in order to operate their businesses.

Gifts, especially pins representing a foreign country or city, are greatly appreciated by all Russians. Hard-to-get items and electronics are also popular gifts and are not considered bribes.

Entertaining

Russians enjoy conducting business informally over lunch or dinner.

An invitation to a Russian home is a great honor. Entertaining in the home is usually done in the kitchen. At home, the Russians are a very sharing and caring people. They enjoy making their guests feel welcome, and it is not unusual to have family and friends drop by unannounced.

When going to a Russian home for dinner, it is customary to bring a gift.

Dinner is usually served around 6:00 p.m.

Be careful not to excessively compliment the host or hostess on something in his/her home, because they might insist on giving it to you.

Toasting is common and frequent during dinner. Russian women do not make toasts but foreign women may do so. Prepare a few toasts beforehand.

Vodka is commonly consumed with all courses during a meal. Do not try to out-drink your Russian counterpart. An empty glass will be refilled. If you do not wish to continue drinking, leave some vodka in your glass. Once a bottle of vodka is opened it must be finished.

All entertaining is done sitting down over a hearty meal. The cocktail-party style of entertaining does not exist in Russia.

In restaurants it is common for there to be a limited selection. Not all items listed on the menu will be offered. If there are no tables available, strangers may share the same table.

Cabbage, beets and potatoes are staples in the Russian diet. Meat is usually difficult to obtain.

SOCIAL VALUES, CUSTOMS AND TIPS

Russians, along with Ukrainians and Byelorussians, are part of the eastern Slavic linguistic group.

Russians have an egalitarian work ethic making them wary of those who achieve great individual success.

Mir, a Russian word meaning village commune, world and peace, was the Russian peasantry's philosophy of life. Many in cities and villages still live by this philosophy. It is the communal, egalitarian idea that preceded the communist communal philosophy.

Russians are heavily steeped in their tradition and turn to new ways slowly.

Since Russian culture is rooted in the extremes of East and West, the Russian character may seem extremist and contradictory.

Throughout Russian history, there have been those who have looked to the West as the ideal, and there have been those who have wished to preserve Russia's unique character free of western influences.

Centuries of autocratic rule have bred a distrust of authority among Russians.

Corruption is prevalent in Russia's new market economy. Necessities are often only available on the black market.

Strong family ties and a network of close friends are of great importance in Russian society.

Family and children are good topics of conversation.

Smoking is very common in Russia, and there are no nonsmoking areas.

Russians remove their shoes upon entering their homes. Although it is not obligatory for a guest to do so, it would be considered a very polite gesture.

Vranyo, the custom of telling fibs, is very common in Russian society. Foreigners should not be alarmed or upset by it. They should be able to recognize and go along with it.

It is unacceptable to wear a coat in a public building, stand with your hands in your pockets or cross your feet to reveal the soles of your shoes.

The "thumbs up" sign is seen as something positive. Whistling on the street is considered rude.

SAUDI ARABIA

Population: 20,785,955 (July 1998 est.); Arab 90%, Afro-Asian 10%

Languages: Arabic

Religions: Muslim 100%

Currency: Saudi riyal

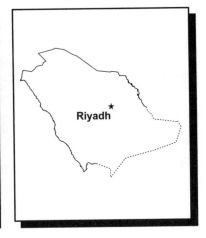

Riyadh ★

HISTORICAL OVERVIEW

- Records indicate that the Arabic peoples originated in the Arabian Peninsula. In the seventh century, Muhammad of the Quraysh family of Mecca began proclaiming the oneness of Allah. He traveled to Medina where he founded Islam, then returned to Mecca and made the two cities the center of Islam. The political center of Islam, however, moved to Damascus, Syria in 66 A.D. and never returned to the Arabian Peninsula again. Mecca and Medina nevertheless remain two of Islam's most holy cities.

- Islam spread throughout the Middle East, North Africa and parts of Asia, and the Arabs established a far-reaching empire, but the Arabian Peninsula remained on the fringes.

- During the Middle Ages, various local and foreign rulers battled over control of Arabia. In 1517, the peninsula fell under Ottoman rule.

- Opposition to Ottoman rule and a growing religious reform movement that sought to purge Islam of outside modern influences developed in the 18th century. Fighting intensified in the 19th century.

- In 1902, the House of Sa'ud, a leading family in the region, recaptured its ancestral home in Riyadh and captured most of central Arabia. Abdul Aziz Al-Sa'ud declared himself king.

- During World War I, King Abdul extended his rule over the western province along the Red Sea. In 1915, Saudi lands became a British protectorate and in 1927, the British granted the kingdom independence. King Ibn Sa'ud, the son of King Abdul, united the warring tribes of the region, and the country was named in his honor. In 1932, the country received the official name of the Kingdom of Saudi Arabia.

- In World War II, Saudi Arabia declared its neutrality, which garnered it U.S. and British subsidies and support. Following the war, Saudi Arabia also came into newfound wealth from the exploitation of its oil fields.

- After King Sa'ud's death, there was a struggle for power between his sons, Sa'ud and Faysal. In the end, Faysal, the more modern of the two, won out. He transformed the Saudi government into a modern bureaucracy.

- In the 1970s, Saudi Arabia was transformed into a modern state, when what Saudi Arabians call *Al Tafra* (The Eruption) occurred. Oil prices rose to unforeseen levels, and Saudi Arabia became a major economic force with the U.S. becoming a close ally. This boom was short-lived. Falling oil prices in the 1980s put the country into a recession from which it is still recovering.

- During the Cold War, Saudi Arabia served as an aid to stability in the region. Although it agreed with its Arab neighbors on the Palestinian cause, it acted as a counter-force to their alliances with the socialist bloc. Saudi Arabia forged strong ties with the U.S. instead.

- In 1982, Prince Fahd became king. He is still the monarch today, although his health began failing in the 1990s.

- Saudi Arabia backed the U.S. in the Gulf War against Iraq in 1991. In 1998, however, ties between Iraq and Saudi Arabia improved, and Saudi Arabia agreed to ease the effects of continued U.S. sanctions by exchanging food for oil.

- Partly in reaction to the Gulf War, there were movements within Saudi Arabia to liberalize economics as well as the political system. Nevertheless, Saudi society remains one of the most conservatively Muslim of all societies in the Arab world.

- Saudi Arabia's oil-based economy has the largest reserves in the world. Economic growth is relatively slow in the late 1990s because oil prices and exports are low. The country is looking to diversify its exports.

BUSINESS PRACTICES

Hours of Business

The average workweek is Saturday through Thursday, 9:00 a.m. to 1:00

p.m. and 4:30 p.m. to 8:00 p.m. During Ramadan the business hours change to 8:00 p.m. to 1:00 a.m.

Dress

Businesswomen should dress very conservatively, wearing long dresses with high necklines and long sleeves. Women should not wear pantsuits.

Men should also be very conservative in their dress. Suits with a buttoned-up collar and long sleeves are appropriate.

Saudi women dress very modestly and foreign women should respect this custom. Women should always completely cover their arms, legs and hair (by wearing, for example, a long skirt, down to the ankles, and a long-sleeved blouse) and dress so as not to attract attention to their bodies.

Appropriate dress for men is conservative, preferably lightweight, suits. In general, people tend to cover themselves, no matter how hot the weather. Shorts should not be worn in public.

Introductions

In Saudi Arabia, it is customary to shake hands lightly but sincerely with everyone in an office when meeting and when departing. The handshake is long and often continues through the entire greeting.

It is likely that you will shake hands frequently, possibly several times a day with the same person. For example, whenever someone enters the room, you should shake hands.

Men who know each other quite well often embrace each other and kiss each other once on each cheek when greeting.

It is extremely unlikely that foreign businessmen will come in contact with Saudi women.

When addressing people, use the titles "Mr.," "Mrs.," "Doctor" (for both M.D. and Ph.D.), *Sheik* (pronounced "shake") if you know that the person is a sheik, "Your Excellency" (for government ministers) or "Your Highness" (for members of the royal family), followed by the last name. Find out which ministers are royal. These ministers should be addressed as "Your Royal Highness" rather than as "Your Excellency."

At a party, expect to be introduced to each person individually. Even if you are not, you should act as if you have been and shake each person's hand.

It is polite to accompany a visitor to the street when the visitor leaves.

Your host may also hold your hand in his as you leave, as a sign of friendship.

Meetings

Bear in mind that European languages are not as widely used in Saudi Arabia as in other Middle Eastern countries. Bring business cards printed in English on one side and in Arabic on the other.

Be aware that people sometimes remove their shoes before entering an office. Check if there is a pile of shoes by the door and then proceed accordingly.

It is not unusual to arrive for a business meeting and find another meeting already underway. It is also common practice for other people to interrupt or to walk in on your meeting and for the meeting to be reconvened several times. The Saudis have a relatively relaxed attitude toward appointments. Be prepared for frequent diversions and waiting. It may, in fact, be impossible to conduct a private meeting.

A business meeting customarily begins with social conversation.

During the course of a meeting, it is customary to drink several cups of tea or coffee.

Business is best conducted face-to-face rather than by mail or telephone. Saudis like to develop long, close business relationships.

Bring many copies of all materials to meetings in the event that your proposal needs to be passed on to others in the decision-making process.

Negotiating

Negotiating and bargaining are traditional Saudi practices. It generally begins with inflated proposals and then proceeds through a series of concessions. The price should be discussed as a matter between friends, establishing trust as you proceed. Take your time in negotiating, and be prepared to discuss many unresolved issues simultaneously.

Business success in Saudi Arabia often depends on who your contact person is. Find someone who has many personal connections. International banks in Saudi Arabia and the U.S. International Trade Administration are useful sources of reliable contacts.

Do not force your Saudi contact into introducing you to the top decision makers right away. He/she will probably introduce you first to Saudis who are most apt to accept your proposal.

The business pace moves more slowly than in the West.

It is best to allow some time for your Saudi business counterparts to deliberate. Do not press for immediate answers or a direct "Yes" or "No."

A Saudi "Yes" does not usually signify definite acceptance of a contract or proposal.

To facilitate communication, eye contact and gestures of openness are important.

You may find it difficult to arrive at a final agreement and you should not confuse courtesy with a decision. Although it is wise to get a written contract, do not be surprised if the deal is renegotiated later. Nothing is final.

Entertaining

Be aware that Saudi Arabian men do not typically socialize with other men outside of the family. Women do not attend social gatherings. From working with western and westernized companies over the past 15 years, however, the Saudis have adapted to the practice of business entertaining.

A Saudi wife should never be included in an invitation to a business meal.

Business entertaining is generally conducted during lunch at a hotel or restaurant. Lunch is usually the largest meal of the day and takes place after the noon prayer.

Do not expect to eat at traditional Saudi restaurants. Restaurants in Saudi Arabia are predominantly Chinese, Korean, Indian, Pakistani or Ethiopian.

No alcohol is served in Saudi Arabia.

If you are invited to a restaurant, you should not argue when your host pays the bill, as your host will be insulted. Reciprocating invitations is not expected, but is appreciated.

Women should not go into restaurants unless accompanied by a couple or a male relative. Most hotels have two restaurants – one for men and one for families. Foreign women should always eat in a family restaurant.

Waiters should be tipped about 15 percent. Be sure to check the bill because a gratuity is sometimes included.

If invited to someone's home, it is suggested that you bring small gifts for the children, but do not bring a gift for the wife, whom you probably will not see. Pastries or imported candies in a box are appropriate gifts.

After meeting with your counterpart two or three times, you may want to present him with a modest gift. It should not advertise anything and should not be very valuable (e.g., desk accessories or small electrical gadgets).

If invited to a Saudi home, expect to be served tea in a sitting room and then be accompanied to another room for the main meal. In fact, if you are invited for dinner for a specific time, the actual meal may not be served until several hours later. It is common to play cards or listen to music before the meal.

At meals in homes, people traditionally sit in a circle on the floor in front of a large mat with food on it. There are no individual plates. When sitting on the floor, sit cross-legged or kneel on one knee. Make sure that your feet are not touching the food mat and that your soles are not facing anybody. Men and women always eat separately.

Before the meal, a basin of water may be passed around for each person to wash his hands.

Handle food with the right hand only. If you are dining at a restaurant, cutlery will probably be available. As a foreign guest, you may be offered a bowl to eat off of, along with a fork and a spoon.

At lunch or dinner, fruit, rice, salad, chicken or fish is usually served. When there are guests present, however, camel, sheep or goat is served because chicken or fish is not considered festive enough. Lamb and chicken are the most popular meats. Dairy products from sheep, goats and camels are also very common in Saudi cooking.

Water and fruit juices are usually served with the meal, while tea, coffee, goat, and camel's milk may be served afterward.

A formal meal may include *khouzi* (stuffed mutton garnished with almonds and eggs), fried shrimp, ragout of okra or *kabsah* (kebabs of lamb with vegetables and rice). Your host will be delighted to explain the ingredients as well as the preparation of the various dishes.

At the end of the meal, you should say *Bismillah* (which means "Thanks to God") or simply "Thank you."

SOCIAL VALUES, CUSTOMS AND TIPS

Saudis tend to stand very close and make direct eye contact when talking to others. This is a sign of courtesy and respect. They may also touch often, in order to heighten communication.

Saudi customs regarding women differ substantially from many other cultures. It is not acceptable to inquire about the adult women (more than 12 years old) in a Saudi man's family. It is acceptable, however, to inquire about a colleague's family in general or about his children. A businesswoman traveling in Saudi Arabia will have to accept the role assigned to women by a very strict Muslim society, including rules about visiting certain places and being in the company of men.

A Saudi appreciates admiring comments about his country, his city, his office or his taste in art. Avoid admiring an individual possession to excess, however, or he will feel obligated to give it to you.

Politics, religion and topics with sexual content or those that are detrimental to Islam or the royal family are best avoided in conversation. If you mention what is usually called the Persian Gulf, you should refer to it as the Arabian Gulf.

Avoid criticizing anyone (Saudi or non-Saudi) publicly. Saudis find this kind of behavior intolerable because it results in a loss of dignity.

Remember to always use the right hand for passing objects, for touching food or for touching other people.

Remove your shoes when entering a home.

In Saudi Arabia, "Yes" may be indicated by swiveling the head from side to side and "No" by tilting the head backwards and clicking the tongue.

You should be aware that Saudis pray five times a day: between 4:30 and 5:00 a.m., around noon, between 2:00 and 4:00 p.m., at sunset and one hour after sunset (although never later than 9:00 p.m.). This schedule varies according to the time of year and the part of the country. At prayer times, all work ceases. You may therefore want to make plans around this prayer schedule.

Be extremely careful when taking photographs. The Koran prohibits the depiction of the human form by graven images. Since Saudi Arabia is the strictest Muslim country, your film may be confiscated or you may be arrested for taking a photograph that includes human figures. You should definitely not photograph women or religious processions.

If your passport contains a "religion" category, it is best that it not read "none" when you are travelling to Saudi Arabia.

Never swear or use obscenities in Saudi Arabia.

Foreigners may not enter mosques in Saudi Arabia.

SENEGAL

Population: 9,723,149 (July 1998 est.); Wolof 36%, Fulani 17%, Serer 17%, Toucouleur 9%, Diola 9%, Mandingo 9%, European and Lebanese 1%, other 2%

Languages: French (official) Wolof, Pulaar, Diola, Mandingo

Religions: Muslim 92%, indigenous beliefs 6%, Christian (mostly Roman Catholic) 2%

Currency: Connunaute Financiere Africaine franc (CFA franc)

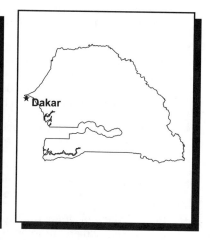

HISTORICAL OVERVIEW

- Great empires and independent kingdoms flourished in modern-day Senegal from 300 A.D. to the 19th century.

- Islamic traders from North Africa made invasions into Senegal in the tenth century. The Tukulor people converted to Islam. Nevertheless, the Tukulor were governed by a series of animist rulers until the 18th century. Today nearly all Senegalese are Muslim.

- Portuguese sailors first traded with the people in this area in the mid-1400s. They were followed by the Dutch and then the French, who set up a trading post in 1638, set up Saint-Louis in 1659 and occupied Gorée Island. Slaves, gum arabic, ivory and gold were the first exports.

- From 1693 to 1841 France and England were both present along the Senegalese coast and vying for its control.

- The French finally gained full control by 1814. They then moved inland, pushed back the Tukulor and instituted French colonial political, economic and educational systems. In 1895, Senegal became part of French West Africa and, in 1902, the Senegalese city of Dakar became the capital of French West Africa. During this period of French rule, peanuts became a major export crop.

- After World War II the movement for independence grew. In 1958, Senegal was made an autonomous republic within the French Community. In 1959, it was made a member of the Mali Federation. It gained full independence in 1960.

- Several famines in the 1970s put a lot of pressure on the economic and political systems. When Senegal entered Gambia in 1981 to help put down a coup, it created a loose federation with Gambia, known as Senegambia. The two nations retained full sovereignty but shared military and economic systems. This alliance was dissolved in 1989.

- Senegal's constitution was amended in 1981 to eliminate restrictions on various political parties, allowing for a more democratic political process than previously. Habib Thiam was elected prime minister in 1991 and reelected in 1993. Abdou Diouf was first elected president in 1981 and has been reelected twice.

- In 1989, Senegal barely avoided war with Mauritania, when the latter's Islamic government expelled over 1,000 people southward into Senegal.

- For the past three decades Senegal's economy has been based on the harvest of peanuts, but the economy has begun to diversify.

- In 1997, the Movement of Democratic Forces of Casamance (MFDC) caused an outbreak of violence in the southern Senegalese province of Casamance. For the past 15 years, this group has been fighting for Casamance's independence. By 1998, the MFDC leader was calling for peace.

- In 1998, Senegal agreed to participate in an African intervention force dedicated to keeping peace throughout Africa. The effort was supported by the UN, Organization for African Unity (OAU), the U.S., France and Britain.

- The per capita income of Senegal remains one of the highest in West Africa.

BUSINESS PRACTICES

Hours of Business

Business hours are from 9:00 a.m. to 1:00 p.m. and from 4:00 to 7:00 p.m., Monday through Saturday. Offices close at midday because of the heat.

Dress

Conservative and elegant dress is appropriate for both women and men, especially when doing business in Dakar. Women should dress modestly, avoiding low necklines and short skirts.

Introductions

Senegalese greetings vary depending on circumstances and how well people are acquainted. Shaking hands and kissing alternate cheeks three times is common.

Traditionally, men would not shake hands with women, but this custom is changing. Whatever greeting is used when meeting is also used when parting.

Meetings

Muslims do not schedule business meetings during prayer times, which take place five times each day. If a meeting runs into prayer time, it might be stopped for a prayer break depending on the region (whether it is traditional or westernized).

Meetings are formal. People do not, for example, roll up their sleeves or remove their jackets during them.

Business is often conducted in either English or French.

Make appointments one week prior to visiting the country. It is best to schedule meetings in the morning.

Avoid making business trips to Senegal during the Muslim fasting month of Ramadan.

Prior to business discussions, it is customary to engage in small talk to establish a personal rapport.

Negotiating

Establishing personal relationships with business colleagues is an important component of Senegalese business transactions.

Maintain your composure at all times, regardless of any feelings of frustration you may have. Displays of irritation or anger are not appropriate.

There are women who hold important positions in Senegal. Sending a woman negotiator should not pose any difficulties. Women, however, should always be very professional and avoid aggressive behavior.

Entertaining

Breakfast is eaten between 6:00 and 9:00 a.m., lunch from noon to 1:30 p.m. and dinner from 8:00 to 9:30 p.m. In traditional homes, the sexes and different age groups eat separately.

The main dish is traditionally served in large bowls that are either placed on mats on the floor or on coffee tables. Several people eat from the same bowl using their fingers or a spoon. Clean hands, eating only from the portion of the communal dish directly in front of a person and avoiding eye contact with people who are still eating are important.

Only the right hand is used when eating. The left can be used only when eating foods that are difficult to handle, such as fruit or meat with bones.

When hosting western visitors, Senegalese will sit at tables, eat from individual plates and use utensils.

Preparing and presenting food are skills that all Senegalese women learn at an early age. Each ethnic group prepares its own traditional dishes and some urban women cook French cuisine as well.

Meals usually consist of one main dish of rice, millet or corn covered by a sauce of vegetables, meat (traditional Muslims do not eat pork), poultry, fish, beans or milk and sugar. One popular dish is *yassa* (rice and chicken covered with a sauce of onions and spices). Another is *thiebou dien*, a meal of fish and rice that is popular for lunch.

SOCIAL VALUES, CUSTOMS AND TIPS

In general, the family is a source of strength and pride for a Senegalese person. In most rural and traditional urban areas, extended families live together in family compounds.

Senegalese enjoy visiting with one another at home. Because most people do not own telephones, dropping by uninvited is acceptable.

Senegalese are hospitable and can make a guest feel comfortable without expecting anything in return.

Foreign visitors should remember not to drink water unless it is bottled. To decline a drink, it is polite to say that one has just finished drinking.

Avoid cigarette smoking in traditional Muslim homes. It is considered especially rude for women to smoke.

Asking personal questions is regarded as impolite. It is considered bad luck to ask specific questions about children, such as when a baby is due, how many children one has or what their ages are.

Few women wear pants or shorts.

In general, Senegalese receive and give objects with their right hand or with both hands.

Scratching in public is impolite, as are public displays of affection.

Eye contact is avoided with a person who is considered to be a superior (in age or status) or with someone of the opposite sex.

SINGAPORE

Population: 3,490,356 (July 1998 est.); Chinese 76.4%, Malay 14.9%, Indian 6.4%, other 2.3%

Languages: Chinese (official), Malay (official and national), Tamil (official), English (official)

Religions: Buddhist, Muslim, Christian, Hindu, Sikh, Taoist, Confucianist

Currency: Singapore dollar

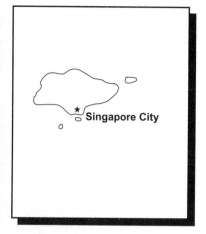

Singapore City

HISTORICAL OVERVIEW

- Singapore is an island nation located off the tip of the Malaysian peninsula. Today it is a city-state without any truly rural areas. Three major cultures (Chinese, Malay and Indian) are represented in Singapore.

- Originally known as Tumasik, it was an outpost of the Sumatran Empire and populated by fishermen and pirates. In the 14th century it passed into Javanese and then Siamese control.

- In the 16th century, the island was controlled by the Portuguese, followed by the Dutch in the 17th century.

- Singapore's strategic location and natural deepwater ports attracted the British in the early 19th century. In 1819, Sir Stamford Raffles established a British trading post on the island and Britain acquired it as a possession in 1824. Britain used Singapore as a center for colonial activities. After the Suez Canal was opened in 1869 and steamships became popular, Singapore experienced an economic boom.

- Britain established a large navy base on Singapore after World War II, but in 1942 the island fell to Japan, which occupied it until 1945. Internal self-rule was granted to Singapore in 1959. In 1963 it became part of Malaysia, but this caused domestic political problems and the island became independent in 1965.

- Lee Kuan Yew became the first prime minister and headed Singapore for 31 years during which time the country became very prosperous. In 1967, it was one of the founding members of the Association of Southeast Asian Nations (ASEAN). Lee resigned in 1990 in favor of a younger man, Goh Chok Tong, who continued Lee's policies.

- In 1993, Singapore reinstated and enhanced the office of the president, to which Ong Teng Cheong was elected later that year. He and Prime Minister Goh have maintained a hard line against anyone critical of Singapore or its government. They believe that authoritarian means are justifiable when the ends are economic prosperity and a safe, clean environment.

- In 1994, Singapore's authoritarian measures caught international attention when several individuals, some of whom were Singaporeans and some of whom were foreign nationalists, received punishments generally considered to be exceedingly severe for their offense. Among them were a Dutch engineer who was hanged for trafficking in heroin and a U.S. teenager who was sentenced to caning and imprisonment for vandalizing cars.

- Singapore's standard of living is very high. The smog and air pollution that have plagued Singapore for several decades are on the decline. The People's Action Party has dominated the country's politics since independence. Although it faces increasingly stronger opposition, it still managed to win the 1997 elections.

BUSINESS PRACTICES

Singapore is a multicultural (approximately 70% Chinese, 15% Malay and 15% Indian) and cosmopolitan society. As a result, social customs and etiquette vary according to the specific situation and the people with whom you are dealing. The business community in Singapore is primarily Chinese. Most of the urban Chinese are Buddhist or Christian. People of Malay heritage are Muslims.

Although western business practices have been adopted, Confucianism still dominates management and business practices in Singapore. Businesses are run like families, and harmony and paternalism are the most important concepts used in running them. Human relations are very important and business is conducted on the basis of trust. The individual defers to the group and to authority.

Hours of Business

Most businesses are open from 8:30 a.m. to 4:30 p.m., Monday through Friday and sometimes from 8:30 a.m. to 12:30 p.m. on Saturday. If a business is open on Sunday, it is required by law to be closed on another day.

Dress

About one-third of the Singaporean labor force is female. Generally, women are treated as equals in business. Because of local religious beliefs, however, foreign businesswomen must be very careful not to offend others by their manner of dress. It is best to dress modestly, conservatively and fashionably. Do not wear short skirts or sleeveless dresses or blouses.

Men should wear a white or light-colored shirt with a tie and pants.

For your general comfort, it is advisable to wear clothes made from natural fabrics such as cotton, linen or silk in the heat and humidity of Singapore. Synthetic fabrics tend to be uncomfortable.

Introductions

In Singapore, greetings vary depending on the age and nationality of the people involved. Most commonly, however, people shake hands when meeting. Men shake hands with both men and women. While women also shake hands, close women friends hold both hands in shaking.

Especially when greeting older or Chinese people, a slight bow may be added to the handshake. In fact, bowing slightly when you enter or leave a room or pass a group shows courtesy.

When being introduced, use the titles "Mr." or "Mrs." ("Ms." is not common) followed by the family name for Chinese and followed by the given name for Indians or Malays. Chinese put their last name first, middle name next and given name last. For example, a Chinese man named Lee Kuan Hock is "Mr. Lee." Malay names are complex. They often attach their father's name after their own. For example, a Malaysian man named Hassan Ahmed is "Mr. Hassan." Most Indians do not have surnames but may use the initial of their father's name in front of their given names.

While various languages are used when greeting, English is acceptable and common.

Business and government officials exchange business cards when greeting each other. The cards should be presented respectfully using both hands.

It is prudent to arrange for a letter of introduction before you arrive. You can contact the trade office in your country for help in finding contacts.

Meetings

Punctuality is valued in Singapore. Visitors are expected to be punctual for business meetings and business entertainment. It is a good idea to make appointments ahead of time.

It is advisable to send your proposal along before making your business trip. In this way, your colleague will be very familiar with it when you meet and will want to discuss it in great detail.

When entering the conference room your delegation should be grouped by seniority with the most highly ranked officials leading the group.

Expect meetings to take place over the course of several months to solidify a deal.

Negotiating

For best results, have your company's delegation headed by someone around the age of 50. Singaporean businesspeople value older, experienced individuals.

Singaporeans value practicality. Negotiations are usually direct and quick. At the same time, Singaporeans may consider aggressive negotiating tactics to be excessively pushy.

Gift-giving among business relations is fairly uncommon in Singapore. A gift could be offensive, as it could be taken as an indication of bribery (especially by government officials). Therefore, remain cautious when giving gifts and only give gifts to individuals you know quite well. Avoid expensive gifts.

Be sure to have all stages of the negotiating process and agreements put in writing. Your Singaporean counterpart will usually have a secretary present during all meetings. Written agreements are generally considered much more binding than verbal ones.

Present a binding contract that details how you intend to maintain contact and form a harmonious business relationship with your representatives in Singapore.

Business is quite fast paced, faster than in other Southeast Asian countries but not as fast as in the United States.

Frequently remind your counterpart of your company's ability to deliver.

Entertaining

Business entertaining usually takes place in a restaurant for lunch or dinner. Business lunches can be long and informal and business can be discussed during the meal. You should wait until you have met someone several times to invite that person to a meal. Be aware that public officials are not allowed to accept invitations.

If you are entertained in someone's home, expect to remove your shoes before entering the house.

When invited to someone's home for a meal, it is appropriate to bring chocolates, flowers or pastries. Be aware that Singaporeans will not open gifts in the presence of the giver. Do not be offended if the gift is not opened in front of you. T-shirts from your home country make good gifts. Gifts should always be given in even pairs, which is a sign of happiness and good luck.

In restaurants, a service charge is usually included in the bill. Even if a service charge is not included, tips are not necessary and may even be discouraged.

Since Singapore has become quite westernized, eating customs and dining etiquette vary according to the type of food being eaten and the culture of the people eating it.

In Singapore, a wide variety of foods are available, including spicy Malaysian foods, Indian curries, Chinese dishes and a number of European foods. Rice and seafood are very popular. Pineapple, papayas, bananas and mangoes are commonly served.

In Singapore, it is customary for the host to be modest and humble. Compliments are appreciated, even though they will be denied for the sake of modesty. Your host will probably apologize for the inferior quality of the food. You should simply reply by saying that the food is good.

While chopsticks are the most popular eating utensil in Singapore, western-style utensils are usually available.

It is considered impolite to refuse food that is offered to you or to not finish the food on your plate. At the same time, you will usually be served very generously. It is polite to finish at least one serving of each food. Then, to indicate that you are finished, place your chopsticks across your dish. Leaving food in your dish – even a small amount – politely indicates that your host was so generous that you could not possibly finish.

The second-to-last dish at a Chinese meal is usually plain, boiled rice. Follow the example of the host. He or she may decline or eat only a little bit. This shows that you have had plenty to eat and are no longer hungry.

Among the Chinese, the host and hostess sit opposite one another. Most guests sit facing the front entrance, with guests of honor to the left of the host and hostess.

Before the meal, the host will invite the guests to drink wine. It is polite to take a sip or at least pretend to, even if you do not wish to drink. Raise your glass with both hands, holding it in your right hand and keeping your left hand under the glass.

Between courses, chopsticks should be laid on the chopstick rest, the soy sauce dish or the bone plate. It is improper to rest them on your dinner plate or on the rice bowl. It is an especially bad omen to place your chopsticks upright in your rice bowl.

Soup should be eaten using the porcelain spoon for the liquid and the chopsticks for the chunks of food. Tilt the soup bowl toward you while eating. Feel free to slurp your soup if you like.

Remove bones from your mouth with the chopsticks, not with your fingers. If there is a bone plate, use it. If one has not been provided, put the bones on your own plate.

Among Indians, it is considered impolite not to wash your hands before eating.

Indians do not always use cutlery. If none has been provided, use your right hand to eat. Never touch food with your left hand.

Although Indian women do not usually drink alcoholic beverages, western women should feel free to accept drinks if they are offered.

Among the Malays, it is customary to entertain at home rather than in restaurants.

The guest of honor is usually seated at the head of the table or to the right of the host.

Hands are washed before the meal at the table. Your host will offer you a small bowl and a towel. It is best to eat and pass food with your right hand only.

Your Malaysian host will be insulted if you refuse any food or drink, whether it is offered during a meal or as a snack. Therefore, take at least a little of what is offered even if only for a taste.

SOCIAL VALUES, CUSTOMS AND TIPS

While it is common for people in Singapore to ask personal questions, it is best if a visitor refrains from asking about a person's family or personal life.

Some good topics of conversation include sports and travel. Water sports, soccer, badminton, tennis, golf and basketball are popular. Martial arts (such as *tae kwon do*) and *taijiquan* (shadowboxing) and the French game of *petanque* are also popular.

Additional conversational topics include your host's success in business and social activities, Singapore's future plans and its economic advances. Movies and books are also good subjects of conversation.

It is best to refrain from discussing religion, politics or the government, even if coaxed. You should also avoid referring to the small size of the country or making comparisons between western standards and those of Singapore. Avoid making jokes until you know someone quite well.

The English language is widely spoken and studied throughout Singapore.

Older people as well as those with seniority are treated with respect in Singapore. Show deference to elders and to those senior in rank in the Asian group by allowing them to go through doors and be seated first.

Singaporean society is very disciplined. Singaporeans avoid showing emotions in public or expressing individualism. The individual defers to authority and to the collective good. Importance is placed on status, which may be indicated by fashionable clothing and lavish entertainment.

Remove your shoes when visiting religious buildings.

It is impolite to cross your legs in front of elders or to put your feet on a chair. Sit in such a way that your legs do not show prominently and be especially careful that the soles of your feet/shoes are not showing. If you do cross your legs, make sure that one knee rests over the other (rather than only placing the ankle of one leg over the knee of the other).

It is considered extremely impolite to touch someone's head.

Finger gestures (e.g., pointing or making the "okay" sign) are considered extremely rude. Beckoning with one finger is considered to be an offensive gesture. When gesturing toward a person, use your whole right hand with the palm facing upward. To summon a person, keep the palm of your hand turned down and wave your hand downward.

The gesture of hitting the fist into a cupped hand is also considered impolite.

Singaporeans tend to laugh when embarrassed or when in a highly emotional situation. Be careful not to misinterpret this behavior.

Be aware that Singapore has very strictly enforced laws regarding minor offenses (littering, jaywalking, etc.) and antisocial behavior (wearing hair too long, chewing gum, etc.)

SLOVAKIA

Population: 5,392,982 (July 1998 est.); Slovak 85.7%, Hungarian 10.7%, Gypsy 1.5%, Czech 1%, Ruthenian 0.3%, Ukrainian 0.3%, German 0.1%, Polish 0.1%, other 0.3%

Languages: Slovak (official), Hungarian

Religions: Roman Catholic 60.3%, atheist 9.7%, Protestant 8.4%, Orthodox 4.1%, other 17.5%

Currency: Slovak koruna

HISTORICAL OVERVIEW

- The first known inhabitants of present-day Slovakia were Illyrian, Celtic and Germanic tribes. By the seventh century A.D., a Slavic tribe, called the Slovaks, had settled in the area.

- A tribe of Avars, meanwhile, had settled in Moravia, the region northwest of Slovakia, and the Slovaks soon came under Avar rule. In the ninth century, Moravia was united with its northern neighbor, Bohemia, to form Great Moravia, and Slovakia, too, was incorporated into the union.

- After 885, the Moravian Empire began to crumble, in part due to invasions by the Hungarian Magyars, and by the 11th century, Slovakia had been fully absorbed into the Kingdom of Hungary.

- Czech religious reformers, known as Hussites, arrived in Slovakia in the 15th century, and many Slovaks became Lutheran or Calvinist over the following century.

- The Austrian Hapsburgs came to the Hungarian throne in 1526, thus also assuming the rule of Slovakia. Slovakia remained a part of the Austo-Hungarian Empire until World War I. Under the Hapsburgs, Roman Catholicism was restored.

- A Slovak nationalist movement briefly took hold among a small group of intellectuals at the end of the 18th century, but it was put down after 1867 when Hungary received direct control of Slovakia once again and pursued a policy of Magyarization.

- When the Austro-Hungarian Empire collapsed after being

defeated in World War I, Czech (Bohemia and Moravia) and Slovak lands were united to form a new Czecho-Slovak state. (The hyphen in the name was dropped in 1923.) Democracy and the economy of the new state flourished.

- In 1938, the Germans marched into Czechoslovakia. Once they had taken Prague in 1939, they set up Slovakia as a Nazi puppet state with nominal independence.

- Slovakia reunited with the Czech lands at the end of World War II, when Czechoslovakia was still under Allied control. The country held elections in 1946 under Soviet auspices, and by 1948, the Communists had seized total control.

- Slovak government officials, who had collaborated with the Nazis, were punished under the Czech-dominated government. Many were sent to work camps. In the 1950s, Slovak Communists were denounced as Titoists and purged from the Communist Party, and in 1962, a newly ratified constitution took away all governmental power from the Slovaks. After an attempt by Czech Communists to liberalize and reform, the government was crushed by the Soviets. In 1968, the Soviets granted Slovaks more power once again.

- In 1989, peaceful demonstrations, known as the "Velvet Revolution," led to the formation of the non-communist state of the Czech and Slovak Federal Republic. Reform-minded Alexander Dubcek, a Slovak, was elected leader of parliament and Vaclav Havel, a Czech dissident playwright, became president in 1990. In that year, the Slovak National Party was created to lobby for an independent Slovakia.

- When full multiparty elections were held in 1992, Vladimir Meciar became prime minister of the Slovak national government. Disagreements between the Slovak and Czech leaders led the two national governments to agree to split the country into two sovereign states in 1993. The breakup was peaceful, and ties between the two nations remain strong.

- Meciar sped up industrial privatization, but he also reduced the language rights of Slovakia's Hungarian minority and allowed Communist leaders to remain in high offices. The economy took a downturn, and in March 1994, Josef Moravcik replaced Meciar as president. The following September, however, Meciar's party regained a majority in parliament.

- In 1997, Slovakia was denied membership in the European Union and NATO, but it has increased its economic ties to the East on the platform of Pan-Slavism.

- In September 1998, Mikulas Dzurinda was elected the new prime minister of Slovakia on a platform of improving diplomatic relations with the Czech Republic and Western Europe.

BUSINESS PRACTICES

Hours of Business

Business hours are usually from 8:00 a.m. until between 3:00 and 5:00 p.m. during the week.

Dress

Business dress is conservative. Businessmen wear dark suits, ties and white shirts, and businesswomen wear dark suits with white blouses or dresses. Follow the lead of your colleagues with regard to removing ties or jackets.

Introductions

Upon introduction, people shake hands firmly and say their last names, followed by a verbal greeting, such as *Tesi mne* (Pleased to meet you) or *Dobry den* (Good day). Women and older people extend their hands first when greeting others.

It is customary to shake hands with everyone present upon both arrival and departure at social and business occasions.

To show respect, it is important to address men and women by their professional titles (Engineer, Doctor, Professor), followed by the last name. If the people you are meeting are not professionals, you may use the titles *Pán* (pronounced "Pahn") which means "Mr.," *Pani* (pronounced "PAH-nee"), which means "Mrs." or *Slecna* (pronounced "SLEH-chnah") which means "Miss."

It is common to precede a professional title with *Pán* or *Pani* when greeting someone. For example, you can say, *Dobry den, Pani Doktorko Cekanova* (Good day, Ms. Dr. Cekan).

Normally, first names are only used among relatives, good friends and young people, who also sometimes hug each other in greeting.

To say good-bye, the formal *Na shledanou* or the informal *Cau* (pronounced "Ciao") are used. *Ahoj* can be used as an informal "Hi" and "Bye."

Meetings

You should avoid planning business trips for July or August, since most people take vacations during the summer months.

Make appointments well in advance (at least ten days), and expect for the meeting to be postponed by your Slovak counterparts.

Negotiating

Eye contact is very important during conversations. Gesturing is also used often for emphasis.

It may take some time for first introductions. If you are sending a letter from abroad, you should send it at least a month in advance. When writing a letter to a Slovak company, you should address the letter to the firm, not to an individual.

Slovaks typically converse about other matters before conducting business. Drinks and coffee are often offered at business meetings. It is polite to accept these refreshments. If a toast is made, it is polite to return it.

It is considered inappropriate to use humor during actual negotiations.

It will take a bit longer to establish a personal relationship with a Slovak business associate than it might in other Slavic countries.

Attempting to negotiate with your Slovak counterparts using the tactic of the "hard sell" will be unsuccessful. Slovaks are reluctant to be pressed into making a decision.

Have business letters sent in English as well as in Slovak to make an extremely good impression.

Keep in mind that English is not widely spoken. Therefore, an interpreter may be needed.

Bring plenty of business cards, as they are used abundantly. It is appreciated if your card is printed in both English and Slovak. Slovaks value education highly. You should be sure to include on your card any degree above a bachelor's level.

Slovaks tend to give small gifts to their foreign associates during negotiations. This is done in the spirit of friendship and should not be taken as a bribe. Acceptable business gifts for your Slovak counterparts include good-quality pens, pocket calculators, cigarette lighters or imported wine or liquor.

Entertaining

Entertaining rarely takes place in the home, since Slovaks consider the home to be strictly private. Normally, people socialize in pubs, coffeehouses and wine bars, and dinners take place in restaurants. If you are invited to a home, even for a drink or coffee, you should consider this an honor.

Do not expect to have much contact with your business associates outside of the office. While Slovaks are very hospitable, it may take a long time to establish a close business relationship. Historically, business meetings have been confined to offices.

Meal reservations should be made in advance since there are only a few good restaurants available for business entertaining.

Business is generally discussed before and after, but not during, a meal.

It is appropriate, but not necessary, to include spouses in invitations.

If you are invited to a home, it is polite to bring flowers. Bring an odd number of flowers (but not 13) to the host, since an even number of flowers is associated with a funeral. Avoid chrysanthemums or calla lilies (which are associated with funerals) and red roses (which are associated with romance). Unwrap the flowers before giving them. Liquor (wine, whiskey or cognac), chocolates or gifts for the children are also appreciated.

At formal parties, your host should introduce you to the other guests. At informal parties, however, it is acceptable to introduce yourself if your host has not introduced you.

Wait until everyone has been served a drink before picking up your glass. Toasting is common both at formal and informal events. As a guest, you should feel free to offer a toast in honor of the celebration.

When dining in a home or a restaurant, men should wear casual slacks, a shirt and a sweater (optional), while women should wear a dress or a skirt and a blouse. In more formal restaurants, men should wear suits and ties.

The tip is usually not included in the bill. The custom is to round the bill up to the nearest whole number or leave a five to ten percent tip at the table.

Slovaks generally eat three meals a day as well as a mid-morning snack. The mid-morning snack, eaten at about 10:00 a.m., usually consists of sandwiches or hot sausages and yogurt. For most people, lunch is the main meal and breakfast and dinner are lighter.

Supper is usually served between 5:30 and 6:30 p.m. If lunch was a full meal, supper will be lighter, often just cheese or meat sandwiches and milk. The meal will be heavier at a dinner party. Dinner usually begins with soup followed by a main course such as roast pork, sauerkraut and dumplings. Turkish coffee generally follows the meal.

Slovaks usually prefer a hot meal to a cold one, even in hot weather.

Plates are usually prepared in the kitchen and are carried to the table. At a dinner, guests are usually served first, although the oldest woman at the table is sometimes served first.

People eat in the continental style, with the fork in the left hand and the knife in the right. You should not put your knife and fork down between bites.

Hands, but not elbows, should be kept above the table during meals (even once the meal has been finished and people are talking).

Conversation is not abundant during meals and is usually only encouraged if guests are present or if the head of the household speaks first. After the meal, people will stay at the table and talk.

Normally, second or third servings are offered. It is not impolite to decline the food graciously. When a second serving is offered, however, it is polite to accept a little food after initially refusing.

When being entertained in a Slovak home, there will be much celebrating and drinking. If you do not wish to be given more food and/or drink, leave something in your glass and/or on your plate to indicate that you have had enough.

To indicate that you have finished, you should place your utensils together at one side of the plate. If you want to signal that you are just taking a break, you should cross your utensils on the plate.

SOCIAL VALUES, CUSTOMS AND TIPS

Slovak is a Slavic language, related to Polish, Croatian and Russian and extremely closely related to Czech. It uses a Latin alphabet. Slovaks also often speak German, Russian or English, depending on their generation. German is the most commonly spoken foreign language.

Due to the difficult transition period to Slovak statehood, some people are extremely sensitive about topics related to independence. They are particularly interested in the way that foreigners view them and are eager to project a positive image.

Sports, especially soccer, tennis and ice hockey, make good conversation topics. The countryside and the area you are staying in are also good topics to discuss since Slovaks have a love for nature and enjoy a number of outdoor activities. Music and other arts also make good topics of conversation. Traditional arts, such as the theater, are close to the hearts of many Slovaks.

If your host brings up political matters, feel free to participate, but avoid criticizing the government.

Speaking loudly is considered impolite.

Slovak folk culture is very colorful and has roots in Hungarian folk culture.

Family and friends are very important to Slovaks.

Women in Slovakia are still expected to fill the traditional roles of keeping a home and working a nonprofessional job, even though many have university degrees.

Janosik, a Slovak Robin Hood, is a frequently encountered symbol of Slovak history.

Avoid taking pictures in museums or galleries and photographing policemen, military installations, airports and railroad stations.

It is acceptable to beckon others and point using the index finger. To gain someone's attention, raise your hand, palm facing out, with only the index finger extended. You should avoid waving.

When sitting, you should cross one knee over the other, rather than resting your ankle on the other knee. You should not prop your feet up on furniture.

It is impolite to converse with your hands in your pockets or while chewing gum.

To wish someone good luck, Slovaks cross their thumbs (they fold the thumb and close the fingers on it).

SOUTH AFRICA

Population: 42,834,520 (July 1998 est.); black 75.2%, white 13.6%, Colored 8.6%, Indian 2.6%

Languages: 11 official languages: Afrikaans, English, Ndebele, Pedi, Sotho, Swazi, Tsonga, Tswana, Venda, Xhosa, Zulu

Religions: Christian 68%, Muslim 2%, Hindu 1.5%, traditional and animistic 28.5%

Currency: rand

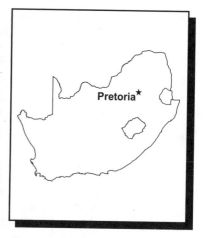

HISTORICAL OVERVIEW

- The earliest known African tribes in South Africa were the San and Khoikhoin.

- In 1652, the Dutch established a colony at the Cape of Good Hope. They became known as Boers and later as Afrikaners on account of their Afrikaans language. French Huguenot refugees joined the Dutch colony in 1688, and Germans arrived later.

- Britain seized control of the Cape Colony in 1806. Many Boers, unhappy with British rule, migrated to the interior of the country starting in the 1830s. This migration, known as the Great Trek, led to war with indigenous tribes as they themselves were pushed further inland. The Boers crushed the Ndebele in 1837 and defeated the Zulu tribe in a series of battles, including the 1838 Battle of Blood River.

- The discovery of gold and diamonds brought great prosperity to the region, especially to the Boer lands. Britain attempted to include parts of Boer territory in a South African confederation in the late 19th century. Tensions between these two groups grew and culminated in the Boer War (1899-1902), in which the Boers were defeated.

- In 1910, Britain combined the two British colonies, Cape and Natal, with the Boer republics of the Orange Free State and Transvaal to create the Union of South Africa. Once united, South African politics centered on keeping power in the hands of the white colonial minority. Blacks soon found themselves prohibited from owning land outside of designated homelands (which comprised no more than ten percent of the land), confined to certain living quarters and greatly restricted in all freedoms.

- A number of organizations, including the African National Congress (ANC), immediately appeared, each attempting to unite black Africans against white rule. The Coloreds, those of mixed black and Afrikaner ancestry, also began to mobilize.

- Tension between Afrikaners and the British population persisted. The Afrikaner population mainly consisted of rural poor who were at a disadvantage as the economy turned to urban industry.

- Beginning in the 1930s the white regime in South Africa instituted a severe system of racial segregation. The white minority retained almost all political and financial power, while Africans, and to a lesser extent Indians and Coloreds, were left with no political or economic power. When the National Party was elected to power in 1948 these discriminatory policies were systematized and given the official name of apartheid.

- South Africa became a republic in 1961.

- The ANC galvanized Africans as well as Indians and Coloreds to participate in passive resistance campaigns in the 1950s and 1960s. When these were met with excessive force on the part of the government, the ANC and other groups turned to violence. Many ANC leaders, including Nelson Mandela, were jailed.

- In the 1970s, the UN officially condemned South Africa and imposed economic embargoes.

- By 1978 it was clear that apartheid was a disastrous means of keeping order in the country. The new president, Pieter W. Botha, made gestures toward reform, but the power relations did not change, and Africans remained poor and disenfranchised.

- During the 1980s, international pressure mounted as foreign countries began imposing trade embargoes. Resistance within the country escalated. Botha responded by declaring a state of emergency and brutally cracking down on all protestors.

- In 1989, F.W. de Klerk replaced Botha as president and began instituting a series of reforms. He freed political prisoners, desegregated public facilities, lifted the state of emergency and granted the ANC legal status. De Klerk also began talks with Mandela and other black leaders.

- These talks, however, were accompanied by growing violence, as the ever more desperate situation in the black community gave rise to militant movements, which did not wish to negotiate with de Klerk. White terrorists also tried to sabotage the talks.

- For the first time, in 1994, general elections were held on the basis of universal suffrage. The task of improving the living standards of blacks and eliminating violence and corruption has proven difficult and slow. Foreign investors have been very wary of investing in the new South Africa.

- In 1996, a new constitution was ratified.

- South Africa's Truth and Reconciliation Commission, led by Desmond Tutu, was formed in order to investigate the political injustices that had taken place under apartheid. In May 1997, Tutu issued a pardon for all those who had committed crimes and were willing to admit to them. Former government employees testified to murderous acts that they had committed under direct orders from their superiors.

BUSINESS PRACTICES

Hours of Business

Business and government offices are usually open from 8:30 a.m. to 5:00 p.m.

Dress

Conservative business clothes, including vested suits for men, are appropriate.

South African men may wear shorts with knee socks instead of pants. Women generally wear comfortable dresses or pants. Indian women often wear the traditional sari. Some rural blacks wear traditional clothing for special occasions as well as for everyday wear.

Introductions

Shake hands at the beginning and at the end of business encounters. Shaking hands is more common among whites but is also a greeting used by other ethnic and tribal groups.

Good friends in some black tribal groups greet each other with an intricate triple handshake.

Because of the ethnic and cultural diversity in South Africa, many different greetings are used. They range from English greetings, such as "Hello" and "Good morning," to Afrikaans (a derivation of Dutch) phrases like *Goeie more* (Good morning), in addition to the Zulu *Sawubona* (Hello). The Xhosa *Molo* and the Sotho or Tswana *Dumela* are similar to "Good morning" and "Hello."

Address people as "Mr.," "Mrs." or "Miss" until you are invited to use first names. Titles are valued.

Meetings

Appointments are required for business and government meetings.

Punctuality is very important.

Negotiating

Status and education are highly valued. Within companies, merit is usually more important than one's personal connections.

Be prepared for bureaucratic delays and red tape.

South Africans of both British and Dutch descent tend to be rather reserved and dislike loud and boisterous behavior.

Many foreign firms print all promotional literature in both Afrikaans and English. English, however, is the predominant language used in business transactions.

The nature and size of the business being conducted will dictate whether junior, middle or senior management will attend initial meetings. Women have made significant inroads into the business community and are achieving top-level positions with firms, as are the nation's black citizens.

Many South Africans do business in a "take it or leave it" manner. Whether they are the buyer or seller, they want you to believe that they are indispensable.

Before beginning negotiations, present an outline of how both sides will benefit from the final deal.

Do not exert pressure by using artificial deadlines. This may result in deliberate delays.

Social relations and interactions are considered a vital element in business negotiations. Take the time to form amicable relations with your counterparts. Socializing before and after meetings is an important part of business interactions.

It is not advisable to bring lawyers to your negotiations. While contracts in South Africa may not be very detailed, South Africans rely on the personal trust established during negotiations to insure that all details agreed upon are adhered to.

Entertaining

Entertaining is generally done in the home and in private clubs. South Africans are very hospitable to guests and they enjoy conversing and socializing. Guests are usually served refreshments.

In an Indian home, it is not polite to refuse refreshments, and it is appropriate to accept second helpings when eating a meal.

Business dinners are more common than business lunches. Barbecues, known as *braaivleis* or *brais*, are also common.

Dinner may be served as early as 5:00 p.m. It is customary to remain for several hours after the meal.

Dinner guests are not expected to bring a gift, but guests often bring something to drink, such as juice or wine.

Etiquette in the home varies between different ethnic and tribal groups, although the continental style of eating, with the fork held in the left hand and the knife in the right, is generally used in South Africa.

After socializing, hosts will usually accompany their guests outside to the gate, car or street when they leave.

South Africa's restaurants serve a cuisine similar to that of North America and Europe. Tipping is at the customer's discretion.

Among the national specialties are *sosaties* (kebab), *bobotie* (minced curried lamb), *bredies* (vegetable and meat casseroles) and South African rock lobster. The Indian population has contributed to the local cuisine with a variety of curries and chutneys.

SOCIAL VALUES, CUSTOMS AND TIPS

English and Afrikaans are the two most frequently spoken official languages. More than 80 percent of white South Africans are bilingual.

You may not be able to avoid a discussion of local politics, particularly the former policy of apartheid. Popular conversation might center on South African taste in art, music, movies and literature, which ranges from popular western to traditional Asian and African cultures.

Soccer, rugby, surfing, swimming and boating are all popular sports. Many people also participate in cricket, squash, lawn bowling, field hockey and tennis. Horse and car racing draw large audiences as well.

Other than eating ice cream or standing at a vendor's stand, South Africans generally do not eat on the street.

When yawning and coughing the mouth is covered.

Among some ethnic and tribal groups, it is not polite to gesture with the left hand, while in others it is polite to receive something with both hands cupped together.

It is considered rude to point at someone using the index finger or to have a conversation with your hands in your pockets.

SOUTH KOREA

Population: 46,416,796 (July 1998 est.); Korean 99.9%, Chinese 0.1%

Languages: Korean (official)

Religions: Buddhist 47%, Christian 49%, Confucianist 3%, pervasive folk religion (shamanism), Chondogyo (Religion of the Heavenly Way) and other 1%

Currency: won

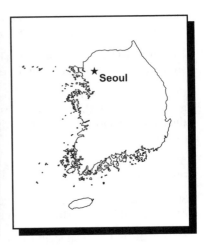

HISTORICAL OVERVIEW

- Although Korean legend places its historical beginnings much further back, modern Korea can trace its history back to the first century B.C., the beginning of the period of the Three Kingdoms of Silla, Koguryo and Paekche. Silla kings conquered the other two kingdoms in 668 A.D., ending centuries of sporadic warfare amongst all three and ushering in an era of Buddhist culture.

- As Silla disintegrated, new states arose and a new kingdom, Koryo, came and unified the peninsula by 936. The name Korea comes from the original name of this kingdom.

- The Mongols controlled Korea for about 100 years beginning in 1259. In 1392, Koryo fell to a former Koryo general who established the Choson (or Yi) Dynasty, which ruled for more than 500 years.

- In the later period of Yi rule, both China and Japan fought to control Korea. After its successful war with China, Japan annexed Korea in 1910. The Japanese ruled Korea almost completely to their own benefit, seizing land and businesses and subjugating the population.

- At the end of World War II, the peninsula was divided at the 38th parallel into two administrative zones, with the Soviet Union in charge to the North and the U.S. in charge to the South.

- In 1948, after attempts at holding nationwide elections failed, a pro-western government was established in the South with

Syngman Rhee as president. Kim Il Sung became head of North Korea. In 1948 the U.S.S.R. withdrew, and in 1949 the U.S. did as well. The governmental systems they had helped establish, however, remained in place.

- In 1950, war broke out between the two newly created states and lasted for three years. The U.S. and the United Nations sent troops to support South Korea. China sent troops to aid North Korea. An armistice but no peace treaty was signed, and violent border incidents occurred over the ensuing years.

- Rhee resigned from office in 1960 under charges of political corruption. South Korea subsequently changed its form of government to a parliamentary one.

- John Chang was elected prime minister of the Second Republic, but his government was ousted by a military coup led by General Park Chung Hee in 1961. Park did away with Chang's reforms, dissolved the National Assembly and banned all political activity. Park ruled the Third Republic until October 1979 when he was assassinated. A military coup followed, and Chun Doo Hwan eventually emerged as president.

- Popular dissatisfaction grew in the 1980s, and a constitution adopted in 1987 established direct presidential elections and protection of human rights. Roh Tae Woo was elected president in that year. This ushered in the Sixth Republic.

- In 1990, the first peace talks since the 1950s were held between the prime ministers of North and South Korea. Talks continued despite tensions over North Korea's possession of nuclear weapons.

- In 1992, Kim Young Sam was elected as the first civilian to occupy the office of president in South Korea in more than 30 years.

- South Korea endured major political shock waves in 1995 when two of its former presidents were convicted on corruption charges.

- Striking among Korea's workforce became common from 1996 onwards. Along with other countries in Asia, Korea faced a severe economic crisis in late 1997, which caused a marked devaluation of its currency and loss of jobs. Strikes escalated in July 1998. The government claimed that these strikes were illegal due to the breach of strike procedure, and warrants were issued for the arrest of union leaders.

BUSINESS PRACTICES

Hours of Business

Businesses are generally open from 8:30 a.m. to 7:00 p.m., six days a week. Banks and government offices close earlier. The average workweek for Koreans is 50 hours, one of the longest in the world.

Dress

Conservative, western-style dresses and business suits are the customary attire. These include fine fabrics, dark colors and white shirts or blouses. Conservative fashion (hemlines, necklines, sleeves and makeup) is especially important for foreign businesswomen. Women should avoid pantsuits. If your Korean counterpart removes his/her jacket, feel free to do so as well.

Women should wear loose skirts or dressy pants when going out with Koreans in the evening. The occasion may include an invitation to a restaurant or coffee shop where guests will be seated on cushions on the floor. A tight skirt would be uncomfortable to sit in under such circumstances.

Introductions

How Koreans greet you depends on your age and social status, relative to the greeter. A bow, usually accompanied by a handshake, is the traditional greeting. During a handshake, the left hand supporting the right arm is a sign of respect. The senior person offers to shake hands first, but the junior person bows first. Men always shake hands. Women only sometimes do. A U.S. businesswoman should extend her hand first to Korean men and women.

Koreans beckon by extending the arm – palm down – and making a scratching motion. Beckoning with the index finger is considered very rude.

When addressing a Korean, use "Mr.," "Miss," "Ms." or "Mrs." and the surname. In business situations, surnames are used. Only the closest of friends within the same peer group are on a first-name basis.

Koreans usually address each other by surname or full name followed by the honorific term *songsaengnim* (pronounced song-sang-nim), which means "respected person." Feel free to use this title, even when addressing someone in English.

Remember that Koreans have three names – first the family name, then the clan name and finally the given name. Some Koreans put their family names last when writing in the Roman alphabet.

Koreans will appreciate it if you show respect by using their business titles, e.g., Manager Kim, Director Lee.

A common greeting is *Annyong haseyo?* meaning "Are you at peace?" To express great respect, the honorific form *Annyong hashimnikka?* is used.

Bring plenty of business cards printed in English on one side and Korean on the other. Business cards are exchanged (presented and accepted) with both hands when professionals meet for the first time. When you receive a business card, keep it on the table in front of you or examine it carefully, then put it in a pocket above the waist as a sign of respect.

It is common to discuss personal subjects when first meeting. You may be asked questions such as "How old are you?," "What degree(s) do you have?," "Are you married?" or "How many children do you have?" People ask your age to fit you into a social hierarchy, as the older you are, the higher you are ranked.

Korean businesspeople maintain tight cultural ties. The best way to introduce yourself prior to traveling to Korea is by making contact with a Korean in your country who can serve as a reference for you. It would then be appropriate to send a letter of introduction.

Meetings

Meetings should be scheduled well in advance with a detailed list of objectives and participants' names sent ahead of time.

In order to feel comfortable with those they are meeting, Koreans tend to ask personal questions before beginning the meeting.

The basis for Korean decision making is consensus, and Koreans respect the ideas of a group. When meeting with Koreans, there should be a group spokesman who represents the ideas of the group as a whole, rather than having several different ideas being expressed by individual people.

Koreans expect others to be punctual for appointments, although many Koreans may not be punctual themselves.

Negotiating

English is widely spoken in Korean business circles, and most correspondence is in English. Catalogs and promotional materials written in English are acceptable. Yet, during important negotiations, it is advisable to have a male interpreter present.

Koreans tend to answer "Yes" frequently because they place great importance on being polite. Thus, questions should be phrased to elicit more than a "Yes" or "No" response. For example, instead of saying "Can the shipment be ready in four weeks?" ask "When can this shipment be ready?"

Expect to repeat answers quite frequently. Koreans want to make sure that they are making the right decision and will deliberate for a relatively long time before a decision is made. Protracted deliberations may also be a way to break down resistance from negotiating partners.

It is common to give gifts in order to obtain favors in return, especially in the workplace. When you accept a gift you must reciprocate. You should wait for Koreans to give you your gift first. Open it only after you have left the group. It is a good idea to bring a gift made in your country, preferably something with your company's emblem or a bottle of Scotch.

Be patient, diplomatic and do not boast about your company while negotiating with Koreans. Respecting their idea of harmony and helping to preserve it will help solidify the deal.

Personal relationships are more important than contracts. Therefore, it is vital to have a long-term perspective in business, with your goal being to maintain and nurture personal contacts.

Interrupting someone while he or she is speaking is considered a desirable sign of eagerness among Koreans. Therefore, do not be insulted if you are interrupted by a Korean colleague while speaking.

Koreans pay particular attention to facial expressions. It is very important to make eye contact.

Entertaining

Most business entertaining in Korea is done in restaurants rather than in private homes.

Guests invited to a home should remove their shoes before entering. Visitors are seated on cushions on *ondol* floors (floors that are heated from below). The guest receives the warmest or best position.

The evening meal usually begins with appetizers. Cocktails are served with food and will not be offered before dinner. *Soju* and *magulli* are common alcoholic drinks served to guests before the main meal.

Each diner sits on an individual cushion, which is placed on a floor mat under a separate low table. Do not sit with your feet straight out in front of you under the table. Men sit cross-legged, and women tuck their legs to one side beneath them.

Korean food is generally hot and spicy. Ginger, chilies and garlic are popular. Koreans appreciate it when Westerners try their food although they are not offended if visitors are unable to eat it.

Rice and *kimch'i* (a spicy pickled cabbage) are staples at almost every meal. Rice is often combined with other ingredients, such as red beans or vegetables. Soups and fish are common. *Bulkogi*, strips of marinated and barbecued beef, is a frequently served delicacy. Barley tea is served with most meals, and fruit is a popular dessert.

Chopsticks and spoons are the most common eating utensils.

When you are offered more food, it is customary to decline politely twice and then accept. If you are entertaining Koreans, be sure to offer more food three times.

People in Korea pour drinks for one another, but never for themselves. If you pour a drink for your Korean friend, he/she will do the same for you. When someone is pouring your drink, lift up your glass. The junior person always pours for the senior (age usually confers seniority). Formerly, drinking alcoholic beverages was only permissible for men, but this tradition is changing in large cities. Women may pour drinks for men, but do not typically pour for other women. It is also polite to fill one's neighbor's small soy sauce dish.

Loud talking and laughter are permissible during business entertaining, although generally not permissible at other times. After dinner there may be singing and laughter. If there is singing after dinner, try to go along with the fun – no matter how poorly you sing!

During dinner, a small communal cup may be passed around. One should drink from the cup and pass it along.

The host accompanies a guest to the door or outside of the house at the end of a visit.

In restaurants, tipping is not expected, as a service charge is usually included in the bill.

SOCIAL VALUES, CUSTOMS AND TIPS

According to the Confucian ethic, status, dignity, courtesy and formality regulate social behavior. Hard work, piety and extreme modesty are valued. In business, the boss is all-powerful.

Since Koreans place great importance on family, especially on sons, the family is an excellent topic of conversation. You may want to ask a Korean man if he is the eldest son in his family. If he is, he will be very proud of his prestigious role.

Public displays of anger are unacceptable in Korea. It is considered better to accept an injustice quietly in order to maintain harmony. Criticism and public disagreements are avoided. Koreans may withhold bad news or disagreement or express such things indirectly.

Koreans can be very direct, depending on their status and the person with whom they are communicating, yet they are also polite and proper. As a result, they sometimes agree with each other simply to preserve harmony. Emotional control and patience are vital.

Koreans are quite friendly and proud of their personal achievements.

Because of their respect for humility, if you offer a compliment to a Korean, expect it to be graciously denied.

Friendship is highly valued and Koreans are quick to make friends. In fact, success depends greatly on social contacts.

The Korean countryside makes for a good conversation topic, as do the country's rapid growth during the past 20 years, Korean food and the 1988 Seoul Olympics. Another good topic of discussion is sports. Soccer is popular in Korea, as are baseball, boxing, basketball, volleyball, tennis and swimming. *Taekwondo* (a form of martial arts) comes from Korea, and a type of wrestling called *sirum* (where contestants are tied together during their match) is unique to Korea. You might want to avoid discussing socialism, communism or Korea's internal politics.

SPAIN

Population: 39,133,996 (July 1998 est.); Spanish (Castilian, Valencian, Andalusian, Asturian) 73%, Catalan 16%, Galician 8%, Basque 2%

Languages: Castilian Spanish 74%, Catalan 17%, Galician 7%, Basque 2%

Religions: Roman Catholic 99%, other 1%

Currency: peseta, euro

HISTORICAL OVERVIEW

- There is evidence that both Phoenicians and Greeks set up small outposts in southern Spain in the eighth and sixth centuries B.C., respectively. Celtic peoples migrated to the northern regions of Spain during the eighth and ninth centuries. Beginning in 218 B.C., Rome extended its control over the Iberian Peninsula, which it lost to invading Visigoths in the fourth century A.D.

- Muslims from North Africa invaded and conquered most of the Iberian Peninsula in the eighth century. The people of the region, who were predominantly Christian, fought the Muslims, and by the late 13th century the two kingdoms of Castile and Aragon emerged as independent. They united in 1479 and conquered the last Muslim kingdom in 1492.

- At the end of the 15th century, Spain began establishing itself as a colonial power in the Americas, and by the middle of the 16th century, it had amassed a large and powerful empire.

- In 1516, King Ferdinand of Aragon was succeeded by his grandson, Hapsburg King Charles I of the Netherlands. Although initially resented by the Spanish, Charles helped substantially expand Spain's influence and holdings in Europe once he became Holy Roman Emperor in 1519.

- Charles' son Phillip II inherited Spain and the Netherlands by 1556. Phillip was a religious zealot who involved Spain in many expensive wars in his efforts to defend Catholicism and eradicate Protestantism.

- After Phillip's rule came to an end, Spain's empire declined. When Hapsburg rule passed to the House of Bourbon in 1700, Spain immediately became embroiled in the war of the Spanish succession (1701-1714) in which it lost Belgium, Luxembourg, Milan, Sardinia and Naples.

- Spain's brief occupation by Napoleon from 1801 to 1814 revealed the monarchy's weakness and encouraged many of Spain's American colonies to declare independence. By 1850, most of Spain's American holdings had been lost, and in 1898 it lost the last of them, the Philippines, to the U.S.

- At the beginning of the 20th century, the Spanish began to call for a republic, causing King Alfonso XIII to abdicate in 1931. In 1936, civil war broke out when the Nationalists, led by Francisco Franco, opposed the Republicans. In 1939, the Nationalists, who had received aid from Hitler's Germany and Mussolini's Italy, were victorious and Franco seized control. He ruled as a dictator until 1975.

- When Franco died in 1975, Juan Carlos de Borbón y Borbón, the designated successor, came to power. Juan Carlos established a constitutional monarchy, naming himself king and restoring democracy. In 1977, the newly formed parliament or *Cortes* established a program of political and economic reform. The government guaranteed human and civil rights, the separation of church and state, and free enterprise.

- The elections of 1982 brought the Socialist Workers' Party to power under Felipe Gonzàlez Márquez. Spain also drew closer to the rest of Western Europe. In 1986, it joined the European Economic Community and NATO.

- Spain celebrated the "Year of Spain" in 1992, commemorating the 500-year anniversary of Columbus' first trip from Spain to the Americas with a world's fair in Seville and the Summer Olympics in Barcelona.

- In 1995, the conservative Popular Party dominated the municipal elections and, in 1996, it narrowly won both houses of Parliament. Its leader, Prime Minister José Maria Aznar, faced the tasks of financial reform and deficit cutting. Political crises and corruption have plagued Spain in the 1990s, but it nevertheless remains a stable, modern democracy.

- In the late 1990s, the Basque separatist's group, seeking independence for the Basque provinces in the northwest of Spain, escalated its violent attacks, increasing the numbers killed and increasing popular antipathy.

BUSINESS PRACTICES

Hours of Business

Most businesses are open Monday through Saturday from 9:00 a.m. to 1:00 p.m. and from 5:00 to 8:00 p.m. From approximately 1:00 to 4:00 p.m., there is a break for the large midday meal and a *siesta* (a rest after the midday meal).

Business trips should not be scheduled between mid-July and the end of August as this is the time when most Spaniards take their vacation.

Dress

Spaniards tend to dress formally and elegantly. Men wear jackets and ties for business even in warm weather. Jackets should be kept buttoned except when sitting. Appropriate business attire for women is a dress or a skirt with a blouse or a conservative pantsuit.

Introductions

When first introduced or when departing, both men and women shake hands.

The Spaniards are a warm and affectionate people. Men who are close friends will embrace when they meet. Women friends kiss each other on both cheeks.

In Spanish, the last name consists of the father's surname followed by the mother's maiden name. When addressing people in conversation, it is polite to use only their first surname (for example, when greeting Mr. Garcia-Lopez, you would call him "Mr. Garcia").

Spaniards have great respect for the elderly and for those of senior status. Although someone older or of higher rank may address you by your first name, this informality is not an invitation for you to do likewise. You should still address that person as "Mr." or "Mrs." (*Señor* or *Señora*) and the last name. In some areas, *Don* and *Doña* are used, followed by the first name, to show special respect and to flatter the person you are greeting.

An unmarried woman is addressed as *Señorita* followed by her first name.

It is customary to address people by their surnames until you have become well acquainted.

Business cards should be presented to all business contacts. They should be printed in both Spanish and English and always be presented with the Spanish side facing up.

Meetings

Appointments should be arranged well in advance. Make appointments between ten days and two weeks ahead of time when doing so by phone. If appointments are being scheduled by mail, allow for three weeks to a month's time. The best time of day to schedule business appointments is early in the day between 10:00 a.m. and 12:30 p.m. Confirm all appointments before arriving in Spain.

It is not unusual for appointments to be scheduled at the last minute or at the same time as another appointment if someone has unexpectedly arrived in town and needs to meet. Do not, therefore, take it amiss if a long-scheduled appointment has been cancelled. Simply return at a later time during the day.

Spaniards have a very fluid orientation toward time. Business is conducted at a very slow pace and punctuality is not expected. It is a customary and an accepted practice to arrive 15 to 30 minutes late for a business meeting.

At the conclusion of a meeting, present your business cards once again to your Spanish counterparts and remember to have the Spanish side facing up.

Negotiating

It is preferred that you write in English when corresponding with Spanish business firms. Most large firms conduct business in both languages. If you send a letter that has been translated into Spanish, it may not seem as formal or descriptive as is the custom in Spain and may therefore offend the recipient.

Correspondence should be formal, even though you may have a casual relationship with your colleague after the first meeting.

It is useful to have a personal contact who can help you cultivate business relationships in Spain. Spaniards value personal influence and it is difficult to accomplish anything on your own. Changing this contact at any time could hurt negotiations because Spaniards place a great deal of value on established relationships.

Before the start of the first business meeting, there is a great deal of small talk. Spaniards prefer to establish a personal rapport with their negotiating partners before initiating business discussions. You may be asked questions about your background, education and interests. Serious discussions can begin after this is completed.

Special care should be taken not to offend your counterpart by implying that he/she is not adequately prepared or by imposing decisions by demand.

When traveling with a senior executive, remember to introduce the person to the senior executives of the Spanish firm. Failure to do so will insult the honor of the Spanish firm and could hamper negotiations.

Use a conservative but highly informative presentation style. Make sure to employ many visual aids.

Spaniards like to review all information relevant to a project before making a decision. It is advisable to translate all materials presented during a meeting into Spanish.

If presenting as a team, it is best to present as a united front. Any contradictions with the team position may be interpreted as signs of weakness or ill preparedness.

During a presentation expect to be interrupted. Voices may be raised and positions may be staked out quite adamantly. Such behavior is not intended to offend anyone, but rather is an expected part of the negotiating style.

Plan on holding several meetings before concluding your deal.

Entertaining

Business lunches and dinners, normally conducted in restaurants, are customary in Spain.

If you are invited to someone's home, it is polite to decline at first, since it may simply be a courtesy. If the host insists, however, accept the invitation.

If several individuals have entertained you, it is appropriate for you to reciprocate by inviting them out to a meal together with their spouses.

If you are a businesswoman entertaining a Spanish businessman, keep in mind that Spanish men always expect to pay for a meal. If you would like to pay for the meal, however, speak to the maitre d' or waiter in advance and arrange to pay with cash or a credit card. In the event that this is not possible, you can discreetly leave the table at the end of the meal to take care of the bill.

Spaniards dress elegantly even for casual occasions. When attending social functions, men should wear jackets with ties and black shoes, and women should wear dresses or skirts with blouses. Formal dress (tuxedos for men and long dresses for women) is only necessary for charity balls or official dinners.

In restaurants, a service charge is usually included in the bill. It is also customary to leave a small tip (about five percent) in addition to the service charge.

Breakfast is the lightest meal of the day consisting of a hot drink and bread with jam. The most substantial meal of the day is at midday and is generally served at about 2:00 p.m. It usually consists of soup, salad, a dish containing fish, a main dish and fresh fruit.

At about 5:00 or 6:00 p.m., Spaniards usually have a *merienda* (snack) which consists of a *bocadillo* (sandwich), sweet bread or crackers with tea or hot milk.

Dinner is served at about 9:00 or 10:00 p.m. In fact, most restaurants remain closed until 9:00 p.m. and do not really get busy until about 11:00 p.m. Dinner is smaller than the midday meal and will often include local specialties such as *paella* (rice with fish and seafood or meat), seafood, sausage, roasted meat or stew.

Adults usually drink wine with their meals, but there is no pressure to drink alcohol, and you may request juice or a soft drink instead. Likewise, if you are not hungry, you will not be pressed to eat. It is preferable to decline food rather than to leave any on your plate.

If you are invited for dinner at a colleague's home, it is customary to bring a gift of flowers, pastries, cookies or chocolates. Do not bring any other type of food. Avoid bringing dahlias or chrysanthemums, as they are associated with funerals. If you are offered a gift, you should open it when presented with it.

If you are invited to a formal dinner, the host will indicate the seating arrangement. The guest of honor is usually seated to the right of the host while the hostess is seated opposite the host.

Cutlery is arranged slightly differently in Spain than in most other European countries. The fruit knife and fork, or other dessert utensils, will be placed above the plate. Two glasses are provided, one for water and one for wine.

The continental style of eating is used with the fork held in the left hand and the knife in the right. Use the knife to push food onto the back of the fork. Neither fingers nor food should ever be used to push food onto the fork.

Wrists should be kept on the table when you are not eating.

When you have completed the meal, place your fork and your knife side by side on the plate. Leaving them on opposite sides of the plate indicates either that you have not finished or that you were not satisfied with your meal.

Spaniards tend to stay and talk after dinner. Plan to stay until around midnight, especially if the conversation is lively.

SOCIAL VALUES, CUSTOMS AND TIPS

Keep in mind that Spaniards are individualists, in both business and social contexts. This individualism translates into a strong sense of personal pride. Treat others with great respect and be careful not to cause them any embarrassment, as it offends their sense of honor.

Many Spaniards feel that one's appearance as well as the projection of affluence are of great importance. Style and quality of clothing are considered signs of social status and respectability.

Spaniards enjoy conversing and giving advice.

In Spain, it is acceptable to discuss politics, but it is best to refrain from making political comparisons between Spain and your country. Other good conversation topics include sports, particularly soccer. It is also appreciated if you express an interest in Spain's history and culture.

Avoid discussing religion or asking too many personal questions about a person's family, job and interests until you are well acquainted. Never make negative comments about bullfighting.

In Spain, it is not considered rude to interrupt someone while conversing. Expect to be interrupted frequently during conversation.

In Spain, eye contact is very important. Women should be wary of eye contact with strangers or acquaintances, however, as returning a gaze could be interpreted as indicating a romantic interest.

In Spain, the family is considered very important. While it is inappropriate to ask Spaniards too many personal questions about their families, you may want to mention your family life. The importance you place on family life will be taken as a sign of your stability as a business partner.

The U.S. "okay" sign, with thumb and index finger forming a circle, is considered a vulgar gesture in Spain.

It is common for Spanish men to call out expressions of admiration as women pass on the street. If they are not acknowledged with a reaction, the woman will not be bothered any longer.

It is considered inappropriate for adults to eat while walking in public.

It is considered polite for men to sit down only after all women in the room have sat down.

It is considered inappropriate for women to cross their legs. Spanish men usually cross their legs at the knees.

To beckon someone, you should wave your fingers or your whole hand with palm facing down.

It is considered rude to chew gum or place your hands in your pockets, especially when conversing with someone.

SRI LANKA

Population: 18,933,558 (July 1998 est.); Sinhalese 74%, Tamil 18%, Muslim 7%, Malay, Burgher and Veddha 1%

Languages: Sinhala (official and national) 74%, Tamil (national) 18%, English 10%

Religions: Buddhist 69%, Hindu 15%, Christian 8%, Muslim 8%

Currency: Sri Lankan rupee

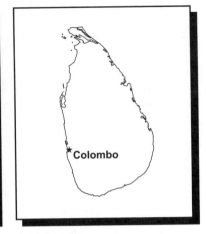

Colombo

HISTORICAL OVERVIEW

- In the fifth century B.C., an Indo-Aryan group led by Prince Vijaya migrated to Sri Lanka and formed a small kingdom. The present-day Sinhalese are descendants of this group. During the third century B.C., Indian Prince Mahinda introduced Buddhism to the Sinhalese population, and Sri Lanka, known as Ceylon at that time, became its stronghold in South Asia.

- The Tamils, another ethnic group, probably emigrated to the island from India in the early centuries A.D.

- The Sinhalese established the Anwadhapura kingdom in the third century B.C. and ruled virtually uninterrupted until 1200 AD. At this time Sinhalese power began moving to Southwestern Ceylon and an Indian dynasty began invading the north. By the 14th century the Indians had established a Tamil kingdom in the north.

- During the 13th, 14th and 15th centuries Ceylon was invaded by India, China and Malaya, and in 1505 the Portuguese landed on the island. The Portuguese began trade and exploited domestic conflicts to slowly gain control of most of Ceylon.

- The Kandyan kingdom solicited the Dutch for help against the Portuguese. Control of Ceylon then passed to the Dutch East India company and, in 1796, to Britain.

- In the 19th century, first coffee and then tea became large-scale plantation crops, vital to Ceylon's economic development.

- In the 20th century, demands for independence grew, and in 1919 the Ceylon National Congress united the Sinhalese and Tamils in part to further this cause.

- In 1948, the island was granted independence from Britain. The United National Party (UNP) then held power until the Sri Lanka Freedom Party (SLFP), a Sinhalese nationalist party, won the elections in 1956. The Tamils objected fiercely, and in 1965 the UNP came to power once again. In response, the SLFP formed a broad Marxist coalition and was reelected. It proclaimed Ceylon the Republic of Sri Lanka in 1972.

- The UNP won the 1977 elections and instituted a new constitution that established a democratic socialist republic and a strong presidency. Relative stability followed until 1981 when Tamil groups seeking an independent Tamil state (called Tamil Eelam) led violent insurgencies against the government.

- Violence continued throughout the 1980s. An unsuccessful attempt was made to introduce Indian troops into the area as a peacekeeping force. Peace existed intermittently throughout early 1990, but by early 1991 the Liberation Tigers of Tamil Eelam had taken control of northern parts of the island. In 1993, President Premadas was killed at a political rally.

- Following the 1994 elections, a leftist government led by Chanrika Kumaratunga came to power and negotiated a ceasefire with the Liberation Tigers, but it quickly disintegrated. President Kumaratunga extended greater autonomy to the Tamils. She also increased privatization and strengthened the military. Yet, after 23 government soldiers were killed in 1997, a new offensive against the Tamil Tigers was undertaken. Despite the conflicting demands of the Sinhalese nationalists and the Tamil Tigers, President Kumaratunga claims that peace is possible. She has refused to comply with Tamil Tiger demands to bring India into civil strife talks. As of 1996, 50,000 people are said to have died due to the conflict.

- In March 1997 parliamentary elections were held. The People's Alliance was victorious and remained in control of the government.

BUSINESS PRACTICES

Hours of Business

Business hours are generally from 8:30 a.m. to 4:30 or 5:00 p.m., Monday through Friday. Be aware that, even if people are seated at their desks, business is not conducted during the morning and afternoon tea break.

Dress

Conservative but lightweight clothing is worn because of the climate. Businessmen rarely wear jackets and ties and businesswomen simply wear a modest, light blouse and skirt.

Introductions

While greetings can vary between different ethnic groups, placing one's palms under the chin and bowing the head slightly is the most common one. Foreigners are not expected to initiate this gesture but it is appreciated if it is returned.

Due to Great Britain's influence on Sri Lanka, the handshake is an acceptable form of greeting for both sexes, especially in business.

Common verbal greetings are *Ayubowan* (pronounced "ah-you-byu-one") in Sinhalese or *Vannakkhan* (one-eh-come) in Tamil. Both expressions mean "May you be blessed with the gift of a long life." If you bow, it may be accompanied by the word *Aaibowan* (in Sinhalese) or *Namaste* (in Tamil), which means "I salute the godlike qualities within you."

Since titles are important to Sri Lankans, it is advisable to use them when addressing acquaintances. English titles, such as "Mr.," "Mrs." or "Miss" are acceptable. It is customary to address a Sinhalese person as *Mahattaya* (Sir) or *Nona* (Madam) following his/her last names or simply by title alone. Tamils, on the other hand, generally do not use titles. Instead, they use *Aiyaa* (father) or *Ammaa* (mother) to show respect when addressing an older person.

At a party, make a point to greet and shake hands with each person in the room.

Business cards are usually exchanged at first meetings. It is appreciated if you have the card printed in English and the local language. This is only a good idea if you can distinguish between Tamil and Sinhalese, however. Otherwise, having the card printed only in English is advisable and perfectly acceptable.

Meetings

It is recommended that you make appointments at least a week in advance. It is advisable to reconfirm those appointments a day or two before the meeting.

Punctuality is valued and expected from Westerners even though Sri Lankans are rarely on time for business appointments. Since Sri Lanka's traffic is very heavy, allocate ample time between appointments.

Many introductory meetings are held over lunch.

Negotiating

Business does not move quickly in Sri Lanka. Delays are common, and several trips may be necessary to finalize a deal. Establishing rapport and a relationship of trust are very important, and negotiations are always preceded by socializing.

For Sri Lankan businesspeople, interpersonal relationships, dictated by tradition and the situation of the moment, are more important than abstract rules and facts.

Both Sinhalese (Buddhists) and Tamils (Hindus) use traditional and religious beliefs, in combination with their personal feelings, as a foundation for determining the truth and making decisions. Do not be surprised if your counterparts consult an astrologer before making significant business commitments.

When making important business decisions, the Sinhalese are concerned with responsibility to the self and to interpersonal relationships. Tamils concern themselves with the individual's responsibility to the group – the family, social group and religion. Thus, Sri Lankan businesspeople tend to place importance on the group and on an individual's position and rank within the group.

It is quite rare to find women in top business positions in Sri Lanka. In neighboring India or Pakistan, however, it is not as unusual. Expect foreign businesswomen to be treated with respect.

Sri Lankans are very hospitable and will always offer refreshments at the beginning of a meeting. This is meant as a sign of good will and it is impolite to refuse. Compliments on the refreshments are welcomed and always appreciated.

Entertaining

Business is mostly discussed over lunch in a restaurant. It is also common to be invited to a Sri Lankan home for either lunch or dinner. Unannounced visits are also acceptable and commonly take place between 4:00 and 7:00 p.m.

The person who initiates an invitation to a restaurant is expected to pay for the entire meal.

If you are invited to a home for a visit or a meal, it is polite to reciprocate by inviting your host(s) to a meal in your hotel's restaurant.

If invited to a home for a meal, a gift is not expected but is appreciated. Good gifts include fruit, expensive chocolates and crafts from your country. It is best to avoid bringing liquor, unless you know that your host drinks alcohol. If you do bring alcohol, imported whiskey is a good choice.

Be aware that there may be as much as two or three hours of socializing before the meal begins in a Sri Lankan home.

In some homes, it is appropriate to remove your shoes before entering. Follow the example of your host or other guests.

Since Sri Lankans of all religious types (Buddhist, Hindu, Muslim or Christian) seek to avoid foods that cause spiritual pollution, what is and is not eaten is determined by the region of the country. Those who adhere strictly to Buddhism do not eat meat of any kind, although some Buddhists will eat fish or eggs. Hindus do not eat beef or pork, and Muslims do not eat pork.

Breakfast is usually eaten between 7:00 and 8:00 a.m. and lunch between noon and 2:00 p.m. Dinner is usually eaten between 7:00 and 10:00 p.m.

Rice is the basic food at all meals in the Sri Lankan diet. A variety of curries (from the Sinhalese) are popular, from mild to very spicy. Sri Lankans typically consume very little meat due to religious restrictions, but eat large amounts of peas, beans and nuts. Tamil cuisine, in particular, often includes beans and peas. The Burghers, an ethnic group in Sri Lanka, are known for their cakes and sweetmeats (another important part of the Sri Lankan diet, consisting of candy and crystallized fruit). Tea is the most common beverage served either with meals or as a refreshment.

At a meal, communal dishes are usually placed in the center of the table and each person serves himself or herself. Remember not to use your left hand when serving food. It is also best not to allow the serving utensils to touch your plate.

Food is always eaten with the right hand. Bread and rice balls are used to scoop up curries and vegetables. Sometimes a plantain leaf is used as a plate. This should not be eaten!

It will be a compliment to your host if you eat more than one serving of food. Therefore, it is advisable to take only small portions at first. If you are full, however, you may politely refuse additional servings.

SOCIAL VALUES, CUSTOMS AND TIPS

About ten percent of the population and most businesspeople and government officials speak English fluently.

Sri Lankans have a relatively open attitude toward foreigners and other ways of life.

Ethnic, religious and social divisions run deep in Sri Lanka. This is in part due to a historic division of society by caste, although the importance of the caste system is declining. It is best to avoid discussing ethnic or religious issues, however, and criticizing the caste system.

Sports make a good topic of conversation. Sri Lankans enjoy a number of sports introduced by the British, including soccer, rugby, cricket, tennis and horse racing. Other good topics of conversation include hobbies, culture, family, schools, your own country and the sights of Sri Lanka.

The left hand is reserved for hygienic purposes and should not be used for touching people or food or for passing objects. Objects are passed with the right hand only or with both hands.

Nonverbal signals of agreement are reversed from those in western countries. Nodding the head means "No" and shaking the head from side to side indicates "Yes."

While western-style clothing is worn, especially in the cities and among the youth, traditional forms of dress also remain popular. Neat, cool clothing is appropriate for casual attire. Shorts and sleeveless, low-cut or revealing clothing and bathing suits are inappropriate for women except at the beach or in resort areas.

As in many other Asian cultures, the head is considered the most sacred part of the body. Therefore, be careful not to touch another person's head.

Do not point the sole of one's foot at anyone or use the foot to move an object or to point at something. Avoid propping your feet up on furniture.

Using the index finger to point or to beckon someone is considered impolite. To beckon someone, wave all fingers with the palm facing down.

A smile is sometimes used instead of saying "Thank you," but women should be aware that smiling can be considered a flirtatious gesture in Sri Lanka.

According to religious beliefs, women are forbidden to touch a Buddhist monk. A monk is forbidden to touch money. Remember to use both hands when giving anything else to a monk.

Remove your shoes and hat before entering a Buddhist temple. An image of Buddha is considered sacred, so never touch, lean on or sit on one.

SWEDEN

Population: 8,886,738 (July 1998 est.); Lappish, foreign-born first generation immigrants (Finnish, Yugoslavian, Danish, Norwegian, Greek, Turkish) 12%

Languages: Swedish, Lapp- and Finnish-speaking minorities

Religions: Evangelical Lutheran 94%, Roman Catholic 1.5%, Pentecostal 1%, other 3.5%

Currency: krona

HISTORICAL OVERVIEW

- Around 12,000 B.C. hunters migrated from Europe to southern Sweden. Two Germanic tribes, the Sviones (Swedes), living in east-central Sweden, and the Goths, inhabiting southern Sweden, conducted trade with the Romans up until 400 A.D.

- While the Norwegian and Danish Vikings sailed westward during the Viking era, the Swedish Vikings went eastward as far as the Black and Caspian seas. They controlled trade routes that extended to Byzantium and the Middle East.

- Sweden resisted conversion to Christianity until the 11th century, when Swedish King Olof Skötkonung was baptized. At the time, Sweden was still a group of loosely confederated regions, and the monarchy's power was frequently threatened by other dynasties and the landed nobility.

- During the 13th and 14th centuries, struggles continued between the monarchy and the nobles. In trying to oppose German expansion, Queen Margrethe I of Denmark united Denmark, Norway and Sweden in the Denmark-based Union of Kalmar in 1397. Her son, Eric of Pomerania, was hailed King of Denmark, Norway and Sweden in that year. He ruled until 1439.

- In 1523, Sweden became an independent kingdom with Gustaf I Vasa as monarch. (The Vasa family remained on the throne until 1720.) The Reformation came to Sweden in the 16th century, and Lutheranism became the state religion. In the following century, Sweden emerged as one of the great powers of Europe, fighting several wars with its neighbors.

- Sweden's terrible defeat at the hands of Russia in 1709 began Sweden's decline. In 1808, Sweden lost Finland to Russia as a consequence of the Napoleonic Wars. A succession crisis led to the appointment of Napoleonic marshal Jean-Baptiste Bernadotte as king. In 1815 he annexed Norway. In 1818 he took the name Charles XIV, beginning a new dynastic line that still rules Sweden today.

- During the 19th century Sweden's position continued to slip as lack of jobs caused many to emigrate in search of work.

- In 1905 Sweden dissolved its union with Norway. During the remainder of the century, Sweden's foreign policy focused on neutrality and nonalignment. The country maintained its neutrality in both World Wars, allowing it to concentrate its resources on developing the economy. The Social Democratic Party came to dominate Swedish politics, and after World War II it instituted a comprehensive and far-reaching welfare state.

- Sweden revised its constitution in 1975 to give greater powers to the parliament and curtail those of the king largely to figurehead. From 1976 to 1982 the Socialists lost to a coalition government dominated by the Center Party.

- When the Socialists gained a majority once again in 1982 it was under Olof Palme, who had been prime minister previously. In 1986 Palme was assassinated, much to the shock of the Swedes, who take great pride in their country's peace and lack of violence.

- Ingvar Carlsson replaced Palme, but Carlsson's austerity measures to help the ailing economy were highly unpopular, and in 1991 Carl Bildt of the right-center Moderate Party formed a coalition government. His administration focused on privatizing the economy and relations with Europe. In 1991 Sweden joined the European Community, and in 1994 it joined NATO and the European Union (EU).

- On 18 September 1994, Swedes returned the Social Democrats to power. The Social Democrats wanted a slower, more managed approach to reforming welfare. Göran Persson, also a Social Democrat, became prime minister in 1996.

- In the late 1990s, most large Swedish firms (Volvo, SAAB, etc.) sold more goods and invested more money abroad than at home.

- During the late 1990s, Sweden experienced a series of bombings set off by "We Who Built Sweden", a local terrorist group, protesting Sweden's bid for the 2004 Summer Olympics.

BUSINESS PRACTICES

Hours of Business

Businesses are usually open from 9:00 a.m. to 5:00 p.m., Monday through Friday. They are sometimes open from 9:00 a.m. to noon on Saturday as well.

Avoid scheduling business trips during the vacation months of June, July and August. All Swedes take five weeks of vacation each year.

Dress

For business, men wear suits and ties while women wear dresses or suits.

Introductions

Swedes commonly shake hands with each person in the room upon meeting and leaving. As a rule, you do not have to shake hands with friends and acquaintances on subsequent meetings, but always shake hands with older people when greeting them and when leaving.

A person's last name preceded by "Mr.," "Mrs." or "Miss" is the appropriate form of address, unless you are a good friend or are invited to use a first name. Try to use professional titles (i.e., Doctor, Engineer, etc.), followed by a surname when appropriate. Using titles may not be necessary with younger people who consider this quite formal.

If there is nobody to introduce you at a meeting or social gathering, introduce yourself by shaking each person's hand.

More formal greetings include *God dag* (Good day) or *God morgon* (Good morning). Most people are more casual, however, and say *Hej* (pronounced "hey" and meaning "Hi").

It is not necessary to send a letter of introduction in order to do business with a Swedish firm.

Meetings

Punctuality is considered important in Sweden. Be on time for all appointments and schedule them well in advance.

It is acceptable to schedule an appointment for any time of the day, except for lunch time (11:30 a.m. to 1:30 p.m.).

Negotiating

Swedish businesspeople conduct business in a serious manner and may seem reserved when you first meet them. Telling humorous stories or joking during negotiations is considered inappropriate.

When making presentations use a conservative and low-key style. Avoid frill and present only concrete data. It is best to keep hand gestures to a minimum.

The pace of business in Sweden is somewhat relaxed. Swedes believe that work breaks are very important for their well-being. They also take very long lunch and coffee breaks. Remember that it is inappropriate to rush Swedish businesspeople since it is interpreted as pushiness.

Swedes avoid direct confrontation when conducting negotiations and will usually not argue with foreign business counterparts.

During a meeting, periods of silence are not uncommon. It is not necessary to fill up that time with talk.

National wines or liquors make good business gifts.

Entertaining

Entertaining is most often done in the home although going out to restaurants is becoming more popular. If you go to someone's home, expect your host's behavior to be quite formal.

Remember that punctuality is very important when invited to someone's home because the meal is served first.

If you are invited to someone's home in the evening, do not presume that it is a dinner invitation unless a meal is specified.

Dress formally for dinner unless you are invited to a picnic. When the invitation specifies formal wear, men should wear tuxedos and women should wear short cocktail dresses in a color other than black.

When visiting the home of a Swedish business colleague, it is appropriate to bring an odd number of flowers or a box of chocolates for the host(s). Flowers should be unwrapped just before presenting them to the host. Liquor or wine is an appreciated gift since alcohol is expensive in Sweden. Candy, but no other kind of food, also makes a suitable gift.

If you choose not to bring a gift, then it is appropriate to send a thank-you card. It is very important to make a point of calling the host the next day to thank him/her for his/her hospitality. The next time you see the person, it is polite to express your appreciation for the meal once again.

Make reservations in advance for business lunches and dinners. Spouses should be included in dinner invitations, but not for business lunches. Formal restaurants, called *Kållare*, are a good choice for such occasions.

When you are in a restaurant, never snap your fingers or yell to get a waiter's attention. It is best to softly call "Sir/Madam" in English.

Be aware that because alcohol is expensive in restaurants, many people have a drink or two at home before going out to dinner.

It is not necessary to leave a tip since a service charge is included in the check. If you wish to leave an additional gratuity, it is advisable not to leave it on the table. Instead, give it to the head waiter.

Swedes eat a light breakfast around 7:00 a.m. and might have a coffee or tea break mid-morning. The main meal is traditionally eaten at midday. Most urban residents have only a light lunch at noon, however, and then eat the main meal in the evening around 6:00 p.m.

The *smørgåsbord* is a lavish buffet eaten on special occasions or at parties. It includes warm and cold dishes.

A popular local drink is called *aquavit*. It is an alcoholic beverage distilled from grain or potatoes and often flavored with caraway seed. It is served extremely cold.

Swedes follow the continental style of eating, with the fork in the left hand and the knife in the right. Separate butter knives are usually provided, and the dinner knife should not be used for spreading butter.

Hands, but not the elbows, should be kept above the table during meals.

The host usually seats all the guests at a dinner. The male guest of honor is seated to the left of the hostess, and the female guest of honor is seated to the left of the host. Husbands and wives are not seated together.

Food is usually placed in serving dishes on the table. It is polite to try a little of everything. Guests usually wait for the host to offer second helpings. It is not impolite to decline food and it is perfectly acceptable to take more.

When you are finished eating, leave the utensils side by side on the plate. It is considered impolite to leave any food on your plate.

It is polite for the guest of honor to make a speech during dessert, elaborating on the meal and the charm of the hostess. Each guest personally thanks the host directly after the meal.

Your host will expect you to stay for coffee and conversation after the meal has concluded. After-dinner conversation may last until 11:00 p.m.

SOCIAL VALUES, CUSTOMS AND TIPS

It is important to make eye contact during conversations. Excessive hand gestures, however, should be avoided.

While Swedes are very friendly, they are also quite reserved. They are sometimes more comfortable speaking with foreigners than talking to other Swedes. They value modesty and material security.

Sweden's economy, the high standard of living and the area in which you are staying are good conversation topics. Swedes are very proud of their nation and its accomplishments. They have developed one of the most egalitarian societies in the world due to a generous social welfare system.

Local patriotism is important. Therefore, be careful not to praise another area over the one being visited. Swedes are pleased if you know something about Swedish history and culture.

Swedes appreciate it if a visitor demonstrates his/her knowledge of the cultural differences between Sweden, Norway, Denmark and Finland.

An interesting topic of conversation is the Nobel prize and prize winners. With the exception of the Nobel Peace Prize (sponsored by Norway), Sweden awards the Nobel prizes each year to significant contributors in the areas of chemistry, literature, medicine and physics. Alfred Bernhard Nobel (1833-96), the inventor of dynamite and a wealthy businessman, was born in Sweden.

Be aware that complimenting people you have just met is regarded as insincere.

Swedes are sports enthusiasts, which makes sports a good topic of conversation. Soccer, skiing, tennis, golf, swimming, ice hockey, bandy (related to ice hockey) and other winter sports are popular. The Swedes also love nature and participate in a lot of nature-related hobbies. Hiking, fishing and bird-watching are enjoyed. Cultural events, opera, ballet and recent books are other good conversation topics.

Avoid discussing prices, sexual attitudes, suicide rates, alcoholism or the country's neutrality during World War II. Comments about any of these topics may be interpreted as criticisms of Sweden, especially if a visitor from the U.S. expresses an opinion.

Traditionally, members of the upper classes refer to each other in the third person. They will avoid using the word "you." For example, in addressing a Mrs. Olson, they might say "How is Mrs. Olson today?" rather than "How are you today?" Although this tradition is changing, it is still appropriate to use this form when speaking to older people.

It is considered impolite to chew gum, yawn or have one's hands in one's pockets when speaking with another person.

It used to be uncommon to see people touching, embracing or putting an arm around someone's shoulder in public. The population is becoming more casual, however, and it is much more common to see displays of friendship or affection. Despite this change in attitude, do not embrace or put your arm around anybody except a close friend.

From a distance, one may nod one's head or raise one's hand to greet someone. Men lift their hats when passing an acquaintance in the street. They also remove their hats when talking to a woman.

It is not uncommon for people to change into their bathing suits on the beach, with or without a towel to hide them.

When waiting for a bus, tickets, etc., lines are respected. Pushing and shoving or barging in line is unacceptable.

SWITZERLAND

Population: 7,260,357 (July 1998 est.); German 65%, French 18%, Italian 10%, Romansch 1%, other 6%
Languages: German, French, Italian, Romansch, other
Religions: Roman Catholic 46.1%, Protestant 40%, other 5%, no religion 8.9%
Currency: Swiss franc

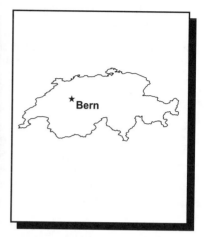

HISTORICAL OVERVIEW

- Before the Christian Era the area was inhabited by farmers, fisherman, hunters and armed warriors. One tribe called the Helvetians tried to move into northern Italy and clashed with the armies of Julius Caesar. The reign then became part of the Roman Empire, serving as a buffer from Germanic tribes in the north. During this time, the Romans set up cities in the region, opening trade and military routes that would later be important to the development of Europe. By the fifth century A.D., the Germanic tribes forced the Romans to withdraw. Burgundian tribes settled in the west and Alemanians in the east. While both groups were Germanic, they and the regions they inhabited developed along different lines.

- In the eighth and ninth centuries, Charlemagne absorbed the area into his empire. In 1273 the cantons of Uri, Schwyz and Unterwalden came under Hapsburg control. In response, these three cantons signed the Perpetual Covenant in 1291, founding the Swiss Confederation, which committed them to mutual assistance against all foreign intrusion. Swiss soldiers gained a reputation for their fighting prowess in their battles with the Austrians as well as with other armies. Luzern, Zurich, Glarus, Bern and Zug all joined the Confederation by 1353. In 1648, the Treaty of Westphalia declared that the 13 cantons of Switzerland were no longer subject to the Holy Roman Empire.

- During the 17th century, Switzerland began to declare itself neutral in the face of conflicts. In 1798, the French occupied much of Switzerland and established the Helvetian Republic. But in 1815, the country was guaranteed permanent neutrality at the Congress of Vienna. The mountains of Switzerland and its well-trained army have helped the country maintain its neutrality. In 1848, Switzerland became a federal state under the constitution. In 1874, direct democracy became part of the constitution.

- Switzerland remained neutral during both World Wars, and it only has observer status at the United Nations. It is not a member of the North Atlantic Treaty Organization (NATO) or the European Union (EU). Nevertheless, it maintains solid relations with many countries.

- Swiss allegiances are much stronger with the canton of origin than with Switzerland as a nation, and Switzerland has resisted the worldwide trend toward government centralization. In 1978, a proposal to create a federal police force was rejected, and Swiss presidents are so inconspicuous that most Swiss are unable to name their own president in any given year.

- The Swiss economy is one of the most efficient and prosperous in the world. While it relies almost entirely on imports to meet its energy and food needs, it is a center of industry, commerce and trade. It has been one of the world's major banking centers since the 16th century, although it has lagged behind New York, Tokyo and London in the 1990s. In the same decade, Switzerland was beset by such problems as political scandals, money laundering and rising drug use.

- In 1996, a controversy began over the role of Swiss banks during the Holocaust. It was found that they held an estimated $7 billion in unclaimed funds and an estimated 263 pounds of gold taken from the Holocaust victims. In 1997 Switzerland agreed to use the unclaimed funds to aid Holocaust survivors.

- For the first time in Swiss history, foreign troops were allowed to cross Swiss territory to another country in 1996 when NATO troops passed through on their way to Bosnia.

BUSINESS PRACTICES

Swiss society is tricultural and trilingual – French, Italian and German. Although there is a common Swiss culture, elements of French, Italian and German culture play a role in social and business etiquette. The specific situation, the region and the individuals with whom you are dealing will dictate appropriate variations in customs and etiquette.

Hours of Business

Business hours are usually from 8:00 a.m. to noon and from 2:00 to

6:00 p.m., Monday through Friday.

It is best to avoid making appointments during the traditional vacation months of July and August.

Dress

The Swiss place a high value on personal cleanliness and neatness. Businesspeople dress conservatively. For business meetings, men wear suits and ties, and women wear dresses or suits. Women can wear slacks, if they conform to business attire.

Introductions

When the Swiss greet or are introduced to someone, they customarily stand and shake hands. Shake hands with each person present when either arriving or departing.

In the French region, women friends embrace and kiss twice (once on each cheek) according to French custom. In the Italian area, women friends embrace but do not kiss when they meet. In both the French and Italian regions, two male friends may embrace if they have not seen each other for a long time. The German region tends to be more reserved. Women may embrace or kiss if they have not seen each other for a long time. Men in this area do not embrace when greeting.

When addressing people, remember to use last names. Using first names is considered very impolite unless you are invited to do so.

Verbal greetings vary according to the time of day and the region of the country, but most Swiss people understand English greetings.

You can use *Herr* and *Frau* to address the German-speaking Swiss, *Monsieur* and *Madame* to address the French-speaking Swiss and *Signor* and *Signora* to address the Italian-speaking Swiss ("Mr." or "Mrs.," respectively).

Exchanging business cards is considered to be an important part of introductions by businesspeople. If your company is very old, have the year of its founding printed on your card. It will impress the Swiss, who respect age.

Meetings

The best time for scheduling business appointments is in the morning after 9:00 a.m.

Appointments can be scheduled by telephone or by mail. If you call, phone three or four days ahead. If you are writing, contact your business associates a minimum of two weeks beforehand to set up an appointment.

The Swiss respect punctuality and are insulted when people are late. It is expected that people be precisely on time for all social and business engagements.

Negotiating

When sending business mail to a specific person in Switzerland, it is best to address the envelope to the company rather than to the individual. The letter itself, however, should be addressed to the individual. Envelopes addressed to an individual will not be opened if the person is away and may seriously delay your business.

Hand your business card to the receptionist, even if you have arranged an appointment in advance. Give a card to the person with whom you are meeting as well.

At business meetings, Swiss people can be direct and may come to the point without any initial small talk. Presentations should be thoroughly prepared, clear and show attention to detail. Know your field very well so that meetings can run efficiently (especially in the German region). In the French and Italian regions, business is generally conducted at a slower and more casual pace than in the German region. Anticipate some opening small talk about your trip to Switzerland, where you are staying, etc.

It is important to realize that Swiss businesspeople are very conservative and value order. Be patient, as they proceed in a very deliberate manner in order to reach a decision. Avoid high-pressure selling techniques. Expect to present all available data on your company (quality control, production and sales figures, profit statistics, etc.). Do not expect this information to be reciprocated.

In Switzerland, business is conducted in a very orderly manner, and decision making is quite centralized. Cultivation of personal relationships will take place only after negotiations are completed. The establishment of relationships will take time, but once established, they are lifelong.

Having a Swiss contact to help explain the rules of each canton's government will be very helpful during negotiations.

The Swiss are not bargainers. State the conditions up front and make your contract as detailed as possible.

It is customary to send a fax or write a follow-up letter summarizing negotiations once they are concluded.

Entertaining

The Swiss are very private and generally entertain visitors in restaurants rather than in their homes. If you are invited to dinner at someone's home, consider it a compliment.

When attending a party, wait for your host to make introductions.

When invited to dinner at someone's home, dress casually – men should wear trousers, shirts and sweaters, and women should wear skirts or slacks with a blouse or sweater.

Formal clothes (tuxedos for men and long dresses for women) are worn to balls, openings of theater or opera, formal weddings or any time the invitation specifies formal wear.

Impersonal gifts such as flowers or candy are popular in Switzerland, and your host would appreciate such a gift. Remember, however, that red roses and carnations are expressions of romantic love, and chrysanthemums and white asters are reserved for funerals. Three flowers or a flowering branch are sufficient. It is not necessary to get a large bunch. If you do not have time to shop in advance, it is acceptable to send flowers the next day. A good bottle of whiskey or cognac is also considered appropriate.

Business dinners are more common than business lunches. When lunching with a businessperson, it is common to be taken to the cafeteria at the workplace.

Include spouses in dinner invitations, unless the sole purpose of the meal is to discuss business.

In restaurants, a service charge is always included in the bill.

The largest meal of the day is the midday meal, which takes place around noon. This meal generally includes soup, a meat dish and fruit. Dinner, which takes place around 6:00 or 7:00 p.m., is a lighter meal. It usually consists of soup followed by salad or bread with cheese or salami.

A meal at a dinner party is often larger than a typical dinner. It consists of soup, a meat dish, vegetables, rice or potatoes and a green salad. The meal usually ends with fruit and cheese, cake or pudding. This may be followed by espresso or after-dinner drinks, such as *grappa* (brandy made from grape skins), cognac, *kirsch* or *pflümwasser* (plum brandy).

A wide variety of cuisines as well as regional specialties are available throughout Switzerland. Cheese dishes and liqueurs are common specialties.

Another popular Swiss dish is fondue – a dish containing melted cheese or gravy placed in the center of the table. Long forks are then used to dip pieces of bread into the cheese or gravy. *Raclettes bagnes* (cheese that has been grilled until it has melted and become crispy, served with cocktail onions and small potatoes) is another local delicacy.

If you are the guest of honor, you will be seated (or should seat yourself) in the middle of the side of the table.

When sitting at the table, never put either hand in your lap. Keep both wrists on the table when not eating.

Wait until the host has proposed a toast before drinking the wine. Then look the host in the eye and say "To your health" in the language appropriate to the region or English. Clink glasses with everyone at the table.

Be aware that Swiss people rarely order drinks before the meal. If drinks are served, they may include beer, wine, Campari, *Cynar* (made from artichokes), *blanc-cassis* (white wine with a blackberry liqueur) or *Pastis* (anise liqueur).

Help yourself to hors d'oeuvres only when offered. Begin eating only after being prompted by your host.

Help yourself to the food passed around the table on serving platters. You are expected to finish everything you put on your plate, so if you are not sure whether you will like something or not, take a very small portion.

Cutlery is arranged with the fork to the left of the plate and the knife and soup spoon to the right. The dessert spoon will be above the plate.

Eat as the Swiss do, with the fork in the left hand and the knife in the right. Use the knife to push the food onto the fork.

Indicate that you are waiting for a second helping by crossing the fork over the knife. The fork should point diagonally to the right, and the knife to the left. To show that you have finished, place the knife and fork horizontally across the plate, with the handles to the right.

Break bread and rolls with your hands, rather than cutting them with a knife.

At a dinner party in a home, it is recommended that you stay until about midnight. You may take the lead from other guests in deciding when to leave, but you should not stay much past midnight. When leaving, shake hands with all family members (including children). It is appropriate to send a thank-you note the next day.

SOCIAL VALUES, CUSTOMS AND TIPS

Swiss-German, French and Italian are spoken in Switzerland. English is widely studied and spoken, however, especially in business circles.

The Swiss take a very long time to establish a relationship, so do not expect people to be friendly immediately. Once you do make a Swiss friend, though, that person will be loyal for life.

Be polite, reserved and sensitive in personal relationships since the Swiss consider courtesy to be very important.

Good topics of conversation are participatory sports such as sailing, hiking and skiing, spectator sports such as soccer and bicycling, your impressions of Switzerland, and your travels in general. The Swiss are particularly proud of their independence and high standard of living.

The Swiss are conservative and reserved, and they dislike displays of wealth. It is best to avoid asking questions about someone's age, family, personal life or profession. Also refrain from comments regarding weight-watching or diets.

Be prepared for serious political discussions, even at parties.

The Swiss are passionate in their opinions about military service. Discussions of this sort could lead to a major argument.

When answering the phone, you may hear a variety of responses. In the French region, people say *Allo*. In the Italian region, people say *Pronto*, and in the German region, people answer with their name.

When meeting an acquaintance on the street, stop and shake hands. It is also customary to shake hands when departing.

In the German region, men tip their hats when they see someone they know on the street.

In a restaurant, it is common practice for strangers to sit in any empty seats remaining at your table, but it is not necessary to strike up a conversation with them.

Sit up straight in public as the Swiss consider sloppy posture rude.

Chewing gum or having your hands in your pockets is considered offensive.

Legs should not be placed on a desk, chair or table. If you cross your legs, you should cross them at the knee.

The Swiss take pride in orderliness and cleanliness; littering is considered to be completely inappropriate behavior.

The elderly are treated with great respect in Switzerland. It is customary to help an elderly person who is getting on or off a bus or carrying heavy bags. Stand and give your seat to the elderly on public transportation.

Shorts and jeans can be worn for casual wear in the country, but avoid wearing shorts in the city.

Expect pushing and shoving when standing in a line.

TAIWAN

Population: 21,908,135 (July 1998 est.); Taiwanese 84%, mainland Chinese 14%, Aborigine 2%

Languages: Mandarin Chinese (official), Taiwanese, Hakka dialects

Religions: Mixture of Buddhist, Confucian and Taoist 93%, Christian 4.5%, other 2.5%

Currency: New Taiwan dollar

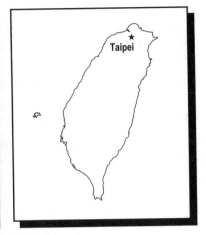

HISTORICAL OVERVIEW

- Chinese immigration to the island of Taiwan began as early as the Tang Dynasty (618-907 A.D.). Yet, major Chinese settlement did not occur until the 17th century.

- The Portuguese arrived in 1590 but did not settle there. The Dutch took control of the island in 1646 and they in turn were ousted by Chinese refugees in 1661. The Manchus ruling China at the time conquered the island in 1683 and made it a province of China.

- Following the Sino-Japanese War (1895), China ceded the island to Japan. It remained under Japanese control until 1945 when it was ceded to China.

- At this time the Nationalists were in power in China. Chiang Kai-shek's Kuomintang (KMT) forces battled Mao Zedong's Communist forces, lost and were forced to flee in 1949. They then established the Republic of China (ROC) on Taiwan. Chiang's government declared itself the legitimate government of all of China and established a policy to eventually reunite with the mainland.

- In 1954, the U.S. signed an agreement to protect Taiwan in case of an attack from mainland China, known as the People's Republic of China (PRC).

- For the next two decades Taiwan was treated as the representative of all China but in 1971 the U.N. ousted Taiwan and the PRC was admitted as the representative. In 1979, the U.S. recognized the PRC as the sole representative of China and broke off diplomatic relations with the ROC. Relations between the U.S. and Taiwan continue on an unofficial basis.

- After Chiang Kai-shek died in 1975, his son Chiang Ching-kuo replaced him as premier.

- The KMT ruled Taiwan as a one-party state under martial law until 1987. Political reforms allowed a multiparty democracy to begin emerging in 1989.

- National elections, held in 1989, elected Lee Teng-hui as president.

- National assembly elections were held in both 1991 and 1992 with the KMT winning a majority both times.

- 1993 pitted President Lee's KMT, which favored a centrist approach, against the Democratic Progressive Party (DPP), which was outspoken in support of independence for Taiwan. Neither party won a plurality in local elections. Premier Hau Pei-tsun also stepped down as premier in favor of Lien Chen. Constitutional amendments were ratified to expand presidential powers.

- Taiwan's first presidential elections were held in March 1996. The incumbent, President Lee, won with 54 percent of the vote. Lee has skillfully raised the international profile of Taiwan.

- Taiwan's economy grew six percent in 1995, slightly less than expected. The infrastructure is weak, and domestic investment is needed. Though birth rates are down, population growth remains an issue.

- Taiwan's government established a new national holiday on 23 February 1997 in order to honor the Taiwanese who died in 1947 at the hand of Chaing Kai-shek's army.

- Negotiations resumed between Taiwan and China after a three-year pause, and during the 1998 U.S.-China Summit, Taiwan was a major topic of discussion for the Chinese.

- In recent years the opposition to the ruling Nationalist Party in Taiwan has been gaining popular support. In contrast to the Nationalist Party, which continues to pay lip service to a united China, the opposition has vocally come forth for outright independence for Taiwan.

BUSINESS PRACTICES

Hours of Business

Businesses are open from about 9:00 a.m. to 5:30 p.m. although many businesspeople work longer hours. Try to set appointments in the morning or after 2:00 p.m., since business lunches usually take place between 12:30 and 2:00 p.m.

Dress

Men are expected to wear a jacket and tie to meetings, even in hot weather. Women are expected to wear suits, dresses or skirts with a blouse. All clothing should be conservative.

Introductions

A smile, with a nod of the head, is both customary and sufficient when greeting someone in Taiwan. A handshake is also very common, however, especially in business circles. Make a point to greet older people first, adding a small bow as a sign of respect.

When a guest, elderly person or someone of higher rank, station or authority enters the room, you should stand up.

First names are rarely used alone. It is more appropriate to address people by title and last name.

In Chinese names, the family name comes first. For example, Chiang Ching-kuo is "Mr. Chiang." It is common to have both an English and a Chinese first name (e.g., Michael Wang Kuo-ching). Since there are many Lis, Wangs, Chiangs and Kuos, many people use their initials placed in front of their last name, according to western customs (e.g., Mr. C.K. Chiang). Remember the initials, especially when you are transacting business with a large family firm in which there are a number of senior people with the same surname.

Common greetings are *Ni hao ma?* (How are you?) and *Ch'ing tso* (Please sit).

To beckon someone, extend your hand and make a waving motion with your fingers with your palm facing downwards.

Exchanging business cards is an important part of introductions among businesspeople. Use both hands when giving and receiving cards. As a sign of respect and sincerity, take a few moments to read both sides of each card that you receive. Do not place cards in your pants pockets.

Meetings

If you arrange appointments yourself, you should make arrangements in advance and then confirm them upon your arrival in Taiwan.

Meetings are usually short and to the point although they may involve customary courtesies (serving of tea or coffee). Accept the beverage offered and begin talking about business only after finishing your drink.

Meetings are usually short at the beginning of the negotiating process. Once a business relationship is established, however, you may be expected to sacrifice some of your personal time to see the deal to its completion. It is not unusual to have to meet in the evenings or to receive phone calls at home at late hours.

In Taiwan the firm that is negotiating a sale chooses the meeting site. If this is your firm, remember to do everything top-shelf. If the finest site and services are not employed the Taiwanese will be insulted. If you are entering into a joint venture with a Taiwanese firm, allow them to choose the meeting site. Do not be surprised if the site is far from your hotel.

Meetings are expected to be free from outside distractions. To this end, they are often scheduled in more secluded areas so that extraneous pressures will not interfere.

After the initial meeting, you will usually be asked to tour the Taiwanese firm's facilities.

Members of a negotiating team are seated hierarchically at meetings.

Negotiating

While both Mandarin Chinese and Taiwanese (a southern Fujian dialect) are spoken in Taiwan, English is also widely used by members of the business community.

Taiwan has a very active, fast-paced business community that devotes a great deal of energy to surpassing the competition and meeting deadlines on a tight schedule. The people of Taiwan view business as essential to growth and stability.

The people of Taiwan, particularly the older generation, value hard work as a virtue. This attitude dominates the business community. People often work ten hours or more per day. Businesspeople of Taiwan are also noted for practicality, simplicity and shrewdness when negotiating.

Foreign businesspeople should be thoroughly prepared, take copious notes at meetings and pay close attention to detail during negotiations since they will be fast-paced.

While negotiating, be aware that, according to the Confucian principle of maintaining harmony, the people of Taiwan are reluctant to say anything that may be construed as negative. Instead of refusing a request, a businessperson from Taiwan might suggest alternatives or say that something is inconvenient. In such cases, pressing the issue will only cause embarrassment.

Other influences of Confucianism on business culture include fostering family networks and connections, fostering small "family-size" businesses and maintaining a slow-paced development of business relationships through the cultivation of personal relationships.

Establishing a business relationship may involve a number of courtesy calls by your Taiwan colleagues. These meetings will be formal and involve polite small talk and even taking photographs to commemorate the event (even if the meeting is unproductive or seemingly banal).

Doing business with a Taiwan-based firm may be time-consuming and may require patience on the part of foreign businesspeople. After initial contact, there is a considerable period during which the business relationship will be strengthened through visits, dinners, gift-giving and small favors. While this process may seem costly, it is vital. Declining gifts or favors is understood as an insult. Also, you should be aware that accepting a gift or favor requires reciprocation at some point in the future.

It is a good idea for a foreign firm to designate one individual to represent the firm on a long-term basis since building long-term relationships between individuals of each firm is an absolute necessity.

Although composing a detailed contract is important, personal commitments may be more important than written ones in the eyes of your Taiwanese counterparts.

It is expeditious to make the initial contact with a Taiwan-based firm through a third party in your home country since business in Taiwan relies on personal contacts and trust.

Bring plenty of business cards, printed in both Chinese and English. Many members of the business community carry two sets of cards – one printed in English and one printed in Chinese – or bilingual business cards. There are many print shops in Taiwan that can fill such an order in two or three days. Try to use a print shop in Taiwan or one run by Taiwanese in your area since there are differences between the PRC and Taiwan writing systems. Some businesspeople in Taiwan consider it tactless to use a card bearing hallmarks of the PRC's writing system.

It is to your advantage to maintain a consistent position. Commitments are taken seriously and are expected to be honored. Even casual business conversations, such as at lunch, are considered part of the negotiating process.

Be sure to negotiate an accounting system that is consistent with that of your home office and domestic tax law. Taiwan is not a member of GAAP (Generally Accepted Accounting Principles).

An interpreter should be in attendance during all stages of negotiations to explain technical terms and to translate when necessary.

Entertaining

The banquet is an important part of the negotiation. Negotiators from Taiwan – particularly the men – like to entertain during the evening in Chinese restaurants. You are not expected to reciprocate. If you do reciprocate, it is most appropriate to invite your guest(s) to a western-style restaurant or to a good Chinese restaurant that knows how to prepare a traditional banquet. The best time to reciprocate is at the conclusion of your business or the evening before you leave Taiwan.

Banquets have their own rules of etiquette. For example, you will be escorted into the dining room only when the entire delegation has arrived. The head of the delegation enters first. Do not be surprised if you are greeted by applause. You will be seated according to a seating arrangement based on rank.

Karaoke (singing along to background music using special audio/ visual equipment) clubs are also popular places for business entertainment.

Dinner usually begins about 6:00 to 7:00 p.m. and can easily continue for two or more hours as your host orders several courses of Chinese food. Ordering is done by the host only.

Business is not usually discussed during meals. If it is, let your host bring up the subject first. Conversation during meals often centers on the meal itself (the ingredients and how the meal was prepared).

Bring a small gift to your business counterpart. Business-related gifts (e.g., a pen, etc.) are appropriate .

It is very unusual to be invited to a home in Taiwan for business entertainment. If you are invited to a home, remember to remove your shoes before entering the house. Bring an appropriate gift, such as a basket of fruit, tea, flowers, foreign liquor, toys for children, perfume for a wife or a memento from your home country.

Be aware that it is polite for the recipient to refuse the gift two or three times before accepting it. You must continue to offer it. It is not necessary for a foreigner to adopt this practice when offered a gift. Also, if the gift is wrapped, your host will not open it in front of you.

A ten percent service charge is usually included in a restaurant bill. It is acceptable, however, to leave an additional gratuity on the table if the service was satisfactory. Restaurant bills are not split.

The people of Taiwan usually drink tea or soft drinks. Occasionally and usually at banquets, they will drink beer, brandy or cognac. Hard alcohol is reserved for toasts.

Your Taiwan hosts may drink a toast to you and then pass you the empty glass. It will then be filled by one of the hosts. You are then expected to toast your hosts and drink the whiskey or wine. The drinking sessions can continue for many hours.

Food is placed in the center of the table. For a formal banquet, it is the host's responsibility to serve the guests. For a family-type (or home) banquet, each person is given a personal bowl of rice in addition to the food. The rice bowl is held near the mouth and chopsticks are used to eat the food. Do not begin to eat until the host urges you to start.

Eat sparingly; there are many courses. Leave a small amount of rice at the bottom of your bowl when you are finished so that your bowl will not be refilled. An empty bowl signals the desire for more rice.

Rice is eaten with nearly every meal. Soup, seafood, pork, chicken, vegetables and fruit are also commonly served. Many foods are stir-fried. Local Taiwanese dishes as well as Peking, Cantonese, Sichuan and other cuisines are available.

SOCIAL VALUES, CUSTOMS AND TIPS

Polite inquiries about health are considered appropriate. Show an appreciation for the significant economic gains that Taiwan has achieved.

Movies, music, baseball and hiking are popular pastimes. Taiwan's Little League champions consistently do well in the Little League World Series. (They were the champs in 1991.)

Loud behavior is inappropriate and considered poor taste.

Although it is an open topic among the people of Taiwan, you should avoid discussions regarding mainland China. The issue of Chinese reunification is very controversial and has great emotional importance.

When conversing with people from Taiwan, the country "Taiwan" should be referred to by its official name, "The Republic of China" (ROC) as opposed to mainland China, which is "The People's Republic of China" (PRC).

THAILAND

Population: 60,037,366 (July 1998 est.) Thai 75%, Chinese 14%, other 11%

Languages: Thai, English

Religions: Buddhist 95%, Muslim 3.8%, Christian 0.5%, Hindu 0.1%, other 0.6%

Currency: baht

HISTORICAL OVERVIEW

- Thailand's early history is linked with that of southern China. The Thai nation was founded in the 13th century, and Buddhism was introduced in the 14th century.

- After a struggle with the Burmese in the 18th century, Rama I founded the Chakri Dynasty and established Bangkok as the capital. The country was then known as Siam. As Siam, the country was ruled by a king and his court until 1932 when King Rama VII accepted a change to a constitutional monarchy. The country was renamed Thailand in 1939.

- Unlike many other countries in southeast Asia, Thailand never came under colonial rule.

- Japan occupied Thailand for a short time during World War II. After the war, Thailand increased its ties with the U.S. and helped to halt the spread of Communism during the 1960s and 1970s.

- Until the 1970s, the Thai army, having been strengthened in response to numerous threats in the 1940s and 1950s, had a virtual monopoly on political power. This gave way, however, to an informal sharing arrangement between the army and civilian politicians and officials. Much of the army leadership did not cooperate, and power shifted between civilian and military-dominated governments. No matter who has been in power, corruption has been a widespread problem.

- A number of military dictators have ruled Thailand over the last few decades. A popular revolt in 1973 overthrew Field Marshal Thanom Kittikachorn and Prapas Charusathiara, who had annulled the constitution and declared martial law two years earlier. A civilian-led government lasted only three years.

- Since 1975, Thailand has been a key destination for many Indochinese refugees.

- In 1976, the military installed General Kriangsak Chomanan as premier. General Prem Tinsulanond succeeded Kriangsak in 1980 and began a slow return to democratic principles. In 1988, Chatichai Choonhavan was elected, but his government was overthrown by a bloodless military coup in 1991, having been discredited by corruption. General Suchinda Kraprayoon became premier after the coup.

- King Rama IX, who has ruled since 1946, forced General Suchinda Kraprayoon's resignation, and popular elections returned a nonmilitary government in September 1992. From 1992 to 1995, the government was ruled by a five-party coalition, which made it difficult to proceed on legislative reform. The current government is led by Prime Minister Banharn Silpa-Archa of the Chart Thai party. Banharn was plagued by allegations of corruption, and a new prime minister, Chavalit Yongchaiyudh, took office in December 1996.

- Although the gap between the rich and the poor is large, the Thai economy is one of the fastest growing in East Asia. The government has taken on environmental problems, and infrastructure development is moving ahead. Another major issue is AIDS, as Thailand has the fastest-growing infected population in Asia.

- In early 1997, problems arose between Myanmar refugees, who have been in Thailand since the mid-1970s, and the army, which is trying to force them leave.

- Due to military conflicts in Cambodia since 1997, the refugee population has risen considerably in Thailand.

- Due to the economic problems in Southeast Asia in early 1998, Thailand was forced to borrow from the World Bank and International Monetary Fund to help decrease its mounting debts.

BUSINESS PRACTICES

Hours of Business

A workweek can be as short as 35 hours or as long as 48 hours depending on the occupation. Businesses are normally open from 8:00 a.m. to 5:00 p.m., Monday to Friday and sometimes for a half-day on Saturday. It is inappropriate to try to make appointments outside of these hours.

The best months for business travel to Thailand are November through March as most business vacations take place during April and May. Also avoid the week before and after Christmas.

Dress

For businessmen, a long-sleeved white shirt, tie, slacks and closed shoes are acceptable. A synthetic-blend suit or a light, wrinkle-resistant jacket adds status. Senior executives generally come to work in lightweight suits. The senior executive may invite the visitor to shed his jacket during a meeting.

Women's clothing should be modest. Skirts are traditional in Thailand, but slacks are acceptable. Women should not wear shorts in public and should avoid sheer dresses or miniskirts, which offend Thailand's Buddhist code of modesty.

Western clothing is very common in most areas, especially in Bangkok. Men and women frequently wear straw hats to shield themselves from the sun. Simple blouses and calf-length loose pants are common for women, as are long wraparound or tube skirts.

The color black is associated with death in Thailand and should be avoided in ordinary dress.

Introductions

The traditional and most common greeting in Thailand is called the *wai*. A person places the palms of the hands together with fingers extended at chest level and bows slightly. Women curtsy. The higher the hands are placed, the greater the respect shown, but the tips of the fingers should not be above eye level. Among adults, it is considered an insult not to return the *wai*. As with the bow in Japan, the *wai* can mean not only "Hello," but also "Thank you" and "I'm sorry." Westerners are greeted with handshakes.

Address people as "Mr.," "Mrs." or "Miss," along with the last name. Thais address each other by their first names, preceded by "Khun" (for example, "Khun Sariya") and reserve surnames for formal occasions.

The Thai given name comes first, followed by the family name.

"Khun" or "Mr.," "Mrs." or "Miss" are often replaced by organizational, professional, occupational, military or noble titles.

Many of the top people in Thailand are relatives of the royal family. A visitor should note certain abbreviations: P.O.C. means the grandchild of a king; M.C. stands for the great-grandchild of a king; and M.R. indicates the great-great-grandchild of a king.

In Thailand, smiling is a way of life. The smile says "hello," "thank you," "yes," "never mind" and "excuse me." It also covers embarrassment. More importantly, a smile forestalls and defuses conflict.

Business cards should be printed in Thai on one side and in English on the other.

Meetings

Be sure to be on time for appointments, but don't be surprised if your Thai counterparts are late.

When scheduling appointments from abroad, it is recommended that you give your Thai business counterpart at least two to three weeks notice.

Be sure to send a list of meeting objectives along with the credentials of those who will be present so that your Thai contacts have time to prepare for the meeting.

The visitor should not schedule very early or very late business appointments, especially in Bangkok. Thai managers often want the freedom to arrive at their desks without having to contend with Bangkok's rush hour traffic.

Meetings generally open with small talk. Discussing business matters without becoming personally acquainted is considered impolite.

Expect frequent interruptions in meetings (e.g., messengers carrying papers in and out, secretaries coming in to consult with their employers, etc.).

Negotiating

Eye contact is not only acceptable but is very important in establishing relationships.

Thais view speaking loudly or showing anger in public as offensive, and such actions may cause loss of respect. English is usually spoken by people in top management in most businesses. When dealing with a smaller company or one outside of Bangkok, however, you may need to hire an interpreter.

Arrange for a letter of introduction. It is best to have an acquaintance, albeit through a third party, with a potential business connection before your arrival. Some small companies, however, will accept visits without appointments.

The foreign visitor must strive to match the hierarchical status of business contacts. For example, a senior vice president – not a sales manager – should meet with the president of a Thai firm.

Thais have an expression, *Mai Pen Rai* (never mind). This characterizes their general attitude that life is to be enjoyed, and that problems and setbacks should not be taken too seriously. This influences Thai behavior in business. While Thais are by no means lazy or unproductive, they are generally happy with the status quo and will rarely engage in radical change or be seriously affected by a setback.

Business tends to be quite slow-paced in Thailand. Thai businessmen usually take a long time to reach a decision. Never show anger or impatience in business negotiations. As a result, Thais tend to think in years when making a business decision and are more concerned with quality and technology than turning a fast profit.

When Thais feel that business negotiations are becoming too intense, they may change the subject. Do not be alarmed, and return to the point at a later time.

Be aware that Thais might make extra concessions or demands that could become detrimental to your company in the long run. This is known as giving a "white elephant."

Have all contracts prepared in Thai and English.

Attempt to learn some basic Thai phrases to show your host that you appreciate the culture.

During negotiations, be aware that, because Thais try to avoid conflict, they will typically avoid saying anything negative, even in response to a request or when questioned about their understanding of an issue. In fact, there isn't a word for "no" in Thai. A Thai "yes" can indicate varying degrees of firmness. Quizzical expressions, suggestions of alternatives by the Thai associates or an indication that something is inconvenient may indicate a lack of understanding or a problem with the request. Also be aware that pressing the issue could lead to embarrassment.

When prices in small shops are not fixed, bargaining is expected, but should be done in good taste because the shop owners make very little profit.

Entertaining

Entertainment is essential to business life. Lunches, dinners and evening entertainment assist in establishing a good social relationship and are an important part of doing business in Thailand.

Let your host bring up the subject of business during a meal.

Home entertaining is rare. If you are invited to a social/business occasion at a Thai home, however, remember to remove your shoes before entering. Dinner at a Thai home will usually be served buffet-style when entertaining guests. Usually, various dishes are placed at the center of the table at dinner, and you then choose a bit of the different foods to eat with rice. Be prepared to sit on the floor to eat. Do not stretch out your feet in front of you during the meal. Women generally tuck their legs to the side and behind them. Men sit cross-legged.

Guests may offer compliments on the home or the children, but should avoid admiring any specific object excessively because the host may feel obligated to present the item as a gift.

Gifts are not necessary when visiting, but it is not uncommon for guests on extended stays to present their hosts with a gift of appreciation.

The rite of gift-giving in Thailand is quite westernized and is generally free of the formalities found elsewhere in Asia, such as Japan and Korea.

In general, Westerners should bring gifts to everyone who is a consistent contact. Gifts can be small (e.g., souvenirs, flowers, books, food baskets, calendars, pens, calculators) and should be wrapped.

Look for symbolic gifts, e.g., white elephants symbolize royalty in Thailand, as do umbrellas since nobles were once sheltered by them. Pewter elephants and nice umbrellas make fine gifts.

Thais generally use forks and spoons. Chopsticks are used in Chinese homes and restaurants. Hold the spoon in the right hand. Use the fork to push food onto the spoon, and then carry it to the rice bowl, where it can be mixed with rice. Serve yourself more rice from the bowl on the table or request an additional portion from a server. When finished, the utensils are placed together on your plate.

Rice is the staple in Thailand. It is usually served with very spicy dishes that consist of meat, vegetables, fish, eggs and fruits. Curries and pepper sauces are popular.

When dining out, foreign men may wear a nice shirt without a tie. A crisp new *batik* (a dyed print) shirt is appropriate, especially for a home visit.

In restaurants, tips are not usually necessary, but some people give a small amount (five to ten percent) to the waiter or waitress for special service.

SOCIAL VALUES, CUSTOMS AND TIPS

Thais are very reserved and usually consider criticism of others to be in poor taste. A sense of humor, laughter and a pleasant, smiling attitude are highly regarded.

Thais love talking about their cultural heritage. Thailand's King and Queen, Buddhism, iconography, Thai food and Thai classical dance are good topics of conversation. Western humor and sarcasm do not translate well across cultures and can be misunderstood.

Thais are proud of their cultural heritage and are often offended by those who see "development" as a need to westernize and change traditional religious and cultural habits.

The King and Queen are the most respected and honored persons in Thailand, and a Thai would be offended by any joke or ill reference to them. There are very strict laws governing the way in which people may refer to royalty.

A good way to start a conversation is to ask a male Thai whether he underwent *phansa*, the three-month period of monkhood that half of all Thai males undergo early in their careers. Most Thai men, especially harried officials and businessmen, carry fond memories of their *phansa* experience and enjoy reliving it through detailed conversation.

Avoid discussions of the AIDS epidemic in Thailand, drug trafficking or regional politics.

Traditionally, success was measured by a person's religious and nationalist attitudes. Today success is measured more according to wealth and education.

Thai families are very close. Several generations may live in the same household. The oldest male is customarily the patriarch of the family. Members of the family (even adults) are usually expected to abide by the advice of their elders, although this is becoming less true today.

Buddhism deeply affects the daily lives of the Thai people. Thailand is the only country on the Pacific Rim that is overwhelmingly Buddhist. Most Thai live by the Buddhist principle of following a middle path. They avoid extremes and see one's well-being as ultimately more important than material success.

Only pass food or touch objects or people with the right hand.

A person's head is considered sacred, and one should neither touch another's head nor pass an object over it.

The bottoms of your feet are considered the least sacred part of your body. Do not cross your legs when sitting, stamp your feet or use them to move or point at objects or other people. When sitting, try to ensure that the sole of your foot is not conspicuous.

Waving at or patting people on the back is unacceptable, particularly in public and especially if the person involved is not of the same gender.

Throwing objects or pointing at someone or something is offensive. To beckon someone, wave your fingers with your palm facing downwards.

Placing one's arm over the back of the chair in which another person is sitting is offensive.

There is more touching in public than in most other Asian countries. While good friends of the same sex may hold hands, however, men and women generally do not touch each other or show affection in public.

Visitors should avoid stepping on the doorsill of a building because Thai tradition says that a soul resides there.

According to religious traditions, women must never touch or offer to shake hands with a Buddhist monk.

It is customary to remove one's shoes when entering a Buddhist temple or a private home.

Bring an envelope containing 100 to 200 baht (Thai currency) when attending a religious ceremony of any kind in Thailand. The gift is for the host at the ceremony to "make merit" with the spirits.

TUNISIA

Population: 9,380,404 (July 1998 est.); Arab 98%, European 1%, Jewish and other 1%

Languages: Arabic (official), French

Religions: Muslim 98%, Christian 1%, Jewish 1%

Currency: Tunisian dinar

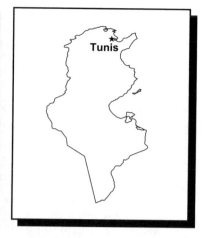

HISTORICAL OVERVIEW

- Tunisia's early history is marked by a series of foreign powers that settled in and dominated the area. During the 12th century B.C. the Phoenicians arrived and set up trading posts. In the eighth century B.C., they founded Carthage in the vicinity of present-day Tunis. Carthage grew into a kingdom of its own that spread out along the North African coast. By the sixth century B.C. the Carthaginian kingdom included most of modern Tunisia.

- After the Punic Wars with Rome, Carthage came under Roman rule in 146 B.C. The Romans were succeeded by Muslim Arabs in the seventh century A.D. The people were converted to Islam, and during the ensuing centuries Tunisia was fought over, won and lost by various Arab ruling dynasties: the Abbasids, the Aghlabids, the Shi'ite Fatimids, the Almohads and the Hafsids. Spain, too, governed Tunisia for a while.

- In 1574, the Ottoman Turks conquered Tunisia and held it until the late 19th century.

- In 1881, much to the dismay of major European powers, who had been vying for Tunisia for several decades, France took over Turkish authority in Tunis, making Tunisia a French protectorate.

- After World War I, nationalist sentiment grew with the formation of the Destour Party (Constitution Party) which called for equal Tunisian control of the country. The Destour leader was arrested soon after for presenting the government with demands for constitutional reforms. In 1934, Habib Bourguiba founded the Neo-Destour Party, which gained popular support despite government suppression. By the end of World War II, tensions between Tunisians and the French had ridden so high that 70,000 French troops were called in to occupy the country.

- France granted full independence to Tunisia in 1956. In 1957, Bourguiba became president, replaced the monarchy with the Constituent Assembly and adopted a new constitution. After being elected to a third term in 1969, Bourguiba was granted presidency for life in 1974.

- Major economic setbacks took place in the 1960s resulting from a severe drought and a failed attempt to redistribute formerly French-owned lands.

- In 1973, a failed attempt by Libya to persuade Tunisia to unite with it led to tensions between the two countries.

- Bourguiba maintained a more open society than other Islamic leaders and instituted a series of social reforms. He granted women the right to vote and to divorce, created a secular educational system and transferred Islamic court powers to the national judiciary.

- Bourguiba was less interested in economic reform, however, and throughout the late 1970s and early 1980s strikes and riots broke out in response to high unemployment and low wages.

- Agitation from Islamic fundamentalist groups grew in the 1980s and 1990s. They resorted to terrorist acts intended to jeopardize Tunisia's large tourist industry.

- In 1993, the Palestine Liberation Organization (PLO) set up its headquarters in Tunisia.

- In 1987, Zine Abidine Ben Ali became president. He was reelected in 1989 and in 1994. Ben Ali softened governmental treatment of Islamic fundamentalists. He nevertheless refused to allow any religious political parties to run in elections.

- In 1997, Tunisia signed the Association Agreement with the European Union. This agreement will permit Tunisia to become an active partner in the European Economic Community after 12 years if it has reached a set level of economic prosperity and stability.

- In 1997, Ben Ali worked together with neighboring North African countries. He revitalized the *Union Maghreb Arabe*, an organization of North African states. Relations with Libya improved through a number of joint economic proposals intended to place Tunisia in the oil exporting sector and increase foreign investment.

BUSINESS PRACTICES

Hours of Business

Offices are open from 8:30 a.m. to 12:30 p.m. and 2:00 to 6:00 p.m., Monday through Friday. Saturday hours are usually 8:30 a.m. to 1:00 p.m.

During the Muslim fasting month of Ramadan, business is limited to morning hours only.

Dress

Business attire includes a suit and tie for men and a dress or skirt for women. Women should dress modestly at all times. Shorts and miniskirts are inappropriate in all environments.

Introductions

Men typically shake hands with both men and women upon greeting. Women exchange either a kiss on both cheeks or a handshake with other women.

French titles are used when initial greetings take place. Use *Monsieur* (Mr.), *Madame* (Mrs.), and *Mademoiselle* (Miss). Professional titles are always used when appropriate.

Most educated Tunisians speak both Arabic and French, although there are some areas of Tunis where you may also find English speakers.

Present your business card first to the highest-ranking representative and then to the others in the group.

Meetings

Avoid making appointments during the weeks surrounding Christmas and Easter. The best time of day to schedule appointments is in the morning between 8:00 a.m. and 12:00 p.m. and in the afternoon from 3:00 to 6:30 p.m.

Schedule appointments prior to entering the country, and reconfirm them upon arrival.

French is the language most commonly used in business. If you need an interpreter, one may be found prior to leaving your country through the Tunisian embassy, or once in Tunisia, through hotels and tourist offices.

Have all materials translated into French.

Arrive on time to all business appointments, as Tunisians value punctuality. Not adhering to this rule could affect your business negatively.

When tea is served, refrain from continuing business discussions.

It is appropriate to give business gifts at the first meeting.

Negotiating

There are many pro-western forces in Tunisia that have pushed for economic development and expansion by establishing more trade and encouraging foreign investment. This attitude makes for a more open business environment. Tunisian businesspeople are familiar with western business practices.

Be aware that the highest-ranking person will heavily influence the decision-making process.

The use of visual aids and charts during presentations is advisable.

Tunisians often do not adhere to fixed deadlines, and business moves at a slower pace than in North America. Do not rush or show impatience.

Although it may require additional meetings and time, building a solid relationship with your business counterparts is necessary for a successful outcome. Good topics of conversation are Tunisian culture and places to visit. Demonstrating an interest in Arabic by learning a few Arabic phrases is always appreciated, and questions about Islam, as long as they remain nonjudgmental, will be well received. Feel free to engage in a discussion of politics if your Tunisian counterpart initiates the conversation, but avoid pro-Israeli or anti-Palestinian remarks.

Tunisian businessmen prefer to negotiate with men. They will however, negotiate with women if necessary. Women still play a limited role in the upper echelons of government and business.

Entertaining

Tunisians regard French culture highly. A French restaurant is generally an appropriate place for a business dinner.

A ten percent tip is appropriate for dining and most other services.

Tunisians will often invite you to their home before inviting you to a restaurant.

When dining at a Tunisian home, appropriate gifts include fruit or cakes. Gold or quality gifts from abroad are also well received. Avoid giving souvenir items as gifts.

Dinner is the main meal of the day and is often not served until 10:00 p.m.

Couscous is the national staple, and it may be prepared with chicken, lamb, beef, chick peas, vegetables, and a variety of other foods. When this dish is served, there are no individual plates and everyone eats off a central platter. Some families may serve wine with meals, while others may serve water or soft drinks.

Tunisian food tends to be very spicy and is often prepared with crushed red pepper.

Traditionally, men and women eat separately. In affluent homes, however, the two sexes may eat together.

Tunisians usually sit on the floor and use their hands while eating. Your host may set up a table for you and supply western eating utensils.

Before eating, a basin of water is passed around, and everyone takes turns washing their hands in front of one another.

It is inappropriate to place your left hand on the table.

Women traditionally stay at home. If you are unsure whether to invite a businessman's wife to dinner, it is appropriate to ask him.

Outside tourist areas, cafés are patronized only by men. Women may feel uncomfortable in such places alone.

Although Tunisia is a predominantly Islamic country, alcohol is not prohibited.

SOCIAL VALUES, CUSTOMS AND TIPS

Informal dress is appropriate when not doing business. When visiting religious monuments, however, respect should be paid to Islamic traditions by covering ankles and shoulders.

The Muslim fasting month of Ramadan is strictly observed in Tunisia. Restaurants will serve foreigners in tourist areas, however.

Tunisian men often hold hands as a gesture of friendship. This has no sexual meaning, and a Tunisian man may be offended if you pull away.

In order to motion someone to come to you, hold your hand out with the palm facing down, and wave your fingers up and down.

The head tossed back together with a clicking sound made by the tongue signifies "No."

The joining of the thumb and index finger signifies a future act of aggression towards the other person.

Both the Western Gregorian calendar and the Muslim calendar are used in Tunisia. The Muslim calendar, based on a 354-day year, is used for official documents and some holidays.

Photographing women is often not appreciated. Ask permission before taking a picture of a run-down house because its owner may be ashamed of its appearance.

TURKEY

Population: 64,566,511 (July 1998 est.); Turkish 80%, Kurdish 20%

Languages: Turkish (official), Kurdish, Arabic

Religions: Muslim 99.8%, other 0.2%

Currency: Turkish lira

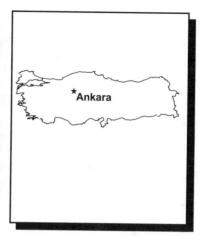

HISTORICAL OVERVIEW

- Around 1900 B.C., the Hittites conquered Anatolia, the Asian portion of Turkey, and established a great empire throughout much of the Middle East, whose center was located near Ankara. The Hittite empire met its demise in the 13th century B.C. Various people subsequently invaded Anatolia, including the Greeks in the fourth century and the Persians in the sixth.

- In the first century B.C., the Romans conquered the area, founding important cities as provincial capitals. In 330 A.D., Emperor Constantine I renamed the city of Byzantium, Constantinople and established it as the capital of the eastern half of the Empire. In 395, the Roman Empire was permanently divided into an eastern and western half, and after the fall of Rome in 476, the eastern half continued to exist as the Byzantine Empire.

- Anatolia was invaded from the East by nomadic Muslim Turkic tribes in the 11th century. Among them were the Kayi who took hold in the eastern and central parts. The Kayi Osman I founded the Ottoman dynasty, which continued to expand westward in a push to spread Islam across the Byzantine Empire.

- In 1543, the Ottoman Turks captured Constantinople. By the 16th century, they had created a vast empire that included the Balkans, large parts of Hungary, most of the Middle East and North Africa.

- The seeds of Ottoman decline were planted in the mid 16th century. By 1718, the Ottomans had lost Hungary to Austria and, in 1783, they lost the Crimea to Russia. Egypt and most of the Balkans were freed from Ottoman control in the 19th century.

- During the 19th century, the system by which religious and ethnic minorities had retained their autonomy under Ottoman rule began to crumble, leading to various ethnic conflicts.

- During World War I, Turkey allied itself with the Central Powers. Their defeat in the war resulted in Turkey's loss of its Arab provinces and part of Anatolia. An ensuing war with Greece coupled by a civil war finally led to the creation of the modern Republic of Turkey in 1923 with Kemal Atatürk as its leader.

- The nation was changed from an Islamic empire to a secular state. Among other major reforms, Atatürk replaced the Arabic alphabet with the Roman one for writing Turkish. Despite periods of unrest, Turkey slowly settled into a multiparty parliamentary government after Atatürk's death in 1938.

- After World War II, Turkey allied itself with Western Europe and the U.S. It joined NATO in 1952 and became an associate member of the European Common Market in 1963.

- Tensions between Greeks and Turks on Cyprus led to a civil war there in 1963. Greece and Turkey got involved, and when a Greek-backed coup in 1974 took over the government, Turkey occupied northern Cyprus in retaliation. Tensions between the two countries, over the island, persist.

- Economic and political problems contributed to domestic terrorism in the late 1970s that paralyzed the government. In 1980, the military restored stability and called for elections in 1983. While the military withdrew from power after the elections, the military commander Kenan Evran was elected president, and Turgut Özal of the Centrist Motherland Party was elected prime minister. Under Özal the country enjoyed peace and prosperity.

- In 1989 and again in 1991, Özal was elected president. In 1993, Demirel became president and Tansu Ciller became the first female prime minister of Turkey.

- A Turkish separatist movement that had coalesced in 1983 stepped up its activities, which included terrorists acts, in the 1990s. At the same time, the pro-Islamic Welfare Party began drawing more support from voters.

- Turkey made a strong economic comeback in the mid-1990s, but the fairly even split in the country between support for the Welfare Party and support for more centrist parties has made for weak parliamentary majorities.

- In 1997, Necmettin Erbakan became the first Welfare Party prime minister. He strengthened Turkey's ties with the Middle East, but in June 1997 Erbakan resigned because of public dissatisfaction with his Islamic policies. Mesut Yilmaz of the Motherland Party succeeded him.

- Turkey has a sizeable Kurdish minority, some of whom are agitating for independence. Turkey refuses to negotiate with them.

BUSINESS PRACTICES

Hours of Business

Businesses are generally open from 9:00 a.m. to 5:00 p.m., Monday through Friday. Some are also open for a half-day on Saturday. Business executives usually arrive at work around 10:00 a.m., leave for lunch at about noon, and return at about 2:30 p.m.

You may want to avoid scheduling business appointments during the months of June, July and August, since these are the months most Turks take vacations.

Dress

Business dress is quite conservative. Western-style clothing is most common. European fashions are especially popular among the young. Men should always wear a suit and tie for business meetings, and women should wear a business suit with high heels.

Introductions

When greeting friends or strangers, one shakes hands and says *Nasılsınız?* (How are you?) or *Merhaba* (Hello). To the first greeting, Turks generally reply *Iyiyim, teshekur ederim* (Fine, thank you very much).

Long-standing friends and acquaintances may clasp hands and kiss both cheeks regardless of gender. To show respect for an elder, a Turk may kiss the elder's hand and touch it to his/her forehead.

Address Turks with "Mr." or "Mrs.," followed by the surname. An occupational title (e.g., *Avokat* for "Lawyer") should be used alone (i.e., not followed by a first or last name). For women, *Bayam* should be added to the occupational title (e.g., *Avokat Bayam*).

Turkish titles follow the first name that is normally used only among Turks. *Hanım* is used for women and *Bay* is used for men among friends or with younger people (e.g., *Leyla Hanım* or *Ismail Bay*). The modern form *Bay* (for men) and *Bayam* (for women), followed by the last name, is used the most in business and social contacts. With older people, *Abla* is used for women and *Aabey* is used for men, after the first name. (These terms mean "sister" and "brother"). If there is a great difference in age, *Teyze* (Aunt) and *Amca* (Uncle) are also used after the first name.

If you enter a room or an office, it is appropriate to say *Günaydin* (Good morning) or *Iyi günler* (Good day).

If you enter a room in which there is a group, greet each person, beginning with the eldest, and shake hands. You need not shake hands with each person when you leave.

Show respect to elders by standing to greet them when they enter a room.

A personal introduction or a letter of introduction from a Turk can be helpful in making an initial contact with a Turkish firm. The best way to assure a personal introduction is to contact a Turkish representative to help you. This can be accomplished through your embassy in Turkey.

Meetings

Appointments are necessary for all commercial and government business. They should be made by mail well in advance. It is acceptable to write business letters in English.

Turkish businessmen appreciate and expect punctuality. Given the traffic in many Turkish cities, they are sympathetic if you arrive late. Government offices, on the other hand, adhere to strict timetables. You are also expected to be on time for dinner invitations.

Business meetings always begin with casual conversations over cups of strong Turkish coffee.

Negotiating

While Turkish, Arabic and some Kurdish are predominantly spoken in Turkey, English is becoming increasingly popular as a second or third language. In particular, it is quite widely spoken in business circles. Many businesspeople also speak French or German. Knowledge of a few words of Turkish is always appreciated.

Turkish society is hierarchical with power flowing from top to bottom. Always try to transact business with the most important person in your field since lower personnel may not have the authority to make decisions.

The senior executives in a Turkish firm will be older gentlemen. It is important always to defer to them, remain calm in their presence and be polite.

In business, as in Turkish society, group orientation is valued over personal assertion or aggressiveness.

Never offer *baksheesh* (tips) in offices. If you recognize an obligation, exchange favors rather than cash.

Turkish names are not always easy to remember or pronounce. Carry plenty of business cards and after exchanging them, try to pronounce the name correctly. Feel free to ask for assistance to make sure that you get it right. Remember to give a business card to the receptionist, to the person you are meeting and to anyone else whom you meet in the course of your appointment. All business cards to be handed out should be printed in Turkish.

If an interpreter is necessary, your Turkish representative can fill this position.

Since small talk is quite common at the onset of a meeting, it could last for a long time. Turkish businesspeople like to get to know those with whom they are conducting business.

Entertaining

Hospitality is vital in Turkish culture. Visiting, even unexpectedly, is common. If you receive an invitation to "drop in," it is always sincere. Visits in homes usually begin around 9:00 p.m. Guests will almost always be invited for something to eat or to drink. It is impolite to decline the refreshments.

In Turkey it is appropriate to include a spouse in an invitation.

In private homes and offices, if you are a man, the host may offer you some cologne to refresh yourself. You should accept, pour a little on your hands and rub it on your face and hands.

Many restaurants in the major cities cater largely to a business clientele for lunch. You can expect to be invited for a leisurely working lunch. A Turkish businessman is more likely to invite you to a restaurant for a leisurely meal than to his home.

In some restaurants, a service charge of ten to 15 percent is automatically added to the bill. If ten percent is included, leave about five percent more on the table for the waiter. If a service charge is not included, a tip of about 15 percent should be given.

Keep in mind that although service in restaurants in Turkey is usually extremely fast, you should not feel "hurried" by the speed with which you are served.

Women may go into coffeehouses only in large cities, and it is recommended that they not go in alone.

If invited to a Turkish home, bring flowers, candy or pastries as a gift. Bring wine only if you know that the family serves alcohol. Other appropriate gifts include books and records in English, which may be hard to find in Turkey. You should expect that, if the gift is wrapped, it will not be opened in front of you.

When you are a guest in a Turkish home, your hosts will work hard to make you feel comfortable. Unpleasant news or problems should not be brought up, and it is best to avoid asking too many personal questions of your host. It is appreciated if you compliment the cook and the meal.

People often smoke between courses, but it is generally a good idea to ask permission first and to conform to what others are doing. At the end of a meal, it is likely that you will be offered a toothpick. If you use a toothpick, be sure to cover your mouth while using it.

If you are visiting a family with children, bring them chocolates or small toys.

Many Turks remove their shoes when entering the home and replace them with slippers. Although hosts may tell foreign visitors that this is unnecessary, you should still insist on removing your shoes.

Breakfast (served about 7:00 a.m.) is usually light, consisting of tea, white cheese, bread, butter, eggplant or fig marmalade, honey and olives. Lunch is a moderately sized meal served about noon. Dinner is the main meal of the day and is served around 7:00 p.m. Meals can be lavish, and Turks are quite proud of their rich cuisine. Staples include lamb and rice. Seafood is popular along the coast. Yogurt is also used abundantly in Turkish cooking.

The thick, sweet coffee called *kahve* is the most popular drink and is served with almost every meal.

Dining customs vary within the provinces. There are some places where it is quite common to eat with one's fingers. In big cities and in most regions, avoid eating with your fingers. Turks use the continental style of eating, with the fork in the left hand and the knife remaining in the right.

Expect your hosts to urge you to eat a great deal.

If you are invited to a meal in a restaurant, you will not be allowed to pay for any part of the check. Similarly, if you invite colleagues to a meal, you will be expected to pay the entire bill. In Turkey, it is not considered appropriate to "split" the bill.

SOCIAL VALUES, CUSTOMS AND TIPS

After years of interaction with both Europe and Asia, the Turkish people have incorporated features from both continents into their lifestyle, customs and thinking. Do not make the mistake of calling Turkey part of the Middle East since Turks consider themselves European. Similarly, do not make the mistake of referring to Turks as Arabs, which they are not.

Turks are proud of their successful modernization efforts as well as the role they played in ancient history. Despite the westernization of Turkish culture, many of the traditional Ottoman and folkloric elements still flourish in the arts, literature, music and everyday life.

It is best to avoid references to or criticisms of past or present political problems, such as the Kurdish rebellion and terrorist violence. Turks often feel misunderstood by western nations because of the publicity these issues have received. They consider their society to be progressive, modern, ethnically diverse, tolerant and democratic.

Honesty, cleverness and a sense of humor (which is considered a sign of intelligence) are very much admired by Turks. They also value a good education, social status and secure employment.

Family is considered very important and, in fact, the primary social unit is the family. In rural areas, traditional values prevail, including the final authority of the father. An individual is loyal to and dependent upon the family.

In Turkey, "No" can be expressed by shaking the head back and forth. However, shaking the head from side to side usually means, "I don't understand." "No" is commonly expressed by lifting the head up and back and raising the eyebrows or closing the eyes momentarily.

Inquiries about someone's health, family and work are appropriate, particularly following a greeting.

Cigarette smoking is common. Avoid insulting your hosts by commenting on this habit.

Should you make a faux pas, a quick apology will be gladly accepted and will end the incident.

Try to pass objects with both hands as it is insulting to more traditional Turks if you use only your left hand.

Demonstrative gestures are used extensively by Turks during conversation to add emphasis or meaning. While gesturing is appropriate, speaking loudly is considered impolite.

Turkish women usually will not converse with a man unless they have been formally introduced.

Avoid sitting with your legs crossed and, in general, when you are seated try to make sure that the sole of your shoe is not conspicuous. It is considered impolite to direct the sole of one's foot at anyone.

It is impolite to smoke or eat on the street.

Islamic cultures generally prohibit overt signs of affection (such as hugging and kissing) in public.

Holding the hand up, palm outward, and slowly bringing the fingers into the thumb in a grasping motion is a gesture unique to Turkey signaling that something is good.

Jerking the forearm up implies strength and has no insulting connotations.

The "thumbs up" signal means "okay." The circle made with the thumb and forefinger, which means "okay" in a number of other countries, means "homosexuality" in Turkey.

Men in Turkey may be seen holding and fingering loops of beads called "worry beads." These are used for relieving tension and have no religious significance.

It is considered rude to have your arms crossed in front of you or to have your hands in your pockets while conversing with someone.

To beckon someone, you should not use your finger. Rather, you should wave your hand up and down with your palm facing downwards.

Due to the significant Muslim population, public prayer takes place five times a day in most parts of Turkey. One of the most important religious holidays is the fasting period of Ramadan. Foreigners are not expected to adhere to the rules of Ramadan, but you may want to avoid eating in public during daylight hours at this time of year.

Expect to remove your shoes when visiting a mosque. In mosques, the doorkeeper will often ask for a small contribution toward maintenance. It is considered rude to refuse.

According to Muslim traditions, women in Turkey should dress modestly, avoiding short skirts or low-cut blouses. When visiting mosques, they should cover their heads and wear long sleeves and pants or skirts. To avoid harassment, women should avoid traveling alone and should always walk purposefully, ignore catcalls and stay away from deserted streets after dark.

Before taking photographs, especially of individuals or a mosque, be sure to ask for permission.

UKRAINE

Population: 50,125,108 (July 1998 est.); Ukrainian 73%, Russian 22%, Jewish 1%, other 4%

Languages: Ukrainian, Russian, Romanian, Polish, Hungarian

Religions: Ukrainian Orthodox–Moscow Patriarchate, Ukrainian Orthodox–Kiev Patriarchate, Ukrainian Autocephalous Orthodox, Ukrainian Catholic, Protestant, Jewish

Currency: hryvina

HISTORICAL OVERVIEW

- It was not until the 20th century that Ukraine existed as an independent entity.

- Various parts of Ukraine were occupied by different peoples at various times during the first millenium Among them, the most important were several Slavic tribes that moved eastward into Ukraine during the fifth and sixth centuries. They would eventually push on north to found Russia and Moscow, and in the seventh century they founded Kiev on the Dnieper River. The state of the Kievan Rus developed around the city and it became a major trading center linking Byzantium and the Baltic. By the 11th century, the Kievan Rus had evolved into an eastern European cultural and political center.

- Thereafter, Kiev declined, however, and in the 13th century it was attacked by Mongols and nearly destroyed. Just a small part of today's Ukraine remained independent.

- Lithuania took most of the Ukraine from the Mongols in the 14th century, but the south remained under Mongol rule and the far west went to Poland. Once Poland and Lithuania were united in 1569, Ukraine was completely under Polish control.

- Ukraine was divided along religious lines between Orthodox Christians and Ukrainian Catholics.

- Religious and social differences caused friction between the Ukrainians and their Polish rulers. In addition, the Zaporozhian

Cossacks, a class of free warriors, which had settled in the region several centuries prior, agitated against the Poles and, in an uprising in 1648, very briefly set up an independent state under their leader, Bogdan Khmelnitsky.

- The Cossacks looked to Russia for assistance against Poland. This caused a war between Russia and Poland that Russia won, making Kiev and the region east of the Dnieper a Russian protectorate. Catherine the Great incorporated this area fully into the Russian Empire. The Cossacks thus lost all political power.

- In the 18th century, the Ukrainian lands west of the Dnieper also became part of the Russian Empire. Austria, however, received Galicia.

- In June 1917, during the turmoil of the Russian Revolution, the Ukraine declared its own *Rada* (council). A struggle for independence ensued but in 1921 the Bolsheviks won.

- In 1924, all of Ukraine became the Ukrainian Soviet Socialist Republic, except Galicia and Volhynia, which remained with Poland. Due to the Language Act of August 1923, Ukrainian was allowed to be the official language of the Ukraine S.S.R., but when Stalin came to power, Russian became the sole official language.

- The Ukrainians suffered greatly under Stalin's industrialization and forced collectivization programs. When peasants resisted Soviet directives, Ukrainian grain was confiscated and five million people died in the resulting famine in the early 1930s.

- While causing the Ukrainians further hardship, World War II also enlarged Ukraine's territories several times. Galicia, Vohynia, northern Bukovina, the Bessarabian area of Hotin and Izamil, Sub-Carpathian Ruthenia and the Crimea were all made part of the Ukraine.

- In 1986, a fire and a partial meltdown occurred at the nuclear power plant near Chernobyl, a town close to Kiev. The nuclear accident caused many thousands of deaths in the ensuing years.

- Ukraine declared its sovereignty in 1990 and its independence in 1991. Communist Party leader Leonid Kravchuk was elected president.

- The government was slow to reform its soviet-style economy, and a high rate of inflation and unemployment resulted.

- In 1994, the Ukrainian legislature ratified a Nuclear Nonproliferation Treaty (NPT). The Friendship Treaty over the Black Sea Fleet was negotiated between Ukraine and Russian in 1997, helping to strengthen relations between the two countries.

BUSINESS PRACTICES

Hours of Business

Businesses are generally open Monday through Friday, 9:00 a.m. to 5:00 p.m.

Dress

Both men and women wear conservative business suits with white blouses and subdued ties.

During the winter months it is important to dress very warmly and to bring a pair of skid-proof boots. It is best to wear layers. Layering is a very good way to keep warm. Layers can be removed in the warm Ukrainian buildings.

Women should avoid wearing heels, because the streets can be uneven, making it difficult to walk in heels.

Weather in the Ukraine is typically warmer then in Russia.

Introductions

Ukrainian names follow the western order, but the middle name is patronymic (father's first name with the suffix "-ovich" for a son or "ovna" for daughter). For example, if a man's name is Vladimir Schenko, son of Ivan, he would be addressed as Vladimir Ivanovich Schenko, or if a woman's name is Maria Romanenko, daughter of Yuri, she would be addressed as Maria Yurinova Romanenko.

First names are not used in Ukraine until a close relationship exists. Mr., Mrs., or a person's title is used followed by the surname. Upon forming a personal relationship, you may begin to call a Ukrainian by his or her first name and patronymic or nickname. At this time you should also allow the Ukrainian to call you by your first name.

The suffix -enko denotes a Ukrainian last name.

It is acceptable to call an older Ukrainian by his/her first name and patronymic when told to do so. Do not be surprised if they ask for your father's name and call you by your first name and patronymic.

Business cards should be presented to everyone with whom you have a business association.

Meetings

Do not make appointments with Ukrainian officials too far in advance, and do not expect them to be on time.

Ukrainians have a fluid, relaxed attitude toward time.

Allot a generous amount of time for meetings as they tend to begin late and to run longer than planned.

Negotiating

Since the dissolution of the U.S.S.R., Ukraine has had a difficult transition to a market economy. Productivity and efficiency are not regarded with the same imperative as in the West.

To expedite negotiations and to ensure that objectives are met, it is best to develop close ties with an Ukrainian official.

Ukrainians prefer to develop a good and lasting relation with their business partners. Taking the time to do so will lay a strong foundation for your venture.

All negotiations should be conducted in person.

The "hard-sell" approach is not appropriate in Ukraine.

Young managers in their 20's or 30's will be best trained in contemporary western business practices and laws. Look to establish contact with them.

Before entering into negotiations with a Ukrainian firm, be sure to review the firm's history carefully and have an expert on Ukrainian law explain the newest and most important laws.

Ask specific questions about your counterpart's firm in order to get a clear and comprehensive picture of its operations. Otherwise you may only hear about what the firm would like to accomplish or what it believes you may want to hear.

Be aware of what are called "Potemkin villages," façades of peace and prosperity created to trick naïve visitors. Such façades derive their name from villages created by Catherine the Great's aide, General Potemkin, on her traveling routes through Russia to illustrate the plentifulness of the Russian lifestyle.

A meeting will usually begin with small talk during which your Ukrainian counterparts will explain their role, as they see it, in the negotiation process. For a Ukrainian, negotiating is a win or lose situation. The western concept of "win-win" is unfamiliar to them.

Ukrainians will always say "No" before they say "Yes".

Taking a tough stance during negotiations and having emotional outbursts are considered acceptable. It is expected that you may do the same or, alternately, that you will take the role of showing unusual forbearance.

You and your team should present your position in a unified manner.

It usually takes several rounds of negotiations before a deal is finalized.

Explain the contract that has been drawn up after negotiations step-by-step so that there are no misunderstandings.

You and your team may be asked to sign a *protokol*, a summary of the day's meeting, after daily negotiations are completed. This is not a formal agreement.

When drawing up a contract, include a clause providing for third-country intervention should there be a disagreement between the Ukrainian firm and your firm at a later date. The most popular country for this task is Sweden.

Joint venture deals are very popular among Ukrainians seeking to do international business.

When a venture needs government approval and is approved, be sure to present the office with a very detailed account of the project. This will reduce bureaucratic problems.

Entertaining

The kitchen is the center of Ukrainian social life.

Most entertaining in Ukraine is done in the home, and it is an honor to receive an invitation to someone's home. When a guest is present, singing and dancing usually follow the meal, and the guest should be prepared to recite folk songs as well.

Alcohol, especially vodka, may be heavily consumed during a meal.

Foreigners are expected to drink along with their Ukrainian hosts because once a bottle of vodka is opened it must be finished, and guests are expected to help.

When going to a Ukrainian home for dinner, it is customary to bring a gift.

Dinner is usually served around 6:00 p.m.

At restaurants, strangers often share the same table if there are no free tables available. Always accept when invited to join a table.

SOCIAL VALUES, CUSTOMS AND TIPS

English is not commonly spoken in Ukraine. Russian and German are the most widely spoken second languages.

Ukrainians should not be confused with Russians. Ukrainian Orthodoxy is actually closer to Greek Orthodoxy than Russian Orthodoxy, and only a certain portion of the Ukrainian Orthodox accepts the partriarchate in Moscow. Others accept the church in Kiev as their patriarchate.

Ukrainians have a strong sense of nationalism and attachment to Europe. They expect their country to be regarded as a new nation in Europe.

Ukrainians are very reserved in public.

Friendship is a lifelong commitment. A Ukrainian will often give unwanted advice as an expression of concern for a person's well-being. Friends will go to great lengths to assist each other in times of need.

Women, though not seen as authority figures, share household responsibilities with their husbands and have always had the opportunity to do many of the same tasks as men. Women are referred to as the backbone of the nation.

In Ukraine friends and families are given highest priority.

Ukrainian folk art is especially colorful.

The Cossacks are considered heroes in Ukrainian history.

Ukrainians stand close to one another when conversing.

The "fig" – a fist with the thumb sticking up between the index and middle finger – means "nothing." It is an acceptable gesture, and the "thumbs up" sign is seen as something positive.

When in a place with public seating by row, always squeeze by in front of Ukrainians facing them. Having your back to them is impolite.

Because of its fertile soil, the Ukraine is considered the breadbasket of Europe.

UNITED ARAB EMIRATES

Population: 2,303,088 (July 1998 est.); Emiri 19%, other Arab and Iranian 23%, South Asian 50%, other expatriates (includes Westerners and East Asians) 8%

Languages: Arabic (official), Persian, English, Hindi, Urdu

Religions: Muslim 96% (Shi'a 16%), Christian, Hindu and other 4%

Currency: Emirian dirham

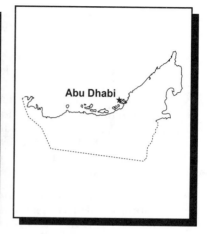

Abu Dhabi

HISTORICAL OVERVIEW

- The region now known as the United Arab Emirates (UAE) began as a group of tribal sheikdoms situated along the southern coast of the Persian Gulf and the northwestern coast of the Gulf of Oman. It shares a history with the other modern Gulf States. Tribal rivalries and warfare were common.

- In the seventh century, Islam swept through the region.

- The Portuguese arrived in the Persian Gulf in the 16th century, and a century later the British East India Company set up business in the UAE.

- The area soon became known as the "Pirate Coast" since frequent raids were conducted from it. The British first attempted to put an end to the raids with the General Treaty of 1820. A further agreement, the Perpetual Maritime Truce in 1853, in which the seven tiny sheikdoms that make up the UAE agreed to abandon piracy for good, bequeathed them with the name of the Trucial Coast or Trucial Oman.

- Trucial Oman was monitored by British India from 1873 to 1947 and thereafter by London. In 1892, the United Kingdom and Trucial Oman concluded a treaty that brought the two much closer together. In reaction to threats from other European powers, Trucial Oman ceded control of its foreign affairs to Britain. The British, in return, agreed to provide protection for the sheikdoms. The Trucial sheikdoms' internal affairs, however, remained autonomous.

- In 1960, the Trucial Council, a local body comprised of the rulers of the seven sheikdoms, was established. The Council was to encourage the adoption of common policies in administrative matters among the component states.

- In 1968, the United Kingdom announced that it would end its treaty relationships with the seven Trucial Sheikdoms as well as with neighboring Bahrain and Qatar. The nine regions attempted to form a union of Arab emirates but were unable to agree on the terms. Bahrain and Qatar declared independence, and when the treaty with Britain expired in 1971, six of the now fully independent Trucial Sheikdoms entered into a union called the United Arab Emirates. A seventh emirate, Ras al-Khaimah, joined in early 1972. While there is a federal government, each of the Emirates – Abu Dhabi, Dubai, Sharjah, Ras Al Khaimah, Fujairah, Umm Al Quwain and Ajman – retains considerable autonomy over local affairs.

- The UAE has contributed large sums of money to other Arab countries, and in 1981, it was a founder of the Gulf Cooperation Council. The Council seeks to achieve greater political and economic integration among the Gulf States.

- In the 1991 Gulf War, together with most Arab states, the UAE supported resistance to Iraqi aggression. Nevertheless, despite UN sanctions against Iraq, the UAE has been a principal destination for Iraqi oil exports. The UAE has also been involved in the Middle East peace process by way of its financial assistance to the Palestinians.

- In 1992, a conflict arose between the UAE and Iran concerning the sovereignty of Abu Musa, an island in the Persian Gulf situated between the two states. Although the issue remains unresolved, tensions were eased in the late 1990s.

- The UAE has an open economy with one of the world's highest per capita incomes. Its wealth is based on oil and gas output and it has a sizeable trade surplus. The government is encouraging increased economic privatization.

- The current leader, Sheikh Zayid, is aging and a new generation of rulers will soon take power.

BUSINESS PRACTICES

Hours of Business

Business hours are from 7:00 or 8:00 a.m. to 1:00 p.m. and 4:00 to 7:00 or 7:30 p.m., Saturday through Wednesday and 7:00 or 8:00 a.m. to 11:00 a.m. or noon on Thursday. As it is throughout the Islamic world, Friday is the day of rest in the UAE.

Government hours are 7:00 or 8:00 a.m. to 1:00 or 2:00 p.m., Saturday through Wednesday and 7:00 or 8:00 a.m. to 11:00 a.m. or noon on Thursday.

Workday hours may vary slightly from summer to winter and among the different emirates.

Banks are open from 8:00 a.m. until noon, Saturday through Thursday.

Dress

Both men and women should dress very conservatively.

Summer clothing, especially lightweight cotton, is worn most of the year. Synthetic fabrics that hold heat should be avoided. Heavier clothing (sweaters, jackets) is needed for the winter months, particularly in the evenings.

Introductions

Sabaah al-khayr yaa (Good morning), *Massa a al-khayr yaa* (Good afternoon) and *Massa a al-khayr yaa* (Good evening) are the usual greetings.

Emiri businesspeople are very friendly and greet each other with a hug or handshake.

Titles are often used. Anyone with a Ph.D will be addressed as *duktoar* (for a man) or *duktoara* (for a woman), meaning "doctor."

Meetings

English is widely used in business circles.

Send a letter to the Federal Chamber of Commerce stating the details of your business visit. You will probably not receive a reply, but this will familiarize the chamber with your company.

Business appointments must be made in advance and the visitor should be punctual even if the host is late.

Bilingual business cards are recommended.

When conducting business in Abu Dhabi, the law requires that you hire an Abu Dhabi national as a contact.

Avoid scheduling business trips during Ramadan, the Muslim holy month of fasting.

Negotiating

Maintain the same negotiator or negotiating team throughout any business transaction. Businesspeople prefer to deal with the same people throughout negotiations.

A level of respect and friendship must be reached before any negotiations can take place. Many meetings may be dedicated to social gatherings, but do not underestimate the importance of such meetings.

Start with high demands and then work your way down from there. Be patient. Bargaining is part of the process of negotiation. Do not be aggressive in your attitude or demand "Yes" or "No" answers.

Time is regarded very flexibly and deadlines are often considered the expression of approximate time.

All contracts should be translated into English and Arabic.

Be patient. Transactions may take a long time to finalize, although there are less formalities than in other Gulf States.

Decisions are made by a few principal people at the top of the company.

Entertaining

It is impolite to refuse coffee or other refreshments offered at meetings.

Keep in mind that a ten percent service charge is usually included in hotel bills.

In restaurants, if the service charge is not added, the recommended tip is roughly ten to 15 percent of the bill.

It is not necessary to tip taxi drivers.

Dining in restaurants tends to be relatively expensive.

Most of the good restaurants in Abu Dhabi are located in the hotels, where alcohol may be served to non-Muslims.

Although there are some good, independent restaurants, Dubai dining is hotel-oriented for the convenience of businesspeople.

Dubai is considered a livelier city than Abu Dhabi and it offers more nightlife. All major hotels have clubs or discos that are open until 2:00 or 3:00 a.m. They also serve alcohol.

SOCIAL VALUES, CUSTOMS AND TIPS

Arabic is the official language. Farsi and Urdu are spoken by many in the expatriate population. English is widely spoken and understood, especially in business.

Bear in mind that 75 percent of the population consists of expatriates.

Standard Arabic is generally understood everywhere. The effort of a visitor to use even a few basic words and phrases, no matter how they are pronounced, is appreciated.

The overall pace of life is slower in the UAE than Westerners may be accustomed to, but any show of impatience or a hurried attitude is considered bad manners.

Do not inquire about family members. Public mention of wives and children is regarded as an invasion of privacy.

Politics are best left undiscussed.

Avoid sitting with the soles of your feet facing anyone.

Do not shake hands, eat food or pass objects with the left hand.

Do not smoke unless the host does so.

Do not excessively admire any of your host's possessions. The host may feel obligated to give you the item as a gift.

Although tap water in Dubai is considered safe, keep in mind that both water and sewage problems do exist. Water at top hotels is treated, but elsewhere it should be filtered and boiled. Bottled mineral water is available.

Women should not go to public beaches alone and they may be excluded from local public events.

Though few Arab women drive, both men and women are permitted to drive in the UAE.

Religious dates vary according to the lunar calendar while national holidays are fixed dates on the solar calendar. These include The Birthday of the Prophet, National Day (December 2), New Year's Day (January 1), National Day (February 13), *Isra' al' Mi' Raj* (Anniversary of the Night Journey), Labor Day (May 1), Ramadan, Accession of the Ruler and Islamic New Year.

During Ramadan, Muslims refrain from eating, consuming beverages and even smoking from sunrise to sunset. Non-Muslims are expected to refrain from eating, consuming beverages or smoking in public during Ramadan, although some restaurants stay open for foreigners, and, of course, hotels serve meals.

UNITED KINGDOM

Population: 58,970,119 (July 1998 est.); English 81.5%, Scottish 9.6%, Irish 2.4%, Welsh 1.9%, Ulster 1.8%, West Indian, Indian, Pakistani and other 2.8%

Languages: English, Welsh, Scottish form of Gaelic

Religions: Christian 90% (Anglican 63%, Roman Catholic 14%, Presbyterian 4%, Methodist 3%, Baptist 1%, Orthodox 1%, other 6%), Muslim 3%, Sikh 1%, Hindu 1%, Jewish 1%, other 1%

Currency: British pound

HISTORICAL OVERVIEW

- The earliest known inhabitants of Britain were Celts. In 54 and 55 B.C., Julius Caesar invaded the island, and the province of Britannia remained part of the Roman Empire until the fifth century when the Germanic Angles, Saxons and Jutes drove out the Romans.

- Christianity made inroads into Britain during the sixth century, and by the seventh century many kingdoms had converted.

- In the eighth and ninth centuries, Vikings began raiding the coasts, prompting England and Scotland toward greater respective unification of their kingdoms. In 1066, William of Normandy conquered England and became William I, thereby establishing the French Norman ruling family. The Norman rulers created a strong central government. French mixed with Anglo-Saxon to form English.

- Ireland was conquered under Henry II (1154-89). His sons, Richard I (1189-99) and John (1199-1216), were confronted by significant challenges to their power from the clergy and noblemen. This led to the signing of the Magna Carta, in 1215, which established that the monarch was also subject to the law of the land. During the 13th century, the English developed the notion of the community of the realm, which ultimately led to the convocation of the first parliament.

- Struggles between the Houses of York and Lancaster over the throne erupted in the War of the Roses in 1455 and lasted until

1485. In the end, Henry Tudor emerged with the crown as Henry VII. His son, Henry VIII, established the Church of England and made the English monarch head of the Church.

- Under the reign of Elizabeth I (1558-1603), England entered into a period of colonial expansion and might. By defeating the Spanish Armada in 1588, England ended Spanish dominance of the high seas and emerged as a major naval power.

- With the ascent of James VI of Scotland to the English throne in 1603, the two kingdoms were joined in a personal union, and in 1707 they officially entered into the Act of Union. In 1801, Ireland joined this union to form the United Kingdom of Great Britain and Ireland (today, the United Kingdom of Great Britain and Northern Ireland).

- Monarchical rule was briefly interrupted in England, between 1649 and 1660, by the rule of Puritan Parliamentarians under Oliver Cromwell and his son.

- The House of Hanover came to the throne in 1714 when George I became king. George III, lost England's American colonies, but during his reign and under the long rule of Queen Victoria (1837-1901), Britain reached the height of its colonial power, gaining colonies in the Mediterranean, Caribbean, Africa and Asia.

- Britain was also the seat of the Industrial Revolution in the late 18th and 19th centuries, making it the most powerful economy in the world during this era. Domestically, the 19th century was a time when parliamentary power grew, under the leadership of such prime ministers as Robert Peel, Benjamin Disraeli and William Gladstone.

- Britain fought on the side of the allies in both World Wars, and it was a major player in World War II under the leadership of Winston Churchill. Meanwhile, it saw its empire decline substantially during the course of the 20th century. In 1921, a revolution in Ireland led to the creation of the dominion of the Irish Free State, which gained full independence as modern-day Ireland after World War II. Some 50 colonies of Britain, including India, gained independence after World War II as well.

- Britain was a founding member of the North Atlantic Treaty Organization (NATO) in 1949, and it joined the European Economic Community in 1973. In the 1970s, Northern Ireland's status became controversial, and Britain sent in troops.

- Britain developed into a modern welfare state during the 20th century, beginning with the Labor ministry of Ramsay MacDonald, who was elected in 1924. In 1945, the Labor Party won an overwhelming majority in Parliament on a socialist platform. It then proceeded to nationalize many industries and set up a national health system and a social insurance plan.

- The election of Conservative Party candidate Margaret Thatcher in 1979 put an end to decades of Labor rule. Under her leadership (1979-1990) and that of her successor, John Major, great economic changes were instituted in favor of private industry. In 1997, Tory rule gave way once more to the Labor Party, which won the elections with Tony Blair as candidate for prime minister.

- Blair is a new brand of Labor politician, called "New Labor," who is friendly to private enterprise, but who simultaneously endorses welfare state institutions.

- In 1998, Great Britain participated in the signing of a peace accord for Northern Ireland. Since then, however, several terrorist attacks have occurred.

BUSINESS PRACTICES

Hours of Business

Most businesses are open from 9:00 a.m. to 5:00 p.m., Monday to Friday. An increasing number of businesses, however, are offering longer hours or are staying open on weekends.

Most businesspeople take a coffee break at about 10:30 a.m. and a tea break at about 3:00 p.m.

Dress

Businessmen should wear dark suits and ties. Businesswomen should wear formal dress suits.

Introductions

When two people are introduced in the United Kingdom, it is customary for both parties to say "How do you do?" (This is a rhetorical question, however, and an answer is not expected.) It is also considered polite to add "Pleased to meet you."

Always address a person as "Mr.," "Mrs.," "Miss" or "Ms." until invited to use a first name. First names may be used after a short acquaintance, although you should take your cue from your English counterpart. Professional titles, such as "Doctor" or "Professor," may also be used, but a surgeon should be addressed as "Mister" rather than "Doctor." Knights and baronets are called "Sir" along with their first names (for example, Sir Francis Chichester becomes "Sir Francis").

Men shake hands. A man should wait for a woman to extend her hand first. Handshakes should be firm but not aggressive.

After people have already been introduced, verbal greetings without a handshake are appropriate upon subsequent meetings.

Among friends, both men and women kiss each other lightly on both cheeks.

It is advisable to have someone introduce you to the U.K. firm, but once negotiations have begun do not continue to use this person as your contact with the firm.

Meetings

Punctuality is highly respected throughout the U.K. It is therefore important to arrive at appointments on time.

Meetings may be scheduled just a few days in advance and confirmed upon arrival in the United Kingdom.

It is suggested that letters be addressed formally, beginning with "Dear Sir" or "Dear Madam" and ending with "Yours faithfully."

Negotiating

The managing director is the head of a British company followed by the deputy, the division officers, then the deputy directors and finally the managers. This is the executive hierarchy of a British firm.

In Britain, the firm's secretary will usually introduce foreign businesspeople to the British executives.

Business communication is conducted in an impersonal and detailed manner. Formal presentations should be understated, thorough and matter-of-fact.

It is wise to have a less aggressive business style with the British than one might have when dealing with U.S. firms. Emphasize short-term gains. Avoid proposing drastic changes. Allow your British counterparts time to think things over and ample opportunity to speak.

British businesspeople prefer to take their time making decisions. In order to help the process along, leave detailed data of your company and a summary of the meeting just conducted with the British executives of your partner firm.

Older executives are more respected than younger ones. Younger executives will usually defer to the older members of the British team to make decisions and to begin and conclude meetings.

During a business meeting, you are likely to be offered coffee or tea. Keep in mind that refreshments are not always served to visitors, but it is not considered impolite to decline them when they are offered.

Entertaining

Throughout the U.K., visitors are entertained both in private homes and in restaurants. If spouses are not present, it is customary practice to discuss business during the meal.

The British enjoy socializing during teatime at about 4:00 p.m. This is a snack of tea, buns (cupcakes) or biscuits (cookies). If a main meat dish is added, the meal then becomes high tea, which is considered a substitute for dinner.

In general, it is best to be conservative in both gift-giving and entertainment to avoid any suggestion that what is given is intended as a bribe. Appropriate gifts include chocolates, flowers or wine.

When invited to someone's home where you will be the only guest, a small gift (flowers or chocolates) is appropriate. It is also proper to send your host a thank-you note the next day.

At a restaurant, a waiter/waitress is summoned by raising the hand. At the end of a meal, the bill is brought on a plate, on which a gratuity of ten to 15 percent should be left.

Certain practices pertain to cutlery. Eating utensils are laid out in the order in which they will be used, starting from the outside in. Hold a fork in the left hand. Soft foods, including omelettes, casseroles and potatoes, are not cut with a knife. Instead, use a fork to separate portions.

Refrain from smoking until the end of the meal. It is also appropriate to ask permission from your host before smoking. If you smoke, you should offer a cigarette to everyone in your group before lighting up.

For a dinner at a restaurant or at someone's home, men should wear a jacket and tie, and women should wear a dress or a blouse and skirt. If an invitation indicates that the event is formal, this term could mean a variety of things. It is suggested that you take the invitation to a formal-wear shop, where they will be able to tell you what attire would be appropriate.

A dinner party usually begins at about 7:00 or 8:00 p.m. The meal starts with cocktails (gin and tonic, sherry or whiskey) and small appetizers. The first course is often a soup or a prawn cocktail. Meat or fish with potatoes and vegetables are then served, accompanied by a salad. Dinner ends with cheese and crackers, dessert, coffee and liqueurs (port, cognac or Grand Marnier). Plan on leaving a dinner party between 11:30 p.m. and midnight.

Traditional English dishes include crumpets, Cornish pastries (turnovers filled with meat and potatoes), bangers-and-mash (sausage and mashed potatoes), cock-a-leekie soup (chicken and leek soup), toad-in-the-hole (sausages baked in pastry), roast beef, Yorkshire pudding (a baked batter usually served in a muffin form), steak or kidney pie and trifle (sponge cake soaked in sherry, topped with custard, fruit and cream). A traditional cooked breakfast may include grilled or fried tomatoes, fried mushrooms or bread.

When you have finished your meal, place your knife and fork on your plate vertically side by side.

SOCIAL VALUES, CUSTOMS AND TIPS

When beginning a conversation with someone whom you have just met, it is suggested that you start with the weather as a safe topic, even if you complain about the British climate. Other good conversation topics include British history, architecture, gardening, the city you are visiting and positive aspects of the British role in world affairs (past and present).

The British are somewhat sensitive about national politics so it is best to avoid a discussion on this topic. Also avoid making negative remarks or jokes about the royal family, the British affection for their dogs, the British work ethic, money and prices, religion, Northern Ireland and England's decline as a world power.

The British are very reserved and respectful of privacy. It is wise to avoid loud or demonstrative behavior as well as personal questions. Personal space is highly respected. If someone stands too close, an English person will interpret this as being intrusive and pushy. Touching is also avoided.

Conversations are conducted in a reserved and somewhat indirect manner. Project your voice to reach only your conversation partner. Gestures are used moderately. When engaged in an argument, the British become cooler and cooler rather than openly angry.

Be aware that British humor tends to be satirical and sarcastic.

Keep in mind that the British tend to end sentences that are really statements with a question. An answer to the question is not expected. For example, a British person may say "The sun rises in the morning, doesn't it?" or "It's a beautiful day, isn't it?"

The British, especially members of the older generation, consider manners to be very important. Visitors are expected to display good manners and courteous behavior.

Be aware that the Scots, Welsh and Irish each have their own cultural identity. They should not be referred to as "English."

People in the U.K. tend to be polite and relatively nonaggressive. At a bus stop, ticket office or shop counter, take your place in line. Refrain from pushing and shoving. Older people should be treated with respect.

Usually men hold doors open for women and stand when a woman enters a room.

Staring at people, shouting or displaying affection in public is inappropriate.

If you see someone in the street whom you know and eye contact has been established, it is appropriate to say "Hello," "Good Morning," "Good Afternoon" or "Good Evening."

"God Save the Queen" is sometimes played at the end of movies or plays. It is recommended that you stand along with the rest of the audience when it is played.

UNITED STATES OF AMERICA

Population: 270,311,756 (July 1998 est.); white 83.4%, black 12.4%, Asian 3.3%, Amerindian 0.8%

Languages: English, Spanish (spoken by a sizeable minority)

Religions: Protestant 56%, Roman Catholic 28%, Jewish 2%, other 4%, none 10%

Currency: U.S. dollar

Washington, D.C.

HISTORICAL OVERVIEW

- Prior to settlement by the Europeans, the North American continent was inhabited by Native American peoples, who were either driven off their land, killed or assimilated into the culture of the Europeans with whom they came into contact.

- First to land in the present-day U.S. were the Spanish, who arrived in 1513. The French began exploring the Mississippi Valley in 1673, and the Russians appeared in Alaska in 1741. The first successful permanent settlement was made by the British at Jamestown, Virginia in 1607.

- A group of Puritans landed in Plymouth, Massachusetts from England in 1620. Most of the rest of New England was subsequently settled by Puritans. New York, New Jersey and Delaware were acquired by the English from the Dutch in 1664. The last of the 13 colonies, Georgia, was established in 1732 as a haven for convicts and debtors.

- Resistance to the British crown's increasingly exploitative economic policies culminated in the Declaration of Independence and a war in 1776. The war ended in 1783, and in 1787 the new United States of America drew up a constitution that established the basic government as it exists today.

- Westward expansion was rapid. In 1803, the United States acquired the western half of the Mississippi River basin from the French, and after the Mexican War (1846-48) the U.S. added the land of seven future states to its territory. With each new acquisition a new flood of pioneers moved westward to explore and settle the land.

- Slavery became hotly contested between the slave-owning agricultural south and the industrializing north. For 50 years compromises held the Union together, but after Abraham Lincoln of the anti-slavery Republican Party was elected president in 1860, ten southern states seceded. This provoked the Civil War (1861-65) in which the Union was victorious.

- Slavery was abolished and former slaves were made citizens. Once northern troops completely withdrew from the south in 1877, however, African-Americans found their civil rights curtailed as segregation was written into law.

- During the 19th century, the U.S. industrialized rapidly. The late 19th and early 20th centuries were also marked by great waves of immigration from Europe. The continued quest for land led many Plains Indians to be driven onto reservations.

- Its territorial and economic expansion pushed the U.S. into the international arena, and in 1917 it was dragged into World War I. Thereafter, it became a force for maintaining the balance of power in Europe.

- In 1929, a great stock market crash and the depression that followed brought an end to economic expansion. In response, the federal government became increasingly involved in providing social services and in setting economic policy under the New Deal plan of President Franklin D. Roosevelt.

- The U.S. entered World War II in 1941 and fought on the side of the Allied forces. At war's end the U.S. emerged as the strongest military and economic power in the West. As such it became heavily involved in European and Japanese post-war recovery and in a 40-year conflict with the Soviet Union, known as the Cold War. The U.S. founded the North Atlantic Treaty Organization in Western Europe in 1949 to act as a counter-force to Soviet expansion in Eastern Europe. It interfered in several conflicts around the world in order to halt what it saw as the expansion of communism. Thus it became engaged in the Korean War (1950-1953) and in the Vietnam War (1955-1973).

- In the 1960s, the U.S. experienced a civil rights movement that sought an end to racial segregation and discrimination against African-Americans throughout American society.

- The U.S. entered into a recession in the 1970s spurred on by a worldwide oil shortage. Trust in government also received a blow with the Watergate scandal and the resulting forced resignation of President Richard Nixon in 1974.

- The 1980s were marked by the economic policies of President Ronald Reagan (1980-1988), who cut taxes to the wealthy in an effort to boost the economy from the top down. Reagan also accelerated the cutting of social programs, which had begun during the Vietnam War. Instead, he put money into the U.S. military in an effort to bankrupt the Soviets in their arms race.

- After 12 years of a Republican Party administration, the U.S. electorate voted for a Democratic Party candidate, Bill Clinton, in 1992. Clinton promised to improve the lot of the average American, whose standard of living had stagnated or declined since the 1970s.

- With the collapse of the Soviet Union in 1991 the Cold War came to an end, and the United States emerged as the world's only superpower. In the same year the U.S. launched the Gulf War on Iraq. Following the war, the U.S. implemented sanctions and initiated a series of U.N. weapons inspections in Iraq, which locked the two countries in a battle of wills. In late 1998 and early 1999 the U.S. bombed Iraq again.

- President Clinton was reelected in 1996, but his second term was marred by a political scandal that erupted over an extramarital affair he had. The debate became highly partisan, and Clinton became the second president in U.S. history ever to be impeached.

BUSINESS PRACTICES

Hours of Business

Business hours are usually 9:00 a.m. to 5:00 p.m., Monday through Friday, with half an hour to an hour off for lunch. In large cities, however, people are frequently in their offices by 8:00 a.m. or earlier, and in industrial towns, especially in the north, the workday may last from 7:00 a.m. to 3:00 p.m.

Bank hours are from 9:00 a.m. to 3:00 p.m., Monday through Friday. Some banks will stay open later one day a week and/or be open on Saturday mornings.

Stores are generally open from 9 or 10:00 a.m. until 5 or 6:00 p.m., Monday through Friday, although many stores are open later several days during the week and stay open for part of the weekend as well.

Dress

A suit of a subdued, usually dark, color and a tie are always acceptable business attire for men. In the spring or summer some men may wear light-colored suits. Businesswomen typically wear a business suit or dress.

Introductions

It is helpful to have a contact person at the firm with which you wish to do business. If you do not, however, it is acceptable to call the company and inquire after a contact person.

Greetings in the U.S. are brief and involve a minimum of physical contact. A firm but quick handshake, accompanied by a smile and direct eye contact, is typical both as a greeting and as a farewell among men and women.

In social situations, women may shake hands less often than men. In business situations, however, a woman will almost always offer her hand, and it is considered rude not to accept.

The standard greeting in the U.S. is a simple "Hello" or "Hi," followed by the question, "How are you?" The expected response is, "Fine, thank you," and not a detailed description of one's state at that moment. This exchange is meant to signal acceptance of the other person across the boundaries of the many cultural heritages present in the U.S. and should not be interpreted as a sign of superficiality.

When meeting someone for the first time Americans will often say "Pleased to meet you." If meeting socially, the person may also ask "What do you do?" In the U.S. this is frequently asked as a topic of conversation.

Using a title (Mr., Mrs., Ms., Dr.) followed by the surname shows respect. It is best to use this form of address when first making contact with another person, whether in writing or in person. A woman executive is usually addressed as Ms. (pronounced "Mizz"), followed by the last name, unless she indicates a preference for another form of address.

Once acquainted, Americans will be quick to address each other by their first names, even when talking with top executives. This informality is intended as a sign of friendliness and equality. If a person is significantly older than you or holds a very high rank, use discretion in switching to a first-name basis.

Bring business cards in English, but do not expect that business cards will be automatically exchanged upon meeting. Most American businesspeople carry business cards, but usually only exchange them if there will be a need to get in touch later on. It is nevertheless a good idea for the visitor to present his/her business card early on.

If there is no one to introduce you at a meeting it is acceptable for you to introduce yourself.

Meetings

Make firm appointments as far in advance as possible. Such appointments may be made by mail, telephone or in person. Clearly state the purpose of your visit.

A U.S. business firm may look into the credentials and experience of their foreign business counterpart as well as the firm they represent. This should not be taken as a personal offense, but as a routine matter of U.S. American procedure.

Time is considered a valuable commodity in the U.S. Although it is acceptable to arrive a few minutes late for a meeting if a delay can not be avoided, it is best to be punctual. Americans expect that people will arrive for appointments on time and that all items on an agenda will be covered according to the schedule that has been set.

It is considered bad management to get behind schedule.

Business meetings usually begin with a formal agenda, outlining the tasks to be accomplished.

If you have arranged the meeting make sure to bring copies of a detailed agenda for all who are present, including topics to be discussed, names of the discussants and objectives for the meeting.

There is very little small talk preceding a business meeting. Americans prefer to begin discussion of business matters almost immediately. This is known as "getting down to business."

Presentations should be direct and to the point, including relevant facts and figures as well as visual aids.

All present are expected to participate, irrespective of rank or status.

Ideas and opinions are expressed openly and directly. Disagreements are common and are openly, sometimes loudly, aired, even when they are with the top decision maker.

Do not be surprised by the degree of informality at a business meeting. Joking and friendly banter are intended to create a relaxed and friendly atmosphere. Men may loosen their ties and take off their jackets.

Meetings are generally only interrupted if some emergency has arisen.

Negotiating

Negotiations in the U.S. are conducted in a relatively confrontational and competitive manner. The desire to win a good deal is a very strong motivating factor, overriding concerns for appearing to be conciliatory and accommodating.

U.S. Americans take a "hard-sell" approach to doing business and may therefore come across as aggressive and tough salesmen.

Positions will be clearly stated, and issues and details of a plan will be openly debated. It is considered important to present one's position with confidence.

U.S. Americans are quite direct in conveying how they feel about a particular proposal. A "No" means no and a "Yes" means yes. Do not be surprised, therefore, at displays of anger, irritation or impatience, or alternately, at displays of pleasure and excitement. U.S. Americans feel free to express such emotions openly in a business context, and they should not be taken as signs of grave disapproval or offense. (Emotions that show the individual as vulnerable, such as sadness, embarrassment or subordination are, however, assiduously avoided.)

Direct eye contact is very important. The failure to make eye contact may be interpreted as a sign of boredom, disinterest, lack of confidence or even of dishonesty.

Although deals may be hammered out aggressively, attacking someone personally, offending or embarrassing someone and making appeals to personal loyalties are always considered completely inappropriate and unprofessional.

Boasting or gloating over having achieved the upper hand is also considered rude and inappropriate.

U.S. Americans like win-win situations best, in which both sides feel that they have gained something from the deal. Compromise is therefore the key to negotiating deals in the U.S., and negotiating is approached as a series of bargaining sessions.

It is assumed that proposals presented will be negotiated on and not simply accepted as is. Thus it is best not to present your final offer in your first proposal.

Show sensitivity to the position of your counterpart, but stand your ground on matters you and your firm cannot compromise on.

Due to the incredibly fast pace of economic life in the U.S., American firms look for profitability above all in a business deal. This is known as looking "at the bottom line." In some instances, the pressure to achieve financial gain quickly will lead to an emphasis on short-term results.

Efficiency and decisiveness are key.

U.S. Americans are quite open to taking risks so long as they are convinced that the project will prove to be profitable in the near future.

Decisions are made quickly, but can also be changed quickly if it appears that things are not working out. Keep in mind that U.S. Americans like to conclude a deal with a minimum expenditure of time and effort.

It is a common business practice in the United States to get everything down on paper, from notes on conversations to a record of events at a meeting, known as "minutes," to all drafts of a proposal. This should not be taken as a sign of distrust nor should you assume that something is binding simply because there is a written record of it. Nothing is considered binding until it has been signed by both parties.

Contracts should be detailed and they should spell out all parts of a deal. A lawyer will assist in navigating through the intricate U.S. legal codes.

Entertaining

As with business meetings, punctuality is expected for social engagements, especially if a meal is being served.

In an office, accepting or rejecting offers of coffee is perfectly proper.

U.S. Americans frequently use mealtimes for business purposes. Business discussions will often take place during lunch or dinner. Business lunches, which are the most common form of business entertainment, take place from about 12:30 to 2:00 p.m. Lunch is usually a light meal. Dinner, the main meal of the day, usually begins between 7:00 and 9:00 p.m. Business luncheon meetings and dinners in restaurants generally require a suit.

Breakfast invitations (at about 7:30 a.m.) are also becoming increasingly common.

Social occasions in the U.S. take several forms. You may be invited to a restaurant for a meal or you may be invited to a home for a formal dinner, an outdoor barbecue or just a few refreshments.

An invitation to a home in the U.S. is relatively rare and should be regarded as a sign of friendship. Similarly, a U.S. American host will usually only invite a colleague to attend a club or theater after a good relationship has developed. Spouses are usually included in these invitations.

Strictly social events are usually casual. If invited to a home inquire as to the appropriate dress.

In restaurants, you may signal to the waiter/waitress that you want the check by making a writing motion in the air. A service charge is generally not included in the bill. A tip of at least 15 percent is highly recommended.

U.S. Americans generally eat with the fork in the right hand. When the knife is not being used for cutting or spreading, it is laid on the plate or the table. If the knife is being used, the fork is switched to the left hand. Bread is often used to push food onto the fork. Some foods, such as french fries, pizza and tacos, are eaten with the hands.

Napkins are usually placed on the lap, and the left hand often rests in the lap as well. It is considered rude to rest one's elbows on the table.

Table manners are informal, and speeches do not usually occur at the table. Toasting is casual and rare, but appreciated.

Drinks may be served before or during a meal. When at someone's home, dessert, coffee and other after-dinner refreshments are often served away from the table. Guests are expected to stay for a moderate period of time after the meal to visit with the host.

Business gift-giving is not common in the U.S. The U.S. has bribery laws that restrict the value of gifts that can be given. Even a modest present may therefore embarrass your American host. If a gift is given, it should be given either at arrival or after negotiations are completed. A token from your home country (a book about the country, a handicraft, a national beverage, etc.) would be most appropriate. Your host may not reciprocate immediately or at all. Many corporations expressly forbid gift-giving in business environments.

Gifts are also not expected when visiting a home, but small gifts such as wine, flowers, candies or a handicraft are appreciated. The most appropriate gesture of gratitude is to send a short, informal note to the hostess after the event.

Due to the variety of backgrounds of people in the U.S., it is difficult to name a national food. Larger cities feature restaurants with cuisine from a wide variety of cultures. Americans will readily try any type of food, and the culture easily adapts to new tastes.

There is an abundance of fast-food restaurants in the United States. The popularity of fast food reflects the often harried pace of life in the country as much as anything else.

SOCIAL VALUES, CUSTOMS AND TIPS

The U.S. is often viewed by other cultures as a relaxed and informal society. This informality reflects an underlying U.S. American belief that hierarchy, and the formality associated with it, are to be overcome. Although in practice all may not be equal in U.S. society, when asked, U.S. Americans will nevertheless cite equality as an ideal.

In businesses, strong hierarchical lines are not drawn. All members of a firm are expected to take initiative and make contributions to the development of a project.

A belief in freedom and self-determination is also at the core of the U.S. cultural outlook. Many of the earliest settlers came seeking religious freedom, and subsequent westward expansion reinforced a sense of limitless freedom. Thus, although U.S. Americans do not inherently object to rules, they are very quick to protest laws or restriction that they view as an infringement upon their personal rights.

Individual initiative and success are greatly valued in the U.S. This is especially so in the business world, where a more junior member of a company may be promoted ahead of a senior colleague if the junior member has proven himself particularly efficient and innovative.

Practicality and efficiency are viewed as essential for the accomplishment of goals. U.S. businesses constantly strive for greater efficiency, speed and practicality in methodology. "Time is money" is a well-worn U.S. American proverb.

Competition is viewed as a further necessary element of free enterprise in the U.S. There is a belief that consumers benefit by the competitive business atmosphere. In order to maintain their share of the market, companies are constantly striving to bring out new and improved products.

The design of most U.S. offices encourages peer/colleague interaction, but Americans tend to avoid close personal relationships at work.

Touching is tolerated socially, but could be construed as sexual harassment in the workplace and should be avoided at all times.

Good topics of social conversation are those that center on persons, rather than business or issues. A visitor might also relate a brief, perhaps humorous, personal experience about his/her travels to and in the U.S.

Very little that one says or does in innocence is taboo in the U.S. The country's broad mixture of peoples and cultures has precluded traditional prohibitions.

Americans are very sensitive to the health risks associated with smoking. It is considered rude to light a cigarette without first asking if anyone objects. Saying frankly that one does object is not considered rude. In many states it is illegal to smoke inside buildings.

It is common for members of the opposite sex to hold hands or show affection in public.

In the U.S., slapping someone's back is a common gesture of friendliness and good humor. Nevertheless, many dislike this gesture or consider it rude, so it is best to avoid it.

A U.S. male might be seen idly swinging his arms and slapping the fist of one hand into the palm of the other. While this gesture might be considered rude in other cultures, it is acceptable in the U.S.

U.S. Americans are very casual when sitting and often will prop their feet up on chairs or place the ankle of one leg on the knee of the other. Crossing legs at the knee is just as common as sitting with legs spread apart. Although poor posture is not considered appropriate or polite, it is quite common.

U.S. Americans stand an arm's length away from each other while conversing.

U.S. Americans respect queues or lines. To shove or push one's way into a line will often result in anger and verbal complaint.

Beckoning is done by raising the index finger and curling it in and out, or by raising the hand and curling the fingers back toward the body.

Using the hand and index finger to point at objects or to point out directions is a common gesture.

The gestures of "thumbs up" or of joining the thumb and forefinger to make a circle (which means "okay" in the U.S.) are acceptable gestures. These gestures do not have the negative connotations that they have in other cultures. Also the "V-for-victory" sign does not have the negative connotations that it has in Britain.

To wish someone good luck, cross the middle finger over the forefinger.

URUGUAY

Population: 3,284,841 (July 1998 est.); European (mainly Spanish and Italian) 88%, mestizo 8%, black 4%

Languages: Spanish, Portunol or Brazilero (Portuguese-Spanish mix on the Brazilian frontier)

Religions: Roman Catholic 66%, Protestant 2%, Jewish 2%, non-professing or other 30%

Currency: Uruguayan peso

Montevideo

HISTORICAL OVERVIEW

- The original inhabitants of the region now known as Uruguay were a group of small, native tribes collectively called the Charrúas.

- In 1516, Spanish explorers came to the area and established their first settlement. Portuguese from Brazil arrived in the area in 1680. They were driven out of Uruguay by the Spanish in 1726. The Spanish pursued colonization aggressively and the native population was almost completely wiped out.

- In 1811, in conjunction with a general uprising throughout South America, a war of independence began. Uruguay was unsuccessful in breaking from Spain despite five years of fighting under José Gervasio Artigas, the leader of the revolt. Artigas is, nevertheless, considered to be the "Father of Uruguay."

- Spanish rule ended in 1820 when the Portuguese from Brazil invaded and overtook the area. Artigas' efforts then inspired another uprising in 1825 when a group of patriots known as the "Thirty-Three Immortals" declared Uruguay an independent republic. Independence from Brazil was granted in 1828.

- A civil war (1839-1851) followed independence. From 1865 until 1870 Uruguay was at war with Paraguay, after which time a dictatorship was implemented and presidential elections were not held until 1903. José Batlle y Ordóñez won this election and served two terms. He then changed the constitution to allow himself to govern until 1929.

- In the first part of the 20th century, the government of Uruguay implemented socialism. It was the first South American government to grant women the right to vote and was among the first to legalize divorce. It was also the first South American country to recognize the rights of trade unions.

- In 1976, terrorist violence and unrest due to economic problems led the government to turn to the military and to ban all political activities in an attempt to regain control. A new president, Aparicio Méndez, was installed.

- In 1980, elections were held to decide if the military should retain control of the government. The vote went against the military, which then simply nullified the results and appointed General Gregorio Alvarez as president in 1981. Reforms during Alvarez's tenure paved the way for general elections in 1984.

- The military stepped down in 1985 and President-elect Julio Maria Sanguinetti was sworn into office. Basic human rights were restored. In 1989, Luis Alberto Lacalle Herrera was elected president and power was transferred democratically for the first time since 1971. Lacalle encouraged the privatization of state companies as a solution to Uruguayan economic problems. This policy led to high inflation in 1993-1994, and in the next election the Uruguayans reelected former President Julio Sanguinetti.

- Sanguinetti's policies focused on reducing inflation, reforming the social security system, and increasing investment in education.

- Uruguay faced a recession in 1996, but pulled out by the beginning of 1997. Continuing drops in inflation and increases in real GDP allowed trade to expand and potential markets to open up through negotiations with neighboring countries and the European Union (EU).

BUSINESS PRACTICES

Hours of Business

Businesses are usually open from 9:00 a.m. to noon and then from 2:30 to 7:00 p.m., Monday through Friday.

The best time to hold business meetings is between May and November, when people are not on vacation or celebrating holidays.

Dress

Business attire in Uruguay tends to be conservative. Men wear dark suits and ties. Women wear white blouses and dark suits or skirts. Normally, women do not wear panty hose in the summer, and men may remove their jackets or loosen their ties. Foreign businesspeople should follow the example of their Uruguayan counterparts in terms of warm-weather dressing.

Introductions

The most common way to greet others is with a warm, firm hand-shake.

Women appear to kiss each other when meeting. They are actually just brushing cheeks and "kissing the air." Men sometimes greet good friends or acquaintances with an *abrazo*, a warm hug.

Verbal greetings depend on the time of the day or the specific situation. A common casual greeting is *¡Hola!* (Hi) and a slightly more formal greeting is *¡Buen día!* (Good day).

Only close friends, family members and children address each other using first names. Professional titles, followed by the last name, should normally be used to show respect. If the person does not have a professional title, use the title *Señor* (Mr.), *Señora* (Mrs.) or *Señorita* (Miss) followed by the last name.

Most Uruguayans have two surnames, one from the father (listed first) and one from the mother. Normally, the father's name is used when addressing someone. For example, Hernan Antonio Martinez Garcia is addressed as *Señor Martinez* and María Elisa Gutierrez Herrera is addressed as *Señorita Gutierrez*. When a woman marries, she usually adds her husband's surname and goes by that surname. For example, if the two people in the above example married, the woman would be known as María Elisa Gutierrez Herrera de Martinez. She would be addressed as *Señora de Martinez* or more informally as *Señora Martinez*.

At a small social function, it is appropriate to greet and shake hands with each person individually. When leaving, also say farewell to each person individually. Group greetings and farewells are considered impolite.

Meetings

Many executives speak English. It is best to check in advance, however, to verify if there may be any obstacles to communication. Arrange for an interpreter, if necessary.

While punctuality is not always practiced by Uruguayans, it is appreciated and is expected of foreigners. The more formal a meeting is, the more important it is to be on time. Even if you are on time, however, do not be surprised if a meeting starts late.

Business meetings tend to be conducted quite formally.

Have your business cards and all presentation materials and brochures translated into Spanish.

Negotiating

When negotiating, be aware that Uruguayans have a spirit of moderation and compromise. They take a pragmatic and materialistic approach to life. At the same time, they extol humanistic and spiritual values, and subjective feelings may play a role in decision making.

While Uruguayans have a strong sense of individualism and individual responsibility, self-identity is determined by one's role in the social system or the group. Expertise is considered to be of less importance than fitting into the group.

The process of finalizing an agreement is usually slow. Many Uruguayan businesspeople are familiar with the pace of business in North America, however, and may speed up the negotiation process.

Personal relationships play a major role in business transactions.

Decisions are usually made by high-level executives.

Do not be surprised if you find highly competent Uruguayan executives working at lower levels than you would expect (e.g., a 40-year-old junior executive). This is likely the result of having been exiled, imprisoned or deemed a "political unreliability" during the 14-year military dictatorship. Avoid asking questions or initiating any discussion on this subject.

Entertaining

It is considered impolite to visit unannounced. Since Uruguayans are concerned with appearance, they prefer to have advance notice of a visit so that the house can be cleaned and refreshments can be prepared.

Business is commonly discussed during lunch, while dinner is primarily a social occasion. Since it might make your host feel uncomfortable, avoid discussing business at a dinner unless your host brings it up first.

It is common for Uruguayan businesspeople to invite their colleagues home for coffee after a dinner. While it is polite to accept, it is best not to stay late if the next day is a business day.

There are many casinos in Uruguay, and it is quite common for Uruguayan businesspeople to invite colleagues to them.

The person who extends an invitation should pay for the meal in full. If you are invited to a meal and would like to reciprocate or split the cost, it is best simply to extend an invitation yourself to your Uruguayan counterpart. It is particularly appreciated if you invite your counterpart to a good-quality French or Chinese restaurant or to a restaurant in an international hotel.

Gift-giving is not a common part of doing business in Uruguay.

If you are invited to a Uruguayan home, you are not expected to bring a gift, but bringing or sending (in advance) a small gift of flowers or chocolates is appreciated. Roses are the most appreciated type of flower.

If you are meeting business associates in a casual situation, avoid wearing jeans. Instead, wear a jacket or blazer and dress slacks. Women should not wear shorts.

To signal a waiter, simply raise your hand. Some Uruguayans make a hissing sound, but it is considered rude.

Although meal habits are changing in the cities due to fast-paced business schedules, the main meal is usually eaten at midday. Some people may even go home for lunch. In the morning a small breakfast is eaten and only a light dinner is served late in the evening (at 9:00 or 10:00 p.m.). Sometimes a snack is eaten at 5:00 p.m.

Roasts, stews and meat pies are popular dishes. Since Uruguay is a cattle producer, some of the best beef in the world is served there.

Uruguayans use the continental style of eating, with the fork held in the left hand and the knife in the right.

Hands, but not elbows, should be kept above the table at all times.

It is polite to take second helpings to show that you like the food.

It is common for people to wipe the plate clean with bread when finishing. Dinner guests remain at the table until everyone is finished eating.

To indicate that you have finished eating, place your utensils side by side on your plate. It is impolite to use a toothpick in public.

SOCIAL VALUES, CUSTOMS AND TIPS

While Italian and other languages are spoken by small minorities, Spanish is the official language and is spoken by most people.

Uruguayans are very proud of their country and they enjoy talking about its history, beautiful sights and culture. Avoid praising other countries over Uruguay.

Sports make a good topic of conversation. *Fútbol* (soccer) is the national sport and basketball, volleyball and swimming are also very popular.

Avoid asking questions about family unless you are prompted by your Uruguayan counterpart, since some family members may have been victims of the military dictatorship that ruled the country for 14 years. It is also best to avoid talking about politics and communism.

Be advised that during Uruguay's military rule, the generals took their economic policy from the "Chicago boys" – free market economic advisors trained by Milton Friedman at the University of Chicago. Many Uruguayans are resentful of this group of advisors and view themselves as having been the subjects of an economics experiment.

Hand gestures are used a great deal in conversation. Do not hide your hands or fidget with them while conversing because you could inadvertently convey unintended messages.

Most Latin Americans stand closer to each other when conversing than U.S. Americans do.

While western-style clothing is worn, clothes tend to be more conservative and very well tailored in Uruguay. Women often wear dresses. Uruguayans also favor subtle colors more so than people in other Latin American countries.

The hand gesture made by joining the tips of the thumb and index finger together to form a "zero," which means "okay" in North America, is extremely rude in Uruguay. Instead, the "thumbs up" gesture is commonly used to show approval.

Brushing the back of the hand under the chin means "I don't know." Raising one's shoulders quickly can mean "What's up?" Curling the fingers around so that they touch the thumb (usually on the right hand) indicates doubt.

Proper posture is considered important. It is rude to rest your feet on a chair, table or any other object. It is also improper to sit on anything other than a chair (i.e., a table or a ledge).

Yawning in public is usually avoided. It will be taken to mean that you are bored or not enjoying your company.

The elderly are respected and deferred to in Uruguayan society. Also, men usually allow women to enter through doorways first and give up their seats to women on public transportation.

U.S. VIRGIN ISLANDS

Population: 118,211 (July 1998 est.); black 80%, white 15%, other 5%

Languages: English (official), Spanish, Creole

Religions: Baptist 42%, Roman Catholic 34%, Episcopalian 17%, other 7%

Currency: United States dollar

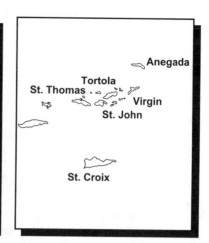

HISTORICAL OVERVIEW

- The U.S. Virgin Islands were originally inhabited by Carib and Arawak Indians. In 1493, the islands were claimed for Spain by Columbus. In 1555, Spanish forces defeated the Carib Indians and, by 1596, the indigenous populations were eradicated.

- The islands were then settled by English and Dutch planters. The islands of St. Thomas and St. John were colonized by the Danish. The first permanent settlement was established in 1672 by the Danes.

- In the mid-17th century, the islands were invaded by the French. Between two periods of French rule, the island of St. Croix was held by the Knights of Malta. France abandoned the region by 1700, leaving it under Danish influence.

- The Danish purchased the island of St. Croix from the French in 1733. The islands of St. Croix, St. Thomas and St. John, all together, then became known as the Dutch West Indies.

- In 1917, the Virgin Islands were purchased by the United States from Denmark for $25 million in a treaty ratified by both nations. This purchase was prompted by the islands' strategic importance, as they control the Anegada Passage from the Atlantic Ocean to the Caribbean Sea and the approach to the Panama Canal.

- In 1927, the Virgin Islands' inhabitants became U.S. citizens although the islands are constitutionally an "unincorporated territory."

- The islands were given a measure of self-government by the 1954 Organic Act, which created an elected 15-member senate. Since 1970, executive authority has been vested in the elected governor and lieutenant-governor. Since 1973, the U.S. Virgin Islands have been represented in the U.S. House of Representatives by one popularly elected delegate, who is permitted to vote only in committees of the House.

- Since 1954, there have been five attempts to redraft the constitution to give the U.S. Virgin Islands greater autonomy, but each draft has been rejected by a referendum. The U.S. has stated that it will welcome reform as long as it is economically feasible and does not affect U.S. national security.

- According to the most recent referendum, which took place in 1993, 80 percent of the inhabitants voted in favor of retaining the islands' existing status. The results of this referendum were invalidated by low voter turnout, however, since only 27 percent of registered voters took part (50 percent participation is required for a referendum to be valid).

- Tourism is the mainstay of the economy, which maintains a very low unemployment rate.

- Roy L. Schneider was elected governor of the Virgin Islands in November 1994, succeeding Alexander A. Farrelly, who had served since 1986.

- During the past several years, hurricanes have been a devastating force on the islands. Unemployment rose in 1996 due to hurricane damage and the subsequent decline in tourism.

- In September 1998, Hurricane George damaged areas of the islands. Fortunately, the major tourist areas were not damaged, although injuries, crop damage, and flooding were reported.

- International business and financial services are a small but growing component of the economy.

- A major economic problem in early 1997 was the more than $1 billion in internal government debts.

BUSINESS PRACTICES

Hours of Business

Business hours are Monday through Friday, 8:00 a.m. to 5:00 p.m.

Dress

Conservative dress is required for business meetings. Men should wear suits. Women should wear suits or dresses.

Introductions

In the U.S. Virgin Islands, greetings extend beyond a mere "Hello." An exchange of pleasantries is expected upon introduction.

Handshakes are appropriate between two men, between men and women but not usually between two women. When friendships develop, men will offer each other a slap on the back while women and men will usually hug one another.

Surnames with the appropriate titles are used, although, due to the large number of U.S. citizens in the Virgin Islands, there is a tendency to use first names, especially among senior managers.

Meetings

It is advisable to make appointments prior to arrival. Confirm the time and place upon arriving.

Business meetings, like most other engagements, begin later than scheduled, but mainland U.S. businesses in the Virgin Islands are usually punctual.

Visiting businesspeople should bring an ample supply of business cards printed in English. Business cards are important for establishing credibility and are used extensively.

Negotiating

Developing a personal understanding and a relationship with business associates is helpful. Islanders tend to be cautious of mainland U.S. citizens because of the transience of many businesses.

Businesspeople in the Virgin Islands practice business at a more relaxed pace than in the U.S. Business often begins with extended social conversation.

Entertaining

Business luncheons are popular. Entertaining in the home is common, however, and not much encouragement is required to have a party.

Exchanging gifts is not required or customary in business settings. If you are invited to a home, however, a gift such as fruit or flowers is appropriate for the host and his/her family.

The preferred style of eating is continental, with the fork held in the left hand and the knife in the right.

The main meal of the day is generally the midday meal.

Conversation at the table is acceptable and may include a number of topics from business to religion.

Table manners are very informal.

SOCIAL VALUES, CUSTOMS AND TIPS

Islanders tend to be gracious but somewhat conservative and undemonstrative.

While English is the prevailing language, Spanish, French, Dutch and several dialects of these languages are also spoken. English is spoken with an accent different from that common in the U.S.

Privacy is cherished.

In the Caribbean, conversations are held in close proximity, especially between friends. One's personal space is not generally held in high regard.

While it is acceptable to discuss the economy, tourism and the weather, it is advisable to avoid discussing local politics, religion and other controversial subjects, particularly race.

Casual warm-weather clothing is acceptable in most areas. It is inappropriate for women and men to dress scantily.

Civility is an important part of interaction. Courtesy and patience are expected.

VENEZUELA

Population: 22,803,409 (July 1998 est.); mestizo 67%, white 21%, black 10%, Amerindian 2%

Languages: Spanish (official), native dialects

Religions: nominally Roman Catholic 96%, Protestant 2%

Currency: bolivar

HISTORICAL OVERVIEW

- Before the arrival of Columbus in 1498, the warrior Carib and peaceable Arawak Indians lived in present-day Venezuela. The Indians fought courageously against the Spaniards but lost.

- Cumaná, Venezuela's first Spanish settlement, was founded in 1520. Caracas, the capital of Venezuela, was founded in 1567.

- In 1564, the area was set up as the Presidency of the Kingdom of Nueva Granada, which controlled present-day Colombia, Panama, Ecuador and Venezuela. The presidency was replaced in 1718 by a viceroyalty at Bogotá, which included Venezuela, thus making it independent from the Viceroyalty of Peru.

- In 1794, Antonio Nariño translated the French Declaration of the Rights of Man into Spanish and set in motion the movement toward independence from Spain.

- In 1808, when Napoleon replaced Ferdinand VII of Spain with his own brother Joseph, there were several revolts in Venezuela. After Napoleon's fall in 1815, Spain unsuccessfully attempted to reassert its authority over Nueva Granada, and in December 1819 Venezuela gained its independence. In 1821 it became a part of the Republic of Gran Colombia, led by President Simón Bolívar.

- Venezuela and Ecuador broke away from the Republic of Gran Colombia in 1830 to form independent republics.

- In the early 20th century, Venezuela was ruled by the dictator Cipriano Castro, who was deposed by Juan Vicente Gómez, whose brutal rule lasted from 1909 to 1935.

- A freely elected president, Rómulo Gallegos, came to power in 1959. He moved too fast on reform, however, and was ousted in a military coup within three months. The new dictator was Marcos Pérez Jiménez, who unleashed a short-lived reign of terror. In 1958, a combined military and civilian committee took over the government. Under the next three presidents, Venezuela enjoyed a period of great prosperity brought by oil revenue. In 1973, Carlos Andrés Péres won the presidential race in a landslide. He quickly launched ambitious agricultural and educational reforms.

- Venezuela was a founding member of OPEC, raising its oil prices by more than 400 percent, which led to windfall profits. This, in turn, caused inflation, but the government was able to channel money overseas and the high income greatly increased Venezuelan influence in South America. The new wealth remained in the hands of a few, however. An international recession and an oil glut beginning in the late 1970s hit the country hard and led the government to institute austerity measures in the mid-1980s.

- Pérez returned to the presidency in 1988. He was impeached after being found guilty of stealing $17 million in public funds. He confronted a failing economy with a national debt of more than half the annual GNP.

- By the end of 1996, the inflation rate was 103 percent. Due to an increase in oil revenues, however, inflation came down by the end of the year. Economic demands came not only from the country's poor, but also from professionals demanding higher wages.

- The prolific oil industry presently attracts foreign investors. Much of the profits, however, are placed in foreign banks or used to support Venezuelans living abroad, and therefore do not benefit the economy as much as one might expect.

- In 1998, tension increased amid the Amazon regions when indigenous groups protested government plans to tear down the rain forests to make way for mining and tourist resorts. The government also faces environmentalists who believe that such actions will prove detrimental to the future of the environment. The government views the Amazon's development as a means of creating jobs and furthering economic growth.

BUSINESS PRACTICES

Hours of Business

Most business meetings take place between 9:00 a.m. and 4:00 p.m., but some take place at night. Weekends (Saturdays and Sundays) are usually free of work responsibilities, except in the case of emergencies.

Most businesses close for two hours at midday (from 12:00 to 2:00 p.m. or from 1:00 to 3:00 p.m.) for a hot lunch.

Stores are open from 9:00 a.m. to 6:00 p.m. but close for one or two hours in the mid-afternoon.

Free time is respected and vacations are planned in advance. Popular periods for taking vacations are during the Christmas holidays (December 15 to January 7), *Carnaval*, Easter, long weekends, and the summer months (usually coinciding with school recess: July, August and September).

Dress

Lightweight, conservative business clothing is required. Men should wear a suit and tie. Women may wear a suit, a dress or a skirt and a blouse. Venezuelan women rarely wear panty hose, but visiting women should wear them when trying to make a good impression.

Introductions

Shake hands both when being introduced to someone and when departing. Venezuelan men greet each other with an *abrazo* (hug). Women greet one another with an embrace and a kiss on the cheek. Always accept or return whatever greeting is offered.

Use titles such as Doctor, Professor, Lawyer, Architect or Engineer. Titles are considered important by Venezuelans.

At large parties, introduce yourself. At smaller gatherings, expect your host to introduce you. Shake hands and say "Good-bye" to each person when you arrive or depart.

Meetings

Do not suggest that a business meeting take place after 4:00 p.m. on a Friday.

The language of business is Spanish. Although many executives speak English, do not assume this to be the case. Have business cards printed in English on one side and Spanish on the other.

Appointments are always necessary. It is preferable to give advance notice of your arrival in the country.

Venezuelans are not punctual. On the contrary, *la hora de espera* (an hour's wait) has been institutionalized. If the appointment is at 9:00 a.m., expect that the meeting will start at 10:00 a.m. This may be changing but it is recommended to allow 60 minutes leeway when scheduling business appointments or meetings.

Translate any materials and specifications you will be using in a presentation into Spanish.

If you have a morning appointment, do not make other plans for lunch. You may be invited to lunch, but may not be asked until you arrive for your appointment.

Expect to be offered a cup of coffee or tea at a meeting. It is wise to accept even if you only sip a little bit. Coffee, fresh-squeezed orange juice and *pastelitos* (stuffed bread with ham, cheese, meat or jam) are fixed items for meetings that take place early in the morning.

Negotiating

Venezuelan executives prefer to negotiate with people they know and prefer to develop a relationship before proceeding with a negotiation. In this context, a sense of familiarity means that the territory is safer and risk taking may be more acceptable. Before a relationship is established, Venezuelan executives may show great caution.

It is common that, in the course of doing business in Venezuela, negotiations with the public sector (i.e., the government) become necessary. It is recommended that you contract the services of a skillful and experienced negotiator, preferably a Venezuelan, and that you delegate this difficult task to him/her.

The negotiating team generally serves as an intermediary, with decisions finalized by higher-level executives who stay behind the scenes.

Take into consideration the disposition of Venezuelans to take advantage of what they believe to be a good deal. Venezuelans like to seize bargains before someone else finds out about them.

Deadlines are not fixed and may be changed unexpectedly. Scheduling appointments far in advance (more than two weeks) may be difficult. Leave reasonable amounts of floating time and allow for a certain degree of flexibility.

Most Venezuelans have a short-term orientation toward planning and aim at quick, profitable results. Most drastic measures are taken as a result of a crisis, rather than as a result of planning and evaluation.

Direct eye contact, open smiles, firm handshakes, and shoulder-slapping greetings are signs that negotiations are going well. Wait until documents are signed, however, before celebrating the close of a deal.

There is a great deal of background noise in most city environments, from honking horns, shouting, noisy vehicles and machinery. Search for secluded areas, away from windows or busy areas, to conduct business.

Do not try to rush a deal or show impatience if your counterpart indicates that some time and thought might be necessary. Any show of irritation is considered rude.

Be aware that you may need to exhibit additional patience when dealing with government officials or offices, due to possibly unavoidable bureaucracy.

Venezuelans do not generally spend a long time socializing before business discussions commence.

Entertaining

Business is sometimes discussed during a meal, but usually after working hours; the business lunch is not common.

Many business deals are discussed at exclusive restaurants. Heavy drinking is customary in the course of negotiation talks.

Venezuelans generally invite only close friends to their homes, but you, as a relative newcomer and business associate, will be invited out to dinner at a restaurant or club.

If invited to someone's home, never arrive empty-handed. Flowers, including an orchid (the national flower), are appreciated.

Do not admire any of your host's possessions excessively; they may insist on giving you the item and you will have to accept.

Do not present a business gift to a Venezuelan executive until a friendly relationship has been established. Gift-giving should follow business, when the setting has become relaxed and less formal. Lunch is usually a good time.

Tailor your gift to the recipient's needs and tastes. If you plan a return trip, ask your Venezuelan colleagues if there is something that they would like you to bring them from your home country. Only give gifts of good quality. Gifts for children from both men and women are greatly appreciated.

Avoid giving 13 of anything (considered bad luck), black or purple items (a reminder of Lent, a somber season), knives (which are thought to symbolize cutting off a relationship) and handkerchiefs (associated with tears).

Women should avoid giving gifts to male colleagues; it could be misconstrued as a personal overture.

Venezuelans dine late, starting at 9:00 p.m. or later. This is usually a lighter meal than lunch. It is not unusual for dinner parties to begin at 11:00 p.m.

The person who suggests the meal is the one who pays. Splitting the bill is simply not done. If a man and woman go out, however, the man always pays.

Women in Venezuela generally do not drink beer or hard liquor.

In elegant restaurants, men must wear a jacket and tie. Women may wear fancy cocktail dresses. Many theaters also require men to wear jackets and ties to evening performances.

In a home, the seats at the head and foot of the table are generally reserved for the mother and father of a family. Wait for your host to seat you.

Always wait until everyone at the table has been served before starting to eat.

Do not feel obligated to finish everything on your plate. Your host will not push you to have extra helpings.

A Venezuelan specialty is *sancocho* (a stew of vegetables, especially yuca, with meat, chicken or fish). Also try *arepas* (a white-corn bread), *cachapas* (a corn pancake wrapped around white cheese), *pabellon* (made of shredded meat, beans, rice and fried plantains) and *empanadas* (corn-flour pies filled with cheese, meat or fish). Two popular desserts are *quesillo* (a flan that is steamed) and *bien-me-sabe de coco* (a cake topped with muscatel wine and coconut cream).

SOCIAL VALUES, CUSTOMS AND TIPS

Venezuelans, especially younger people, are quite fashion conscious. The latest European fashions are popular. People generally dress rather formally in cities.

Shorts and beachwear are worn only at beaches or recreational spots, not in the cities.

People stand very close to each other when having a conversation. It is best not to back away.

Good topics of conversation include people's jobs, local sights, art and literature. Venezuelans are usually very interested in visitors' views of their country.

Avoid discussing politics and telling political jokes.

It is advisable not to ask personal questions (such as whether someone is married or has a family) until you know the person fairly well.

Venezuelan businesspeople are well educated and sophisticated.

Baseball is the major spectator sport. The playing season is from October through February. Some U.S. major leaguers play "winter ball" in Venezuela. Other popular spectator sports are boxing, horse racing and bullfighting.

Most Venezuelans are not terribly concerned with privacy and do not mind being photographed.

When entering a shop or an office, always say *Buenos dias.* Say *Adios* when leaving.

VIETNAM

Population: 76,236,259 (July 1998 est.); Vietnamese 85-90%, Chinese 3%, Muong, Thai, Meo, Khmer, Man, Cham

Languages: Vietnamese (official), Chinese, English, French, Khmer, Tribal languages

Religions: Buddhist, Taoist, Muslim, Roman Catholic, Hoa Hao, Cao Dai, Protestant, indigenous beliefs

Currency: new dong

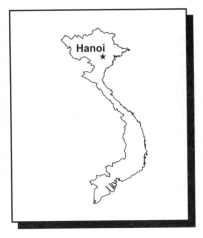

HISTORICAL OVERVIEW

- By 200 B.C., when the kingdom of Nam Viet was annexed to China, Nam Viet had a distinct ethnic group with its own languages. In 939 the northern part of what is today Vietnam was liberated from Chinese rule, and in the 13th century the Vietnamese resisted three Mongol invasions only to be conquered by the Chinese in the early 1400s. In 1428 Vietnam finally achieved permanent independence from China.

- A succession of Vietnamese dynasties followed until France established colonial rule in the late 19th century. The French ruled Vietnam first as a colony (1883-1939) and then under Japanese occupation during World War II. Toward the end of the war the French were ousted completely and a Vietnamese emperor, Boa Dai, was allowed to declare his country independent with real power still exercised by the Japanese. In the meantime, the Communist Party was growing in Vietnam under the leadership of Ho Chi Minh. When the war ended Ho wrested powers from Boa Dai in Hanoi.

- The French, however, were determined to restore colonial rule and took control of Southern Vietnam. The First Indochina War ensued, which the Vietnamese won in 1954. The country was then temporarily divided into a communist, Soviet-supported north and a southern part supported by the U.S. When North Vietnamese guerillas became active in South Vietnam, the U.S. intervened, leading to the Second Indochina War or Vietnam War (1955-1975). The war spread to Laos and Cambodia and claimed many lives.

- The war ended with the withdrawal of U.S. troops and the fall of Saigon (now Ho Chi Minh City) in April 1975. Vietnam, as well as Laos and Cambodia, came under communist rule. Thousands of people fled the area. For those who remained, difficult years of repression, poverty and isolation followed.

- Vietnam was officially reunited in 1976 as the Socialist Republic of Vietnam. The U.S. refused to recognize the new government and did not establish diplomatic ties. This kept Vietnam relatively isolated from western nations.

- In 1979, Vietnam invaded Cambodia, deposed the Pol Pot regime and installed a government loyal to Hanoi. Vietnam then fought off a Chinese invasion. In 1989, Vietnam withdrew from Cambodia.

- The Communist leaders of Vietnam introduced market reforms in 1986 and stepped up efforts to improve relations with their non-communist neighbors as well as with the West.

- The peace treaty with Cambodia led the U.S. to renew relations with Vietnam. The U.S. opened a diplomatic office in Hanoi in 1991 to coordinate the search for American MIAs and to pave the way to better relations. Economic sanctions were lifted on 4 February 1994 and full diplomatic relations were announced in July 1995.

- In July 1997 elections were held for the National Assembly and the Communists once again won a clear majority, although many who ran for seats were non-Communist Party members. A new president and a new prime minister were appointed. This was long awaited and a much-welcomed move.

- 16 March 1998 marked the 30th anniversary of the My Lai Massacre, in which U.S. troops killed innocent Vietnamese. Both Vietnamese and American military men and veterans were in attendance at the memorial service in Vietnam.

BUSINESS PRACTICES

Hours of Business

The average workweek is six days, Monday through Saturday.

The typical workday is from 7:00 a.m. to noon and from 2:00 p.m. to 4:30 p.m. The Vietnamese people have a strong work ethic and many people hold two or three jobs.

Dress

It is best to err on the formal side in attire. The north, which is cooler, tends to be more formal. Men should wear suits, and women should cover their shoulders and knees. Designer labels should not be visible on clothing.

Everyday attire for both men and women is generally slacks worn with a casual cotton or knit blouse or sport shirt.

Shorts are not worn in public except at the beach.

Introductions

Introductions are usually facilitated by a third party. It is best not to directly approach someone whom you want to meet. Rather, it is appropriate to find someone to introduce you.

Vietnamese people generally shake hands when greeting and saying good-bye. The use of both hands shows respect for the individual. Bowing the head slightly while shaking hands also indicates respect.

Women usually bow their heads slightly instead of shaking hands.

The Vietnamese address each other by their given names, but add a title signifying their relationship to the other person. The younger of two colleagues might combine the given name with the title of *Ahn* (older brother).

Xin chao (seen-chow) is a basic greeting. Because Vietnamese is a tonal language, this phrase could have several different meanings depending on how it is pronounced.

In formal meetings, people may exchange business cards while greeting each other.

Vietnamese names begin with the family name and are then followed by the given name.

Meetings

An initial business meeting may begin with light conversation over tea or coffee and fruit or sweets.

Punctuality is generally appreciated.

Important meetings should be scheduled in the morning as the afternoon is usually reserved for managing and supervising operations.

Before arriving, confirm your meeting in Vietnam via fax. When you land, reconfirm your meeting schedule by phone.

Mail or fax a detailed document outlining the matters to be discussed, along with a hierarchical list of the team members who will be visiting. Include their titles (use Mr., Mrs. and Miss – never Ms.), their roles on the team and photographs, if possible. Identify the team leader by putting his or her name at the top and by including more information about him or her than any of the others. This information will help the Vietnamese prepare their own materials.

Negotiating

Personal contacts are crucial and the establishment of trust and friendship precedes doing business. Discuss business only when your host is ready.

If using a translator, focus your eyes and attention on the person with whom you are meeting, not the translator.

Start with the basics when discussing business in Vietnam. Do not assume that your counterpart will fill in any missing information.

Attempting to learn a few words of Vietnamese demonstrates interest in Vietnam and will please your Vietnamese counterparts.

Always have your own interpreter present. This will help negotiations go more smoothly.

Displays of emotion are not considered appropriate to a business setting. Remember that the Vietnamese display great patience and little emotion in public.

Make sure that you understand every item in your contract.

Due to bureaucracy, red tape is very common in Vietnam, and it is often used to break down negotiations or cause delays. Tell your counterparts that if business can not be concluded in the time allotted, then the negotiations will not continue after the initial meetings.

Showing anger or frustration is not advised, even as a tactic. Courtesy is important and one should not cause someone to "lose face" in front of his/her peers.

Entertaining

Gifts are not required, but are appreciated. Flowers, incense or tea may be appropriate gifts for the host. A small gift for the children of the host or his/her elderly parents is appreciated.

Business dinners will usually not occur until a partnership has developed.

It is important to make formal, courteous toasts before a meal. Once the party is underway, alcohol usually flows freely and things can get rowdy. Men are expected to participate for a couple of drinks, while women can easily refuse drinking if they prefer.

Rice is the staple of Vietnam. Vietnamese people use chopsticks and rice bowls at most meals. The rice bowl is held in the hand; it is considered lazy to eat from a rice bowl that is on the table. Food is placed on dishes in the center of the table and each person helps himself or herself. The host might serve guests, but usually simply invites them to help themselves.

Nuoc mam (a fermented fish sauce) is the main seasoning used to flavor dishes. Special foods are also dipped in the sauce.

The most common beverages served are hot tea, coffee and beer. Often beverages are not served until the meal is finished.

Tips are not expected in restaurants.

The Vietnamese have a keen sense of humor and will often order or serve exotic dishes, such as snake blood, to a foreign guest, whose reaction rarely fails to entertain.

When eating in someone's home, the oldest man usually sits near the door. You will, most probably, be shown where to sit.

It is polite to rest one's chopsticks on top of, rather than in, one's bowl. Leaving rice in one's bowl is considered wasteful.

The Vietnamese are relatively noisy eaters.

SOCIAL VALUES, CUSTOMS AND TIPS

It is inappropriate to visit a home without being invited. The Vietnamese have a great sense of hospitality and feel embarrassed if they cannot show their guest full respect with proper preparation.

Use both hands to pass an object to another person.

Do not touch the head of a young child as it is considered a sensitive spiritual area.

It is considered rude to summon someone with the index finger. Instead, wave all four fingers with the palm facing down.

While men and women generally do not show affection in public, members of the same sex often hold hands when walking together in public.

Most Vietnamese families have an altar for ancestor worship. Fruit and/or flowers are placed there twice in each lunar month. Incense is burned and prayers are made to ancestors for support in overcoming misfortune and for achieving good luck and good health.

The Vietnamese enjoy team sports such as volleyball and soccer. In urban areas, it is common to see people out early in the morning for various exercises such as jogging, tai chi, yoga or group calisthenics.

ZIMBABWE

Population: 11,044,147 (July 1998 est.); African 98% (Shona 71%, Ndebele 16%, other 11%), white 1%, mixed and Asian 1%

Languages: English (official), Shona, Sindebele (the language of the Ndebele, sometimes called Ndebele), numerous minor tribal dialects

Religions: syncretic (part Christian part indigenous beliefs) 50%, Christian 25%, indigenous beliefs 24%, Muslim and other 1%

Currency: Zimbabwean dollar

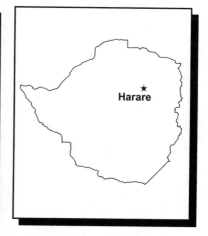

HISTORICAL OVERVIEW

- Bantu migration into the area comprising present-day Zimbabwe began perhaps as early as the fourth century A.D. The Zimbabwe ruins, the only remnants of pre-European architecture found in sub-Saharan Africa, are dated to some time between the sixth and 13th centuries A.D. The buildings were constructed by the Mashona or Shona peoples.

- In the early 19th century, the area was visited by a second wave of migration of Bantu-speakers fleeing a Zulu chief. Among them were the Ndebele, who dominated over the Shona. At the same time, British and Afrikaner traders, prospectors, hunters and missionaries were spreading out into the area.

- The British commissioned the British South Africa Company in 1889. Led by Cecil Rhodes, the company founded the town of Salisbury in what was then known as Mashonaland.

- The settlement of Rhodesia (the name given by white settlers to the area) was slow, because it was believed that diamonds and gold were to be found only to the south in present-day South Africa. In 1923, the white government of Southern Rhodesia was granted independence from Britain and became an autonomous commonwealth. White control was further strengthened by the passage of the Land Apportionment Act of 1931, which gave one-half of the best land to the 150,000 whites in the country and relegated the three million blacks to the other half.

- By the end of World War II, the city of Salisbury had become a cosmopolitan center that attracted a large number of white Europeans.

- In 1953, Rhodesia joined a federation with Northern Rhodesia (present-day Zambia) and Malawi. The Africans, who had been restricted to poorer lands, rose in protest during the ten years of the federation. In the early 1960s, nationalist movements in Malawi and Northern Rhodesia resulted in independence from Britain. Southern Rhodesia, however, returned to colonial status.

- In 1965, the white Rhodesian government, under Ian Smith, unilaterally declared independence from Britain, bringing on U.N. and U.K. sanctions.

- The Zimbabwe African People's Union (ZAPU) and the Zimbabwe African National Union (ZANU) were two black guerrilla organizations established in Zambia and Mozambique, from where they staged attacks on Rhodesia. A third group within Rhodesia, the United African National Council, led by Bishop Abel Muzorewa, was less radical and more interested in developing a relationship between blacks and whites for the future.

- The sporadic warfare that went on over the next ten years claimed many lives and left almost one million homeless.

- In a 1979 referendum, white voters approved a new constitution that granted majority rule. Bishop Muzorewa's party won the elections in that year. The rebel groups, however, would not accept the new government and renewed warfare erupted. In 1980, the ZANU gained a majority of parliamentary seats. They installed Marxist Robert Mugabe as prime minister. The country, which had recently been renamed, was officially recognized as an independent nation on 18 April 1980.

- The calm was short-lived as ZANU forces went to war against the ZAPU. White-owned newspapers were taken over by the government, and whites began leaving the country in great numbers. This, plus drought conditions, did much damage to the economy.

- Throughout the 1980s and 1990s, Mugabe's government engaged in the systematic persecution of members and supporters of ZAPU. Mugabe also moved quickly to redress discrimination against blacks. In the early 1990s, he began to redistribute land to poor blacks by seizing white holdings.

- AIDS and government corruption have been two major problems confronting Zimbabwe in the 1990s.

- Mugabe was reelected in 1996 but renewed protests broke out because of dissatisfaction with his regime. Although the government redistributed land to appease protesters, hunger riots broke out in January 1998. As a result, prices rose and military troops were deployed.

BUSINESS PRACTICES

Hours of Business

In cities, businesses, government offices and shops are open Monday through Friday from 8:00 or 8:30 a.m. to 5:00 or 5:30 p.m. Banks close at 2:00 p.m. most days and at noon on Wednesdays.

It is best to avoid business trips during June. Many businesses close during this month.

Dress

When conducting business, men should wear suits and ties, and women should wear modest suits or dresses.

Introductions

A handshake is common when greeting. "Good morning, how are you?" and "Hello" are the usual greetings and are understood by all language groups.

Three-part handshakes are often used. First, the two people shake hands in a standard fashion. Then the fingers are bent and linked, with the up-pointing thumbs touching. Finally, another standard handshake is given.

Common Shona (a native language) greetings include *Manguanani* (Good morning), *Masikati* (Good day) and *Maneru* (Good evening).

Greetings among friends may include lengthy inquiries about one's family. A person claps hands when asking how things are. Traditionally, passing a stranger without a word is considered bad manners. In cities, however, it is now acceptable to do so.

Zimbabweans do not commonly address each other by title, except in urban areas where people often follow English customs.

Meetings

Punctuality is expected in most business-related circumstances.

Socializing over tea is common after business meetings. You should build this into your schedule of appointments.

Negotiating

Locate contacts through the chief public relations officer at the Zimbabwe Chamber of Commerce, the Ministry of Industry and Commerce or the Confederation of Zimbabwe Industries.

Take time to build relationships with your Zimbabwean colleagues. Socializing is an important part of the negotiating process.

Be patient with bureaucratic procedures. Government officials should be dealt with pragmatically, as they have the potential to become a formidable obstacle to your business goals if they are treated poorly.

Decision-making is done by consensus. Therefore, the negotiation process may take a long time. Build solid relationships with Zimbabweans on all levels because they all may influence the final outcome.

Entertaining

Patience and politeness are important assets in relationships with Zimbabweans.

When guests are entertained, the host usually serves each plate, and it is polite to leave a little food behind to show that one is not greedy.

Guests are expected to arrive on time.

Tea is popular with meals as well as in the office.

In rural areas, unannounced visits are common, and schedules are flexible.

A person asks permission of others to leave the table when finished eating.

In cities, people tend to follow a more western diet, including meat and potatoes or rice.

People eat breakfast before beginning work, a light lunch during the day and the main meal after work.

Guests wait for an invitation from the host before being seated. In villages, people may seat themselves without waiting for an invitation.

Sadza, a stiff porridge made from maize (cornmeal) is the staple of most Zimbabweans and is served at nearly every meal. Various local vegetables are served as a garnish, and meat is eaten when it is available.

While many people use utensils, in rural areas it is also common to eat with the fingers.

In a private home, water or beer is often served in a communal cup.

SOCIAL VALUES, CUSTOMS AND TIPS

Zimbabweans are generally friendly, cheerful, optimistic and courteous. While open and enthusiastic among friends, they are more cautious and reserved with strangers.

In urban areas, private cars are relatively common and are often used for taxi service (although this practice is illegal). People rely heavily on the rail system when traveling from one city to another.

English is the official language in Zimbabwe and is spoken by most educated people. In rural areas, people speak in their native language.

Many people speak more than one language and mix parts of other native languages together while conversing.

Due to years of colonial rule, Zimbabweans are sensitive to racism and to discrimination.

The concept of a nursing home is highly offensive. The elderly are considered a family treasure, and there is always room for them in one's home. Children are expected to obey without question.

Urban families often have electricity and running water. Some rural families, however, continue to live a more traditional life in thatched-roof homes without modern conveniences.

Sports are very important to Zimbabweans. Among the most popular are soccer, cricket, polo, bowling, field hockey, squash, golf and horse racing. People also enjoy watching television and going to the movies.

Dressing neatly in clean clothes is very important. Zimbabweans wear western-style clothing, as traditional African dress is reserved for special occasions.

Direct eye contact during conversation is considered rude, principally in rural areas, because it connotes a lack of respect.

A person may clap hands as a gesture of gratitude or politeness. Women and girls, especially in rural areas, often curtsy as a gesture of politeness.

It is rude to decline a gift.

For minor things, such as a store clerk giving you change, you can show thanks by receiving with the right hand while touching the left hand to the right elbow. Spoken thanks are uncommon, and if you use them often you will be considered odd.

Regardless of how people eat, they first wash their hands. Rural families may eat from a communal dish, depending on the food served.

Traditionally, one gives and accepts items with both hands.

The national holidays in Zimbabwe include New Year's Day, Easter (Good Friday and Easter Monday), Independence Day (18th April), Workers Day (1st May) and Christmas.

REGIONAL MAPS

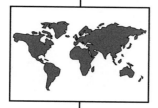

EUROPE

AFRICA

SOUTHWESTERN ASIA

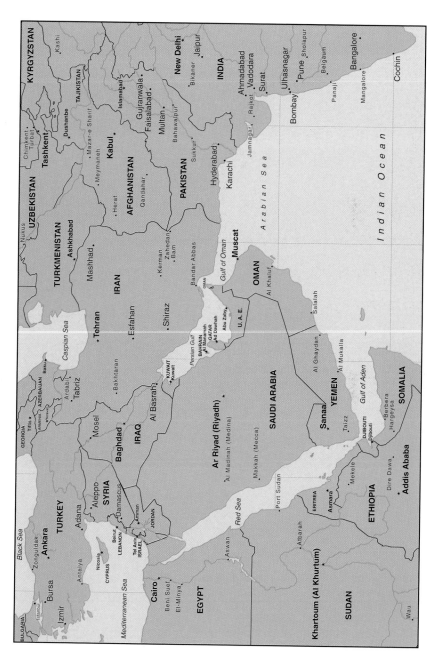

CENTRAL ASIA

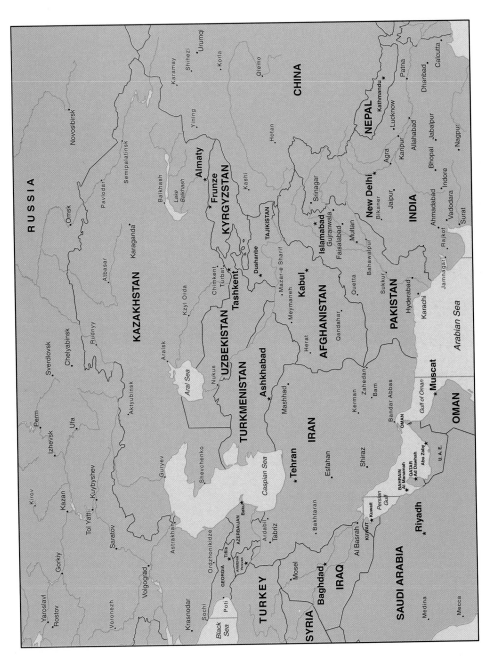

SOUTHERN ASIA

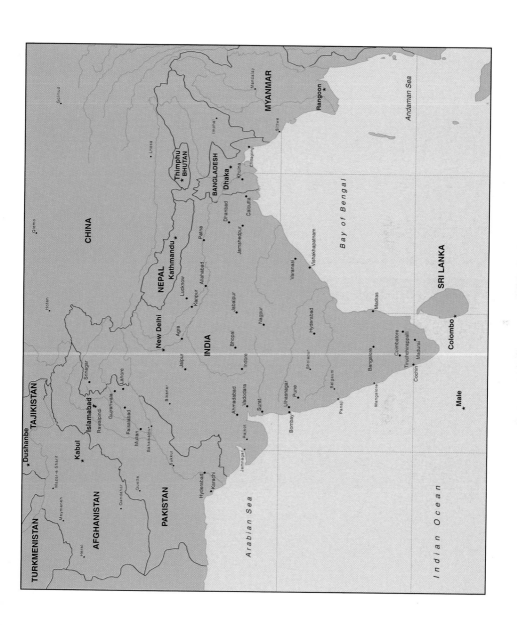

EASTERN ASIA

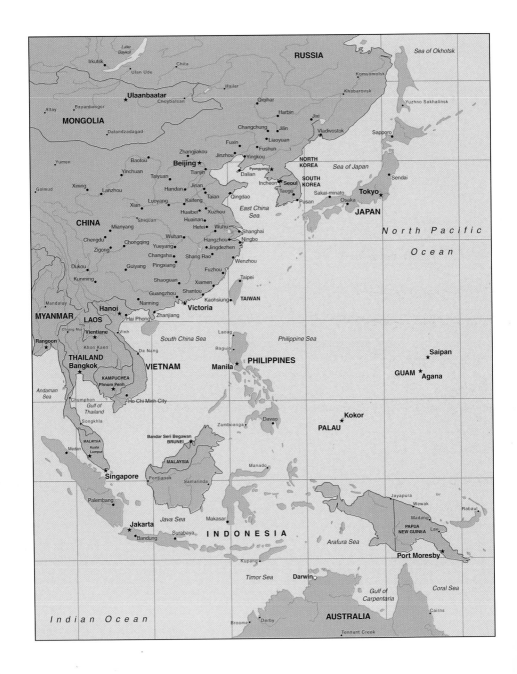

NORTH AMERICA

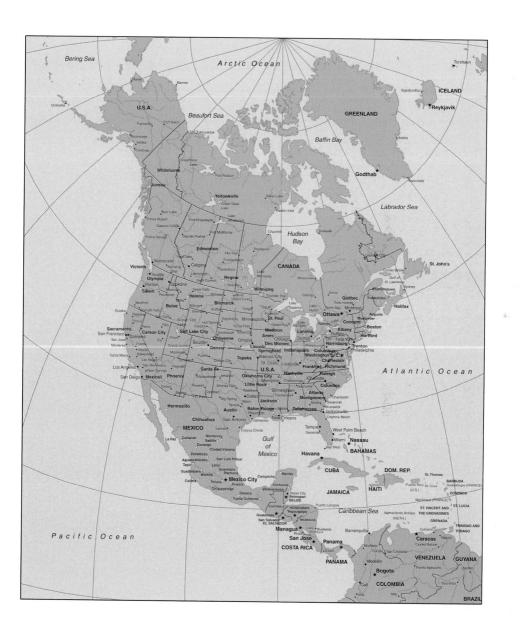

SOUTH AMERICA

Caribbean Sea

NICARAGUA
Managua
Bluefields
San Jose
COSTA RICA
Panama
PANAMA
Kingstown
Castries
St. George's
Barranquilla
Valencia
Caracas
Cucuta
VENEZUELA
Medellin
Bogota
Puerto Ayacucho
Georgetown
Paramaribo
GUYANA
SURINAME
FRENCH GUIANA
Cayenne
COLOMBIA
Boa Vista
Camopi
Pasto
Mitu
Serro Do Navio
Quito
ECUADOR
Baquerizo Moreno
Guayaquil
Cuenca
Iquitos
Tefe
Macapa
Manaus
Santarem
Belem
Sao Luis
Fortaleza
Talara
PERU
Orellana
Jacareacanga
Sao Goncalo
Teresina
Imperatriz
Chiclayo
Trujillo
Tarauaca
Porto Velho
Cachimbo
Recife
Huaraz
Rio Branco
Maceio
Huanuco
Cerro De Pasco
BRAZIL
Gurupi
Alvorada
Barreiras
Aracaju
Huancayo
Ayacucho
Lima
Ica
Cuzco
BOLIVIA
La Paz
Cuiaba
Brasilia
Salvador
Canavieiras
Puno
Santa Cruz
Goiania
Arica
Sucre
Belo Horizonte
Iquique
Tarija
Campo Grande
Boa Vista
Vitoria
Antofagasta
PARAGUAY
Asuncion
Campinas
Rio De Janeiro
Sao Paulo
Curitiba
Salta
San Miguel De Tucuman
CHILE
Florianopolis
Resistencia
Porto Alegre
Cordoba
Tacuarembo
Valparaiso
Santiago
Rosario
URUGUAY
Durazno
Buenos Aires
Montevideo
Concepcion
ARGENTINA
Neuquen
Bahia Blanca
Mar Del Plata
Valdivia
San Carlos de Bariloche
Puerto Montt
Rawson
Comodoro Rivadavia
Puerto Santa Cruz
Rio Gallegos
FALKLAND ISLANDS
Port Stanley
Ushuaia
SOUTH GEORGIA ISLAND

612

ADDITIONAL INFORMATION FOR INTERNATIONAL BUSINESS

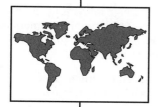

This section of the Resource Book leaves you with some helpful information when conducting business internationally. This information allows you to become familiar with the background and key provisions of the Foreign Corrupt Practices Acts (FCPA). It also offers some sound practical advice on the use of agents and intermediaries if you should require such services. General gift-giving guidelines provide a handy reference when doing business with other cultures. We offer suggestions for working with interpreters, language insights for native English speakers and international business card exchange.

FOREIGN CORRUPT PRACTICES ACT (FCPA)

> **Note:** This section contains background information on the
> Foreign Corrupt Practices Act (FCPA). It does not provide
> legal advice. Specific legal interpretations of the FCPA
> should be attained from legal counsel.

Introduction

- U.S. firms seeking to do business in foreign markets must be
  familiar with the FCPA. In general, the FCPA prohibits American
  companies from making corrupt payments to foreign officials for
  the purpose of obtaining or keeping business.

- The Department of Justice is the chief enforcement agency, with
  a coordinate role played by the Securities and Exchange Commission (SEC).

Background

Post Watergate Environment
- Moral fiber of nation thought to be in jeopardy.

Mid 1970s – SEC Investigation
- U.S. companies using corporate funds to influence foreign
  officials in order to obtain or retain business overseas.

  - Some practices were legal under local law, others were not

  - Customary "grease" payments e.g., clearing a ship for off-
    loading

  - Bribes to government officials to influence official policy

  - Political contributions – some legal under local law, others
    not

- Use of special funds ("slush funds"), sales agents, foreign subsidiaries.

  - Extortion by foreign officials

  - U.S. initiatives

- Over 400 U.S. companies disclosed substantial bribery activities,
  admitting to making illegal payments in excess of $300 million to
  foreign government officials. 117 of the companies were on the
  Fortune 500 list.

- Revelations rocked governments of Japan and Netherlands.

May 12, 1976 – SEC Report
- Report on questionable and illegal corporate payments and practices submitted to Senate Committee on Banking, Housing and Urban Affairs. Recommended legislation to ensure accountability for disclosure of future payments of these kinds.

- 94th Congress (1976) approved legislation for a direct ban on overseas bribes.

- December 19, 1977 Foreign Corrupt Practices Act became law.

1988 – Omnibus Trade and Competitive Act
- Amendments made to remove ambiguities, facilitate prosecutions and increase penalties upon conviction.

Foreign Policy
- Questionable payment practices of private multinational corporations had created risks for U.S. political relations with important foreign countries, at times and places outside the control of United States governmental authorities.

  - Complications arose with governments of Japan, Italy, Korea and the Netherlands

Economics
- Was argued that bribery introduces inefficient, non-market distortions into sales considerations, raising the cost of transactions to the consumer.

Ethics
- Senate report stated, "…bribery is simply unethical. It is counter to the moral expectations and values of the American public, and it erodes public confidence in the integrity of the free market system."

- Congress enacted the FCPA to bring a halt to bribery of foreign officials and restore public confidence in the character of the American business system.

Provisions

Major provisions
- Anti-Bribery

- Record-Keeping and Internal Control

Anti-Bribery

- Anti-Bribery provisions apply to certain issuers of registered securities, issuers required to file periodic SEC reports, and those referred to as "domestic concerns."

- It is a crime for a bribe to be made to:

  - A foreign official

  - A foreign political party

  - Party officials

  - Candidates for political office

    for the purpose of obtaining or retaining business, or directing business to another person.

- It is a crime if the bribe is paid directly to a third-party agent, consultant or intermediary with the purpose of being passed on – in whole or in part – to a foreign official, foreign political party, party official or candidate for political office.

- It is also a crime to make a payment to any person, while knowing the payment will be offered or promised , directly or indirectly, to any foreign official, foreign political party, party official or candidate for purposes of obtaining or retaining business.

Note: A "bribe" is defined broadly. The definition is such that it makes it a crime for any public corporation, or any officer, director, employee, agent or stockholder acting on behalf of the company, to make use of the mails or any means or instrumentality of interstate commerce corruptly in furtherance of an offer, payment, promise to pay, or authorization of the payment of any money, or offer, gift, promise to give, or authorization of the giving of anything of value to foreign officials, political parties, party officials or candidates.

Elements of An Offense

- There are five elements which must be met, under basic prohibition, to constitute a violation of the Act:

  1. Who— The FCPA applies to any individual firm, officer, director, employee, or agent of the firm and any stockholder acting on behalf of the firm.

  2. Corrupt intent— The person making or authorizing the payment must have a corrupt intent, and the payment must be intended to persuade the recipient to misuse his/her

official position in order wrongfully to direct business to the payor.

3. Payment— The FCPA prohibits paying, offering and promising to pay money or anything of value.

4. Recipient— The prohibition extends exclusively to corrupt payments to a foreign official, a foreign political party, or any candidate for foreign political office.

5. Business Purpose Test— The FCPA prohibits payments made in order to assist the firm in obtaining, or retaining business for or with, or directing business to, any person.

- Penalties are severe:

  -- Companies which violate the Act can be fined up to 2,000,000.

  - Individuals may be fined up to $100,000 and imprisoned for up to 5 years.

Note: Any willful violation by a corporate employee or agent is punishable as a felony, irrespective of the firms adjudicated guilt or lack thereof.

  - Individual fines cannot be paid by the company.

Note: There is no threshold amount to trigger the statute. Any payment qualifies, if it is made with a corrupt purpose.

- Payments for routine governmental action by a foreign official, political party or party official are allowed. Such payments are known as "facilitating," "expediting" or "grease" payments. The Act specifies what type of action is considered routine:

  - Dispensing permits, licenses and other official documents needed to qualify to do business in a foreign country.

  - Processing visas, work orders and other governmental papers.

  - Providing police protection, mail service and scheduling inspections related to contract performance or transporting goods in a foreign country.

  - Providing utilities (phone, power and water), loading and unloading cargo and protecting perishables from deterioration.

> **Note:** Any decision made or encouraged by a foreign official with respect to whether or on what terms new businesses will be awarded, or business continued with a particular party, is definitely not routine governmental action.

Record Keeping and Internal Control

- Every SEC-reporting company must make and keep books, records and accounts that accurately and fairly reflect both the transactions and resulting dispositions of the company's assets.

- Quantitative and qualitative aspects of transactions must be recorded.

- The parent company is responsible for the books and records of subsidiaries.

- Every SEC reporting company must devise and maintain a system of internal accounting controls that meets four objectives:

  1. All transactions will be executed in accordance with management directives (i.e., the schedule of authorizations).

  2. The method of recording transactions will facilitate the preparation of financial statements according to generally accepted accounting principles (GAAP).

  3. Access to corporate assets will be safeguarded by management.

  4. Recorded and existing assets will be compared at reasonable intervals and discrepancies resolved.

> **Note:** Only the anti-bribery provisions of the Act specify that violations are punishable as crimes; however, failure to observe the accounting requirements may also lead to criminal prosecutions.

Also note that falsification of financial records subjects you to criminal exposure. The willful violation of any rule or regulation under the Exchange Act of 1934 is a felony punishable by five years in prison and/or a fine of $10,000.

Some Open Issues/Problem Areas

- When does a facilitating payment become a bribe?

  Guideline: If the action you're paying for is routine and has no bearing on the obtaining or retaining of business, you're okay.

- Who – or who isn't – a foreign government official?

  Guideline: Don't assume! Find out!

- How successfully can it be determined when a corporation should have "reason to know" that funds are being used in a prohibited fashion, especially when intervening parties such as agents or dealers may be involved?

  Guideline: It's your responsibility to know. Ignorance is no defense.

- Is extortion a legitimate defense when it has been used to extract payment from a company?

  Guideline: If you give in to extortion, then you may have more problems than you bargained for.

Ethical Decision-Making Questions

Regarding the Foreign Corrupt Practices Act

- Does the questionable situation involve making payments to a foreign official, foreign political party, official of a foreign political party, candidate for foreign political office or any third party who will forward the payment(s), in part or in whole, to any of the above categories of individuals?

- Does the situation in question involve giving anything of value (payments, offers, promises to pay, gifts, etc.) for the purpose of obtaining or retaining business or directing business to another person?

- If a situation involves making payments, would the payments be for routine governmental action (as defined in the Act) or for "facilitating" the decision-making process with respect to the awarding or retaining of business?

- Do you record both quantitative and qualitative aspects of transactions?

- Does your company – and the foreign subsidiaries of your company – use a system of internal accounting controls that fulfills the guidelines set forth in the FCPA?

- Do the records of your company – and the foreign subsidiaries of your company – accurately reflect both the transactions and resulting disposition of assets?

Regarding Corporate Codes of Conduct

- Does the situation involve compromising the standards of conduct as outlined by your company?

- Does the dilemma involve using corporate funds or resources for the support of political parties or candidates?

- Does the situation in question involve accepting gifts of other than nominal value, loans, personal favors, services, special privileges or unusual hospitality?

- Would the activity in question create a conflict of interest?

- Would providing the gift or entertainment in question to a customer create unfair obligation on the part of the customer?

- Would it give the perception that favorable treatment was sought?

- If the dilemma under scrutiny involves a third-party consultant, representative or agent, is the third-party individual acting in any manner that is inconsistent with company policies?

Guidance from the Government

- The Dept. of Justice is establishing a revised FCPA Opinion Procedure by which any party will be able to request a statement of the Justice Department's present enforcement intentions under the anti-bribery provisions of the FCPA regarding any proposed business conduct.

USING AGENTS AND INTERMEDIARIES

The following suggestions should guide you if you require the services of a business agent or intermediary while conducting business abroad.

- Ask your prospective agent, intermediary, consultant – even your prospective legal counsel or banker – for references; you are entitled to know if they have done this kind of work before and, if so, for whom.

- Get an estimate of the charges involved for each discrete aspect of the work to be done and make sure you receive an itemized bill.

- If you are considering engaging a business representative to act as a commission agent, be sure of the following:

  - Be certain the agreement with the agent is made on the basis of a written contract; unwritten understandings, on the basis of which an enterprising representative will undertake discussions on your behalf, are an invitation to real trouble.

  - Review the agent's list of clients or at least obtain a written assurance that it does not include any of your competitors.

  - Your agent is presumably selling an ability to help you succeed, so try to fix compensation on the basis of success achieved – if possible, solely on the basis of a commission for sales actually made, or a project successfully undertaken. If a monthly retainer must be paid, try to keep it low, and as an advance against any future commissions payable.

  - Every agent has expenses, and you will very likely be expected to cover money advanced for what your agent does for your company alone (e.g., travel and telecommunication expenses). Control these expenses by setting a ceiling on what expenses the agent can incur without first obtaining your approval.

  - Most agents want exclusivity; that is, they want to be your sole representative for a fixed period of time. If you are willing to agree to an exclusive arrangement, be certain it does not foreclose your company from seeking to make its own contacts in the given country.

  - Provide terms for cancelling your agent's services with or without cause, at your sole discretion.

  - Require activity reports, if not progress reports, to be sure that your agent keeps your project moving forward.

GIFT-GIVING

General Guidelines

Whether gifts are business or social, an understanding of cultural differences is the key to selecting a successful gift and avoiding embarrassment. Appreciation of cultural differences will also expand your ability to be effective in dealing with foreign businesspeople, both here and abroad, and help you avoid common gift-giving mistakes.

Each country has its own seasons and symbols for giving. Be careful to study the specific country and/or culture you will be doing business in so that you can tailor your gift-giving for maximum effect. Some factors that must be taken into account include such influences as:

- the local and national economy

- social customs

- religious customs and holidays

- political concerns

While gift-giving may appear to be as complex a task as learning a foreign language, certain general characteristics apply everywhere. The following list of questions will help businesspeople from American companies in deciding an appropriate gift for international gift-giving.

- Is the gift within the guidelines prescribed by your company's Code of Business Conduct?

- Is the gift made in the United States?

  In a study conducted by Dr. Kathleen Kelley Reardon (Dept. of Communication Sciences, University of Connecticut) on international gift-giving practices, investigators found that 95 percent of the executives surveyed felt that it was somewhat or very important that an international business gift be distinctly American. Famous brand names usually get a warm reception. Gifts that reflect some part of America or distinctly American culture (i.e., pictures of the Old West, American magazines, maple syrup, cowboy hats, U.S. coins, etc.) are also appreciated.

- Does the gift have conversational value?

  In the research study mentioned above, 84 percent of those surveyed said that it was somewhat or very important that a business gift have conversational value (i.e., that the gift be unique or unavailable in the recipient's country).

- Is the gift practical or useful?

- Does the gift have an internationally respected designer name?

  With a name like Gucci, Tiffany, Hermès, etc. on the label, the thought is often as significant as the content. Designer-made products are universally appreciated.

- Could your gift be considered an invasion of the recipient's private life? (i.e., a gift for your counterpart's wife or husband could be seen as an inappropriate intrusion of their private lives.)

- Is your gift appropriate to the status of the person who receives it?

- Does your gift show good taste and thoughtfulness for the intended recipient?

While following the above guidelines won't answer all of your questions, they do help serve as an overall framework for international gift-giving.

Cultural Differences and Perceptions

What American businesspeople consider a bribe is considered good will and custom in many other countries. For example, consider the following scenario told by guide and translator Niu Ching-Lu to writer Bart Jackson:

"The Japanese will come to negotiate a $10 million deal with a Chinese firm. The corporate principal will personally present each Chinese committee member with a color television. Through the day the deal gets rougher, looks like it will fall through. The Japanese call for a lunch break. They return with a motorbike for each member of the committee. The deal goes through. The Americans, for the same deal, send a lawyer. He brings out just one matching pen and pencil – I have seen this – and gives it to the head committee man. The deal dies."

This scenario typifies cultural – and legal – differences between American businesspeople and their foreign colleagues. Whereas many Americans flatly refuse to receive or give any gift at all, most people in other cultures enjoy and expect gifts. Furthermore, they see gift-giving as an important part in establishing long-term good will. For them, gift-giving is not a means to personal profit, but rather is a polite ritual that serves as a platform for mutual, profitable, enduring business.

Western interest is dependent upon business; non-Western, in forming bonds so that business can begin. Westerners seek to discharge obligations; non-Westerners, to create them. Americans focus on producing short-term profits; non-Westerners focus on generating favors.

Note that in developing countries, western-trained and educated nationals are simultaneously drawn to both indigenous and western ideals. This means that they may have internalized the western norms of personal enrichment along with those of modern commerce, while simultaneously adhering to indigenous traditions by fulfilling communal obligations. Requests for payoffs may spring from both these ideals, and American corporate responses must be designed to satisfy them both.

What is of great importance is considering the request for a gift or money in its local context. In nations where gifts generate a sense of obligation, it may prove best to give them, thereby creating "inner debts" among key foreign colleagues in the belief that they will repay them over time.

Gift or Bribe?

This question has puzzled travelers for centuries, so if you are ever confronted with an outright bribe, you might as well know the terminology.

* *Mordida* (mor-DEE-da) is a Spanish term for bribe, popularly known in Mexico. The literal meaning is "a little bite."

* *Grease* (greese) indicates "facilitating payments," specifically referring to legal and permitted payments of modest sums to foreign officials for speedy action of their normal duties. It is common almost everywhere, including the U.S.

* *Kumshaw* (KUM-shaw) is a Southeast Asian term for bribe.

In most cultures, gift-giving is an established business custom that often yields tangible – sometimes extraordinary – results. No line exists dividing gifts from bribes, however. It seems that direct solicitation of gifts involves smaller amounts, while larger ones require go-betweens. Furthermore, while smaller gifts may signal a desire to work with the local business circles, a company that supplies larger sums could violate both local anti-payoff statutes and the Foreign Corrupt Practices Act.

With most business dealings, an agreeable middle path can be found that cuts successfully between rudeness and outright bribery, a path in which one can maintain personal and company ethics without rejecting other countries' cultural norms. In order to do so, you need to verify that:

- The gift-giving won't be in conflict with the law of the United States;

- Gift giving is a custom in your host country;

- Your gift is not a cash payment;

- Your company's gift-giving is part of the overall strategy and is part of your company's budget.

Sources: "Giving Abroad: Separating Gifts from Gaffes," Richard D. Smith, US 1, September 12, 1990; "Do's and Taboos Around the World," Parker Pen Co., John Wiley & Sons, 1985; "Beware the Purple Pigskin Clock," Dawn Bryan, Sales & Marketing Management, August 1990; "A Traveler's Guide to Gifts and Bribes," Jeffrey A. Fadiman, Harvard Business Review, July-August 1986.

WORKING WITH INTERPRETERS

1. Brief your interpreter in advance about the subject and your objectives.

2. Speak clearly, slowly and concisely.

3. Avoid little-known or difficult words.

4. Explain your major idea two or three different ways, as your point may be lost if expressed only once.

5. Do not talk more than a minute or two without breaking for interpretation.

6. Do not depend on your foreign counterpart's interpreter to effectively communicate your messages. If you need an interpreter, hire and brief one for yourself.

7. Allow time for the interpreter to clarify obscure points.

8. Never interrupt the interpreter.

9. Avoid long sentences, double negatives or negative wordings when a positive form could be used.

10. When speaking, always look at your foreign counterpart.

11. During meetings, write out the main points agreed upon so that both parties can check their understandings.

12. Ask the interpreter for advice if communication problems arise.

13. Allow your interpreter adequate rest periods.

14. Consider using two interpreters if interpreting is to last into the evening.

15. Be understanding if it develops that the interpreter has made a mistake.

Adapted from "Managing Cultural Differences" by P. Harris and R. Moran, Gulf Publishing Co., 1987

DO'S AND DON'TS

Do's:

- Speak plainly, clearly and slowly, but not loudly.

- Present only one point at a time.

- Paraphrase what has been said by asking, "Did I understand you to say that…"

- Confirm phone conversations by fax or telex.

- Use visual aids and printed matter wherever possible and follow up any meeting with a written summary.

- Learn the basics of your foreign associate's language (verbal and nonverbal) and use both languages, yours and theirs, when presenting material.

- Watch what others do and how they say things, and take your cues from them.

Don'ts:

- Do not use slang, jargon, colloquialisms, regional expressions or sports talk.

- Be wary of using American humor; it may not translate well.

- Do not use numerals unless you write them out.

- Do not rush negotiations or "push" the American way of doing things on your foreign associate.

- Do not interrupt a foreign associate when he or she is speaking.

- Never say "You're not making yourself clear."

LANGUAGE INSIGHTS FOR NATIVE ENGLISH SPEAKERS

Most Americans are unable to conduct business in a language other than English. While it is desirable to speak in the language(s) of those from the country with which you are dealing, the following suggestions may help you communicate with non-native English speakers.

1. Practice using the most common 3,000 words in English; that is, those words typically learned by non-native speakers in their first two years of language study. Avoid uncommon or esoteric words and use simple words instead.

2. Restrict your use of English words to their most common meaning. Many words have multiple meanings, and non-native speakers are most likely to know the first or second most common meanings. For example, "to address" to mean "to send" (rather than "to consider") and "impact" to mean "the force of a collision" (rather than "effect").

3. Whenever possible, select an action-specific verb (e.g., "ride the bus"). Verbs to avoid include "do," "make," "get," "have," "be" and "go." For example, the verb "get" can have at least five meanings – buy, borrow, steal, rent, retrieve – as in, "I'll get a car and meet you in an hour."

4. In general, select a word with few alternate meanings (such as "accurate," which has one meaning) rather than a word with many alternate meanings (such as "right," which has 27 meanings).

5. Become aware of words whose primary meaning is restricted elsewhere. For example, outside of the United States, "check" most commonly means a financial instrument and is frequently spelled "cheque."

6. Become aware of alternate spellings of commonly used words and the regions where those spellings are used: for example, colour/color, organisation/organization, centre/center.

7. Resist changing a word's part of speech from its most common usage; for example, avoid saying "a warehousing operation" or "attachable assets."

8. Conform to basic grammar rules more strictly than is common in everyday conversation. Make sure that sentences express a complete thought, that pronouns and antecedents are used correctly, and that subordination is accurately expressed. For example, the sentence, "No security regulations shall be distributed to personnel that are out of date," needs to be rewritten as "Do not distribute out-of-date security regulations to personnel."

9. Clarify the meaning of modal auxiliaries; for example, be sure that the reader will understand whether "should" means moral

obligation, expectation, social obligation or advice.

10. Avoid "word pictures," constructions that depend for their meaning on invoking a particular mental image (e.g., "run that by me," "wade through these figures," "slice of the free world pie"). A particular form of mental imagery likely to cause misunderstandings is the use of assumptions contrary to fact (e.g., "suppose you were me," "suppose there were no sales").

11. Avoid terms borrowed from sports (e.g., "struck out," "field that question," "touchdown," "can't get to first base," "ballpark figure") Also, avoid terms borrowed from literature (e.g., "catch-22") and the military (e.g., "run it up the flagpole," "run a tight ship").

12. When writing to someone you do not know well, use his or her last name and keep the tone formal while expressing personal interest or concern. Initial sentences can express appreciation (e.g., "We are extremely grateful to your branch...") or personal connection (e.g., "Mr. Ramos has suggested...") Closing phrases can express personal best wishes (e.g., "With warmest regards, I remain sincerely yours...").

13. Whenever the cultural background of your reader is known, try to adapt your tone to the manner in which such information – apology, suggestion, refusal, thanks, request, directive – is usually conveyed in his or her culture. For example, apologies may need to be sweeping and unconditional (e.g., "My deepest apologies for any problems..."). Refusals may need to be indirect (e.g., "Your proposal contains some interesting points that we need to study further...").

14. If possible, determine and reflect the cultural values of your reader on such dimensions as espousing control versus adaptation to one's environment, emphasizing individual versus collective accomplishments, or focusing on quantitative versus qualitative changes. When in doubt, include a variety of value orientations: "I want to thank you [individual] and your department [collective]...."

15. When the cultural background of your reader is known, try to capture the flavor of his or her language. For example, communications to Spanish speakers would be more flowery and lengthy than those to German speakers.

16. Whenever possible, adopt the reasoning style of your reader or present information in more than one format. For example, the following sentence contains both a general position statement and inductive reasoning: "Trust among business partners is essential; and our data show that our most successful joint ventures are those in which we invested initial time building a personal trusting relationship."

Adapted from "The Journal of Language for International Business," Spring 1985, D.I. Riddle and Z.D. Lanham. "International Written Business English."

INTERNATIONAL BUSINESS CARD EXCHANGE

- Overall, the tone of the business card exchange should be slow, deliberate and formal. Quick motions and speech can signify disrespect.

- Give your business card with one hand and receive business cards with both hands.

- After you have received a business card, study it carefully. Immediately pocketing the card would be considered an insult. Handle the card formally. Do not flip, stroke or put the card into your rear pants pocket.

- Make certain your own cards are in prime condition.

- It is appropriate to ask the giver how to pronounce his or her name. Card exchange is the proper time to inquire about pronunciation.

- It is not inappropriate for you to exchange cards with a person a second time if any information on your card has been changed.

- Make certain you have a sufficient supply of cards. Japanese businessmen, in particular, claim that Americans often say they've "just run out."

- Never inflate your job title.

- Consider having your card translated into the language of people you are visiting or hosting.

SOURCE MATERIALS AND USEFUL RESOURCES

The potential list of useful cross-cultural materials is enormous. We have selected a sample that offers sound, practical advice for the business person.

You will learn best when you have a specific need, e.g., business trip or overseas assignment. Even on these occasions, however, you will learn more efficiently and effectively if you have maintained an on-going interest in cross-cultural business issues. Make your own additions to our list of resources; maintain a personal file of articles, reports, etc. *As the world gets smaller, your international files should be getting bigger.*

SOURCE MATERIALS

The following publications served as source material for the development of this book.

Acuff. Frank L., *How to Negotiate Anything with Anyone Anywhere Around the World*, New York: American Management Association (AMACOM), 1993.

Adler, N.J., "Women in International Management: Where Are They?," *California Management Review*, vol. 26, no. 4, Summer 1984, pp. 78-89.

Adler, Nancy, *International Dimensions of Organizational Behavior*, Boston: Kent Publishing, 1986.

Adler, Nancy J., "Pacific Basin Managers: A Gaijin, Not a Woman," *Human Resource Management*, vol. 26, Summer 1987, p. 169 (23).

Althen, G., *American Ways, A Guide for Foreigners in the United States*, Yarmouth, ME: Intercultural Press, 1988.

Axtell, R., *Do's and Taboos Around the World*, 3rd Edition, New York: John Wiley & Sons, 1993.

Axtell, R., *Do's and Taboos of Hosting International Visitors*, New York: John Wiley & Sons, 1989.

Barker, Joel Arthur, *Discovering the Future: The Business of Paradigms*, St. Paul, MN: ILI Press, 1989.

Bartlett, Christopher and Sumatra Ghoshal, *Managing Across Borders: The Transnational Solution*, Cambridge, MA: Harvard Business School Press, 1989.

Bartlett, Christopher and Sumatra Ghoshal, "Matrix Management: Not a Structure, a Frame of Mind," *Harvard Business Review*, July-August 1990, pp. 138-45.

Bartlett, Christopher and Sumatra Ghoshal, "Organizing for Worldwide Effectiveness: The Transnational Solution," *California Management Review*, vol. 31, no. 1 (1988).

Baskerville, Dawn M., et. al., "21 Women of Power and Influence in Corporate America," *Black Enterprise*, vol. 22, no. 1, pp. 39-90, Aug. 1991.

Brake, Terence, Danielle Medina Walker, and Thomas D. Walker, *Doing Business Internationally: The Guide to Cross-Cultural Success*, New York: McGraw-Hill, 1994.

Brake, Terence and Danielle Walker, *Doing Business Internationally: The Workbook to Cross-Cultural Success*, Princeton, NJ: Princeton Training Press, 1994.

Bridges, William, *The Character of Organizations* (a diagnostic testing instrument), Palo Alto, CA: Consulting Psychologists Press, 1992.

Broganti, Nancy L. and Elizabeth Devine, *The Traveler's Guide to European Customs & Manners,* Deephaven, MN: Meadowbrook, Inc., 1984.

Carney, Larry S. and Charlotte G. O'Kelly, "Barriers and Constraints to the Recruitment and Mobility of Female Managers in the Japanese Labor Force," *Human Resource Management,* vol. 26, Summer 1987, p. 193 (24).

Central Intelligence Agency, *The World Factbook 1997,* Washington, DC: U.S. Government Printing Office, 1997.

Central Intelligence Agency, *The World Factbook 1998,* Washington DC: US Government Printing Office, 1998.

Chesanow, Neil, *The World Class Executive: How to Do Business Like a Pro Around the World,* New York: Bantam Books, 1985.

Clutterbuck, D., "Dow Makes the Most of Womanpower," *International Management,* vol. 31, no. 11, Nov. 1976, pp. 27-8.

Condon, J. C., *Good Neighbors: Communicating with Mexicans,* Yarmouth, ME: Intercultural Press, 1985.

Condon, J. C., *With Respect to the Japanese: A Guide for Americans,* Yarmouth, ME: Intercultural Press, 1984.

Copeland, Lennie and Lewis Griggs, *Going International: How to Make Friends and Deal Effectively in the International Marketplace,* New York: Random House, 1985.

Crystal, David, *The Cambridge Factfinder,* Cambridge: Cambridge University Press, 1998.

Cutter, Charles H., *Africa 1998,* Baltimore, MD: Stryker-Post Publications, 1998.

Devine, Elizabeth and Nancy L. Broganti, *The Traveler's Guide to African Customs and Manners,* New York: St. Martin's Press, 1985.

Devine, Elizabeth and Nancy L. Broganti, *The Traveler's Guide to Latin American Customs & Manners,* New York: St. Martin's Press, 1988.

Devine, Elizabeth and Nancy L. Broganti, *The Traveler's Guide to Middle Eastern and North African Customs and Manners,* New York: St. Martin's Press, 1991.

Doing Business in Chile, U.S.A.: Price Waterhouse, 1994

Doing Business in Venezuela, Philadelphia, PA: Price Waterhouse, 1990.

Doz, Yves, *Strategic Management in International Companies,* New York: Pergamon Press, 1986.

Drucker, Peter F., *Managing in Turbulent Times*, New York: Harper & Row, 1980.

Drucker, Peter F., *The Changing World of the Executive*, New York: Times Books, 1985.

Drucker, Peter F., *The New Realities*, New York: Harper & Row, 1989.

Elledge, Robin and Steven Phillips, *Teambuilding Sourcebook*, San Diego, CA: University Associates Press, 1989.

Encyclopaedia Britannica Online. [http://www.eb.com:180]. Encyclopaedia Britannica, Inc., 1994-1999.

Engholm, Christopher, *When Business East Meets Business West: The Guide to Practice and Protocol in the Pacific Rim*, New York: John Wiley & Sons, 1991.

Evans, Paul, Yves Doz, and Andre Laurent, eds., *Human Resource Management in International Firms: Change, Globalization, Innovation*, New York: St. Martin's Press, 1990.

Far Eastern Review: Asia 1995 Yearbook, Hong Kong: Review Publishing Company Ltd, 1995.

Feig, John Paul, *A Common Core: Thais and Americans*, Yarmouth, ME: Intercultural Press, 1989.

Ferguson, Henry, *Tomorrow's Global Executive*, Homewood, IL: Dow Jones-Irwin, 1988.

Fisher, Glen, *Mindsets: The Role of Culture and Perception in International Relations*, Yarmouth, ME: Intercultural Press, 1988.

Foster, Dean Allen, *Bargaining Across Borders: How to Negotiate Business Successfully Anywhere in the World*, New York: McGraw-Hill, 1992.

Funakawa, Atsushi, *Transcontinental Management*, San Francisco: Jossey-Bass Publishers, 1997.

George III, Munchus, "Discrimination Against Working Women in Japan," *Women in Management Review*, vol. 8, no. 1, pp. 9-14, 1993.

Ghadar, Fariborz, Phillip D. Grub, Robert T. Moran, and Marshall Geer, *Global Business Management in the 1990s*, Washington DC: Beacham Publishing, Inc., 1990.

Gibbs, Paul, *The Largest Market in the World*, Holbrook, MA: Bob Adams, Inc., 1990.

Global Road Warrior: 85-Country Handbook for the International Business Traveler, San Rafael, CA: World Trade Press, 1999.

Gross, Thomas, Ernie Turner, and Lars Cederholm, "Building Teams for Global Operations," *Management Review*, June 1987, pp. 32-36.

Hall, Edward T., *Beyond Culture*, Garden City, NY: Anchor/Doubleday, 1976.

Hall, Edward T., *The Hidden Dimension*, New York: Anchor Press, 1966.

Hall, Edward T., *The Silent Language*, New York: Doubleday & Company, 1959.

Hall, E.T. and M.R. Hall, *Hidden Differences: Doing Business with the Japanese*, New York: Doubleday, 1987.

Hall, E.T. and M.R. Hall, *Understanding Cultural Differences: Germans, French, and Americans*, Yarmouth, ME: Intercultural Press, 1990.

Harris, Phillip R. and Robert T. Moran, *Managing Cultural Differences* (Third Edition), Houston, TX: Gulf Publishing, 1991.

Harris, Philip and Robert Moran, *Managing Cultural Differences* (Second Edition), Houston, TX: Gulf Publishing, 1987.

Harris, Philip R., and Dorothy L. Harris, "Women Managers and Professionals Abroad," *Journal of Managerial Psychology*, vol. 3, no. 4, pp. i-ii, 1988.

Heger, Kyle, "A Tale of Two Lucys," *Communication World*, vol. 6, Jan. 1989, p. 32 (4).

Hendon, Donald W. and Rebecca Angeles Hendon, *World Class Negotiating: Deal Making in the Global Marketplace*, New York: John Wiley, 1990.

Hersey, Paul and Kenneth Blanchard, *The Management of Organizational Behavior* (Third Edition), Englewood Cliffs, NJ: Prentice Hall, 1976.

Hoecklin, Lisa Adent, "Managing Cultural Differences for Competitive Advantage," Special Report No. P. 656, London: The Economist Intelligence Unit, 1993.

Hoffman, J., *The International Assignment: Is It For You?*, Foster City, CA: D.C.W. Research Associate Press, 1982.

Hofstede, Geert, *Culture's Consequences: International Differences in Work-Related Values*, Beverly Hills, CA: Sage Publishing, 1980.

Hofstede, Geert, *Cultures and Organizations: Software of the Mind*, London: McGraw-Hill, 1991.

Hoopes, David, *Global Guide to International Relations: The International Business Source Book*, New York: Facts on File Publications, 1983.

Imai, Masaaki, *Kaizen: The Key to Japan's Competitive Success*, New York: Random House, 1986.

Izraeli, D.N., et. al., "Women Executives in MNC Subsidiaries," *California Management Review*, vol. 23, no. 1, Fall 1980, pp. 53-63, Bibliog. 41.

Keirsey, David and Marilyn Bates, *Please Understand Me: Character and Temperament Types,* Del Mar, CA: Prometheus Nemesis Book Company, 1984.

Kluckhohn, Florence and Frederick L. Strodtbeck, *Variations in Value Orientations,* Evanston, IL: Row, Peterson and Company, 1956.

Kohls, L. R., *Survival Kit for Overseas Living* (Second Edition), Yarmouth, ME: Intercultural Press, 1984.

Korn/Ferry International and Columbia School of Business, *21st Century Report: Reinventing the CEO,* New York: Korn/Ferry International, 1989.

Kras, E., *Management in Two Cultures: Bridging the Gap Between U.S. and Mexican Managers,* Yarmouth, ME: Intercultural Press, 1989.

Kupfer, Andre, "How to be a Global Manager," *Fortune,* March 14, 1988, pp. 43-48.

Lanier, Alison R., *The Rising Sun on Main Street: Working With the Japanese,* Yardley, PA: International Information Associates, 1990.

Lansing, Paul, and Kathryn Ready, "Hiring Women Managers in Japan: An Alternative for Foreign Employers," *California Management Review,* vol. 30, Spring, 1988, p. 112 (16).

Laurent, Andre, "The Cross-Cultural Puzzle of Human Resource Management," *Human Resource Management,* vol. 25, no. 1, (Spring 1986), pp. 91-102.

Leaptrott, Nan, *Rules of the Game: Global Business Protocol,* Cincinnati, Ohio: Thompson Executive Press, 1996.

Lee, S. K. Jean, and Tan Hwee Hoon, "Rhetorical Vision of Men and Women Managers in Singapore," *Human Relations,* vol. 46, no. 4, pp. 527-42, April 1993.

Leibo, Steven A., *East, Southeast Asia, and the Western Pacific 1998,* Baltimore, MD: Stryker-Post Publications, 1998.

Levitt, Theodore, "The Globalization of Markets," *Harvard Business Review,* May-June 1983, pp. 92-102.

Lobel, Sharon A., "Global Leadership Competencies: Managing to a Different Drumbeat," *Human Resource Management,* vol. 29, no. 1 (Spring 1990), pp. 39-47.

Maddock, Su, and Di Parkin, "Gender Cultures: Women's Choices and Strategies at Work," *Women in Management Review,* vol. 8, no. 2, pp. 3-9, 1993.

Mead, Richard, *Cross-Cultural Management Communication,* New York: John Wiley, 1990.

Mole, John, *Mind Your Manners: Culture Clash in the Single European Market*, London: The Industrial Society, 1990.

Moran, Robert T. and William G. Stripp, *Dynamics of Successful International Business Negotiations*, Houston, TX: Gulf Publishing, 1991.

Morrison, Terri, Wayne A. Conoway and George A. Bordon, *Kiss Bow, or Shake Hands: How to do Business in Sixty Countries*, Holbrook, MA: Bob Adams Inc., 1994..

The New Encyclopaedia Britannica. Edited by Philip W. Goetz. 32 vols. Chicago: Encyclopaedia Britannica, Inc., 1991.

Nydell, Margaret K., *Understanding Arabs: A Guide for Westerners*, Yarmouth, ME: Intercultural Press, 1987.

Ohmae, Kenichi, *The Borderless World*, New York: Harper Business Press, 1990.

Ohmae, Kenichi, "The Logic of Strategic Alliances," *Harvard Business Review*, March-April 1989, pp. 143-54.

"Other Men's Shoes – Gill Lewis – A Toast to A Modern Marketing Success," *The Director*, vol. 30, no. 10, April 1978, p. 25.

Perlmutter, Howard V. and David A. Heenan, "Cooperate to Compete Globally," *Harvard Business Review*, March-April 1986.

Peters, Thomas, *Thriving on Chaos: Handbook for a Management Revolution*, New York: Harper & Row, 1988.

Porter, Michael, ed., *Competition in Global Business*, Cambridge, MA: Harvard Business School Press, 1986.

Povall, M., "Overcoming Barriers to Women's Advancement In European Organizations," City University, *Personnel Review*, vol. 13, no. 1, 1984, pp. 32-40.

Povall, M., et. al., "Banking on Women Managers," *Management Today*, Feb. 1982, pp. 50-3, 108.

Prahalad, C.K. and Yves Doz, *The Multinational Mission: Balancing Local Demands and Global Vision*, New York: Free Press, 1987.

Quelch, John A. and Edward J. Hoff, "Customizing Global Marketing," *Harvard Business Review*, May-June 1986, pp. 59-86.

Reich, Robert B., "Who is Them?" *Harvard Business Review*, March-April 1991, pp. 77-88.

Reich, Robert B., "Who is Us?" *Harvard Business Review*, January-February 1990, pp. 53-64.

Reier, S., "The Feminine Mystique," *Institutional Investor*, vol. 18, no. 7, July 1984, pp. 223-4, 226.

Rhinesmith, Stephen H., "Americans in the Global Learning Process," *The Annals of the American Academy of Political and Social Science*, vol. 442 (March 1979), pp. 98-108.

Rhinesmith, Stephen H., *A Manager's Guide to Globalization: Six Keys to Success in a Changing World*, New York: McGraw-Hill, 1993. (Co-published with the American Society for Training and Development, Alexandria, VA)

Rhinesmith, Stephen H., "An Agenda for Globalization," *Training and Development Journal*, February 1991, pp. 22-29.

Rhinesmith, Stephen H., *Cultural-Organizational Analysis: The Interrelationship Between Value Orientations and Managerial Behavior*, Cambridge, MA: McBer and Company, 1971.

Rhinesmith, Stephen H., "Going Global from the Inside Out," *Training and Development Journal*, November 1991, pp. 42-47.

Rhinesmith, Stephen H., John N. Williamson, David M. Ehlen, and Denise S. Maxwell, "Developing Leaders for a Global Enterprise," *Training and Development Journal*, April 1989, pp. 24-34.

Richmond, Yale, *From Da to Yes: Understanding the East Europeans*, Yarmouth, ME Intercultural Press, 1995

Richmond, Yale, *From Nyet to Da: Understanding the Russians*, Yarmouth, ME: Intercultural Press, 1996.

Ricks, D., et al., *International Business Blunders*, Washington, DC: Transemantics, 1974.

Rossman, Marlene, *The International Businesswoman of the 1990s*, New York: Praeger Publishers, 1990.

Russell, Malcom B., *The Middle East and South Asia 1998*, Baltimore, MD: Stryker-Post Publications, 1998.

Schein, Edgar H., *Organizational Culture and Leadership*, San Francisco: Jossey-Bass, 1989.

Shaeffer, Ruth G., "Building Global Teamwork for Growth and Survival," *The Conference Board Research Bulletin*, no. 228, 1989.

Shoemaker, M. Wesley, *Russia, Eurasian States, and Eastern Europe 1998*, Baltimore MD: Stryker-Post Publications, 1998.

Singer, Marshall R., *Intercultural Communication: A Perceptual Approach*, Englewood Cliffs, NJ: Prentice Hall (Simon & Schuster), 1987.

Skabelund, Grant Paul, (managing ed.), *Culturgrams* , Provo, UT: Brigham Young University, David M. Kennedy Center for Int'l Studies, 1997.

SRI International Business Intelligence Program, "More About Strategic Alliances," D88-1256, 1988.

SRI International Business Intelligence Program, "Strategic Partnering: Keys to Success in the 1990s," D88-1255, 1988.

Steingraber, Fred G., "Managing in the 1990s," *Business Horizons,* January-February 1990, pp. 49-61.

Stewart, E. C. and M.J. Bennett, *American Cultural Patterns: A Cross-Cultural Perspective* (Revised Edition), Yarmouth, ME: Intercultural Press, 1991.

Taylor, Lee, "Developing an Organizational Strategy for Equal Opportunities: A Case Study From the Open University, UK," *Women in Management Review,* vol. 8, no. 2, pp. 24-8, 1993.

Taylor, William, "The Logic of Global Business: An Interview with ABB's Percy Barnevik," *Harvard Business Review,* March-April 1991, pp. 91-105.

Terpstra, Vern and Kenneth David, *The Cultural Framework of International Business* (Second Edition), Pelham Manor, NY: South-Western Publishing, 1985.

Thompson, Wayne C., *Canada 1998,* Balitmore, MD: Stryker- Post Publications, 1998.

Thompson, Wayne C., *Western Europe,* Baltimore, MD: Stryker-Post Publications, 1998.

Tiglao, Rigaberto, *Far Eastern Economic Review,* January 30, 1997, p. 17.

Wolniansky, Natalia, "International Training for Global Leadership," *Management Review,* May 1992.

Yoon, Julie, and Brian H. Kleiner, *What Companies Can Do For Women,* Equal Opportunities International, vol. 12, no. 1, 1993.

OTHER:

Economist Intelligence Unit: *How-to Guides for International Managers*

- Reports on business strategies from leading international companies

Contact: Business International Corp., 215 Park Avenue South, New York, NY 10003

Intercultural Press: *Current Intercultural Resources*

- Listing of cross-cultural books, videos and other materials

Contact: Intercultural Press, 16 US Route One, P.O. Box 700, Yarmouth, Maine 04096

BESTSELLERS

Doing Business Internationally: The Resource for Business and Social Etiquette

by Training Management Corporation
646 pages   ISBN: 1-882390-16-4 $48.00 U.S.

The Resource Book is the capstone of the *Doing Business Internationally* series. It provides information on protocol, business and social practices and communication for 100 countries around the world. The Resource Book serves as a simple frame of reference for profiling and understanding the major characteristics of cultures around the globe in order to make life easier for both traveling and home-based personnel. It is a comprehensive source when doing business in a culture other than your own. The information in the Resource Book will benefit readers when:

- They are planning a business trip to a foreign culture and need information on protocol, business and social practices.

- They are puzzled by a foreign colleague/employee's behavior.

- They are thinking of expanding business overseas and want a quick overview of some of the challenges they may face.

Doing Business Internationally: The Workbook to Cross-Cultural Success

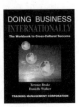

by Training Management Corporation
269 pages   ISBN: 1-882390-00-8 $49.50 U.S.

The workbook is the companion, self-paced manual for TMC's popular international business seminar, *Doing Business Internationally*. It was designed to complement *The Guide to Cross-Cultural Success*, although each can be used independently as a learning tool. It is intended for those who cannot fit a full seminar into their schedules and are looking for independent study. The book is organized into four modules:

- Global Business Thinking
- Cross-Cultural Awareness
- Communication
- Working and Managing

This workbook presents a program for building the knowledge and skills that will help executives and managers operate effectively in a variety of cultural settings and achieve cross-cultural success.

Doing Business Internationally: The Guide to Cross-Cultural Success

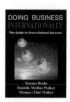

by Terence Brake, Danielle Medina Walker, Tim Walker

284 pages   ISBN: 0-7863-0117-1   **$25.00 U.S.**

This hardcover book provides executives and managers with the knowledge and skills they will need to compete in today's global marketplace. This is the ideal guide for executives and managers who are seeking to leverage culture and turn it into competitive advantage. The guide establishes the key principles of communication and negotiation across cultural lines and identifies the dynamics and scope of today's global workforce. It represents a rich composite of research, interviews and training guidelines based on the authors' 25 years of experience in the global business environment. Executives and managers with, or likely to have, international responsibilities, will need the information presented in this book in order to succeed. The book includes information necessary to:

- Analyze key global trends and their impact on business practices.

- Recognize the impact of cultural differences on business practices.

- Adapt key business skills to achieve better results when working with different cultures.

- Identify the critical success factors needed by managers operating across borders.

ON-LINE RESOURCES

R-BASE™—The Resource For Business and Social Etiquette

R-BASE™ is a powerful database available on the Internet that provides easy access to essential information for conducting business in cultures around the world.

R-BASE™ features easy access to:

- Country-specific information on over 90 countries

- Essential material about each country, revised and updated annually

Country-specific subjects for over 90 countries include:

- Historical overview
- Business practices
- Hours of business
- Dress
- Introductions
- Meetings
- Negotiating
- Entertaining
- Social Values, customs and tips
- Regional maps and country flags

And much more

General guidelines for doing business internationally include:

- The Foreign Corrupt Practices Act
- Using agents and inter-mediaries
- Gift giving guidelines
- Working with interpreters
- Language insights for native English speakers
- International business card exchange

And others

INSTRUMENTS & RELATED PRODUCTS

Cultural Orientations Indicator (COI)™

By Training Management Corporation
Completion Time: 20 minutes $25.00 U.S. ea.

Culture strongly influences how people behave and how they understand the behavior of others. Culture also influences the behaviors people view as proper and acceptable as well as what they view as unacceptable.

The Cultural Orientations Indicator (COI)™ is a cross-cultural self-assessment instrument that allows individuals to assess their personal cultural preferences and compare them with generalized profiles of other cultures. The COI™ draws on work done by experts in the field of anthropology, cross-cultural psychology and international business management and integrates this research into TMC's perspective on how executives learn to understand the essential areas of human values as they affect the workplace.

The COI™ provides respondents with a personal cultural profile based on ten dimensions that have particular application in the business world. Insights into your cultural orientations are especially useful for understanding differences between yourself and others from different cultural or national backgrounds. The understanding gained from your personal profile can be applied to the development of specific business, management, sales, marketing, negotiation and leadership skills among others when you apply them in multicultural situations.

Application

The COI™ is a comprehensive tool that can be employed by a variety of users in organizations of all sizes, in all industries and at all levels to improve multicultural effectiveness. TMC offers data comparisons of personal cultural orientations with a number of demographic and organizational parameters.

Any individual or organization interacting with others from different cultures will benefit from the information produced by the COI™. The instrument enables users to understand better the subtle, yet critical, impact that culture can have on a variety of management interactions and development activities. These include teambuilding, interpersonal communication, problem solving, decision making, strategy and tactic implementation, internal consulting and pre-departure assessment, among other multicultural objectives.

Feedback reports are generated for a multitude of end-users from individuals to large group applications. Results from the data can also be aggregated upwards based on any single parameter or multiple combinations of information contained on the instrument's demographic data/response sheet. Statistical analysis can thus be provided at the business unit, organizational, national or other levels.

Administration, Scoring & Feedback Procedures

The COI™ is a self-administered, forced-choice questionnaire consisting of a demographic data sheet, an answer sheet, 90 items and several additional items being studied for future application. Administration takes approximately 20 minutes. Answer sheets are forwarded to TMC for scoring and analysis.

After data analysis, each respondent receives a personal Profile Summary sheet indicating the individual's preferences along the ten dimensions and 36 orientations featured in the **Cultural Orientations Model (COM)™**. An additional feedback piece is available that compares the individual's preferences with those of a selected country.

As with other self-assessments, there is no "correct" profile. Results are currently presented to respondents by TMC-certified facilitators, often within the context of a development program.

COM™/COI™ Certification

Certification is available to corporate trainers, human resource executives and OD consultants to use the COM™ and administer the COI™ directly in their initiatives. The certification process is designed to ensure that the COM™/COI™ is properly administered and professionally debriefed by facilitators who have demonstrated a proficiency in cross-cultural understanding and who possess an in-depth knowledge of the underlying principles upon which the COI™ is based. Certification does not authorize individuals or organizations to reproduce or score the COI™.

Availability of the COI™ and Pricing Information

The COI™ can be purchased only by TMC-certified professionals. The COI™, consisting of a questionnaire booklet, response form, data processing and analysis and preparation of individual profiles costs $25 U.S. each, and the accompanying COI™ explanatory booklet, the **Cultural Orientations Guide (COG)**, costs $49 U.S. a copy. Composite group reports are also available for $500 U.S. each.

Cultural Orientations Model (COM)™

By Training Management Corporation
PTP stock no. COM $3.00 U.S. ea.

Anyone who has traveled abroad understands the feeling of disorientation that can occur when coming into contact with cultural differences. Usually referred to as "culture shock," this phenomenon may cause feelings of depression, aggressiveness, resentment, superiority, inferiority, curiosity, excitement, loneliness, fear, frustration and so on. To avoid such unpleasant feelings, individuals need to be able to get their bearings by relating themselves to specific features in the environment. When trying to adjust to a new culture, travelers can also pay attention to a number of key features – the dominant value orientations of the culture.

An important question is "value orientations toward what?" Given the findings of anthropologists, cross-cultural psychologists, communication experts and TMC's own experiences, TMC has developed the Cultural Orientations Model (COM)™. The COM™ was designed to help individuals traveling abroad understand the new culture. Through this model, TMC has defined ten major cultural dimensions and 36 associated cultural orientations that are highly valuable to international businesspeople in distinguishing between cultures and guiding key decisions. The COM™ is the model upon which the COI™ is based and can be used as a quick reference tool when traveling abroad.

Cultural Orientations Guide (COG): A Framework for Developing Cross-Cultural Effectiveness

By Training Management Corporation
PTP stock no. COG $49.00 U.S. ea.

Culture is an increasingly important dimension in interactions between individuals in a world that is characterized by the constant movement of people across national borders, the globalization of business and widespread social, economic and political change. A high degree of contact and exchange between cultures is redefining our world and posing enormous personal, social and business challenges. While organizations need to leverage culture to establish and maintain a competitive advantage, individuals need to become more flexible in adapting customs and adjusting to practices that differ from those of their own culture in order to ensure their personal and professional success.

The COG is designed to complement the COI™ and assist in building intercultural effectiveness by helping individuals understand and explore culture. It is an introduction to building cross-cultural skills and engaging in global learning.

ORDER FORM

5 Easy Ways to Order:

TEL: (609) 951-9319   **FAX:** (609) 951-0395   **EMAIL:** cpalmquist@tmcorp.com
WEB: http://www.tmcorp.com   **MAIL:** PTP 600 Alexander Rd Princeton, NJ 08540 USA

Training key personnel in your company to compete in the global marketplace is a sound investment. You can further optimize the use of your training dollars by contracting with Training Management Corporation to:

❑ Customize any of the Global Leadership courses listed below
❑ Deliver the program via our experienced international business trainers

Global Leadership Series:

❑ Doing Business Internationally   ❑ Cross-Cultural Presentation Skills
❑ Cultural Orientations at Work   ❑ Global Diversity and Culture
❑ Global Leadership   ❑ Leadership for the 21st Century
❑ Effective Global Management   ❑ Managing for Competitive Advantage
❑ Doing Business in Targeted Region/Country ❑ Project Management Fundamentals
❑ Negotiating Across Cultures   ❑ Project Team Management
❑ Multicultural Teamwork   ❑ Project Management for Global Teams

Name _____   Title _____

Company _____   Purchase Order # _____

Address _____

City _____   State _____   Zip _____

Phone _____   Fax _____

❑ **American Express** _____
                          Card #

_____   _____
          Signature   Expiration Date

Qty	Title	Unit Price	Price
	Doing Business Internationally: Business and Social Etiquette	$48.00 US	
	Doing Business Internationally: The Guide to Cross-Cultural Success	$25.00 US	
	Doing Business Internationally: The Workbook to Cross-Cultural Success	$49.50 US	
	Doing Business Internationally Series (all 3 DBI titles) 20% Discount	$98.00 US	
	Cultural Orientations Model (COM)™ card	$ 3.00 US	

Subtotal	
NJ Residents Only—6% Tax	
Shipping & Handling (see chart)	
Total	

US Orders: Orders will be shipped via UPS standard GroundTrac unless otherwise requested by the customer.

First item: $5.00
Each additional item: $2.00

Rush delivery options:
UPS 3 Day Select: add $5.50
UPS 2nd Day Air: add $7.50

International Orders: Payment must be made in U.S. dollars. Please contact PTP at (609) 951-9319 for more information on shipping options and costs.

Thank You For Your Order!